The Guide to
Executive Recruiters

D1365932

The Guide to Executive Recruiters

Michael Betrus

New and Updated Edition

McGraw-Hill
New York   San Francisco   Washington, D.C.   Auckland   Bogotá
Caracas   Lisbon   London   Madrid   Mexico City   Milan
Montreal   New Delhi   San Juan   Singapore
Sydney   Tokyo   Toronto

International Standard Serial Number:
Guide to Executive Recruiters
ISSN 1083-6152

McGraw-Hill

A Division of The McGraw·Hill Companies

1 2 3 4 5 6 7·8 9 0   DOC/DOC   9 0 2 1 0 9 8 7

ISBN 0-07-006280-3

The sponsoring editor for this book was Betsy Brown, the editing supervisor was Jane Palmieri, and the production supervisor was Claire Stanley. It was set by Carol Woolverton Studio.

Printed and bound by R. R. Donnelley & Sons Company.

McGraw-Hill books are available at special quantity discounts to use as premiums and sales promotions, or for use in corporate training programs. For more information, please write to the Director of Special Sales, McGraw-Hill, 11 West 19th Street, New York, NY 10011. Or contact your local bookstore.

To update an entry included in this edition or to have an entry included in the next edition, please complete the form at the back of the book.

This book is printed on recycled, acid-free paper containing a minimum of 50% recycled, de-inked fiber.

Contents

Acknowledgments

I would like to thank the following people who contributed both directly and indirectly in making this Guide possible: Lawrence LoPrete, Conrad Lee, Calvin Beals, Shawn Bising, William Gutierrez, Jay Block, Patti Burns, Dick Erlanger, Jeffrey Page, Al Hunt, Tracey Testa, Mark Young, and Lori Harding, as well as Betsy Brown and her associates at McGraw-Hill.

The Guide to
Executive Recruiters

Background
of the Recruiting
Industry

When you begin your job campaign, you must investigate, follow up, and exploit every opportunity available. The recruiting industry is one of the best ways to uncover a hidden job opportunity. Jay Block, a Certified Résumé Professional, said the role of recruiting will increase as administrative support is decreased in companies and it's no longer practical to advertise for a position. What is a recruiter? You may know them as executive recruiters, professional recruiters, executive search consultants, or headhunters. Whatever you call them, recruiters are people who are paid to fill positions.

Search firms are categorized according to their fee arrangement with the client company as being either retainer-based or contingency-based. Retained search firms are paid in advance by a client company to find someone to fill a position. Generally, the position is for a candidate earning $75,000 per year or higher. The search firm receives from 20 to 35 percent of that position's first-year salary as an up-front fee to find a candidate. The recruiter is paid whether a successful placement is made or not. Generally, a successful placement is made unless the position requirements are very narrow. In this sense a retainer-based firm is like an employee: someone hired to perform a specific function. A retained firm is usually exclusive in searching to fill a given position. In contrast, a contingency firm may be one of two or three firms trying to fill a position.

Contingency firms search to fill positions paying from the high teens to over $100,000. They are more likely than retained firms to work with less specialized placements, such as sales staff, accounting and finance, or engineering disciplines, but this category is by no means restrictive. Contingency firms are paid by the client company, generally 20 percent of the first-year salary. They are paid only when the position has been successfully filled by the search firm. Suppose two different contingency firms are trying to fill a controller position. Each may send three candidates to be interviewed and of the six, one may be hired. The firm whose candidate was not selected receives no compensation.

The contingency firm may even market strong candidates to companies where no formal search has been undertaken. For this reason you will achieve greater success soliciting a contingency firm over a retained firm. However, *both* are worth contacting as a potential opportunity.

There are thousands of recruiters across the country specializing in just about every imaginable industry and discipline. In fact, there are many added and subtracted to this list each year. This directory lists 6860 firms, with about one-third classified as generalists. Generalists will conduct searches in a variety of disciplines and industries. Other firms are dedicated to specific specialties, like law, engineering, healthcare, etc. One important thing to remember is potential crossovers between industries and disciplines. Suppose you work in finance. If you are currently an analyst for an HMO, you should contact finance, accounting, banking, healthcare, and generalist recruiters. That is a lot of contacts, and recruiters are already inundated with unsolicited résumés and phone inquiries. But, nearly every recruiter interviewed for this guide conceded it is in the job seeker's best interest to try everything and contact as many people as possible.

Here is a simplified overview of the recruiting process. First, the search firm receives a job order from a client company. If it is a retained search, then the firm receives its fee in advance to try to fill the position. If it is a contingency search, then the firm enters into an agreement with a client company that if it provides a candidate selected for hire, the search firm is paid a predetermined fee.

To find a candidate, the search firm will first research its database for a potential match. This is where the term *head-hunting* comes from. For example, if Pepsico is seeking a new vice president of marketing with a specific program in mind, the recruiter may seek out the marketing people in charge of a similarly successful program, perhaps from General Electric, Nike, or some other well-known company.

If that method is ineffective, the firm may place an advertisement for the position. That ad may be in a local paper, a national paper like *The Wall Street Journal*, trade journals, an on-line service (especially for technical disciplines), or other sources.

Once the firm finds a potential candidate, the recruiter will interview him or her and sometimes do a preliminary reference check. The recruiter will set up an interview and coach the candidate prior to the meeting. If the interview is successful, the recruiter will negotiate with both sides for the compensation terms. If a hire is made, the recruiter will generally guarantee its success for some period of time, usually a few months to a year. If the hire doesn't work out, the firm will replace that hire at no charge.

Recruiters place from small locales to an international scope. Should you contact every recruiter in the book for your research? No. An approach that most recruiters agreed on is to contact all recruiters that specialize in your specific industry or discipline on a national basis, and all generalists and specialists within your local area. It is important to contact all recruiters nationally that specialize in your area of expertise because they are the most likely to have a job order that will be a potential match for you. For example, if your field is engineering, contacting all firms with that recruiting specialty will likely yield more opportunities than contacting firms that specialize in accounting or sales. However, contacting the generalists nationally may be worth your while, too.

It is also to your advantage to contact *all* recruiters in your geographic area. From time to time recruiters that specialize in one or two disciplines or industries will have repeat business from clients. A client may mention another position needed outside the recruiting firm's specialty that the recruiter should keep in mind. The recruiters interviewed did say this was rare, but the possibility of uncovering a local opportunity or gaining some inside advice is certainly worth the effort. Even though this strategy may cause some of them to get an increased number of solicitations from prospective job seekers, they all agreed you should invest the time to call everyone possible.

2

Working with Recruiters

USING THE DIRECTORY TO CONTACT RECRUITERS

Once you have decided that contacting recruiters will help your job search (and presumably you have by purchasing this book), you must decide who should be contacted and how. This user-friendly guide, containing thousands of firms, will help you make that decision. The firms are listed alphabetically by location (state and city). They are then cross-referenced by their recruiting specialty, specific industry, or discipline. Though in the past recruiting was presumed to be for senior-level professionals, you will notice the minimum salary level for placements ranges from about $20,000 per year to the level of the chairman of the board. All of the firms listed are fee-paid by the employer; there are no career marketing firms listed here. There are some temporary placement firms listed, primarily in professional disciplines like accounting or MIS.

Who should you contact, and how? First we'll go over who to contact. Any given search firm may have between two and fifteen searches concurrently, depending on the size of the firm. However, contacting 7000 firms is

unrealistic, and unnecessary. Determine if you have a geographic require-
ment. If you live in Cincinnati and are determined to stay there, contact
every recruiter in that metropolitan area. Though a recruiter specializing in
MIS will not be able to match you to a current search if your field is consumer products packaging, you may pick up a networking tip or hit the low
percentage chance that the firm is searching out of its specialty. Next, contact
most of the recruiters in Ohio, especially those in Cleveland, Lexington, and
Louisville (KY). Concentrate on those recruiters specializing in your industry
or discipline and on the generalists. Finally, review the firms listed in the
cross-reference index by industry at the back of this book under consumer
products, packaging, or anything else you see that relates to your experience,
and contact all firms in the country in those categories. You will notice many
different specialties, and that about a third of the firms listed classify them-
selves as generalists. Be analytical when examining recruiting specialties. They
come in a variety of disciplines and industries, which differ. Generally, a func-
tional specialty, like accounting, can span all industries. However, an industry
like banking can reflect many disciplines in banking, like marketing, portfolio
analysis, sales, loan specialists, MIS, or any other discipline.

Now, how do you contact the recruiters? You have two options. You can
send a general unsolicited letter or you can call them. I interviewed many
different recruiters and industry specialists and asked them what the
thought was the most effective method *for the job seeker—you*. Every o'
conceded that an *initial phone call* was the best method. Even though tak'
additional phone calls means more work for the recruiters, just about ev
one felt it was the most productive means for the prospective candidate.

Recruiters have a vested interest in finding out if you are a potenti;
didate. They will need a résumé eventually, so when the time is righ
one ready and send it. Another advantage of calling first is the
industry or local insight you may gain. If you send out 500 résu;
few will be responded to and you will have gained nothing from
did not respond. If you call, your odds are the same and you may
mation which could be a good lead. A recruiter may not have
which you are matched but may know another recruiter who (
offer an inside industry tip.

THE CALL

When you are ready to call, have a one-minute backg
pared that is concise and clear but not too narrow in scop
appear marketable and professional. Smile (even on the
astic and act positive, relax, and above all approach it
tion. A relaxed, conversational tone can be achieved i'

you are talking about and well prepared. Shawn Bising, a generalist recruiter interviewed, says that candidates should be conscious of how they talk on the phone. "Do not be pushy," she cautions, "and above all else, make the recruiter like you."

The recruiter will want to hear about specific qualities early in the conversation so that he or she can make a decision about working with you quickly. Approach all calls with the same vigor and enthusiasm. Remember, you are calling to discuss yourself—a subject on which you should be well-informed, confident, and enthusiastic. To prepare for the initial description of yourself, you will need to list the best elements of your personality, key accomplishments, special skills, and any other key traits you possess that will create interest on the part of the person hearing this information. Jay Block emphasizes the importance of having a script and adds, "If you don't have a script written out, it should at the very least be clear in your mind."

Here is a sample of the way a successful initial contact should flow. Bob is a prospective candidate with ten years' experience as a controller. He is contacting a recruiter specializing in accounting and finance for the first time:

Recruiter: *(Phone rings) "Hello. Dave Parker's office. May I help you?"*

Bob: *"Hello, my name is Bob Richardson. I hope you can help me. I understand you specialize in the search of professionals in the finance and accounting areas. Is that true?"*

Recruiter: *"Yes. What can I do for you?"*

Bob: *"Mr. Parker, I am currently going through a career transition and would like to ask you a couple of questions about it. Do you have a couple of minutes now?"*

Recruiter: *"Yes, but I only have a couple of minutes. What's your background in, Bob?"*

Bob: *"Thanks. I've been a controller for a paging company for the last six years. Prior to that I worked with Taylor-Hunder in accounting for three years. The paging company I work for has experienced growth of over 30 percent per year and my staff is up to eleven people. Last year our gross revenues were $9 million. Of all our company's regional locations ours achieved the highest profit margin, lowest receivables, and highest sales in the country. Part of that was due to the sales staff's ability to take me on necessary sales calls and require a 24-hour return call policy for both the finance department and all customer service people, who also report to me. My financial skills are solid, and I also have good field experience with sales and resolving customer service problems. My company appears to be a*

takeover target. What do you think of the local market based on your business and exposure to other companies?"

Recruiter: *"Well, we've seen fair movement in the last year. Things have definitely gotten stronger the last year or two. Our business has gotten stronger in the last year or so too. A couple of years ago we were even placing a few temporary positions because some of our clients were not ready to hire permanent people. Now we have several searches from staff accountants to a CFO position with a growing healthcare firm. Do you have a résumé prepared?"*

Bob: *"Yes. Would you like to see it?"*

Recruiter: *"Yes. Drop it in the mail or fax it over. I'd like to take a look at it. I don't know if we have anything now, but I'd like to see your résumé and maybe talk more."*

Bob: *"Okay. I am assuming this will be confidential. I'll put it in the mail this week, and give you a call next week to talk in more detail. Thanks for the talk, Dave."*

You can see from this call that early in the conversation the recruiter will take control and ask a couple of qualifying questions. At this point or in the follow-up phone call, ask the recruiter what you can expect in this process. Shawn Bising feels the candidate should know what to expect. By asking this the candidate is leaving little to question. If a recruiter has a problem with this question (asked nicely and professionally), then you will know not to expect too much from this contact. The recruiter will then let you continue, and ask for your résumé, or he or she may not be able to help you, but hopefully refer you to a colleague who can.

THE RÉSUMÉ

Much has been written about résumés. The comments here are a summation of the views of many recruiters on how to make initial contacts and what the content should be. Should you write first? The drawback of writing first is that it's difficult to customize the letter/résumé and then you're categorized as another unsolicited résumé. One recruiter interviewed for this book, who has a two-person office in Florida, said he receives over 75 unsolicited résumés a day! Certainly yours should reflect a previous contact and remind the recruiter that this is requested information.

There are different opinions on which is better, the résumé and cover letter or the broadcast/résumé letter. The broadcast/résumé letter is résumé information presented in letter form, allowing you to explain your background, qualifications, and aspirations on one page. It is also designed to whet the reader's appetite, without giving detailed information that might eliminate you from consideration before you ever get the interview.

Most recruiters prefer the conventional résumé and cover letter. Why? Because they're going to need it anyway. One recruiter said, "It just adds an extra step in the process and wastes time."

Lawrence LoPrete, president of Kenmore Executives Inc., had this to say about résumés:

> *The potential employer or recruiter is looking for someone to fill a certain position. People have to direct a résumé to what they're looking for, not what they did. They have to recognize what they have to put in a résumé to achieve their objectives and what the reader is looking for.*

Now let's assume you have an interview set up through a recruiter. The recruiter will set up the appointment and likely prep you for it. Whatever you do, be relaxed and confident. You're there to sell yourself, so don't be passive or unprepared. Whatever happens, walk out of that interview knowing you did the best job you could presenting yourself. If you are really interested in the position you are interviewing for, tell that to the interviewer and ask if you can meet any other key or necessary people in the organization. And above all, *close the sale* before you leave.

Job hunting is never simple, but having good tools to work with can make it easier and more rewarding. Recruiters play a vital role in successful career management. You will surely be conducting a more comprehensive and ultimately more successful job search to reach your next level when you use this guide.

Executive Recruiter Directory

Alphabetic Listing by State and City

A L A B A M A

ANNISTON

Search South, Inc.
P.O. Box 2224
Anniston, AL 36202
(205) 820-7268
Contact: Arthur Young
Minimum Salary Placed: $30,000
Recruiting Specialty: General

Scott Watson & Associates, Inc.
P.O. Box 1307
Anniston, AL 36202
(205) 237-5020
Contact: Mr. Scott Watson
Minimum Salary Placed: $40,000
Recruiting Specialty: Banking and finance

BIRMINGHAM

JR Adams and Associates
3000 Riverchase Galleria, Suite 800
Birmingham, AL 35244
(205) 985-3116
Contact: Jerry Adams
Minimum Salary Placed: $25,000
Recruiting Specialty: General

Blanton & Company
P.O. Box 94041
Birmingham, AL 35220
(205) 836-3063
Contact: Ms. Julia Blanton
Minimum Salary Placed: $50,000
Recruiting Specialty: General

Dunhill Personnel
2738 South 18th Street
Birmingham, AL 35209
(205) 877-4580
Contact: Ms. Peggy Clarke
Minimum Salary Placed: $25,000
Recruiting Specialty: General

General Personnel Corporation
616 Gadsen Highway, Suite B
Birmingham, AL 35235
(205) 833-3467
Contact: Jim Gilbert
Minimum Salary Placed: $30,000
Recruiting Specialty: General

Langford Search
2025 3rd Avenue North
Birmingham, AL 35203
(205) 328-5477
Contact: Ann Langford
Minimum Salary Placed: $20,000
Recruiting Specialty: General

Management Recruiters
101 Carnoustie
Birmingham, AL 35242
(205) 871-3550
Contact: Mr. Glenn Estess
Minimum Salary Placed: $25,000
Recruiting Specialty: General

McJunkin Group, Inc.
P.O. Box 19649
Birmingham, AL 35226
(205) 942-7611
Contact: Ms. JoAnn McJunkin
Minimum Salary Placed: $25,000
Recruiting Specialty: Engineering

Personnel World, Inc.
3125 Montgomery Highway, Suite 119
Birmingham, AL 35209
(205) 870-5862
Contact: Dee Dee Sullivan
Recruiting Specialty: Office support

RHS Associates, Inc.
1 Perimeter Park South, Suite 400-N
Birmingham, AL 35243
(205) 969-1099
Contact: Mr. Russell Stanley
Minimum Salary Placed: $35,000
Recruiting Specialty: General

Robert Half and Associates
600 Luckie Drive
Birmingham, AL 35223
(205) 879-8889
Contact: C. Sigler
Minimum Salary Placed: $25,000
Recruiting Specialty: Finance and ac-
counting

Sales Consultants
2 Office Park Circle, Suite 106
Birmingham, AL 35223
(205) 871-1128
Contact: Mr. Glenn Estess
Minimum Salary Placed: $20,000
Recruiting Specialty: Sales

J.L. Small & Associates
P.O. Box 157
Birmingham, AL 35201
(205) 252-9933
Contact: Mr. James Small
Minimum Salary Placed: $30,000
Recruiting Specialty: General

Snelling Personnel
200 Vestavia Parkway, Suite 221
Birmingham, AL 35216
(205) 822-7878
Contact: Ms. Joanna Bosko
Minimum Salary Placed: $20,000
Recruiting Specialty: General

Trace Associates
2678 Altadena Road
Birmingham, AL 35243
(205) 967-5927
Contact: Mr. Robert McArdle
Minimum Salary Placed: $35,000
Recruiting Specialty: Communications

DAPHNE

Millman Search Group, Inc.
28651 U.S. Highway 98, Suite A5
Daphne, AL 36526
(334) 626-5513
Contact: Ms. Cheryl Kamitz
Minimum Salary Placed: $20,000
Recruiting Specialty: Retailing

DECATUR

Professional Search Associates, Inc.
P.O. 1108
Decatur, AL 35602
(205) 355-0315
Contact: Mr. John Hilburn
Minimum Salary Placed: $30,000
Recruiting Specialty: Manufacturing

ENTERPRISE

Merritt Enterprise
111 College Plaza
Enterprise, AL 36330
(334) 393-4502
Contact: Mr. R. Merritt
Minimum Salary Placed: $25,000
Recruiting Specialty: General

HOMEWOOD

VIP Personnel, Inc.
478 Palisades Boulevard
Homewood, AL 35244
(205) 879-8889
Contact: Ms. Bonnie Wainwright
Recruiting Specialty: Office support

HUNTSVILLE

Fortune Personnel Consultants
3311 Bob Wallace Avenue, Suite 204
Huntsville, AL 35805
(205) 534-7282
Contact: Mr. Robert Langford
Minimum Salary Placed: $30,000
Recruiting Specialty: General

Information Technology Services
P.O. Box 7107
Huntsville, AL 35807
(205) 533-9800
Contact: Mr. Robert Taylor
Minimum Salary Placed: $25,000
Recruiting Specialty: Data processing

Personnel Inc.
P.O. Box 1413
Huntsville, AL 35807
(205) 536-4431
Contact: Mr. Bill Breen
Minimum Salary Placed: $25,000
Recruiting Specialty: Technical disciplines and engineering

Snelling and Snelling
1813 University Drive NW
Huntsville, AL 35801
(205) 533-1410
Contact: George Barnes
Minimum Salary Placed: $20,000
Recruiting Specialty: General

MOBILE

Clark Personnel Service
4315 Downtowner Loop North
Mobile, AL 36609
(334) 342-5511
Contact: Ms. Donna Clark
Minimum Salary Placed: $25,000
Recruiting Specialty: General

Cornelius and Associates
4555 Cindy Drive
Mobile, AL 36619
(334) 666-3505
Minimum Salary Placed: $25,000
Recruiting Specialty: General

Hughes and Associates
3737 Government Boulevard, Suite 304B
Mobile, AL 36693
(334) 661-8888
Contact: Mr. Tim Hughes
Minimum Salary Placed: $25,000
Recruiting Specialty: Engineering, pulp and paper and chemicals

Management Recruiters
3263 Demetropolis Road, Suite 6C
Mobile, AL 36693
(334) 602-0104
Contact: Mr. Rufus Brock
Minimum Salary Placed: $25,000
Recruiting Specialty: Engineering, nurses and MIS

Snelling Temporaries
3100 Cottage Hill Road, Suite 113
Mobile, AL 36606
(205) 473-1001
Contact: Mr. G. Huth
Recruiting Specialty: Office support

MONTGOMERY

Job Referrals
3606 Debby Drive
Montgomery, AL 36111
(334) 288-2080
Contact: Mr. C. Jones
Recruiting Specialty: General

Locke & Associates
4144 Carmichael Road, Suite 20
Montgomery, AL 36106
(334) 272-7400
Contact: Mr. Glen Pruitt
Minimum Salary Placed: $50,000
Recruiting Specialty: General

Murkett Associates
1653 S. Perry Street
Montgomery, AL 36101
(334) 265-5531
Contact: Mr. Philip Murkett
Minimum Salary Placed: $35,000
Recruiting Specialty: General

Snelling Personnel
3001 Zelda Road
Montgomery, AL 36106
(334) 270-0100
Contact: Mr. W. Mahoney
Minimum Salary Placed: $25,000
Recruiting Specialty: General

MOUNTAIN BROOK

Sawyer, Simril and Associates
3248 Overton Road
Mountain Brook, AL 35223
(205) 967-8865
Minimum Salary Placed: $25,000
Recruiting Specialty: General

NORTHPORT

Mary Cheek and Associates
11991 Knollwood Road
Northport, AL 35476
(205) 333-8550
Contact: Ms. Mary Cheek
Minimum Salary Placed: $30,000
Recruiting Specialty: Engineering, manufacturing and automotive

A L A S K A

ANCHORAGE

Alaska Executive Search
821 N. Street, Suite 204
Anchorage, AK 99501
(907) 276-5707
Contact: Mr. Robert Bulmer
Minimum Salary Placed: $25,000
Recruiting Specialty: General

Growth Company
2221 Northern Lights Boulevard,
  Suite 107
Anchorage, AK 99508
(907) 276-4769
Contact: Ms. Lynn Curry-Swann
Minimum Salary Placed: $25,000
Recruiting Specialty: General

Personnel Plus Employment Agency
701 E. Tudor Road, Suite 160
Anchorage, AK 99503
(907) 563-7587
Contact: Ms. C. Schebler
Minimum Salary Placed: $25,000
Recruiting Specialty: General

A R I Z O N A

CHANDLER

Electronic Power Source
1507 W. Loughlin Drive
Chandler, AZ 85224
(602) 821-1946
Contact: Mr. Gary Moore
Minimum Salary Placed: $25,000
Recruiting Specialty: Technical disciplines in power supplies and analog design

GLENDALE

Elliot Associates, Inc.
5227 W. Acapulco Lane
Glendale, AZ 85306
(602) 978-0218
Contact: Ms. Libby Gordon
Minimum Salary Placed: $15,000
Recruiting Specialty: Hospitality

GREEN VALLEY

Gaudette & Company
980 W. Paseo Del Cilantro
Green Valley, AZ 85614
(602) 648-1963
Contact: Mr. Charles Gaudette
Minimum Salary Placed: $40,000
Recruiting Specialty: Insurance and Finance in Healthcare

Holden and Associates
P.O. Box 1317
Green Valley, AZ 85622
(602) 648-3624
Contact: Mr. Dan Zelenkin
Minimum Salary Placed: $20,000
Recruiting Specialty: Sales and engineering

LAKE HAVASU CITY

Search by Design
P.O. Box 3316
Lake Havasu, AZ 85405
(520) 855-2121
Contact: Mr. Dayton VanSlyke
Recruiting Specialty: Building products - wood, pulp, and paper

MESA

Paul Dicken Associates
1930 S. Alma School Road, Suite D-207
Mesa, AZ 85210
(602) 345-2036
Contact: Mr. James Hoefer
Recruiting Specialty: Technical, electronics, and full service temporary

Robert Half Accountemps
1811 South Alma School Road, Suite 205
Mesa, AZ 85210
(602) 820-4641
Contact: Mr. Aylward
Minimum Salary Placed: $20,000
Recruiting Specialty: Accounting and finance

World Wide Executive Search
Westcoast Hospitality Search
1839 S. Alma School Road, Suite 115
Mesa, AZ 85210
(602) 491-3737
Contact: Mr. Jim Gunther
Recruiting Specialty: Hospitality, sales, marketing, accounting, retail, and human resources

NOGALES

Management Recruiters
235 N. Freeport Drive, Suite 6
Nogales, AZ 85621
(520) 281-9440
Contact: Mr. Joseph Garcia
Minimum Salary Placed: $60,000
Recruiting Specialty: Recruiting for positions in Mexico

PHOENIX

Accountants Executive Search
2111 East Highland Avenue, Suite D420
Phoenix, AZ 85016
(602) 957-1400
Contact: Mr. Stu Libes
Minimum Salary Placed: $30,000
Recruiting Specialty: Accounting

Accountants On Call
Park One, Suite B-360
Phoenix, AZ 85016
(602) 957-1200
Contact: Mr. John Kuzmick
Recruiting Specialty: Accounting and
bookkeeping

Accountemps
100 W. Clarendon Avenue, Suite 1150
Phoenix, AZ 85013
(602) 265-5455
Contact: Ms. K. Norris
Minimum Salary Placed: $20,000
Recruiting Specialty: Accounting and
bookkeeping

**Accounting & Bookkeeping Personnel,
Inc.**
1702 E. Highland Avenue, Suite 200
Phoenix, AZ 85016
(602) 277-3700
Contact: Mr. Michael Nolan
Minimum Salary Placed: $15,000
Recruiting Specialty: Accounting and
bookkeeping

Asosa Personnel
8027 North Black Canyon Highway,
  Suite 402
Phoenix, AZ 85021
(602) 246-7024
Contact: Ms. Katie McCauley
Minimum Salary Placed: $20,000
Recruiting Specialty: General

B&B Employment
7250 N. 16th Street
Phoenix, AZ 85020
(602) 277-3381
Contact: Mr. Paul Smith
Recruiting Specialty: General, property
management

Career Transition Center
2910 E. Camelback Road, Suite 230
Phoenix, AZ 85016
(602) 955-7002
Contact: Mr. Richard Davis
Minimum Salary Placed: $20,000
Recruiting Specialty: General

Catalina Professional
7600 N. 15th Street, Suite 210
Phoenix, AZ 85020
(602) 331-1655
Contact: Ms. Joan Pearson
Minimum Salary Placed: $60,000
Recruiting Specialty: Physicians

Cizek Associates, Inc.
2390 E. Camelback Road, Suite 300
Phoenix, AZ 85016
(602) 553-1066
Contact: Ms. Marti Cizek
Minimum Salary Placed: $60,000
Recruiting Specialty: General

Clifford & Associates
16042 N. 32nd Street, Suite D-18
Phoenix, AZ 85032
(602) 992-1477
Contact: Mr. Dennis Clifford
Recruiting Specialty: Automotive

Douglas, Richmond & Grice
3002 E. Weldon
Phoenix, AZ 85016
(602) 955-8230
Contact: Mr. Ron Sampson
Recruiting Specialty: Sales, marketing
and MIS

Duffy Research
610 E. Bell Road
Phoenix, AZ 85022
(602) 942-7112

Contact: Ms. Kathleen Duffy
Minimum Salary Placed: $20,000
Recruiting Specialty: General

Executemp Southwest
7330 N. 16th Street, Suite C117
Phoenix, AZ 85020
(602) 861-1200
Contact: Ms. Rose Skladowski
Minimum Salary Placed: $35,000
Recruiting Specialty: Financial services,
real estate, medical and data processing

Finance Support
2198 E. Camelback Road, Suite 348
Phoenix, AZ 85016
(602) 553-0833
Contact: Ms. Robin Bumgarner
Minimum Salary Placed: $20,000
Recruiting Specialty: Credit, collections,
and customer service

Fishel HR Associates
5125 N 16th Street, Suite D125
Phoenix, AZ 85016
(602) 604-6100
Contact: Richard Fishel
Minimum Salary Placed: $40,000
Recruiting Specialty: Human resource,
engineering, accounting, and management

Harris Kovacs Alderman
4636 E. University Drive, Suite 105
Phoenix, AZ 85034
(602) 894-8440
Contact: Mr. B. Evans
Minimum Salary Placed: $75,000
Recruiting Specialty: Physicians

Phyllis Hawkins & Associates, Inc.
3550 N. Central Avenue, Suite 1400
Phoenix, AZ 85012
(602) 263-0248
Contact: Ms. Phyllis Hawkins
Minimum Salary Placed: $50,000
Recruiting Specialty: Attorneys and physi-
cians

Health Search USA
7220 E. 16th Street, Suite F
Phoenix, AZ 85020
(602) 921-0705
Contact: Ms. P. Owens
Minimum Salary Placed: $20,000
Recruiting Specialty: Healthcare

Health Staffing Alternatives
706 E. Bell Road, Suite 116
Phoenix, AZ 85022
(602) 788-1700
Contact: Ms. Marcia Davis
Recruiting Specialty: Medical and clerical

Intersource, LTD
515 Carefree Highway, P.O. Box
  42033-138
Phoenix, AZ 85080
(602) 780-4540
Contact: Ms. Belinda Jones
Recruiting Specialty: Finance, audit, accounting, and human resources

A.T. Kearney Executive Search
2141 E. Highland, Suite 135
Phoenix, AZ 85016
(602) 994-3032
Contact: Ms. Jill Faber
Minimum Salary Placed: $60,000
Recruiting Specialty: General

Key Personnel
1600 W. Camelback, Suite 1K
Phoenix, AZ 85015
(602) 263-8356
Contact: Ms. Phyllis Regnier
Recruiting Specialty: General

McDonald Ledterman Executive Search
2425 E. Camelback Road, Suite 375
Phoenix, AZ 85016
(602) 955-2733
Contact: Mr. John McDonald
Minimum Salary Placed: $50,000
Recruiting Specialty: Technical disciplines in high technology

O'Connor & Associates
12601 N. Cave Creek, Suite 109
Phoenix, AZ 85022
(602) 788-5890
Contact: Mr. Kevin O'Connor
Recruiting Specialty: Automotive

PDS Technical Services
3737 E. Bonanza Way, Suite 100
Phoenix, AZ 85034
(602) 231-0026
Contact: Ms. Mari Hellriegel
Recruiting Specialty: Aircraft, manufacturing, semiconductor, municipalities, and electronics

Perfect Match Personnel
5080 N. 40th Street, Suite 360
Phoenix, AZ 85018
(602) 952-2065
Contact: Ms. Susan Thomas
Recruiting Specialty: Office and clerical, support and administrative

Personalized Management Assoc.
One East Camelback, Suite 550
Phoenix, AZ 85012
(602) 222-9499
Contact: Mr. Dave Hottle
Recruiting Specialty: Retail, restaurant, and sales management

Professionals Placement Inc./Pro Tem
3900 E. Camelback, Suite 500
Phoenix, AZ 85018
(602) 955-0870
Contact: Mr. Jeff Seifert
Recruiting Specialty: Office, accounting, sales, and technical

Professional Search
4250 E Camelback Road, Suite 156K
Phoenix, AZ 85018
(602) 952-2500
Contact: Ms. J. Beauvais
Minimum Salary Placed: $20,000
Recruiting Specialty: Data processing

Roberts & Michaels International
3875 N. 44th Street, Suite 300
Phoenix, AZ 85018-5435
(602) 808-5510
Contact: Mr. Bob Schurman
Recruiting Specialty: Human resources, attorneys, and accountants

SS & A Executive Search Consultants
4350 E. Camelback Road, Suite B200
Phoenix, AZ 85018
(602) 998-1744
Contact: Ms. Susan Shultz
Minimum Salary Placed: $40,000
Recruiting Specialty: General

Source Services
5343 N. 16th Street, Suite 270
Phoenix, AZ 85016
(602) 230-0220
Minimum Salary Placed: $25,000
Recruiting Specialty: Computers

Southland Group
3218 East Bell Road, Suite 220
Phoenix, AZ 85032
(602) 581-6633
Contact: Mr. Scott Grant
Minimum Salary Placed: $30,000
Recruiting Specialty: Healthcare

Squaw Peak Personnel
5151 N. 16th Street, Suite 234
Phoenix, AZ 85020
(602) 279-5662
Contact: Ms. Sue B. Morton
Recruiting Specialty: Legal

Staffing Solutions
1181 N. Tatum Boulevard, Suite 3051
Phoenix, AZ 85028
(602) 953-1969
Contact: Ms. Debbie DeWitt
Recruiting Specialty: Insurance and medical, some general

Linda J. Staneck & Associates
4537 N. 106th Drive
Phoenix, AZ 85037
(602) 877-9601
Contact: Ms. Lin Staneck
Recruiting Specialty: Consulting engineers, architects, and environmental

Technical Search Service
2425 E. Camelback Road
Phoenix, AZ 85016
(602) 955-7000

Minimum Salary Placed: $25,000
Recruiting Specialty: Technical disciplines

Universal Search
1944 W. Thunderbird Road, Suite 5
Phoenix, AZ 85022
(602) 863-0037
Contact: Mr. M. Shunk
Minimum Salary Placed: $20,000
Recruiting Specialty: High technology engineering

Ward Howell International, Inc.
2525 E. Arizona Biltmore Circle,
  Suite 124
Phoenix, AZ 85016
(602) 955-3800
Contact: Mr. Vance Howe
Minimum Salary Placed: $75,000
Recruiting Specialty: General

Western Connections Limited
802 E. Brook Hollow Drive
Phoenix, AZ 85022
(602) 375-9272
Contact: Mr. S. Cannon
Minimum Salary Placed: $20,000
Recruiting Specialty: General

Western Staff Services
202 E. Earle, Suite 175
Phoenix, AZ 85012
(602) 264-3928
Minimum Salary Placed: $18,000
Recruiting Specialty: General

Donald Williams Associates, Inc.
4350 E. Camelback Road, Suite 140E
Phoenix, AZ 85018
(602) 952-8620
Minimum Salary Placed: $200,000
Recruiting Specialty: General

Witt/Kieffer, Ford, Hadelman & Lloyd
432 N. 44th Street, Suite 360
Phoenix, AZ 85008
(602) 267-1370
Contact: Mr. Michael Meyer
Minimum Salary Placed: $75,000
Recruiting Specialty: General

SCOTTSDALE

Austin Michaels Limited
8687 East Via De Ventura, Suite 303
Scottsdale, AZ 85258
(602) 483-5000
Contact: Mr. Frank O'Brien
Minimum Salary Placed: $30,000
Recruiting Specialty: Electronics and computers

BJB Medical Association
10245 E. Via Linda
Scottsdale, AZ 85258
(602) 451-0922
Contact: Mr. B. Biagini
Minimum Salary Placed: $20,000
Recruiting Specialty: Healthcare

Bartholdi & Company, Inc.
8260 E. Raintree Drive, Suite 212
Scottsdale, AZ 85260
(602) 502-2178
Contact: Mr. Theodore Bartholdi
Minimum Salary Placed: $70,000
Recruiting Specialty: General

The Bren Group
7320 E. Shoeman Lane
Scottsdale, AZ 85251
(602) 970-1091

Contact: Ms. Brenda Rowenhorst
Minimum Salary Placed: $25,000
Recruiting Specialty: Hospitality and entertainment

Dynamic Computer Consultants, Inc.
6390-1 E. Thomas Road, Suite 210
Scottsdale, AZ 85251
(602) 990-8179
Contact: Mr. Roc Rogers
Recruiting Specialty: Data processing, midrange, and computers

EFL International
8777 E. Via De Ventura, Suite 330
Scottsdale, AZ 85258
(602) 483-0496
Contact: Mr. William Franquemont
Minimum Salary Placed: $50,000
Recruiting Specialty: General

Energetix
8655 E. Via De Ventura, Suite 209
Scottsdale, AZ 85250
(602) 922-9522
Contact: Ms. Mary Jo Fraipont
Recruiting Specialty: Software professionals

R.E. Foley and Company
12215 N. 60th Street
Scottsdale, AZ 85254
(602) 991-7771
Contact: Mr. Rich Foley
Minimum Salary Placed: $30,000
Recruiting Specialty: Public accounting

Lynn Greenburg Associates Inc.
9067 East Evans Drive
Scottsdale, AZ 85260
(602) 391-9074

Contact: Ms. Lynn Greenburg
Minimum Salary Placed: $50,000
Recruiting Specialty: Scientists in pharmaceuticals and biotechnology

Halden & Associates
8711 E. Pinnacle Peak Road, Box 328
Scottsdale, AZ 85255
(602) 488-9634
Contact: Mr. Kermit Halden
Minimum Salary Placed: $50,000
Recruiting Specialty: Wholesale, retail and hospitality

Christopher J. Hoffman Associates, Inc.
5833 E. Sandra Terrace
Scottsdale, AZ 85254-1299
(602) 971-4628
Contact: Mr. Chris Hoffman
Recruiting Specialty: Chemical industry - distribution and logistics

Jackson & Coker
6609 N. Scottsdale, Road Suite 102
Scottsdale, AZ 85250
(800) 638-7335
Contact: Mr. Paul Byerlein
Minimum Salary Placed: $60,000
Recruiting Specialty: Physicians

LCC Company
7975 N. Hayden, Suite D290
Scottsdale, AZ 85258
(602) 483-5660
Contact: Ms. Cheryl DeBerry
Recruiting Specialty: Information systems

Lappe and Associates
8202 North 53rd Street
Scottsdale, AZ 85253
(602) 991-3321

Contact: Mr. Mark Lappe
Minimum Salary Placed: $80,000
Recruiting Specialty: High technology

Reynolds Lebus Associates
P.O. Box 9177
Scottsdale, AZ 85252
(602) 946-6929
Contact: Mr. Reynolds Lebus
Minimum Salary Placed: $30,000
Recruiting Specialty: Product and marketing managers in consumer products

Management Recruiters
6900 E. Camelback Road, Suite 935
Scottsdale, AZ 85251
(602) 941-1515
Contact: Mr. Dick Govig
Minimum Salary Placed: $20,000
Recruiting Specialty: General

Len Oppenheimer and Associates
8626 E. Mackenzie Drive
Scottsdale, AZ 85251
(602) 990-1220
Contact: Mr. Len Oppenheimer
Minimum Salary Placed: $20,000
Recruiting Specialty: General

The Phoenix Health Search Group
8300 N. Hayden Road, Suite 207
Scottsdale, AZ 85258
(602) 443-4994
Contact: Mr. Gregory Erstling
Minimum Salary Placed: $35,000
Recruiting Specialty: Healthcare

Power Source Systems Inc.
14700 N. Airport Drive, Suite 202
Scottsdale, AZ 85260
(602) 951-6212

Contact: Mr. D. Miller
Minimum Salary Placed: $20,000
Recruiting Specialty: Mining, cement and chemicals

Rand-Curtis Resources
8507 N. Farview Drive
Scottsdale, AZ 85258
(602) 948-5400
Contact: Ms. Judy Kapulos
Minimum Salary Placed: $40,000
Recruiting Specialty: General

Roberson & Company
10752 N. 89th Place, Suite 202
Scottsdale, AZ 85260
(602) 391-3200
Contact: Mr. Steve Silvas
Recruiting Specialty: Medical, sales and marketing, finance and accounting, and manufacturing

The Rubicon Group
P.O. Box 2159
Scottsdale, AZ 85252-2159
(602) 423-9280
Contact: Mr. Martin Jacobs
Minimum Salary Placed: $40,000
Recruiting Specialty: Attorneys, engineers, actuaries, and healthcare

Sales Consultants
4300 N. Miller Road, Suite 110
Scottsdale, AZ 85251
(602) 946-1609
Contact: Mr. Albert Britten
Minimum Salary Placed: $25,000
Recruiting Specialty: Sales

Robert Saxon and Associates
7419 E. Onyx Court
Scottsdale, AZ 85258
(602) 991-4460
Contact: Mr. Bob Saxon
Minimum Salary Placed: $20,000
Recruiting Specialty: Data processing

Spectra Professional Search
6991 East Camelback, Suite B-305
Scottsdale, AZ 85251
(602) 481-0411
Contact: Ms. Sybil Goldberg
Minimum Salary Placed: $30,000
Recruiting Specialty: General

Swartz & Associates, Inc.
P.O. Box 14167
Scottsdale, AZ 85267
(602) 998-0363
Contact: Mr. William Swartz
Minimum Salary Placed: $100,000
Recruiting Specialty: General

Susan Swenson & Associates
8502 E. Cholla Street
Scottsdale, AZ 85260
(602) 948-3330
Contact: Ms. Sue Swenson
Recruiting Specialty: Electronics, semiconductor, and automated test equipment

Telesolutions of Arizona, Inc.
8655 E. Via De Ventura
Scottsdale, AZ 85258
(602) 483-1300
Contact: Ms. C. Wichansky
Minimum Salary Placed: $25,000
Recruiting Specialty: Engineering

Torrance Recruiting
P.O. Box 1984
Scottsdale, AZ 85252
(602) 946-9024
Contact: Mr. M. Torrance
Minimum Salary Placed: $20,000
Recruiting Specialty: Printing, ink and paper

VZ International
3080 North Civic Center Plaza, Suite 20
Scottsdale, AZ 85251
(602) 596-1859
Contact: Mr. Bill Van Zanten
Minimum Salary Placed: $50,000
Recruiting Specialty: High technology and semi-conductors

Weinman and Associates
7100 E. McDonald, Suite B6
Scottsdale, AZ 85254
(602) 483-2132
Minimum Salary Placed: $20,000
Recruiting Specialty: Hotels

SEDONA

Search Masters International
500 Foothills South, Suite 2
Sedona, AZ 86336
(602) 282-3553
Contact: Mr. David Jensen
Minimum Salary Placed: $50,000
Recruiting Specialty: Technical disciplines in biotechnology

TEMPE

Confidential Search International
6115 South Kyrene Road, Suite 201
Tempe, AZ 85283
(602) 820-6883
Contact: Mr. M. Catena
Minimum Salary Placed: $20,000
Recruiting Specialty: General

Express Personnel
11 W. Baseline
Tempe, AZ 85283
(602) 413-1200
Contact: Ms. Judy Taylor
Recruiting Specialty: Generalist

Integrated Management Resource
51 W. Elliott, Suite 108
Tempe, AZ 85284
(602) 460-4422
Contact: Mr. B. Franklin
Minimum Salary Placed: $40,000
Recruiting Specialty: Finance

Richard Wayne and Roberts
4625 S. Wendler Drive, Suite 111
Tempe, AZ 85282
(602) 438-1496
Contact: Mr. Mike Coltrane
Minimum Salary Placed: $20,000
Recruiting Specialty: Telecommunications

TAD Resources
125 S. 52nd Street
Tempe, AZ 85280
(602) 267-7254
Contact: Mr. Bryan Patrick
Recruiting Specialty: Computer and software, electronics, aerospace, manufacturing, and automotive

Rice Associates
7670 E. Broadway Boulevard, Suite 106
Tucson, AZ 85710
(520) 298-8989
Contact: Ms. G. Rice
Minimum Salary Placed: $20,000
Recruiting Specialty: Semi-conductors

Robert Half International
1760 E. River Road
Tucson, AZ 85718
(602) 628-8367
Minimum Salary Placed: $20,000
Recruiting Specialty: Accounting and finance

Spectrum Consultants
6879 E. Dorado Court
Tucson, AZ 85715
(520) 721-4304
Contact: Mr. Aram Tootelian
Minimum Salary Placed: $50,000
Recruiting Specialty: High technology

Wien and Associates
655 N. Alvernon Way, Suite 120
Tucson, AZ 85711
(520) 323-3402
Contact: Mr. Terry Wien
Minimum Salary Placed: $30,000
Recruiting Specialty: General

YUMA

Search By Design
P.O. Box 5702
Yuma, AZ 85366
(602) 782-4041
Contact: Mr. Dayton VanSlyke
Minimum Salary Placed: $30,000
Recruiting Specialty: Wood and building products

ARKANSAS

CONWAY

John C. Zopolos and Associates
P.O. Box 386
Conway, AR 72033
(501) 327-2572
Contact: Mr. John Zopolos
Minimum Salary Placed: $25,000
Recruiting Specialty: General

FAYETTEVILLE

Management Recruiters
10121 S. Whitehouse Road
Fayetteville, AR 72701
(501) 643-3305
Contact: Mr. Steven Bulla
Minimum Salary Placed: $20,000
Recruiting Specialty: General

Professional Connections
3358 N. College, Suite 4
Fayetteville, AR 72703
(501) 442-7892
Contact: Ms. Cindy Cope
Minimum Salary Placed: $50,000
Recruiting Specialty: Banking

FORT SMITH

Dunhill Personnel Agency
P.O. Box 6149
Fort Smith, AR 72906
(501) 646-1413
Contact: Mr. Gary Foster
Minimum Salary Placed: $35,000
Recruiting Specialty: Data processing

TUCSON

Accounting & Bookkeeping Personnel, Inc.
4400 E. Broadway, Suite 600
Tucson, AZ 85711
(520) 323-3600
Contact: Mr. Duane Etter
Minimum Salary Placed: $15,000
Recruiting Specialty: Accounting and bookkeeping

Asosa Acustaff
1016 E. Broadway Boulevard
Tucson, AZ 85719
(520) 792-0622
Contact: Mr. P. Payne
Recruiting Specialty: General

Calver Associates, Inc.
7360 N. Yucca Via
Tucson, AZ 85704
(520) 297-8361
Contact: Mr. Jon Calver
Recruiting Specialty: Plastics

Circuit Technology Inc.
610 E. Delano Street
Tucson, AZ 85705
(520) 623-7070
Contact: Mr. R. Greenwald
Minimum Salary Placed: $20,000
Recruiting Specialty: Printed circuit boards

Coburn Scientific Search
3343 E. Glenn
Tucson, AZ 85716
(520) 881-0084
Contact: Ms. Ann Coburn
Minimum Salary Placed: $35,000
Recruiting Specialty: Scientific and technical disciplines

Computer Strategies Inc.
5620 N. Kolb Road, Suite 225
Tucson, AZ 85750
(520) 721-9544
Contact: Ms. Debbie Brodie
Minimum Salary Placed: $20,000
Recruiting Specialty: Computers

CS Associates
P.O. Box 30926
Tucson, AZ 85751
(520) 327-7999
Contact: Mr. Joe Connelly
Minimum Salary Placed: $45,000
Recruiting Specialty: Engineering

Employment Hotline
3210 E. Fort Lowell Road, Suite 110
Tucson, AZ 85716
(520) 795-1907
Contact: Ms. B. McClure
Minimum Salary Placed: $20,000
Recruiting Specialty: General

Industry Consultants, Inc.
5055 E. Broadway
Tucson, AZ 85711
(520) 750-9400
Contact: Mr. Jim Corey
Minimum Salary Placed: $45,000
Recruiting Specialty: Engineers

Medical Executive Search Associat
3250 N. Riverbend Circle East
Tucson, AZ 85715
(520) 885-2552
Contact: Mr. William Piatkiewicz
Minimum Salary Placed: $30,000
Recruiting Specialty: Medical produ

Express Personnel Services
1217 S. Waldron Road
Fort Smith, AR 72903
(501) 452-8925
Contact: Mr. P. Magee
Minimum Salary Placed: $25,000
Recruiting Specialty: Manufacturing

Moore and Associates
5111 Rogers Avenue, Suite 514
Fort Smith, AR 72903
(501) 478-7052
Contact: Mr. Noel Moore
Minimum Salary Placed: $25,000
Recruiting Specialty: All disciplines in
manufacturing

Search Associates
P.O. Box 10703
Fort Smith, AR 72917
(501) 452-0005
Contact: Ms. Jennie Little
Minimum Salary Placed: $20,000
Recruiting Specialty: General

HOT SPRINGS VILLAGE

John Anderson Associates
81 Murillo Lane
Hot Springs Village, AR 71909
(501) 922-5999
Contact: Mr. John Anderson
Minimum Salary Placed: $25,000
Recruiting Specialty: Services and fuel en-
gineering

LITTLE ROCK

Alynco Personnel Agency Inc.
10709 Platte Valley Drive
Little Rock, AR 72212
(501) 221-0066
Contact: Mr. Andy Fausett
Minimum Salary Placed: $30,000
Recruiting Specialty: Distribution logis-
tics

Executive Recruiters Agency, Inc.
14 Office Park Drive, Suite 100
P.O. Box 21810
Little Rock, AR 72221
(501) 224-7000
Contact: Mr. Greg Downs
Minimum Salary Placed: $35,000
Recruiting Specialty: General

Management Recruiters
1701 Centerview Drive, Suite 314
Little Rock, AR 72211
(501) 224-0801
Contact: Mr. Noel Hall
Minimum Salary Placed: $20,000
Recruiting Specialty: General

Rottman Group Inc.
8201 Cantrell Road, Suite 240
Little Rock, AR 72227
(501) 228-4433
Contact: Mr. Dan Rottman
Minimum Salary Placed: $25,000
Recruiting Specialty: Healthcare

**Turnage Employment Service Group,
Inc.**
1225 Breckenridge Drive, Suite 206
Little Rock, AR 72205
(501) 224-6870

Contact: Mr. Tom Symons
Minimum Salary Placed: $25,000
Recruiting Specialty: General

MAUMELLE

Herring and Associates
600 Pine Forrest Drive, Suite 130
Maumelle, AR 72113
(501) 851-1234
Contact: Mr. B. Herring
Minimum Salary Placed: $25,000
Recruiting Specialty: General

MOUNTAIN HOME

Kromenaker & Associates
277 Crestview Drive
Mountain Home, AR 72653
(501) 424-6990
Contact: Mr. Robert Kromenaker
Minimum Salary Placed: $30,000
Recruiting Specialty: Manufacturing

NORTH LITTLE ROCK

Employment World
5111 JFK Boulevard
North Little Rock, AR 72116
(501) 758-7307
Contact: Mr. Wade Althen
Minimum Salary Placed: $25,000
Recruiting Specialty: General

PARAGOULD

Management Recruiters
402 Linwood Drive, Suite 1
Paragould, AR 72450
(501) 236-1800
Contact: Ms. Lawanda Hooten
Minimum Salary Placed: $20,000
Recruiting Specialty: General

ROGERS

Dunhill Personnel
102 N. First Street
P.O. Box 1570
Rogers, AR 72757
(501) 636-8578
Contact: Mr. A. Dwayne Owens
Minimum Salary Placed: $30,000
Recruiting Specialty: Metals and manufacturing

Sales Consultants
1623 S. Dixieland Road
Rogers, AR 72756
(501) 631-4045
Contact: Mr. Daniel Morris
Minimum Salary Placed: $45,000
Recruiting Specialty: Sales

C A L I F O R N I A

AGOURA HILLS

Interstate Recruiters
5126 Clareton Drive
Agoura Hills, CA 91301
(818) 706-3737
Contact: Mr. Richard Alsberry
Minimum Salary Placed: $30,000
Recruiting Specialty: General

Rosenstein Associates
191 Parkview Drive
Agoura Hills, CA 91301
(818) 865-9400
Recruiting Specialty: Medical sales and marketing

F. B. Schmidt International
30423 Canwood Place, Suite 239
Agoura Hills, CA 91301
(818) 706-0500
Contact: Mr. Frank Schmidt
Minimum Salary Placed: $60,000
Recruiting Specialty: Advertising and marketing

Signore Group
5699 Kanan Road, Suite 290
Agoura Hills, CA 91301
(818) 706-3131
Contact: Mr. Tom Signore
Recruiting Specialty: General

United Comtec Service
28310 Roadside Drive
Agoura Hills, CA 91301
(818) 991-2285
Recruiting Specialty: General

ALAMEDA

Deborah Bishop & Associates
1070 Marina Village Parkway, Suite 203
Alameda, CA 94501
(510) 523-2305
Contact: Ms. Deborah Bishop
Minimum Salary Placed: $85,000
Recruiting Specialty: High technology

ALAMO

Alamo Management Group, Inc.
P.O. Box 375
Alamo, CA 94507
(510) 837-4708
Contact: Ms. Jan Robinson
Recruiting Specialty: General

Brody & Associates
P.O. Box 522
Alamo, CA 94507
(510) 838-8898
Contact: Mr. Steve Brody
Minimum Salary Placed: $85,000
Recruiting Specialty: Marketing and advertising in computer software applications

Stuart H. Pike & Associates
2538 Rolling Hills Court
Alamo, CA 94507
(510) 831-9181
Contact: Mr. Stuart Pike
Minimum Salary Placed: $70,000
Recruiting Specialty: Environmental and hazardous waste

ALISO VIEJO

Bakehorm Enterprises, Inc.
27 Santa Clara
Aliso Viejo, CA 92656
(800) 853-1676
Contact: Mr. Thomas Bakehorn
Minimum Salary Placed: $60,000
Recruiting Specialty: Computer, software, telecommunications, and commercial high technology

ANAHEIM

McGladrey & Pullen
222 S. Harbor Boulevard, Suite 800
P.O. Box 200
Anaheim, CA 92815
(714) 520-9561
Contact: Ms. Diane Johnson
Minimum Salary Placed: $30,000
Recruiting Specialty: General

Search Alternatives
P.O. Box 17025
Anaheim, CA 92817
(714) 998-6200
Minimum Salary Placed: $30,000
Recruiting Specialty: Marketing in consumer products

ANAHEIM HILLS

Warring & Associates
5673 Stetson Court
Anaheim Hills, CA 92807
(714) 998-8228
Contact: Mr. J. T. Warring
Minimum Salary Placed: $150,000
Recruiting Specialty: General

ANTIOCH

Parker-Smith Personnel Inc.
23 W. 6th Street
Antioch, CA 94509
(510) 754-9675
Contact: Beverly Sperry-Fernandez
Recruiting Specialty: Office support

APPLE VALLEY

Studwell Associates
P.O. Box 579
Apple Valley, CA 92307
(619) 242-8949
Contact: Ms. Barbara Bowen
Minimum Salary Placed: $50,000
Recruiting Specialty: General

APTOS

Management Recruiters
15 Seascape Village, Suite 15
Aptos, CA 95003
(408) 688-5200
Contact: Ms. Cathy Henderson
Minimum Salary Placed: $30,000
Recruiting Specialty: General

ARCADIA

K & C Associates
290 Oakhurst Lane, Suite A
Arcadia, CA 91007
(818) 445-1961
Contact: Mr. Bob Kuhnmuench
Minimum Salary Placed: $30,000
Recruiting Specialty: Manufacturing and distribution of machinery

AUBURN

Paul Norsell & Associates, Inc.
P.O. Box 6686
Auburn, CA 95604
(916) 269-0121
Contact: Mr. Paul Norsell
Minimum Salary Placed: $100,000
Recruiting Specialty: General

BAKERSFIELD

Careers in Finance
1601 N. Chester, Suite A
Bakersfield, CA 93308
(805) 393-8374
Contact: Mr. S. Florence
Minimum Salary Placed: $25,000
Recruiting Specialty: Finance

Larry Combs Executive Search
4909 Stockdale Highway, Suite 289
Bakersfield, CA 93309
(805) 831-0149
Contact: Mr. Larry Combs
Minimum Salary Placed: $25,000
Recruiting Specialty: General

Rand Personnel
1200 Truxtun Avenue, Suite 130
Bakersfield, CA 93301
(805) 325-0751
Contact: Ms. S. Simrin
Minimum Salary Placed: $25,000
Recruiting Specialty: General

BEAUMONT

Betty Kemp
P.O. Box 3104
Beaumont, CA 92223
(909) 845-6276
Contact: Ms. Betty Kemp
Minimum Salary Placed: $25,000
Recruiting Specialty: Healthcare

BELMONT

The Simmons Group
951-2 Old County Road, Suite 136
Belmont, CA 94002
(415) 592-3775
Contact: Mr. Noel Simmons
Minimum Salary Placed: $50,000
Recruiting Specialty: High technology

Jack Willis and Associates
1281 5th Avenue
Belmont, CA 94002
(415) 654-0620
Contact: Mr. Jack Willis
Recruiting Specialty: General

BELVEDERE TIBURON

Walker and Torrente
1640 Tiburon Boulevard
Belvedere Tiburon, CA 94920
(415) 435-9178
Contact: Mr. Bill Walker
Minimum Salary Placed: $25,000
Recruiting Specialty: Financial institutions

BENICIA

Leonard Associates
1090 Adams, Suite H
Benicia, CA 94510
(707) 747-1290
Contact: Joe
Minimum Salary Placed: $50,000
Recruiting Specialty: High technology

Marathon Search
555 1st Street, Suite 305
Benicia, CA 94510
(707) 747-5250
Contact: Mr. Carl Rowe
Minimum Salary Placed: $25,000
Recruiting Specialty: Hospitality

BERKELEY

Art Links
1450 4th Street, Suite 10
Berkeley, CA 94710
(510) 528-2668
Contact: Mr. Marti Stites
Recruiting Specialty: Arts, graphic design, multimedia

Barry C. Kleinman and Associates
2550 9th Street
Berkeley, CA 94710
(510) 549-7300
Contact: Mr. Barry Kleinman
Minimum Salary Placed: $25,000
Recruiting Specialty: General

Management Recruiters
2150 Shattuck Avenue, Suite 704
Berkeley, CA 94704
(510) 486-8100

Contact: Mr. Richard Howard
Minimum Salary Placed: $40,000
Recruiting Specialty: General

BEVERLY HILLS

Attorney Search International
8500 Wilshire Boulevard
Beverly Hills, CA 90210
(310) 855-1682
Minimum Salary Placed: $50,000
Recruiting Specialty: Attorneys

Chiu Miranda
9538 Brighton Way
Beverly Hills, CA 90210
(310) 274-0051
Minimum Salary Placed: $25,000
Recruiting Specialty: Art directors and writers in advertising

Douglas Dorflinger and Associates
9171 Wilshire Boulevard
Beverly Hills, CA 90210
(310) 276-7091
Contact: Mr. D. Dorflinger
Recruiting Specialty: Construction

Goldstein and Associates Personnel
8601 Wilshire Boulevard, Suite 1101
Beverly Hills, CA 90210
(310) 657-7161
Contact: Ms. Debra Goldstein
Minimum Salary Placed: $25,000
Recruiting Specialty: General

Groenekamp & Associates
P.O. Box 2308
Beverly Hills, CA 90213
(310) 855-0119

Contact: Mr. William Groenekamp
Minimum Salary Placed: $40,000
Recruiting Specialty: General

Sabine McManus and Associates
433 N. Camden Drive
Beverly Hills, CA 90210
(310) 205-2006
Contact: Ms. Sabine McManus
Minimum Salary Placed: $25,000
Recruiting Specialty: Healthcare, accounting and finance

Morgan Samuels Company Inc.
9171 Wilshire Boulevard, Suite 428
Beverly Hills, CA 90210
(310) 278-9660
Contact: Mr. Richard Morgan
Minimum Salary Placed: $85,000
Recruiting Specialty: Environmental and agri-business

Stanford & Associates
200 N Robertson Boulevard
Beverly Hills, CA 90211
(310) 271-6870
Recruiting Specialty: Medical

Paster and Associates
200 N. Robertson Boulevard, 3rd Floor
Beverly Hills, CA 90211
(310) 273-5424
Contact: Mr. Steve Paster
Minimum Salary Placed: $25,000
Recruiting Specialty: Medical sales and management

J.D. Ross International
9595 Wilshire Boulevard, Suite 800
Beverly Hills, CA 90212
(310) 859-9484

Contact: Ms. Alicia Sullivan
Minimum Salary Placed: $100,000
Recruiting Specialty: General

The Stevenson Group
9744 Wilshire Boulevard, Suite 205
Beverly Hills, CA 90212
(310) 285-0003
Contact: Mr. Simon Baitler
Minimum Salary Placed: $70,000
Recruiting Specialty: Life insurance

Western Secretaries
280 S. Beverly Drive, Suite 307
Beverly Hills, CA 90212
(310) 274-0439
Contact: Ms. E. Sachtjen
Minimum Salary Placed: $18,000
Recruiting Specialty: Office support

BREA

Culver Personnel Service
3 Pointe Drive, Suite 100
Brea, CA 92621
(714) 990-4459
Contact: Ms. T. Sullivan
Minimum Salary Placed: $30,000
Recruiting Specialty: Sales

Larson Associates
P.O. Box 9005
Brea, CA 92822
(714) 529-4121
Contact: Mr. Ray Larson
Minimum Salary Placed: $50,000
Recruiting Specialty: Chemical, environmental and industrial

RSR International Agency
749 S Brea Boulevard
Brea, CA 92621
(714) 529-9480
Recruiting Specialty: Computer information systems and manufacturing housing

BUELLTON

Sarver & Carruth Associates
P.O. Box 1967
Buellton, CA 93427
(805) 686-4425
Contact: Ms. Catherine Sarver
Minimum Salary Placed: $40,000
Recruiting Specialty: General

BURBANK

Accountants Executive Search
3500 W. Olive Avenue, Suite 550
Burbank, CA 91505
(818) 505-0171
Contact: Mr. William DeMario
Minimum Salary Placed: $25,000
Recruiting Specialty: Accounting

Accountants Executive Search
3500 W. Olive Avenue
Burbank, CA 91505
(818) 845-6700
Recruiting Specialty: Accounting and finance

Mark Nine Systems Inc.
333 N. Glenoaks Boulevard
Burbank, CA 91502
(818) 972-2452
Minimum Salary Placed: $25,000
Recruiting Specialty: Data processing

Patrick Associates
1621 N. Niagra
Burbank, CA 91505
(818) 848-0188
Contact: Mr. Ron Coyne
Minimum Salary Placed: $25,000
Recruiting Specialty: General

Renard International Hospitality
3601 Empire Avenue
Burbank, CA 91505
(818) 565-5530
Contact: Mr. T. Hamill
Minimum Salary Placed: $25,000
Recruiting Specialty: Hospitality

BURLINGAME

Accountants Inc.
111 Anza Boulevard, Suite 400
Burlingame, CA 94010
(415) 343-5111
Contact: Ms. D. Burr Justus
Minimum Salary Placed: $25,000
Recruiting Specialty: Finance and accounting

Culver Personnel Service
1555 Bayshore Highway
Burlingame, CA 94010
(415) 692-9090
Contact: Mr. P. Ravetti
Minimum Salary Placed: $25,000
Recruiting Specialty: Sales

Lonnie French Executive Recruiters
1204 Burlingame Avenue
Burlingame, CA 94010
(415) 375-0700

Contact: Ms. Lonnie French
Minimum Salary Placed: $25,000
Recruiting Specialty: General

Steffin Kutzman and Associates
533 Airport Boulevard
Burlingame, CA 94010
(415) 375-7835
Contact: Mr. Steffin Kutzman
Minimum Salary Placed: $25,000
Recruiting Specialty: Medical sales

CALABASAS

Cohen Associates
23801 Calabasas Road
Calabasas, CA 91302
(818) 222-6600
Contact: Ms. N. Cohen
Minimum Salary Placed: $40,000
Recruiting Specialty: Microwave engineering and other high-technology disciplines

Data Center Agency
24007 Ventura Boulevard, Suite 240
Calabasas, CA 91302-1458
(818) 225-2830
Contact: Mr. Jim Auld
Recruiting Specialty: Data processing

Extract & Associates
26540 Agoura Road
Calabasas, CA 91302
(818) 880-5590
Contact: Roy
Recruiting Specialty: General

Hildreth and Cleveland
23901 Calabasas Road
Calabasas, CA 91302
(818) 222-4619
Contact: Ms. L. Rawding
Minimum Salary Placed: $30,000
Recruiting Specialty: Banking

Fred L. Hood and Associates
23801 Calabasas Road
Calabasas, CA 91302
(818) 222-6222
Contact: Mr. Fred Hood
Minimum Salary Placed: $40,000
Recruiting Specialty: High technology

Information Resource Inc.
23801 Calabasas Road, Suite 2007
Calabasas, CA 91302
(818) 225-5800
Contact: Mr. G. McPike
Minimum Salary Placed: $35,000
Recruiting Specialty: Information sys-
tems and data processing

Med-Exec International
23679 Calabasas Road
Calabasas, CA 91302
(818) 225-1206
Contact: Ms. Emily Outhwaite
Recruiting Specialty: Healthcare and hospital, medical equipment

Montenido Associates
481 Cold Canyon Road
Calabasas, CA 91302
(818) 222-2744
Contact: Mr. Stephen Wolf
Minimum Salary Placed: $50,000
Recruiting Specialty: MIS, sales, and mar-
keting in computers and services

Villanti and Company
23801 Calabasas Road
Calabasas, CA 91302
(818) 591-9491
Contact: Ms. D. Villanti
Minimum Salary Placed: $40,000
Recruiting Specialty: High technology

Wingate Dunross Inc.
5000 N. Parkway Calabasas
Calabasas, CA 91302
(818) 222-9800
Minimum Salary Placed: $25,000
Recruiting Specialty: Healthcare, engineering and legal

CAMPBELL

The Bradbury Management Group, Inc.
1901 S. Bascom Avenue, Suite 1005
Campbell, CA 95008
(408) 377-5400
Contact: Mr. Paul Bradbury
Minimum Salary Placed: $80,000
Recruiting Specialty: High technology

Essential Solutions, Inc.
2542 South Bascom Avenue, Suite 225
Campbell, CA 95008
(408) 369-9500
Contact: Mr. Aaron Woo
Minimum Salary Placed: $45,000
Recruiting Specialty: Wireless communications

Quest Search Associates Inc.
1901 S. Bascom Avenue
Campbell, CA 95008
(408) 371-8313

Contact: Mr. J. Newman
Minimum Salary Placed: $40,000
Recruiting Specialty: General

Semiconductor Search Associates
51 E. Campbell Avenue
Campbell, CA 95008
(408) 866-4444
Contact: Mr. C. Robert
Minimum Salary Placed: $35,000
Recruiting Specialty: High technology

CANOGA PARK

Independent Resource Systems
22122 Sherman Way
Canoga Park, CA 91303
(818) 999-5690
Contact: Mr. D. Speth
Minimum Salary Placed: $35,000
Recruiting Specialty: High technology engineering and sales

Search Information Service
21044 Sherman Way
Canoga Park, CA 91303
(818) 888-7068
Contact: Mr. Marty Keller
Minimum Salary Placed: $25,000
Recruiting Specialty: General

CARLSBAD

Accountants Inc.
2011 Palomar Airport Road
Carlsbad, CA 92009
(619) 431-1101
Recruiting Specialty: Accounting

Tom Conway International
6965 El Camino Real, Suite 105
Carlsbad, CA 92009
(619) 436-8400
Contact: Mr. Thomas Conway
Recruiting Specialty: Sales, marketing
and technical disciplines in computers
and high technology

Fell & Nicholson Technology
1921 Palomar Oaks Way
Carlsbad, CA 92008
(619) 929-9200
Recruiting Specialty: High technology

Global Search
5355 Avenida Encinas
Carlsbad, CA 92008
(619) 431-4771
Contact: Mr. M. Burnett
Minimum Salary Placed: $25,000
Recruiting Specialty: Environmental

Healthcare Recruiters
701 Palomar Airport Road, Suite 300
Carlsbad, CA 92009
(619) 931-9877
Minimum Salary Placed: $25,000
Recruiting Specialty: Healthcare

Leaders
6120 Paseo del Norte
Carlsbad, CA 92009
(619) 431-5700
Contact: Mr. J. Rucks
Minimum Salary Placed: $30,000
Recruiting Specialty: General; military officers

Moore and Associates
5411 Avenida Encinas
Carlsbad, CA 92008
(619) 931-6607
Contact: Ms. M. Moore
Minimum Salary Placed: $25,000
Recruiting Specialty: Real estate development and construction

National Search Association
2035 Corte Del Nogul
Carlsbad, CA 92009
(619) 431-1115
Contact: Mr. P. Peluso
Minimum Salary Placed: $25,000
Recruiting Specialty: Computers, pharmaceuticals and biotechnology

CARMEL

J. H. Dugan & Associates, Inc.
225 Crossroads Boulevard, Suite 416
Carmel, CA 93923
(408) 625-5880
Contact: Mr. John Dugan
Minimum Salary Placed: $50,000
Recruiting Specialty: Chemicals, plastics
and packaging

Charles A. Skorina and Company
P.O. Box 22556
Carmel, CA 93922
(408) 624-2330
Contact: Mr. Charles Skorina
Minimum Salary Placed: $25,000
Recruiting Specialty: General

CARSON

Great 400 Group International
500 E. Carson Street, Suite 105
Carson, CA 90745
(310) 518-9627
Recruiting Specialty: Engineering, high
technology, and computer

CENTURY CITY

McMorrow Associates Inc.
1901 Avenue of the Stars, 18th Floor
Century City, CA 90067
(310) 556-0158
Contact: Ms. R. McMorrow
Minimum Salary Placed: $45,000
Recruiting Specialty: Attorneys

CERRITOS

Abigail Abbott Staffing Services
18000 Studebaker Road, Suite 610
Cerritos, CA 90701
(714) 995-1177
Contact: Mr. Jade Jenkins
Recruiting Specialty: General

CHATSWORTH

Kizer Ashlyn Executive Search
21032 Devonshire Street
Chatsworth, CA 91311
(818) 709-9821
Contact: Mr. L. Kizer
Minimum Salary Placed: $25,000
Recruiting Specialty: Financial institutions

Lifter and Associates
10918 Lurline Avenue
Chatsworth, CA 91311
(818) 885-5797
Contact: Ms. Barbara Lifter
Minimum Salary Placed: $25,000
Recruiting Specialty: General

Al Ponaman Company
10041-5 Larwin Avenue
Chatsworth, CA 91311
(818) 993-9100
Contact: Mr. Albert Ponaman
Minimum Salary Placed: $25,000
Recruiting Specialty: General

Quality Search Unlimited
21323 Lemarsh Street, Suite 119
Chatsworth, CA 91311
(818) 822-9017
Contact: Ms. Linda Lee Green
Recruiting Specialty: Insurance

CHICO

Sales Consultants
55 Independence Circle, 108
Chico, CA 95973
(916) 892-8880
Contact: Mr. K.L. Johnson
Minimum Salary Placed: $20,000
Recruiting Specialty: Sales

CITRUS HEIGHTS

Management Recruiters
7777 Greenback
Citrus Heights, CA 95610
(916) 729-7700

Contact: Mr. Ken McCollum
Minimum Salary Placed: $20,000
Recruiting Specialty: General

**WBS Network Professional &
Executive Search**
P.O. Box 346
Citrus Heights, CA 95611
(916) 966-7194
Contact: Mr. W. Barry Spiller
Minimum Salary Placed: $35,000
Recruiting Specialty: General

CLAREMONT

Hartman and Company
415 W. Foothill Boulevard
Claremont, CA 91711
(909) 621-0117
Contact: Mr. Dan Hartman
Minimum Salary Placed: $30,000
Recruiting Specialty: Forestry products
and building materials

Princeton Corporate Consultant
630 S. Indian Hill Boulevard
Claremont, CA 91711
(909) 625-3007
Contact: Mr. V. Ventura
Minimum Salary Placed: $25,000
Recruiting Specialty: General

Search One
976 W. Foothill Boulevard, Suite 270
Claremont, CA 91711
(909) 629-2998
Contact: Mr. R. Gaikar
Minimum Salary Placed: $35,000
Recruiting Specialty: Electronics, DSP,
telecommunications and wireless communications

CLOVIS

Carver Search Consultants
9303 E. Bullard Avenue, Suite 1
Clovis, CA 93611
(209) 298-7791
Contact: Mr. Michael Cavolina
Minimum Salary Placed: $50,000
Recruiting Specialty: Technical industries
and start-up/turnaround operations

Management Recruiters
150 Clovis Avenue, Suite 205
Clovis, CA 93612
(209) 299-7992
Contact: Mr. Gary Hendrickson
Minimum Salary Placed: $20,000
Recruiting Specialty: General

Management Resource Service
1626 Bliss Avenue
Clovis, CA 93611
(209) 323-0381
Contact: Mr. Mike Stevens
Minimum Salary Placed: $35,000
Recruiting Specialty: IBM mid-range
and data processing

CONCORD

Daley Consulting and Search
1866 Clayton Road, Suite 211
Concord, CA 94520
(510) 798-3866
Contact: Mr. Mike Daley
Minimum Salary Placed: $50,000
Recruiting Specialty: Data processing
and MIS

William Estes & Associates
4480 Treat Boulevard, Suite 128
Concord, CA 94521
(510) 930-6050
Contact: Mr. Bill Estes
Recruiting Specialty: Finance and accounting and data processing

CORTE MADERA

Forkin and Associates
100 Tamal Plaza
Corte Madera, CA 94925
(415) 987-7282
Contact: Mr. Jim Forkin
Minimum Salary Placed: $25,000
Recruiting Specialty: General

Schweichler Associates, Inc.
200 Tamal Vista, Suite 100, Building 200
Corte Madera, CA 94925
(415) 924-7200
Contact: Mr. Lee Schweichler
Minimum Salary Placed: $100,000
Recruiting Specialty: General

COSTA MESA

Markar Associates
940 South Coast Drive, Suite 175
Costa Mesa, CA 92626
(714) 433-0100
Contact: Ms. Ani or Mike Chitjian
Recruiting Specialty: Accounting, finance, environmental, and office support

McCormack & Farrow
695 Town Center Drive, Suite 660
Costa Mesa, CA 92626
(714) 549-7222
Contact: Mr. Jerry Farrow
Minimum Salary Placed: $65,000
Recruiting Specialty: General

Pacific Shore Resources
575 Anton Boulevard, Suite 300
Costa Mesa, CA 92692
(714) 432-6414
Contact: Ms. Cathy Ashbaugh
Recruiting Specialty: Data processing

Gene Phelps Associates
650 Town Center Drive, Suite 1900
Costa Mesa, CA 92626
(714) 755-8015
Contact: Mr. Gene Phelps
Minimum Salary Placed: $25,000
Recruiting Specialty: General

Resource Perspectives, Inc.
535 Anton Boulevard, Suite 860
Costa Mesa, CA 92626
(714) 662-4967
Contact: Mr. Donald DeLany
Minimum Salary Placed: $40,000
Recruiting Specialty: Manufacturing

Telford & Company, Inc.
650 Town Ctr. Drive, Suite 850-A
Costa Mesa, CA 92626
(714) 850-4309
Contact: Mr. John Telford
Minimum Salary Placed: $75,000
Recruiting Specialty: General

CULVER CITY

Management Recruiters
300 Corporate Pointe, Suite 100
Culver City, CA 90230
(213) 670-3040
Contact: Mr. Joe Ruzich
Minimum Salary Placed: $20,000
Recruiting Specialty: General

CUPERTINO

Adia Personnel Services
10055 Miller Avenue, Suite 103
Cupertino, CA 95014
(408) 257-4408
Contact: Ms. Alison Pollack
Recruiting Specialty: General

SK Writers
20430 Town Center Lane, Suite 5E-1
Cupertino, CA 95014
(408) 252-4818
Contact: Ms. Shirley Krestas
Recruiting Specialty: General

Stanley Barber Southard Brown
10050 N. Wolfe Road
Cupertino, CA 95014
(408) 725-1440
Contact: Sandy
Minimum Salary Placed: $25,000
Recruiting Specialty: General

Technique Executive Search
P.O. Box 456
Cupertino, CA 95015
(408) 257-5888
Contact: Mr. Gene Kayes
Minimum Salary Placed: $35,000
Recruiting Specialty: Networking, sales
and marketing

DANVILLE

Badger Group
4125 Blackhawk Plaza Circle, Suite 270
Danville, CA 94506
(510) 736-5553
Contact: Mr. F. Badger
Minimum Salary Placed: $100,000
Recruiting Specialty: High technology

Lynn Dwigans & Company
1610 Lawrence Road
Danville, CA 94506
(510) 736-4208
Contact: Mr. Lynn Dwigans
Minimum Salary Placed: $70,000
Recruiting Specialty: Finance and high
technology

Executive Recruiters
3840 Blackhawk Road
Danville, CA 94506
(510) 736-2262
Recruiting Specialty: Retail

Pat Newton
3860 Blackhawk Road, Suite 130
Danville, CA 94506
(510) 736-6166
Recruiting Specialty: Accounting and finance

DAVIS

Abbott Associates
225 B Street
Davis, CA 95616
(916) 757-2770
Contact: Ms. Brenda Abbott
Minimum Salary Placed: $60,000
Recruiting Specialty: General

DEL MAR

Carolyn Smith Paschal International
1155 Camino Del Mar, Suite 506
Del Mar, CA 92014
(619) 587-1366
Contact: Ms. Carolyn Smith Paschal
Minimum Salary Placed: $35,000
Recruiting Specialty: Fund raising, public
relations, marketing and investor relations

Warren Morris and Madison Ltd.
2190 Carmel Valley Road
Del Mar, CA 92014
(619) 481-3388
Contact: Mr. C. Morris
Minimum Salary Placed: $25,000
Recruiting Specialty: Cable television and
telecommunications

DIAMOND BAR

Vestex
706 N. Diamond Bar Boulevard, Suite B
Diamond Bar, CA 91765
(909) 396-5266
Contact: Sherry
Minimum Salary Placed: $25,000
Recruiting Specialty: General

DOVE CANYON

Dzierzynski and Associates
5 Columbine
Dove Canyon, CA 92679
(714) 589-0484
Contact: Mr. R. Dzierzynski
Minimum Salary Placed: $25,000
Recruiting Specialty: Tax

DOWNEY

Mitchell Personnel Services
8615 Florence Ave., Suite 369
Downey, CA 90241
(310) 861-9716
Contact: Ms. Carol Lee Kratzert
Recruiting Specialty: General

EL CAJON

Carter and Associates
P.O. Box 21444
El Cajon, CA 92021
(619) 588-5339
Contact: Mr. D. Carter
Minimum Salary Placed: $25,000
Recruiting Specialty: Media

EL CERRITO

Lander International
P.O. Box 1370
El Cerrito, CA 94530
(510) 232-4264
Contact: Mr. Richard Tuck
Recruiting Specialty: Data processing

EL GRANADA

Andrew Consulting
P.O. Box 2088
El Granada, CA 94018
(415) 726-3233
Minimum Salary Placed: $25,000
Recruiting Specialty: General

EL SEGUNDO

D.P. Specialists, Inc.
2141 Rosecrans, Suite 5100
El Segundo, CA 90245
(310) 416-9846
Contact: Mr. Ed Myers
Minimum Salary Placed: $40,000
Recruiting Specialty: Computer programming and MIS

EL TORO

Eaton and Associates
23161 Lake Center Drive, Suite 201
El Toro, CA 92630
(714) 586-3898
Contact: Mr. K. Eaton
Minimum Salary Placed: $25,000
Recruiting Specialty: Plastics and mental health

ELK GROVE

Agri-Search
P.O. Box 775
Elk Grove, CA 95759
(916) 689-6400
Contact: Mr. K. Yelle
Minimum Salary Placed: $25,000
Recruiting Specialty: Agriculture

EMERYVILLE

Accountants Inc.
2000 Powell Street, Suite 111
Emeryville, CA 94608
(510) 652-5627

Contact: Ms. D. McMahon
Minimum Salary Placed: $25,000
Recruiting Specialty: Finance and accounting

Management Recruiters
2000 Powell Street, Suite 1200
Emeryville, CA 94608
(510) 658-1405
Contact: Mr. Mark Hoffman
Minimum Salary Placed: $20,000
Recruiting Specialty: General

ENCINITAS

Elsie Chan & Associates
132 N. El Camino Real, Suite 514
Encinitas, CA 92024
(619) 944-9478
Contact: Ms. Elsie Chan
Minimum Salary Placed: $30,000
Recruiting Specialty: Data processing and MIS

Fortune Personnel Consultants
543 Encinitas Boulevard
Encinitas, CA 92024
(619) 944-8980
Contact: Ms. Donna Derario
Minimum Salary Placed: $25,000
Recruiting Specialty: Biomedical and pharmaceuticals

Glen Lee Associates
2611 S. Highway 101
Encinitas, CA 92024
(619) 634-1903
Recruiting Specialty: Management consulting

Systems Research Group
162 S. Rancho Santa Fe Road, Suite 880
Encinitas, CA 92024
(619) 436-1575
Contact: Mr. S. Gebler
Minimum Salary Placed: $25,000
Recruiting Specialty: Software

ENCINO

Advancement Personnel Service
16055 Ventura Boulevard
Encino, CA 91436
(818) 990-2800
Contact: Ms. C. Hulfish
Minimum Salary Placed: $25,000
Recruiting Specialty: General

Bogard Staffing Services
16501 Ventura Boulevard, Suite 104
Encino, CA 91436
(818) 905-5522
Contact: Ms. Iris Bogard Lampel
Recruiting Specialty: General

Career Spectrum Group
6345 Balboa Boulevard
Encino, CA 91316
(818) 776-0350
Contact: Mr. David Shotland
Minimum Salary Placed: $25,000
Recruiting Specialty: General

J. Carson & Associates
16200 Ventura Boulevard, Suite 228
Encino, CA 91436
(818) 906-3312
Contact: Ms. Jeannea Nightingale
Recruiting Specialty: Marketing research

Marsha Fox Career Resources
16133 Ventura Boulevard
Encino, CA 91436
(818) 783-1107
Contact: Ms. Marsha Fox
Minimum Salary Placed: $25,000
Recruiting Specialty: General

Healthcare Executive Recruiter
17003 Ventura Boulevard
Encino, CA 91316
(818) 788-0150
Contact: Ms. S. Fleischer
Minimum Salary Placed: $25,000
Recruiting Specialty: Healthcare

Management Recruiters
16027 Ventura Boulevard, Suite 320
Encino, CA 91436
(818) 906-3155
Contact: Ms. Loren Kaun
Minimum Salary Placed: $20,000
Recruiting Specialty: General

Merex Company
18801 Ventura Boulevard
Encino, CA 91356
(818) 774-9974
Minimum Salary Placed: $25,000
Recruiting Specialty: Sales and marketing
in electronics

Princeton Corporate Consultants
16830 Ventura Boulevard
Encino, CA 91436
(818) 784-8989
Minimum Salary Placed: $25,000
Recruiting Specialty: General

Sales Consultants
16027 Ventura Boulevard, Suite 320
Encino, CA 91436
(818) 906-3155
Contact: Mr. Hector Alaniz
Minimum Salary Placed: $20,000
Recruiting Specialty: Sales

The Shotland Group
6345 Balboa Boulevard, Suite 370
Encino, CA 91316
(818) 995-1501
Contact: Mr. David Shotland
Minimum Salary Placed: $50,000
Recruiting Specialty: General

Ward Howell International, Inc.
16255 Ventura Boulevard, Suite 400
Encino, CA 91436
(818) 905-6010
Contact: Mr. Nil Maslan
Minimum Salary Placed: $75,000
Recruiting Specialty: General

EUREKA

Sequoia Personnel Service
2930 E Street
Eureka, CA 95501
(707)445-9641
Contact: Ms. Liana Simpson
Recruiting Specialty: General

FAIR OAKS

DP Technical Search
10217 Fair Oaks Boulevard
Fair Oaks, CA 95628
(916) 863-7138
Contact: Mr. Doug Pechstein
Minimum Salary Placed: $25,000
Recruiting Specialty: Computers

Daley Technical Search
4227 Sunrise Boulevard, Suite 220
Fair Oaks, CA 95628
(916) 863-7111
Contact: Vicki
Minimum Salary Placed: $25,000
Recruiting Specialty: Information systems

Rowland Associates
7840 Madison Avenue, Suite 185
Fair Oaks, CA 95628
(916) 961-3632
Contact: Mr. J. Rowland
Minimum Salary Placed: $25,000
Recruiting Specialty: General

K.K. Walker Professional Recruitment
P.O. Box 1558
Fair Oaks, CA 9528
(916) 863-6363
Contact: Ms. Karen Walker
Recruiting Specialty: Healthcare

FAIRFAX

Paul Herrerias
P.O. Box 537
Fairfax, CA 94978
(415) 398-1001

Contact: Mr. Paul Herrerias
Minimum Salary Placed: $25,000
Recruiting Specialty: Accounting and finance

FOLSOM

Opportunities, Ink.
110 Eveland Court
Folsom, CA 95630
(916) 353-1515
Contact: Ms. Deborah Costa
Recruiting Specialty: Entertainment, software and computer

FOSTER CITY

ASAP Employment Service
13 Commons Lane
Foster City, CA 94404
(415) 345-2727
Contact: Ms. Bonnie Marsh
Minimum Salary Placed: $25,000
Recruiting Specialty: General

FOUNTAIN VALLEY

Frontline Executive Search
9550 Warner Avenue, Suite 250
Fountain Valley, CA 92708
(714) 968-7797
Contact: Ms. Ann Barr
Minimum Salary Placed: $30,000
Recruiting Specialty: Sales in office products and machinery

FREEDOM

Doering & Associates
24 Airport Road, P.O. Box 30
Freedom, CA 95019
(408) 728-1293
Contact: Mr. Louis Doering
Minimum Salary Placed: $25,000
Recruiting Specialty: General

FREMONT

Accountants Inc.
39350 Civic Center Drive, Suite 411
Fremont, CA 94538
(510) 791-7111
Contact: Ms. J. Terwilliger
Minimum Salary Placed: $25,000
Recruiting Specialty: Finance and accounting

Engineering Solutions
39210 State Street, Suite 213
Fremont, CA 94538
(510) 505-9755
Contact: Mr. Mark Cunningham
Minimum Salary Placed: $30,000
Recruiting Specialty: Engineering

Leading Edge
174 Doe Court
Fremont, CA 94539
(408) 353-8535
Minimum Salary Placed: $25,000
Recruiting Specialty: General

Management Recruiters of Fremont
3100 Mowry Avenue, Suite 206
Fremont, CA 99538
(510) 505-5125

Contact: Mr. Jim Anderson
Minimum Salary Placed: $40,000
Recruiting Specialty: Accounting and finance

Predictor Systems Corp.
39350 Civic Center Drive
Fremont, CA 94538
(510) 713-0840
Contact: Mr. Larry Dillon
Minimum Salary Placed: $65,000
Recruiting Specialty: General

Scandling Resources International
4480 Red Oak Common
Fremont, CA 94538
(510) 440-0404
Contact: Mr. David Scandling
Minimum Salary Placed: $40,000
Recruiting Specialty: Technical disciplines in computers and communications

Staff Search
39159 Paseo Padre, Suite 106
Fremont, CA 94536
(510) 790-3611
Contact: Ms. Adelia
Minimum Salary Placed: $18,000
Recruiting Specialty: General

Synapse
39210 State Street
Fremont, CA 94538
(510) 744-2100
Contact: Research Department
Recruiting Specialty: Technical

FRESNO

Denham Temporary Service
1520 E. Shaw Avenue, Suite 109
Fresno, CA 93710
(209) 222-5284
Contact: Mr. D. Denham
Recruiting Specialty: Office support

Pat DiFuria and Associates
790 W, Shaw Avenue
Fresno, CA 93704
(209) 222-5426
Contact: Mr. Pat DiFuria
Minimum Salary Placed: $25,000
Recruiting Specialty: Food and agriculture

Quickstaff
1044 E. Herndon, Suite 106
Fresno, CA 93720
(209) 261-9566
Contact: Mr. Cedric Reese
Recruiting Specialty: Finance and accounting

Cedric L. Reese's Inc.
1044 E. Herndon
Fresno, CA 93711
(209) 261-9566
Recruiting Specialty: Technical

Robert Half International
5250 N. Palm Avenue, Suite 305
Fresno, CA 93704
(209) 439-4861
Contact: Ms. P. Nelson
Minimum Salary Placed: $25,000
Recruiting Specialty: Accounting and finance

Rowland Associates
5588 N. Palm Avenue
Fresno, CA 93704
(209) 431-9229
Minimum Salary Placed: $35,000
Recruiting Specialty: General

Sales Consultants/Management Recruiters
114 E. Shaw, Suite 207
Fresno, CA 93710
(209) 226-5578
Contact: Mr. Ron Johnson
Minimum Salary Placed: $30,000
Recruiting Specialty: General

Search Consultants
4123 W. Los Altos Avenue
Fresno, CA 93722
(209) 432-1350
Contact: Ms. Stephanie MacDonald
Minimum Salary Placed: $100,000
Recruiting Specialty: High technology

Selective Staffing
4905 N. West Avenue, Suite 115
Fresno, CA 93710
(209) 227-9159
Contact: Ms. Jane Small
Minimum Salary Placed: $25,000
Recruiting Specialty: Insurance and high technology

Sherwood-Lehman Inc.
3455 W. Shaw Avenue, Suite 107
Fresno, CA 93711
(209) 276-8572
Contact: Mr. B. Sherwood
Minimum Salary Placed: $35,000
Recruiting Specialty: General

FULLERTON

Accounting Network
2501 E. Chapman Avenue, Suite 100
Fullerton, CA 92631
(714) 879-2660
Contact: Mr. Dean Gavello
Recruiting Specialty: Accounting and finance

DEC & Associates
2555 E. Chapman Avenue, Suite 300
Fullerton, CA 92631
(714) 447-0826
Contact: Ms. Diane Skullr
Recruiting Specialty: Healthcare, hospital, and medical equipment

Paules Associates
3231 La Loma Place
Fullerton, CA 92635
(714) 738-3518
Contact: Mr. Paul Paules
Minimum Salary Placed: $25,000
Recruiting Specialty: General

GARDEN GROVE

Barry M. Gold & Co.
12459 Lewis Street, Suite 102
Garden Grove, CA 92640
(714) 740-1414
Contact: Mr. Barry Gold
Recruiting Specialty: Insurance and legal

Professional Search Associates
12459 Lewis Street, Suite 102
Garden Grove, CA 92640
(714) 740-0919

Contact: Ms. Mary K. Dowell
Minimum Salary Placed: $20,000
Recruiting Specialty: General

GARDENIA

Source EDP
879 W. 190th Street, Suite 250
Gardenia, CA 90248
(310) 323-6633
Contact: Mr. Joe Gendron
Minimum Salary Placed: $20,000
Recruiting Specialty: Computers, programming and MIS

GLENDALE

London Agency
550 N. Brand Boulevard, Suite 1660
Glendale, CA 91203
(818) 240-9620
Contact: Ms. Candi Sisk
Recruiting Specialty: General

Med-Exec International
100 N. Brand Boulevard
Glendale, CA 91203
(818) 552-2036
Contact: Ms. R. Christopher
Minimum Salary Placed: $25,000
Recruiting Specialty: Healthcare

GLENDORA

Management Recruiters
P.O. Box 1998
Glendora, CA 91741
(818) 963-4503
Contact: Mr. Matt Albanese
Minimum Salary Placed: $20,000
Recruiting Specialty: General

GRANITE BAY

Genesis Recruiting
P.O. Box 2388
Granite Bay, CA 95746
(916) 652-8615
Contact: Mr. Jerry Kleames
Minimum Salary Placed: $40,000
Recruiting Specialty: Technical disciplines in paper, chemical and metals

GREENBRAE

Eagle Search Associates
336 Bon Air Center
Greenbrae, CA 94904
(415) 398-6066
Contact: Mr. Mark Gideon
Minimum Salary Placed: $35,000
Recruiting Specialty: Computers and sales in high technology

Kearney Boyle & Associates
336 Bon Air Center, Suite 106
Greenbrae, CA 94904
(415) 925-0397
Contact: Ms. Debra Boyle
Recruiting Specialty: General

Pierce and Crow
100 Drakes Landing Road, Suite 300
Greenbrae, CA 94904
(415) 925-1191
Contact: Mr. Richard Pierce
Minimum Salary Placed: $120,000
Recruiting Specialty: Computers

HACIENDA HEIGHTS

Shaffer Consulting Group
15742 Caracol Drive
Hacienda Heights, CA 91745
(818) 968-5955
Contact: Mr. Ken Finlay
Minimum Salary Placed: $50,000
Recruiting Specialty: Science-oriented
disciplines and higher education

HALF MOON BAY

Colucci, Blendow & Johnson
445 Greenbrier Road
Half Moon Bay, CA 94019
(415) 712-0103
Contact: Mr. Bart Colucci
Minimum Salary Placed: $60,000
Recruiting Specialty: Healthcare products

Perry-D'Amico and Associates
2181 Saint Andrews Road
Half Moon Bay, CA 94019
(415) 726-3132
Contact: Mr. L. Perry
Minimum Salary Placed: $25,000
Recruiting Specialty: Healthcare

HAYWARD

Sterling Personnel Service
26250 Industrial Boulevard, Suite 29
Hayward, CA 94545
(510) 782-6187
Contact: Ms. Ute Julson
Recruiting Specialty: General

HUNTINGTON BEACH

J.D. Caron & Associates, Inc.
P.O. Box 819
Huntington Beach, CA 92648
(714) 536-8603
Contact: Ms. Jill D. Caron
Minimum Salary Placed: $30,000
Recruiting Specialty: Insurance

Impact Search Consultants
P.O. Box 4305
Huntington Beach, CA 92605
(714) 890-9255
Contact: Ms. Tere Ann Newman
Recruiting Specialty: General

Jatinen & Associates
20422 Beach Boulevard, Suite 235
Huntington Beach, CA 92648
(714) 960-9082
Contact: Mr. Dave Jatinen
Recruiting Specialty: Insurance

Mason, Band and Nicastri
9121 Atlanta Avenue, Suite 336
Huntington Beach, CA 92646
(310) 573-7577
Minimum Salary Placed: $25,000
Recruiting Specialty: Restaurant

NJ Solutions
9082 Rhodesia Drive
Huntington Beach, CA 92646
(714) 963-9913
Contact: Ms. Gail Johnston
Recruiting Specialty: Engineering, environmental, sales and marketing

INDIAN WELLS

Mixtec Group
75355 St. Andrews Court
Indian Wells, CA 92210
(619) 773-0717
Contact: Mr. Don Thomas
Minimum Salary Placed: $70,000
Recruiting Specialty: Food, medical, telecommunications and engineering

INGLEWOOD

The Century Group
9800 La Cienega Boulevard, Suite 904
Inglewood, CA 90301
(310) 216-2100
Contact: Mr. Harry Boxer
Minimum Salary Placed: $25,000
Recruiting Specialty: Accounting and finance

IRVINE

Actuarial Connection
4199 Campus Drive, Suite 550
Irvine, CA 92715
(714) 509-6511
Contact: Ms. Carol Zadek
Recruiting Specialty: Insurance

Barrett Hospitality Search
7700 Irvine Center Drive, Suite 800
Irvine, CA 92718
(714) 458-6789
Contact: Mr. Peter Barrett
Minimum Salary Placed: $50,000
Recruiting Specialty: General

Boyle Ogata
18301 Von Karman Avenue, Suite 810
Irvine, CA 92715
(714) 474-6855
Contact: Mr. Mark Bregman
Recruiting Specialty: Senior management positions

Burriston Company
19000 Macarthur Boulevard
Irvine, CA 92715
(714) 476-4588
Contact: Mr. Rob Burrington
Minimum Salary Placed: $25,000
Recruiting Specialty: General

CJA Associates, Inc.
111 Pacifica
Irvine, CA 92718
(714) 731-0867
Contact: Mr. Louis Adler
Minimum Salary Placed: $50,000
Recruiting Specialty: General

California Search Agency Inc.
111 Pacifica, Suite 250
Irvine, CA 92718
(714) 727-2482
Contact: Mr. D. Crane
Minimum Salary Placed: $25,000
Recruiting Specialty: Engineering and manufacturing

Coelyn Miller Phillip & Associates
1 Park Plaza
Irvine, CA 92714
(714) 261-6600
Minimum Salary Placed: $25,000
Recruiting Specialty: General

**Dunhill Professional Search
Irvine/Newport**
9 Executive Circle, Suite 240
Irvine, CA 92714
(714) 474-6666
Contact: Mr. David Vaughan
Minimum Salary Placed: $30,000
Recruiting Specialty: General

EN Search
14 Rockrose Way
Irvine, CA 92715
(714) 262-1100
Contact: Ms. Denise Crofoot
Minimum Salary Placed: $40,000
Recruiting Specialty: Healthcare

Executive Medical Search
111 Pacifica
Irvine, CA 92718
(714) 770-9022
Contact: Ms. Diane Brewer
Minimum Salary Placed: $25,000
Recruiting Specialty: Medical and health-
care

Fortune Personnel
18552 Macarthur Boulevard, Suite 345
Irvine, CA 92715
(714) 250-0650
Contact: Mr. S. Pandolfo
Minimum Salary Placed: $25,000
Recruiting Specialty: Communications

GM Associates
15375 Barranca Parkway
Irvine, CA 92718
(714) 753-9107
Contact: Mr. Gary Malyzurek
Minimum Salary Placed: $25,000
Recruiting Specialty: EDP auditors, ac-
counting, finance and data processing

Richard Gast and Associates
15550-B Rockfield Boulevard, Suite 100
Irvine, CA 92718
(714) 472-1130
Contact: Mr. Dick Gast
Minimum Salary Placed: $25,000
Recruiting Specialty: Human resources

Harrigan Associates
111 Pacifica, Suite 250
Irvine, CA 92718
(714) 727-0784
Contact: Mr. Emmitt Harrington
Minimum Salary Placed: $50,000
Recruiting Specialty: Supermarket indus-
try

Heritage Pacific Corporation
14172 Klee Drive
Irvine, CA 92714
(714) 768-4501
Contact: Mr. Gary Draper
Recruiting Specialty: Pulp and paper

Human Resource Bureau
P.O. Box 19793-403
Irvine, CA 92713
(714) 660-7966
Contact: Ms. Joyce Newberry
Minimum Salary Placed: $40,000
Recruiting Specialty: General

JM Associates
2222 Martin Drive, Suite 255
Irvine, CA 92715
(714) 260-9200
Contact: Mr. Merry Neitlich
Minimum Salary Placed: $60,000
Recruiting Specialty: Attorneys

Jennings Company
2010 Main Street, Suite 1070
Irvine, CA 92714
(714) 474-5080
Contact: Ms. Kathryn Jennings
Recruiting Specialty: General

John Kurosky & Associates
3 Corporate Park Drive, Suite 210
Irvine, CA 92714
(714) 851-6370
Contact: Mr. John Kurosky
Minimum Salary Placed: $60,000
Recruiting Specialty: High technology

Legal Network Inc.
2151 Michelson Drive, Suite 135
Irvine, CA 92715
(714) 752-8800
Contact: Ms. Carol Wampole
Minimum Salary Placed: $60,000
Recruiting Specialty: Legal

Lucas Associates
2302 Martin Street, Suite 200
Irvine, CA 92715
(714) 660-9450
Contact: Mr. Tony Tomarello
Minimum Salary Placed: $40,000
Recruiting Specialty: Sales and marketing

M F Associates
15041 Bake Parkway
Irvine, CA 92718
(714) 380-8990
Contact: Mr. Mark Fierle
Recruiting Specialty: General

Management Search International
15375 Barranca Parkway, Suite B-205
Irvine, CA 92718
(714) 727-4343
Contact: Mr. Scott Sawyer
Minimum Salary Placed: $35,000
Recruiting Specialty: General

C Newell & Associates
18101 Von Karman Ave
Irvine, CA 92715
(714) 251-6560
Recruiting Specialty: Attorneys and general

Pan Group
4330 Barranca Parkway, Suite 101-181
Irvine, CA 92714
(714) 552-9453
Contact: Ms. Lea Timmons
Recruiting Specialty: Healthcare, hospital and medical equipment

Phoenix Professionals
2646 Dupont Drive, Suite 20314
Irvine, CA 92715
(714) 493-2747
Contact: Ms. Sheryl Wayne
Minimum Salary Placed: $25,000
Recruiting Specialty: General

Search Group
2082 Michelson Drive
Irvine, CA 92715
(714) 752-0519
Minimum Salary Placed: $25,000
Recruiting Specialty: General

Select Temporary Service
16525 Von Karman Avenue, Suite 3D
Irvine, CA 92714
(714) 476-2817
Contact: Ms. D. Cary
Recruiting Specialty: General

Source EDP
One Park Plaza, Suite 560
Irvine, CA 92714
(714) 660-1666
Contact: Mr. Bob Gennawey
Minimum Salary Placed: $20,000
Recruiting Specialty: Computers, programming and MIS

Technology
7700 Irvine Drive, Suite 245
Irvine, CA 92718
(714) 453-1533
Minimum Salary Placed: $25,000
Recruiting Specialty: Software development

D. L. Weiss & Associates
18500 Von Karman Avenue, Suite 410
Irvine, CA 92715
(714) 724-1502
Contact: Mr. David Weiss
Minimum Salary Placed: $100,000
Recruiting Specialty: General; high technology

Witt/Kieffer, Ford, Hadelman & Lloyd
1920 Powell Street, Suite 310
Irvine, CA 94608
(510) 420-1370
Contact: Mr. James Gauss
Minimum Salary Placed: $65,000
Recruiting Specialty: General

KELSEYVILLE

Horizons Unlimited
9385 Tenaya Way
Kelseyville, CA 95451
(707) 277-9744
Contact: Mr. Bruce Van Buskirk
Minimum Salary Placed: $40,000
Recruiting Specialty: Technical disciplines in chemicals and petroleum

LA COSTA

Sales Consultants
6994 El Camino Real, Suite 208
La Costa, CA 92009
(619) 438-7771
Contact: Mr. Jim Yager
Minimum Salary Placed: $20,000
Recruiting Specialty: Sales

LA JOLLA

Accountants Inc. Temporary Service
4225 Executive Square
La Jolla, CA 92037
(619) 452-7111
Recruiting Specialty: Finance and accounting

Alfred Daniels & Associates
5795 Waverly Avenue
La Jolla, CA 92037
(619) 459-4009
Contact: Mr. Alfred Daniels
Minimum Salary Placed: $50,000
Recruiting Specialty: Banking and financial institutions

J.S. Bollinger and Associates
7817 Ivanhoe Avenue, Suite 300
La Jolla, CA 92037
(619) 456-2900
Contact: Mr. Jeff Bollinger
Minimum Salary Placed: $35,000
Recruiting Specialty: Hospitality

ET Search Inc.
1250 Prospect Street, Suite 101
La Jolla, CA 92037
(619) 459-3443
Contact: Ms. Kathleen Jennings
Minimum Salary Placed: $40,000
Recruiting Specialty: Taxation

Global Resources Group
4225 Executive Square, Suite 390
La Jolla, CA 92037
(619) 455-8008
Contact: Mr. Donn Bleau
Minimum Salary Placed: $60,000
Recruiting Specialty: Human resources

John Anthony and Associates
P.O. Box 12291
La Jolla, CA 92037
(619) 457-1116
Contact: Mr. John Muller
Minimum Salary Placed: $75,000
Recruiting Specialty: General

Klein and Associates Inc.
7825 Fay Avenue
La Jolla, CA 92037
(619) 456-2820
Contact: Mr. N. Klein
Minimum Salary Placed: $40,000
Recruiting Specialty: Real estate

James Smith and Company
4275 Executive Square
La Jolla, CA 92037
(619) 546-2811
Contact: Mr. James Smith
Minimum Salary Placed: $25,000
Recruiting Specialty: General

LA PALMA

Accountants Overload
6 Centerpointe Drive, Suite 250
La Palma, CA 90623
(310) 924-7318
Contact: Ms. P. Baggott
Minimum Salary Placed: $25,000
Recruiting Specialty: Finance and accounting

LA QUINTA

W. F. Hay and Company
78080 Calle Estado, Suite 2A
La Quinta, CA 92253
(619) 777-0220
Contact: Mr. W. Hay
Minimum Salary Placed: $35,000
Recruiting Specialty: Entertainment

William C. Houze & Company
48249 Vista De Nopal
La Quinta, CA 92253
(619) 564-6400
Contact: Mr. William Houze
Minimum Salary Placed: $90,000
Recruiting Specialty: General

LAFAYETTE

Accro Personnel Service
1654 Foothill Park Circle
Lafayette, CA 94549
(510) 937-3387
Contact: Mr. Harry Coyle, Jr.
Recruiting Specialty: Environmental

Berger & Associates
47 Lafayette
Lafayette, CA 94549
(510) 946-9667
Contact: Mr. Alan Berger
Minimum Salary Placed: $30,000
Recruiting Specialty: MIS, accounting
and finance

Dunhill Professional Search
3732 Mt. Diablo Boulevard, Suite 375
Lafayette, CA 94549
(510) 283-5300
Contact: Mr. John Tierney
Minimum Salary Placed: $30,000
Recruiting Specialty: General

Perkiss and Associates
3470 Mount Diablo Boulevard,
 Suite A150
Lafayette, CA 94549
(510) 284-5310
Contact: Mr. Dave Perkiss
Minimum Salary Placed: $25,000
Recruiting Specialty: Sales

LAGUNA BEACH

Don Zee Associates
6 South Portola
Laguna Beach, CA 92651
(714) 499-0917

Contact: Mr. Don Zee
Minimum Salary Placed: $25,000
Recruiting Specialty: General

Sanford Rose Associates
580 Broadway, Suite 226
Laguna Beach, CA 92651
(714) 497-5728
Contact: Mr. Bob Dudley
Recruiting Specialty: Management,
manufacturing, transportation, and logistics

LAGUNA HILLS

Management Recruiters
23461 S. Pointe Drive, Suite 390
Laguna Hills, CA 92653
(714) 768-9112
Contact: Mr. Thomas Toole
Minimum Salary Placed: $30,000
Recruiting Specialty: General

O'Connor Group
24162 Laguna Hills Mall
Laguna Hills, CA 92653
(714) 582-5111
Contact: Mr. B. O'Connor
Minimum Salary Placed: $25,000
Recruiting Specialty: Technical disciplines in manufacturing

Roberts and Sellers Agency
25231 Paseo De Alicia, Suite 220
Laguna Hills, CA 92653
(714) 380-8350
Contact: Mr. E. Roberts
Minimum Salary Placed: $25,000
Recruiting Specialty: Computer programming

Victor White Inc.
23332 Mill Creek Drive, Suite 120
Laguna Hills, CA 92653
(714) 380-4800
Contact: Mr. Victor Chapa
Minimum Salary Placed: $50,000
Recruiting Specialty: Medical technology
development

West-Pacific Search Group
23421 South Point, Suite 270
Laguna Hills, CA 92653
(714) 830-8780
Contact: Mr. Glen Burnett
Minimum Salary Placed: $25,000
Recruiting Specialty: Insurance

LAGUNA NIGUEL

Advanced Medical Recruiters
26012 Campeon
Laguna Niguel, CA 92677
(714) 364-1916
Contact: Donald Ropain
Recruiting Specialty: Healthcare, hospital, and medical equipment

D.S. Allen Associates
7 Pointe San Pablo, Suite 400
Laguna Niguel, CA 92677
(714) 363-1505
Contact: Ms. Muriel Levitt
Minimum Salary Placed: $40,000
Recruiting Specialty: General

W.R. Bielfeldt and Company
30092 Ivy Glenn Drive
Laguna Niguel, CA 92677
(619) 442-7866
Minimum Salary Placed: $25,000
Recruiting Specialty: General

Clancy Associates
28241 Crown Valley Parkway
Laguna Niguel, CA 92677
(714) 364-0755
Contact: Mr. D. Marro
Minimum Salary Placed: $40,000
Recruiting Specialty: Biotechnology,
computer electronics and high technology

Metro Tech Consultants
30101 Town Center Drive, Suite 213
Laguna Niguel, CA 92677
(714) 249-8885
Contact: Mr. Ben Garfinkle
Minimum Salary Placed: $35,000
Recruiting Specialty: Communications

Peter Joseph Associates
25281 Via Poedra Blanca
Laguna Niguel, CA 92677
(714) 495-1714
Contact: Mr. P. Lorusso
Minimum Salary Placed: $25,000
Recruiting Specialty: Hospitality

LAKE FOREST

Hayes Medical Personnel
21932 Bellcroft Drive
Lake Forest, CA 92630
(714) 855-2707
Contact: Ms. Debra Mahon
Recruiting Specialty: Healthcare, hospital, and medical equipment

Risher Associates
22865 Lake Forest Drive, Suite 52
Lake Forest, CA 92630
(714) 455-9777
Minimum Salary Placed: $30,000
Recruiting Specialty: Retail

SMC Group
26772 Vista Terrace Drive
Lake Forest, CA 92630
(714) 855-4545
Contact: Ms. S. Shafahni
Minimum Salary Placed: $30,000
Recruiting Specialty: Sales and marketing in data communications

LAKEPORT

Bernes-McAllister Inc.
514 Lakeport Boulevard
Lakeport, CA 95453
(707) 263-9181
Contact: Mr. D. Dolan
Minimum Salary Placed: $50,000
Recruiting Specialty: Semi-conductors

LAKEWOOD

Rollins and Associates
4010 Watson Plaza Drive, Suite 105
Lakewood, CA 90712
(310) 421-6649
Contact: Ms. Jill Rollins
Minimum Salary Placed: $25,000
Recruiting Specialty: General

LANCASTER

Richard Marie Staffing Center
200 W. Pondera
Lancaster, CA 93534
(805) 942-0466
Contact: Mr. Lon McCracken
Recruiting Specialty: General

LARKSPUR

Hokenstad and Company
700 Larkspur Landing Circle
Larkspur, CA 94939
(415) 461-5250
Contact: Mr. J. Hokenstad
Minimum Salary Placed: $50,000
Recruiting Specialty: Biotechnology

LOMITA

Wayne S. Chamberlain & Associates
25835 Narbonne Avenue, Suite 280-C
Lomita, CA 90717
(310) 534-4840
Contact: Mr. Wayne Chamberlain
Minimum Salary Placed: $35,000
Recruiting Specialty: Manufacturing, electronic connectors

LONG BEACH

Culver Personnel Inc.
3447 Atlantic Avenue, Suite 190
Long Beach, CA 90807
(310) 427-0069
Contact: Mr. T. Culver
Minimum Salary Placed: $25,000
Recruiting Specialty: Sales

Houze, Shourds & Montgomery, Inc.
Greater LA World Trade Center,
 Suite 800
Long Beach, CA 90831
(310) 495-6495
Contact: Mr. James Montgomery
Minimum Salary Placed: $90,000
Recruiting Specialty: General

PIPS Personnel Service
5000 E. Spring St., Suite 380
Long Beach, CA 90815
(310) 435-3030
Contact: Mr. Ernest Davis
Recruiting Specialty: General

LOS ALTOS

Busch International
One First Street, Suite 6
Los Altos, CA 94022
(415) 949-1115
Contact: Mr. Jack Busch
Minimum Salary Placed: $75,000
Recruiting Specialty: High technology
and biotechnology

Furlong Search, Inc.
505 Tyndall Street, Suite 11
Los Altos, CA 94022
(415) 856-8484

Contact: Mr. James Furlong
Minimum Salary Placed: $40,000
Recruiting Specialty: High technology
and consumer electronics

Hockett Associates Inc.
P.O. Box 1765
Los Altos, CA 94023
(415) 941-8815
Contact: Mr. Bill Hockett
Minimum Salary Placed: $100,000
Recruiting Specialty: Life sciences

Planting and Associates
220 State Street, Suite H
Los Altos, CA 94022
(415) 949-2002
Contact: Mr. D. Planting
Minimum Salary Placed: $30,000
Recruiting Specialty: MIS and software
engineering

Sales Consultants
4970 El Camino Real, Suite 230
Los Altos, CA 94022
(415) 691-0104
Contact: Mr. Tak Tsukuda
Minimum Salary Placed: $20,000
Recruiting Specialty: Sales

Trattner Network
170 State Street, Suite 240
Los Altos, CA 94022
(415) 949-9555
Contact: Mr. Jim Trattner
Minimum Salary Placed: $30,000
Recruiting Specialty: Technical disciplines

LOS ANGELES

Accountants Executive Search
10960 Wilshire Boulevard, Suite 1115
Los Angeles, CA 90024
(310) 553-3111
Contact: Mr. Steve Shapiro
Minimum Salary Placed: $18,000
Recruiting Specialty: Finance and accounting

Actuarial Search Associates
1107 Venice Boulevard
Los Angeles, CA 90036
(310) 391-0313
Recruiting Specialty: Actuaries

Advanced Information Management
900 Wilshire Boulevard, Suite 1424
Los Angeles, CA 90017
(213) 243-9236
Contact: Ms. Karen Flanders
Recruiting Specialty: Library research and reference work

Affiliates, The Legal Staffing Division
1901 Avenue of the Stars, Suite 350
Los Angeles, CA 90067
(310) 557-2334
Contact: Ms. Laura Miller
Recruiting Specialty: Legal

Alexander & Collins
1888 Century Park East, Suite 1900
Los Angeles, CA 90067
(310) 277-4656
Contact: Ms. Sara Collins
Minimum Salary Placed: $80,000
Recruiting Specialty: General

Altschuler Company
3311 W. 3rd Street
Los Angeles, CA 90020
(213) 380-1270
Contact: Mr. Harry Altschuler
Minimum Salary Placed: $40,000
Recruiting Specialty: Chemical engineering

Ashley Taylor Company
11845 W. Olympic Boulevard
Los Angeles, CA 90064
(310) 444-5969
Contact: Mr. P. Hagopian
Minimum Salary Placed: $40,000
Recruiting Specialty: General

BDO Seidman
1900 Avenue of the Stars, 11th Floor
Los Angeles, CA 90067
(310) 557-0300
Minimum Salary Placed: $70,000
Recruiting Specialty: General

Banner Personnel Service
2049 Century Park East, Suite 1200
Los Angeles, CA 90067
(310) 556-0662
Contact: Ms. K. Carver
Minimum Salary Placed: $25,000
Recruiting Specialty: General

Bast & Associates, Inc.
11726 San Vicente Boulevard, Suite 200
Los Angeles, CA 90049
(310) 207-2100
Contact: Mr. Larry Bast
Minimum Salary Placed: $50,000
Recruiting Specialty: Sales and marketing in consumer products

Bench International Search, Inc.
116 N. Robertson Boulevard, Suite 503
Los Angeles, CA 90048
(310) 854-9900
Contact: Ms. Denise DeMan
Minimum Salary Placed: $50,000
Recruiting Specialty: Food, drugs and healthcare

Berkhemer/Clayton Inc.
800 N Alameda Street
Los Angeles, CA 90012
(213) 621-2300
Recruiting Specialty: General, executive senior level

Billington & Associates, Inc.
3250 Wilshire Boulevard, Suite 900
Los Angeles, CA 90010
(213) 386-7511
Contact: Mr. Brian Billington
Minimum Salary Placed: $50,000
Recruiting Specialty: Finance and accounting

Jerold Braun & Associates
P.O. Box 67C13
Los Angeles, CA 90067
(310) 203-0515
Contact: Mr. Jerold Braun
Recruiting Specialty: General

Brentwood International
9841 Airport Boulevard, Suite 420
Los Angeles, CA 90045
(310) 216-0033
Contact: Mr. James Keenan
Minimum Salary Placed: $50,000
Recruiting Specialty: High technology

Bristol Associates
5757 W Century Boulevard
Los Angeles, CA 90045
(310) 216-4070
Recruiting Specialty: General

Brown/Bernardy, Inc.
12100 Wilshire Boulevard, Suite M-40
Los Angeles, CA 90025
(310) 826-5777
Contact: Mr. Buzz Brown
Minimum Salary Placed: $30,000
Recruiting Specialty: Marketing and advertising

Business and Professional
3255 Wilshire Boulevard, 17th Floor
Los Angeles, CA 90010
(213) 380-8200
Contact: Ms. LaPerch
Minimum Salary Placed: $25,000
Recruiting Specialty: General

CJA Associates, Inc.
11835 West Olympic Boulevard,
 Suite 834
Los Angeles, CA 90064
(310) 478-9556
Contact: Mr. Barry Deutsch
Minimum Salary Placed: $50,000
Recruiting Specialty: General

Cadillac Associates
8033 Sunset Boulevard, Suite 5200
Los Angeles, CA 90046
(213) 385-9111
Recruiting Specialty: Healthcare and some general

Robert Caldwell & Associates
12021 Wilshire Boulevard, Suite 650
Los Angeles, CA 90025
(310) 454-1946
Contact: Mr. Robert Caldwell
Minimum Salary Placed: $100,000
Recruiting Specialty: General

Carlson and Associates
11444 W. Olympic Boulevard, Suite 1051
Los Angeles, CA 90064
(310) 312-9546
Contact: Mr. P. Carlson
Minimum Salary Placed: $25,000
Recruiting Specialty: Healthcare

Carson-Thomas Personnel
900 Wilshire Boulevard
Los Angeles, CA 90017
(213) 489-4480
Contact: Ms. Sandra Carson
Recruiting Specialty: General

Colt Systems Professional Personnel Services
1880 Century Park E., Suite 208
Los Angeles, CA 90067
(310) 277-4741
Contact: Mr. Sheldon Arons
Minimum Salary Placed: $30,000
Recruiting Specialty: Accounting, finance, FIS and data processing

The Corporate Source Group
11601 Wilshire Boulevard, Suite 500
Los Angeles, CA 90025
(310) 575-4863
Contact: Ms. Susanne Crocker
Minimum Salary Placed: $60,000
Recruiting Specialty: General

Curphey and Malkin Associates Inc.
13011 W. Washington Boulevard
Los Angeles, CA 90066
(310) 822-7555
Contact: Mr. J. Curphey
Minimum Salary Placed: $25,000
Recruiting Specialty: Computer systems and sales

DBL Associates
11835 West Olympic Boulevard,
 Suite 835
Los Angeles, CA 90064
(310) 575-9202
Contact: Mr. David Long
Minimum Salary Placed: $50,000
Recruiting Specialty: Finance and accounting

Davidson and Associates
1453 N. Benton Way
Los Angeles, CA 90026
(213) 413-2613
Contact: Mr. Tom Davidson
Minimum Salary Placed: $150,000
Recruiting Specialty: Attorneys

Dellon and Taras Partners
1801 Avenue of the Stars
Los Angeles, CA 90067
(310) 286-0625
Minimum Salary Placed: $30,000
Recruiting Specialty: Real estate

Druthers Agency Inc.
12621 Rose Avenue, Suite A
Los Angeles, CA 90066
(310) 451-2331
Contact: Mr. Jeffery Harris
Minimum Salary Placed: $25,000
Recruiting Specialty: Healthcare administration

Dunhill Personnel Service
5657 Wilshire Boulevard, Suite 200
Los Angeles, CA 90036
(213) 931-1311
Contact: Mr. Ray Cech
Minimum Salary Placed: $30,000
Recruiting Specialty: General

Egon Zehnder International Inc.
300 S. Grand Avenue, Suite 2625
Los Angeles, CA 90071
(213) 621-8900
Contact: Mr. John Derning
Minimum Salary Placed: $80,000
Recruiting Specialty: Mergers and acquisitions and start-up organizations

Executive Careers
1801 Avenue of the Stars, Suite 640
Los Angeles, CA 90067
(310) 306-0360
Contact: Ms. Annette Segil
Minimum Salary Placed: $50,000
Recruiting Specialty: Retailing of textiles

Executive Network Group
1233 Daniels Drive
Los Angeles, CA 90035
(310) 286-7055
Contact: Ms. Margaret Zito
Recruiting Specialty: Accounting and finance

Finders International
2999 Overland Avenue, Suite 204
Los Angeles, CA 90064
(310) 841-2280
Contact: Mr. J. King
Minimum Salary Placed: $25,000
Recruiting Specialty: General

Ford Payton and Davis
900 Wilshire Boulevard, Suite 820
Los Angeles, CA 90017
(213) 624-1297

Contact: Mr. L. Cacciotti
Minimum Salary Placed: $40,000
Recruiting Specialty: Finance

Fortune Personnel Consultants
5300 West Century Boulevard, Suite 208
Los Angeles, CA 90045
(310) 410-9662
Contact: Mr. Marc Kasten
Minimum Salary Placed: $40,000
Recruiting Specialty: Medical, biotechnology and pharmaceuticals

Fox Meyers & Associates
800 S. Figueroa Street, Suite 900
Los Angeles, CA 90017
(213) 622-5000
Contact: Mr. Jim Johnson
Minimum Salary Placed: $35,000
Recruiting Specialty: General

Future Personnel Agency, Inc.
4727 Wilshire Boulevard, Suite 200
Los Angeles, CA 90010
(213) 936-1799
Contact: Ms. Linda Lea McGuire
Recruiting Specialty: General

N.W. Gibson International
5900 Wilshire Boulevard, Suite 760
Los Angeles, CA 90036
(213) 930-1100
Contact: Mr. Nelson Gibson
Minimum Salary Placed: $100,000
Recruiting Specialty: General

Barry Goldberg & Associates, Inc.
2049 Century Park East, Suite 1100
Los Angeles, CA 90067
(310) 277-5800
Contact: Mr. Barry Goldberg
Minimum Salary Placed: $80,000
Recruiting Specialty: Attorneys

M. Greenwood and Associates
P.O. Box 46067
Los Angeles, CA 90046
(213) 656-9458
Contact: Mr. M. Greenwood
Minimum Salary Placed: $45,000
Recruiting Specialty: Real estate and accounting

Alice Gunderson Associates
5757 W. Century Boulevard, Suite 700
Los Angeles, CA 90045
(310) 216-0157
Contact: Ms. Alice Gunderson
Minimum Salary Placed: $25,000
Recruiting Specialty: General

Haffner Group
1901 Avenue of the Stars
Los Angeles, CA 90067
(310) 551-0300
Contact: Ms. Nancy Haffner
Recruiting Specialty: Attorneys

Harrison and Hunt
11444 W. Olympic Boulevard, 10th Floor
Los Angeles, CA 90064
(310) 445-8815
Contact: Mr. G. Hunt
Minimum Salary Placed: $50,000
Recruiting Specialty: General

The Hawkins Company
5455 Wilshire Boulevard, Suite 1406
Los Angeles, CA 90036
(213) 933-3337
Contact: Mr. William Hawkins
Minimum Salary Placed: $60,000
Recruiting Specialty: General, and some non-profit

Heidrick & Struggles, Inc.
300 S. Grand Avenue, Suite 2400
Los Angeles, CA 90071
(213) 625-8811
Contact: Mr. Thomas Mitchell
Minimum Salary Placed: $60,000
Recruiting Specialty: High technology, manufacturing, higher education and hospitals

Helstrom Turner and Associates
624 S. Grand Avenue
Los Angeles, CA 90017
(213) 688-8778
Contact: Ms. K. Turner
Minimum Salary Placed: $30,000
Recruiting Specialty: Retail and consumer products

Hemingway Personnel
2040 Avenue of the Stars, 4th Floor
Los Angeles, CA 90067
(310) 226-8530
Contact: Ms. Alessa Powell
Recruiting Specialty: Accounting and finance

Hochman and Associates
1801 Avenue of the Stars
Los Angeles, CA 90067
(310) 552-0662
Contact: Ms. Judy Hochman
Minimum Salary Placed: $25,000
Recruiting Specialty: General

Intersearch Chrisman & Company, Inc.
350 South Figueroa Street, Suite 550
Los Angeles, CA 90071
(213) 620-1192
Contact: Mr. Timothy Chrisman
Minimum Salary Placed: $60,000
Recruiting Specialty: General

The Jameson Group
1900 Avenue of the Stars, Suite 200
Los Angeles, CA 90067
(310) 286-0220
Contact: Mr. John Jameson
Minimum Salary Placed: $60,000
Recruiting Specialty: Attorneys

Ronald S. Johnson Associates, Inc.
11661 San Vicente Boulevard, Suite 400
Los Angeles, CA 90049
(310) 820-5855
Contact: Mr. Ronald Johnson
Minimum Salary Placed: $100,000
Recruiting Specialty: High technology

Karsch Card
2049 Century Park E. Suite 1200
Los Angeles, CA 90067
(310) 556-8866
Contact: Ms. E. Karsch
Minimum Salary Placed: $30,000
Recruiting Specialty: Advertising

Kass/Abell & Associates, Inc.
10780 Santa Monica Boulevard,
  Suite 200
Los Angeles, CA 90025
(310) 475-4666
Contact: Mr. Peter Redgrove
Minimum Salary Placed: $70,000
Recruiting Specialty: Legal

A T Kearney Executive Search
500 S Grand Avenue, Suite 1780
Los Angeles, CA 90071
(213) 624-8328
Contact: Research Department
Minimum Salary Placed: $50,000
Recruiting Specialty: General

Kinzer Corporation
6033 West Century Boulevard
Los Angeles, CA 90045
(310) 417-8577
Contact: Ms. Arlene Dickey
Minimum Salary Placed: $35,000
Recruiting Specialty: Retail, wholesale
and manufacturing

Korn/Ferry International
1800 Century Park E., Suite 900
Los Angeles, CA 90067
(310) 552-1834
Contact: Ms. Caroline Nahas
Minimum Salary Placed: $100,000
Recruiting Specialty: General

Korn/Ferry International
601 S. Figueroa, Suite 1900
Los Angeles, CA 90017
(213) 624-6600
Contact: Mr. Peter Kelly
Minimum Salary Placed: $100,000
Recruiting Specialty: General

Evie Kreisler Associates Inc.
8655 S. Figuerda Street, Suite 950
Los Angeles, CA 90014
(213) 622-8994
Contact: Ms. Mary Windle
Minimum Salary Placed: $25,000
Recruiting Specialty: Garment and fashion industry

Jeff Kroh Associates
11400 W. Olympic Boulevard
Los Angeles, CA 90064
(310) 445-8804
Contact: Mr. Jeff Kroh
Minimum Salary Placed: $35,000
Recruiting Specialty: Engineering and
other technical disciplines

Marvin Laba & Associates
6255 Sunset Boulevard, Suite 617
Los Angeles, CA 90028
(213) 464-1355
Contact: Mr. Marvin Laba
Minimum Salary Placed: $35,000
Recruiting Specialty: Retail and Wholesale

The LaBorde Group
5410 Wilshire Boulevard, Suite 206
Los Angeles, CA 90036
(213) 938-9007
Contact: Mr. John LaBorde
Minimum Salary Placed: $60,000
Recruiting Specialty: Engineering in construction and transportation

Larsen Zilliacus & Associates, Inc.
601 W. Fifth Street, Suite 710
Los Angeles, CA 90071
(213) 243-0033
Contact: Mr. Richard Larsen
Minimum Salary Placed: $55,000
Recruiting Specialty: General

Legal Placements International
1901 Avenue of the Stars
Los Angeles, CA 90067
(310) 551-0300
Contact: Ms. N. Haffner
Minimum Salary Placed: $30,000
Recruiting Specialty: Legal

Legal Works Inc.
1875 Century Park E., Suite 1200
Los Angeles, CA 90067
(310) 277-8998
Contact: Ms. R. Frisch
Minimum Salary Placed: $30,000
Recruiting Specialty: Legal

Michael Levine & Associates
1999 Avenue of the Stars, Suite 1150
Los Angeles, Ca 90067
(310) 282-0787
Recruiting Specialty: Executive assistants—administrative

Lipson & Company
1900 Avenue of the Stars, Suite 2810
Los Angeles, CA 90067
(310) 277-4646
Contact: Mr. Howard Lipson
Minimum Salary Placed: $50,000
Recruiting Specialty: General

London Agency
3250 Wilshire Boulevard, Suite 1403
Los Angeles, CA 90039
(213) 384-8881
Contact: Ms. lleene Bernard
Recruiting Specialty: General

MSI International/MSI Physician Recruiters
2049 Century Park East, Suite 1010
Los Angeles, CA 90067
(310) 286-0222
Contact: Mr. Greg Inguagiato
Minimum Salary Placed: $25,000
Recruiting Specialty: Healthcare

Management Recruiters
3800 Barham Boulevard, Suite 405
Los Angeles, CA 90068
(213) 876-6700
Contact: Mr. Jeffrey Merino
Minimum Salary Placed: $20,000
Recruiting Specialty: General

Brad Marks International
1888 Century Park East
Los Angeles, CA 90067
(310) 286-0600
Contact: Mr. Brad Marks
Minimum Salary Placed: $25,000
Recruiting Specialty: Media and entertainment

J. Martin & Associates
10820 Holman Avenue, Suite 103
Los Angeles, CA 90024
(310) 475-5380
Contact: Ms. Judy Martin
Minimum Salary Placed: $70,000
Recruiting Specialty: High technology and healthcare

Kevin E. McCarthy and Associates
9800 Sepulveda Boulevard, Suite 720
Los Angeles, CA 90045
(310) 568-4070
Contact: Mr. Kevin McCarthy
Minimum Salary Placed: $40,000
Recruiting Specialty: Financial services

McCormack & Associates
201 N. Figueroa Street, Suite 700
Los Angeles, CA 90012
(213) 975-1585
Contact: Mr. Joseph McCormack
Minimum Salary Placed: $70,000
Recruiting Specialty: Non-profit and liberal causes and organizations

McMorrow Associates Inc.
1901 Avenue of the Stars
Los Angeles, CA 90067
(310) 556-0158
Contact: Ms. S. McClure
Minimum Salary Placed: $45,000
Recruiting Specialty: Attorneys

Ober & Company
11777 San Vicente Boulevard, Suite 860
Los Angeles, CA 90049
(310) 207-1127
Contact: Ms. Lynn Ober
Minimum Salary Placed: $65,000
Recruiting Specialty: General

The Odessa Group
523 W. 6th Street, Suite 807
Los Angeles, CA 90014
(213) 629-9181
Contact: Mr. Odessa Felactu
Minimum Salary Placed: $75,000
Recruiting Specialty: General

Omega Tech
3551 Grand View Boulevard
Los Angeles, CA 90066
(310) 390-7907
Contact: Mr. D. Rojas
Minimum Salary Placed: $30,000
Recruiting Specialty: Computers: 400 and LAN series systems

Pathfinder Enterprises
624 S. Grand Avenue
Los Angeles, CA 90017
(213) 627-2222
Contact: Mr. F. Spain
Minimum Salary Placed: $100,000
Recruiting Specialty: Investment management

Paul Ray Berndtson
2029 Century Park East, Suite 1000
Los Angeles, CA 90067
(310) 557-2828
Contact: Mr. David Radden
Minimum Salary Placed: $90,000
Recruiting Specialty: General

Pierce Associates
1888 Century Park East, 21st Floor
Los Angeles, CA 90067
(310) 282-7171
Contact: Ms. Lisa Pierce
Minimum Salary Placed: $75,000
Recruiting Specialty: Attorneys

Poirier, Hoevel & Company
12400 Wilshire Boulevard, Suite 1250
Los Angeles, CA 90025
(310) 207-3427
Contact: Mr. Michael Hoevel
Minimum Salary Placed: $75,000
Recruiting Specialty: General

Purcell Group
1640 S. Sepulveda Boulevard, Suite 208
Los Angeles, CA 90025
(310) 477-4433
Contact: Mr. F. Purcell
Minimum Salary Placed: $25,000
Recruiting Specialty: General

Raber Associates
523 W. 6th Street
Los Angeles, CA 90014
(213) 622-0505
Contact: Mr. C. Raber
Minimum Salary Placed: $35,000
Recruiting Specialty: Convention and
tourism

Rivera Legal Search, Inc.
P.O. Box 63343
Los Angeles, CA 90063
(213) 780-0000
Contact: Mr. Al Rivera
Minimum Salary Placed: $80,000
Recruiting Specialty: Attorneys

Robert Half International
1901 Avenue of the Stars
Los Angeles, CA 90067
(310) 286-6800
Contact: Mr. T. Barao
Minimum Salary Placed: $25,000
Recruiting Specialty: Accounting and fi-
nance

Norman Roberts & Associates, Inc.
1800 Century Park East, Suite 430
Los Angeles, CA 90067
(310) 552-1112
Contact: Mr. Norman Roberts
Minimum Salary Placed: $70,000
Recruiting Specialty: Public sector

Robinson Company
11444 W. Olympic Boulevard
Los Angeles, CA 90064
(310) 914-0110
Contact: Ms. Pamela Robinson
Minimum Salary Placed: $100,000
Recruiting Specialty: Entertainment

R. Rollo Associates
725 Figueroa Street, Suite 3230
Los Angeles, CA 90017
(213) 688-9444
Contact: Mr. Robert Rollo
Minimum Salary Placed: $75,000
Recruiting Specialty: General

Russell Reynolds Associates, Inc.
333 S. Grand Avenue, Suite 3500
Los Angeles, CA 90071
(213) 489-1520
Contact: Mr. Richard Krell
Minimum Salary Placed: $100,000
Recruiting Specialty: General

Ryan, Miller & Associates
4601 Wilshire Boulevard, Suite 225
Los Angeles, CA 90010
(213) 938-4768
Contact: Mr. Lee Ryan
Minimum Salary Placed: $30,000
Recruiting Specialty: Accounting and finance

Search Group
1328 Sierra Alta Way
Los Angeles, CA 90069
(310) 550-0292
Contact: Ms. Yardena Keren
Minimum Salary Placed: $25,000
Recruiting Specialty: Engineering

Search West, Inc.
2049 Century Park East, Suite 650
Los Angeles, CA 90067
(310) 284-8888
Contact: Mr. Robert Cowan
Minimum Salary Placed: $50,000
Recruiting Specialty: General

Seltzer-Fontaine Beckwith
2999 Overland Avenue, Suite 203
Los Angeles, CA 90064
(310) 839-6000
Contact: Ms. Valerie Fontiane
Recruiting Specialty: Attorneys

David Shiplacoff & Associates
2030 Fairburn Avenue, Suite 100
Los Angeles, CA 90025
(310) 474-3600
Contact: Mr. David Shiplacoff
Minimum Salary Placed: $60,000
Recruiting Specialty: General

Smith & Associates
3826 Monteith Drive, Suite 300
Los Angeles, CA 90043
(213) 295-8198
Contact: Mr. Darrell Smith
Minimum Salary Placed: $50,000
Recruiting Specialty: General

Spectrum Search Associates, Inc.
1888 Century Park East, 3rd Floor
Los Angeles, CA 90067
(310) 286-6920
Contact: Mr. Nick Roberts
Minimum Salary Placed: $25,000
Recruiting Specialty: Accounting and finance

Spencer Stuart
555 S. Flower Street, Suite 4455
Los Angeles, CA 90071
(213) 620-0814
Contact: Mr. Anthony Pfannkuche
Minimum Salary Placed: $75,000
Recruiting Specialty: General

Stanton Chase International
10866 Wilshire Boulevard, Suite 870
Los Angeles, CA 90024
(310) 474-1029
Contact: Mr. Edward Savage
Minimum Salary Placed: $60,000
Recruiting Specialty: Communications and entertainment

Russell Stephens, Inc.
445 S Figueroa St., Suite 2600
Los Angeles, CA 90071
(213) 612-7711
Contact: Mr. Carl Miller
Recruiting Specialty: Accounting, finance and banking

Stone and Associates Executive Search
10850 Wilshire Boulevard
Los Angeles, CA 90067
(310) 475-7433
Contact: Ms. Diane Stone
Minimum Salary Placed: $35,000
Recruiting Specialty: Insurance

Technical Connections, Inc.
11400 Olympic Boulevard, Suite 770
Los Angeles, CA 90064
(310) 479-8830
Contact: Ms. Helen MacKinnon
Minimum Salary Placed: $35,000
Recruiting Specialty: Computers

Thor, Inc.
4201 Wilshire Boulevard, Suite 105
Los Angeles, CA 90010
(213) 932-7200
Contact: Mr. Terry Thormodsgaard
Minimum Salary Placed: $25,000
Recruiting Specialty: General

Thornton Associates
2040 Avenue of the Stars
Los Angeles, CA 90067
(310) 553-1773
Contact: Ms. Rathaelle Thornton
Minimum Salary Placed: $25,000
Recruiting Specialty: General

Time Engineering
P.O. Box 25845
Los Angeles, CA 90025
(310) 478-0591
Contact: Mr. D. Anderson
Minimum Salary Placed: $30,000
Recruiting Specialty: Engineering

Villasenor & Associates
6546 San Vicente Boulevard
Los Angeles, CA 90048
(213) 936-4880
Contact: Mr. Hector Villasenor
Recruiting Specialty: Attorneys

Ronald Walden and Associates Inc.
2049 Century Park East, Suite 2050
Los Angeles, CA 90067
(310) 552-3174
Contact: Mr. Ronald Walden
Minimum Salary Placed: $25,000
Recruiting Specialty: General

Waldorf Associates, Inc.
11400 W. Olympic Boulevard, 2nd Floor
Los Angeles, CA 90064
(310) 445-8886
Contact: Mr. Michael Waldorf
Recruiting Specialty: Attorneys

Whitney Associates
601 S. Figueroa Street, Suite 3400
Los Angeles, CA 90017
(213) 688-7508
Contact: Mr. William Whitney
Minimum Salary Placed: $60,000
Recruiting Specialty: Hospitality and entertainment

Daniel Wier & Associates
333 S. Grand Avenue, Suite 2980
Los Angeles, CA 90071
(213) 628-2580
Contact: Mr. Daniel Wier
Minimum Salary Placed: $85,000
Recruiting Specialty: General

Wollborg Michelson Personnel
1901 Avenue of the Stars, Suite 1232
Los Angeles, CA 90067
(310) 788-3400
Contact: Ms. Joan Van Donge
Recruiting Specialty: General

Ziskind Greene and Augustine
2566 Overland Avenue, Suite 600
Los Angeles, CA 90064
(310) 841-2240
Contact: Mr. G. Zisking
Minimum Salary Placed: $40,000
Recruiting Specialty: Attorneys

LOS GATOS

The Advisory Group, Inc.
266 Los Gatos-Saratoga Road
Los Gatos, CA 95030
(408) 395-5960
Contact: Mr. George Vaccaro
Minimum Salary Placed: $70,000
Recruiting Specialty: High technology

Devine and Virnig
718 University Avenue, Suite 110
Los Gatos, CA 95030
(408) 354-3400
Minimum Salary Placed: $75,000
Recruiting Specialty: General

Lexington Co.
24323 Mountain Chalie Rd
Los Gatos, CA 95030
(408) 353-5200
Recruiting Specialty: General

Markus Executive Search
215 N Santa Cruz Ave
Los Gatos, CA 95030
(408) 399-4400
Contact: David
Recruiting Specialty: High technology

RESULTS Recruiting
136 Belglen Way
Los Gatos, CA 95032
(408) 356-0412
Contact: Mr. Paul Lotz
Recruiting Specialty: Technical

Splaine & Associates, Inc.
15951 Los Gatos Boulevard, Suite 13
Los Gatos, CA 95032
(408) 354-3664
Contact: Mr. Charles Splaine
Minimum Salary Placed: $70,000
Recruiting Specialty: High technology
and computers

M. Stahl, Inc.
20 S. Santa Cruz, Suite 312
Los Gatos, CA 95030
(408) 354-5654
Contact: Ms. Mary Stahl
Minimum Salary Placed: $80,000
Recruiting Specialty: Technical

Dick Wray & Consultants, Inc.
540 N. Santa Cruz, Suite 269
Los Gatos, CA 95030
(408) 436-9729
Contact: Mr. Dick Wray
Minimum Salary Placed: $50,000
Recruiting Specialty: Restaurants

MANHATTAN BEACH

Fisher Personnel Management Services
1219 Morningside Drive
Manhattan Beach, CA 90266
(310) 546-7507
Contact: Mr. Neal Fisher
Minimum Salary Placed: $60,000
Recruiting Specialty: High technology,
industrial materials, computers, trucks
and equipment

Marino & Associates
3601 Aviation Boulevard, Suite 1500
Manhattan Beach, CA 90266
(310) 643-7501
Contact: Ms. Cheryl Marino
Recruiting Specialty: General

J. L. Mark Associates, Inc.
1219 Morningside Drive
Manhattan Beach, CA 90266
(310) 545-7833
Contact: Mr. John Mark
Recruiting Specialty: General

Amy Zimmerman & Associates, Inc.
111 N. Sepulveda Boulevard, Suite 243
Manhattan Beach, CA 90266
(310) 798-6979
Contact: Ms. Amy Zimmerman
Recruiting Specialty: General

MARINA DEL REY

Holland Executive Search
P.O. Box 9774
Marina Del Rey, CA 90295
(310) 459-1802
Contact: Ms. R. Holland
Minimum Salary Placed: $25,000
Recruiting Specialty: General

Leading Edge Consulting Inc.
13763 Fiji Way
Marina Del Rey, CA 90292
(310) 822-7557
Contact: Ms. S. Brainin
Minimum Salary Placed: $25,000
Recruiting Specialty: Data processing

MENLO PARK

Brown Venture Associates
3000 Sand Hill Road, Suite 110
Menlo Park, CA 94025
(415) 233-0205
Contact: Mr. Jerry Brown
Minimum Salary Placed: $85,000
Recruiting Specialty: Growth organiza-
tions and high technology

Heidrick & Struggles, Inc.
2740 Sand Hill Road
Menlo Park, CA 94025
(415) 854-9300
Contact: Mr. David Kixmiller
Minimum Salary Placed: $60,000
Recruiting Specialty: General

Howe-Lewis International, Inc.
1010 El Camino Real, Suite 360
Menlo Park, CA 94025
(415) 324-4430
Contact: Mr. John Taylor
Minimum Salary Placed: $80,000
Recruiting Specialty: Biotechnology and
pharmaceuticals

Thomas A. Kelley and Associates
3000 Sand Hill Road
Menlo Park, CA 94025
(415) 854-3247
Contact: Mr. Tom Kelly
Minimum Salary Placed: $75,000
Recruiting Specialty: High technology

Kerwin Associates
633 Menlo Avenue
Menlo Park, CA 94025
(415) 326-6565
Contact: Ms. A. Kerwin
Minimum Salary Placed: $55,000
Recruiting Specialty: Attorneys

Korn/Ferry International
2180 Sand Hill, Suite 440
Menlo Park, CA 94025
(415) 529-1834
Contact: Mr. Mel Connet
Minimum Salary Placed: $100,000
Recruiting Specialty: General

Mason & Associates
3000 Sand Hill Road, Building 1,
  Suite 290
Menlo Park, CA 94025
(415) 322-5288
Contact: Mr. Robert Mason
Minimum Salary Placed: $70,000
Recruiting Specialty: General

Michael Parcells and Associates
2200 Sand Hill Road
Menlo Park, CA 94025
(415) 854-9833
Contact: Mr. Michael Parcells
Minimum Salary Placed: $80,000
Recruiting Specialty: High technology

Spencer Stuart
3000 Sand Hill Road, Building 2,
  Suite 175
Menlo Park, CA 94025
(415) 688-1285
Contact: Mr. Brad Stirn
Minimum Salary Placed: $75,000
Recruiting Specialty: High technology

Tirocchi, Wright, Inc.
1120 Crane Street
Menlo Park, CA 94025
(415) 369-6033
Contact: Mr. Fred Tirocchi
Minimum Salary Placed: $70,000
Recruiting Specialty: General

The Ultimate Source
2147 Avy
Menlo Park, CA 94025
(415) 854-1849
Contact: Ms. Jean Martin
Minimum Salary Placed: $65,000
Recruiting Specialty: High technology

MERCED

Toconis and Associates
470 W. Main Street
Merced, CA 95340
(209) 384-1555
Contact: Ms. P. Toconis
Recruiting Specialty: General

MILL VALLEY

J. Blakslee International, Ltd.
49 Hillside Avenue
Mill Valley, CA 94941
(415) 389-7300

Contact: Mr. Jan Blakslee
Minimum Salary Placed: $100,000
Recruiting Specialty: Pharmaceuticals

Block & Associates
20 Sunnyside Avenue, Suite A 332
Mill Valley, CA 94941
(415) 389-9710
Contact: Mr. Randall Block
Minimum Salary Placed: $90,000
Recruiting Specialty: High technology

Chancellor and Chancellor
P.O. Box 999
Mill Valley, CA 94941
(415) 332-0123
Contact: Mr. A. Goeree
Minimum Salary Placed: $25,000
Recruiting Specialty: General

Computing Professionals Inc.
358 Strawberry Drive
Mill Valley, CA 94941
(415) 383-0817
Contact: Mr. Paul Hodge
Minimum Salary Placed: $35,000
Recruiting Specialty: Computers

Management Recruiters
591 Redwood Highway, Suite 2225
Mill Valley, CA 94941
(415) 383-7044
Contact: Mr. Eric Wheel
Minimum Salary Placed: $50,000
Recruiting Specialty: High technology

Pat Franklyn Associates, Inc.
655 Redwood Highway, Suite 350
Mill Valley, CA 94941
(415) 388-1894
Contact: Rhona or Suzanne
Recruiting Specialty: Legal and technical
disciplines in construction, chemical and
high technology

Shannahan & Company, Inc.
655 Redwood Highway, Suite 133
Mill Valley, CA 94941
(415) 381-3613
Contact: Mr. Peter Shannahan
Minimum Salary Placed: $50,000
Recruiting Specialty: General

Sheffield Consulting Group
591 Redwood Highway, Suite 3210
Mill Valley, CA 94941
(415) 381-6600
Contact: Mr. Roger Norton
Recruiting Specialty: General

MILLBRAE

Maciejewski and Associates
348 Broadway
Millbrae, CA 94030
(415) 692-8803
Contact: Mr. J. Maciejewski
Minimum Salary Placed: $30,000
Recruiting Specialty: Hardware, program-
ming analysts and MIS

George Sardonis
4 Hazel Ave.
Millbrae, CA 94030
(415) 692-4810
Contact: Mr. George Sardonis
Recruiting Specialty: Engineering and insurance

MISSION VIEJO

Auerbach Hotel Associates
27281 Las Ramblas, Suite 200
Mission Viejo, CA 92691
(714) 582-1887

Contact: Mr. Mark Auerbach
Minimum Salary Placed: $25,000
Recruiting Specialty: Hospitality

C & C Associates
27001 E. La Paz Road, Suite 400
Mission Viejo, CA 92691
(714) 859-6733
Contact: Mr. Tim Korg
Minimum Salary Placed: $25,000
Recruiting Specialty: Sales and customer service

Computer Network Resources, Inc.
28231 Tinajo
Mission Viejo, CA 92692
(714) 951-5929
Contact: Mr. Kenneth Miller
Minimum Salary Placed: $40,000
Recruiting Specialty: MIS and FIS in finance and insurance

Corporate Resources
2728 Las Ramblas, Suite 200
Mission Viejo, CA 92691
(714) 582-1277
Contact: Mr. N. McClurg
Minimum Salary Placed: $45,000
Recruiting Specialty: Computer programming

Cramer & Associates
26005 Orbita
Mission Viejo, CA 92691
(714) 360-0992
Contact: Ms. Barbara Cramer
Recruiting Specialty: Healthcare, hospital and medical equipment

Executive Resource Systems
27281 Las Ramblas, Suite 200
Mission Viejo, CA 92691
(714) 496-4300
Contact: Mr. Stephen Brody
Minimum Salary Placed: $40,000
Recruiting Specialty: Accounting, finance, and systems positions

Healthcare Recruiters
26400 La Alameda, Suite 204
Mission Viejo, CA 92691
(714) 367-7888
Contact: Ms. Carol Raia
Minimum Salary Placed: $25,000
Recruiting Specialty: Healthcare

JPM International
26060 Acero, Suite 100
Mission Viejo, CA 92691
(714) 955-2545
Contact: Ms. Trish Ryan
Recruiting Specialty: Healthcare and hospitals

Richard E. Rigler & Associates
23120 Alicia Parkway
Mission Viejo, CA 92692
(714) 837-6999
Contact: Mr. Dick Rigler
Minimum Salary Placed: $40,000
Recruiting Specialty: General

MODESTO

Automation Technology Search
7309 Del Cielo Way
Modesto, CA 95356
(209) 545-4500

Contact: Mr. Ralph Becker
Minimum Salary Placed: $30,000
Recruiting Specialty: Computer programming

Availability Personnel Service
2813 Coffee Road, Building A
Modesto, CA 95355
(209) 527-7878
Contact: Ms. N. Rasmussen
Recruiting Specialty: Office support and accounting

Sales Consultants
1101 Sylvan Avenue, Suite B-20
Modesto, CA 95350
(209) 529-5051
Contact: Mr. James Ortman
Minimum Salary Placed: $30,000
Recruiting Specialty: Sales

MONTEREY

Corporate Solutions
1173 Ninth Street
Monterey, CA 93940
(408) 646-0779
Contact: Ms. Judy Marra
Recruiting Specialty: Accounting and finance

David Fockler & Associates, Inc.
25944 Paseo Estribo
Monterey, CA 93940
(408) 649-6666
Contact: Mr. David Fockler
Minimum Salary Placed: $50,000
Recruiting Specialty: Consumer products, sales and marketing

Gibson & Company, Inc.
P.O. Box 1547
Monterey, CA 93942
(408) 373-3600
Contact: Mr. Bruce Gibson
Minimum Salary Placed: $125,000
Recruiting Specialty: General

Management Recruiters
494 Alvarado Street, Suite F
Monterey, CA 93940
(408) 649-0737
Contact: Mr. Richard Kashinsky
Minimum Salary Placed: $35,000
Recruiting Specialty: General

MORAGA

Madden Associates
P.O. Box 6775
Moraga, CA 94570
(510) 284-3634
Contact: Ms. Linda Madden
Recruiting Specialty: Real estate and consulting engineering

MOSS BEACH

Ballantyne & Associates
P.O. Box 810
Moss Beach, CA 94038
(415) 495-4641
Contact: Mr. Tom Ballantyne
Minimum Salary Placed: $55,000
Recruiting Specialty: Sales and marketing in manufacturing

MOUNTAIN VIEW

Adler-Brown Associates
2672 Bayshore Parkway, Suite 524
Mountain View, CA 94043
(415) 960-7101
Minimum Salary Placed: $25,000
Recruiting Specialty: Computer networks
and data communications

Bryson Myers Company
2083 Old Middlefield Way, Suite 206
Mountain View, CA 94043
(415) 964-7600
Contact: Mr. C. Myers
Minimum Salary Placed: $25,000
Recruiting Specialty: High technology

Tech Systems Research
1928 Old Middlefield Way
Mountain View, CA 94043
(415) 321-1216
Minimum Salary Placed: $30,000
Recruiting Specialty: Technical disciplines

Warren Wicke and Company
625 Ellis Street
Mountain View, CA 94043
(415) 962-1184
Contact: Mr. Warren Wicke
Minimum Salary Placed: $25,000
Recruiting Specialty: Accounting and fi-
nance

NAPA

Alkar Personnel Services
3273 Claremont Way, Suite 104
Napa, CA 94558
(707) 224-5468
Contact: Ms. Liz Pridmore
Recruiting Specialty: General

J.H. Lindell and Company
1420 3rd Street
Napa, CA 94559
(707) 259-1771
Minimum Salary Placed: $30,000
Recruiting Specialty: Real estate

Prouty and Associates
1339 Pearl Street
Napa, CA 94559
(707) 253-9037
Contact: Mr. Dennis Prouty
Minimum Salary Placed: $150,000
Recruiting Specialty: Electronics

NEVADA CITY

Kremple Consulting
222 Reward Street
Nevada City, CA 95959
(916) 478-9050
Contact: Mr. Bob Kremple
Minimum Salary Placed: $50,000
Recruiting Specialty: General

NEWARK

Pro Staff
5600 Morvry School Road, Suite 305
Newark, CA 94560
(510) 657-7900
Recruiting Specialty: General

Spectra West
39899 Ballantine, Suite 218
Newark, CA 94560
(415) 594-1444
Contact: Mr. Fred Arredondo
Minimum Salary Placed: $50,000
Recruiting Specialty: Computers and
high technology

NEWPORT BEACH

Accountants On Call
5000 Birch Street, Suite 550
Newport Beach, CA 92660
(714) 955-0100
Contact: Ms. Janet Tyler
Recruiting Specialty: Finance and accounting

Ankenbrandt Group
4685 Macarthur Court, Suite 480
Newport Beach, CA 92660
(714) 955-1455
Contact: Mr. David Ankenbrandt
Minimum Salary Placed: $35,000
Recruiting Specialty: General

Arboit Associates
5020 Campus
Newport Beach, CA 92660
(714) 833-8186
Contact: Mr. Bob Arboit
Minimum Salary Placed: $25,000
Recruiting Specialty: General

California Management Enterprises
2700 W. Coast Highway, Suite 230
Newport Beach, CA 92663
(714) 642-8510
Minimum Salary Placed: $25,000
Recruiting Specialty: General

Career Consultants International
620 Newport Center Drive, 11th Floor
Newport Beach, CA 92660
(714) 347-8414
Contact: Mr. George Vasu
Minimum Salary Placed: $25,000
Recruiting Specialty: Finance and accounting

Career Development Service
309 Promontory Drive East
Newport Beach, CA 92660
(714) 673-1107
Contact: Mr. Bruce Bollen
Recruiting Specialty: General

Cliff Schacht Company
P.O. Box 7966
Newport Beach, CA 92658
(714) 759-8966
Minimum Salary Placed: $30,000
Recruiting Specialty: Flexible packaging and paper

Corporate Careers
1500 Quail St., Suite 290
Newport Beach, CA 92660
(714) 476-7007
Contact: Ms. Dolores Cronin
Recruiting Specialty: Sales and marketing

Cory Associates Agency
1401 Dove Street, Suite 230
Newport Beach, CA 92660
(714) 261-1988
Contact: Mr. Tom Cory
Recruiting Specialty: Sales and marketing

Jacqueline Dey Company
110 Newport Center Drive
Newport Beach, CA 92660
(714) 760-9449
Contact: Ms. Jackie Dey
Minimum Salary Placed: $35,000
Recruiting Specialty: Real estate development

Drake & Associates
5100 Birch Street
Newport Beach, CA 92660
(714) 222-0711

Contact: Tom
Minimum Salary Placed: $50,000
Recruiting Specialty: General

The Enghauser Group
111 Newport Center Drive, Suite 200
Newport Beach, CA 92660
(714) 760-8118
Contact: Mr. Paul Enghauser
Minimum Salary Placed: $25,000
Recruiting Specialty: General

Hemingway Personnel, Inc.
1301 Dove Street, Suite 960
Newport Beach, CA 92660
(714) 851-1228
Contact: Mr. Arne Beruldsen
Minimum Salary Placed: $35,000
Recruiting Specialty: Accounting and finance

International Staffing Consultants, Inc.
610 Newport Center Drive, Suite 31040
Newport Beach, CA 92660
(714) 721-7990
Contact: Mr. James Gettys
Minimum Salary Placed: $25,000
Recruiting Specialty: Technical disciplines and human resources

Korn/Ferry International
1300 Dove Street, Suite 300
Newport Beach, CA 92660
(714) 851-1834
Contact: Mr. Elliot Gordon
Minimum Salary Placed: $100,000
Recruiting Specialty: General

O'Shea, Divine & Company, Inc.
610 Newport Center Drive, Suite 450
Newport Beach, CA 92660
(714) 720-9070
Contact: Mr. Robert Divine
Minimum Salary Placed: $75,000
Recruiting Specialty: General

Robert Ottke Associates
P.O. Box 7553
Newport Beach, CA 92660
(714) 759-1515
Contact: Mr. Robert Ottke
Minimum Salary Placed: $50,000
Recruiting Specialty: General

Prosearch
4500 Campus Drive, Suite 130
Newport Beach, CA 92660
(714) 757-0135
Contact: Ms. Sharon Dodson
Minimum Salary Placed: $25,000
Recruiting Specialty: General

Emery A. Rose & Associates
110 Newport Center Drive, Suite 200
Newport Beach, CA 92660
(714) 640-7370
Contact: Mr. Emery Rose
Minimum Salary Placed: $30,000
Recruiting Specialty: High technology and defense-related industries

W. Shryock & Company
160 Newport Center Drive, Suite 100
Newport Beach, CA 92660
(714) 759-7600
Contact: Mr. William Shryock
Minimum Salary Placed: $75,000
Recruiting Specialty: Real estate

Vlcek & Company, Inc.
620 Newport Center Drive, 11th Floor
Newport Beach, CA 92660
(714) 752-0661
Contact: Mr. Thomas Vlcek
Minimum Salary Placed: $60,000
Recruiting Specialty: General

West Coast Hospitality Search
620 Newport Center Drive, 11th Floor
Newport Beach, CA 92660
(714) 721-6603
Contact: Mr. Jim Ginther
Minimum Salary Placed: $30,000
Recruiting Specialty: Hospitality

Wright and Company
2103 Yacht Grayling
Newport Beach, CA 92660
(714) 759-7056
Contact: Mr. Jack Wright
Minimum Salary Placed: $35,000
Recruiting Specialty: General

NEWPORT COAST

EXSEL International, Inc.
4 Morning View Drive, Suite 200
Newport Coast, CA 92657
(714) 497-1775
Contact: Mr. James Smith
Minimum Salary Placed: $40,000
Recruiting Specialty: Finance disciplines
in finance, service, healthcare and insurance

NORCO

Presley Consultants, Inc.
812 Third Street
Norco, CA 91760
(909) 734-2237
Contact: Mr. Philip Presley
Minimum Salary Placed: $50,000
Recruiting Specialty: Hospitality

NORTH HOLLYWOOD

Green Trice Company
13366 Camarillo Street
North Hollywood, CA 91602
(818) 985-6200
Contact: Mr. James Trice
Minimum Salary Placed: $100,000
Recruiting Specialty: Stock brokerage
and some general

NORTHRIDGE

Furlong Search, Inc.
19312 Romar Street
Northridge, CA 91324
(818) 885-7044
Contact: Mr. James Furlong
Minimum Salary Placed: $60,000
Recruiting Specialty: Consumer electronics and semi-conductors

Keyth Hart Inc.
19312 Romar Street
Northridge, CA 91324
(818) 773-0475
Contact: Ms. Keyth Hart
Minimum Salary Placed: $75,000
Recruiting Specialty: Attorneys

NOVATO

Robert Beech Inc.
100 Montura Way
Novato, CA 94949
(415) 884-2600
Contact: Mr. Robert Beech
Minimum Salary Placed: $40,000
Recruiting Specialty: High technology,
data and telecommunications

Core Group
630 Davidson Street
Novato, CA 94945
(415) 899-3171
Contact: Mr. David Lego
Minimum Salary Placed: $25,000
Recruiting Specialty: General

Data Graph Executive Search
P.O. Box 1772
Novato, CA 94948
(415) 898-3171
Contact: Mr. B. Costigan
Minimum Salary Placed: $25,000
Recruiting Specialty: Data processing

Harreus & Associates, Inc.
2250 Vineyard Road
Novato, CA 94947
(415) 898-7879
Contact: Mr. Charles Harreus
Minimum Salary Placed: $60,000
Recruiting Specialty: Marketing and advertising in consumer products and services

Insearch Management Consultant
250 Bel Marin Keys Boulevard
Novato, CA 94949
(415) 884-2700

Contact: Mr. Michael Huskins
Recruiting Specialty: Multimedia and entertainment

Matthews, Barkin and Associates
1701 Novato Boulevard
Novato, CA 94947
(415) 899-1100
Contact: Mr. Ken Barkin
Minimum Salary Placed: $25,000
Recruiting Specialty: General

Robert Half Accountemps
100 Roland Way
Novato, CA 94945
(415) 892-9563
Contact: Ms. Susan Farrow
Recruiting Specialty: Accounting and finance

Schalich and Company
51 Oak Valley Drive
Novato, CA 94947
(415) 899-1193
Contact: Ms. Beverly Schalich
Minimum Salary Placed: $25,000
Recruiting Specialty: General

Search Solutions
695 De Long Avenue
Novato, CA 94945
(415) 898-1800
Contact: Mr. M. Robbins
Minimum Salary Placed: $25,000
Recruiting Specialty: Sales and marketing in computers

Spelman & Associates
444 Alameda De La Loma
Novato, CA 94949
(415) 382-8228
Recruiting Specialty: Biotech scientists

Thomas Associates
127 Cobblestone Court
Novato, CA 94945
(415) 331-8700
Contact: Mr. Tom Marino
Minimum Salary Placed: $40,000
Recruiting Specialty: High technology

OAKLAND

Accountants Executive Search
7677 Oakport Street
Oakland, CA 94621
(510) 633-1665
Contact: Ms. J. Herbert
Minimum Salary Placed: $25,000
Recruiting Specialty: Finance and accounting

Accountants On Call
7677 Oakport Street, Suite 180
Oakland, CA 94621
(510) 633-1665
Contact: Ms. Julie Herberth
Recruiting Specialty: Finance and accounting

Accountemps
1999 Harrison Street
Oakland, CA 94612
(510) 839-2100
Contact: Ms. S. Lowder
Recruiting Specialty: Finance and accounting

Bay Resources Inc.
519 17th Street
Oakland, CA 94612
(510) 465-2781
Contact: Ms. A. Adams
Minimum Salary Placed: $25,000
Recruiting Specialty: Accounting and finance

CRI Professional Search
1784 Leimert Boulevard
Oakland, CA 94602
(510) 531-1681
Contact: Mr. Charles Acridge
Minimum Salary Placed: $35,000
Recruiting Specialty: Healthcare

K.E.Y Resources
505 - 14th St., Suite 820
Oakland, CA 94612
(510) 522-8080
Contact: Mr. Mike Binder
Recruiting Specialty: General

Romac and Associates
2101 Webster Street, Suite 1500
Oakland, CA 94612
(510) 451-5956
Contact: Mr. J. McLaughlin
Minimum Salary Placed: $25,000
Recruiting Specialty: Accounting and finance

Ryals and Associates Inc.
505 14th Street, Suite 330
Oakland, CA 94612
(510) 839-5330
Contact: Ms. B. Ryals
Recruiting Specialty: Technical and finance

Sales Consultants
480 Roland Way, Suite 103
Oakland, CA 94621
(510) 569-6231
Contact: Mr. Tom Thrower
Minimum Salary Placed: $35,000
Recruiting Specialty: Sales

OCEANSIDE

California Search Consultants
2103 S. El Camino Real
Oceanside, CA 92054
(619) 439-5511
Contact: Mr. J. Morris
Minimum Salary Placed: $35,000
Recruiting Specialty: Engineering and science

Open Systems Consultants
P.O. Box 1218
Oceanside, CA 92051-1218
(619) 967-9600
Contact: Mr. Gary Schlageter
Recruiting Specialty: General

OJAI

Scott-Marlow Agency
1919 Meiners Road
Ojai, CA 93023
(805) 646-5609
Contact: Mr. Dan Komiako
Recruiting Specialty: Accounting and finance

ONTARIO

Search West, Inc.
3401 Centrelake Drive, Suite 600
Ontario, CA 91764
(909) 390-1966
Contact: Mr. Nate Reddicks
Minimum Salary Placed: $25,000
Recruiting Specialty: General

ORANGE

Clanton & Company
1095 North Main Street, Suite M
Orange, CA 92667
(714) 532-5652
Contact: Ms. Diane Clanton
Minimum Salary Placed: $35,000
Recruiting Specialty: Sales in food and related industries

Discovery Staffing
1820 Orangewood Avenue, Suite 204
Orange, CA 92868
(714) 771-6686
Contact: Mr. R. Shuler
Minimum Salary Placed: $35,000
Recruiting Specialty: General

Fox-Morris Associates, Inc.
1940 E. Orangewood Avenue, Suite 207
Orange, CA 92668
(714) 634-2600
Minimum Salary Placed: $35,000
Recruiting Specialty: General

Management Recruiters/Sales Consultants
One City Boulevard West, Suite 710
Orange, CA 92668
(714) 978-0500
Contact: Ms. Pat Gregg
Minimum Salary Placed: $20,000
Recruiting Specialty: General

Frank Parillo & Associates
1801 E. Heim Avenue, Suite 200
Orange, CA 92665
(714) 921-8008
Contact: Mr. Frank Parillo
Minimum Salary Placed: $50,000
Recruiting Specialty: Biotechnology and healthcare

Physicians Search Associates Agency
1224 E. Katella Avenue, Suite 202
Orange, CA 92667
(714) 288-8350
Contact: Mr. Clifford Rauch
Minimum Salary Placed: $50,000
Recruiting Specialty: Physicians

Professional Health Care Search
210 City Boulevard, West, Suite 118
Orange, CA 92668
(714) 634-4613
Contact: Mr. Eden Dankowski
Recruiting Specialty: General

Search West, Inc.
750 The City Drive South, Suite 100
Orange, CA 92668
(714) 748-0400
Contact: Mr. Robert Cowan
Minimum Salary Placed: $25,000
Recruiting Specialty: General

Unisearch
790 The City Drive South, Suite 150
Orange, CA 92667
(714) 748-0700
Contact: Mr. J. Rose
Minimum Salary Placed: $25,000
Recruiting Specialty: General

Walker Stephens Company
1038 N. Tustin Avenue
Orange, CA 92667
(714) 997-4380
Contact: Mr. Hugh Walker
Minimum Salary Placed: $45,000
Recruiting Specialty: Computer graphics

ORINDA

J. J. Professional Services
12 Orinda Way, Suite 12-C
Orinda, CA 94563
(510) 254-3011
Contact: Ms. Aimee Johnson
Recruiting Specialty: Electronics, environmental, and manufacturing

OXNARD

Lincoln International
999 West 7th Street
Oxnard, CA 93030
(805) 487-3236
Contact: Mr. Scott Lincoln
Minimum Salary Placed: $30,000
Recruiting Specialty: General

PACIFIC GROVE

Cameron Consulting Group
1112 Austin Avenue
Pacific Grove, CA 93950
(408) 646-8415
Contact: Mr. James Cameron
Minimum Salary Placed: $60,000
Recruiting Specialty: General

Herlien Search Consultants
P.O. Box 51246
Pacific Grove, CA 93950
(408) 373-1331
Contact: Ms. Pauline Herlien
Minimum Salary Placed: $35,000
Recruiting Specialty: Engineering, marketing and sales in high technology

PACIFIC PALISADES

Hill & Associates
860 Via de la Paz Suite E-2
Pacific Palisades, CA 90272
(310) 573-1261
Contact: Mr. Tom Hill
Minimum Salary Placed: $50,000
Recruiting Specialty: General

Kremple & Meade, Inc.
P.O. Box 426
Pacific Palisades, CA 90272
(310) 459-4221
Contact: Ms. Jeannette Clemens
Minimum Salary Placed: $100,000
Recruiting Specialty: General

PALM DESERT

Bolen and Associates
73710 Fred Warning Drive
Palm Desert, CA 92260
(619) 773-3723
Contact: Mr. Dan Bolen
Minimum Salary Placed: $25,000
Recruiting Specialty: Rotation equipment and computers

C-E Search
42335 Washington Street, Suite E120
Palm Desert, CA 92211
(619) 568-3060
Contact: Mr. Jim Brown
Minimum Salary Placed: $30,000
Recruiting Specialty: Industrial construction

PALM SPRINGS

Cadillac Associates
100 South Sunrise Way, Suite 353
Palm Springs, CA 92262
(619) 327-0920
Contact: Mr. Dwight Hanna
Recruiting Specialty: Healthcare and some general

Jerry Pollack & Associates
2343E Miramonte Circle West
Palm Springs, CA 92264
(619) 328-0921
Contact: Mr. Jerry Pollack
Minimum Salary Placed: $40,000
Recruiting Specialty: Chain store retailing

Pursuant Legal Consultants
P.O. Box 1781
Palm Springs, CA 92263
(619) 325-2953
Contact: Mr. Allen Norman
Minimum Salary Placed: $50,000
Recruiting Specialty: Legal

Thomas Magnum Company
2469 Cahuilla Hills Road
Palm Springs, CA 92264
(619) 325-0700
Contact: Mr. William Magnum
Minimum Salary Placed: $75,000
Recruiting Specialty: General

PALMDALE

Vic Perkins Management Consultants
310 E. Palmdale Boulevard, Suite K-2
Palmdale, CA 93550
(805) 267-2240
Contact: Mr. Vic Perkins
Recruiting Specialty: Electronics, engineering, and software development

PALO ALTO

Accountants Inc.
175 Forest Avenue
Palo Alto, CA 94301
(415) 325-1411

Contact: Ms. D. Passen
Minimum Salary Placed: $25,000
Recruiting Specialty: Finance and accounting

Accountants On Call
525 University Avenue, Suite 23
Palo Alto, CA 94301
(415) 328-8400
Contact: Mr. David Mason
Recruiting Specialty: Finance and accounting

Ames & Ames
P.O. Box 7404
Palo Alto, CA 94026
(415) 322-4000
Contact: Mr. Andrew Ames
Minimum Salary Placed: $100,000
Recruiting Specialty: High technology medical products.

Avery Group
444 Ramona Street
Palo Alto, CA 94301
(415) 688-7900
Contact: Ms. K. Avery
Minimum Salary Placed: $40,000
Recruiting Specialty: Technical disciplines for software

C.R. Associates
378 Cambridge Avenue, Suite D
Palo Alto, CA 94306
(415) 324-9000
Contact: Mr. Harold Stephenson
Minimum Salary Placed: $30,000
Recruiting Specialty: Banking

Fell and Nicholson Technology
1731 Embarcadero Road
Palo Alto, CA 94303
(415) 856-9200
Contact: Mr. J. Nicholson
Minimum Salary Placed: $40,000
Recruiting Specialty: Technical disciplines in communications, networks and high technology

Charlotte Germane Legal Search
394 University Avenue, P.O. Box 292
Palo Alto, CA 94302
(415) 326-3084
Contact: Ms. Charlotte Germane
Minimum Salary Placed: $50,000
Recruiting Specialty: Attorneys in copyright, trademark and patent law

Haley Associates, Inc.
526 Ramona Street
Palo Alto, CA 94301
(415) 323-0456
Contact: Mr. Timothy Haley
Minimum Salary Placed: $150,000
Recruiting Specialty: High technology

Hemenway Associates
607 St. Claire Drive
Palo Alto, CA 94306
(415) 424-9230
Contact: Mr. Scott Hemenway
Minimum Salary Placed: $50,000
Recruiting Specialty: Software engineering and telecommunications

International Research Group
345 Manvanita Avenue
Palo Alto, CA 94303
(415) 833-1050

Contact: Ms. Sherrie Wilkins
Minimum Salary Placed: $60,000
Recruiting Specialty: Chemicals, soap, perfume and pharmaceuticals

Donovan Martin & Associates
1000 Elwell Court, Suite 217
Palo Alto, CA 94303
(415) 969-8235
Contact: Mr. Donovan Martin
Minimum Salary Placed: $70,000
Recruiting Specialty: General

Douglas Owen Search Consultants
2814 South Court Street
Palo Alto, CA 94306
(415) 321-0193
Contact: Mr. Douglas Owen
Minimum Salary Placed: $80,000
Recruiting Specialty: Technical disciplines

Rusher, Loscavio & LoPresto
2479 E. Bayshore Road, Suite 700
Palo Alto, CA 94303
(415) 494-0883
Contact: Mr. Robert LoPresto
Minimum Salary Placed: $100,000
Recruiting Specialty: General

Adele Steinmetz Techniquest
711 Colorado Avenue
Palo Alto, CA 94303
(415) 321-3723
Contact: Ms. Adele Steinmetz
Minimum Salary Placed: $30,000
Recruiting Specialty: General

TASA Executive Search
430 Cowper Street, Suite 206
Palo Alto, CA 94301
(415) 323-0202
Contact: Mr. Herman DeKesel
Minimum Salary Placed: $120,000
Recruiting Specialty: General

Transpacific Group
935 Middlefield Road
Palo Alto, CA 94301
(415) 327-8801
Minimum Salary Placed: $65,000
Recruiting Specialty: Software

Yelverton Executive Search
2465 E. Bayshore Road, Suite 301
Palo Alto, CA 94303
(415) 354-0231
Contact: Mr. Jack Yelverton
Minimum Salary Placed: $75,000
Recruiting Specialty: High technology

PALOS VERDES ESTATES

Finnegan Associates
P.O. Box 1183
Palos Verdes Estates, CA 90274
(310) 375-8555
Contact: Mr. Richard Finnegan
Minimum Salary Placed: $100,000
Recruiting Specialty: General

PASADENA

Austin and Associates
215 North Marengo Avenue
Pasadena, CA 91101
(818) 793-4807
Contact: Mr. Chris Austin
Minimum Salary Placed: $30,000
Recruiting Specialty: General

J. Kevin Coleman & Associates, Inc.
2609 E. Colorado Boulevard
Pasadena, CA 91117
(818) 792-0533
Contact: Mr. J. Kevin Coleman
Minimum Salary Placed: $60,000
Recruiting Specialty: Finance, manufacturing and communications

General Management Resources
201 S. Lake Avenue
Pasadena, CA 91101
(818) 304-9337
Contact: Mr. M. Wood
Minimum Salary Placed: $60,000
Recruiting Specialty: MIS and finance

Gary Kaplan & Associates
201 S. Lake Avenue, Suite 600
Pasadena, CA 91101
(818) 796-8100
Contact: Mr. Gary Kaplan
Minimum Salary Placed: $70,000
Recruiting Specialty: General

Allen McDonald Associates, Inc.
1 S. Fair Oaks Avenue, Suite 303
Pasadena, CA 91105
(818) 405-0026
Contact: Mr. Bob Allen McDonald
Recruiting Specialty: General

Morris & Berger
201 South Lake Avenue, Suite 700
Pasadena, CA 91101
(818) 795-0522
Contact: Ms. Kristine Morris
Minimum Salary Placed: $50,000
Recruiting Specialty: General

Ott & Hansen, Inc.
136 S. Oak Knoll, Suite 300
Pasadena, CA 91101
(818) 578-0551
Contact: Mr. David Hansen
Minimum Salary Placed: $100,000
Recruiting Specialty: General

Protocol Inc.
300 N. Lake Avenue, Suite 208
Pasadena, CA 91101
(818) 449-2214
Contact: Mr. Robert Sparks
Minimum Salary Placed: $40,000
Recruiting Specialty: General

The Repovich - Reynolds Group
709 E. Colorado Boulevard, Suite 200
Pasadena, CA 91101
(818) 584-4853
Contact: Ms. Smooch Reynolds
Minimum Salary Placed: $70,000
Recruiting Specialty: General

Ryan, Miller & Associates
790 E. Colorado
Pasadena, CA 91101
(818) 567-4150
Contact: Mr. Roger Miller
Minimum Salary Placed: $30,000
Recruiting Specialty: Accounting and finance

David Shiplacoff & Associates
621 S. Pasadena Avenue, Suite 4
Pasadena, CA 91105
(818) 568-9830
Contact: Ms. Elaine Lissy
Minimum Salary Placed: $60,000
Recruiting Specialty: General

Tax Executive Search
1 W. California Boulevard
Pasadena, CA 91105
(818) 577-1120
Contact: Mr. C. Heil
Minimum Salary Placed: $25,000
Recruiting Specialty: Taxation

Melissa Turner and Associates
778 E. California Boulevard, Suite 2
Pasadena, CA 91106
(818) 793-0550
Contact: Ms. Melissa Turner
Minimum Salary Placed: $30,000
Recruiting Specialty: Finance and accounting

PASO ROBLES

Executive Consulting
1007 Riverside Drive, Suite 501
Paso Robles, CA 93446
(805) 238-5224
Contact: Ms. J. Mason
Minimum Salary Placed: $30,000
Recruiting Specialty: Healthcare

PESCADERO

Molton Associates
P.O. Box 130
Pescadero, CA 94060
(415) 434-0360
Contact: Ms. Shelly Molton
Recruiting Specialty: Financial services
and bank brokerage

PETALUMA

Ensearch Management Consultants
921 Transport Way, Suite 4
Petaluma, CA 94954
(707) 778-8252
Contact: Mr. Tim Mattis
Minimum Salary Placed: $50,000
Recruiting Specialty: Healthcare

Executive Search Consultants
2108 Appaloosa Circle
Petaluma, CA 94954
(707) 763-0100

Contact: Ms. Peg Iverson
Minimum Salary Placed: $40,000
Recruiting Specialty: Software development and product marketing

PLACENTIA

Robert Powers & Associates
P.O. Box 1085
Placentia, CA 92670
(714) 524-7279
Contact: Mr. Robert Powers
Minimum Salary Placed: $25,000
Recruiting Specialty: General

PLEASANT HILL

Wollborg Michelson Personnel
3480 Buskirk Road, Suite 100
Pleasant Hill, CA 94523
(510) 946-0200
Contact: Ms. Phyllis Raposa
Recruiting Specialty: General

PLEASANTON

Bay Area Executive Resources
5820 Stoneridge Mall Road, Suite 212
Pleasanton, CA 94588
(510) 734-8754
Contact: Mr. J. Glickman
Minimum Salary Placed: $25,000
Recruiting Specialty: General

Management Recruiters
4125 Mohr Avenue, Suite M
Pleasanton, CA 94566
(510) 462-8579
Contact: Mr. Mike Machi
Minimum Salary Placed: $20,000
Recruiting Specialty: General

Robert Half International
7901 Stoneridge Drive
Pleasanton, CA 94588
(510) 460-0888
Contact: Ms. R. Steel
Minimum Salary Placed: $25,000
Recruiting Specialty: Accounting and finance

Snelling Personnel
5000 Hopyard Road, Suite 420
Pleasanton, CA 94588
(510) 463-1900
Minimum Salary Placed: $20,000
Recruiting Specialty: General

Dick Williams & Associates
2557 Glen Isle Avenue
Pleasanton, CA 94588
(510) 426-6707
Contact: Mr. Dick Williams
Minimum Salary Placed: $75,000
Recruiting Specialty: Chemical and high technology

Wollborg Michelson Personnel
4637 Chabot Drive, Suite 101
Pleasanton, CA 94588
(510) 847-7300
Contact: Ms. Amy Pike
Recruiting Specialty: General

PORTOLA VALLEY

Strategic Alternatives
3 Portola Road
Portola Valley, CA 94028
(415) 851-2211
Contact: Mr. Ira Marks
Minimum Salary Placed: $80,000
Recruiting Specialty: General

RANCHO CORDOVA

System 1
2724 Kilgore Road, Suite 8
Rancho Cordova, CA 92670
(916) 635-4800
Contact: Laurie
Minimum Salary Placed: $30,000
Recruiting Specialty: Medical

RANCHO CUCAMONGA

Fortune Personnel Consultants
9330 Baseline Road, Suite 205
Rancho Cucamonga, CA 91701
(909) 941-9964
Contact: Mr. E. David Barker
Minimum Salary Placed: $35,000
Recruiting Specialty: General

RANCHO SANTA FE

Village Employment Agency
6002 El Tordo, Suite A
Rancho Santa Fe, CA 92067
(619) 756-4226
Contact: Ms. F. Beachy
Minimum Salary Placed: $25,000
Recruiting Specialty: Domestic services

RANCHO SANTA MARGARITA

Sterling Group
30021 Tomas
Rancho Santa Margarita, CA 92688
(714) 459-2110
Contact: Mr. Ron Henry
Minimum Salary Placed: $25,000
Recruiting Specialty: General

REDLAND

Management Recruiters, Inland Empire Agency
19 E. Citrus Avenue, Suite 201
Redland, CA 92373
(909) 335-2055
Contact: Mr. Maurice Meyers
Minimum Salary Placed: $20,000
Recruiting Specialty: Construction

REDONDO BEACH

Executive Quest
936 Calle Miramar
Redondo Beach, CA 90277
(310) 378-2959
Contact: Mr. P. McGregor
Minimum Salary Placed: $25,000
Recruiting Specialty: Software and computers

Hollander Horizon International
1617 S. Pacific Coast Highway, Suite C
Redondo Beach, CA 90277
(310) 540-3231
Contact: Mr. Arnold Zimmerman
Minimum Salary Placed: $30,000
Recruiting Specialty: Food and consumer products

Raycor Group
1874 Pacific Coast Highway, Suite 180
Redondo Beach, CA 90277
(310) 791-5090
Minimum Salary Placed: $25,000
Recruiting Specialty: General

REDWOOD CITY

A.T. Kearney Executive Search
3 Lagoon Drive, Suite 160
Redwood City, CA 94065
(415) 637-0620

Contact: Mr. Carl Olsen
Minimum Salary Placed: $70,000
Recruiting Specialty: General

Peden and Associates
2000 Broadway Street
Redwood City, CA 94063
(415) 367-1181
Contact: Ms. Ann Peden
Minimum Salary Placed: $30,000
Recruiting Specialty: High technology and software

REDWOOD SHORES

Advanced Technology Staffing
220 Twin Dolphin Drive
Redwood Shores, CA 94065
(415) 324-3222
Contact: Mr. D. Black
Minimum Salary Placed: $35,000
Recruiting Specialty: Computers

RESEDA

Lynn Borne and Company
6934 Canby Avenue, Suite 109
Reseda, CA 91335
(818) 881-9353
Contact: Ms. Lynn Borne
Minimum Salary Placed: $25,000
Recruiting Specialty: Accounting

RIO LINDA

Jim Reed
521 W. Ascot Avenue
Rio Linda, CA 95673
(916) 991-6464
Contact: Mr. Jim Reed
Minimum Salary Placed: $45,000
Recruiting Specialty: Banking and mortgage banking

RIVERSIDE

Accountants On Call
1650 Spruce Street, Suite 210
Riverside, CA 92507
(909) 686-2100
Contact: Mr. Vic Schneider
Recruiting Specialty: Finance and accounting

MacNaughton Associates
3600 Lime Street, Suite 232
Riverside, CA 92506
(909) 788-4951
Contact: Mr. Sperry MacNaughton
Minimum Salary Placed: $40,000
Recruiting Specialty: Higher education

Riverside Personnel Service
3590 Central Avenue, Suite 200
Riverside, CA 92506
(909) 788-7900
Contact: Ms. Kathleen Harman
Recruiting Specialty: General

ROHNERT PARK

Harvey Bell and Associates
700 Lindsay Avenue
Rohnert Park, CA 94928
(707) 795-0650
Contact: Mr. Harvey Bell
Minimum Salary Placed: $25,000
Recruiting Specialty: General

ROLLING HILLS ESTATES

Don Gertner and Associates
27520 Hawthorne Boulevard, Suite 150
Rolling Hills Estates, CA 90285
(310) 544-7145

Contact: Mr. Don Gertner
Minimum Salary Placed: $25,000
Recruiting Specialty: General

Global Resources
27520 Hawthorne Boulevard, Suite 285
Rolling Hills Estates, CA 90274
(310) 544-7144
Recruiting Specialty: General

ROSEVILLE

Tirocchi, Wright, Inc.
3017 Douglas Boulevard, Suite 300
Roseville, CA 95661
(916) 624-1700
Contact: Ms. Paula Wright
Minimum Salary Placed: $70,000
Recruiting Specialty: General

ROSS

A. William Smyth, Inc.
P.O. Box 380
Ross, CA 94957
(415) 457-8383
Contact: Mr. William Smyth
Minimum Salary Placed: $50,000
Recruiting Specialty: Consumer packaged goods, entertainment and hospitality

ROWLAND HEIGHTS

Accountants Executive Search
17700 Castleton Street, Suite 265
Rowland Heights, CA 91748
(818) 966-2929
Minimum Salary Placed: $25,000
Recruiting Specialty: Finance and accounting

SACRAMENTO

Management Recruiters
915 L Street, Suite 110
Sacramento, CA 95814
(916) 442-9116
Contact: Ms. Beth Dinse
Minimum Salary Placed: $20,000
Recruiting Specialty: General

Robert Half International
2180 Harvard Street, Suite 250
Sacramento, CA 95815
(916) 441-4562
Contact: Ms. R. Bollinger
Minimum Salary Placed: $25,000
Recruiting Specialty: Accounting and finance

Sales Consultants
4320 Auburn Boulevard, Suite 2100
Sacramento, CA 95841
(916) 481-7000
Contact: Mr. Larry Williams
Minimum Salary Placed: $20,000
Recruiting Specialty: Sales

Tonik Search
2100 Watt Avenue, Suite 130
Sacramento, CA 95825
(916) 488-5300
Contact: Mr. Nick Past
Minimum Salary Placed: $25,000
Recruiting Specialty: General

Wilcox Bertoux & Miller
601 University Avenue, Suite 236
Sacramento, CA 95825
(916) 929-7723
Contact: Mr. Fred Wilcox
Minimum Salary Placed: $45,000
Recruiting Specialty: General

Jay Wren & Associates
6355 Riverside Boulevard, Suite P
Sacramento, CA 95831
(916) 424-8614
Contact: Mr. Jay Wren
Minimum Salary Placed: $50,000
Recruiting Specialty: Sales

SAINT HELENA

JMC Partners
2930 Silverado Trail North
St. Helena, CA 94574
(707) 963-3353
Contact: Mr. Jerry McQuiddy
Minimum Salary Placed: $25,000
Recruiting Specialty: Construction, engineering and design

SALINAS

Career Connections
P.O. Box 2552
Salinas, CA 93902
(408) 757-8756
Contact: Ms. D. Pope
Minimum Salary Placed: $25,000
Recruiting Specialty: Accounting and medical

Marlene Critchfield Company Career
150 W. Gabilan, Suite 2
Salinas, CA 93901
(408) 753-2466
Contact: Ms. Marlene Critchfield
Minimum Salary Placed: $50,000
Recruiting Specialty: Produce and accounting

Marshall Group
1000 South Main, Suite 687
Salinas, CA 93901
(408) 484-1144
Contact: Ms. Lois Marshall
Minimum Salary Placed: $50,000
Recruiting Specialty: Franchising

J.W. Silvera and Company Search
523 Pajaro Street
Salinas, CA 93901
(408) 758-0808
Contact: Mr. Jim Silvera
Minimum Salary Placed: $25,000
Recruiting Specialty: General

SAN CARLOS

The Corporate Staff, Inc.
P.O. Box 1082
San Carlos, CA 94070
(415) 344-2613
Contact: Mr. Stephen Pickford
Minimum Salary Placed: $50,000
Recruiting Specialty: General

Med Quest
655 Sky Way
San Carlos, CA 94070
(415) 593-3103
Contact: Ms. Lynn Bradhead
Minimum Salary Placed: $30,000
Recruiting Specialty: Medical

Silicon Valley Software
953 Washington St.
San Carlos, CA 94070
(415) 596-1127
Contact: Mr. Steve Vizena
Recruiting Specialty: Software development

SAN CLEMENTE

Aaron Jensen Associates Inc.
275 N. Ola Vista
San Clemente, CA 92672
(714) 498-6050
Contact: Ms. E. Korsen
Minimum Salary Placed: $25,000
Recruiting Specialty: Pulp and paper

IPR, Inc.
302 N. El Camino Real, Suite 200
San Clemente, CA 92672
(714) 361-7800
Contact: Mr. Gordon Thomas
Recruiting Specialty: General

Jeff McDermott and Associates
521 West Lobos Marinos
San Clemente, CA 92672
(714) 366-1517
Contact: Mr. Jeff McDermott
Minimum Salary Placed: $40,000
Recruiting Specialty: Healthcare

Tom Pezman and Associates
P.O. Box 3175
San Clemente, CA 92674
(714) 661-6637
Contact: Mr. Tom Pezman
Minimum Salary Placed: $25,000
Recruiting Specialty: General; publishing

Teleforce International
P.O. Box 3175
San Clemente, CA 92674
(714) 661-3337
Contact: Mr. Joe Barritas
Recruiting Specialty: Telecommunications

SAN DIEGO

Abcow Services
2525 Camino Del Rio South
San Diego, CA 92108
(619) 291-7000
Contact: Mr. J. Gilbert
Minimum Salary Placed: $20,000
Recruiting Specialty: Accounting and bookkeeping

Accounting Resources International, Inc.
409 Camino del Rio South, Suite 205
San Diego, CA 92108
(619) 291-7990
Contact: Mr. T. Robert Storevik
Minimum Salary Placed: $30,000
Recruiting Specialty: Finance and accounting

Automotive + Agency
P.O. Box 17808
San Diego, CA 92177
(619) 273-5638
Contact: Ms. Marie Valdisera
Recruiting Specialty: General

The Bencom Group
4350 Executive Drive, Suite 200
San Diego, CA 92121
(619) 453-8651
Contact: Mr. Mark Gamboa
Minimum Salary Placed: $50,000
Recruiting Specialty: Healthcare

Dick Berg & Associates
P.O. Box 927171
San Diego, CA 92192
(619) 452-2745
Contact: Mr. Richard Lechtenberg
Recruiting Specialty: General

David S. Burt Associates
17161 Alva Road, Suite 3123
San Diego, CA 92127
(619) 673-4381
Contact: Mr. David Burt
Minimum Salary Placed: $30,000
Recruiting Specialty: Chemicals

Coastal Legal Consultants
701 Kettner Boulevard
San Diego, CA 92101
(619) 232-5537
Contact: Ms. Suzanne White
Minimum Salary Placed: $35,000
Recruiting Specialty: Legal

Communications Pro Search
9285 Dowdy Drive, Suite 207
San Diego, CA 92126
(619) 695-8202
Contact: Mr. G. Welch
Minimum Salary Placed: $25,000
Recruiting Specialty: Cable television

Creative Leadership Consultant
11777 Bernardo Plaza Court
San Diego, CA 92128
(619) 592-0506
Contact: Mr. Bob Spence
Minimum Salary Placed: $50,000
Recruiting Specialty: General

Culver Executive Search Group
6610 Flanders Drive
San Diego, CA 92121
(619) 587-9600
Contact: Mr. T. Culver
Recruiting Specialty: Sales and marketing

The Eastridge Group
2355 Northside Drive, Suite 180
San Diego, CA 92108
(619) 260-2085
Contact: Ms. Nanci Porter
Minimum Salary Placed: $30,000
Recruiting Specialty: Environmental

Executive Group
9191 Towne Centre Drive, Suite 105
San Diego, CA 92122
(619) 457-8100
Contact: Mr. Paul Bouzan
Minimum Salary Placed: $60,000
Recruiting Specialty: General

Fargo Search Inc.
7801 Mission Center Court
San Diego, CA 92108
(619) 299-9734
Contact: Ms. Joan Davis
Minimum Salary Placed: $25,000
Recruiting Specialty: General

French and Associates
P.O. Box 152565
San Diego, CA 92195
(619) 565-2988
Contact: Mr. Dick Taylor
Minimum Salary Placed: $40,000
Recruiting Specialty: Manufacturing and operations

GSW Consulting Group, Inc.
5510 Morehouse Drive, Suite 260
San Diego, CA 921213
(619) 457-7500
Contact: Mr. Joel Winitz
Minimum Salary Placed: $60,000
Recruiting Specialty: General

Gavin Forbes and Associates
2207 Garnet Avenue, Suite F
San Diego, CA 92109
(619) 483-6696
Contact: Mr. D. Price
Minimum Salary Placed: $25,000
Recruiting Specialty: General

Michael R. Guerin Company
16368 Avenida Suavidad
San Diego, CA 92128
(619) 675-0395
Contact: Mr. Michael Guerin
Minimum Salary Placed: $60,000
Recruiting Specialty: Software

Harmenling and Associates
3232 Governor Drive
San Diego, CA 92122
(619) 455-6212
Contact: Mr. H. Harmeling
Minimum Salary Placed: $40,000
Recruiting Specialty: Retail and shopping-center development

Hawkins and Associates
2420 University Avenue
San Diego, CA 92104
(619) 294-2320
Contact: Mr. Edwin Hawkins
Minimum Salary Placed: $25,000
Recruiting Specialty: General

Health Care Professional Search
6065 Mission Gorge Road, Suite 173
San Diego, CA 92120
(619) 562-6564
Contact: Ms. Patti Carpenter
Recruiting Specialty: Healthcare

Image Support Systems Agency
950 Hotel Circle North
San Diego, CA 92108
(619) 220-0644
Contact: Mr. Wally Smith
Minimum Salary Placed: $30,000
Recruiting Specialty: General

Intech Summit Group, Inc.
5075 Shoreham Place, Suite 280
San Diego, CA 92122
(619) 452-2100
Contact: Mr. Robert Cohen
Minimum Salary Placed: $40,000
Recruiting Specialty: General

Roye Johnston Associates, Inc.
16885 W. Bernardo Drive, Suite 270
San Diego, CA 92127
(619) 487-5200
Contact: Ms. Roye Johnston
Recruiting Specialty: Physicians and
healthcare

E. Keith and Associates
4420 Hotel Circle Court, Suite 250
San Diego, CA 92108
(619) 294-4294
Contact: Mr. Rich Harold
Minimum Salary Placed: $30,000
Recruiting Specialty: General

LaCosta & Associates
6727 Flanders Drive, Suite 108
San Diego, CA 92121
(619) 457-1377
Contact: Mr. Paul LaCosta
Minimum Salary Placed: $25,000
Recruiting Specialty: General

**Management Recruiters/Sales
Consultants**
9455 Ridgehaven Court, Suite 205
San Diego, CA 92123
(619) 565-6600
Contact: Mr. Harvey Baron
Minimum Salary Placed: $35,000
Recruiting Specialty: General

Beverly Nelson & Associates Inc.
3727 Camino Del Rio S., Suite 200
San Diego, CA 92108
(619) 281-2727
Contact: Ms. Beverly Nelson
Minimum Salary Placed: $25,000
Recruiting Specialty: Insurance and high
technology

P & E Search
7710 Balboa Avenue, Suite 223B
San Diego, CA 92108
(619) 495-0025
Contact: Mr. Duane Kuperus
Minimum Salary Placed: $35,000
Recruiting Specialty: Power plant and en-
vironmental engineering

Jules Pincus and Associates
7801 Mission Center Court, Suite 200
San Diego, CA 92108
(619) 291-8079
Contact: Ms. Jules Pincus
Minimum Salary Placed: $25,000
Recruiting Specialty: Retailing

**Pro. Inc./Professional Recruiting
Office**
9191 Town Center Drive, Suite 102
San Diego, CA 92122
(619) 587-1313

Contact: Mr. Erwin Schneekluth
Minimum Salary Placed: $35,000
Recruiting Specialty: Healthcare and in-surance

Progressive Search Associates
12526 High Bluff Drive
San Diego, CA 92130
(619) 457-7818
Contact: Ms. M. Schmerling
Minimum Salary Placed: $25,000
Recruiting Specialty: General

Radosevic Associates
4350 La Jolla Village Drive, Suite 870
San Diego, CA 92122
(619) 642-0900
Contact: Mr. Frank Radosevic
Minimum Salary Placed: $50,000
Recruiting Specialty: General

Robert Half International
409 Camino Del Rio South, Suite 305
San Diego, CA 92108
(619) 291-7990
Contact: Mr. K. Norris
Minimum Salary Placed: $25,000
Recruiting Specialty: Accounting and fi-nance

Roberta Rea and Company
4510 Executive Drive
San Diego, CA 92121
(619) 457-3566
Minimum Salary Placed: $30,000
Recruiting Specialty: Retail and shopping center development

Larry Rosenthal and Associates
2820 Camino Del Rio South, Suite 160
San Diego, CA 92108
(619) 298-5825

Contact: Mr. Larry Rosenthal
Minimum Salary Placed: $25,000
Recruiting Specialty: General

Ryan-Allen & Associates, Inc.
732 Devon Court
San Diego, CA 92109
(619) 576-0737
Contact: Ms. Sheila Hawley
Minimum Salary Placed: $30,000
Recruiting Specialty: Accounting, fi-nance, banking and human resources

Search Dynamics
8765 Aero Drive
San Diego, CA 92123
(619) 292-5567
Minimum Salary Placed: $25,000
Recruiting Specialty: General

The Search Network
5755 Oberlin Drive, Suite 312
San Diego, CA 92121
(619) 535-0015
Contact: Ms. Liz Henderson
Minimum Salary Placed: $45,000
Recruiting Specialty: High technology

Sears & Associates
16776 Bernardo Center Drive,
 Suite 110B
San Diego, CA 92128
(619) 673-7000
Contact: Mr. Jerry Sears
Minimum Salary Placed: $80,000
Recruiting Specialty: Attorneys

Source EDP
4510 Executive Drive, Suite 211
San Diego, CA 92121
(619) 552-0300

Contact: Ms. Laurie Levenson
Minimum Salary Placed: $20,000
Recruiting Specialty: Computers, programming and MIS

Spectrum Consultants
12625 High Bluff Drive, Suite 215
San Diego, CA 92130
(619) 259-3232
Contact: Mr. G. W. Christiansen
Minimum Salary Placed: $70,000
Recruiting Specialty: High technology, engineering and manufacturing

Stephens and Associates
2168 Balboa Avenue, Suite 3
San Diego, CA 92109
(619) 270-8800
Contact: Mr. Lee Stephens
Minimum Salary Placed: $25,000
Recruiting Specialty: General

Strategic Search
4350 La Jolla Village Drive
San Diego, CA 92122
(619) 546-4400
Contact: Mr. Phillip Coelyn
Minimum Salary Placed: $25,000
Recruiting Specialty: Life sciences

Judy Thompson & Associates, Inc.
3727 Camino Del Rio S., Suite 200
San Diego, CA 92108
(619) 281-2626
Contact: Ms. Judy Thompson
Minimum Salary Placed: $25,000
Recruiting Specialty: Accounting and finance

R.J. Watkins and Company
625 Broadway, Suite 1210
San Diego, CA 92101
(619) 239-3094
Contact: Mr. R. Watkins
Minimum Salary Placed: $100,000
Recruiting Specialty: General

WestCare Executive Search
11535 Eaglesview Court, Suite 2E
San Diego, CA 92127
(619) 487-0909
Contact: Ms. Lisa West
Minimum Salary Placed: $40,000
Recruiting Specialty: Healthcare

SAN FRANCISCO

ABA Personnel Service Inc.
690 Market Street
San Francisco, CA 94104
(415) 434-4222
Contact: Melissa
Minimum Salary Placed: $25,000
Recruiting Specialty: General

Access Staffing
100 Pine
San Francisco, CA 94111
(415) 788-1200
Minimum Salary Placed: $25,000
Recruiting Specialty: General

Accountants Executive Search
44 Montgomery Street
San Francisco, CA 94104
(415) 398-3800
Contact: Mr. S. Libes
Minimum Salary Placed: $25,000
Recruiting Specialty: Finance and accounting

Accountants Inc.
555 Montgomery Street, Suite 811
San Francisco, CA 94111
(415) 434-1411
Contact: Ms. D. Burr
Minimum Salary Placed: $25,000
Recruiting Specialty: Finance and accounting

Accountants On Call
44 Montgomery Street, Suite 1250
San Francisco, CA 94104
(415) 398-3366
Contact: Ms. Sara Boyd
Recruiting Specialty: Finance and accounting

Accounting & Office Concepts
50 First Street, Suite 401
San Francisco, CA 94105-2413
(415) 995-9858
Contact: Mr. Bruce Zelony
Recruiting Specialty: Finance and accounting

Jeffrey Adams and Company
455 Market Street, 19th Floor
San Francisco, CA 94105
(415) 546-4150
Contact: Mr. Jeff Adams
Minimum Salary Placed: $25,000
Recruiting Specialty: General

Allard Associates
44 Montgomery Street, Suite 500
San Francisco, CA 94104
(415) 433-0500
Contact: Ms. Susan Allard
Minimum Salary Placed: $50,000
Recruiting Specialty: Banking and consumer credit

Allied Search Inc.
2030 Union Street, Suite 206
San Francisco, CA 94123
(415) 921-2200
Contact: Mr. D. May
Minimum Salary Placed: $25,000
Recruiting Specialty: General

Alper and Associates
353 Sacramento, Suite 1760
San Francisco, CA 94111
(415) 397-6611
Contact: Ms. Diane Alper
Recruiting Specialty: General

Amato & Associates, Inc.
388 Market Street, Suite 500
San Francisco, CA 94111
(415) 781-7664
Contact: Mr. Joseph D. Amato
Minimum Salary Placed: $50,000
Recruiting Specialty: Sales and marketing in insurance

Avis-Caravello Inc.
50 California, Suite 1500
San Francisco, CA 94111
(415) 979-0200
Contact: Mr. S. Barnett
Minimum Salary Placed: $60,000
Recruiting Specialty: Attorneys

Bascom & Associates
717 Market Street, Suite 306
San Francisco, CA 94103
(415) 896-5991
Contact: Ms. Betty Williams
Recruiting Specialty: General

Edward Bell Associates
50 1st Street
San Francisco, CA 94105
(415) 442-0270
Contact: Mr. Ed Bell
Minimum Salary Placed: $25,000
Recruiting Specialty: Accounting, finance
and technical disciplines in computers

Berger and Leff
1 Sansome Street
San Francisco, CA 94104
(415) 951-4750
Contact: Ms. L. Leff
Minimum Salary Placed: $25,000
Recruiting Specialty: Tax, accounting
and finance

Bioquest Inc.
100 Spear Street
San Francisco, CA 94105
(415) 777-2422
Contact: Mr. Roger Anderson
Minimum Salary Placed: $70,000
Recruiting Specialty: Pharmaceuticals
and biotechnology

Blue Garni and Company
Pier One
San Francisco, CA 94011
(415) 986-1110
Contact: Ms. P. Blue
Minimum Salary Placed: $70,000
Recruiting Specialty: General

Boyden
275 Battery Street, Suite 420
San Francisco, CA 94111
(415) 981-7900
Contact: Mr. Putney Westerfield
Minimum Salary Placed: $90,000
Recruiting Specialty: General

Business Specialists
655 Montgomery Street, Suite 515
San Francisco, CA 94111
(415) 421-9400
Contact: Mr. Gregory Foss
Recruiting Specialty: General

Interim Search Solutions
600 Montgomery Street, 37th Floor
San Francisco, CA 94111
(415) 788-7800
Contact: Mr. C. Juntunen
Minimum Salary Placed: $75,000
Recruiting Specialty: General

Bullis & Company, Inc.
120 Quintara Street
San Francisco, CA 94116
(415) 753-6140
Contact: Mr. Richard Bullis
Minimum Salary Placed: $75,000
Recruiting Specialty: General

L.R. Burke and Associates Inc.
2833 Sacramento Street
San Francisco, CA 94115
(415) 771-2552
Contact: Ms. L. Burke
Minimum Salary Placed: $25,000
Recruiting Specialty: General

CCIA Personnel
220 Montgomery Street
San Francisco, CA 94104
(415) 398-3894
Contact: Ms. S. Long
Recruiting Specialty: Paralegals and office support

Career Consociates
220 Montgomery Street, Penthouse
  Suite 2
San Francisco, CA 94104
(415) 398-3894
Contact: Ms. Sharron Long
Recruiting Specialty: General

Chartwell Partners International, Inc.
275 Battery Street, Suite 2180
San Francisco, CA 94111
(415) 296-0600
Contact: Mr. David deWilde
Minimum Salary Placed: $75,000
Recruiting Specialty: General

Chefs Agency
870 Market Street, Suite 863
San Francisco, CA 94102
(415) 392-1563
Minimum Salary Placed: $25,000
Recruiting Specialty: Culinary and hospitality

China Professional Resources
1 Maritime Plaza, Suite 850
San Francisco, CA 94111
(415) 544-9200
Contact: Ms. M. Chen
Minimum Salary Placed: $25,000
Recruiting Specialty: General

Colton Bernard Inc.
870 Market Street, Suite 822
San Francisco, CA 94102
(415) 399-8700
Contact: Mr. Harry Bernard
Minimum Salary Placed: $75,000
Recruiting Specialty: Apparel and retail

Concept Corporation
260 California Street, Suite 300
San Francisco, CA 94011
(415) 332-7373
Contact: Mr. R. Miner
Minimum Salary Placed: $30,000
Recruiting Specialty: Sales, marketing
and engineering in plastics and packaging

De Snoo Marianne
675 Madrid Street
San Francisco, CA 94112
(415) 337-9409
Contact: Ms. N. De Snoo Marianne
Minimum Salary Placed: $25,000
Recruiting Specialty: General

The Domann Organization
One Sansome Street, 19th Floor
San Francisco, CA 94104
(800) 923-6626
Contact: Mr. William Domann
Minimum Salary Placed: $60,000
Recruiting Specialty: General

Dougherty and Associates
447 Battery Street, Suite 300
San Francisco, CA 94111
(415) 773-8280
Contact: Ms. D. Dougherty
Minimum Salary Placed: $25,000
Recruiting Specialty: Paralegals and attorneys

Dunhill Personnel System
220 Montgomery Street, Suite 1085
San Francisco, CA 94104
(415) 956-3700
Contact: Mr. George Curtiss
Minimum Salary Placed: $30,000
Recruiting Specialty: General

Egon Zehnder International Inc.
100 Spear Street, Suite 920
San Francisco, CA 94105
(415) 904-7800
Contact: Mr. S. Ross Brown
Minimum Salary Placed: $80,000
Recruiting Specialty: Mergers and acquisitions and start-up organizations

Engineering Network Inc.
55 New Montgomery Street
San Francisco, CA 94105
(415) 543-4400
Minimum Salary Placed: $35,000
Recruiting Specialty: Engineering

Ethos Consulting, Inc.
100 Pine Street, Suite 750
San Francisco, CA 94111
(415) 397-2211
Contact: Mr. Conrad Prusak
Minimum Salary Placed: $100,000
Recruiting Specialty: General

Executive Direction
369 Pine Street
San Francisco, CA 94104
(415) 956-7070
Contact: Mr. F. Naderi
Minimum Salary Placed: $25,000
Recruiting Specialty: High technology

Leon A. Farley Associates
468 Jackson Street
San Francisco, CA 94111
(415) 989-0989
Contact: Mr. Creighton Barton
Minimum Salary Placed: $100,000
Recruiting Specialty: General

Ferneborg & Associates
388 Market Street, Suite 860
San Francisco, CA 94111
(415) 543-4181
Contact: Mr. John Ferneborg
Minimum Salary Placed: $80,000
Recruiting Specialty: General

Financial Resources Group
750 Bay Street
San Francisco, CA 94109
(415) 563-0466
Contact: Mr. Rob Thorpe
Minimum Salary Placed: $25,000
Recruiting Specialty: Finance

Neil Fink & Associates
900 N. Point Street, Suite 410
San Francisco, CA 94109
(415) 441-3777
Contact: Mr. Neil Fink
Recruiting Specialty: Multi-media, computers and audio-video

Garrison-Randall Inc.
1 Sansome Street, Suite 2100
San Francisco, CA 94104
(415) 433-2330
Contact: Ms. Rita Fornino
Minimum Salary Placed: $25,000
Recruiting Specialty: Medical

Geneva Group International
4 Embarcadero Center, Suite 3470
San Francisco, CA 94111
(415) 433-4646
Contact: Mr. Igor Sill
Minimum Salary Placed: $80,000
Recruiting Specialty: High technology

Tom Gilbert Associates
353 Sacramento Street
San Francisco, CA 94111
(415) 546-0112
Contact: Mr. Tom Gilbert
Minimum Salary Placed: $25,000
Recruiting Specialty: General

Robert Grant Associates, Inc.
100 Pine Street, Suite 2225
San Francisco, CA 94111
(415) 981-7424
Contact: Mr. Robert Grant
Minimum Salary Placed: $50,000
Recruiting Specialty: Financial services,
healthcare, food and beverage, data telecommunications

Heidrick & Struggles, Inc.
Four Embarcadero Center, Suite 3570
San Francisco, CA 94111
(415) 981-2854
Contact: Mr. Robert Saydah
Minimum Salary Placed: $70,000
Recruiting Specialty: General

Helstrom Turner and Associates
1750 Montgomery Street
San Francisco, CA 94111
(415) 921-0663
Contact: Mr. Doug Perlstadt
Minimum Salary Placed: $25,000
Recruiting Specialty: Retail, marketing
and multi-media

Bruce Hendry Associates
465 California Avenue
San Francisco, CA 94104
(415) 398-6540
Contact: Mr. Bruce Hendry
Minimum Salary Placed: $25,000
Recruiting Specialty: Healthcare

Hill Allyn Associates
P.O. Box 15247
San Francisco, CA 94115
(415) 922-8797
Contact: Ms. Gayle Hill
Minimum Salary Placed: $25,000
Recruiting Specialty: Accounting and fi-
nance

Holman Group Inc.
1592 Union Street, Suite 239
San Francisco, CA 94123
(415) 751-2700
Contact: Mr. John Holman
Minimum Salary Placed: $25,000
Recruiting Specialty: General

H. Hunter and Company
1177 California Street
San Francisco, CA 94108
(415) 776-5124
Contact: Ms. Susan Goldstein
Minimum Salary Placed: $25,000
Recruiting Specialty: General

Innovations PSI
345 California Street, Suite 1750
San Francisco, CA 84104
(415) 392-4022
Contact: Ms. P. Todd
Minimum Salary Placed: $25,000
Recruiting Specialty: Financial services

Interim Accounting Personnel
44 Montgomery Street
San Francisco, CA 94104
(415) 391-0200
Contact: Ms. Stephanie Greenburg
Minimum Salary Placed: $30,000
Recruiting Specialty: Accounting and fi-
nance

Johnson, Smith and Knisely
44 Montgomery, Suite 3060
San Francisco, CA 94104
(415) 397-0846
Contact: Ms. Sarah Ashby
Minimum Salary Placed: $90,000
Recruiting Specialty: General

Joseph Michaels Company
120 Montgomery, Suite 1260
San Francisco, CA 94104
(800) 786-1099
Contact: Mr. J. Pelayo
Minimum Salary Placed: $35,000
Recruiting Specialty: Accounting

KVB Partners Inc.
235 Pine Street
San Francisco, CA 94104
(415) 777-2199
Contact: Mr. S. King
Minimum Salary Placed: $25,000
Recruiting Specialty: High technology

Kaye and Company
30 Sonoma Street
San Francisco, CA 94133
(415) 398-2007
Contact: Ms. Andrea Kaye
Minimum Salary Placed: $25,000
Recruiting Specialty: General

K.E.Y. Resources
101 California Street, Suite 650
San Francisco, CA 94111
(415) 986-6700
Contact: Ms. Ginny Kim-Kennedy
Recruiting Specialty: General

Jeffrey Knapp Legal Search
100 Bush Street, Suite 1100
San Francisco, CA 94104
(415) 399-8734
Contact: Mr. Jeff Knapp
Minimum Salary Placed: $25,000
Recruiting Specialty: General

Korn/Ferry International
600 Montgomery Street, 31st Floor
San Francisco, CA 94111
(415) 956-1834
Contact: Mr. Buzz Schulte
Minimum Salary Placed: $100,000
Recruiting Specialty: General

Kronman Matthew and Associates
220 Montgomery Street, Suite 398
San Francisco, CA 94104
(415) 296-0494
Contact: Mr. R. Kronman
Minimum Salary Placed: $25,000
Recruiting Specialty: General

Larkin & Company
582 Market, Suite 1115
San Francisco, CA 94104
(415) 433-5338
Contact: Mr. Dick Larkin
Minimum Salary Placed: $70,000
Recruiting Specialty: High technology,
engineering, environmental

Ricci Lee Associates
100 Stear Street, Suite 1810
San Francisco, CA 94104
(415) 247-2980
Contact: Ms. Ricci Lee
Minimum Salary Placed: $25,000
Recruiting Specialty: Marketing and advertising

Levin Storm Company
1301 Page Street
San Francisco, CA 94117
(415) 552-9522
Contact: Ms. B. Levin
Minimum Salary Placed: $130,000
Recruiting Specialty: Pharmaceuticals,
biotechnology and medical devices

LifeScience Network, Inc.
1 Sansome Street, 21st Floor
San Francisco, CA 94104
(415) 951-1030
Contact: Mr. Randall Boris
Minimum Salary Placed: $60,000
Recruiting Specialty: Healthcare

Kathy MacDonald Associates
555 California, Suite 4490
San Francisco, CA 94140
(415) 433-0700
Contact: Ms. Kathy MacDonald
Minimum Salary Placed: $75,000
Recruiting Specialty: General

Maczkov-Biosciences
289 World Trade Center
San Francisco, CA 94111
(415) 312-0440
Contact: Mr. N. Maczkov
Minimum Salary Placed: $25,000
Recruiting Specialty: Biotechnology

Madsen Personnel Services
220 Sansome Street, 8th Floor
San Francisco, CA 94104
(415) 433-1018
Contact: Mr. Peter Fodor
Recruiting Specialty: General

Major, Wilson & Africa
655 Commercial Street
San Francisco, CA 94111
(415) 956-1010
Contact: Ms. Martha Fay Africa
Minimum Salary Placed: $40,000
Recruiting Specialty: Attorneys

McFeely Wackerle Shulman
425 California Street
San Francisco, CA 94104
(415) 398-3488
Contact: Mr. Mel Shulman
Minimum Salary Placed: $150,000
Recruiting Specialty: General

Edward Meister Executive
100 Bush, Suite 2309
San Francisco, CA 94111
(415) 362-6262
Contact: Mr. Ed Meister
Minimum Salary Placed: $25,000
Recruiting Specialty: Finance

Metz Dominguez and Associates
12 Geary Street
San Francisco, CA 94108
(415) 765-1505
Contact: Ms. N. Metz
Minimum Salary Placed: $25,000
Recruiting Specialty: Retail and finance

Joseph Michaels, Inc.
120 Montgomery Street, Suite 1260
San Francisco, CA 94104
(800) 786-1099
Contact: Mr. Joe Pelayo
Recruiting Specialty: Accounting and finance

Montgomery Resources, Inc.
555 Montgomery Street, Suite 1650
San Francisco, CA 94104
(415) 956-4242
Contact: Mr. Roger Lee
Minimum Salary Placed: $30,000
Recruiting Specialty: Finance and accounting

James Moore and Associates
90 Montgomery Street
San Francisco, CA 94105
(415) 392-3933
Contact: Mr. L. Fenyzes
Minimum Salary Placed: $25,000
Recruiting Specialty: Computers

Naughton Sheehan and Monfredini
601 Montgomery Street, Suite 1200
San Francisco, CA 94111
(415) 296-9800
Contact: Mr. P. Sheehan
Minimum Salary Placed: $25,000
Recruiting Specialty: Finance, accounting, auditing and banking

PFC Inc.
455 Market Street, Suite 1850
San Francisco, CA 94105
(415) 957-1400
Contact: Ms. Nina Manson
Minimum Salary Placed: $25,000
Recruiting Specialty: Data processing and MIS

PHR Group
100 1st Street
San Francisco, CA 94105
(415) 882-6221
Contact: Mr. Pat Haro
Minimum Salary Placed: $50,000
Recruiting Specialty: General; Asia

Pacific Rim Human Resource
690 Market Street, Suite 625
San Francisco, CA 94104
(415) 956-6250
Contact: Ms. Ruth Breslin
Recruiting Specialty: Bilingual - Japanese and English

Partner Search Catalyst
580 California Street
San Francisco, CA 94108
(415) 956-1600
Contact: Mr. John Kenney
Recruiting Specialty: General

Katharine Patterson Consulting
235 Montgomery, Suite 1850
San Francisco, CA 94104
(415) 398-2622
Contact: Ms. K. Patterson
Minimum Salary Placed: $60,000
Recruiting Specialty: Attorneys, patents

Pearson, Caldwell and Farnsworth
One California Street, Suite 1950
San Francisco, CA 94111
(415) 982-0300
Contact: Mr. John Pearson
Recruiting Specialty: Financial services

Placement Dynamics
690 Market Street, Suite 800
San Francisco, CA 94105
(415) 442-0700
Contact: Mr. Ran Hobbs
Minimum Salary Placed: $25,000
Recruiting Specialty: General

Prism Group
475 Sansome Street, Suite 1850
San Francisco, CA 94104
(415) 394-7171
Contact: Ms. N. Agatiello
Minimum Salary Placed: $25,000
Recruiting Specialty: Computer

ProServ
110 Sutter Street, Suite 600
San Francisco, CA 94104
(415) 781-6100
Contact: Ms. Judy Litteer
Recruiting Specialty: General

Pryor and Associates
100 Pine Street, Suite 1660
San Francisco, CA 94111
(415) 989-9890
Contact: Ms. J. Pryor
Minimum Salary Placed: $25,000
Recruiting Specialty: Insurance

RGA Associates
465 California, Suite 830
San Francisco, CA 94111
(415) 397-4646
Contact: Mr. R. Englehart
Minimum Salary Placed: $30,000
Recruiting Specialty: Software and engineering

Raleigh and Company
611 Washington Street
San Francisco, CA 94111
(415) 362-7550
Contact: Mr. Mike Raleigh
Minimum Salary Placed: $25,000
Recruiting Specialty: General

Edward Rast and Company
235 Montgomery Street
San Francisco, CA 94104
(415) 986-1710
Contact: Mr. Ed Rast
Minimum Salary Placed: $25,000
Recruiting Specialty: General

Robert Half International
388 Market Street, Suite 1400
San Francisco, CA 94111
(415) 434-1900
Contact: Mr. A. Boris
Minimum Salary Placed: $25,000
Recruiting Specialty: Accounting and finance

Romac & Associates
180 Montgomery Street, Suite 1860
San Francisco, CA 94104
(415) 788-2815
Contact: Mr. John McLaughlin
Recruiting Specialty: MIS, finance and accounting

Rusher, Loscavio & LoPresto
180 Montgomery
San Francisco, CA 94104
(415) 391-0430
Contact: Mr. J. Michael Loscavio
Recruiting Specialty: Life insurance, high technology and non-profit

Russell Staffing
120 Montgomery Street
San Francisco, CA 94104
(415) 781-1444
Contact: Ms. Carol Russell
Minimum Salary Placed: $25,000
Recruiting Specialty: General

Russell Reynolds Associates, Inc.
101 California Street, Suite 3140
San Francisco, CA 94111
(415) 392-3130
Contact: Mr. P. Anthony Price
Minimum Salary Placed: $100,000
Recruiting Specialty: General

Sabourin Associates
237 Upper Terrace
San Francisco, CA 94117
(415) 957-1001
Contact: Mr. Alan Sabourin
Minimum Salary Placed: $25,000
Recruiting Specialty: General

Sales Professionals Personnel Services
595 Market Street, Suite 2500
San Francisco, CA 94105
(415) 543-2828
Contact: Mr. Sheldon Israel
Minimum Salary Placed: $20,000
Recruiting Specialty: Sales

Schatter and Associates
388 Market Street, Suite 400
San Francisco, CA 94111
(415) 433-8100
Contact: Mr. Craig Schatter
Minimum Salary Placed: $25,000
Recruiting Specialty: Accounting and finance

Search Consortions
44 Montgomery Street
San Francisco, CA 94104
(415) 955-0500
Contact: Mr. Rod Ramsey
Minimum Salary Placed: $45,000
Recruiting Specialty: General

The Search Firm Inc.
595 Market Street, Suite 1400
San Francisco, CA 94105
(415) 777-3900
Contact: Mr. Heinz Bartesch
Recruiting Specialty: General

Search One
649 Mission Street
San Francisco, CA 94105
(415) 495-2801
Minimum Salary Placed: $25,000
Recruiting Specialty: Graphic arts

Search West
100 Pine Street, Suite 2500
San Francisco, CA 94111
(415) 788-1770
Contact: Ms. Ellen Williams
Minimum Salary Placed: $25,000
Recruiting Specialty: General

Secura/Burnett Partners
555 Montgomery Street, Suite 3950
San Francisco, CA 94108
(415) 398-0700

Contact: Mr. Louis Burnett
Recruiting Specialty: Finance

Seitchik, Corwin & Seitchik Inc.
3443 Clay Street
San Francisco, CA 94118
(415) 928-5717
Contact: Mr. Blade Corwin
Recruiting Specialty: General

M.B. Shattuck & Associates, Inc.
100 Bush Street, Suite 1675
San Francisco, CA 94104
(415) 421-6264
Contact: Mr. M. B. Shattuck
Minimum Salary Placed: $75,000
Recruiting Specialty: General

Simon and Ryan Inc.
235 Montgomery Street
San Francisco, CA 94104
(415) 956-3550
Minimum Salary Placed: $25,000
Recruiting Specialty: Banking and financial intermediaries

Singer Strouse
1865 California Street
San Francisco, CA 94109
(415) 781-6444
Minimum Salary Placed: $25,000
Recruiting Specialty: Corporate tax

Source EDP
425 California Street, Suite 1200
San Francisco, CA 94104
(415) 434-2410
Contact: Mr. Jim Kosturos
Minimum Salary Placed: $20,000
Recruiting Specialty: Computers, programming and MIS

Source Finance
425 California Street, Suite 1200
San Francisco, CA 94104
(415) 956-4740
Contact: Mr. B. Mensik
Minimum Salary Placed: $25,000
Recruiting Specialty: Finance and accounting

Spencer Stuart
525 Market Street, Suite 3700
San Francisco, CA 94105
(415) 495-4141
Contact: Mr. Jeffrey Hodge
Minimum Salary Placed: $75,000
Recruiting Specialty: General

Stansbury Staffing Consultants
100 Bush Street, Suite 900
San Francisco, CA 94104
(415) 677-0167
Contact: Ms. Patricia Stansbury
Recruiting Specialty: Accounting, finance, and data processing

Systems Careers
211 Sutter Street, Suite 607
San Francisco, CA 94108
(415) 434-4770
Contact: Mr. A. Wayne Sarchett
Minimum Salary Placed: $60,000
Recruiting Specialty: Software

TSS Personnel Agency
605 Market Street, Suite 1250
San Francisco, CA 94105
(415) 543-4545
Contact: Ms. Cynthia Fassier
Recruiting Specialty: General

Tanzi Executive Search
110 Sutter, Suite 414
San Francisco, CA 94104
(415) 391-9991
Contact: Mr. Richard Meyerhoff
Minimum Salary Placed: $40,000
Recruiting Specialty: General

Target Research Corporation
3 Embarcadero Center
San Francisco, CA 94111
(415) 391-3556
Contact: Ms. Dina Kuntz
Minimum Salary Placed: $25,000
Recruiting Specialty: General

Tech Source
101 California Street, Suite 2050
San Francisco, CA 94111
(415) 439-6400
Minimum Salary Placed: $25,000
Recruiting Specialty: Technical disciplines

Tetsell Group Company
1 Maritime Plaza, Suite 1919
San Francisco, CA 94111
(415) 392-4000
Contact: Mr. R. Tetsell
Minimum Salary Placed: $30,000
Recruiting Specialty: Insurance

The Thomas Tucker Company
425 California Street
San Francisco, CA 94104
(415) 693-5900
Contact: Mr. Thomas Tucker
Minimum Salary Placed: $150,000
Recruiting Specialty: General

Mel White Associates
44 Montgomery Street
San Francisco, CA 94105
(415) 955-2740
Minimum Salary Placed: $25,000
Recruiting Specialty: Banking

S. White Consulting
2185 Union Street
San Francisco, CA 94123
(415) 346-4475
Contact: Ms. S. White
Minimum Salary Placed: $35,000
Recruiting Specialty: High technology

Wilkinson & Ives
One Bush Street, Suite 550
San Francisco, CA 94104
(415) 834-3100
Contact: Ms. Suzanne Snyder
Minimum Salary Placed: $120,000
Recruiting Specialty: General

Winguth, Donahue & Company
220 Montgomery, Suite 303
San Francisco, CA 94104
(415) 854-5300
Contact: Mr. Ed Winguth
Minimum Salary Placed: $70,000
Recruiting Specialty: General

Wollborg Michelson Personnel
120 Montgomery Street, Suite 2460
San Francisco, CA 94104
(415) 391-7600
Contact: Mr. Todd Witkin
Recruiting Specialty: Accounting and finance

SAN JOSE

Accountants Executive Search
2099 Gateway Place, Suite 440
San Jose, CA 95110
(408) 437-9779
Contact: Mr. Mendie Cohen
Minimum Salary Placed: $25,000
Recruiting Specialty: Finance and accounting

Alphanumeric Inc.
2635 N. 1st Street
San Jose, CA 95134
(408) 954-1600
Contact: Ms. B. Sherman
Minimum Salary Placed: $35,000
Recruiting Specialty: Engineering

Career Search Personnel Agency
3097 Moorpark Avenue, Suite 130
San Jose, CA 95128
(408) 296-7711
Contact: Ms. Barbara Templeman Shandera
Recruiting Specialty: General

Design Automation Consultants
2635 N. 1st Street
San Jose, CA 95134
(408) 428-9300
Contact: Mr. R. Goldstein
Minimum Salary Placed: $35,000
Recruiting Specialty: Engineering

Devlin and Associates
1762 Technology Drive
San Jose, CA 95110
(408) 453-7845
Contact: Mr. Dick Devlin
Minimum Salary Placed: $40,000
Recruiting Specialty: Sales and engineering

Dunhill Professional Search
1190 Saratoga Avenue, Suite 210
San Jose, CA 95129
(408) 236-3262
Contact: Mr. Kevin Keifer
Minimum Salary Placed: $30,000
Recruiting Specialty: General

Fisher and Associates
1063 Lenor Way
San Jose, CA 95128
(408) 554-0156
Minimum Salary Placed: $25,000
Recruiting Specialty: Marketing, sales, software and engineering

Hall Kinton
5300 Stevens Creek Boulevard, Suite 320
San Jose, CA 95129
(408) 241-6602
Contact: Ms. B. Hall
Minimum Salary Placed: $20,000
Recruiting Specialty: Engineering and office support

Interim Search Solutions
2150 N. 1st Street, Suite 250
San Jose, CA 95131
(408) 436-2900
Contact: Mr. C. Juntunen
Minimum Salary Placed: $25,000
Recruiting Specialty: General

Cindy Jackson Search International
3031 Tisch Way
San Jose, CA 95128
(408) 247-6767
Contact: Ms. Cindy Jackson
Minimum Salary Placed: $40,000
Recruiting Specialty: Sales, marketing
and technical disciplines in computers

Josephine's Personnel Services, Inc.
1731 Technology Drive, Suite 870
San Jose, CA 95110
(408) 441-9941
Contact: Ms. Josephine Hughes
Recruiting Specialty: Office support,
sales and marketing

MIS Search
2099 Gateway Place
San Jose, CA 95110
(408) 437-0800
Contact: Mr. Lou Schuckman
Minimum Salary Placed: $30,000
Recruiting Specialty: MIS and accounting

Management Recruiters Inc.
2055 Gateway Place, Suite 420
San Jose, CA 95110
(408) 453-9999
Contact: Mr. Ron Whitney
Minimum Salary Placed: $30,000
Recruiting Specialty: Computer and electronic engineers, healthcare and environmental

Management Solutions, Inc.
99 Almaden Boulevard, Suite 600
San Jose, CA 95113
(408) 292-6600
Contact: Mr. Richard Williams
Minimum Salary Placed: $35,000
Recruiting Specialty: Finance and ac-
counting

Joseph J. McTaggart
5710 Arapah Drive
San Jose, CA 95123
Phone withheld at recruiters request
Contact: Mr. Joseph McTaggart
Minimum Salary Placed: $80,000
Recruiting Specialty: General

NAB Engineering
3031 Tisch Way
San Jose, CA 95128
(408)296-3930
Minimum Salary Placed: $30,000
Recruiting Specialty: Engineering

Pencom Systems Inc.
1731 Technology Drive, Suite 840
San Jose, CA 95110
(408) 452-8888
Contact: Mr. Edgar Saadi
Minimum Salary Placed: $35,000
Recruiting Specialty: UNIX program-
ming and MIS

Robert Half International
333 W. Santa Clara
San Jose, CA 95113
(408) 293-9040
Contact: Mr. D. Arnold
Minimum Salary Placed: $25,000
Recruiting Specialty: Accounting and fi-
nance

Sage Technologies
5190 Harwood Road
San Jose, CA 95131
(408) 448-4304
Contact: Mr. Mitch Levy
Minimum Salary Placed: $25,000
Recruiting Specialty: Biotechnology and
pharmaceuticals

Sales Consultants
2055 Gateway Place, Suite 420
San Jose, CA 95110
(408) 453-9999
Contact: Mr. Ron Whitney
Minimum Salary Placed: $20,000
Recruiting Specialty: Sales

Sequoia Partners
922 Saratoga Avenue
San Jose, CA 95128
(408) 244-2999
Contact: Mr. Don Fernanadez
Minimum Salary Placed: $25,000
Recruiting Specialty: Computers

R. W. Stearns
333 W. San Carlos Street
San Jose, CA 95110
(408) 297-4220
Contact: Mr. R. Stearns
Minimum Salary Placed: $35,000
Recruiting Specialty: Electronics

Target Personnel Services
3031 Tisch Way Suite 701
San Jose, CA 95128
(408) 261-1122
Contact: Ms. Vicki Bartelt
Recruiting Specialty: Accounting and finance, legal, and office support

Techniquest
55 South Market Street, Suite 1001
San Jose, CA 95113
(408) 748-1122
Contact: Ms. C. Lindquist
Minimum Salary Placed: $35,000
Recruiting Specialty: Technical disciplines

Wendell Associates
P.O. Box 7376
San Jose, CA 95150
(408) 266-9643
Minimum Salary Placed: $25,000
Recruiting Specialty: Electronics

SAN JUAN CAPISTRANO

Kuhn Med-Tech
27128-B Paseo Espada, Suite 623
San Juan Capistrano, CA 92675
(714) 496-3500
Contact: Mr. Otis Archie
Minimum Salary Placed: $30,000
Recruiting Specialty: Medical device and biotechnology

Intelli Sourte Computer Couriers, Ltd.
27921 Via Estancia
San Juan Capistrano, CA 92675
(714) 496-7927
Contact: Mr. Mark Rinovato
Minimum Salary Placed: $30,000
Recruiting Specialty: Computers

SAN LEANDRO

Susan Riskind Executive Search
182 Sunnyside Drive
San Leandro, CA 94577
(510) 638-6903
Contact: Ms. Susan Riskind
Minimum Salary Placed: $25,000
Recruiting Specialty: Information systems

SAN MARCOS

Kathy Clayton & Associates
1930 W San Marcos Boulevard,
   Suite 399A
San Marcos, CA 92069
(619) 598-3344
Contact: Ms. Kathy Clayton
Recruiting Specialty: Insurance and title
insurance

J. Jackson and Associates
1046 Commerce Street
San Marcos, CA 92069
(619) 744-7115
Minimum Salary Placed: $25,000
Recruiting Specialty: General

The Niemond Corporation
P.O. Box 4106
San Marcos, CA 92069
(619) 591-4127
Contact: Ms. Nancy Niemond
Minimum Salary Placed: $100,000
Recruiting Specialty: General

SAN MATEO

Abington Associates Inc.
P.O. Box 6955
San Mateo, CA 94403
(704) 254-1914
Contact: Ms. S. Abington
Minimum Salary Placed: $25,000
Recruiting Specialty: General

Bowman Associates
1660 S. Amphlett Boulevard
San Mateo, CA 94402
(415) 573-0188

Contact: Mr. Dan Bowman
Minimum Salary Placed: $25,000
Recruiting Specialty: Hospitality and lei-
sure services

Howard Karr & Associates, Inc.
1777 Borel Place, Suite 408
San Mateo, CA 94402
(415) 574-5277
Contact: Ms. Cynthia Karr
Minimum Salary Placed: $75,000
Recruiting Specialty: General

Management Recruiters
1900 S. Norfolk Street, Suite 318
San Mateo, CA 94403
(415) 548-4800
Contact: Mr. Don Hirschbein
Minimum Salary Placed: $20,000
Recruiting Specialty: Technical

Next Step Recruiting
3130 La Selva, Suite 105
San Mateo, CA 94403
(415) 364-6398
Contact: Mr. Jeffrey Spingler
Recruiting Specialty: High technology
and business services

Robert Half International
941 Mariners Island Boulevard, Suite 610
San Mateo, CA 94404
(415) 574-8200
Contact: Ms. J. Carroll
Minimum Salary Placed: $25,000
Recruiting Specialty: Accounting and fi-
nance

Sales Consultants
1900 S. Norfolk Street, Suite 318
San Mateo, CA 94403
(415) 571-5611

Contact: Mr. Donald Hirschbein
Minimum Salary Placed: $20,000
Recruiting Specialty: Sales

The Winchester Group
100 S. Ellsworth Avenue, Suite 400
San Mateo, CA 94401
(415) 696-3266
Contact: Mr. J. Barry Ryan
Minimum Salary Placed: $70,000
Recruiting Specialty: General

SAN PEDRO

The Wentworth Company, Inc.
479 W. 6th Street, Suite 211
San Pedro, CA 90731
(310) 519-0113
Contact: Mr. John Wentworth
Recruiting Specialty: General; high technology

SAN RAFAEL

Accounting Additions
851 Irwin Street, Suite 302
San Rafael, CA 94901
(415) 459-2300
Contact: Ms. D. Kreuzberger
Minimum Salary Placed: $25,000
Recruiting Specialty: Finance and accounting

Accountants Plus
4270 Redwood Highway
San Rafael, CA 94903
(415) 479-5124
Minimum Salary Placed: $25,000
Recruiting Specialty: Accounting

Bayland Associates
4286 Redwood Highway
San Rafael, CA 94903
(415) 499-8111
Contact: Mr. Tom Kunkle
Minimum Salary Placed: $35,000
Recruiting Specialty: Medical devices

CN Associates
4040 Civic Center Drive
San Rafael, CA 94903
(415) 883-1114
Contact: Mr. Charles Nicolosi
Minimum Salary Placed: $40,000
Recruiting Specialty: Sales and marketing in high technology

Coast to Coast Executive Search
4040 Civic Center Drive, Suite 200
San Rafael, CA 94903
(415) 492-2870
Contact: Mr. Horowitz
Minimum Salary Placed: $25,000
Recruiting Specialty: General

The Goodman Group
P.O. Box 150960
San Raphael, CA 94915
(415) 455-15000
Contact: Mr. Lion Goodman
Minimum Salary Placed: $40,000
Recruiting Specialty: Medical, healthcare and computers

Hire Resources Group
7 Mount Lassen Drive
San Rafael, CA 94903
(415) 491-6444
Minimum Salary Placed: $25,000
Recruiting Specialty: General

Barry Jacobs Associates
1010 B. Street
San Rafael, CA 94901
(415) 456-2828
Contact: Mr. Barry Jacobs
Recruiting Specialty: Attorneys

Longo Associates
12 Northview Court
San Rafael, CA 94903
(415) 472-1400
Contact: Mr. Roger Longo
Minimum Salary Placed: $25,000
Recruiting Specialty: General

J.R. Morrison and Associates Inc.
2169 Francisco Boulevard East
San Rafael, CA 94901
(415) 457-4600
Contact: Mr. Jack Morrison
Minimum Salary Placed: $25,000
Recruiting Specialty: General

Nelson Personnel Service
4270 Redwood Highway
San Rafael, CA 94903
(415) 479-5101
Contact: Ms. L. McGuinness
Recruiting Specialty: General

SAN RAMON

Schlueter Executive Search
2 Annabel Lane
San Ramon, CA 94583
(510) 866-8660
Contact: Ms. A. Schlueter
Minimum Salary Placed: $25,000
Recruiting Specialty: Packaging, processing and machinery in foods and pharmaceuticals

SANTA ANA

Gorelick and Associates
1971 E. 4th Street, Suite 100
Santa Ana, CA 92705
(714) 667-5050
Contact: Ms. S. Gorelick
Minimum Salary Placed: $25,000
Recruiting Specialty: Consumer products

Ziskind Greene
2700 N. Main Street
Santa Ana, CA 92701
(714) 541-9903
Contact: Mr. Ziskind Greene
Minimum Salary Placed: $50,000
Recruiting Specialty: Attorneys

Lending Personnel Service
2938 Daimler Street, Suite 107
Santa Ana, CA 92705
(714) 250-8133
Contact: Ms. C. Bloch
Minimum Salary Placed: $25,000
Recruiting Specialty: General

McKinstry Consultants
534 W. 17th Street
Santa Ana, CA 92706
(714) 543-9363
Contact: Frank Weidner
Minimum Salary Placed: $25,000
Recruiting Specialty: Medicine and accounting

Craig Miller Associates
1720 E. Garry Avenue, Suite 207
Santa Ana, CA 92705
(714) 261-6246
Contact: Mr. Craig Miller
Minimum Salary Placed: $25,000
Recruiting Specialty: High technology
and computers

Scott-Thaler Associates Agency, Inc.
86 Brookhollow Drive
Santa Ana, CA 92705
(714) 966-1671
Contact: Mr. Brian Thaler
Minimum Salary Placed: $30,000
Recruiting Specialty: General

D.L. Weaver & Associates
6 Hutton Center Drive, Suite 1150
Santa Ana, CA 92707
(714) 979-2900
Contact: Ms. Doris Weaver
Minimum Salary Placed: $20,000
Recruiting Specialty: General

SANTA BARBARA

Brooks Associates
610 Anacapa
Santa Barbara, CA 93101
(805) 963-5858

Contact: Mr. James Brooks
Minimum Salary Placed: $25,000
Recruiting Specialty: Marketing and sales

Garland Associates
1727 State Street
Santa Barbara, CA 93101
(805) 563-2398
Contact: Mr. R. Darryl Garland
Minimum Salary Placed: $55,000
Recruiting Specialty: Manufacturing and
energy

KABL Ability Network
1727 State Street,
Santa Barbara, CA 93101
(805) 563-2398
Contact: Mr. Brad Naegle
Minimum Salary Placed: $40,000
Recruiting Specialty: General

Sanford Rose Associates
101 E. Victoria Street, Suite 22
Santa Barbara, CA 93101
(805) 966-1846
Contact: Mr. James Myatt
Minimum Salary Placed: $50,000
Recruiting Specialty: General

Santa Barbara Placement
1300 Santa Barbara Street, Suite B
Santa Barbara, CA 93101
(805) 965-0511
Minimum Salary Placed: $25,000
Recruiting Specialty: General

SANTA CLARA

Accountants Inc.
3945 Freedom Circle Drive, Suite 110
Santa Clara, CA 95054
(408) 986-8110
Contact: Ms. B. Tilbrooke
Minimum Salary Placed: $25,000
Recruiting Specialty: Finance and accounting

Richard Beckstead and Associates
4677 Old Ironsides Drive
Santa Clara, CA 95054
(408) 727-2456
Contact: Mr. Richard Beckstead
Minimum Salary Placed: $35,000
Recruiting Specialty: Telecommunications, data communications and computers

Brandenburg Smith and Associates
4633 Old Ironsides, Suite 400
Santa Clara, CA 95054
(408) 727-5554
Contact: Mr. Gary Brandenburg
Minimum Salary Placed: $25,000
Recruiting Specialty: General

Financial Staff Resources
4699 Old Ironsides Drive, Suite 230
Santa Clara, CA 95054
(408) 492-9301
Contact: Mr. J. Silver
Minimum Salary Placed: $25,000
Recruiting Specialty: Finance

High Tech Ventures
3945 Freedom Circle, Suite 120
Santa Clara, CA 95054
(408) 562-0740

Contact: Mr. E. Takacs
Minimum Salary Placed: $25,000
Recruiting Specialty: Software engineering

Holland, McFadzean & Assoc., Inc.
2901 Tasman Drive, Suite 204
Santa Clara, CA 95054
(408) 496-0775
Contact: Mr. James McFadzean
Minimum Salary Placed: $75,000
Recruiting Specialty: High technology and office machinery and products

Mackauf and Company
3333 Bowers Avenue, Suite 130
Santa Clara, CA 95054
(408) 727-7472
Contact: Mr. Ed Mackauf
Minimum Salary Placed: $25,000
Recruiting Specialty: General

Management Associates
2700 Augustine Drive, Suite 255
Santa Clara, CA 95054
(408) 727-4717
Contact: Mr. Val Baldwin
Minimum Salary Placed: $40,000
Recruiting Specialty: Engineering and marketing

Nadzam, Lusk & Horgan
3211 Scott Boulevard, Suite 205
Santa Clara, CA 95054
(408) 727-6601
Contact: Mr. Theodore Lusk
Minimum Salary Placed: $100,000
Recruiting Specialty: General

Netsoft Inc.
2727 Walsh Avenue
Santa Clara, CA 95051
(408) 562-2080
Contact: Eric
Minimum Salary Placed: $25,000
Recruiting Specialty: Computers

Oryx Executive Search Inc.
3235 Kifer Road, Suite 340
Santa Clara, CA 95051
(408) 481-0100
Contact: Mr. B. Russell
Minimum Salary Placed: $25,000
Recruiting Specialty: General

John Velcamp & Associates
3333 Bowers Avenue, Suite 130
Santa Clara, CA 95054
(408) 986-9343
Contact: Mr. John Velcamp
Minimum Salary Placed: $100,000
Recruiting Specialty: High technology

SANTA MONICA

Christopher Bryant
2716 Ocean Park Boulevard, Suite 3001
Santa Monica, CA 90405
(310) 314-2424
Minimum Salary Placed: $25,000
Recruiting Specialty: Non-profit

Demery Associates
201 Wilshire Boulevard
Santa Monica, CA 90401
(310) 393-3900
Contact: Mr. J. Demery
Minimum Salary Placed: $25,000
Recruiting Specialty: General

Joanne Dunn and Associates
2001 Wilshire Boulevard, Suite 600
Santa Monica, CA 90403
(310) 315-2787
Contact: Ms. Joanne Dunn
Minimum Salary Placed: $25,000
Recruiting Specialty: General

Dynamic Synergy Corporation
631 Wilshire Boulevard, Suite 209
Santa Monica, CA 90401
(310) 576-7600
Contact: Mr. Mark Landau
Minimum Salary Placed: $70,000
Recruiting Specialty: General

Garb & Associates
2001 Wilshire Boulevard, Suite 510
Santa Monica, CA 90403
(310) 998-3388
Contact: Ms. Sheila Garb
Minimum Salary Placed: $50,000
Recruiting Specialty: Attorneys

Krakower Group Inc.
233 Wilshire Boulevard, Suite 600
Santa Monica, CA 90403
(310) 829-7022
Contact: Mr. B. Krakower
Minimum Salary Placed: $80,000
Recruiting Specialty: High technology
and biotechnology

Larkin Group
604 Santa Monica Boulevard
Santa Monica, CA 90401
(310) 829-2800
Contact: Ms. Susan Silver
Minimum Salary Placed: $100,000
Recruiting Specialty: General

SANTA ROSA

Master Search
P.O. Box 9070
Santa Rosa, CA 95405
(707) 538-4000
Contact: Mr. Greg Masters
Minimum Salary Placed: $25,000
Recruiting Specialty: General

Personnel Perspective
575 W. College Avenue, Suite 101A
Santa Rosa, CA 95401
(707) 576-7653
Contact: Ms. C. Silvestri
Minimum Salary Placed: $25,000
Recruiting Specialty: General

Real Estate Executive Search, Inc.
P.O. Box 40
Santa Rosa, CA 95402
(707) 525-4591
Contact: Mr. Erik Kempinski
Minimum Salary Placed: $50,000
Recruiting Specialty: Finance, banking
and real estate

Strada Corporation
50 Old Courthouse Square, Suite 300
Santa Rosa, CA 95401
(707) 575-1122
Contact: Mr. P. Boldt
Minimum Salary Placed: $25,000
Recruiting Specialty: Data processing

S.R. Wilson, Inc.
520 Mendocino Avenue, Suite 200
Santa Rosa, CA 95401
(707) 571-5990
Contact: Mr. Stoney Wilson
Recruiting Specialty: Attorneys in manufacturing

SANTEE

Southwest Search Association
10226 Buena Vista Avenue
Santee, CA 92071
(619) 562-1103
Contact: Ms. Linda Shaw
Recruiting Specialty: Engineering

SARATOGA

Pinsker and Company, Inc.
P.O. Box 3269
Saratoga, CA 95070
(408) 867-5161
Contact: Mr. Richard Pinsker
Minimum Salary Placed: $75,000
Recruiting Specialty: General

SAUSALITO

Anabus International
507 Main Street
Sausalito, CA 94965
(415) 289-7420
Contact: Ms. Iris Bieri
Minimum Salary Placed: $50,000
Recruiting Specialty: Software engineer-
ing; general

Thomas Beck Inc.
P.O. Box 789
Sausalito, CA 94966
(415) 331-1555
Contact: Mr. Tom Beck
Minimum Salary Placed: $25,000
Recruiting Specialty: Semi-conductors

Bialla & Associates, Inc.
4000 Bridgeway, Suite 201
Sausalito, CA 94965
(415) 332-7111
Contact: Mr. Vito Bialla
Minimum Salary Placed: $80,000
Recruiting Specialty: Sales, marketing
and advertising

Candidate Referral Network
P.O. Box 2522
Sausalito, CA 94966
(415) 332-3265
Recruiting Specialty: Equipment leasing

Mata and Associates
180 Harbor Drive, Suite 208
Sausalito, CA 94965
(415) 332-2893
Minimum Salary Placed: $30,000
Recruiting Specialty: Data processing

Physician Search Group
475 Gate 5 Road
Sausalito, CA 94965
(415) 289-8610
Contact: Mr. K. Baker
Minimum Salary Placed: $75,000
Recruiting Specialty: Physicians

Tech Search
2015 Bridgeway, Suite 301
Sausalito, CA 94965
(415) 332-1282
Contact: Mr. Roger King
Minimum Salary Placed: $40,000
Recruiting Specialty: MIS and IT

SEBASTOPOL

Bankert-Samuel
380 Sexton Road
Sebastopol, CA 95472
(707) 824-9420
Minimum Salary Placed: $25,000
Recruiting Specialty: General

SHERMAN OAKS

Cory Associates Agency
15303 Ventura Boulevard
Sherman Oaks, CA 91403
(818) 995-7755
Contact: Mr. Tom Cory
Recruiting Specialty: Sales and marketing

Culver Personnel Service Inc.
15301 Ventura Boulevard, Suite 410
Sherman Oaks, CA 91403
(818) 788-7550
Contact: Ms. L. Dia
Minimum Salary Placed: $25,000
Recruiting Specialty: Sales

Executive Registry
15315 Magnolia Boulevard
Sherman Oaks, CA 91403
(818) 501-8088
Minimum Salary Placed: $25,000
Recruiting Specialty: Home healthcare,
biotechnology and software

Focus Agency
15300 Ventura Boulevard, Suite 207
Sherman Oaks, CA 91403
(818) 981-9519
Contact: Ms. Kathryn Shepherd
Recruiting Specialty: Management, sales,
and marketing

Fred J. Goldsmith Associates
14056 Margate Street
Sherman Oaks, CA 91401
(818) 783-3931
Contact: Mr. Fred Goldsmith
Minimum Salary Placed: $50,000
Recruiting Specialty: Computer, food and beverage and energy

William Guy & Associates, Inc.
P.O. Box 57407
Sherman Oaks, CA 91413
(818) 763-2514
Contact: Mr. C. William Guy
Minimum Salary Placed: $50,000
Recruiting Specialty: General

Seymour and Associates
13948 Moorpark, Suite H
Sherman Oaks, CA 91403
(818) 906-0755
Contact: Mr. R. Eidman
Minimum Salary Placed: $25,000
Recruiting Specialty: Food service and packaging

Source EDP
15260 Ventura Boulevard, Suite 380
Sherman Oaks, CA 91403
(818) 905-1500
Contact: Ms. Vicki Girdziunas
Minimum Salary Placed: $20,000
Recruiting Specialty: Computers, programming and MIS

SIMI VALLEY

Advanced Corporate Search
660 D Baywood Lane
Simi Valley, CA 93065
(805) 522-1997

Contact: Ms. Jan Gibson
Minimum Salary Placed: $35,000
Recruiting Specialty: General

Search for Excellence
2828 Cochran Street, Suite 118
Simi Valley, CA 93065
(805) 527-6146
Contact: Mr. Andrew Smith
Minimum Salary Placed: $40,000
Recruiting Specialty: General

SOLANA BEACH

Carolyn Smith Paschal International
225 Stevens Avenue
Solana Beach, CA 92075
(619) 587-1366
Contact: Ms. Carolyn Smith Paschal
Minimum Salary Placed: $25,000
Recruiting Specialty: Fundraising, communications and public relations

SOLVANG

Hergenrather & Company
3125 Riley Road, P.O. Box 1100
Solvang, CA 93464
(805) 686-2018
Contact: Mr. Ed Hergenrather
Minimum Salary Placed: $60,000
Recruiting Specialty: General

SOMIS

Sales Consultants
P.O. Box 115
4892 North Street, Suite 6
Somis, CA 93066
(805) 386-5200

Contact: Mr. Len Rosson
Minimum Salary Placed: $20,000
Recruiting Specialty: Sales

SONOMA

Zanne Clark and Company
757 2nd Street East
Sonoma, CA 95476
(415) 392-4544
Contact: Ms. Zanne Clark
Minimum Salary Placed: $25,000
Recruiting Specialty: General

SOQUEL

J.M. Meredeth and Associates
2240 N. Rodeo Gulch Road
Soquel, CA 95073
(408) 479-7522
Minimum Salary Placed: $25,000
Recruiting Specialty: High technology

STOCKTON

Robert Half International
1776 W. March Lane
Stockton, CA 95207
(209) 474-6731
Contact: Ms. K. Branstetter
Minimum Salary Placed: $25,000
Recruiting Specialty: Accounting and finance

Search Resources
10082 E. Eight Mile Road
Stockton, CA 95212
(209) 931-0102
Contact: Mr. C. Blackburn
Minimum Salary Placed: $25,000
Recruiting Specialty: Foods

STUDIO CITY

Hicks Group
12190 1/2 Ventura Boulevard, Suite 714
Studio City, CA 91604
(310) 201-0688
Contact: Ms. Helen Hicks
Minimum Salary Placed: $40,000
Recruiting Specialty: Attorneys

SUNNYVALE

Abdo and Associates
1310 Hollenbeck Avenue
Sunnyvale, CA 94087
(408) 736-0650
Contact: Mr. Ron Abdo
Minimum Salary Placed: $25,000
Recruiting Specialty: General

Christian & Timbers, Inc.
1250 Oakmead Parkway, Suite 210
Sunnyvale, CA 94088
(408) 730-6864
Contact: Mr. Jeffrey Christian
Minimum Salary Placed: $75,000
Recruiting Specialty: General

Complimate, Inc.
150 West Iowa Ave., Suite 203
Sunnyvale, CA 94085
(408) 773-8994
Contact: Mr. Ted Doyle
Recruiting Specialty: Data processing, management, and software development

Corporate Technology Inc.
P.O. Box 70310
Sunnyvale, CA 94086
(408) 735-1690

Contact: Mr. J. Reinhardt
Minimum Salary Placed: $35,000
Recruiting Specialty: Semi-conductors
and computers

Daggett & Kvistad
1095 East Duane Avenue, Suite 100
Sunnyvale, CA 94086
(408) 736-8990
Contact: Mr. James Daggett
Minimum Salary Placed: $45,000
Recruiting Specialty: General

Emerson, Brooks and Associates
1030 E. Camino Real, Suite 228
Sunnyvale, CA 94057
(408) 297-3067
Contact: Mr. Richard Girard
Minimum Salary Placed: $30,000
Recruiting Specialty: Computers

Plum Write Tech Writing Service
333 Cobalt Way, Suite 107
Sunnyvale, CA 94086
(408) 730-4650
Contact: Mr. C. Balalis
Minimum Salary Placed: $25,000
Recruiting Specialty: Technical writers

Source Engineering
1290 Oakmead Parkway, Suite 318
Sunnyvale, CA 94086
(408) 738-8440
Contact: Mr. David Pregeant
Minimum Salary Placed: $30,000
Recruiting Specialty: Engineering

SYLMAR

Pocrass Associates
13190 Telfair Avenue
Sylmar, CA 91342
(818) 364-8300
Contact: Ms. Nancy Gilmore
Minimum Salary Placed: $75,000
Recruiting Specialty: General

TARZANA

Anderson Sterling Associates
18623 Ventura Boulevard, Suite 207
Tarzana, CA 91356
(818) 996-0920
Contact: Mr. Victor Goodman
Recruiting Specialty: General

Brennan Associates
19528 Ventura Boulevard, Suite 503
Tarzana, CA 91356
(818) 881-3046
Contact: Mr. Mike Brennan
Minimum Salary Placed: $25,000
Recruiting Specialty: Real estate

Paul Gregory and Associates
18455 Burbank Boulevard
Tarzana, CA 91356
(818) 342-0075
Contact: Mr. Paul Gregory
Minimum Salary Placed: $30,000
Recruiting Specialty: Insurance

Thomas Gregory and Associates
18600 Palomino Drive
Tarzana, CA 91356
(818) 609-1794

Contact: Mr. Tom Gregory
Minimum Salary Placed: $30,000
Recruiting Specialty: Finance and insurance

United Franchise Consultants
3955 El Enita Avenue
Tarzana, CA 91356
(818) 705-8555
Minimum Salary Placed: $40,000
Recruiting Specialty: Franchising

TEMECULA

National Resources
41661 Enterprise Circle North, Suite 113
Temecula, CA 92590
(909) 694-5577
Contact: Mr. Gene Jenkins
Minimum Salary Placed: $30,000
Recruiting Specialty: MIS and data processing

THOUSAND OAKS

Chase Morgan and Associates Inc.
1269 Valley High Avenue
Thousand Oaks, CA 91362
(805) 373-1289
Contact: Mr. T. Feldman
Minimum Salary Placed: $35,000
Recruiting Specialty: Insurance and gaming

Dove Medical System Inc.
1342 Calle Pecos
Thousand Oaks, CA 91360
(805) 375-8436
Contact: Ms. J. Piccioni
Minimum Salary Placed: $25,000
Recruiting Specialty: Healthcare

Job Search
137 E. Thousand Oaks Boulevard
Thousand Oaks, CA 91360
(805) 492-0562
Contact: Mr. P. Wolf
Minimum Salary Placed: $25,000
Recruiting Specialty: General

Management Recruiters
325 East Hillcrest Drive, Suite 160
Thousand Oaks, CA 91360
(805) 495-5544
Contact: Mr. John Dempster
Minimum Salary Placed: $30,000
Recruiting Specialty: General

Tangent Associates
P.O. Box 3054
Thousand Oaks, CA 91362
(805) 496-2555
Contact: Ms. N. Biederman
Minimum Salary Placed: $25,000
Recruiting Specialty: Banking

TIBURON

Montague Enterprises
1630 Tiburon Boulevard
Tiburon, CA 94920
(415) 435-5123
Contact: Mr. R.M. Thomas
Minimum Salary Placed: $90,000
Recruiting Specialty: General

TORRANCE

Accountants On Call
970 West 190th Street, Suite 420
Torrance, CA 90502
(310) 527-2777

Contact: Ms. Diane O'Meally
Recruiting Specialty: Finance and accounting

IMCOR, Inc.
970 W. 190th Street, Suite 425
Torrance, CA 90505
(310) 791-2033
Contact: Mr. Michael Hagerthy
Minimum Salary Placed: $90,000
Recruiting Specialty: General

Alan Israel Executive Search
3820 Del Amo Boulevard
Torrance, CA 90503
(310) 370-0144
Contact: Mr. Alan Israel
Minimum Salary Placed: $25,000
Recruiting Specialty: Computers

David James Search
4001 Pacific Coast Highway, Suite 101
Torrance, CA 90505
(310) 791-0789
Contact: Mr. David James
Minimum Salary Placed: $100,000
Recruiting Specialty: General

Lockhart Group
970 W 190th Street, Suite 600
Torrance, CA 90503
(310) 660-0330
Recruiting Specialty: Computers

Meng, Finseth & Associates, Inc.
3858 Carson Street, Suite 202
Torrance, CA 90503
(213) 316-0706
Contact: Ms. Cameron Meng
Minimum Salary Placed: $75,000
Recruiting Specialty: General

Robert Half International
990 W. 190th Street
Torrance, CA 90502
(310) 719-1400
Contact: Ms. P. Hawkins
Minimum Salary Placed: $25,000
Recruiting Specialty: Accounting and finance

Search 21 Inc.
1455 Crenshaw Boulevard
Torrance, CA 90501
(310) 212-7212
Contact: Mr. T. Tamba
Minimum Salary Placed: $30,000
Recruiting Specialty: International business; general

The Tibbetts Group Ltd.
1455 Crenshaw Boulevard, Room 105
Torrance, CA 90501
(310) 782-0771
Contact: Mr. Charles Tibbetts
Minimum Salary Placed: $25,000
Recruiting Specialty: General

Wollborg Michelson Personnel
3625 Del Amo Boulevard, Suite 270
Torrance, CA 90503
(310) 793-8600
Contact: Ms. Joan Van Donge
Recruiting Specialty: General

TURLOCK

Multisearch Recruiters
2851 Geer Road, Suite G
Turlock, CA 95382
(209) 634-5814
Contact: Mr. D. Gallagher
Minimum Salary Placed: $25,000
Recruiting Specialty: General

TUSTIN

Abigail Abbott Staffing Services
660 West First Street
Tustin, CA 92680
(714) 731-7711
Contact: Ms. Donna Averill
Recruiting Specialty: General

American Executive Service
17300 17th Street, Suite J262
Tustin, CA 92680
(714) 998-6599
Minimum Salary Placed: $25,000
Recruiting Specialty: General

Blackhawk Advantage, Inc.
1100 Irvine Boulevard, Suite 340
Tustin, CA 92670
(714) 731-9400
Contact: Mr. Phil Andersen
Minimum Salary Placed: $40,000
Recruiting Specialty: Accounting and finance

William Hogan and Associates Inc.
100 W. Main Street, Suite 8
Tustin, CA 92680
(714) 544-3881
Contact: Mr. Bill Hogan
Minimum Salary Placed: $35,000
Recruiting Specialty: Technical disciplines in computers and engineering

UKIAH

Worldwide Medical Services
617 S. State Street
Ukiah, CA 95487
(707) 463-0948
Contact: Mr. John Paju
Recruiting Specialty: General

VALENCIA

Selective Search Inc.
23822 Valencia Boulevard, Suite 304
Valencia, CA 91355
(805) 222-3150
Contact: Mr. Michael Schneider
Recruiting Specialty: Accounting

VAN NUYS

Pathfinders
13615 Victory Boulevard, Suite 225
Van Nuys, CA 91401
(818) 902-9910
Contact: Mr. Adam Silbar
Minimum Salary Placed: $35,000
Recruiting Specialty: Healthcare

VENTURA

Dr. Jim Campell
674 County Square Drive
Ventura, CA 93003
(805) 650-1817
Contact: Dr. Jim Campell
Recruiting Specialty: Medical and healthcare

Management Recruiters
1727 Mesa Verde Avenue, Suite 203
Ventura, CA 93003
(805) 650-1716
Contact: Mr. Bob Packer
Minimum Salary Placed: $20,000
Recruiting Specialty: General

Shaffer Consulting Group
2437 Grand Avenue, Suite 255
Ventura, CA 93003
(805) 642-3808

Contact: Mr. Bradford Shaffer
Minimum Salary Placed: $75,000
Recruiting Specialty: General

Survival Systems Staffing Center
2419 Portola Road
Ventura, CA 93003
(805) 650-8888
Contact: Mr. Dennis Nickerson
Recruiting Specialty: General

VISTA

Aadnesen & Associates
420 Hutchison St.
Vista, CA 92084
(619) 726-9418
Contact: Ms. Mary Anne Aadnesen
Recruiting Specialty: Healthcare, hospital, and medical equipment

WALNUT CREEK

Accountants Inc.
100 Pringle Avenue, Suite 330
Walnut Creek, CA 94596
(510) 946-1411
Minimum Salary Placed: $25,000
Recruiting Specialty: Finance and accounting

Accountants On Call
2175 N. California Boulevard, Suite 615
Walnut Creek, CA 94596
(510) 937-1000
Contact: Ms. Kathleen Waxman
Recruiting Specialty: Finance and accounting

Bernard Haldane Associates
1333 North California Boulevard,
 Suite 510
Walnut Creek, CA 94596
(510) 945-0776
Contact: Ms. S. Bianco
Minimum Salary Placed: $25,000
Recruiting Specialty: General

William Estes and Associates
1615 Bonanza Street
Walnut Creek, CA 94596
(510) 930-6050
Contact: Mr. Bill Estes
Minimum Salary Placed: $25,000
Recruiting Specialty: Finance, accounting and data processing

Charles Fralick Associates
1766 Lacassie
Walnut Creek, CA 94596
(510) 946-0817
Contact: Mr. Chuck Fralick
Minimum Salary Placed: $25,000
Recruiting Specialty: Computers

Goldstein and Company
1700 N. Broadway, Suite 307
Walnut Creek, CA 94596
(510) 935-6360
Contact: Mr. M. Goldstein
Minimum Salary Placed: $25,000
Recruiting Specialty: Graphic arts

Interim Accounting Personnel
200 Pringle Avenue, Suite 325
Walnut Creek, CA 94596
(510) 934-7092
Contact: Ms. Nancy Nolan
Minimum Salary Placed: $30,000
Recruiting Specialty: Accounting and finance

Kelch and Shea Associates
1717 N. California, Boulevard, Suite 3B
Walnut Creek, CA 94596
(510) 932-6011
Contact: Ms. L. Kelch
Minimum Salary Placed: $25,000
Recruiting Specialty: Automotive dealers, data processing, software and engineering

K.E.Y. Resources
1850 Mt. Diablo Boulevard, Suite 470
Walnut Creek, CA 94596
(510) 934-1311
Contact: Mr. Mike Binder
Recruiting Specialty: General

Madsen Personnel Services
710 S. Broadway, Suite 212
Walnut Creek, CA 94596
(510) 945-1444
Contact: Ms. Kerry Teakle
Recruiting Specialty: General

Miles O'Connor and Associates
3420 Deerpark Drive
Walnut Creek, CA 94598
(510) 932-6638
Contact: Mr. Miles O'Connor
Minimum Salary Placed: $25,000
Recruiting Specialty: Forestry, food, and manufacturing

Progressive Search and Consulting
1320 Mount Diablo Boulevard, Suite D
Walnut Creek, CA 94596
(510) 930-6340
Contact: Mr. D. Shank
Minimum Salary Placed: $25,000
Recruiting Specialty: General

Sales Solutions
P.O. Box 3557
Walnut Creek, CA 94598
(510) 932-8900
Contact: Mr. Bill Schmeh
Recruiting Specialty: Sales and marketing

System 1 Search - System 1 Temps
3021 Citris Circle, Suite 230
Walnut Creek, CA 94598
(510) 932-8801
Contact: Mr. David Doyle
Recruiting Specialty: Data processing, engineering, and management

Taylor and Company
500 Ignacio Valley Road, Suite 390
Walnut Creek, CA 94596
(510) 935-9566
Contact: Ms. P. Taylor
Recruiting Specialty: Telecommunications and computers

WEST COVINA

Lund & Associates, Inc.
1300 Hollencrest Drive
West Covina, CA 91791
(818) 918-0670
Contact: Mr. J. Kenneth Lund
Minimum Salary Placed: $50,000
Recruiting Specialty: High technology and manufacturing

WESTLAKE VILLAGE

Byron Leonard International, Inc.
2659 Townsgate Road, Suite 100
Westlake Village, CA 91361
(805) 373-7500

Contact: Mr. Leonard Linton
Minimum Salary Placed: $60,000
Recruiting Specialty: Manufacturing and high technology

Robert W. Dingman Company, Inc.
32129 West Lindero Canyon Road, Suite 206
Westlake Village, CA 91361
(818) 991-5950
Contact: Mr. Robert Dingman
Minimum Salary Placed: $95,000
Recruiting Specialty: General

Genel Associates
223 East Thousand Oaks Boulevard
Westlake Village, CA 91360
(805) 374-8737
Contact: Mr. George Genel
Minimum Salary Placed: $30,000
Recruiting Specialty: General

Harmon & Associates International, Inc.
2500 Townsgate, Suite 1
Westlake Village, CA 91361
(805) 371-4404
Contact: Mr. George Harmon
Recruiting Specialty: General

Klenin Group
32107 W. Lindero Canyon Road, Suite 218
Westlake Village, CA 91361
(818) 597-3434
Contact: Mr. Klenin
Minimum Salary Placed: $30,000
Recruiting Specialty: General

Mixtec Group
31255 Cedar Valley Drive, Suite 327
Westlake Village, CA 91362
(818) 889-8819

Contact: Mr. Ward Fredericks
Minimum Salary Placed: $70,000
Recruiting Specialty: Food and medical

Protocol Inc.
650 Hampshire Boulevard, Suite 208
Westlake Village, CA 91361
(805) 371-0069
Contact: Mr. Chris Salcido
Recruiting Specialty: MIS

Sales Consultants
5655 Lindero Canyon Road, Suite 423
Westlake Village, CA 91362
(818) 889-9926
Contact: Mr. Donald Vezina
Minimum Salary Placed: $20,000
Recruiting Specialty: Sales

Search West
340 N. Westlake Boulevard, Suite 320
Westlake Village, CA 91362-3761
(805) 496-6811
Contact: Mr. Mike Begun
Recruiting Specialty: General

Peggy Shea and Associates
5655 Lindero Canyon Road
Westlake Village, CA 91362
(818) 889-5350
Contact: Ms. Peggy Shea
Recruiting Specialty: Administrative support in healthcare

Venture Resources, Inc.
2659 Toronsgate Road, Suite 119
Westlake Village, CA 91361
(806) 371-3600
Contact: Mr. William White
Minimum Salary Placed: $100,000
Recruiting Specialty: General

Wilkins and Associates
2334 Bayside Court
Westlake Village, CA 91361
(805) 496-9595
Minimum Salary Placed: $40,000
Recruiting Specialty: Biotechnology and
healthcare

WHITTIER

Comet Employment Agency
14831 E Whittier Boulevard
Whittier, CA 90605
(310) 945-2347
Contact: Ms. Joanne Klemm
Recruiting Specialty: Accounting and finance, data processing, and office support

WOODLAND HILLS

Accountants Executive Search
21800 Oxnard Street
Woodland Hills, CA 91367
(818) 992-7676
Contact: Mr. R. Maynard
Minimum Salary Placed: $25,000
Recruiting Specialty: Finance and accounting

Accounts Overload
21550 Oxnard Street
Woodland Hills, CA 91367
(818) 713-0553
Contact: Ms. B. Sanders
Minimum Salary Placed: $25,000
Recruiting Specialty: Finance and accounting

Brooke-Blair Ltd. Agency
4819 Poe Avenue
Woodland Hills, CA 91367
(818) 704-8284
Minimum Salary Placed: $35,000
Recruiting Specialty: General

Buff and Associates
21024 Victory Boulevard
Woodland Hills, CA 91367
(818) 340-6300
Contact: Mr. J.T. Buff
Minimum Salary Placed: $30,000
Recruiting Specialty: Home and office
furnishings

Chaitin and Associates
22543 Ventura Boulevard, Suite 220
Woodland Hills, CA 91364
(818) 225-8655
Contact: Mr. Dick Chaitin
Minimum Salary Placed: $25,000
Recruiting Specialty: Accounting, marketing and retail

Computer Recruiters, Inc.
22276 Buenaventura Street
Woodland Hills, CA 91364
(818) 704-7722
Contact: Mr. Bob Moore
Minimum Salary Placed: $25,000
Recruiting Specialty: Computers

Mel Frazer & Associates
20350 Chapter Drive
Woodland Hills, CA 91364
(818) 703-0040
Contact: Mr. Mel Frazer
Minimum Salary Placed: $40,000
Recruiting Specialty: Medical products

Madeleine Lav & Associates
5703 Califa Place, Suite 333
Woodland Hills, CA 91367
(818) 887-2409
Contact: Ms. Madeleine Lav
Minimum Salary Placed: $60,000
Recruiting Specialty: General

Mahl and Associates Inc.
22647 Ventura Boulevard
Woodland Hills, CA 91364
(818) 591-3866
Contact: Mr. Marshall Mahl
Minimum Salary Placed: $40,000
Recruiting Specialty: General

The Morgan/Geoffries Group
21755 Ventura Boulevard, Suite 450
Woodland Hills, CA 91364
(818) 704-1100
Contact: Mr. J. Lawrence Pepin
Minimum Salary Placed: $100,000
Recruiting Specialty: Manufacturing and
high technology

**Mortgage & Financial Personnel
Services**
5850 Canoga Avenue, Suite 400
Woodland Hills, CA 91367
(818) 710-7133
Contact: Mr. Robert Sherman
Minimum Salary Placed: $25,000
Recruiting Specialty: General

Profit Pros, Inc.
21695 Yucatan Avenue
Woodland Hills, CA 91364
(818) 888-6362
Contact: Mr. B. Allen
Minimum Salary Placed: $50,000
Recruiting Specialty: General

RJ Associates
23730 Canzonet Street
Woodland Hills, CA 91367
(818) 715-7121
Contact: Ms. Judith Fischer
Minimum Salary Placed: $50,000
Recruiting Specialty: MIS, finance and ac-
counting

M. H. Springer & Associates
5855 Topanga Canyon Boulevard,
 Suite 230
Woodland Hills, CA 91367
(818) 710-8955
Contact: Mr. Mark Springer
Minimum Salary Placed: $75,000
Recruiting Specialty: Finance and high
technology

The Stevens Group, Inc.
P.O. Box 367
Woodland Hills, CA 91365
(818) 712-0242
Contact: Ms. Martha Stevens
Minimum Salary Placed: $40,000
Recruiting Specialty: Accounting, finance
and human resources

Zeiger Technical Careers, Inc.
20969 Ventura Boulevard, Suite 217
Woodland Hills, CA 91364
(818) 999-9394
Contact: Mr. Stephen Zeiger
Minimum Salary Placed: $45,000
Recruiting Specialty: Technical disci-
plines in computer and communications

WOODSIDE

David Powell, Inc.
2995 Woodside Road, Suite 150
Woodside, CA 94062
(415) 851-6000
Contact: Mr. David Powell
Minimum Salary Placed: $100,000
Recruiting Specialty: General

YORBA LINDA

Paar and Associates
17451 Bastanchury Road, Suite 204
Yorba Linda, CA 92686
(714) 579-1465
Contact: Mr. Fred Paar
Minimum Salary Placed: $25,000
Recruiting Specialty: General

Gerald Reynolds
20335 Via La Vieja
Yorba Linda, CA 92587
(714) 693-7018
Contact: Mr. G.L. Reynolds
Recruiting Specialty: General

C O L O R A D O

ARVADA

Bridge
P.O. Box 740297
Arvada, CO 80006
(303) 422-1900
Contact: Mr. Alex Wilcox
Minimum Salary Placed: $30,000
Recruiting Specialty: General

AURORA

Daniel J. Kerstein
14338 E. Baltic Circle
Aurora, CO 80014
(303) 695-1114
Contact: Mr. Daniel Kerstein
Minimum Salary Placed: $60,000
Recruiting Specialty: General

National Affirmative Action
4255 South Buckley Road, Suite 299
Aurora, CO 80013
(303) 699-8599
Contact: Mr. Calvin Booker
Minimum Salary Placed: $25,000
Recruiting Specialty: General

Princeton Associates
13791 E. Rice Place
Aurora, CO 80015
(303) 699-4230
Contact: Mr. Tom Boyer
Minimum Salary Placed: $25,000
Recruiting Specialty: General

BOULDER

Carlson Bentley Associates
3889 Promontory Court
Boulder, CO 80304
(303) 443-6500
Contact: Mr. Don Miller
Minimum Salary Placed: $25,000
Recruiting Specialty: Data processing,
specifically the IBS AS400

Corporate Search Partners
1050 Walnut Street, Suite 212
Boulder, CO 80302
(303) 444-3678
Contact: Mr. John Horn
Minimum Salary Placed: $25,000
Recruiting Specialty: General

Executive Search Placements
P.O. Box 17403
Boulder, CO 80308
(303) 776-0094
Contact: Mr. Richard Bagert
Minimum Salary Placed: $75,000
Recruiting Specialty: Investment banking

Front Range Personnel
1800 30th Street, Suite 311
Boulder, CO 80301
(303) 443-4730
Contact: Mr. Tim Donovan
Minimum Salary Placed: $20,000
Recruiting Specialty: General

Kutt, Inc.
2336 Canyon Boulevard
Boulder, CO 80302
(303) 440-6111
Contact: Mr. David Huff
Recruiting Specialty: Printing

Management Recruiters
P.O. Box 4657
Boulder, CO 80306
(303) 447-9900
Contact: Ms. Sharon Hunter
Minimum Salary Placed: $25,000
Recruiting Specialty: Microwave engineering and MIS

Mountain States Personnel
2850 Iris Avenue
Boulder, CO 80301
(303) 444-5770
Contact: Mr. Fred Clark
Minimum Salary Placed: $20,000
Recruiting Specialty: Hospitality and retailing

NCS, INC.
2897 Mapleton Avenue, Suite 1A
Boulder, CO 80301
(303) 440-5110
Recruiting Specialty: Accounting, banking, and finance

Young and Thulin
555 Clover Lane
Boulder, CO 80303
(303) 499-7242

Contact: Mr. William Young
Minimum Salary Placed: $75,000
Recruiting Specialty: General

CASTLE ROCK

Miller Denver
P.O. Box 340
Castle Rock, CO 80104
(303) 688-6630
Contact: Mr. Eric Miller
Minimum Salary Placed: $35,000
Recruiting Specialty: Technical disciplines and engineering

COLORADO SPRINGS

Alexander Group
4575 Hilton Parkway, Suite 201
Colorado Springs, CO 80907
(719) 528-5700
Contact: Mr. John Parabek
Minimum Salary Placed: $25,000
Recruiting Specialty: Data processing

Dunhill Personnel
1215 N. Nevada Avenue
Colorado Springs, CO 80903
(719) 473-7273
Minimum Salary Placed: $40,000
Recruiting Specialty: Chemicals, refining, oil and gas, technical and manufacturing

Health Care Dimensions
7150 Campus Drive, Suite 320
Colorado Springs, CO 80920
(800) 373-3401
Contact: Ms. Christine Carter
Minimum Salary Placed: $50,000
Recruiting Specialty: Rehabilitation, long-term care and sub-acute

Management Recruiters
10 Boulder Crescent, Suite 302B
Colorado Springs, CO 80903
(719) 389-0600
Contact: Mr. Bud Reynolds
Minimum Salary Placed: $20,000
Recruiting Specialty: General

Omni Executive Recruiters
2860 S. Circle Drive, Suite GL22
Colorado Springs, CO 80903
(719) 576-0779
Contact: Mr. Bud Nott
Minimum Salary Placed: $30,000
Recruiting Specialty: Mining

Peak Limited Executive Recruiters
118 N. Tejon, Suite 205F
Colorado Springs, CO 80903
(719) 578-1814
Contact: Mr. B. Casterline
Minimum Salary Placed: $30,000
Recruiting Specialty: Insurance

Robert Half International
105 E. Vermiso, Suite 550
Colorado Springs, CO 80903
(719) 577-4499
Minimum Salary Placed: $25,000
Recruiting Specialty: Accounting and finance

Rubicon HRT
225 S. Academy
Colorado Springs, CO 80910
(719) 574-8802
Contact: Theresa
Minimum Salary Placed: $25,000
Recruiting Specialty: Technical disciplines and engineering

Team Resources Inc.
6180 Lehman Drive
Colorado Springs, CO 80918
(719) 594-4747
Contact: Mr. Jim Schroeder
Minimum Salary Placed: $50,000
Recruiting Specialty: General

Technical Recruiters of Colorado
3322 Water Street
Colorado Springs, CO 80904
(719) 632-3835
Contact: Mr. Greg McGannon
Minimum Salary Placed: $40,000
Recruiting Specialty: Engineering

CONIFER

Mycoff and Associates
26689 Pleasant Park Road, Suite 260
Conifer, CO 80433
(303) 838-7445
Contact: Mr. C. Mycoff
Minimum Salary Placed: $25,000
Recruiting Specialty: Utilities

DENVER

Abacus Consultants
1777 S. Harrison, Suite 404
Denver, CO 80210
(303) 759-5064
Contact: Mr. Stephen Kukoy
Minimum Salary Placed: $30,000
Recruiting Specialty: MIS

Accountants On Call
1200 17th Street, Suite 2160
Denver, CO 80282
(303) 571-1110

Contact: Mr. Mark Rahe
Recruiting Specialty: Accounting

Accounting Solutions
410 17th Street
Denver, CO 80210
(303) 534-1950
Contact: Mr. E. Olsen
Minimum Salary Placed: $25,000
Recruiting Specialty: Accounting and finance

Aim Executive Consulting Services
1 Tabor Center
Denver, CO 80202
(303) 893-0146
Contact: Mr. Fred Holt
Minimum Salary Placed: $70,000
Recruiting Specialty: General

American Medical Recruiters
325 Krameria Street
Denver, CO 80220
(303) 393-0791
Contact: Ms. Gayle Berouist
Minimum Salary Placed: $30,000
Recruiting Specialty: Healthcare

William B. Arnold Associates, Inc.
600 S. Cherry Street, Suite 1105
Denver, CO 80222
(303) 393-6662
Contact: Mr. William Arnold
Minimum Salary Placed: $60,000
Recruiting Specialty: General

Attorney Service Center/ASC Inc.
2135 South Cherry Street, Suite 111
Denver, CO 80222
(303) 691-2278

Contact: Ms. Karen Erfman
Minimum Salary Placed: $18,000
Recruiting Specialty: Legal—secretaries, paralegals, and administrative

C.S. Barnes
650 South Cherry Street, Suite 102
Denver, CO 80222
(303) 320-3727
Contact: Ms. Colleen S. Barnes
Minimum Salary Placed: $18,000
Recruiting Specialty: Accounting and finance, legal, and real estate

Boling and Associates
55 Madison Avenue
Denver, CO 80206
(303) 320-4755
Contact: Ms. Robin Curry
Recruiting Specialty: General

CLGS
730 17th Street, Suite 220
Denver, CO 80202
(303) 571-4800
Contact: Mr. P. Rubin
Minimum Salary Placed: $45,000
Recruiting Specialty: Healthcare

Careers Limited
1700 Lincoln Street
Denver, CO 80203
(303) 832-5200
Contact: Mr. G. Peay
Minimum Salary Placed: $25,000
Recruiting Specialty: General

Cochran, Cochran & Yale, Inc.
1333 West 120th Ave, Suite 311
Denver, CO 80234
(303) 252-4600
Contact: Mr. Chet Marino
Recruiting Specialty: General

Continental Quest
2140 S, Ivanhoe Street
Denver, CO 80222
(303) 782-9648
Contact: Ms. Candice Koch
Minimum Salary Placed: $25,000
Recruiting Specialty: General

Daniels & Patterson Corporate Search, Inc.
1732 Marion Street
Denver, CO 80218
(303) 830-1230
Contact: Ms. Ruby Patterson
Minimum Salary Placed: $25,000
Recruiting Specialty: Computer Science and telecommunications

DiMarchi Partners
1225 17th Street
Denver, CO 80202
(303) 292-9300
Contact: Mr. Paul DiMarchi
Minimum Salary Placed: $75,000
Recruiting Specialty: General

Executive Search and Consulting
1685 Steele, Suite 9
Denver, CO 80206
(303) 220-1230
Contact: Mr. John Moreno
Minimum Salary Placed: $25,000
Recruiting Specialty: General

Ford Personnel, Inc.
650 South Cherry Street, Suite 1011
Denver, CO 80222
(303) 322-2317
Contact: Ms. Ginny Ford
Minimum Salary Placed: $20,000
Recruiting Specialty: Legal

Gimble and Nicol Executive Search
1675 Broadway
Denver, CO 80203
(303) 892-6400
Recruiting Specialty: Attorneys and mining engineers

Hallmark Personnel Systems Inc.
6825 E. Tennessee Avenue
Denver, CO 80224
(303) 388-6190
Contact: Ms. G. Sweeney
Minimum Salary Placed: $25,000
Recruiting Specialty: General

David W. Hebble Management Group
5031 S. Uester, Suite 370
Denver, CO 80237
(303) 779-4466
Contact: Mr. David Hebble
Minimum Salary Placed: $25,000
Recruiting Specialty: Cable television

JFI - Jobs For Industry
1888 Sherman Street, Suite 500
Denver, CO 80203
(303) 831-0048
Contact: Mr. Kevin Courtney
Minimum Salary Placed: $20,000
Recruiting Specialty: Distribution and packaging

Karam Group
1675 Larimer Street, Suite 310
Denver, CO 80202
(303) 436-1884
Contact: Mr. Richard Karam
Minimum Salary Placed: $60,000
Recruiting Specialty: General

A.T. Kearney Executive Search
1200 17th Street, Suite 950
Denver, CO 80202
(303) 572-6175
Contact: Ms. Marcia Pryde
Minimum Salary Placed: $60,000
Recruiting Specialty: General

LD Placements, Inc.
621 17th Street, Suite 2000
Denver, CO 80293
(303) 298-7373
Contact: Ms. Rie Kenkel
Minimum Salary Placed: $20,000
Recruiting Specialty: Accounting and finance

Preferred Leads, Inc.
1660 South Albion, Suite 812
Denver, CO 80222
(303) 782-5447
Contact: Ms. Susie Thorpe
Minimum Salary Placed: $20,000
Recruiting Specialty: Property management and real estate

Management West
470 22nd Street
Denver, CO 80205
(303) 388-2888
Contact: Mr. Mike Waterman
Minimum Salary Placed: $25,000
Recruiting Specialty: Construction

R.J. Masek and Associates
875 Colorado Boulevard
Denver, CO 80222
(303) 744-7870
Contact: Mr. R. Masek
Minimum Salary Placed: $25,000
Recruiting Specialty: Accounting and finance

Pendleton Resources
1301 Pennsylvania Street
Denver, CO 80203
(303) 832-8100
Contact: Mr. M. Jacobs
Minimum Salary Placed: $25,000
Recruiting Specialty: Environmental

Phillips Personnel/Search
1675 Broadway, Suite 2410
Denver, CO 80202
(303) 893-1850
Contact: Mr. Phil Heinschel
Minimum Salary Placed: $45,000
Recruiting Specialty: General

Prime Consultants
410 17th Street
Denver, CO 80202
(303) 592-1900
Contact: Mr. Tom McAleer
Recruiting Specialty: Financial services

Rocky Mountain Recruiters, Inc.
1801 Broadway, Suite 810
Denver, CO 80202
(303) 296-2000
Contact: Mr. Michael Turner
Minimum Salary Placed: $30,000
Recruiting Specialty: Accounting and finance

Scheer and Associates
1873 S. Bellaire Street
Denver, CO 80222
(303) 757-7357
Contact: Mr. Roger Scheer
Minimum Salary Placed: $25,000
Recruiting Specialty: General

Sklar Resource Group, Inc.
1776 S. Jackson, Suite 905
Denver, CO 80210
(303) 753-9401
Contact: Mr. Ron Lee
Recruiting Specialty: Credit, collections
and receivables

Snelling Personnel Service
655 Broadway
Denver, CO 80203
(303) 534-3581
Contact: Ms. B. Strawn
Recruiting Specialty: General

Travel Careers, Inc.
300 South Jackson Street, Suite 540
Denver, CO 80209
(303) 355-9004
Contact: Ms. Anne DiCicco
Minimum Salary Placed: $18,000
Recruiting Specialty: Travel

Van Dernoot and Associates
50 S. Steele Street, Suite 222
Denver, CO 80209
(303) 322-1202
Recruiting Specialty: General

EDGEWATER

Douglas, Richmond & Grice
2474 Newland, Suite 100
Edgewater, CO 80214
(303) 233-3369

Contact: Mr. Rick Grice
Recruiting Specialty: MIS and environmental

EDWARDS

Goodwin and Associates
1061 June Creek Road
Edwards, CO 81632
(970) 926-1883
Contact: Ms. Linda Goodwin
Minimum Salary Placed: $30,000
Recruiting Specialty: Food

ENGLEWOOD

Access Personnel Services, Inc.
8100 East Arapahoe Road, Suite 206
Englewood, CO 80112
(303) 694-3499
Contact: Ms. Dana Elwess
Minimum Salary Placed: $18,000
Recruiting Specialty: Accounting and finance, sales

Bennett & Curran, Inc.
1545 W. Tufts Avenue, Suite M
Englewood, CO 80110
(303) 783-2255
Contact: Mr. Jeffrey Stephenson
Minimum Salary Placed: $40,000
Recruiting Specialty: General

Career Consultants Inc.
Englewood, CO
(303) 741-2501
Contact: Ms. C. Kelly
Minimum Salary Placed: $25,000
Recruiting Specialty: Technical disciplines in computers and electronics

Dunhill Professional Search
P.O. Box 4905
Englewood, CO 80155
(303) 755-7466

Contact: Mr. John Lippe
Minimum Salary Placed: $25,000
Recruiting Specialty: Technical disciplines in consumer products, food and beverages and pharmaceuticals

Dunhill Professional Search
6909 S. Holly Circle, Suite 305
Englewood, CO 80112
(303) 721-0525
Contact: Mr. Leon Parnes
Recruiting Specialty: Healthcare, credit cards and medical information systems

EFL Associates
7120 E. Orchard, Suite 240
Englewood, CO 80111
(303) 779-1724
Contact: Mr. Jeffrey Riley
Minimum Salary Placed: $60,000
Recruiting Specialty: General

Health Industry Consultants, Inc.
9250 E. Costilla Avenue, Suite 600
Englewood, CO 80112
(303) 790-2009
Contact: Mr. Jon Fitzgerald
Minimum Salary Placed: $55,000
Recruiting Specialty: Biotechnology and pharmaceuticals

Health Technology, Inc.
7502 S. Willow Circle, Suite D
Englewood, CO 80112
(303) 322-6226
Contact: Mr. Thomas Miller
Minimum Salary Placed: $50,000
Recruiting Specialty: Biotechnology and pharmaceuticals

David L. Henson Inc.
P.O. Box 5324
Englewood, CO 80155
(303) 741-4211
Contact: Mr. David Henson
Minimum Salary Placed: $25,000
Recruiting Specialty: General

Integrity Network Inc.
5445 DTC Boulevard
Englewood, CO 80111
(303) 220-9752
Contact: Ms. Judy Kennelley
Minimum Salary Placed: $25,000
Recruiting Specialty: General

Management Recruiters
9350 E. Arapahoe Road, Suite 480
Englewood, CO 80112
(303) 799-8188
Contact: Mr. Kent Milius
Recruiting Specialty: General

Medical Personnel Resources, Inc.
3333 South Bannock, Suite 530
Englewood, CO 80110
(303) 762-0806
Contact: Mr. Ronald J. Robacker
Minimum Salary Placed: $20,000
Recruiting Specialty: Medical

MedQuest Associates
9250 E. Costilla Avenue, Suite 600
Englewood, CO 80112
(303) 790-2009
Contact: Ms. Judy Stiles
Minimum Salary Placed: $30,000
Recruiting Specialty: Medical products

National Executive Resources
5455 DTC Parkway, Suite 4
Englewood, CO 80111
(303) 721-7672
Contact: Mr. Alan Pike
Minimum Salary Placed: $25,000
Recruiting Specialty: Engineering, mining and refining

M. S. Pickert and Associates
8050 S. Jasmine Circle
Englewood, CO 80112
(303) 337-3708
Contact: Ms. Marti Pickert
Minimum Salary Placed: $25,000
Recruiting Specialty: Medical sales

The Pinnacle Source, Inc.
9250 E. Costille Avenue, Suite 603
Englewood, CO 80112
(303) 792-5300
Contact: Mr. Jordan Greenberg
Minimum Salary Placed: $55,000
Recruiting Specialty: Sales and MIS in communications and high technology

Premier Consulting
8301 East Prentice Avenue
Englewood, CO 80111
(303) 779-1006
Contact: Ms. J. Hanbery
Minimum Salary Placed: $25,000
Recruiting Specialty: Computers

Professional Search, Inc.
7909 S. Monaco Court
Englewood, CO 80112
(303) 694-1210
Contact: Mr. Lawrence Jock
Minimum Salary Placed: $30,000
Recruiting Specialty: General

Sigma Group International
6551 S. Revere 3 Parkway, Suite 125
Englewood, CO 80111
Contact: Mr. George Reisinger
Minimum Salary Placed: $90,000
Recruiting Specialty: General

Source EDP
7730 E. Belleview Avenue
Englewood, CO 80111
(303) 773-3700
Recruiting Specialty: Computer programming and MIS

Source Finance
7730 East Belleview Avenue, Suite 302
Englewood, CO 80111
(303) 773-3799
Contact: Mr. B. Francis
Minimum Salary Placed: $25,000
Recruiting Specialty: Finance and accounting

Summit Medical Consultants
7400 E. Orchard Road, Suite 290
Englewood, CO 80111
(303) 798-6610
Recruiting Specialty: Physicians

Trish & Associates
7120 East Orchard Road, Suite 250
Englewood, CO 80111
(303) 220-0700
Contact: Ms. Patricia Dill
Recruiting Specialty: Sales and some general

EVERGREEN

Management Recruiters
27972 Meadow Drive Street, Suite 110
Evergreen, CO 80439
(303) 863-7400
Contact: Mr. Pete Neumann
Minimum Salary Placed: $25,000
Recruiting Specialty: Healthcare

FORT COLLINS

Dunhill Professional Search
2120 S. College Avenue, Suite 3
Fort Collins, CO 80525
(970) 221-5630
Contact: Mr. Jerold Lyons
Minimum Salary Placed: $25,000
Recruiting Specialty: Agriculture, micro-electronics and semi-conductors

GLENWOOD SPRINGS

Alpha Group, Inc.
311½ Eighth Street, Suite 600
Glenwood Springs, CO 81601
(970) 945-2338
Contact: Mr. J. Astrach
Recruiting Specialty: High technology, plastics, metals and environmental

GOLDEN

SEI, Inc.
14818 West 6th Avenue, Suite 17A
Golden, CO 80401
(303) 271-9554

Contact: Mr. Gene Scott
Minimum Salary Placed: $30,000
Recruiting Specialty: Computer, engineering, environmental, and manufacturing

GRAND JUNCTION

Carlsen Resources, Inc.
388 Ridgeway Drive, 2nd Floor
Grand Junction, CO 81503
(970) 242-9462
Contact: Ms. Ann Carlsen
Minimum Salary Placed: $50,000
Recruiting Specialty: Telecommunications and cable

GREELEY

York and Associates
1019 9th Street
Greeley, CO 80631
(970) 352-3086
Contact: Ms. Terry York
Minimum Salary Placed: $25,000
Recruiting Specialty: General

GREENWOOD VILLAGE

Career Marketing Associates, Inc.
7100 E. Belleview Avenue, Suite 102
Greenwood Village, CO 80111
(303) 779-8890
Contact: Mr. Jan Sather
Minimum Salary Placed: $35,000
Recruiting Specialty: General

Eleventh Hour Personnel
8577 East Arapahoe Road, Suite A
Greenwood Village, CO 80111
(303) 220-8892
Contact: Ms Mary Smith
Recruiting Specialty: Accounting and finance, insurance, and office administration and support staff

R.L. Plimpton Associates, Inc.
5655 S. Yosemite Street, Suite 410
Greenwood Village, CO 80111
(303) 771-1311
Contact: Mr. Ralph Plimpton
Minimum Salary Placed: $70,000
Recruiting Specialty: General

Skupsky & Associates
5600 S. Quebec Street, Suite C-250
Greenwood Village, CO 80111
(303) 290-9480
Contact: Ms. Lorraine Skupsky
Recruiting Specialty: Physicians

HIGHLANDS RANCH

Chapman Tierney Search
P.O. Box 4310
Highlands Ranch, CO 80126
(303) 791-8027
Contact: Ms. K. Chapman-Tierne
Minimum Salary Placed: $75,000
Recruiting Specialty: General

LAKEWOOD

The Human Resource Consulting Group, Inc.
165 S. Union Boulevard, Suite 456
Lakewood, CO 80228
(303) 987-8888

Contact: Mr. Joseph Zaccaro
Minimum Salary Placed: $50,000
Recruiting Specialty: General

Management Recruiters
12600 W. Colfax Avenue, Suite C-440
Lakewood, CO 80215
(303) 233-8600
Contact: Mr. Rodney Bonner
Minimum Salary Placed: $20,000
Recruiting Specialty: Engineers: medical and electrical

PC Associates
2682 S. Holman Street
Lakewood, CO 86228
(303) 986-4111
Contact: Mr. Paul Cochlan
Minimum Salary Placed: $35,000
Recruiting Specialty: General

Sterling Recruiters and Consultants
1880 S. Pierce Street, Suite 16E
Lakewood, CO 80232
(303) 934-7343
Contact: Ms. D. Brown
Minimum Salary Placed: $25,000
Recruiting Specialty: Hospitality

US Envirosearch
445 Union Boulevard, Suite 225
Lakewood, CO 80228
(303) 980-6600
Contact: Mr. P. Lake
Minimum Salary Placed: $30,000
Recruiting Specialty: Environmental

LEADVILLE

Bartholdi & Company
156 Elk Road
Leadville, CO 80461
(719) 486-2918
Contact: Ms. Terry Stevenson
Minimum Salary Placed: $70,000
Recruiting Specialty: General

LITTLETON

Corporate Technologies
9244 Ritenour Court
Littleton, CO 80124
(303) 290-9282
Contact: Mr. Teddy Pendergast
Minimum Salary Placed: $30,000
Recruiting Specialty: Banking

Fortune Consultants
7800 South Elati Street
Littleton, CO 80120
(303) 795-9210
Contact: Mr. J. Dorfman
Minimum Salary Placed: $25,000
Recruiting Specialty: General

I. J. and Associates
679 W. Littleton Boulevard, Suite 108
Littleton, CO 80120
(303) 798-5393
Contact: Ms. Diana Larson
Minimum Salary Placed: $35,000
Recruiting Specialty: Software and data
processing

Recruiting Resources, Inc.
26 W. Dry Creek Circle, Suite 600
Littleton, CO 80120
(303) 797-2575
Contact: Ms. Monica Zorens
Minimum Salary Placed: $30,000
Recruiting Specialty: Construction, engi-
neering and architecture

Ruppert Comann Associates, Inc.
8151 Saint Paul Way
Littleton, CO 80122
(303) 488-0108
Contact: Mr. William Ruppert
Minimum Salary Placed: $70,000
Recruiting Specialty: Mining, minerals
and cement

The Search Network, Inc.
6901 South Pierce Street, Suite 100
Littleton, CO 80123
(303) 932-1024
Contact: Ms. Jan Giles Huszcza
Minimum Salary Placed: $30,000
Recruiting Specialty: Engineering

LOUISVILLE

MPI Associates
761 W. Birch Court
Louisville, CO 80027
(303) 666-4195
Contact: Mr. Frank Welzig
Minimum Salary Placed: $35,000
Recruiting Specialty: Computer engineer-
ing and high technology

MONUMENT

TransAmerica Network
215 Jack Boot Way
Monument, CO 80132
(719) 481-2799
Contact: Mr. Don Wunder
Minimum Salary Placed: $35,000
Recruiting Specialty: Technical disciplines in manufacturing and processing

Woodmoor Group
P.O. Box 1383
Monument, CO 80132
(719) 488-8589
Contact: Mr. Mike Gleim
Minimum Salary Placed: $35,000
Recruiting Specialty: Engineering,
R & D and manufacturing

NAIWOT

Dunhill Personnel
6897 Paiute
Naiwot, CO 80544
(303) 444-5531
Contact: Mr. Fran Boruff
Minimum Salary Placed: $25,000
Recruiting Specialty: General

PARKER

MESA, Inc.
6019 Belmont Way
Parker, CO 80134
(303) 841-4512
Contact: Mr. Dennis Cook
Minimum Salary Placed: $80,000
Recruiting Specialty: Manufacturing and
high technology

Omniquest, Inc.
19201 East Main Street, Suite 203
Parker, CO 80134
(303) 840-9200
Contact: Mr. Pat Clark
Minimum Salary Placed: $20,000
Recruiting Specialty: Home care, medical, and sales

PUEBLO

Check Mate Careers
147 Macneil Road
Pueblo, CO 81001
(719) 543-2277
Minimum Salary Placed: $30,000
Recruiting Specialty: Data processing

TELLURIDE

Karen Haddy and Associates
P.O. Box 1616
Telluride, CO 81435
(970) 728-3004
Contact: Ms. Karen Haddy
Minimum Salary Placed: $25,000
Recruiting Specialty: General

WHEATRIDGE

Career Forum Inc.
4350 Wadsworth Boulevard, Suite 300
Wheatridge, CO 80033
(303) 425-8721
Contact: Mr. Steve Grebe
Minimum Salary Placed: $20,000
Recruiting Specialty: General

C O N N E C T I C U T

AVON

DKC Associates, Inc.
P.O. Box 1473
Avon, CT 06001
(860) 678-1555
Contact: Dan Correia
Minimum Salary Placed: $75,000
Recruiting Specialty: Sales and marketing, executives in high technology

KC Hale Inc.
20 Avon Meadow Lane
Avon, CT 06001
(860) 677-7511
Recruiting Specialty: Financial services, insurance, and healthcare

Horton International
10 Tower Lane
Avon, CT 06001
(203) 674-8701
Contact: Mr. C. Edward Snyder
Minimum Salary Placed: $100,000
Recruiting Specialty: General

Knight Group
10 Tower Lane
Avon, CT 06001
(203) 674-1024
Contact: Mr. John Fisher
Minimum Salary Placed: $60,000
Recruiting Specialty: General

People Management Northeast, Inc.
1 Darling Drive
Avon, CT 06001
(203) 678-8900

Contact: Mr. Steven Darter
Minimum Salary Placed: $75,000
Recruiting Specialty: General

RCI-Horton International
10 Tower Lane
Avon, CT 06001
(203) 674-8701
Contact: Mr. Robert Horton
Minimum Salary Placed: $60,000
Recruiting Specialty: General

Roberts Personnel Svc. Inc.
34 E. Main Street
Avon, CT 06001
(860) 677-5915
Contact: Mr. Bob Fishberg
Recruiting Specialty: Engineering

Snyder & Company
35 Old Avon Village, Route 44, Suite 185
Avon, CT 06001
(203) 521-9760
Contact: Mr. James Snyder
Recruiting Specialty: General

BISHOPS CORNER

ARC Associates LTD
69 Mohawk Drive
Bishops Corner, CT 06117
(860) 233-8820
Recruiting Specialty: Attorneys

Gene Wittenberg & Associates
2446 Albany Avenue
Bishops Corner, CT 06117
(860) 232-9700
Recruiting Specialty: Insurance

BLOOMFIELD

Insurance Career Center, Inc.
1280 Blue Hills Avenue
Bloomfield, CT 06002
(203) 726-9133
Contact: Ms. Linda Kiner
Minimum Salary Placed: $25,000
Recruiting Specialty: Insurance

BRANFORD

Ryan Abbott Search Associates, Inc.
250 W. Main Street
Branford, CT 06405
(203) 488-7245
Contact: Mr. Eugene McGetrick
Minimum Salary Placed: $30,000
Recruiting Specialty: Pharmaceuticals

CANTON

Dillon and Company
101 River Road
Canton, CT 06019
(203) 693-9600
Contact: Mr. John Dillon
Minimum Salary Placed: $30,000
Recruiting Specialty: General

CHESHIRE

Development Systems Inc.
402 Highland Avenue
Cheshire, CT 06410
(203) 272-1117
Contact: Mr. Arnold Bernstein
Minimum Salary Placed: $50,000
Recruiting Specialty: Retail and wholesale

Napolitano and Wulster
311 S. Main Street
Chesire, CT 06410
(203) 272-2820
Contact: Mr. Anthony Napolitano
Minimum Salary Placed: $25,000
Recruiting Specialty: Pharmaceuticals

COLLINSVILLE

Richard Wright Company
P.O. Box 127, 7 Shingle Mill Drive
Collinsville, CT 06022
(203) 693-1822
Contact: Mr. Richard Eickenhorst
Minimum Salary Placed: $40,000
Recruiting Specialty: Insurance

COS COB

Flexible Resources
399 E. Putnam Avenue
Cos Cob, CT 06807
(203) 629-3255
Contact: Ms. Nadine Mockler
Recruiting Specialty: General

The Hyde Group, Inc.
209 Palmer Point, River Road
Cos Cob, CT 06807
(203) 661-0413
Contact: Ms. Anne Hyde
Minimum Salary Placed: $80,000
Recruiting Specialty: General

COVENTRY

Confidential Search Company
98 Timber Trail
Coventry, CT 06238
(203) 742-1555
Contact: Mr. Matthew Brien
Minimum Salary Placed: $20,000
Recruiting Specialty: General

CROMWELL

Management Recruiters
154 West Street, Building 3, Unit C
Cromwell, CT 06416
(203) 635-0612
Contact: Mr. Leslie Cole
Recruiting Specialty: Consumer products

DANBURY

Abraham & London Ltd.
7 Old Sherman Turnpike, Suite 209
Danbury, CT 06810
(203) 798-7537
Contact: Mr. Stuart Laub
Minimum Salary Placed: $30,000
Recruiting Specialty: Sales in healthcare,
communications and high technology

Argus National, Inc.
98 Mill Plain Road, Suite 301
Danbury, CT 06811
(203) 790-8420
Contact: Ms. Constance Gruen
Minimum Salary Placed: $50,000
Recruiting Specialty: General

Dunhill Personnel System
40 Richbury Road
Danbury, CT 06810
(203) 743-6994
Contact: Ms. Joanne DiAntonio
Minimum Salary Placed: $30,000
Recruiting Specialty: General

E O Technical
57 North Street
Danbury, CT 06810
(203) 797-2653
Contact: Ms. Jeanette Petroski
Recruiting Specialty: General

Wendall L. Johnson Associates
12 Grandview Drive
Danbury, CT 06811
(203) 743-4112
Contact: Mr. Wendall Johnson
Minimum Salary Placed: $20,000
Recruiting Specialty: General

DARIEN

Academy Graduates Executive
576 Post Road
Darien, CT 06820
(203) 656-0404
Contact: Mr. Nathaniel Gallagher
Minimum Salary Placed: $20,000
Recruiting Specialty: General

Anderson and Company
980 Post Road
Darien, CT 06820
(203) 655-9337
Contact: Ms. Jane Anderson
Minimum Salary Placed: $80,000
Recruiting Specialty: Financial services

Cosco Resources Inc.
980 Post Road
Darien, CT 06820
(203) 655-7787
Contact: Ms. Suzanne Cosco
Minimum Salary Placed: $40,000
Recruiting Specialty: Finance

Lindsey & Company, Inc.
P.O. Box 1273
Darien, CT 06820
(203) 655-1590
Contact: Mr. Lary Lindsey
Minimum Salary Placed: $50,000
Recruiting Specialty: General

W. D. Nolte & Company
6 Middlesex Road
Darien, CT 06820
(203) 323-5858
Contact: Mr. William Nolte
Minimum Salary Placed: $60,000
Recruiting Specialty: General

RX Executive Search
70 Arrowhead Way
Darien, CT 06820
(203) 655-6528
Contact: Ms. E. Lyons
Minimum Salary Placed: $25,000
Recruiting Specialty: Pharmaceuticals

EAST HARTFORD

Source EDP
111 Founders Plaza, Suite 1501
East Hartford, CT 06108
(203) 528-0300
Minimum Salary Placed: $25,000
Recruiting Specialty: Computer hardware and software

EAST HAVEN

Marge Dana Association
4 Lynn Court
East Haven, CT 06512
(203) 467-7893
Contact: Ms. Marge Dana
Minimum Salary Placed: $75,000
Recruiting Specialty: General

ESSEX

Ullstein Association
6 Hanna Lane
Essex, CT 06426
(203) 767-8449
Contact: Hans Ullstein
Minimum Salary Placed: $75,000
Recruiting Specialty: General

FAIRFIELD

C. A. Durakis Association, Inc.
1 Post Road
Fairfield, CT 06430
(203) 255-5567
Contact: Mr. Charles Durakis
Minimum Salary Placed: $80,000
Recruiting Specialty: General

Robert Lacey and Associates
583 Jefferson Street
Fairfield, CT 06430
(203) 373-0733
Contact: Mr. Robert Lacey
Minimum Salary Placed: $20,000
Recruiting Specialty: General

Management Recruiters
140 Sherman Street
Fairfield, CT 06430
(203) 255-2299
Contact: Mr. R. Rush Oster
Minimum Salary Placed: $40,000
Recruiting Specialty: Healthcare and consumer products

Tucker Group
111 Reef Road
Fairfield, CT 06430
(203) 256-3789
Recruiting Specialty: Sales & marketing and healthcare

FARMINGTON

Thomas Byrne Associates
7 Melrose Drive
Farmington, CT 06032
(203) 676-2468
Contact: Mr. Thomas Byrne
Minimum Salary Placed: $30,000
Recruiting Specialty: Accounting, finance and MIS

GLASTONBURY

Alexander Research Services
140 Heywood Drive
Glastonbury, CT 06033
(203) 657-1458
Contact: Ms. Holly Alexander
Minimum Salary Placed: $70,000
Recruiting Specialty: Information systems

R. C. Handel Association Inc.
117 New London Turnpike
Glastonbury, CT 06033
(203) 633-3900
Contact: Mr. Richard Handel
Minimum Salary Placed: $50,000
Recruiting Specialty: General

Richard L. Mather & Associates
P.O. Box 1183
Glastonbury, CT 06033
(203) 633-8130
Contact: Mr. Richard Mather
Minimum Salary Placed: $35,000
Recruiting Specialty: High technology

GREENWICH

John A. Bennett
34 E. Putnam Avenue
Greenwich, CT 06830
(203) 629-3953
Contact: Mr. John Bennett
Recruiting Specialty: General

Blackshaw, Olmstead & Lynch
60 Arch Street
Greenwich, CT 06830
(203) 869-7727
Contact: Mr. John Lynch
Minimum Salary Placed: $70,000
Recruiting Specialty: General

Catania and Associates
100 Melrose Avenue
Greenwich, CT 06830
(203) 869-3330
Contact: Mr. C. Catania
Minimum Salary Placed: $25,000
Recruiting Specialty: General

David Chambers & Association, Inc.
2 Greenwich Plaza, Suite 100
Greenwich, CT 06830
(203) 622-1333
Contact: Mr. David Chambers
Minimum Salary Placed: $100,000
Recruiting Specialty: General

Datapath Search Group
32 Sherwood Place
Greenwich, CT 06830
(203) 869-3536
Contact: Mr. Steve Silvi
Minimum Salary Placed: $40,000
Recruiting Specialty: Data processing,
sales and human resources

Erlanger Association
2 Pickwick Plaza
Greenwich, CT 06830
(203) 629-5410
Contact: Mr. Richard Erlanger
Minimum Salary Placed: $160,000
Recruiting Specialty: Investor's portfolio
companies

Heidrick & Struggles, Inc.
Greenwich Office Park, Building 3
Greenwich, CT 06830
(203) 629-3200
Contact: Mr. Ray Foote
Minimum Salary Placed: $60,000
Recruiting Specialty: General

Livingston, Robert & Company
2 Greenwich Plaza, Suite 100
Greenwich, CT 06830
(203) 622-4901
Contact: Mr. Peter Livingston
Minimum Salary Placed: $100,000
Recruiting Specialty: General

Matte & Company, Inc.
124 W. Putnam Avenue
Greenwich, CT 06830
(203) 661-2224
Contact: Mr. Norman Matte
Minimum Salary Placed: $75,000
Recruiting Specialty: General

Online Marketing Company, Inc.
P.O. Box 1608
Greenwich, CT 06830
(203) 625-9292
Contact: Ms. Margareta Sjolund
Recruiting Specialty: Scandinavian re-
cruiting

Search Solutions Inc.
3 Lewis Street
Greenwich, CT 06830
(203) 869-0972
Recruiting Specialty: Retained executive
search

Smith Hanley Associates
71 Arch Street
Greenwich, CT 06830
(203) 869-6660
Recruiting Specialty: Risk management,
insurance

William Willis Worldwide Inc.
164 Mason Street
Greenwich, CT 06830
(203) 661-4500
Contact: Mr. William Willis
Minimum Salary Placed: $85,000
Recruiting Specialty: General

GUILFORD

Anderson Group
741 Boston Post Road
Guilford, CT 06437
(203) 458-7060
Contact: Mr. Jim Anderson
Minimum Salary Placed: $25,000
Recruiting Specialty: General

Dunsmore and Associates
87 Whitfield Street
Guilford, CT 06437
(203) 453-3942
Contact: Mr. Joseph Dunsmore
Minimum Salary Placed: $25,000
Recruiting Specialty: Market research
and strategic planning

Galen Giles Group
635 Nut Plains Road
Guilford, CT 06437
(203) 453-5511
Contact: Mr. David Johnson
Minimum Salary Placed: $30,000
Recruiting Specialty: General

JFW Associates
44 Long Hill Road, P.O. Box 267
Guilford, CT 06437
(203) 453-1415
Contact: Mr. John Wilbur
Recruiting Specialty: Computers and MIS

HAMDEN

MRG Search & Placement
2693 Whitney Avenue
Hamden, CT 06518
(203) 624-0161
Contact: Mr. Gary Clark
Minimum Salary Placed: $25,000
Recruiting Specialty: Computers and MIS

HARTFORD

Accountants On Call
100 Constitution Place, Suite 957
Hartford, CT 06103
(203) 246-4200
Contact: Mr. Bernard Simon
Recruiting Specialty: Accounting

S. W. Delano & Company
750 Main Street, 2nd Floor
Hartford, CT 06103
(203) 278-5186
Contact: Mr. Steven Delano
Minimum Salary Placed: $60,000
Recruiting Specialty: Financial services

High-Tech Recruiters
30 High Street, Suite 104A
Hartford, CT 06103
(203) 527-4262

Contact: Mr. Clement Williams
Minimum Salary Placed: $30,000
Recruiting Specialty: MIS, finance and
telecommunications

Robert Half Accountemps
100 Pearl Street
Hartford, CT 06103
(203) 278-7170
Contact: Mr. Greg Laines
Recruiting Specialty: Accounting, finance
and administration

Howard W. Smith Associates
Old State House Station
P.O. Box 230877
Hartford, CT 06123-0877
(860) 549-2060
Contact: Mr. Howard Smith
Minimum Salary Placed: $70,000
Recruiting Specialty: Financial services,
non-profit

Stewart Associates
410 Asylum Street
Hartford, CT 06103
(203) 548-1388
Contact: Mr. Phil Stewart
Minimum Salary Placed: $20,000
Recruiting Specialty: Data processing

MADISON

Dussick Management Associates
149 Durham Road
Madison, CT 06443
(203) 245-9311
Contact: Mr. Vince Dussick
Minimum Salary Placed: $45,000
Recruiting Specialty: Marketing and sales

ESA
141 Durham Road
Madison, CT 06443
(203) 245-1983
Contact: Mr. Barry Dicker
Minimum Salary Placed: $40,000
Recruiting Specialty: High technology

MANCHESTER

Corporate Staffing Systems
150 North Main Street
Manchester, CT 06040
(203) 647-8004
Contact: Mr. Walter Roser
Minimum Salary Placed: $40,000
Recruiting Specialty: General

Lutz Associates
9 Stephen Street
Manchester, CT 06040
(203) 647-9338
Contact: Mr. Allen Lutz
Minimum Salary Placed: $35,000
Recruiting Specialty: Engineering and
manufacturing

MILFORD

Management Recruiters
61 Cherry Street
Milford, CT 06460
(203) 876-8755
Contact: Ms. Sandy Campbell
Minimum Salary Placed: $20,000
Recruiting Specialty: General

Carol A. McInnis and Associates
203 Broad Street, Suite 6
Milford, CT 06460
(203) 876-7110

Contact: Ms. Carol McInnis
Minimum Salary Placed: $30,000
Recruiting Specialty: Medical and scientific products

Sales Consultants
326 W. Main Street, Suite 202
Milford, CT 06460
(203) 876-4949
Contact: Mr. Ronald Fink
Minimum Salary Placed: $20,000
Recruiting Specialty: Sales

MONROE

Lee Ann Lee
P.O. Box 234
Monroe, CT 06468
(203) 377-3677
Recruiting Specialty: General

Tidewater Group Inc.
115 Main
Monroe, CT 06468
(203) 459-2500
Contact: Mr. John Kalas
Minimum Salary Placed: $40,000
Recruiting Specialty: General

NEW CANAAN

Baldwin Associates, Inc.
39 Locust Avenue
New Canaan, CT 06840
(203) 966-5355
Contact: Mr. Max Baldwin
Minimum Salary Placed: $100,000
Recruiting Specialty: General

Emmons Association, Inc.
226 Lost District Drive
New Canaan, CT 06840
(203) 966-4584
Contact: Mr. William Emmons
Minimum Salary Placed: $100,000
Recruiting Specialty: Computers and communications

JT Associates
89 Comstock Hill Road
New Canaan, CT 06840
(203) 966-6311
Contact: Mr. Joe Fazio
Minimum Salary Placed: $40,000
Recruiting Specialty: General

Alan Perry Associates
9 Whiffle Tree Lane
New Canaan, CT 06840
(203) 966-8432
Contact: Mr. Alan Perry
Minimum Salary Placed: $20,000
Recruiting Specialty: General

J. D. Walsh & Company
456 Lost District Drive
New Canaan, CT 06840
(203) 966-2893
Contact: Mr. John Walsh
Minimum Salary Placed: $50,000
Recruiting Specialty: Telecommunications and information services

NEW HARTFORD

Blackwood Associates
100 Business Park Drive, Suite 3
New Hartford, CT 06057
(860) 489-0494

Contact: Mr. Jeffrey Blackwood
Minimum Salary Placed: $20,000
Recruiting Specialty: Medical (medical assistants, therapists) and banking & finance

NEW HAVEN

Dunhill Search International
59 Elm Street
New Haven, CT 06510
(203) 562-0511
Contact: Mr. Donald Kaiser
Minimum Salary Placed: $30,000
Recruiting Specialty: International placement, marketing and sales

Robert Half International
555 Long Wharf, Suite 9H
New Haven, CT 06510
(203) 562-9262
Contact: Ms. S. Growney
Minimum Salary Placed: $25,000
Recruiting Specialty: Accounting and finance

NEWINGTON

Julian Association, Inc.
162 Willard Avenue
Newington, CT 06111
(203) 232-7876
Contact: Mr. Julian Brownstein
Minimum Salary Placed: $30,000
Recruiting Specialty: Advertising and public relations

NEWTOWN

Riswold and Associates
6 Hall Lane
Newtown, CT 06470
(203) 426-9960

Contact: Mr. Irving Riswold
Minimum Salary Placed: $25,000
Recruiting Specialty: Petroleum

NORWALK

Creative Options Inc.
50 Washington Street
Norwalk, CT 06854
(203) 854-9393
Contact: Mr. Karl Heine
Recruiting Specialty: Advertising and design

Fairfaxx Corporation
17 High Street
Norwalk, CT 06851
(203) 838-8300
Contact: Mr. Jeffrey Thomas
Minimum Salary Placed: $75,000
Recruiting Specialty: Apparel and textile

Goodrich & Sherwood
401 Merritt 7 Corporate Park
Norwalk, CT 06851
(203) 847-2525
Recruiting Specialty: General

Grey Associates
21 Eastwood Road
Norwalk, CT 06851
(203) 849-9291
Contact: Mr. R. Scoggins
Minimum Salary Placed: $20,000
Recruiting Specialty: General

Harris Heery & Association, Inc.
One Norwalk West, 40 Richards Avenue
Norwalk, CT 06854
(203) 857-0808
Contact: Mr. William Heery
Minimum Salary Placed: $50,000
Recruiting Specialty: General

Higbee Associates Inc.
112 Rowayton Avenue
Norwalk, CT 06853
(203) 853-7600
Recruiting Specialty: Management consulting

William W. Kenney Inc.
188 W. Norwalk Road
Norwalk, CT 06850
(203) 831-8144
Contact: Mr. William Kenney
Minimum Salary Placed: $30,000
Recruiting Specialty: Insurance

Marks & Company, Inc.
324 Main Avenue, Suite 364
Norwalk, CT 06851
(203) 849-0888
Contact: Ms. Sharon Marks
Recruiting Specialty: Computers

Montaigne Association, Inc.
83 East Avenue, Suite 115
Norwalk, CT 06851
(203) 838-7948
Contact: Mr. Stellan Wollmar
Minimum Salary Placed: $60,000
Recruiting Specialty: Finance; international

O'Connell, Mann and Fitzpatrick
71 East Avenue
Norwalk, CT 06851
(203) 838-6400
Contact: Mr. Brian O'Connell
Minimum Salary Placed: $30,000
Recruiting Specialty: Sales and marketing

Barry Persky & Company, Inc.
301 Merritt 7 Corporate Park
Norwalk, CT 06851
(203) 849-0300
Contact: Mr. Barry Persky
Minimum Salary Placed: $50,000
Recruiting Specialty: General

The Resource Group
26 Pearl Street
Norwalk, CT 06850
(203) 846-3333
Contact: Mr. Christopher Mangieri
Minimum Salary Placed: $50,000
Recruiting Specialty: Marketing, sales and advertising

Ross Personnel Consultants, Inc.
161 East Avenue, Suite 105
Norwalk, CT 06851
(203) 866-2033
Contact: Mr. Anthony Barca
Minimum Salary Placed: $30,000
Recruiting Specialty: Marketing, sales and advertising

Frank Wilkinson & Co
105 Rowayton Avenue
Norwalk, CT 06853
(203) 866-7300
Recruiting Specialty: Financial

Weatherby Healthcare
25 Van Zant Street
Norwalk, CT 06855
(203) 866-1144
Contact: Mr. Joseph Pendergast
Recruiting Specialty: Healthcare

OLD GREENWICH

Halbrecht & Company
P.O. Box 324
Old Greenwich, CT 06870
(203) 637-5815
Contact: Mr. Thomas Kubiak
Minimum Salary Placed: $30,000
Recruiting Specialty: MIS and sales in
high technology

REDDING

Schreuder Randall Corporation
50 Deerhill Road
Redding, CT 06896
(203) 938-3860
Contact: Mr. A. Leo Schreuder
Minimum Salary Placed: $45,000
Recruiting Specialty: Environmental, en-
gineering, manufacturing and utilities

RIDGEFIELD

Foy & Foy
P.O. Box 1200
Ridgefield, CT 06877
(203) 438-5115
Minimum Salary Placed: $75,000
Recruiting Specialty: General

P.J. Lynch Association
P.O. Box 967
Ridgefield, CT 06877
(203) 438-8475
Contact: Mr. Patrick Lynch
Minimum Salary Placed: $65,000
Recruiting Specialty: General

Maiorino & Weston Association, Inc.
90 Grove Street, Suite 205
Ridgefield, CT 06877
(203) 431-0600
Contact: Mr. Robert Maiorino
Minimum Salary Placed: $50,000
Recruiting Specialty: Marketing and sales

Ridgefield Search International
224 Barlow Mountain Road
Ridgefield, CT 06877
(203) 438-8000
Contact: Mr. Ralph Bailey
Minimum Salary Placed: $60,000
Recruiting Specialty: Consumer products, healthcare and industrial in international placements

RIVERSIDE

Robert Edwards
10 Field Road
Riverside, CT 06878
(203) 622-6298
Contact: Robert Edwards
Minimum Salary Placed: $50,000
Recruiting Specialty: Financial services

Lamay Association, Inc.
P.O. Box 517
Riverside, CT 06878
(203) 637-8440
Contact: Mr. Lawrence Mayers
Minimum Salary Placed: $40,000
Recruiting Specialty: General

ROCKY HILL

Sales Consultants
P.O. Box 658
Rocky Hill, CT 06067
(203) 563-2301
Contact: Mr. Fred Raley
Minimum Salary Placed: $20,000
Recruiting Specialty: Sales

Sales Opportunities
1800 Silas Deane Highway, Suite 32
P.O. Box 521
Rocky Hill, CT 06067
(203) 563-2301
Contact: Mr. Joel Molchan
Minimum Salary Placed: $20,000
Recruiting Specialty: Sales

ROWAYTON

Higbee Association, Inc.
112 Rowayton Avenue
Rowayton, CT 06853
(203) 853-7600
Contact: Mr. R. W. Higbee
Minimum Salary Placed: $50,000
Recruiting Specialty: Finance and MIS

Frank Wilkinson & Company
105 Rowayton Avenue
Rowayton, CT 06853
(203) 866-7300
Contact: Mr. Frank Wilkinson
Minimum Salary Placed: $50,000
Recruiting Specialty: Finance and health-
care

ROXBURY

Kronfeld Associates
47 South Street
Roxbury, CT 06783
(860) 355-3111
Contact: Mr. John Kronfeld
Recruiting Specialty: General

SHELTON

Source EDP
1 Corporate Park, Suite 215
Shelton, CT 06484
(203) 944-9001
Contact: Mr. Bob Macaluso
Minimum Salary Placed: $25,000
Recruiting Specialty: Computer hard-
ware and software

SIMSBURY

The Hudson Group
P.O. Box 263
Simsbury, CT 06070
(203) 658-0245
Contact: Mr. Paul Hudson
Minimum Salary Placed: $35,000
Recruiting Specialty: Technical disciplines

W. R. Lawry, Inc.
6 Wilcox Street, P.O. Box 832
Simsbury, CT 06070
(203) 651-0281
Contact: Mr. William Lawry
Minimum Salary Placed: $40,000
Recruiting Specialty: General

Nocton Associates
48 Simsbury Landing
Simsbury, CT 06070
(860) 651-4843
Recruiting Specialty: Attorneys, investment and marketing

SOUTHBURY

Hunter International Inc.
262 S. Britain Road
Southbury, CT 06488
(203) 264-1000
Recruiting Specialty: General

Research Department
262 S. Britain Road
Southbury, CT 06488
(203) 264-2600
Recruiting Specialty: General

SOUTHINGTON

Peter M. Cahill Association, Inc.
P.O. Box 401, 100 Main Street
Southington, CT 06489
(203) 628-3963
Contact: Mr. Peter Cahill
Minimum Salary Placed: $40,000
Recruiting Specialty: General

Hobson Association
293 Spring Street
Southington, CT 06489
(203) 621-3651
Contact: Mr. Danny Cahill
Recruiting Specialty: General

SOUTHPORT

John O'Keefe & Association, Inc.
P.O. Box 1092
Southport, CT 06490
(203) 254-2544
Contact: Ms. Kathy O'Keefe
Minimum Salary Placed: $50,000
Recruiting Specialty: Consumer products

PFS Smith Associates
3280 Post Road
Southport, CT 06490
(203) 254-3999
Contact: Hank
Minimum Salary Placed: $20,000
Recruiting Specialty: Financial services

STAMFORD

AST / Bryant
1 Atlantic Street
Stamford, CT 06901
(203) 975-7188
Contact: Mr. Steven Ast
Minimum Salary Placed: $75,000
Recruiting Specialty: Fund-raising and non-profit—institutions, museums, universities

Accountants On Call
2777 Summer Street
Stamford, CT 06905
(203) 327-5100
Contact: Mr. Marvin Sternlicht
Recruiting Specialty: Accounting

Atlantic Search Group, Inc.
1100 Summer Street
Stamford, CT 06905
(203) 356-9540
Contact: Mr. Jim Baker
Minimum Salary Placed: $30,000
Recruiting Specialty: MIS and market research

Career Consulting Group, Inc.
1100 Summer Street
Stamford, CT 06905
(203) 975-8800
Contact: Mr. Gerald Kanovsky
Minimum Salary Placed: $35,000
Recruiting Specialty: Marketing and legal

Howard Chase Enterprises
77 3rd Street
Stamford, CT 06903
(203) 324-9908
Recruiting Specialty: Public relations and strategic planning

Curran Partners, Inc.
One Landmark Square, 18th Floor
Stamford, CT 06901
(203) 363-5350
Contact: Mr. Michael Curran
Recruiting Specialty: General

DAL Associates
2777 Summer Street, 2nd Floor
Stamford, CT 06905
(203) 961-8777
Contact: Mr. Donald Lotufo
Recruiting Specialty: General

DeFlores International Group
999 Summer Street, Suite 200
Stamford, CT 06905
(203) 359-9339
Contact: Elaine DeFlorres
Minimum Salary Placed: $30,000
Recruiting Specialty: Finance

Fleming Energy Group
One Landmark Square, Suite 805
Stamford, CT 06901
(203) 324-1153

Contact: Mr. Robert Burr
Minimum Salary Placed: $60,000
Recruiting Specialty: Energy, utility, environmental and construction

Flynn, Hannock, Kennan, Inc.
P.O. Box 8027
Stamford, CT 06905
(203) 357-0009
Contact: Mr. Richard Sandor
Minimum Salary Placed: $50,000
Recruiting Specialty: Insurance, banking and manufacturing

D.E. Foster & Partners, L.P.
3001 Summer Street
Stamford, CT 06905
(203) 356-9800
Contact: Mr. Robert Hart
Minimum Salary Placed: $75,000
Recruiting Specialty: General

Halbrecht Lieberman Association, Inc.
1200 Summer Street
Stamford, CT 06905
(203) 327-5630
Contact: Ms. Beverly Lieberman
Minimum Salary Placed: $90,000
Recruiting Specialty: MIS

Robert Half International
3001 Summer Street
Stamford, CT 06905
(203) 324-3399
Contact: Ms. Ruth Goldstein
Minimum Salary Placed: $25,000
Recruiting Specialty: Accounting and finance

Hipp Waters, Inc.
777 Summer Street
Stamford, CT 06901
(203) 357-8400
Contact: Mr. Louis Hipp
Recruiting Specialty: General

IMCOR, Inc.
100 Prospect Street, North Tower
Stamford, CT 06901
(203) 975-8000
Contact: Mr. David Thorpe
Minimum Salary Placed: $75,000
Recruiting Specialty: General

A.T. Kearney Executive Search
1 Landmark Square, Suite 302
Stamford, CT 06901
(203) 969-2222
Contact: Ms. Laura Copeland
Minimum Salary Placed: $60,000
Recruiting Specialty: General

Korn/Ferry International
1 Landmark Square
Stamford, CT 06901
(203) 359-3350
Contact: Mr. Duke Foster
Minimum Salary Placed: $100,000
Recruiting Specialty: General

MGA Inc.
24 Richmond Hill Avenue
Stamford, CT 06901
(203) 325-1010
Recruiting Specialty: General

Management Recruiters
2001 West Main Street
Stamford, CT 06902
(203) 324-2232

Contact: Ms. Lorraine Dennen
Minimum Salary Placed: $20,000
Recruiting Specialty: General

Masserman & Associates
30 Myano Lane, Suite 36
Stamford, CT 06902
(203) 323-4006
Contact: Mr. Bruce Masserman
Recruiting Specialty: MIS and computers

Mirtz Morice, Inc.
One Dock Street, 3rd Floor
Stamford, CT 06902
(203) 964-9266
Contact: Mr. P. John Mirtz
Minimum Salary Placed: $75,000
Recruiting Specialty: General

Moyer, Sherwood Association, Inc.
65 High Ridge Road, Suite 502
Stamford, CT 06905
(203) 656-2220
Contact: Mr. David Moyer
Minimum Salary Placed: $75,000
Recruiting Specialty: Advertising and
public relations

Norman Broadbent International
100 Prospect Street, 2nd Floor
South Building
Stamford, CT 06901
(203) 358-0010
Minimum Salary Placed: $100,000
Recruiting Specialty: General

Object Resources International
14 Cresthill Place
Stamford, CT 06902
(203) 325-1919

Contact: Mr. Kent Straat
Minimum Salary Placed: $60,000
Recruiting Specialty: Sales, marketing
and MIS

Opalka Dixon
72 Cummings Point Road
Stamford, CT 06902
(203) 977-1135
Minimum Salary Placed: $80,000
Recruiting Specialty: Direct marketing

P.R.H. Management, Inc.
2777 Summer Street
Stamford, CT 06905
(203) 327-3900
Contact: Mr. Peter Hendelman
Minimum Salary Placed: $50,000
Recruiting Specialty: Telecommunications and sales in high technology

Plummer & Association, Inc.
30 Myano Lane, Suite 36
Stamford, CT 06902
(203) 965-7878
Contact: Mr. John Plummer
Minimum Salary Placed: $100,000
Recruiting Specialty: General

Romac & Association
500 Summer Street, Suite 503
Stamford, CT 06901
(203) 358-8155
Contact: Mr. Ron Pascale
Minimum Salary Placed: $40,000
Recruiting Specialty: Finance and accounting

Sales Consultants
111 Prospect Street
Stamford, CT 06901
(203) 327-3270

Contact: Mr. Jim Burt
Minimum Salary Placed: $20,000
Recruiting Specialty: Sales

Search Advisors
29 Bank Street
Stamford, CT 06901
(203) 359-8999
Contact: Mr. Mark Strom
Minimum Salary Placed: $50,000
Recruiting Specialty: General

Spencer Stuart
695 E. Main Street, Financial Centre
Stamford, CT 06901
(203) 324-6333
Contact: Mr. Robert Benson
Minimum Salary Placed: $75,000
Recruiting Specialty: General

Edward Stewart and Company
1200 Summer Street
Stamford, CT 06905
(203) 325-000
Contact: Mr. Edward Stewart
Minimum Salary Placed: $25,000
Recruiting Specialty: Finance, accounting, and tax

Strategic Executives, Inc.
6 Landmark Square, 4th Floor
Stamford, CT 06901
(203) 359-5757
Contact: Mr. Randolph Gulian
Minimum Salary Placed: $80,000
Recruiting Specialty: General

Sullivan-Murphy Association
6 Landmark Square, Suite 406
Stamford, CT 06901
(203) 323-3800

Contact: Mr. R. Blair Murphy
Minimum Salary Placed: $100,000
Recruiting Specialty: General

Ward Howell International, Inc.
One Landmark Square, Suite 1810
Stamford, CT 06901
(203) 964-1481
Contact: Mr. George Atkeson
Minimum Salary Placed: $75,000
Recruiting Specialty: General

Westend Group, Inc.
1372 Summer Street
Stamford, CT 06905
(203) 353-0777
Contact: Mr. Michael Nardella
Minimum Salary Placed: $20,000
Recruiting Specialty: Computers

STRATFORD

Tryg R. Angell Ltd.
4021 Main Street
Stratford, CT 06497
(203) 377-4541
Contact: Mr. Tryg Angell
Recruiting Specialty: Sales and product
development in construction products

Kensington Management Consultants, Inc.
200 Watson Boulevard
Stratford, CT 06497
(203) 386-9304
Contact: Ms. Ann Fimmano-Scheuer
Minimum Salary Placed: $40,000
Recruiting Specialty: General

TRUMBULL

ESI
45 Stonehouse Road
Trumbull, CT 06611
(203) 268-8889
Minimum Salary Placed: $20,000
Recruiting Specialty: General

Huntington Group
6527 Main Street
Trumbull, CT 06611
(203) 261-1166
Contact: Mr. John Boehmer
Minimum Salary Placed: $35,000
Recruiting Specialty: General

Lineal Recruiting Services
46 Copper Kettle Road
Trumbull, CT 06611
(203) 386-1091
Contact: Ms. Lisa Lineal
Recruiting Specialty: Technical disciplines in electrical apparatus and equipment

PD Sierra Association
14 Ascolese Road
Trumbull, CT 06611
(203) 452-0078
Contact: Ms. Patricia Sierra
Minimum Salary Placed: $25,000
Recruiting Specialty: MIS and computers

UNIONVILLE

McIntyre Association
P.O. Box 533
Unionville, CT 06085
(203) 673-0030
Contact: Mr. Jeffrey McIntyre
Minimum Salary Placed: $60,000
Recruiting Specialty: Technical disciplines in biotechnology

WALLINGFORD

MJF Associates
P.O. Box 132
Wallingford, CT 06492
(203) 284-9878
Contact: Mr. Matt Furman
Recruiting Specialty: Sales and engineering in manufacturing and high technology

WATERBURY

Wallace Associates
49 Leavenworth Street, Suite 200
P.O. Box 11294
Waterbury, CT 06703
(203) 879-2011
Contact: Mr. Gregory Gordon
Minimum Salary Placed: $40,000
Recruiting Specialty: Manufacturing and engineering

WEST HARTFORD

D.F. Fenton Associates
8 North Main Street, Suite 207
West Hartford, CT 06107
(860) 523-1214
Contact: Mr. Don Fenton
Minimum Salary Placed: $20,000
Recruiting Specialty: General

Flynn, Hannock, Inc.
1001 Farmington Avenue
West Hartford, CT 06107
(203) 521-5005
Contact: Mr. Elwin Hannock
Minimum Salary Placed: $50,000
Recruiting Specialty: Insurance, banking and manufacturing

Industrial Recruiters Association, Inc.
20 Hurlbut
West Hartford, CT 06110
(203) 953-3643
Contact: Mr. Len Baron
Minimum Salary Placed: $20,000
Recruiting Specialty: General

The Stevenson Group Inc.
836 Farmington Avenue, Suite 223
West Hartford, CT 06119
(203) 232-3393
Contact: Mr. James Johnston
Minimum Salary Placed: $70,000
Recruiting Specialty: Insurance and financial services

Vezan Associates
117 Garfield Road
West Hartford, CT 06107
(203) 521-8848
Contact: Mr. Henry Vezan
Minimum Salary Placed: $30,000
Recruiting Specialty: Healthcare

Gene Wittenberg and Associates
2446 Albany Avenue
West Hartford, CT 06117
(203) 232-9700
Contact: Mr. Gene Wittenberg
Minimum Salary Placed: $50,000
Recruiting Specialty: Insurance

WEST HAVEN

Harvard Aimes Group
6 Holcomb Street, P.O. Box 16006
West Haven, CT 06516
(203) 933-1976
Contact: Mr. James Gunther
Minimum Salary Placed: $50,000
Recruiting Specialty: General

WESTON

Barry Persky & Company
5 Oak Lane
Weston, CT 06883
(203) 454-4500
Recruiting Specialty: General

WESTPORT

Barrer Legal Search
578 Post Road East, Suite 530
Westport, CT 06880
(203) 454-9773
Contact: Ms. Nancy Barrer
Minimum Salary Placed: $20,000
Recruiting Specialty: Legal

Bond and Company
10 Saugatuck Avenue
Westport, CT 06880
(203) 454-2340

Contact: Mr. Mike Burke
Minimum Salary Placed: $60,000
Recruiting Specialty: Finance

Bonnell Association Ltd.
One Morningside Drive North
Westport, CT 06880
(203) 226-2624
Contact: Mr. William Bonnell
Recruiting Specialty: General

The Cambridge Group Ltd.
830 Post Road East
Westport, CT 06880
(203) 226-4243
Contact: Mr. Michael Salvagno
Minimum Salary Placed: $80,000
Recruiting Specialty: General

Chaves and Associates
7 Whitney Extension
Westport, CT 06880
(203) 222-2222
Contact: Mr. V. Chaves
Minimum Salary Placed: $20,000
Recruiting Specialty: Computers

David - Kris Associates, Inc.
225 Main Street, P.O. Box 5051
Westport, CT 06881
(203) 227-4206
Contact: Mr. Michael Dellacato
Minimum Salary Placed: $40,000
Recruiting Specialty: Banking and finance

Harrison Associates
5 Hawthorne Lane
Westport, CT 06880
(203) 227-1138
Contact: Mr. Ray Harrison
Minimum Salary Placed: $60,000
Recruiting Specialty: Insurance and risk
management

J. G. Hood Association
599 Riverside Avenue, Suite 2
Westport, CT 06880
(203) 226-1126
Contact: Ms. Joyce Hood
Recruiting Specialty: General

Jansen Associates
34 Warnock Drive
Westport, CT 06880
(203) 221-9149
Contact: Ms. Joan Jansen
Minimum Salary Placed: $30,000
Recruiting Specialty: Pharmaceutical industry

Kennedy Group
26 imperial Avenue
Westport, CT 06880
(203) 226-7443
Contact: Mr. Louis Reda
Minimum Salary Placed: $20,000
Recruiting Specialty: General

Lack and Daily, Inc.
253 Post Road West
Westport, CT 06880
(203) 227-5913
Contact: Mr. Joe Lack
Minimum Salary Placed: $20,000
Recruiting Specialty: General

The McLeod Group, Inc.
253 Post Road West
Westport, CT 06880
(203) 454-1234
Contact: Mr. Anthony Schenck
Minimum Salary Placed: $100,000
Recruiting Specialty: General

James Mead & Company
164 Kings Highway North
Westport, CT 06880
(203) 454-5544
Contact: Mr. James Mead
Minimum Salary Placed: $75,000
Recruiting Specialty: Sales and marketing in consumer products

Phase II Management
25 Stonybrook Road
Westport, CT 06880
(203) 226-7252
Contact: Mr. Richard Fincher
Minimum Salary Placed: $60,000
Recruiting Specialty: Healthcare, electrical, industrial distribution and manufacturing

Pine Tree Inc.
21 Charles Street
Westport, CT 06880
(203) 222-0106
Contact: Mr. E. Nichols
Minimum Salary Placed: $25,000
Recruiting Specialty: General

R. C. Associates
72 Kings Highway South
Westport, CT 06880
(203) 454-2920
Contact: Ms. Rosemary Cass
Minimum Salary Placed: $40,000
Recruiting Specialty: Healthcare

Research Associates, Inc.
6 Whipper Will
Westport, CT 06880
(203) 454-2040
Recruiting Specialty: General

Ross & Company
One Gorham Island
Westport, CT 06880
(203) 221-8200
Contact: Mr. H. Lawrence Ross
Minimum Salary Placed: $125,000
Recruiting Specialty: General

Sound Management Inc.
500 E. Post Road
Westport, CT 06880
(203) 222-7006
Contact: Mr. R. Ernst
Minimum Salary Placed: $25,000
Recruiting Specialty: General

J. Stroll Associates, Inc.
980 Post Road East, Suite 3
Westport, CT 06880
(203) 227-3688
Contact: Ms. Betty St. George
Minimum Salary Placed: $60,000
Recruiting Specialty: Life sciences

Sturges House Inc.
191 Post Road West
Westport, CT 06880
(203) 221-2680
Contact: Mr. Phil Decocco
Minimum Salary Placed: $30,000
Recruiting Specialty: General

Ward Liebelt Association Inc.
50 Riverside Avenue
Westport, CT 06880
(203) 454-0414
Contact: Mr. Anthony Ward
Minimum Salary Placed: $75,000
Recruiting Specialty: Consumer products

Wittlan Group
181 Post Road West
Westport, CT 06880
(203) 227-2455
Contact: Ms. R. Wittlan
Minimum Salary Placed: $20,000
Recruiting Specialty: Graphic arts and promotions

WETHERSFIELD

Availability of Hartford, Inc.
936 Silas Deane Highway, Suite 112
Wethersfield, CT 06109
(860) 529-1688
Contact: Mr. David Roser
Recruiting Specialty: Engineering

WILTON

Johnson & Company
11 Grumman Hill Road
Wilton, CT 06897
(203) 761-1212
Contact: Mr. Stanley Johnson
Minimum Salary Placed: $75,000
Recruiting Specialty: General

K/N International
P.O. Box 073
Wilton, CT 06897
(203) 834-0587
Contact: Mr. Edgar Newman
Minimum Salary Placed: $30,000
Recruiting Specialty: General

Knapp Consultants
184 Old Ridgefield Road
Wilton, CT 06897
(203) 762-0790
Contact: Mr. Ronald Knapp
Minimum Salary Placed: $90,000
Recruiting Specialty: High technology
and manufacturing

Management Recruiters
57 Danbury Road
Wilton, CT 06897
(203) 834-1111
Contact: Mr. Robert Schmidt
Minimum Salary Placed: $20,000
Recruiting Specialty: General

Ross-Richter
195 Danbury Road
Wilton, CT 06897
(203) 834-0174
Contact: Mr. E. Perlman
Minimum Salary Placed: $25,000
Recruiting Specialty: Sales

D I S T R I C T
O F
C O L U M B I A

Blake, Hansen & Nye, Ltd.
1155 Connecticut Avenue NW, Suite 400
Washington, DC 20036
(202) 429-6611
Contact: Mr. David Nye
Minimum Salary Placed: $65,000
Recruiting Specialty: General

Boulware & Associates, Inc.
1850 M Street NW, Suite 440
Washington, DC 20036
(202) 785-8630
Contact: Ms. Linda Henderson
Minimum Salary Placed: $50,000
Recruiting Specialty: General

Brubach Corporation
1776 Eye Street
Washington, DC 20006
(202) 861-0590
Contact: Ms. B. Brubach
Minimum Salary Placed: $20,000
Recruiting Specialty: General

Development Resource Group
1629 K Street NW, Suite 802
Washington, DC 20006
(202) 223-6528
Recruiting Specialty: Non-profit

Financial Placement Network
1625 K Street NW, Suite 735
Washington, DC 20006
(202) 728-5901
Contact: Mr. Barry Goldstein
Minimum Salary Placed: $30,000
Recruiting Specialty: Finance and MIS

Finn & Schneider Associates, Inc.
1730 Rhode Island Avenue NW,
 Suite 1212
Washington, DC 20036
(202) 822-8400
Contact: Ms. Susan Schneider
Recruiting Specialty: Attorneys

D.E. Foster & Partners, Ltd.
2001 M Street NW
Washington, DC 20036
(202) 467-3630
Contact: Mr. Dann Stringer
Minimum Salary Placed: $75,000
Recruiting Specialty: General

Goodwin and Company
1320 19th Street NW, Suite 801
Washington, DC 20036
(202) 785-9292
Contact: Mr. Tom Goodwin
Minimum Salary Placed: $50,000
Recruiting Specialty: General

Bruce W. Haupt Associates
P.O. Box 21599, Kalorama Station NW
Washington, DC 20009
(202) 462-1524
Contact: Mr. Bruce Haupt
Minimum Salary Placed: $60,000
Recruiting Specialty: MIS and legal

Heidrick & Struggles, Inc.
1301 K Street NW
Washington, DC 20006
(202) 466-5410
Contact: Mr. Eugene Rackley
Minimum Salary Placed: $60,000
Recruiting Specialty: General

The Interface Group, Ltd./Boyden
2828 Pennsylvania Avenue NW, Suite 305
Washington, DC 20006
(202) 342-7200
Contact: Mr. William Marumoto
Minimum Salary Placed: $75,000
Recruiting Specialty: General

John Michael Associates
P.O. Box 17130
Washington, DC 20041
(703) 471-6300
Contact: Mr. Gary Fossett
Minimum Salary Placed: $80,000
Recruiting Specialty: Legal

Klein, Landau, Romm & North
1725 K Street NW, Suite 602
Washington, DC 20006
(202) 728-0100
Contact: Mr. Gary Ethan Klein
Minimum Salary Placed: $80,000
Recruiting Specialty: Legal

Korn/Ferry International
900 19th Street NW
Washington, DC 20006
(202) 822-9444
Contact: Mr. Ron Walker
Minimum Salary Placed: $75,000
Recruiting Specialty: General

M & M Management
National Press Building, Suite C1060
Washington, DC 20045
(202) 737-4530
Contact: Mr. Mekonen
Minimum Salary Placed: $25,000
Recruiting Specialty: Hospitality

McBride Associates, Inc.
1511 K Street NW
Washington, DC 20005
(202) 638-1150
Contact: Mr. Jonathan McBride
Minimum Salary Placed: $120,000
Recruiting Specialty: General

McPherson Square Associates, Inc.
805 15th Street NW, Suite 701
Washington, DC 20005
(202) 737-8777
Contact: Mr. Ronald Russell
Minimum Salary Placed: $70,000
Recruiting Specialty: Attorneys

Mee Derby & Company
1522 K Street NW, Suite 704
Washington, DC 20005
(202) 842-8442
Contact: Ms. Robin Mee
Recruiting Specialty: Sales

Morrison Associates
1730 Rhode Island Avenue, Suite 712
Washington, DC 20036
(202) 223-6523
Contact: Ms. Anne Morrison
Minimum Salary Placed: $40,000
Recruiting Specialty: Non-profit

NRI Staffing Resources
1899 L Street, NW, Suite 301
Washington, DC 20036
(202) 466-2160
Contact: Mr. Robert Mulberger
Minimum Salary Placed: $20,000
Recruiting Specialty: General

National Attorney Placement
1010 Vermont Avenue NW, Suite 408
Washington, DC 20005
(202) 393-1550
Contact: Mr. Charlie Valender
Minimum Salary Placed: $50,000
Recruiting Specialty: Attorneys

Pierce Associates
1815 Pennsylvania Avenue NW, Suite 900
Washington, DC 20006
(202) 835-1776
Minimum Salary Placed: $50,000
Recruiting Specialty: Attorneys

R. H. Perry & Associates, Inc.
2607 31st Street, NW
Washington, DC 20008
(202) 965-6464
Contact: Mr. R. H. Perry
Minimum Salary Placed: $70,000
Recruiting Specialty: Higher education

Rurak & Associates, Inc.
1350 Connecticut Avenue NW, Suite 801
Washington, DC 20036
(202) 293-7603
Contact: Mr. Zbigniew Rurak
Minimum Salary Placed: $100,000
Recruiting Specialty: General

Russell Reynolds Associates, Inc.
1700 Pennsylvania Avenue NW, Suite 850
Washington, DC 20006
(202) 628-2150
Contact: Mr. Eric Vautou
Minimum Salary Placed: $100,000
Recruiting Specialty: General

Savoy Partners, Ltd.
1620 L Street NW, Suite 801
Washington, DC 20036
(202) 887-0666
Contact: Mr. Robert Brudno
Minimum Salary Placed: $100,000
Recruiting Specialty: General

Robert Sellery Associates, Ltd.
1155 Connecticut Avenue NW, Suite 500
Washington, DC 20036
(202) 331-0090
Contact: Mr. Robert Sellery
Recruiting Specialty: General

Source EDP
1667 K Street NW
Washington, DC 20006
(202) 293-9255
Contact: Mr. Paul Villella
Recruiting Specialty: Computer hardware and software

Spivak Director and Sitcov
1900 L Street NW, Suite 250
Washington, DC 20036
(202) 828-5600
Contact: Mr. C. Sitcov
Minimum Salary Placed: $50,000
Recruiting Specialty: Attorneys

Mark Stanley & Company
1629 K Street, Suite 1100
Washington, DC 20006
(202) 785-6716
Recruiting Specialty: General

Thomas, Whelan Associates, Inc.
P.O. Box 40237
Washington, DC 20016
(202) 833-8980
Contact: Ms. Cheryl Molliver Ross
Minimum Salary Placed: $35,000
Recruiting Specialty: Accounting and finance

Travaille Executive Search
1730 Rhode Island Drive NW, Suite 401
Washington, DC 20036
(202) 463-6342
Contact: Mr. Benjamin Long
Recruiting Specialty: Marketing and corporate communications

D E L A W A R E

CLAYMONT

J.B. Groner Executive Search, Inc.
2616 D Philadelphia Pike, Suite 101
Claymont, DE 19703
(302) 792-9228
Contact: Mr. J.B. Groner
Minimum Salary Placed: $30,000
Recruiting Specialty: MIS, data processing, engineering

HOCKESSIN

E.W. Hodges and Associates
3 McCormick Drive
Hockessin, DE 19707
(302) 995-6022
Contact: Mr. Ed Hodges
Minimum Salary Placed: $75,000
Recruiting Specialty: General

NEW CASTLE

Healthcare Network
38 W. 4th Street
New Castle, DE 19720
(302) 322-9396
Contact: Ms. J. Smith
Minimum Salary Placed: $25,000
Recruiting Specialty: Healthcare

NEWARK

Fortune Personnel Inc.
205 Topkis Building
Newark, DE 19702
(302) 453-0404
Contact: Mr. L. Weston
Minimum Salary Placed: $40,000
Recruiting Specialty: General

WILMINGTON

ACSYS Resources, Inc.
1300 Market Street, Suite 501
Wilmington, DE 19801
(302) 658-6181
Contact: Mr. Domenic Vacca
Minimum Salary Placed: $25,000
Recruiting Specialty: Accounting, finance and banking

CRI Temps
1200 Pennsylvania Avenue, Suite 101
Wilmington, DE 19806
(302) 478-9655
Contact: Ms. D. Berry
Recruiting Specialty: General

Discovery Staffing Specialists, Inc.
3519 Silverside Road, Suite 102
Wilmington, DE 19810
(302) 477-0680
Contact: Mr. Fran DeMichele
Minimum Salary Placed: $20,000
Recruiting Specialty: Credit and collections and finance

Gilbert Tweed Associates, Inc.
3411 Silverside Road
Wilmington, DE 19810
(302) 479-5144
Contact: Mr. Robert Templin
Minimum Salary Placed: $70,000
Recruiting Specialty: Healthcare and physicians

HR Inc.
3225 Cardiff, Suite 201A
Wilmington, DE 19810
(302) 479-9813
Contact: Mr. Dick Burkhard
Minimum Salary Placed: $35,000
Recruiting Specialty: Human resources

Hornberger Management Company
1 Commerce Center, 7th Floor
Wilmington, DE 19801
(302) 573-2541
Contact: Mr. Frederick Hornberger
Minimum Salary Placed: $75,000
Recruiting Specialty: Construction

Network Personnel
1700 Shallcross Avenue
Wilmington, DE 19806
(302) 656-5555
Contact: Mr. Ed Griffin
Minimum Salary Placed: $25,000
Recruiting Specialty: General

F L O R I D A

ALTAMONTE SPRINGS

Advanced Marketing
1180 Spring Centre South Boulevard
Altamonte Springs, FL 32714
(813) 579-4004
Recruiting Specialty: General

A.M. Auster Association
498 Palm Springs Drive, Suite 100
Altamonte Springs, FL 32701
(407) 831-2400
Contact: Mr. A. Marc Auster
Minimum Salary Placed: $80,000
Recruiting Specialty: General

Financial Resource Association, Inc.
105 West Orange Street
Altamonte Springs, FL 32714
(407) 869-7000
Contact: Mr. John Cannavino
Minimum Salary Placed: $30,000
Recruiting Specialty: Lending and financial institutions

Fiordalis Associates, Inc.
498 Palm Springs Drive, Suite 100
Altamonte Springs, FL 32701
(407) 830-4444
Contact: Mr. Stuart Fiordalis
Minimum Salary Placed: $75,000
Recruiting Specialty: Healthcare

Quality Career Center
499 N. State Road 434
Altamonte Springs, FL 32714
(407) 869-6979
Minimum Salary Placed: $25,000
Recruiting Specialty: General

Snelling and Snelling
222 South Westmonte Drive
Altamonte Springs, FL 32714
(407) 788-7300
Contact: Ms. Judy Kirby
Minimum Salary Placed: $20,000
Recruiting Specialty: General

APOPKA

Nolan and Nolan
802 Pink Camelia Court
Apopka, FL 32712
(407) 884-8339
Recruiting Specialty: Physicians

BOCA RATON

Benson & Associates
551 NW 77th Street, Suite 102
Boca Raton, FL 33487
(561) 997-1600
Contact: Mr. Lou Benson
Recruiting Specialty: Upper management and financial

Buckley Group
7000 W. Palmetto Park Road, Suite 302
Boca Raton, FL 33433
(561) 392-4575
Contact: Mr. Richard Dodge
Minimum Salary Placed: $40,000
Recruiting Specialty: Programming, sales, marketing and MIS in computers and other high technology

Career Associates
7777 Glades Road, Suite 212
Boca Raton, FL 33434
(561) 487-4800

Contact: Mr. Andrew Pober
Recruiting Specialty: Accounting and finance

Curtiss International
301 Yamato Road, Suite 2112
Boca Raton, FL 33431
(561) 997-0011
Contact: Mr. William Frank
Minimum Salary Placed: $75,000
Recruiting Specialty: General

Daudlin, De Beaupre & Co., Inc.
20423 State Road 7, Suite 425
Boca Raton, FL 33498
(561) 477-9118
Contact: Ms. Gale Freidenreich
Minimum Salary Placed: $50,000
Recruiting Specialty: Healthcare

David Wood Personnel
1300 N. Federal Highway
Boca Raton, FL 33432
(561) 392-9050
Contact: Ms. S. Thaler
Minimum Salary Placed: $25,000
Recruiting Specialty: General

E.G. Todd Physicians Search
7700 West Camino Real
Boca Raton, FL 33433
(561) 338-9822
Contact: Ms. Lauren Simon
Minimum Salary Placed: $75,000
Recruiting Specialty: Physicians

Jon Harvey Associates
1300 North Federal Highway, Suite 105
Boca Raton, FL 33432
(561) 368-5900
Contact: Mr. S. Mersand
Minimum Salary Placed: $25,000
Recruiting Specialty: Computers

Kenmore Executives Inc.
1 South Ocean Boulevard, Suite 306
Boca Raton, FL 33432
(561) 392-0700
Contact: Mr. Lawrence Loprete
Minimum Salary Placed: $40,000
Recruiting Specialty: Management consulting

Konstroffer & Partner Marketing Inc.
4400 N Federal Highway, Suite 210
Boca Raton, FL 33431
(561) 394-9966
Contact: Christiana
Recruiting Specialty: International

La Morte Search Associates
3003 Yamato Road
Boca Raton, FL 33433
(561) 997-1100
Contact: Mr. W. La Morte
Minimum Salary Placed: $30,000
Recruiting Specialty: Insurance

The Conrad Lee Company
7280 West Palmetto Park Road, Suite 208
Boca Raton, FL 33433
(561) 347-2980
Contact: Mr. Conrad Lee
Minimum Salary Placed: $50,000
Recruiting Specialty: General

Management Recruiters
370 W. Camino Real
Boca Raton, FL 33432
(561) 393-3991
Contact: Mr. Ernie Labadie
Minimum Salary Placed: $40,000
Recruiting Specialty: Chemicals

Management Resource Associates, Inc.
P.O. Box 3266
Boca Raton, FL 33427
(561) 852-5650
Contact: Mr. Gerald Schneiderman
Minimum Salary Placed: $50,000
Recruiting Specialty: High technology
and finance

Richard L. Morgenstern International, Inc.
299 West Camino Gardens Boulevard,
  Suite 206
Boca Raton, FL 33432
(561) 994-5070
Contact: Mr. Richard Morgenstern
Minimum Salary Placed: $50,000
Recruiting Specialty: General

Daniel Silverstein Association, Inc.
5355 Town Center Road, Suite 1001
Boca Raton, FL 33486
(561) 391-0600
Contact: Mr. Daniel Silverstein
Minimum Salary Placed: $100,000
Recruiting Specialty: Pharmaceuticals,
healthcare and some general

Southport International Association Inc.
562011 Arbor Club Way
Boca Raton, FL 33433
(561) 393-6320
Contact: Ms. Kit Stelika
Minimum Salary Placed: $50,000
Recruiting Specialty: Telecommunica-
tions and MIS

Tricor Inc.
1355 W. Palmetto Park Road, Suite 101
Boca Raton, FL 33486
(561) 395-8255

Contact: Mr. S. Smith
Minimum Salary Placed: $40,000
Recruiting Specialty: Attorneys

BONITA SPRINGS

J. Krauss Associates
28091 Winthrop Circle SW
Bonita Springs, FL 33923
(941) 947-8320
Contact: Mr. Jack Krauss
Minimum Salary Placed: $35,000
Recruiting Specialty: General

Management Recruiters
9240 Bonita Beach Road, Suite 3307
Bonita Springs, FL 33923
(941) 495-7885
Contact: Mr. Gary Shearer
Minimum Salary Placed: $20,000
Recruiting Specialty: General

BOYNTON BEACH

Allan Hechtman Inc.
2240 Woolbright, Suite 338
Boynton Beach, FL 33426
(561) 374-6111
Contact: Mr. Allan Hechtman
Minimum Salary Placed: $35,000
Recruiting Specialty: Marketing and ad-
vertising

Alan Lerner Associates
6 Eastgate Drive, Suite C
Boynton Beach, FL 33436
(561) 735-3550
Contact: Mr. Alan Lerner
Recruiting Specialty: Retail

BRADENTON

The Hillary Group
6417 Quail Hollow Place, Suite B
Bradenton, FL 34210
(941) 753-9926
Contact: Mr. John Faucher
Minimum Salary Placed: $50,000
Recruiting Specialty: High technology

Management Recruiters
3005 26th Street West, Suite C
Bradenton, FL 34205
(941) 753-5837
Minimum Salary Placed: $20,000
Recruiting Specialty: General

Ron Stevens & Associates, Inc.
4501 Galloway Boulevard
Bradenton, FL 34210
(800) 458-1611
Contact: Mr. Ron Stevens
Minimum Salary Placed: $35,000
Recruiting Specialty: Paper processing,
chemical, manufacturing

CAPE CORAL

Anmar Executive Search Group
4518 Del Prado Boulevard, Suite 5
Cape Coral, FL 33904
(941) 574-2100
Minimum Salary Placed: $30,000
Recruiting Specialty: Sales, marketing
and engineering in telecommunications

CLEARWATER

The Butlers Company Insurance Recruiters
2753 State Road 580, Suite 103
Clearwater, FL 34621
(813) 725-1065
Contact: Mr. Kirby Butler
Minimum Salary Placed: $30,000
Recruiting Specialty: Insurance

DSI Staff RX
1940 Drew Street
Clearwater, FL 34625
(813) 461-9642
Contact: Ms. Phyllis Bracken
Recruiting Specialty: Healthcare

Fortune Personnel Consultants
2531 Landmark Drive
Clearwater, FL 34621
(813) 797-9577
Contact: Mr. T. Brill
Minimum Salary Placed: $25,000
Recruiting Specialty: General

Healthcare Recruiters
3000 Gulf to Bay Boulevard
Clearwater, FL 34619
(813) 725-5770
Contact: Mr. T. Fleury
Minimum Salary Placed: $25,000
Recruiting Specialty: General

Merrill Wasson Recruiting
3036 Haverford Drive
Clearwater, FL 34621
(813) 796-3455
Contact: Mr. Merrill Wasson
Minimum Salary Placed: $40,000
Recruiting Specialty: Manufacturing and
production

Management Recruiters
P.O. Box 7711
Clearwater, FL 34618
(813) 791-3277
Contact: Ms. Helen Gleason
Minimum Salary Placed: $20,000
Recruiting Specialty: General

Tech Consulting
50 South Belcher Road, Suite 113
Clearwater, FL 34625
(813) 443-5335
Contact: Mr. Mark Bavli
Minimum Salary Placed: $30,000
Recruiting Specialty: Technical disciplines in high technology

CORAL GABLES

Accountants Executive Search
1 Alhambra Plaza, Suite 1435
Coral Gables, FL 33134
(305) 443-9333
Contact: Ms. Daniel Perron
Minimum Salary Placed: $25,000
Recruiting Specialty: Accounting

Farwell Group Inc.
1 Alhambra Plaza, Suite 1425
Coral Gables, FL 33134
(305) 529-4811
Contact: Ms. Sondra Farwell
Minimum Salary Placed: $25,000
Recruiting Specialty: Banking, finance and accounting

Mark Stanley & Company
2 Alhambra Plaza, Suite 1106
Coral Gables, FL 33134
(305) 444-1612

Contact: Mr. John Ramsey
Minimum Salary Placed: $80,000
Recruiting Specialty: General

Robert Half International
2655 S. Le Jeune Road, Suite 1000
Coral Gables, FL 33134
(305) 447-1757
Contact: Mr. Lee Elkinson
Minimum Salary Placed: $25,000
Recruiting Specialty: Accounting and finance

Sales Consultants
1320 South Dixie, Suite 941
Coral Gables, FL 33146
(305) 666-5991
Contact: Mr. Dennis McCarthy
Minimum Salary Placed: $25,000
Recruiting Specialty: Sales

Tai and Associates Inc.
2100 Ponce De Leon Boulevard,
  Suite 1050
Coral Gables, FL 33134
(305) 444-3340
Contact: Mr. Thomas Bello
Minimum Salary Placed: $30,000
Recruiting Specialty: General

CORAL SPRINGS

Gerrish Associates, Inc.
8222 Wiles Road, Suite 223
Coral Springs, FL 33075
(305) 340-1250
Contact: Mr. Stuart Gerrish
Recruiting Specialty: Computer and software hardware

Bert Buckley and Associates
9337 W. Sample Road
Coral Springs, FL 33065
(954) 346-9800
Contact: Mr. Bert Buckley
Minimum Salary Placed: $25,000
Recruiting Specialty: Medical

Koerner Group
9900 W. Sample Road, Suite 300
Coral Springs, FL 33065
(954) 755-6676
Contact: Mr. D. Koerner
Minimum Salary Placed: $25,000
Recruiting Specialty: Accounting and finance

NPF Association Ltd., Inc.
1999 University Drive, Suite 405
Coral Springs, FL 33071
(954) 753-8560
Contact: Mr. Nick Fischler
Minimum Salary Placed: $40,000
Recruiting Specialty: General

National Search, Inc.
2816 University Drive
Coral Springs, FL 33065
(954) 755-4355
Recruiting Specialty: Insurance and medical

Sales Consultants
9900 West Sample Road, Suite 407
Coral Springs, FL 33065
(954) 340-8000
Contact: Mr. Frank Braile
Minimum Salary Placed: $25,000
Recruiting Specialty: Sales

Search Enterprises, Inc.
12358 Wiles Road
Coral Springs, FL 33076
(954) 755-3121
Contact: Mr. Gary Runge
Minimum Salary Placed: $45,000
Recruiting Specialty: Technical disciplines in manufacturing, engineering and environmental

Searchworks
3111 University Drive
Coral Springs, FL 33065
(954) 340-1000
Contact: Mr. Schindell
Minimum Salary Placed: $30,000
Recruiting Specialty: Medical

CRYSTAL RIVER

Nature Coast Employment
326 N. Suncoast Boulevard
Crystal River, FL 34429
(352) 795-6038
Contact: Ms. K. Warrington
Recruiting Specialty: General

DADE CITY

ESP
14028 5th Street
Dade City, FL 33525
(904) 567-3353
Contact: Mr. J. Botto
Minimum Salary Placed: $25,000
Recruiting Specialty: Electrical utilities

DAVIE

Gene Rogers Associates Inc.
13211 SW 32nd Court
Davie, FL 33330
(954) 476-0221
Contact: Mr. Gene Rogers
Minimum Salary Placed: $40,000
Recruiting Specialty: Banks and trusts

DAYTONA BEACH

Heller Kil Associates, Inc.
123 Green Heron Court
Daytona Beach, FL 32119
(904) 761-5100
Contact: Mr. Phillip Heller
Minimum Salary Placed: $40,000
Recruiting Specialty: Manufacturing in automobiles and parts

DEERFIELD BEACH

Career Search USA
10 Fairway Drive, Suite 225
Deerfield Beach, FL 33441
(954) 570-9478
Contact: Ms. Debi Kaye
Minimum Salary Placed: $20,000
Recruiting Specialty: General

Medexec USA Inc.
1701 West Hillsboro Boulevard
Deerfield Beach, FL 33442
(954) 360-9980
Contact: Mr. Richard Myers
Minimum Salary Placed: $30,000
Recruiting Specialty: Home healthcare and temporary executives

The Ryan Charles Group, Inc.
2151 West Hillsboro Boulevard,
 Suite 203
Deerfield Beach, FL 33442
(954) 421-9112
Contact: Mr. Norman St. Jean
Minimum Salary Placed: $40,000
Recruiting Specialty: General

DELAND

Alpha Search
P.O. Box 1379
Deland, FL 32721
(904) 734-0776
Contact: Mr. Bob Stillings
Minimum Salary Placed: $30,000
Recruiting Specialty: Food service, wholesale grocery and supermarkets

DELRAY BEACH

Andrews and Wald
5344 Monterey Circle, Suite 88
Delray Beach, FL 33484
(561) 496-2931
Contact: Mr. Steve Wald
Minimum Salary Placed: $40,000
Recruiting Specialty: Sales and marketing

Specialized Search Associates
15200 Carter Road
Delray Beach, FL 33446
(407) 499-3711
Contact: Mr. Leonard Morris
Minimum Salary Placed: $60,000
Recruiting Specialty: Construction and engineering for the construction industry

DESTIN

Porter & Associates, Inc.
P.O. Box 6217
Destin, FL 32541
(904) 654-9300
Contact: Mr. Nancy Porter
Minimum Salary Placed: $40,000
Recruiting Specialty: Retail

DUNNELLON

Zackrison Associates, Inc.
P.O. Box 1808
Dunnellon, FL 34430
(352) 489-2215
Contact: Mr. Walter Zackrison
Minimum Salary Placed: $60,000
Recruiting Specialty: Physicians and scientists in pharmaceuticals and healthcare

ENGLEWOOD

Hansen Group, Ltd.
1920 Bayshore Drive
Englewood, FL 34223
(941) 475-1300
Contact: Mr. Ty Hansen
Minimum Salary Placed: $70,000
Recruiting Specialty: High technology

International Corporate Senators Association
1920 Bayshore Drive
Englewood, FL 34223
(813) 475-3400
Contact: Mr. Ty Hansen
Minimum Salary Placed: $40,000
Recruiting Specialty: Aviation and aerospace

FORT LAUDERDALE

Accountants Express
5200 NW 33rd Avenue, Suite 220
Fort Lauderdale, FL 33309
(954) 486-8585
Contact: Mr. S. Sloan
Minimum Salary Placed: $25,000
Recruiting Specialty: Accounting and general

American Executive Search
800 West Cypress Creek Road, Suite 460
Fort Lauderdale, FL 33309
(954) 771-6663
Contact: Mr. Carl Carieri
Minimum Salary Placed: $30,000
Recruiting Specialty: Sales, engineering and manufacturing

B&B Associates
1120 S. Federal Highway
Fort Lauderdale, FL 33315
(954) 761-1220
Contact: Mr. William Gutierrez
Minimum Salary Placed: $25,000
Recruiting Specialty: Accounting and finance

DHR International, Inc.
2810 East Oakland Park Boulevard,
  Suite 104
Fort Lauderdale, FL 33306
(954) 564-6110
Contact: Mr. Victor Viglino
Minimum Salary Placed: $50,000
Recruiting Specialty: General

Franklin Search Group
5632 SW 88th Terrace
Fort Lauderdale, FL 33328
(954) 434-5332
Contact: Dr. Franklin Heasley
Minimum Salary Placed: $50,000
Recruiting Specialty: Pharmaceuticals,
biopharmaceuticals, diagnostics and
biotechnology

Gimble and Associates
201 NE 2nd Street
Fort Lauderdale, FL 33301
(954) 525-7000
Contact: Mr. M. Gimble
Minimum Salary Placed: $25,000
Recruiting Specialty: Accounting, fi-
nance, MIS and data processing

Heim Management
9330 NW 48th Street
Fort Lauderdale, FL 33351
(954) 524-0052
Contact: Mr. D. Heimmermann
Minimum Salary Placed: $25,000
Recruiting Specialty: General

Kelley & Keller, Inc.
2518 Key Largo
Fort Lauderdale, FL 33312
(954) 791-4900
Contact: Mr. Verne Kelley
Minimum Salary Placed: $50,000
Recruiting Specialty: Marketing in con-
sumer services

R.H. Larsen & Associates, Inc.
1401 East Broward Boulevard
Fort Lauderdale, FL 33301
(954) 763-9000

Contact: Mr. Robert Larsen
Minimum Salary Placed: $50,000
Recruiting Specialty: General

Lasher Associates
1200 South Pine Island Road, Suite 370
Fort Lauderdale, FL 33324
(954) 472-5658
Contact: Mr. Charles Lasher
Minimum Salary Placed: $75,000
Recruiting Specialty: High technology
and development

Management Recruiters
1500 NW 49th Street, Suite 500
Fort Lauderdale, FL 33309
(954) 776-4477
Contact: Mr. Joel Dickstein
Minimum Salary Placed: $20,000
Recruiting Specialty: General

Mankuta, Gallagher and Associates
8333 W. McNab Road, Suite 231
Fort Lauderdale, FL 33211
(954) 344-1935
Contact: Dr. Michael Gallagher
Minimum Salary Placed: $50,000
Recruiting Specialty: Pharmaceuticals,
biopharmaceuticals, diagnostics and
biotechnology

Marc Joseph Consultants
1802 University Drive, Suite 203L
Fort Lauderdale, FL 33301
(954) 370-5151
Contact: Mr. Joseph Cavanaugh
Minimum Salary Placed: $25,000
Recruiting Specialty: Real estate

Merit Group, Inc.
108 SE 8th Avenue, Suite 112
Fort Lauderdale, FL 33301
(954) 779-7747
Contact: Mr. Edward Cripe
Minimum Salary Placed: $40,000
Recruiting Specialty: Human relations and personnel development

Omni Partners
7770 W Oakland Park Boulevard
Fort Lauderdale, FL 33351
(954) 748-9800
Recruiting Specialty: General

Perfect Search
2400 E. Commercial Boulevard,
  Suite 702
Fort Lauderdale, FL 33308
(954) 776-7533
Contact: Ms. R. Callicott
Minimum Salary Placed: $35,000
Recruiting Specialty: Healthcare

Pro-Search
6896 NW 29th Avenue
Fort Lauderdale, FL 33309
(954) 977-9794
Contact: Mr. G. Turnball
Minimum Salary Placed: $25,000
Recruiting Specialty: Property and casualty insurance

Retail Executive Search
4620 N. State Road 7, Suite 212
Fort Lauderdale, FL 33319
(954) 731-2300
Contact: Mr. Manuel Kaye
Minimum Salary Placed: $20,000
Recruiting Specialty: Retail

Robert Half International
200 E. Las Olas Boulevard, Suite 1650
Fort Lauderdale, FL 33301
(954) 761-3811
Contact: Ms. Lori Harding
Minimum Salary Placed: $25,000
Recruiting Specialty: Accounting and finance

Romac & Associates, Inc.
500 W. Cypress Creek Road, Suite 200
Fort Lauderdale, FL 33309
(954) 928-0811
Contact: Mr. Howard Sutter
Recruiting Specialty: General

Ropes Association, Inc.
333 North New River Drive East,
  3rd Floor
Fort Lauderdale, FL 33301
(954) 525-6600
Contact: Mr. John Ropes
Minimum Salary Placed: $75,000
Recruiting Specialty: Commercial and residential real estate development

Ruden Barnett McClosky Smith
200 E Broward Boulevard, Floor 16
Fort Lauderdale, FL 33301
(954) 761-2919
Contact: Mr. Vallenti
Recruiting Specialty: Laterals for all areas of law

Sales Consultants
100 West Cypress Creek Road, Suite 965
Fort Lauderdale, FL 33309
(954) 772-5100
Contact: Mr. Jeff Taylor
Minimum Salary Placed: $25,000
Recruiting Specialty: Sales in healthcare, MIS and FIS

Allan Stolee Inc.
6278 N. Federal Highway, Suite 450
Fort Lauderdale, FL 33308
(954) 564-9111
Contact: Mr. Allan Stolee
Minimum Salary Placed: $100,000
Recruiting Specialty: General

Summit Healthcare Inc.
1975 East Sunrise Boulevard
Fort Lauderdale, FL 33304
(954) 522-7210
Contact: Ed
Minimum Salary Placed: $30,000
Recruiting Specialty: Medical

Taman-Haider Inc.
1451 W. Cypress Creek Road
Fort Lauderdale, Fl 33309
(954) 776-1907
Contact: Ms. A. Tatarka
Minimum Salary Placed: $25,000
Recruiting Specialty: Insurance

Technisource
1901 W. Cypress Creek Road, Suite 401
Fort Lauderdale, FL 33309
(954) 493-8601
Contact: Mr. J. Collard
Minimum Salary Placed: $25,000
Recruiting Specialty: Engineering and
software

Weatherby Healthcare
3230 Commercial Boulevard, Suite 240
Fort Lauderdale, FL 33309
(954) 730-3340
Contact: Mr. Michael Pendergast
Minimum Salary Placed: $25,000
Recruiting Specialty: Healthcare

FORT MYERS

J. R. Akin & Company
7181 College Parkway, Suite 30
Fort Myers, FL 33907
(941) 395-1575
Contact: Mr. J. R. Akin
Minimum Salary Placed: $75,000
Recruiting Specialty: General

Management Recruiters
4100 Center Pointe Drive, Suite 105
Fort Myers, FL 33916
(941) 939-2223
Contact: Mr. Calvin Beals
Minimum Salary Placed: $30,000
Recruiting Specialty: Banking, trusts and
building materials

ME Redding Associates
5647 Shaddelee Lane W
Fort Myers, FL 33919
(941) 433-0222
Contact: Malcolm
Minimum Salary Placed: $50,000
Recruiting Specialty: General

GAINESVILLE

Career Concepts
2770 NW 43rd Street, Suite N
Gainesville, FL 32606
(352) 377-5760
Contact: Ms. Wendel Smith
Minimum Salary Placed: $25,000
Recruiting Specialty: General

B.L. Handley and Associates
10009 SW 44th Lane
Gainesville, FL 32608
(352) 337-9660

Contact: Mr. Brian Handley
Minimum Salary Placed: $25,000
Recruiting Specialty: General

Personnel Center
927 NW 13th Street
Gainesville, FL 32601
(352) 372-6377
Contact: Ms. Marriane Voyles
Recruiting Specialty: General

GULF BREEZE

Terik Company
83 Bay Bridge Drive
Gulf Breeze, FL 32561
(904) 932-4474
Contact: Mr. Tom Williams
Minimum Salary Placed: $25,000
Recruiting Specialty: General

Media Management Resources
31 B Gulf Breeze Parkway
Gulf Breeze, FL 32561
(904) 934-4880
Recruiting Specialty: Telecommunications and media

HEATHROW

Pulp and Paper International
1570 Farrindon Circle
Heathrow, FL 32746
(407) 444-9960
Contact: Mr. Phil Riesling
Minimum Salary Placed: $30,000
Recruiting Specialty: Pulp and paper

HIALEAH

H. Hertner & Associates, Inc.
6600 Cow Pen Road
Hialeah, FL 33014
(305) 556-8882
Recruiting Specialty: Attorneys

Management Recruiters
8181 NW 154th Street
Hialeah, FL 33016
(305) 828-2887
Recruiting Specialty: Medical device

HOLLYWOOD

Caruso and Associates
2131 Hollywood Boulevard, Suite 202
Hollywood, FL 33020
(954) 923-3477
Contact: Mr. D. Caruso
Minimum Salary Placed: $25,000
Recruiting Specialty: Real estate

Steven Douglas Associates
3850 Hollywood Boulevard
Hollywood, FL 33021
(954) 381-8100
Contact: Mr. S. Sadaka
Minimum Salary Placed: $25,000
Recruiting Specialty: Accounting, finance and MIS

First Recruiters Group Inc.
1922 Tyler Street
Hollywood, FL 33020
(954) 373-3113
Contact: Ms. Ginger Cielo
Minimum Salary Placed: $20,000
Recruiting Specialty: General

Wilcoxen, Blackwell, Niven & Associates
1926 Hollywood Boulevard, Suite 220
Hollywood, FL 33020
(954) 922-4569
Contact: Mr. C. E. Wilcoxen
Minimum Salary Placed: $50,000
Recruiting Specialty: Hospitality and travel

JACKSONVILLE

Bill Bishop & Associates
9511 Abbey Way
Jacksonville, FL 32650
(904) 642-5063
Contact: Mr. Bill Bishop
Recruiting Specialty: Healthcare

Chatham Personnel Consultants
2110 Park Street
Jacksonville, FL 32204
(904) 384-0076
Contact: Ms. Stephanie Schwader
Minimum Salary Placed: $20,000
Recruiting Specialty: General

Florida Legal Search, Inc.
1301 Gulf Life Drive, Suite 2214
Jacksonville, FL 32207
(904) 396-1101
Contact: Mr. Jim Valenti
Minimum Salary Placed: $30,000
Recruiting Specialty: Legal

Fortune Personnel Consultants
3830 Crown Point Road, Suite E
Jacksonville, FL 32257
(904) 398-1688

Contact: Mr. Bob Pepple
Minimum Salary Placed: $25,000
Recruiting Specialty: Engineering, quality and manufacturing

Heidrick & Struggles, Inc.
76 S. Laura Street, Suite 2110
Jacksonville, FL 32202
(904) 355-6674
Contact: Mr. Charles Hoskins
Minimum Salary Placed: $60,000
Recruiting Specialty: General

Hospitality Search Inc.
6251 Phillips Highway
Jacksonville, FL 32216
(904) 730-0133
Contact: Mr. L. Luthra
Minimum Salary Placed: $25,000
Recruiting Specialty: Hospitality

Insurance Consultants
3268 Marbon Road
Jacksonville, FL 32223
(904) 292-9752
Minimum Salary Placed: $25,000
Recruiting Specialty: Insurance

Kellogg, Kessler, Wellington & Co.
7077 Bonneval Road, Suite 650
Jacksonville, FL 32216
(800) 296-0896
Contact: Mr. Steven Highfill
Minimum Salary Placed: $25,000
Recruiting Specialty: Legal and healthcare

Jim King Company
1301 Riverplace, Suite 700
Jacksonville, FL 32207
(904) 398-5464
Contact: Mr. Jim King
Minimum Salary Placed: $30,000
Recruiting Specialty: Clerical

Kirschner Resource Group Inc.
51116 Baymeadows Road, Suite 6
Jacksonville, FL 32217
(904) 292-1717
Minimum Salary Placed: $30,000
Recruiting Specialty: General

Management Recruiters
3840-1 Williamsburg Park Boulevard
Jacksonville, FL 32257
(904) 448-5200
Contact: Mr. Charles Hansen
Minimum Salary Placed: $30,000
Recruiting Specialty: Manufacturing

Management Recruiters, Inc.
4231 Walnut Bend, Suite 1-D
Jacksonville, FL 32257
(904) 260-4444
Contact: Mr. Robert Lee
Minimum Salary Placed: $40,000
Recruiting Specialty: Business development and engineering in manufacturing

Management Recruiters
4231 Walnut Bend, Suite 1-D
Jacksonville, FL 32257
(904) 260-4444
Contact: Mr. Robert Lee
Minimum Salary Placed: $20,000
Recruiting Specialty: General

Marathon Group
2320 South 3rd Street
Jacksonville, FL 32256
(904) 270-2121
Contact: Mr. Michael Moore
Minimum Salary Placed: $40,000
Recruiting Specialty: Bar code data collection, packaging and paper

McGinnis and Associates
701 San Marco Boulevard
Jacksonville, FL 32207
(904) 398-1378
Contact: Mr. Fred McGinnis
Minimum Salary Placed: $25,000
Recruiting Specialty: General

RAS Service of Jacksonville
P.O. Box 56106
Jacksonville, FL 32241
(904) 730-4162
Contact: Mr. Mel Sanders
Minimum Salary Placed: $30,000
Recruiting Specialty: Manufacturing

Robinson Personnel Service
4000 Saint Johns Avenue, Suite 35
Jacksonville, FL 32205
(904) 388-5111
Contact: Ms. Annette Robinson
Minimum Salary Placed: $20,000
Recruiting Specialty: General; physical and occupational therapists

Sales Consultants
9471 Baymeadows Road, Suite 204
Jacksonville, FL 32216
(904) 737-5770
Contact: Mr. Scott Sheridan
Minimum Salary Placed: $25,000
Recruiting Specialty: Sales

Doug Sears and Associates
6339 Argyle Forest Boulevard
Jacksonville, FL 32244
(904) 573-6919
Contact: Mr. Doug Sears
Minimum Salary Placed: $30,000
Recruiting Specialty: General

Southwestern Professional Services
9485 Regency Square Boulevard,
 Suite 110
Jacksonville, FL 32225
(904) 725-9200
Contact: Mr. Mark Langley
Minimum Salary Placed: $30,000
Recruiting Specialty: Sales

JACKSONVILLE BEACH

PMR Search Consultants Inc.
428 B Osceola Avenue
Jacksonville Beach, FL 32250
(904) 270-0505
Contact: Mr. P. Gurtenstien
Minimum Salary Placed: $40,000
Recruiting Specialty: Attorneys

JUNO BEACH

Select Personnel Service
13205 US Highway 1, Suite 530
Juno Beach, FL 33408
(561) 626-9637
Contact: Ms. Shawn Bising
Recruiting Specialty: General

JUPITER

Chase America, Inc.
1001 N US Highway 1
Jupiter, FL 33477
(561) 744-6670
Recruiting Specialty: Sports industry

KEY BISCAYNE

Dunhill Professional Search
240 Crandon Boulevard, Suite 115
Key Biscayne, FL 33149
(305) 365-0400
Contact: Mr. Charles Parsons
Minimum Salary Placed: $50,000
Recruiting Specialty: General

LAKE PLACID

Tully- Woodemansee International
1088 US Highway 27 North
Lake Placid, FL 33852
(941) 465-1024
Contact: Ms. Margo Tully
Minimum Salary Placed: $40,000
Recruiting Specialty: General

LAKELAND

Evans and Associates
6700 South Florida Avenue, Suite 25
Lakeland, FL 33941
(941) 646-2984
Contact: Mr. Charles Terry Evans
Minimum Salary Placed: $20,000
Recruiting Specialty: General

Meads & Associates
6700 South Florida Avenue, Suite 4
Lakeland, FL 33941
(941) 644-0411
Contact: Mr. Walter Meads
Minimum Salary Placed: $50,000
Recruiting Specialty: Advertising

Jim Parham & Associates, Inc.
6700 S. Florida Avenue, Suite 33
Lakeland, FL 33941
(941) 644-7097
Contact: Mr. Jim Parham
Minimum Salary Placed: $30,000
Recruiting Specialty: Freight

Rita Temporaries
5150 S. Florida Avenue
Lakeland, FL 33941
(941) 646-5021
Contact: Mr. J. Dayvault
Recruiting Specialty: General

LARGO

Dunhill of St. Petersburg
1915 East Bay Drive, Suite 3B
Largo, FL 34641
(813) 585-0000
Contact: Mr. Richard Williams
Minimum Salary Placed: $25,000
Recruiting Specialty: General

HLM Recruiters
9242 100 23rd Avenue N, Suite 100
Largo, FL 33773
(813) 586-6989
Contact: Mr. Perry Ellie
Recruiting Specialty: Healthcare

McConnell, Mae & Miller, Inc.
3665 E. Bay Drive, Suite 204-286
Largo, FL 33771
(813) 524-1051
Contact: Ms. Jeannie Abston
Recruiting Specialty: Sales, human resources, and food & beverage

LONGBOAT KEY

Curl and Associates
2241 Harbourside Drive
Longboat Key, FL 34228
(941) 383-6497
Contact: Mr. Joe Curl
Minimum Salary Placed: $30,000
Recruiting Specialty: Healthcare

LONGWOOD

MSI Chase Morgan
2170 West State Road 434, Suite 454
Longwood, FL 32779
(407) 788-7700
Contact: Ms. Vicki Cox
Minimum Salary Placed: $25,000
Recruiting Specialty: Healthcare

The Primary Group, Inc.
P.O. Box 916160
Longwood, FL 32791
(407) 869-4111
Contact: Mr. Ken Friedman
Minimum Salary Placed: $50,000
Recruiting Specialty: Finance, insurance, paper, chemicals and environmental

Raymond Thomas & Associates
407 Wekiva Springs Road, Suite 221
Longwood, FL 32779
(407) 774-8300
Contact: Mr. Ray Huegel
Minimum Salary Placed: $50,000
Recruiting Specialty: Manufacturing of metals

Weiss & Associates, Inc.
P.O. Box 915656
Longwood, FL 32791
(407) 774-1212
Contact: Mr. Terry Weiss
Minimum Salary Placed: $50,000
Recruiting Specialty: Legal and taxation

The Witt Group
P.O. Box 521281
Longwood, FL 32752
(407) 324-4137
Contact: Mr. Gerald Witt
Minimum Salary Placed: $50,000
Recruiting Specialty: Technical disciplines in pharmaceuticals and chemicals

LUTZ

Business Partners, Inc.
1531 No. Dale Mabrey Highway,
  Suite 102
Lutz, FL 33549
(813) 948-1440
Contact: Mr. Joe Johnson
Minimum Salary Placed: $20,000
Recruiting Specialty: Database management and MIS

MADEIRA BEACH

Therapy, Staff Service, Inc.
4300 Duhme Road
Madeira Beach, FL 33708
(813) 391-2000
Contact: Ms. Lois Conger
Recruiting Specialty: Physicians and therapists

MAITLAND

Management Recruiters
2600 Maitland Center Parkway, Suite 295
Maitland, FL 32751
(407) 660-0089
Contact: Mr. Tom Brown
Minimum Salary Placed: $20,000
Recruiting Specialty: General

Tina Morbitzer & Associates
668 N. Orlando Ave, Suite 105
Maitland, FL 32751
(407) 539-1000
Contact: Ms. Tina Morbitzer
Recruiting Specialty: Commercial real estate development

Sales Consultants
2600 Maitland Center Parkway, Suite 295
Maitland, FL 32751
(407) 660-0089
Contact: Ms. Arlene Brown
Minimum Salary Placed: $25,000
Recruiting Specialty: Sales

MIAMI

Accutemps Inc.
1801 Coral Way, Suite 405
Miami, FL 33145
(305) 285-9606
Contact: Ms. O. Febles
Recruiting Specialty: Office support

Ad Hoc Law Association Inc.
444 Brickell Avenue, Suite 611
Miami, FL 33131
(305) 381-9600
Contact: Ms. Suzanne Pallot
Minimum Salary Placed: $50,000
Recruiting Specialty: Attorneys

American Medical Consultants
11625 SW 110th Road
Miami, FL 33176
(305) 271-9225
Contact: Mr. Martin Osinski
Minimum Salary Placed: $80,000
Recruiting Specialty: Healthcare and physicians

American Recruiters Inc.
3900 NW 79th Avenue, Suite 401
Miami, FL 33166
(305) 592-1455
Contact: Ms. Gina Meloche
Minimum Salary Placed: $30,000
Recruiting Specialty: General

Kay Apfel Hancock Search
777 Brickell Avenue, Suite 1130
Miami, FL 33131
(305) 371-7298
Contact: Ms. Kay Apfel
Minimum Salary Placed: $50,000
Recruiting Specialty: Banking

Brickell Personnel Consultants
1110 Brickell Avenue
Miami, FL 33131
(305) 371-6187
Contact: Ms. N. Torres
Minimum Salary Placed: $25,000
Recruiting Specialty: General

Career X-Change
220 Miracle Mile, Suite 203
Miami, FL 33134
(305) 529-0064
Contact: Ms. S. Romanos
Recruiting Specialty: General

Corporate Advisors
250 NE 27th Street
Miami, FL 33137
(305) 573-7753
Contact: Ms. M. Kurtzman
Minimum Salary Placed: $30,000
Recruiting Specialty: General

Crume Bailey and Company
3021 Oak Avenue
Miami, FL 33133
(305) 444-7200
Contact: Mr. John Crume
Minimum Salary Placed: $90,000
Recruiting Specialty: General

Global Search
1451 S. Miami Avenue, Suite A
Miami, FL 33130
(305) 374-8277
Contact: Mr. M. Tannhauser
Minimum Salary Placed: $35,000
Recruiting Specialty: Productions discipline in finance, banking and brokerages

Griffith & Werner, Inc.
10691 N. Kendall Drive, Suite 212
Miami, FL 33144
(305) 553-9700
Contact: Mr. Warland Griffith
Minimum Salary Placed: $75,000
Recruiting Specialty: General

Lydia Harrison and Associates Inc.
1550 Madruga Avenue
Miami, FL 33146
(305) 667-7455
Contact: Ms. Lydia Harrison
Minimum Salary Placed: $25,000
Recruiting Specialty: General

Hastings and Hastings Inc.
1001 S. Bayshore Drive
Miami, FL 33131
(305) 374-2255
Contact: Ms. R. Cox
Minimum Salary Placed: $25,000
Recruiting Specialty: General

A.T. Kearney Executive Search
201 South Biscayne Boulevard,
 Suite 3180
Miami, FL 33131
(305) 577-0046
Contact: Mr. John Mestepey
Minimum Salary Placed: $60,000
Recruiting Specialty: General

MD Resources, Inc.
9360 Sunset Drive, Suite 250
Miami, FL 33173
(305) 271-9213
Contact: Ms. Judith Berger
Minimum Salary Placed: $80,000
Recruiting Specialty: Physicians and
healthcare

Management Recruiters
2121 Ponce De Leon Boulevard,
 Suite 220
Miami, FL 33134
(305) 448-1608
Contact: Mr. Joe Mullings
Minimum Salary Placed: $20,000
Recruiting Specialty: General

Management Recruiters
815 NW 57th Avenue, Suite 110
Miami, FL 33126
(305) 264-4212
Contact: Mr. Del Diaz
Minimum Salary Placed: $20,000
Recruiting Specialty: General

Marin Associates
1420 S. Bayshore Drive, Suite 208
Miami, FL 33131
(305) 374-4665
Contact: Ms. M. Drescher
Minimum Salary Placed: $50,000
Recruiting Specialty: International banking

Maxecon Executive Search Consultants
9500 South Dadeland Boulevard,
 Suite 601
Miami, FL 33156
(305) 670-1933
Contact: Mr. Ronald Gerstl
Minimum Salary Placed: $50,000
Recruiting Specialty: Foreign placement
with American companies operating
abroad

Professional Recruiting Services
121 SE 1st Street, Suite 817
Miami, FL 33131
(305) 372-3611
Contact: Ms. Sylvia Hernandez
Minimum Salary Placed: $40,000
Recruiting Specialty: Telecommunications

Snelling and Snelling
8685 NW 53rd Terrace
Miami, FL 33166
(305) 761-3408
Contact: Ms. S. Lewis
Minimum Salary Placed: $25,000
Recruiting Specialty: General

Universal Consultants Inc.
13911 SW 108th Street
Miami, FL 33186
(305) 382-5088
Contact: Mr. S. Silverstein
Minimum Salary Placed: $50,000
Recruiting Specialty: Trust banking

Universal Search Inc.
1460 Brickell Avenue
Miami, FL 33131
(305) 374-1922
Contact: Larry
Minimum Salary Placed: $20,000
Recruiting Specialty: General

Walley Chesson Associates
P.O. Box 960876
Miami, FL 33296
(305) 255-3736
Contact: Mr. Randy Walley
Minimum Salary Placed: $35,000
Recruiting Specialty: Apparel, sewn products and textiles

MIAMI BEACH

Parker Page Group
6924 Trouville Esplanave
Miami Beach, FL 33141
(305) 892-2822
Contact: Mr. Harry Harfenist
Minimum Salary Placed: $40,000
Recruiting Specialty: Hospitality, finance, healthcare and high technology

Summit Executive Search Consultants, Inc.
420 Lincoln Road, Suite 265
Miami Beach, FL 33139
(305) 672-5008

Contact: Mr. Alfred Holzman
Minimum Salary Placed: $35,000
Recruiting Specialty: General

MIAMI LAKES

Crawford and Crofford
15327 NW 60th Avenue
Miami Lakes, FL 33014
(305) 820-0855
Contact: Ms. Greer Jensen
Minimum Salary Placed: $30,000
Recruiting Specialty: General

First Employment Consultants
6175 NW 153rd Street, Suite 121
Miami Lakes, FL 33014
(305) 825-8900
Minimum Salary Placed: $25,000
Recruiting Specialty: Construction in the Middle East

Management Recruiters
8181 NW 154th Street
Miami Lakes, FL 33014
(305) 828-2887
Minimum Salary Placed: $20,000
Recruiting Specialty: General

Source EDP
15600 NW 67th Avenue, Suite 201
Miami Lakes, FL 33014
(800) 733-0002
Minimum Salary Placed: $25,000
Recruiting Specialty: MIS

MIRAMAR

Lloyd Personnel Consultants
305 Gulfstream Drive
Miramar, FL 33023
(954) 491-8404
Contact: Mr. K. Banks
Minimum Salary Placed: $25,000
Recruiting Specialty: General

MILTON

Management Recruiters
5652-B Highway 90
Milton, FL 32583
(904) 626-3303
Contact: Ms. Karen Brand
Minimum Salary Placed: $20,000
Recruiting Specialty: Managed healthcare

MOUNT DORA

Management Recruiters
117 North Donnelly Street
Mount Dora, FL 32757
(352) 383-7101
Contact: Mr. Roger Holloway
Minimum Salary Placed: $25,000
Recruiting Specialty: General

NAPLES

C. A. Durakis Associates, Inc.
3003 Gulf Shore Boulevard
Naples, FL 33940
(941) 262-5306
Contact: Mr. Charles Durakis
Minimum Salary Placed: $80,000
Recruiting Specialty: General

Management Recruiters
1300 3rd Street South, Suite 301-A
Naples, FL 33940
(941) 261-8800
Contact: Mr. Dan Ressler
Minimum Salary Placed: $20,000
Recruiting Specialty: Automotive and
medical device

NEW SMYRANA BEACH

Page Associates
P.O. Box 217
New Smyrna Beach, FL 32170
(904) 427-9908
Contact: Jack Page
Recruiting Specialty: Plastics, manufacturing, engineering, and operations

ORANGE PARK

Brian and Associates
1279 Kingsley Avenue, Suite 114
Orange Park, FL 32073
(904) 745-5255
Contact: Mr. Dave Jackson
Minimum Salary Placed: $25,000
Recruiting Specialty: General

Exclusive Search Inc.
P.O. Box 1424
Orange Park, FL 32607
(904) 276-1479
Contact: Ms. B. Horn
Minimum Salary Placed: $25,000
Recruiting Specialty: Graphic arts

ORLANDO

Accountemps
225 E. Robinson, Suite 545
Orlando, FL 32801
(407) 422-2275
Contact: Ms. Linda Harrington
Minimum Salary Placed: $25,000
Recruiting Specialty: Accounting and
MIS

Executive Search International
733 N. Magnolia Avenue
Orlando, FL 32803
(407) 425-6000
Contact: Mr. B. Wosgien
Minimum Salary Placed: $50,000
Recruiting Specialty: Hotels

International Recruiting Services
P.O. Drawer 533976
Orlando, FL 32753
(407) 896-9606
Contact: Mr. Mell Leonard
Minimum Salary Placed: $45,000
Recruiting Specialty: Agriculture, horti-
culture and floral cultures

Kias Klaus Idhe and Associates
1202 Lake Willisara Circle
Orlando, FL 32806
(407) 422-0772
Minimum Salary Placed: $30,000
Recruiting Specialty: Hospitality

McGuire Executive Search, Inc.
1650 Sand Lake Road, Suite 302
Orlando, FL 32809
(407) 857-6100
Contact: Mr. Harry McGuire
Minimum Salary Placed: $30,000
Recruiting Specialty: Hospitality

Mitchell and Associates
P.O. Box 124
Orlando, FL 32802
(407) 228-6881
Contact: Ms. Sheri Mitchell
Minimum Salary Placed: $25,000
Recruiting Specialty: Sales and marketing

Romac International
111 North Orange Avenue, Suite 1150
Orlando, FL 32801
(407) 843-0765
Contact: Ms. Kate Grantham
Recruiting Specialty: Accounting and finance

PALM BAY

McMillan Associates, Inc.
P.O. Box 062005
Palm Bay, FL 32940
(407) 254-4423
Contact: Mr. John McMillan
Recruiting Specialty: Materials manage-
ment, purchasing and logistics

R. B. Jones Corporation
1334 Golf Cista Court NE
Palm Bay, FL 32905
(407) 722-2949
Contact: Mr. Brad Jones
Minimum Salary Placed: $50,000
Recruiting Specialty: Legal and technical

PALM BEACH

Management Recruiters
350 South County Road, Suite 126
Palm Beach, FL 33480
(561) 659-5001

Contact: Mr. Tom Johanskey
Minimum Salary Placed: $20,000
Recruiting Specialty: General

Recruiters Network
2875 South Ocean Boulevard
Palm Beach, FL 33480
(407) 586-7111
Contact: Mr. Tom Allen
Minimum Salary Placed: $30,000
Recruiting Specialty: General

PALM BEACH GARDENS

L. Battalin & Company
P.O. Box 31815
Palm Beach Gardens, FL 33410
(561) 627-0042
Contact: Mr. Laurence Battalin
Minimum Salary Placed: $50,000
Recruiting Specialty: Sales and marketing
in food and beverages

Vento Associates
4521 PGA Boulevard, Suite 340
Palm Beach Gardens, FL 33403
(407) 625-9660
Contact: Mr. Joseph Vento
Minimum Salary Placed: $40,000
Recruiting Specialty: High technology

PALM CITY

Management Recruiters
1151 SW 30th Street
Palm City, FL 34990
(407) 287-9700
Contact: Mr. William Hollinger
Minimum Salary Placed: $30,000
Recruiting Specialty: Medical management

PALM HARBOR

Career Images
P.O. Box 1777
Palm Harbor, FL 34682
(813) 786-9334
Contact: Ms. Debbie Hunkins
Recruiting Specialty: Environmental,
health, and safety & occupational health

Davis-Hill Company
2706 US Highway 19 Alt. N., Suite 204
Palm Harbor, FL 34683
(813) 787-3550
Contact: Mr. Mark Davis
Minimum Salary Placed: $30,000
Recruiting Specialty: Insurance

**Environmental, Health & Safety
Search Associates**
P.O. Box 1325
Palm Harbor, FL 34682
(813) 787-3225
Contact: Mr. Randy Williams
Minimum Salary Placed: $40,000
Recruiting Specialty: Industrial hygiene
and environmental

Kay & Associates
P.O. Box 4825
Palm Harbor, FL 34685
(800) 879-5850
Contact: Ms. Heidi Kay
Recruiting Specialty: High technology

Sales Consultants
2706 Alternate U.S. 19N, Suite 223
Palm Harbor, FL 34683
(813) 787-3656
Contact: Mr. Steve Fox
Recruiting Specialty: Sales

PANAMA CITY

Cantrell and Associates
433 Harrison Avenue, Suite 1A
Panama City, FL 32401
(904) 784-1680
Contact: Mr. T. Cantrell
Minimum Salary Placed: $35,000
Recruiting Specialty: Engineering

Physician Trust
100 Camelot Circle
Panama City, FL 32405
(904) 785-6236
Contact: Ms. B. Sample
Minimum Salary Placed: $100,000
Recruiting Specialty: Physicians

PENSACOLA

Management Recruiters
603 East Government Street
Pensacola, FL 32501
(904) 434-6500
Contact: Mr. Ken Kirchgessner
Minimum Salary Placed: $30,000
Recruiting Specialty: Paper and plastic
products manufacturing

Reinhardt and Associates
1175 College Boulevard
Pensacola, FL 32504
(904) 478-8449
Contact: Mr. M. Reinhardt
Minimum Salary Placed: $25,000
Recruiting Specialty: General

PLANTATION

Focus Consulting
1507 S. University Drive
Plantation, FL 33324
(954) 476-0411
Contact: Ms. L. Moss
Minimum Salary Placed: $25,000
Recruiting Specialty: Benefits consulting

**Networking Unlimited of New
Hampshire, Inc.**
1810 SW 51st Terrace
Plantation, FL 33317
(954) 792-3767
Contact: Ms. Kristina Fabian
Minimum Salary Placed: $50,000
Recruiting Specialty: Healthcare

Omni Partners
8211 W. Broward Boulevard
Plantation, FL 33324
(954) 452-0400
Contact: Mr. M. Cohen
Minimum Salary Placed: $40,000
Recruiting Specialty: Retail

PONTE VEDRA BEACH

Dobson and Associates
4 Sawgrass Village Drive, Suite 110A
Ponte Vedra Beach, FL 32802
(904) 285-9500
Contact: Mr. Dave Dobson
Minimum Salary Placed: $25,000
Recruiting Specialty: Data processing

Stewart Group
4 Sawgrass Village Drive
Ponte Vedra Beach, FL 32082
(904) 285-6622

Contact: Mr. Jim Stewart
Minimum Salary Placed: $25,000
Recruiting Specialty: General

PORT ST. LUCIE

Heritage Search Group, Inc.
7687 Wyldwood Way, Suite 100
Port St. Lucie, FL 34986
(407) 489-5300
Contact: Mr. Philip Tripician
Minimum Salary Placed: $40,000
Recruiting Specialty: Marketing in food
and beverages and consumer packaging

Management Recruiters
558 SE Port St. Lucie Boulevard
Port St. Lucie, FL 34984
(407) 879-2400
Contact: Mr. Arthur Sheehan
Minimum Salary Placed: $30,000
Recruiting Specialty: Healthcare

Management Recruiters
570 SE Port St. Lucie Boulevard
Port St. Lucie, FL 34984
(407) 871-1100
Contact: Mr. Larry Breault
Minimum Salary Placed: $30,000
Recruiting Specialty: Sales and marketing
in MIS and financial services

SAFETY HARBOR

Helffrich International
132 10th Avenue North
Safety Harbor, FL 34695
(813) 725-5525

Contact: Mr. A. Helffrich
Minimum Salary Placed: $30,000
Recruiting Specialty: Environmental
health and safety engineers

SAINT PETERSBURG

Construction Resources Group
466 94th Avenue North
St. Petersburg, FL 33702
(813) 578-1962
Contact: Ms. C. Harris
Minimum Salary Placed: $25,000
Recruiting Specialty: Construction

Management Recruiters
9500 Koger Boulevard, Suite 203
St. Petersburg, FL 33702
(813) 577-2116
Contact: Mr. Robert Raffin
Minimum Salary Placed: $30,000
Recruiting Specialty: General

Management Recruiters
4020 Park Street
St. Petersburg, FL 33709
(813) 345-8811
Contact: Ms. Jean Hand
Minimum Salary Placed: $30,000
Recruiting Specialty: General

Dennis Wynn Associates, Inc.
P.O. Box 7100
St. Petersburg, FL 33734
(813) 823-2042
Contact: Mr. Dennis Wynn
Recruiting Specialty: Data processing

SANFORD

Florapersonnel, Inc.
1740 Lake Markham Road
Sanford, FL 32771
(407) 682-5151
Contact: Ms. Judy Devine
Minimum Salary Placed: $25,000
Recruiting Specialty: Horticulture

SARASOTA

DP Search
2477 Stickney Point Road, Suite 201B
Sarasota, FL 34231
(941) 925-3503
Minimum Salary Placed: $25,000
Recruiting Specialty: General

Dunhill of Sarasota
5053 Ocean Avenue, Suite 59
Sarasota, FL 34242
(941) 349-6200
Contact: Mr. John Olson
Minimum Salary Placed: $25,000
Recruiting Specialty: General

Fortune Personnel Consultants
98 Sarasota Center Boulevard, Suite C
Sarasota, FL 34240
(941) 378-5262
Contact: Mr. Arthur Grindlinger
Minimum Salary Placed: $30,000
Recruiting Specialty: Manufacturing

Franstaff Inc.
73 S. Palm Avenue, Suite 219
Sarasota, FL 34236
(941) 952-9555
Minimum Salary Placed: $30,000
Recruiting Specialty: Franchising

Management Recruiters
7737 Holiday Drive
Sarasota, FL 34231
(941) 923-3671
Contact: Dr. David Lechner
Recruiting Specialty: Medical, insurance
and environmental

Sales Consultants
1343 Main Street, Suite 600
Sarasota, FL 34236
(941) 365-5151
Contact: Mr. Donald Mattran
Minimum Salary Placed: $25,000
Recruiting Specialty: Sales

SINGER ISLAND

The Andre Group, Inc.
2655 N. Ocean Drive, Suite 300
Singer Island, FL 33404
(561) 844-9008
Contact: Michael
Minimum Salary Placed: $50,000
Recruiting Specialty: Human resources
and therapists

SOUTH MIAMI

Stat Healthcare RC
6438 Manor Lane
South Miami, FL 33143
(305) 667-6549
Contact: Mr. Gary Gorski
Minimum Salary Placed: $40,000
Recruiting Specialty: Physicians and
other healthcare

SPRING HILL

Nationwide Recruiters Inc.
5327 Commercial Way
Spring Hill, FL 34606
(352) 597-5950

Minimum Salary Placed: $25,000
Recruiting Specialty: Corrugated and metals

Roberts Ryan & Bentley
420 Silas Court
Spring Hill, FL 34609
(352) 686-3610
Contact: Mr. Mark Lorenzetti
Minimum Salary Placed: $50,000
Recruiting Specialty: General

STUART

RIC Corporation
900 Ocean Boulevard, Suite 32
Stuart, FL 34994
(407) 287-5409
Contact: Mr. R. Thomas Welch
Minimum Salary Placed: $75,000
Recruiting Specialty: General

TALLAHASSEE

Management Recruiters
1406 Hays Street, Suite 7
Tallahassee, FL 32301
(904) 656-8444
Contact: Ms. Kittie Carter
Minimum Salary Placed: $30,000
Recruiting Specialty: Insurance and plastic injection molding

Stanewick, Hart & Associates, Inc.
7829 Briarcreek Road
Tallahassee, FL 32312
(904) 893-7849
Contact: Mr. David Hunter
Minimum Salary Placed: $40,000
Recruiting Specialty: MIS and logistics

TAMARAC

Executive Career Strategies
7900 N. University Drive, Suite 201
Tamarac, FL 33321
(954) 720-9764
Contact: Mr. R. Bernstein
Minimum Salary Placed: $25,000
Recruiting Specialty: Insurance

TAMPA

Accountants On Call
1715 N. Westshore Boulevard, Suite 460
Tampa, FL 33607
(813) 289-0051
Contact: Mr. Jeffrey Waldon
Recruiting Specialty: Accounting and finance

Carter-Evdemon & Associates
777 South Harbour Island Boulevard, Suite 930
Tampa, FL 33602
(813) 229-2220
Contact: Mr. Jeffrey Carter
Minimum Salary Placed: $30,000
Recruiting Specialty: Insurance

Century Consultants
2910 W. Bay Boulevard
Tampa, FL 33629
(813) 831-1697
Minimum Salary Placed: $30,000
Recruiting Specialty: General

Colli Associates
P.O. Box 2865
Tampa, FL 33601
(813) 681-2145
Contact: Mr. Ben Colli
Minimum Salary Placed: $30,000
Recruiting Specialty: Electrical, chemical and manufacturing

The Corporate Source Group
4830 West Kennedy Boulevard, Suite 495
Tampa, FL 33609
(813) 286-4422
Contact: Mr. Mark Hausherr
Minimum Salary Placed: $70,000
Recruiting Specialty: General

Dunhill Personnel
4350 West Cypress Street, Suite 814
Tampa, FL 33607
(813) 872-8118
Contact: Mr. Donald Kramer
Minimum Salary Placed: $25,000
Recruiting Specialty: Healthcare and
auditing

Executive Sales Registry
14029 N. Dale Mabry Highway
Tampa, FL 33618
(813) 879-1324
Contact: Sue
Minimum Salary Placed: $35,000
Recruiting Specialty: Consumer products
and medical sales

Ken Goodwin and Associates
10014 N. Dale Mabry Highway
Tampa, FL 33618
(813) 962-2611
Contact: Mr. Ken Goodwin
Minimum Salary Placed: $25,000
Recruiting Specialty: General

Bob Graham and Associates
5401 W. Kennedy Boulevard
Tampa, FL 33609
(813) 282-4623
Contact: Mr. Bob Graham
Minimum Salary Placed: $30,000
Recruiting Specialty: Engineering and
computers

Judge Inc. of Florida
500 N. Westshore Boulevard, Suite 850
Tampa, FL 33609
(813) 877-7000
Minimum Salary Placed: $30,000
Recruiting Specialty: Manufacturing

Lamalie Amrop International
3903 Northdale Boulevard, Suite 220
Tampa, FL 33624
(813) 961-7494
Contact: Mr. Jack Wissman
Minimum Salary Placed: $50,000
Recruiting Specialty: General

Lloyd Prescott Associates, Inc.
4902 Eisenhower Boulevard, Suite 185
Tampa, FL 33634
(813) 881-1110
Contact: Mr. Sheldon Ginsberg
Minimum Salary Placed: $60,000
Recruiting Specialty: General

Management Recruiters
4012 Gunn Highway, Suite 140
Tampa, FL 33624
(813) 264-7165
Contact: Mr. Gary King
Minimum Salary Placed: $30,000
Recruiting Specialty: Medical sales and
pharmaceuticals

Management Recruiters
2909 Bay to Bay Boulevard, Suite 302
Tampa, FL 33609
(813) 875-7374
Contact: Mr. Rudy Koletic
Minimum Salary Placed: $35,000
Recruiting Specialty: Engineering and
sales

Management Recruiters
4200 West Cypress Street, Suite 640
Tampa, FL 36607
(813) 876-1151
Contact: Mr. Ron Cottick
Minimum Salary Placed: $30,000
Recruiting Specialty: General

Robert Murphy Associates
6305 Songbird Way
Tampa, FL 33625
(813) 962-3300
Contact: Mr. Robert Murphy
Minimum Salary Placed: $75,000
Recruiting Specialty: General

National Engineering Consultants
2700 N. MacDill AU, Suite 215
Tampa, FL 33607-2273
(813) 348-0522
Contact: Ms. Carolyn E. Nicholson
Recruiting Specialty: Mechanical & electrical product design development

Physician Executive Management Center
4014 Gunn Highway, Suite 160
Tampa, FL 33624
(813) 963-1800
Contact: Mr. David Kirschman
Minimum Salary Placed: $90,000
Recruiting Specialty: Physicians

Priority Executive Search, Inc.
2805 W. Busch Boulevard, Suite 105
Tampa, FL 33618
(813) 933-0082
Contact: Ms. Arlen Crittenden
Recruiting Specialty: Healthcare and sales

Roth Young of Tampa
5201 West Kennedy Boulevard, Suite 506
Tampa, FL 33609
(813) 289-6556
Contact: Mr. P. Barry Cushing
Minimum Salary Placed: $25,000
Recruiting Specialty: General

Sales Consultants
4200 West Cypress Street, Suite 640
Tampa, FL 33607
(813) 876-1151
Contact: Mr. Dave Peterson
Minimum Salary Placed: $30,000
Recruiting Specialty: Sales

Search Advisors
777 South Harbour Island Boulevard
Tampa, FL 33602
(813) 221-7555
Contact: Mr. Mark Strom
Minimum Salary Placed: $70,000
Recruiting Specialty: General

Southern Research Services
3837 Northdale Boulevard, Suite 364
Tampa, FL 33624
(813) 269-9595
Contact: Mr. Thomas Bloch
Minimum Salary Placed: $45,000
Recruiting Specialty: High technology and healthcare manufacturing

Sun Personnel West
5444 Bay Center Drive South, Suite 215
Tampa, FL 33609
(813) 286-2009
Contact: Ms. G. De Cruse
Minimum Salary Placed: $25,000
Recruiting Specialty: Sales

Sweeney Harbert & Mummert, Inc.
777 South Harbour Island Boulevard,
  Suite 130
Tampa, FL 33602
(813) 229-5360
Contact: Mr. David Harbert
Minimum Salary Placed: $70,000
Recruiting Specialty: General

VENICE

Management Recruiters
996-B Laguna Drive
Venice, FL 34285
(941) 484-3900
Contact: Mr. Walt Taylor
Minimum Salary Placed: $40,000
Recruiting Specialty: General

VERO BEACH

The Brand Co., Inc.
8402 Red Bay Court
Vero Beach, FL 32963
(407) 231-1807
Contact: Mr. J. Brand Spangenberg
Minimum Salary Placed: $75,000
Recruiting Specialty: General

Executive Recruiters
P.O. Box 3447
Vero Beach, FL 32964
(407) 234-5253
Contact: Mr. Miles O'Brien
Minimum Salary Placed: $50,000
Recruiting Specialty: Insurance

Hutton Group
815 Live Oak Road, Suite A
Vero Beach, FL 32963
(561) 234-7333
Contact: Ms. Joan Hutton
Minimum Salary Placed: $25,000
Recruiting Specialty: Healthcare

WEST PALM BEACH

Career Development Associates
2300 Palm Beach Lakes Boulevard
West Palm Beach, FL 33409
(561) 686-5098
Contact: Ms. Maria Greco
Minimum Salary Placed: $25,000
Recruiting Specialty: General

Career Planners Inc.
5730 Corporate Way, Suite 100
West Palm Beach, FL 33561
(561) 683-8785
Contact: Ms. D. Finley
Recruiting Specialty: General

Erlanger Associates, Inc.
777 South Flagler Drive, 8th Floor
West Palm Beach, FL 33401
(561) 820-9461
Contact: Ms. Lynn Hayden
Minimum Salary Placed: $130,000
Recruiting Specialty: Investors portfolio
companies

Howard Williams Associates
105 South Narcissus Avenue, Suite 806
West Palm Beach, FL 33401
(561) 833-4888
Contact: Mr. George Howard
Minimum Salary Placed: $35,000
Recruiting Specialty: Legal

Stan Reiff Associates
1499 Forest Hill Boulevard, Suite 103
West Palm Beach, FL 33406
(561) 433-9434
Contact: Mr. Stan Reiff
Minimum Salary Placed: $25,000
Recruiting Specialty: General

**Robert Half
International/Accountemps**
1645 Palm Beach Lakes Boulevard
West Palm Beach, FL 33401
(561) 684-8500
Contact: Ms. M. Murasko
Recruiting Specialty: Accounting

Search Inc.
2708 N. Australian Avenue
West Palm Beach, FL 33561
(561) 832-7213
Contact: Mr. R. Butler
Minimum Salary Placed: $45,000
Recruiting Specialty: Attorneys

Snelling Personnel
2161 Palm Beach Lakes Boulevard
West Palm Beach, FL 33409
(561) 689-5400
Contact: Ms. Jane Wohlorn
Minimum Salary Placed: $25,000
Recruiting Specialty: General

WINTER PARK

Accountants Executive Search
1801 Lee Road, Suite 375
Winter Park, FL 32789
(407) 629-2999
Contact: Mr. Donald Phillips
Minimum Salary Placed: $25,000
Recruiting Specialty: Accounting and finance

Career Choice Inc.
1035 S. Semoran Boulevard
Winter Park, FL 32792
(407) 679-5150
Minimum Salary Placed: $25,000
Recruiting Specialty: Entertainment, hospitality, sales and marketing

Cary & Associates
P.O. Box 2043
Winter Park, FL 32790
(407) 647-1145
Contact: Mr. Con Cary
Minimum Salary Placed: $35,000
Recruiting Specialty: General

Gwen Dycus & Associates
P.O. Box 5210
Winter Park, FL 32793
(407) 629-4010
Contact: Ms. Gwen Dycus
Minimum Salary Placed: $30,000
Recruiting Specialty: Retail development

GEORGIA

ALPHARETTA

Agri-Associates Inc.
895B Macfarland Road
Alpharetta, GA 30201
(770) 475-2201
Contact: Mr. M. Deal
Minimum Salary Placed: $25,000
Recruiting Specialty: Agricultural

DBC Recruiting Network
4840 Agate Drive
Alpharetta, GA 30202
(770) 729-0990
Contact: Ms. Debbie Brooks
Recruiting Specialty: Sales and marketing
in computers and high technology

Doctor's Choice, Inc.
5250-A Highway
Alpharetta, GA 30201
(770) 475-0504
Minimum Salary Placed: $20,000
Recruiting Specialty: Medical

Elliot Associates, Inc.
131 Roswell Street, Suite B
Alpharetta, GA 30201
(770) 664-5354
Contact: Ms. Joan Williams Ray
Recruiting Specialty: Hospitality

Thomas E. Hardee & Associates, Inc.
5675 Commons Lane
Alpharetta, GA 30202
(770) 475-7436
Contact: Mr. Tom Hardee
Recruiting Specialty: Marketing, sales,
and human resources

Management Recruiters
21 North Main Street, Suite 204
Alpharetta, GA 30201
(770) 664-5512
Contact: Mr. John Harvey
Recruiting Specialty: Finance and pulp
and paper

Philo & Associates
2024 Eagle Glen Road, Suite A
Alpharetta, GA 30202
(770) 993-0550
Contact: Mr. David Philo
Minimum Salary Placed: $40,000
Recruiting Specialty: Packaging, food
and beverages

Richey and Associates
520 Chimney Bluff
Alpharetta, GA 30202
(770) 998-4709
Contact: Mr. Jack Richey
Minimum Salary Placed: $65,000
Recruiting Specialty: Interiors, textiles
and furniture

ARLINGTON

Jubilee, Inc.
P.O. Box 340
Arlington, GA 31713
(912) 725-4500
Contact: Mr. William Gleaton
Recruiting Specialty: MIS, accounting
and finance

ATHENS

Sanford Rose Association
2500 W. Broad Street, Suite 106
Athens, GA 30605
(706) 548-3942
Contact: Mr. Art Weiner
Recruiting Specialty: Manufacturing

ATLANTA

A.D. & Associates
5589 Woodsong Drive, Suite 100
Atlanta, GA 30338
(770) 393-0021
Contact: Mr. Dwight Hawksworth
Minimum Salary Placed: $45,000
Recruiting Specialty: General

AMD & Associates
1872-A Independence Square
Atlanta, GA 30338
(770) 395-1202
Contact: Ms. Anna Marie Denman
Minimum Salary Placed: $30,000
Recruiting Specialty: General

AMD Consulting Service
210 Interstate Parkway NW, Suite 700
Atlanta, GA 30339
(770) 980-6744
Contact: Mr. Ted Lakes
Minimum Salary Placed: $25,000
Recruiting Specialty: Accounting

Accountants On Call
3355 Lenox Road NE, Suite 630
Atlanta, GA 30326
(404) 261-4800
Contact: Ms. Sherry Pontious
Recruiting Specialty: Accounting and finance

Accountants One
1870 Independence Square
Atlanta, GA 30338
(770) 457-6969
Contact: Mr. B. Erling
Recruiting Specialty: Accounting

Accurate Group
5046 Chestnut Forrest Lane
Atlanta, GA 30360
(770) 452-0443
Minimum Salary Placed: $25,000
Recruiting Specialty: General

Ad Temps
3355 Lenox Road, Suite 750
Atlanta, GA 30326
(404) 467-9800
Minimum Salary Placed: $25,000
Recruiting Specialty: Marketing

Aggressive Corporation
8300 Dunwoody Place, Suite 140
Atlanta, GA 30350
(770) 998-0500
Contact: Mr. Rick Stradtman
Minimum Salary Placed: $50,000
Recruiting Specialty: Manufacturing

Agri-Personnel
5120 Old Bill Cook Road
Atlanta, GA 30349
(404) 768-5701
Contact: Mr. David Wicker
Minimum Salary Placed: $40,000
Recruiting Specialty: Agri-business

Allen and Associates
200 Galleria Parkway NW, Suite 350
Atlanta, GA 30339
(770) 916-1999

Contact: Ms. Karen Battoe
Minimum Salary Placed: $20,000
Recruiting Specialty: General

Allen Personnel Consultants
5881 Glenridge Drive NE, Suite 100
Atlanta, GA 30328
(404) 843-2955
Contact: Mr. Robert Allen
Minimum Salary Placed: $25,000
Recruiting Specialty: Manufacturing

Anderson, Watson and Associates
1872 Independence Square
Atlanta, GA 30338
(770) 393-3431
Contact: Mr. Bill Watson
Minimum Salary Placed: $25,000
Recruiting Specialty: General

Ashford Management Group
2295 Parklake Drive NE
Atlanta, GA 30345
(770) 938-6260
Recruiting Specialty: Executive retail
management

Atwood Group
3343 Peachtree Road NE
Atlanta, GA 30326
(404) 261-4484
Contact: Mr. C. Atwood
Minimum Salary Placed: $75,000
Recruiting Specialty: General

B A Associates, Inc.
5881 Glenridge Drive NE
Atlanta, GA 30328
(404) 843-2955
Contact: Ms. Jan Spannow
Recruiting Specialty: Manufacturing and
high technology

Bell Oaks Company
3390 Peachtree Road NE, Suite 1124
Atlanta, GA 30326
(404) 261-2170
Contact: Ms. Amy Brown
Minimum Salary Placed: $25,000
Recruiting Specialty: General

Bellon & Associates, Inc.
1175 Peachtree Street NE
100 Colony Square, Suite 1920
Atlanta, GA 30361
(404) 881-1153
Contact: Ms. Lee Ann Bellon
Minimum Salary Placed: $60,000
Recruiting Specialty: Attorneys

Best Agency
2971 Flowers Road South, Suite 139
Atlanta, GA 30341
(770) 452-1732
Contact: Mr. John Williams
Minimum Salary Placed: $25,000
Recruiting Specialty: General

Betty Thomas Associates
2020 Howell Mill Road, Suite C-283
Atlanta, GA 30318
(404) 352-2569
Minimum Salary Placed: $35,000
Recruiting Specialty: Healthcare

Blackshaw, Olmstead & Lynch
3414 Peachtree Road NE
1010 Monarch Plaza
Atlanta, GA 30326
(404) 261-7770
Contact: Mr. Brian Blackshaw
Minimum Salary Placed: $75,000
Recruiting Specialty: General

Boreham International
275 Carpenter Drive NE
Atlanta, GA 30328
(404) 252-2199
Minimum Salary Placed: $25,000
Recruiting Specialty: General

Bradley-Morris Inc.
200 Galleria Parkway, Suite 220
Atlanta, GA 30339
(770) 612-4950
Contact: Mr. Bill Basnett
Minimum Salary Placed: $25,000
Recruiting Specialty: Manufacturing, engineering and operations

Brandt and Associates
1390 Mile Post Drive
Atlanta, GA 30338
(770) 396-0505
Contact: Mr. Fred Brandt
Minimum Salary Placed: $25,000
Recruiting Specialty: General

Brock and Associates
3190 Northeast Expressway, Suite 210
Atlanta, GA 30341
(404) 525-2525
Contact: Ms. Pam Griggs
Minimum Salary Placed: $25,000
Recruiting Specialty: General

Broward-Dobbs, Inc.
1532 Dunwoody Village Parkway,
  Suite 200
Atlanta, GA 30338
(770) 399-0744
Contact: Mr. W. Luke Greene
Minimum Salary Placed: $35,000
Recruiting Specialty: High technology, utilities, telecommunications and manufacturing

Business Professional Group
3490 Piedmont Road, Suite 212
Atlanta, GA 30305
(404) 262-2577
Minimum Salary Placed: $25,000
Recruiting Specialty: General, some engineering

Calland and Company
2296 Henderson Mill Road NE
Atlanta, GA 30345
(770) 270-9100
Minimum Salary Placed: $25,000
Recruiting Specialty: Healthcare

Churchill Group
100 Galleria Parkway NW
Atlanta, GA 30339
(770) 980-0068
Contact: Mr. Richard Reagan
Minimum Salary Placed: $75,000
Recruiting Specialty: General

Commonwealth Consultants
4840 Roswell Road, Suite C302
Atlanta, GA 30342
(404) 256-0000
Contact: Mr. David Aiken
Minimum Salary Placed: $30,000
Recruiting Specialty: Computers

Comprehensive Search
2050 Eldorado Drive
Atlanta, GA 30345
(404) 686-8236
Contact: Ms. Gail Standard
Minimum Salary Placed: $25,000
Recruiting Specialty: General

Computer Search Associates
P.O. Box 8403
Atlanta, GA 30308
(404) 231-0965
Contact: Ms. Norma Rayburn
Minimum Salary Placed: $30,000
Recruiting Specialty: Computers

Comms People, Inc.
3340 Peachtree Road, Suite 1410
Atlanta, GA 30326
(404) 812-7600
Contact: Ms. Roberta Fried
Minimum Salary Placed: $25,000
Recruiting Specialty: Telecommunications

David C. Cooper and Associates Temps
Suite 5 Concourse Parkway, Suite 2700
Atlanta, GA 30346
(770) 395-0014
Contact: Mr. David Cooper
Recruiting Specialty: Accounting and finance

Corporate Development Services, Inc.
400 Perimeter Center Terrace, Suite 900
Atlanta, GA 30346
(770) 392-4295
Minimum Salary Placed: $25,000
Recruiting Specialty: General

Corporate Personnel, Inc.
1148 Hampton Hall Drive
Atlanta, GA 30319
(404) 252-3292
Contact: Mr. A.H. Sautter
Minimum Salary Placed: $30,000
Recruiting Specialty: Manufacturing

The Crawford Group
100 Colony Square, Box 326
Atlanta, GA 30361
(404) 872-8500
Contact: Mr. Tom Crawford
Minimum Salary Placed: $40,000
Recruiting Specialty: Marketing and advertising

Creative Search
887 W. Marietta Street, Suite N-109
Atlanta, GA 30309
(404) 892-7475
Recruiting Specialty: Art directors and writers

DDS Staffing Resources
863 Holcomb Bridge Road, Suite 230
Atlanta, GA 30076
(770) 998-7779
Minimum Salary Placed: $25,000
Recruiting Specialty: Medical and dental

Dalley Hewitt Company
1401 Peachtree Street NE, Suite 500
Atlanta, GA 30309
(404) 885-6642
Contact: Ms. Rives Hewitt
Minimum Salary Placed: $40,000
Recruiting Specialty: General

Ray Dankel and Company
400 Colony Square NE
Atlanta, GA 30361
(404) 872-8620
Contact: Mr. Ray Dankel
Minimum Salary Placed: $25,000
Recruiting Specialty: General

Dunhill of Atlanta
3340 Peachtree Road NE, Suite 2570
Atlanta, GA 30326
(404) 261-3751
Contact: Mr. Marvin Bearman
Recruiting Specialty: General

Dunhill Professional Search
2110 Powers Ferry Road, Suite 110
Atlanta, GA 30339
(770) 952-0009
Contact: Mr. Jon Harvill
Minimum Salary Placed: $30,000
Recruiting Specialty: Manufacturing

Eastman & Beaudine, Inc.
1 Ravinia, Suite 1110
Atlanta, GA 30346
(770) 390-2720
Contact: Mr. Frank Beaudine
Minimum Salary Placed: $60,000
Recruiting Specialty: General

Egon Zehnder International, Inc.
1201 West Peachtree Street NE
3000 IBM Tower
Atlanta, GA 30309
(404) 875-3000
Contact: Mr. Joel Koblentz
Minimum Salary Placed: $80,000
Recruiting Specialty: General

ExecuSource Associates, Inc.
3232 Cobb Parkway, Suite 227
Atlanta, GA 30339
(770) 943-4254
Contact: Mr. Melvin Larry
Minimum Salary Placed: $25,000
Recruiting Specialty: General

Executive Placement Services
5901-C Peachtree Dunwoody Road,
  Suite 498
Atlanta, GA 30328
(770) 396-9114
Minimum Salary Placed: $25,000
Recruiting Specialty: Gaming, hospitality
and retail

Executive Resource Group
127 Peachtree Street, Suite 922
Atlanta, GA 30303
(404) 522-0888
Contact: Mr. Robert Pauley
Minimum Salary Placed: $25,000
Recruiting Specialty: Healthcare, finance
and gaming

Executive Search Corporation
6075 Roswell Road NE
Atlanta, GA 30328
(404) 303-0003
Minimum Salary Placed: $60,000
Recruiting Specialty: General

Executive Source International
550 Pharr Road, Suite 840
Atlanta, GA 30305
(404) 231-3783
Contact: Mr. Lance Coachman
Minimum Salary Placed: $60,000
Recruiting Specialty: General

Focus Enterprises, Inc.
3 Corporate Square, Suite 340
Atlanta, GA 30329
(404) 321-5400
Minimum Salary Placed: $25,000
Recruiting Specialty: Data processing

D.E. Foster & Partners
303 Peachtree Street NE, Suite 2000
Atlanta, GA 30308
(404) 222-3440
Contact: Mr. Gerald Bump
Minimum Salary Placed: $50,000
Recruiting Specialty: General

Fox-Morris Associates, Inc.
9000 Central Park West, Suite 150
Atlanta, GA 30328
(770) 393-0933
Contact: Mr. Ty Smith
Minimum Salary Placed: $20,000
Recruiting Specialty: General

GKR Americas
100 Galeria Parkway, Suite 1100
Atlanta, GA 30339
(770) 955-9550
Contact: Mr. Charles Chalk
Minimum Salary Placed: $90,000
Recruiting Specialty: General

Garrett Associates Inc.
P.O. Box 190189
Atlanta, GA 31119
(404) 364-0001
Contact: Mr. Donald Garrett
Minimum Salary Placed: $40,000
Recruiting Specialty: Healthcare and human resources

Genovese & Company
455 Otter Creek NE
Atlanta, GA 30328
(770) 671-8330
Contact: Mr. Donald Genovese
Minimum Salary Placed: $70,000
Recruiting Specialty: MIS, FIS, and EDP

George Martin Associates, Inc.
12 Executive Park Drive NE
Atlanta, GA 30329
(404) 325-7101
Minimum Salary Placed: $25,000
Recruiting Specialty: Data processing

Grapevine Group, Inc.
3355 Lenox Road, Suite 670
Atlanta, GA 30326
(404) 365-8472
Minimum Salary Placed: $25,000
Recruiting Specialty: Retail

Harris, Kovacs, Alderman and Associates
4170 Ashford Dunwoody Road NE
Atlanta, GA 30319
(404) 252-7987
Contact: Mr. C. Harris
Minimum Salary Placed: $60,000
Recruiting Specialty: Physicians

Hayman, Daughtery and Associates Inc.
2849 Paces Ferry Road NE
Atlanta, GA 30339
(770) 435-2922
Contact: Ms. K. Daughtery
Minimum Salary Placed: $50,000
Recruiting Specialty: Physicians

Heidrick & Struggles, Inc.
303 Peachtree Street, Suite 3100
Atlanta, GA 30308
(404) 577-2410
Contact: Mr. Patrick Pittard
Minimum Salary Placed: $50,000
Recruiting Specialty: General

Robert Howe & Associates
35 Glenlake Parkway, Suite 164
Atlanta, GA 30328
(770) 390-0030
Contact: Mr. Robert Hamill
Minimum Salary Placed: $50,000
Recruiting Specialty: General and manufacturing

Hughes & Sloan, Inc.
1360 Peachtree Street NE, Suite 490
Atlanta, GA 30309
(404) 873-3421
Contact: Ms. Melba Hughes
Recruiting Specialty: Attorneys

IPR Group, Inc.
8097 B Roswell Road
Atlanta, GA 30350
(770) 396-7500
Contact: Mr. Richard Gay
Minimum Salary Placed: $30,000
Recruiting Specialty: Human resources and insurance

Inroads Atlanta Inc.
100 Peachtree Street NW
Atlanta, GA 30303
(404) 586-0352
Recruiting Specialty: Engineering in business or computers, technical

Innovative Search Inc.
8097 Roswell Road, Suite 101
Atlanta, GA 30350
(770) 399-9093
Minimum Salary Placed: $30,000
Recruiting Specialty: General

JES Search Firm, Inc.
3475 Lenox Road, Suite 970
Atlanta, GA 30326
(404) 262-7222
Contact: Ms. Brenda Evers
Minimum Salary Placed: $25,000
Recruiting Specialty: Data processing

Jackson & Coker
115 Perimeter Center Place, Suite 380
Atlanta, GA 30346
(800) 888-8821
Contact: Ms. Crissy Jester
Recruiting Specialty: Physicians and healthcare

Jacobson Associates
1775 The Exchange, Suite 240
Atlanta, GA 30339
(770) 952-3877
Contact: Mr. John Baumann
Recruiting Specialty: Healthcare and insurance

Jordan & Champagne Intersearch
12 Piedmont Center NE, Suite 115
Atlanta, GA 30305
(404) 262-0691
Recruiting Specialty: Senior level only

Kauffman & Company
P.O. Box 53218
Atlanta, GA 30355
(404) 233-3530

Contact: Mr. Christopher Kauffman
Minimum Salary Placed: $100,000
Recruiting Specialty: Restaurants

A.T. Kearney Executive Search
1100 Abernathy Road, Suite 900
Atlanta, GA 30328
(770) 393-9900
Contact: Mr. James Riddle
Recruiting Specialty: Physicians and
healthcare

Kenzer Corporation
1600 Parkwood Circle, Suite 310
Atlanta, GA 30339
(770) 955-7210
Contact: Ms. Marie Powell
Minimum Salary Placed: $50,000
Recruiting Specialty: Physicians and
healthcare, and some general

Key Professionals Search
4015 Peachtree Road NE
Atlanta, GA 30326
(404) 233-1476
Contact: Ms. B. Reaid
Minimum Salary Placed: $25,000
Recruiting Specialty: Physicians and
healthcare

King Personnel Consultants
3390 Peachtree Road NE
Atlanta, GA 30326
(404) 266-1800
Contact: Mr. N. Traves
Minimum Salary Placed: $30,000
Recruiting Specialty: Fast food

Korn/Ferry International
303 Peachtree Street NE, Suite 1600
Atlanta, GA 30308
(404) 577-7542

Contact: Mr. Al Neely
Recruiting Specialty: Physicians and
healthcare

Evie Kreisler Association Inc.
2575 Peachtree Road, Suite 300
Atlanta, GA 30305
(404) 262-0599
Contact: Ms. Debbi Kreisler
Recruiting Specialty: Consumer retail,
and some general

Lamalie Amrop International
191 Peachtree Street, NE
Atlanta, GA 30303
(404) 688-0800
Contact: Mr. Joe Goodwin
Minimum Salary Placed: $75,000
Recruiting Specialty: General

Lanzi and Associates
2900 Chamblee Tucker Road
Atlanta, GA 30341
(404) 414-8512
Minimum Salary Placed: $25,000
Recruiting Specialty: General

Lawrence-Balakonis & Associates, Inc.
P.O. Box 888241
Atlanta, GA 30356
(770) 587-2342
Contact: Mr. Charles Balakonis
Minimum Salary Placed: $40,000
Recruiting Specialty: Consumer goods

Lectra Search
4900 Parliament Way, Suite 250
Atlanta, GA 30338
(770) 394-4727

Contact: Mr. Henry Catherman
Minimum Salary Placed: $70,000
Recruiting Specialty: Marketing in high technology

Lloyd Association
35 Glenlake Parkway, Suite 164
Atlanta, GA 30328
(770) 390-0001
Contact: Ms. Carolyn Lloyd
Minimum Salary Placed: $50,000
Recruiting Specialty: General

Lovewell & Associates Inc.
P.O. Box 724197
Atlanta, GA 31139
(404) 436-3398
Contact: Mr. Hubart Lovewell
Minimum Salary Placed: $50,000
Recruiting Specialty: General

Lucas Associates
3384 Peachtree, Suite 700
Atlanta, GA 30328
(404) 901-5570
Contact: Ms. Cathy deMartino
Minimum Salary Placed: $40,000
Recruiting Specialty: General

MRI and Sales Consultants
5901-C Peachtree-Dunwoody NE, Suite 370
Atlanta, GA 30328
(770) 394-1300
Minimum Salary Placed: $30,000
Recruiting Specialty: General

MSI International
200 Galleria Parkway, Suite 1610
Atlanta, GA 30339
(770) 951-1208

Contact: Mr. James Cox
Recruiting Specialty: General

MacFarlane & Company, Inc.
1 Park Place, Suite 450
Atlanta, GA 30318
(404) 352-2290
Contact: Mr. Ian MacFarlane
Minimum Salary Placed: $60,000
Recruiting Specialty: General

Bob Maddox Associates
3134 W. Roxboro Road NE
Atlanta, GA 30324
(404) 231-0558
Contact: Mr. Bob Maddox
Minimum Salary Placed: $30,000
Recruiting Specialty: Sales and marketing

Major, Hagen & Africa
1355 Peachtree Street, Suite 1125
Atlanta, GA 30309
(404) 875-1070
Contact: Mr. Wes Dobbs
Recruiting Specialty: Attorneys

Management Recruiters
2625 Cumberland Parkway, Suite 485
Atlanta, GA 30339
(770) 433-8330
Contact: Mr. Richard Holland
Recruiting Specialty: General

Management Search International
200 Galleria Parkway NW, Suite 1610
Atlanta, GA 30339
(770) 951-1208
Recruiting Specialty: Construction, plastics, and manufacturing

Marcomm Connection, Inc.
3355 Lenox Road, Suite 750
Atlanta, GA 30326
(404) 262-1022
Contact: Ms. Lorice Bland
Minimum Salary Placed: $25,000
Recruiting Specialty: Marketing and communications

Matrix Resources, Inc.
115 Perimeter Center Place, Suite 1099
Atlanta, GA 30346
(770) 393-9933
Contact: Ms. Emily Ingram
Minimum Salary Placed: $25,000
Recruiting Specialty: Data processing

McHale & Associates
5064 Roswell Road NE
Atlanta, GA 30342
(404) 252-9020
Recruiting Specialty: General

Jon McRae & Associates, Inc.
1930 North Druid Hills Road NE,
 Suite 200
Atlanta, GA 30319
(404) 325-3252
Contact: Mr. O. Jon McRae
Recruiting Specialty: Finance

Med Pro Personnel, Inc.
1955 Cliff Valley Way, Suite 116
Atlanta, GA 30329
(404) 633-8280
Minimum Salary Placed: $35,000
Recruiting Specialty: Medical and physicians

Mercer Group Inc.
990 Hammond Drive NE, Suite 510
Atlanta, GA 30328
(770) 551- 0403
Contact: Mr. Jim Mercer
Minimum Salary Placed: $50,000
Recruiting Specialty: Local government

Mirus Resources
35 Glenlake Parkway NE
Atlanta, GA 30328
(770) 393-2551
Contact: Ms. Robin Stevens
Minimum Salary Placed: $25,000
Recruiting Specialty: High technology

More Personnel Services, Inc.
4501 Circle 75 Parkway, Suite A-1190
Atlanta, GA 30339
(770) 955-0885
Minimum Salary Placed: $25,000
Recruiting Specialty: General

National Personnel Recruiters
6520 Powers Ferry Road NW, Suite 150
Atlanta, GA 30339
(770) 955-4221
Contact: Mr. J. Haly
Minimum Salary Placed: $25,000
Recruiting Specialty: Sales, food manufacturing and retail

Norrell Financial Staffing
3535 Piedmont Road NE
Atlanta, GA 30305
(404) 240-3816
Contact: Mr. Andy MacLean
Minimum Salary Placed: $25,000
Recruiting Specialty: Accounting and finance

North Group
1925 Century Blvd. NE, Suite 4
Atlanta, GA 30345
(404) 325-3110
Recruiting Specialty: Executive search for
data and communication

Omega Executive Search
2033 Monroe Drive
Atlanta, GA 30324
(404) 873-2000
Contact: Mr. D. Dorries
Minimum Salary Placed: $25,000
Recruiting Specialty: Hospitality

Packaged Solutions
2 Piedmont Center, Suite 300
Atlanta, GA 30305
(770) 671-1107
Contact: Mr. Jerry Paine
Recruiting Specialty: Information technology

Perimeter Placement, Inc.
24 Perimeter Center East, Suite 2417
Atlanta, GA 30346
(770) 393-0000
Minimum Salary Placed: $25,000
Recruiting Specialty: General

Personnel Opportunities Inc.
5064 Roswell Road NW, Suite D301
Atlanta, GA 30342
(404) 252-9484
Minimum Salary Placed: $25,000
Recruiting Specialty: General

Richard Peterson & Associates, Inc.
5064 Roswell Road, Suite C-201
Atlanta, GA 30342
(404) 256-1661
Contact: Mr. Richard Peterson
Minimum Salary Placed: $35,000
Recruiting Specialty: General

Phoenix Partners, Inc.
5600 Roswell Road NE, Suite 280
Atlanta, GA 30342
(404) 250-1133
Contact: Mr. Donald Addington
Recruiting Specialty: High Technology

Physicians Pro Tem
1000 Abernathy Road NE
Atlanta, GA 30328
(770) 698-0200
Contact: Ms. Naomi Meadows
Minimum Salary Placed: $25,000
Recruiting Specialty: Healthcare

Proquest Inc.
77 East Andrews Drive, Suite 184
Atlanta, GA 30305
(404) 239-0480
Contact: Mr. Donald Powell
Minimum Salary Placed: $50,000
Recruiting Specialty: Operations manage-
ment and medical products manufacturing

RDR Associates
3436 Breton Circle
Atlanta, GA 30319
(404) 843-0263
Contact: Mr. Rod Deremer
Recruiting Specialty: Healthcare

Rannou and Associates
1900 The Exchange NW
Atlanta, GA 30339
(770) 956-8225
Contact: Mr. Frank Rannou
Minimum Salary Placed: $25,000
Recruiting Specialty: Corrugated

Paul Ray & Berndtson
191 Peachtree Street, NE Suite 3800
Atlanta, GA 30303
(404) 215-4600
Recruiting Specialty: Computers

P J Reda & Associates
1955 Cliff Valley Way NE, Suite 117
Atlanta, GA 30329
(404) 325-8812
Recruiting Specialty: Restaurant management

Retail Executive Placement Services
5901-A Peachtree Dunwoody Road,
  Suite 498
Atlanta, GA 30328
(770) 396-9114
Contact: Mr. John Weiss
Minimum Salary Placed: $30,000
Recruiting Specialty: Retail

Retail Executive Search
2295 Parklake Drive NE
Atlanta, GA 30345
(770) 938-6260
Contact: Ms. J. Martinez
Recruiting Specialty: Retail

The Reynolds Group, Inc.
2323 Dunwoody Crossing, Suite E
Atlanta, GA 30338
(770) 454-8272
Contact: Mr. Jerry Reynolds
Minimum Salary Placed: $40,000
Recruiting Specialty: General

Rita Corporation
5600 Glenridge Drive NE, Suite 170W
Atlanta, GA 30342
(404) 250-3760
Contact: Ms. Rita Johnson
Minimum Salary Placed: $50,000
Recruiting Specialty: General

Romac International
3 Ravinia Drive NE
Atlanta, GA 30346
(770) 604-3880
Contact: Mr. Gary Campbell
Minimum Salary Placed: $25,000
Recruiting Specialty: Accounting and data processing

Rowland Mountain and Associates
4 Executive Park East, Suite 100
Atlanta, GA 30329
(404) 325-2189
Minimum Salary Placed: $25,000
Recruiting Specialty: Sales

Russell Reynolds Associates, Inc.
50 Hurt Plaza, Suite 600
Atlanta, GA 30303
(770) 577-3000
Contact: Mr. Joseph Spence
Minimum Salary Placed: $100,000
Recruiting Specialty: General

Sales Consultants
5901-C Peachtree-Dunwoody Road,
  Suite 370
Atlanta, GA 30328
(404) 394-1300
Contact: Mr. Jeff Ram
Minimum Salary Placed: $20,000
Recruiting Specialty: Sales

Salesforce
3294 Woodrow Way NE
Atlanta, GA 30319
(404) 252-8566
Contact: Mr. Fred Shankweiler
Minimum Salary Placed: $25,000
Recruiting Specialty: Sales

Schuyler, Frye & Baker, Inc.
1100 Abernathy Road NE, Suite 1825
Atlanta, GA 30328
(770) 804-1996
Contact: Mr. Lambert Schuyler
Minimum Salary Placed: $75,000
Recruiting Specialty: General and education

Search Group Capital Inc.
3131 Piedmont Road NE
Atlanta, GA 30305
(404) 231-0088
Contact: Mr. Keith Fedder
Minimum Salary Placed: $25,000
Recruiting Specialty: Finance and brokerages

Shoemaker & Association
1862 Independence Square, Suite A
Atlanta, GA 30338
(770) 395-7225
Contact: Mr. Larry Shoemaker
Minimum Salary Placed: $60,000
Recruiting Specialty: General

Arthur Sloan and Associates
8283 Dunwoody Place, Northridge 400
Atlanta, GA 30358
(770) 393-1040
Contact: Mr. Arthur Sloan
Minimum Salary Placed: $25,000
Recruiting Specialty: Accounting, finance, tax and auditing

James F. Smith & Associates
4651 Roswell Road NE, Suite B102
Atlanta, GA 30342
(404) 256-6408
Contact: Mr. James Smith
Minimum Salary Placed: $30,000
Recruiting Specialty: General

Source EDP
4170 NE Ashford Dunwoody Road,
  Suite 285
Atlanta, GA 30319
(404) 255-2045
Contact: Mr. Tom Freeh
Recruiting Specialty: Computers

Special Counsel
1201 West Peachtree Street, Suite 4830
Atlanta, GA 30309
(404) 872-6672
Contact: Ms. Judith Serio
Recruiting Specialty: Legal

Specialty Employment Group
7390 Twin Branch Road
Atlanta, GA 30328
(770) 399-9350
Minimum Salary Placed: $25,000
Recruiting Specialty: Travel industry

Spencer Stuart
1201 West Peachtree Street, Suite 3230
Atlanta, GA 30309
(404) 892-2800
Contact: Mr. William Reeves
Minimum Salary Placed: $75,000
Recruiting Specialty: General

Stuart Compton Associates
1355 Peachtree, Suite 104
Atlanta, GA 30309
(404) 872-7600
Contact: Mr. Richard Gallow
Minimum Salary Placed: $60,000
Recruiting Specialty: General

Thalatta Corporation
P.O. Box 76643
Atlanta, GA 30358
(770) 396-1725
Contact: Mr. Wallace Webb
Minimum Salary Placed: $50,000
Recruiting Specialty: General

Tyler & Company
1000 Abernathy Road NE, Suite 1400
Atlanta, GA 30328
(770) 396-3939
Contact: Mr. J. Larry Tyler
Minimum Salary Placed: $60,000
Recruiting Specialty: Physicians and
healthcare

Vickers Chambliss Managed Search
3343 Peachtree Road NE
Atlanta, GA 30326
(404) 365-0377
Contact: Mr. Vickers Chambliss
Minimum Salary Placed: $40,000
Recruiting Specialty: Healthcare

Ward Howell International, Inc.
3350 Peachtree Road NE, Suite 1600
Atlanta, GA 30326
(404) 261-6532
Contact: Mr. Ernest Taylor
Minimum Salary Placed: $75,000
Recruiting Specialty: General

R. A. Wells Company
P.O. Box 723-232
Atlanta, GA 31139
(770) 424-8493
Contact: Mr. Robert Wells
Minimum Salary Placed: $30,000
Recruiting Specialty: Packaging

Whittaker & Associates, Inc.
2675 Cumberland Parkway
Suite 263, Atlanta, GA 30339
(770) 434-3779
Contact: Ms. Millie Boatman
Minimum Salary Placed: $30,000
Recruiting Specialty: Food, meat and
dairy products in production

Anne Williams and Associates
3475 Lenox Road NE, Suite 400
Atlanta, GA 30326
(404) 266-2663
Contact: Ms. Anne Williams
Minimum Salary Placed: $25,000
Recruiting Specialty: Insurance, legal and
office support

Worth Group
1925 Century Boulevard NE
Atlanta, GA 30345
(404) 325-3050
Contact: Mr. Brett Buckwald
Minimum Salary Placed: $25,000
Recruiting Specialty: Data processing
and telecommunications

Zay & Company
1360 NE Peachtree Street, Suite 1740
Atlanta, GA 30309
(404) 876-9986
Contact: Mr. Thomas Zay
Minimum Salary Placed: $75,000
Recruiting Specialty: General

AUGUSTA

Dunhill of Augusta, Inc.
801 Broad Street, Suite 411
Augusta, GA 30901
(706) 722-5741
Contact: Mr. Frederick Gehle
Recruiting Specialty: General

MAU, Inc.
500 Hatcher Building
501 Greene Street
Augusta, GA 30901
(706) 722-6806
Minimum Salary Placed: $25,000
Recruiting Specialty: Accounting, engineering and technical

Sizemore Personnel Services
1369 Reynolds Street
Augusta, GA 30901
(706) 724-5629
Minimum Salary Placed: $20,000
Recruiting Specialty: General

BIG CANOE

The Castle Group
665 Big Canoe
Big Canoe, GA 30143
(706) 579-1333
Minimum Salary Placed: $25,000
Recruiting Specialty: Engineering and marketing

BRUNSWICK

Career Placements
777 Gloucester Street, Suite 204
Brunswick, GA 31520
(912) 264-3401
Contact: Ms. Pam McGeachy
Minimum Salary Placed: $25,000
Recruiting Specialty: General

CANYERS

Oliver Search
P.O. Box 81092
Canyers, GA 30208
(770) 760-7661
Contact: Mr. Tim Oliver
Minimum Salary Placed: $25,000
Recruiting Specialty: Food industry

COLUMBUS

Access Career Associates
P.O. Box 8022
Columbus, GA 31908
(706) 322-9699
Minimum Salary Placed: $25,000
Recruiting Specialty: General

Management Recruiters
233 12th Street, Suite 818A
Columbus, GA 31901
(706) 571-9611
Contact: Mr. Mike Silverstein
Recruiting Specialty: EDP, MIS, and data programming

Southern Employment SVC
5617 Princeton Avenue
Columbus, GA 31904
(706) 327-6533

Recruiting Specialty: Programmers, accountants and office support

COMMERCE

Chandler Consultants
P.O. Box 741
Commerce, GA 30529
(706) 335-7994
Contact: Mr. Harvey Chandler
Minimum Salary Placed: $25,000
Recruiting Specialty: Insurance

CUMMING

Christou and Associates, Inc.
6530 Crossroads Road
Cumming, GA 30131
(770) 887-9877
Contact: Ms. Anne Marie Christou
Minimum Salary Placed: $25,000
Recruiting Specialty: Data processing

Management Recruiters
600 Peachtree Parkway, Suite 108
Cumming, GA 30131
(770) 889-5250
Contact: Mr. Dan Barrett
Recruiting Specialty: General

DAHLONEGA

William M. Halderson Associates
P.O. Box 566
Dahlonega, GA 30533
(706) 864-5800
Contact: Mr. William Halderson
Minimum Salary Placed: $25,000
Recruiting Specialty: Medical and healthcare

DALTON

Management Recruiters
415 East Walnut Avenue, Suite 314
Dalton, GA 30721
(706) 226-8550
Contact: Ms. Verna Webb
Recruiting Specialty: Plastics

DAWSONVILLE

Applied Search Association, Inc.
P.O. Box 1207
Dawsonville, GA 30534
(706) 265-2530
Contact: Mr. Richard Rockwell
Minimum Salary Placed: $30,000
Recruiting Specialty: General

DECATUR

R.A. Clark Consulting
823 N. Superior Avenue
Decatur, GA 30033
(404) 982-0495
Contact: Mr. Richard Clark
Minimum Salary Placed: $25,000
Recruiting Specialty: Human resources
and some general

Healthcare Management Resource
1894 Ludovie Lane, Suite 200
Decatur, GA 30033
(404) 329-9314
Contact: Ms. S. Locktov
Minimum Salary Placed: $25,000
Recruiting Specialty: Healthcare

Medical Care Associates
3500 Kensington Road
Decatur, GA 30032
(404) 299-6111
Minimum Salary Placed: $25,000
Recruiting Specialty: Medical and nursing

DULUTH

C.G. and Associates
P.O. Box 956066
Duluth, GA 30136
(770) 564-0031
Contact: Ms. Connie Gerdts
Minimum Salary Placed: $25,000
Recruiting Specialty: Sales in electrical
and technical industries

Harry Fields Search
P.O. Box 188
Duluth, GA 30136
(770) 495-7334
Minimum Salary Placed: $25,000
Recruiting Specialty: Hospitality

Industry Consultants, Inc.
5805 State Bridge R, Suite G-277
Duluth, GA 30155
(770) 623-9400
Contact: Mr. Joseph Corey
Minimum Salary Placed: $50,000
Recruiting Specialty: Manufacturing

Management Recruiters
3700 Crestwood Parkway, Suite 320
Duluth, GA 30136
(770) 925-2266
Contact: Mr. David Riggs
Recruiting Specialty: General

National Sales Network Inc.
3761 Venture Drive
Duluth, GA 30136
(770) 813-1040
Recruiting Specialty: Medical and consumer products

WMA Associates
5310 Twillingate Place
Duluth, GA 30136
(770) 729-8268
Contact: Mr. Bill Adams
Minimum Salary Placed: $25,000
Recruiting Specialty: Pulp and paper

DUNWOODY

Brandt and Associates
3 Dunwoody Park
Dunwoody, GA 30338
(770) 399-0490
Contact: Mr. Reggie Bradford
Minimum Salary Placed: $25,000
Recruiting Specialty: Sales and marketing
in consumer products

H.O. Catherman Inc.
4900 Parliament Way
Dunwoody, GA 30338
(770) 394-4727
Contact: Mr. Hal Catherman
Minimum Salary Placed: $25,000
Recruiting Specialty: General

Management Decisions Inc.
1867 Independence Square
Dunwoody, GA 30338
(770) 512-0006
Contact: Ilene
Recruiting Specialty: Data processing

Robert Half International
1816 Independence Square
Dunwoody, GA 30338
(770) 392-0540
Recruiting Specialty: Accounting and
data processing

Wileman and Associates
4720 Chamblee-Dunwoody Road
Dunwoody, GA 30338
(770) 642-4026
Contact: Ms. S. Wileman
Minimum Salary Placed: $25,000
Recruiting Specialty: Insurance

ELLENWOOD

Charlotte Cody Consultants
1487 Panola Road
Ellenwood, GA 30049
(770) 981-0431
Contact: Ms. Charlotte Cody
Minimum Salary Placed: $20,000
Recruiting Specialty: Retail

FAYETTEVILLE

The CARVIR Group
P.O. Box 125
Fayetteville, GA 30214
(770) 460-8272
Contact: Mr. Virgil Fludd
Minimum Salary Placed: $40,000
Recruiting Specialty: General

Excel Executive Recruiters
140 Wynchase Lane
Fayetteville, GA 30215
(770) 719-9745
Contact: Kevin
Recruiting Specialty: Telecommunication
and high technology

GAINESVILLE

Lanier Employment Services
P.O. Box 699
631 Spring Street
Gainesville, GA 30503
(770) 536-2884
Minimum Salary Placed: $20,000
Recruiting Specialty: General

Snelling Personnel Services
502 S. Enota Drive NE
Gainesville, GA 30501
(770) 534-0001
Contact: Ms. J. Harrison
Recruiting Specialty: General

HAMILTON

Ward and Associates
851 W. Cedar Drive
Hamilton, GA 31811
(706) 596-0575
Contact: Ms. Barbara Ward
Minimum Salary Placed: $25,000
Recruiting Specialty: General

KENNESAW

Cubbage and Associates
3590 Cherokee Street
Kennesaw, GA 30144
(770) 424-6361
Contact: Mr. R. Cubbage
Minimum Salary Placed: $25,000
Recruiting Specialty: General

Knight and Associates
P.O. Box 248
Kennesaw, GA 30144
(770) 423-9836
Contact: Ms. Pat Knight
Minimum Salary Placed: $25,000
Recruiting Specialty: Environmental

Nell J. Rich and Associates
2864 Jim Owens Road NW
Kennesaw, GA 30144
(770) 974-7567
Contact: Mr. Nell Rich
Minimum Salary Placed: $20,000
Recruiting Specialty: General

LA GRANGE

Comprehensive Search
316 South Lewis Street
La Grange, GA 30240
(706) 884-3232
Contact: Mr. Jeffrey Brown
Minimum Salary Placed: $25,000
Recruiting Specialty: Home furnishings

Dunhill Search of La Grange, Inc.
301 Broome Street, Suite 100
La Grange, GA 30240
(706) 882-0497
Contact: Mr. Dee Woodward
Recruiting Specialty: General

LAWRENCEVILLE

Hillary Group
1550 Ashwood Way
Lawrenceville, GA 30243
(770) 338-4555
Minimum Salary Placed: $25,000
Recruiting Specialty: Medical

Pete Spain Associates
1131 Heather Winn Circle
Lawrenceville, GA 30243
(770) 995-9095
Contact: Mr. Pete Spain
Minimum Salary Placed: $25,000
Recruiting Specialty: Textiles and apparel

Tanner Personnel
698 Highway 120
Lawrenceville, GA 30245
(770) 682-5646
Minimum Salary Placed: $20,000
Recruiting Specialty: Medical

LILBURN

Emerson & Company
449 Pleasant Hill Road, Suite 315
Lilburn, GA 30247
(770) 564-3215
Contact: Mr. Harold Popham
Minimum Salary Placed: $25,000
Recruiting Specialty: Manufacturing

Thomas Executive Search
713 Lanford Springs Drive SW
Lilburn, GA 30247
(770) 381-1181
Contact: Mr. Tom Gryzinski
Minimum Salary Placed: $25,000
Recruiting Specialty: General

LITHIA SPRINGS

Management Recruiters of Atlanta West, Inc.
685 Thorton Way
Lithia Springs, GA 30057
(404) 948-5560
Contact: Mr. Gene Brown
Recruiting Specialty: General

LITHONIA

Atlantek Network Inc.
940 Timberclair Way, Suite 200
Lithonia, GA 30058
(770) 484-8104
Recruiting Specialty: Computer and tele-communications

MARIETTA

Bradshaw and Associates
1850 Parkway Place, Suite 420
Marietta, GA 30067
(770) 426-5600
Contact: Ms. Jennifer Bobbitt
Minimum Salary Placed: $30,000
Recruiting Specialty: General

Dixie Search Association
501 Village Trace, Building 9
Marietta, GA 30067
(770) 252-8800
Contact: Mr. Clifford Fill
Minimum Salary Placed: $30,000
Recruiting Specialty: Food and beverages

Eden Group Inc.
1837 Mallard Lake Drive
Marietta, GA 30068
(770) 640-9577
Contact: Ms. Suzanne Fehr
Minimum Salary Placed: $40,000
Recruiting Specialty: Investments, brokering and sales

Eggleston Consulting International
500 Brookhollow Circle
Marietta, GA 30067
(770) 804-1212
Contact: Mr. G. Dudley Eggleston
Minimum Salary Placed: $100,000
Recruiting Specialty: Real estate

Bruce Eide and Associates
256 Woods Edge Court
Marietta, GA 30068
(770) 977-5800
Contact: Mr. Bruce Eide
Minimum Salary Placed: $25,000
Recruiting Specialty: General

Engineering Placement
2715 Bridgegate Cove
Marietta, GA 30068
(770) 565-2346
Contact: Mr. Paul Banks
Minimum Salary Placed: $30,000
Recruiting Specialty: Manufacturing, including engineering, cost accounting and sales

Evans & James Executive Search
P.O. Box 862232
Marietta, GA 30062
(770) 992-4299
Contact: Mr. Jim Ingram
Recruiting Specialty: Packaging, plastics, coatings, adhesives and machinery

FSA, Inc.
P.O. Box 448
Marietta, GA 30061
(770) 427-8813
Contact: Ron
Minimum Salary Placed: $25,000
Recruiting Specialty: Insurance

Graphic Resources
2265 Roswell Road, Suite 100
Marietta, GA 30062
(770) 509-2295
Contact: Mr. Jeff Gord
Minimum Salary Placed: $25,000
Recruiting Specialty: Multi-media, packaging and printing

W.L. Handler & Associates
3200 Windy Hill Road, Suite 1410
Marietta, GA 30067
(770) 850-6220
Contact: Mr. William Handler
Minimum Salary Placed: $50,000
Recruiting Specialty: Technical disciplines

Harmon Double & Company
P.O. Box 672642
Marietta, GA 30067
(770) 977-1378
Contact: Mr. Jerry Harmon
Minimum Salary Placed: $30,000
Recruiting Specialty: MIS, FIS and data
communications

**Healthcare Recruiters/Executive
Resource Group**
2470 Windy Hill Road
Marietta, GA 30067
(770) 984-0094
Contact: Ms. P. Zacharchuck
Minimum Salary Placed: $25,000
Recruiting Specialty: Healthcare

Home Health and Hospital Recruiters
2858 Johnson Ferry Road, Suite 250
Marietta, GA 30062
(770) 993-2828
Contact: Mr. Barry Savransky
Minimum Salary Placed: $25,000
Recruiting Specialty: Healthcare

David Houser and Associates
660 Village Trace NE
Marietta, GA 30067
(770) 951-1335
Contact: Mr. David Houser
Minimum Salary Placed: $25,000
Recruiting Specialty: General

Huey Gerald Associates
3636 Autumn Ridge Parkway, Suite 100
Marietta, GA 30066
(770) 973-8944
Minimum Salary Placed: $25,000
Recruiting Specialty: Data processing

Hygun Group Incorporated
3020 Roswell Road
Marietta, GA 30062
(770) 973-0838
Minimum Salary Placed: $25,000
Recruiting Specialty: General

JSA, Inc.
2900 Dalk Road, Suite 700-290
Marietta, GA 30067
(770) 973-7771
Contact: Mr. Jim Scapin
Minimum Salary Placed: $70,000
Recruiting Specialty: Data processing
and engineering

Kentshire Group
133 Johnson Ferry Road
Marietta, GA 30068
(770) 952-4555
Contact: Mr. Leon Waller
Minimum Salary Placed: $25,000
Recruiting Specialty: General

Lowderman and Haney
3939 Roswell Road NE
Marietta, GA 30062
(770) 977-3020
Contact: Mr. D. Haney
Recruiting Specialty: Healthcare

Malcom Group
1973 Sherwood Drive
Marietta, GA 30067
(770) 565-5213
Contact: Mr. C. Malcom
Minimum Salary Placed: $25,000
Recruiting Specialty: Insurance

Management Recruiters
3115 Roswell Road, Suite 205
Marietta, GA 30062
(770) 509-9055
Contact: Mr. Lawrence Dougherty
Minimum Salary Placed: $45,000
Recruiting Specialty: MIS, logistics, transportation and distribution

Management Recruiters
274 North Marietta Parkway NE, Suite C
Marietta, GA 30060
(770) 423-1443
Contact: Mr. Jim Kirby
Recruiting Specialty: General

Omni Resources
1950 Spectrum Circle, Suite A-400
Marietta, GA 30067
(770) 988-2788
Contact: Ms. Judy Paul
Minimum Salary Placed: $30,000
Recruiting Specialty: Sales

Personalized Management Associates, Inc.
1950 Spectrum Circle, Suite B-310
Marietta, GA 30067
(770) 916-1668
Contact: Bill or Bonnie Lins
Minimum Salary Placed: $25,000
Recruiting Specialty: Hospitality, foods, and retail

Peters Engineering Environmental
2155 Denson Lane
Marietta, GA 30060
(770) 419-2594
Contact: Ms. Cheryl Peters
Minimum Salary Placed: $25,000
Recruiting Specialty: Engineering and environmental

Phoenix Group
2619 Sandy Plains Road
Marietta, GA 30066
(770) 971-5430
Contact: Mr. Neal Smith
Minimum Salary Placed: $25,000
Recruiting Specialty: Data processing

P.J. Reda & Associates, Inc.
1090 Northchase Parkway South,
 Suite 200
Marietta, GA 30067
(770) 984-3238
Contact: Ms. Pat Reda
Recruiting Specialty: General

Nell Rich and Associates
P.O. Box 6363
Marietta, GA 30065
(770) 974-7567
Contact: Mr. Nell Rich
Minimum Salary Placed: $25,000
Recruiting Specialty: Construction, finance and real estate development

Russell Rose and Associates
141 Village Parkway NE, Building 5
Marietta, GA 30067
(770) 952-0081
Contact: Mr. M. Mauldin
Minimum Salary Placed: $25,000
Recruiting Specialty: General

Search Atlanta Inc.
3200 Windy Hill Road
Marietta, GA 30067
(770) 984-0880
Contact: Mr. Bill Parks
Recruiting Specialty: Engineering

Windward Executive Search, Inc.
58 South Park Square, Suite B
Marietta, GA 30060
(770) 425-6788
Contact: Mr. Tom Arnette
Minimum Salary Placed: $45,000
Recruiting Specialty: Technical and sales
disciplines in paper mill manufacturing

Steve Wyman and Associates
4201 Fairgreen Terrace NE
Marietta, GA 30068
(770) 977-4410
Contact: Mr. Steve Wyman
Minimum Salary Placed: $40,000
Recruiting Specialty: Radio and television

MORROW

President Group
1590 Adamson Parkway
Morrow, GA 30260
(404) 762-5300
Contact: Mr. Ormond Curl
Recruiting Specialty: General

NEWMAN

LCM Associates
30 Spring Ridge Court
Newman, GA 30265
(770) 254-8777
Contact: Ms. Terry Michalewicz
Minimum Salary Placed: $25,000
Recruiting Specialty: Actuaries

NORCROSS

Barrington Associates Ltd.
3949 Holcomb Bridge Road
Norcross, GA 30092
(770) 447-0100
Minimum Salary Placed: $25,000
Recruiting Specialty: General

Brannon and Tully
3690 Holcomb Bridge Road, Suite 100
Norcross, GA 30092
(770) 447-8773
Minimum Salary Placed: $25,000
Recruiting Specialty: Data processing

Bridgers, Goeltz and Associates
5335 Triangle Parkway, Suite 510
Norcross, GA 30092
(770) 368-9835
Contact: Mr. J. Bridgers
Minimum Salary Placed: $25,000
Recruiting Specialty: Insurance

Cella Associates of Atlanta
4045 Wetherburn Way, Suite 4
Norcross, GA 30092
(770) 242-3040
Contact: Mr. Jim Compton
Minimum Salary Placed: $25,000
Recruiting Specialty: Food industry

Data Processing Services, Inc.
5855 Jimmy Carter Boulevard, Suite 260
Norcross, GA 30071
(770) 368-1300
Minimum Salary Placed: $25,000
Recruiting Specialty: Data processing

Engineering Group
3000 Langford Road, Suite 700
Norcross, GA 30071
(770) 441-2729
Contact: Mr. J. May
Minimum Salary Placed: $30,000
Recruiting Specialty: Engineering and other technical disciplines

Forbes Enterprises
6045 Atlantic Boulevard
Norcross, GA 30071
(770) 662-1547
Contact: Ms. Kathy Forbes
Minimum Salary Placed: $25,000
Recruiting Specialty: Computers and medical

Fortune Personnel Consultants
6825 Jimmy Carter Boulevard
Norcross, GA 30071
(770) 246-9757
Contact: Mr. J. Deavours
Minimum Salary Placed: $30,000
Recruiting Specialty: General

The Horizon Healthcare Group, Inc.
3150 Holcomb Bridge Road, Suite 310
Norcross, GA 30071
(770) 417-2160
Contact: Mr. Joe Stork
Recruiting Specialty: Physicians

IMCOR, Inc.
5431 Clinchfield Trail
Norcross, GA 30092
(770) 449-9069
Contact: Mr. Joseph Negley
Minimum Salary Placed: $75,000
Recruiting Specialty: Senior level temporary assignments; general

Management Decisions Inc.
3060 Holcomb Bridge Road, Suite J
Norcross, GA 30071
(770) 416-7949
Recruiting Specialty: Information technology professionals

Medical Employment Group
4056 Wetherburn Way, Suite 1
Norcross, GA 30092
(770) 662-8700
Minimum Salary Placed: $35,000
Recruiting Specialty: Medical

Northside Personnel, Inc.
5151 Brook Hollow Parkway NW, Suite 140
Norcross, GA 30071
(770) 368-8400
Minimum Salary Placed: $25,000
Recruiting Specialty: Medical

Peachtree Peopleware, Inc.
One Meca Way
Norcross, GA 30093
(770) 564-5585
Minimum Salary Placed: $25,000
Recruiting Specialty: General

Pro Source Recruiting
P.O. Box 922275
Norcross, GA 30092
Contact: Mr. Tom Williams
Recruiting Specialty: I/T, sales, aerospace, factory automation, food, personnel

Sanford Rose Association
3525 Holcomb Bridge Road, Suite 2B
Norcross, GA 30092
(770) 449-7200

Contact: Mr. Donald Patrick
Minimum Salary Placed: $45,000
Recruiting Specialty: Telecommunications

Carrie York Associates
5696 Peachtree Parkway
Norcross, GA 30092
(770) 263-3747
Contact: Ms. Carrie York
Minimum Salary Placed: $20,000
Recruiting Specialty: Accounting

PERRY

Management Recruiters
P.O. Box 1455
Perry, GA 31069
(912) 988-4444
Contact: Mr. Tom Baird
Recruiting Specialty: Apparel and home furnishings

POWDER SPRINGS

Gerard and Associates
400 Collegiate Drive
Powder Springs, GA 30073
(770) 514-8840
Contact: Mr. Ed Gerard
Minimum Salary Placed: $25,000
Recruiting Specialty: Legal

RICHMOND HILL

Sales Consultants
40 Ford Avenue, Unit 1, Suite B
Richmond Hill, GA 31327
(912) 756-5060
Contact: Mr. David Pearl
Minimum Salary Placed: $20,000
Recruiting Specialty: Sales

RIVERDALE

Career Image Inc.
8060 Woodlake Drive
Riverdale, GA 30274
(770) 473-4741
Contact: Mr. Buddy Day
Minimum Salary Placed: $25,000
Recruiting Specialty: Retail

IMPD Associates, Inc.
6255 Georgia Highway 85, Suite 2-A
Riverdale, GA 30274
(770) 997-4637
Recruiting Specialty: Medical and dental

Management Recruiters
6724 Church Street, Suite 5
Riverdale, GA 30274
(770) 991-1703
Contact: Mr. Ron Wise
Recruiting Specialty: General

ROSWELL

Barton Executive Search
150 Willow Brook Drive
Roswell, GA 30076
(770) 518-9443
Contact: Mr. Tom Barton
Minimum Salary Placed: $25,000
Recruiting Specialty: General

Beall & Company, Inc.
535 Colonial Park Drive
Roswell, GA 30075
(770) 992-0900
Contact: Mr. Charles Beall
Minimum Salary Placed: $60,000
Recruiting Specialty: High technology
and some general

Cubbage and Associates
11285 Elkins Road
Roswell, GA 30076
(770) 442-8870
Contact: Mr. Larry Turner
Minimum Salary Placed: $25,000
Recruiting Specialty: General

Emerging Technology Search
1080 Holcomb Bridge Road
Building 100, Suite 300
Roswell, GA 30076
(770) 643-4994
Minimum Salary Placed: $25,000
Recruiting Specialty: Communications
and data processing

Howie & Associates, Inc.
875 Old Roswell Road, F-100
Roswell, GA 30076
(770) 998-0099
Contact: Ms. Ellen Brown
Recruiting Specialty: Data processing

Intersource, Ltd.
72 Sloan Street
Roswell, GA 30075
(770) 645-0015
Minimum Salary Placed: $25,000
Recruiting Specialty: Human resources

Management Recruiters
30 Woodstock Street
Roswell, GA 30075
(770) 998-1555
Contact: Mr. Art Katz
Recruiting Specialty: Healthcare, foods
and MIS

McLaughlin Group
3812 Glengarry Way
Roswell, GA 30076
(770) 640-6722
Contact: Mr. Paul McLaughlin
Minimum Salary Placed: $25,000
Recruiting Specialty: General

Peachtree Executive Search
10930 Crabapple Road, Suite 6
Roswell, GA 30075
(770) 998-2272
Contact: Mr. Mark Snoddy
Minimum Salary Placed: $70,000
Recruiting Specialty: General

Plemmons Associates, Inc.
535-B Colonial Park Drive, Suite 202
Roswell, GA 30075
(770) 993-6073
Contact: Mr. Patrick Plemmons
Recruiting Specialty: Healthcare

RCI-Horton International
33 Sloan Street
Roswell, GA 30075
(770) 640-1533
Contact: Mr. David Reddick
Minimum Salary Placed: $70,000
Recruiting Specialty: General

Sondra Search
P.O. Box 101
Roswell, GA 30077
(770) 552-1910
Contact: Sondra
Minimum Salary Placed: $25,000
Recruiting Specialty: Sales

Tennant and Associates
11285 Elkins Road
Roswell, GA 30076
(770) 740-1609
Contact: Mr. Ken Tennant
Minimum Salary Placed: $25,000
Recruiting Specialty: Computers and tele-communications

TOAR Consulting Inc.
1176 Grimes Bridge Road, Suite 200
Roswell, GA 30075
(770) 993-7663
Contact: Mr. Herschal Hill
Recruiting Specialty: General

SANDY SPRINGS

Dorothy Long Search
6065 Roswell Road NE
Sandy Springs, GA 30328
(404) 252-3787
Contact: Ms. Dorothy Long
Minimum Salary Placed: $25,000
Recruiting Specialty: General

SAVANNAH

Coastal Employment
409 E. Montgomery Crossroads
Savannah, GA 31405
(912) 355-8009
Contact: Ms. G. Padgett
Minimum Salary Placed: $25,000
Recruiting Specialty: General

Fortune Personnel Consultants
7 E. Congress Street, Suite 712
Savannah, GA 31401
(912) 233-4556

Contact: Mr. C. Smith
Minimum Salary Placed: $25,000
Recruiting Specialty: General

Management Recruiters
2431 Habersham Street, 2nd Floor
Savannah, GA 31401
(912) 232-0132
Contact: Mr. Ron McElhaney
Recruiting Specialty: Chemicals

QVS International
349 Mall Boulevard, Suite 217
Savannah, GA 31406
(912) 353-7773
Contact: Mr. B. Cooper
Minimum Salary Placed: $50,000
Recruiting Specialty: General and management consulting

Sales Consultants
2431 Habersham Street
Savannah, GA 31401
(912) 232-0132
Contact: Mr. Cal Bridgett
Minimum Salary Placed: $20,000
Recruiting Specialty: Sales

Smith and Associates
5513 Woodland Drive
Savannah, GA 31406
(912) 354-7472
Contact: Mr. Ray Smith
Minimum Salary Placed: $75,000
Recruiting Specialty: Healthcare, special nursing and home care

SMYRNA

Management Consultants Group
2400 Lake Park Drive, Suite 170
Smyrna, GA 30080
(770) 438-1177

Contact: Mr. S. Bliss
Minimum Salary Placed: $25,000
Recruiting Specialty: General

STATESBORO

Rivers End Associates
27 S. Zetterower, Suite C
Statesboro, GA 30458
(912) 489-5801
Contact: Mr. Bryan Bree
Minimum Salary Placed: $30,000
Recruiting Specialty: Hospitality

STONE MOUNTAIN

Claremont-Branan, Inc.
1298 Rockbridge Road, Suite B
Stone Mountain, GA 30087
(770) 925-2915
Contact: Mr. Phil Collins
Minimum Salary Placed: $40,000
Recruiting Specialty: Architecture and engineering

TUCKER

Atlanta Division of Software
2163 Northlake Parkway, Suite 100
Tucker, GA 30084
(770) 934-5138
Contact: Mr. L. Okeson
Minimum Salary Placed: $25,000
Recruiting Specialty: Programmers and analysts in software

Corporate Plus
3145 Tucker-Norcross Road, Suite 206
Tucker, GA 30084
(770) 934-5101
Minimum Salary Placed: $25,000
Recruiting Specialty: General

Leader Institute, Inc.
340 Interstate North Highway, Suite 250
Atlanta, GA 30339
(770) 984-2700
Contact: Mr. Richard Zabor
Recruiting Specialty: Engineering, MIA and high technology

MD Solutions
100 Crescent Centre Parkway, Suite 360
Tucker, GA 30084
(770) 723-3783
Minimum Salary Placed: $50,000
Recruiting Specialty: Healthcare and medical

Software Search
2163 Northlake Parkway, Suite 100
Tucker, GA 30084
(770) 934-5138
Minimum Salary Placed: $40,000
Recruiting Specialty: Computer programming

Summit Group International, Inc.
100 Crescent Centre Parkway, Suite 300
Tucker, GA 30084
(770) 493-1441
Contact: Mr. Dotson Benefield
Minimum Salary Placed: $35,000
Recruiting Specialty: General

WOODSTOCK

Rollins Search Group
216 Parkway 575
Woodstock, GA 30188
(770) 516-6042
Contact: Mr. Jay Rollins
Minimum Salary Placed: $25,000
Recruiting Specialty: Actuaries, insurance and data processing

Search America
180 Plantation Trace
Woodstock, GA 30188
(770) 751-3920
Contact: Mr. Robert Carlisle
Minimum Salary Placed: $25,000
Recruiting Specialty: General

Workman and Associates, Inc.
223 Brolley Woods Drive
Woodstock, GA 30188
(770) 926-8892
Contact: Mr. J. Workman
Minimum Salary Placed: $35,000
Recruiting Specialty: Trust and banking

H A W A I I

AIEA

Maresca and Associates
98-1961 B Kaahumanu
Aiea, HI 96701
(808) 531-0461
Contact: Ms. S. Maresca
Minimum Salary Placed: $70,000
Recruiting Specialty: General

HONOLULU

Associated Employment Service
1141 Union Mall, Suite 41
Honolulu, HI 96812
(808) 537-3381
Contact: Mr. H. Yokoyama
Minimum Salary Placed: $25,000
Recruiting Specialty: General

Beneficial Employment Service
841 Bishop Street, Suite 904
Honolulu, HI 96813
(808) 526-4121
Contact: Ms. K. Yamata
Minimum Salary Placed: $25,000
Recruiting Specialty: General

Dunhill Professional Search
841 Bishop Street, Suite 420
Honolulu, HI 96813
(808) 524-2550
Contact: Ms. Nadine Calizo-Stollenmaier
Minimum Salary Placed: $20,000
Recruiting Specialty: General

James P. Ellis & Associates
700 Richards Street, Suite 2503
Honolulu, HI 96813
(808) 526-3812
Contact: Mr. James Ellis
Minimum Salary Placed: $60,000
Recruiting Specialty: General

Executive Support Hawaii
745 Fort Street, 10th Floor
Honolulu, HI 96813
(808) 521-5911
Contact: Ms. K. Scheffer
Minimum Salary Placed: $25,000
Recruiting Specialty: General

M.J. Freitas Associates Ltd.
P.O. Box 25849
Honolulu, HI 96813
(808) 536-3667
Contact: Mr. M. Freitas
Minimum Salary Placed: $25,000
Recruiting Specialty: General

**Human Resources Management
Hawaii, Inc.**
210 Ward Avenue, Suite 126
Honolulu, HI 96814
(808) 536-3438
Contact: Mr. Mike Elinski
Minimum Salary Placed: $40,000
Recruiting Specialty: MIS, engineering,
and some general

Lam Associates
P.O. Box 75113, Eaton Square
Honolulu, HI 96836
(808) 947-9815
Contact: Ms. Pat Lambrecht
Minimum Salary Placed: $45,000
Recruiting Specialty: Technical disci-
plines in construction, manufacturing and
environmental

Management Recruiters

33 South King Street, Suite 514
Honolulu, HI 96813
(808) 524-1190
Contact: Mr. Paul Reagan
Minimum Salary Placed: $20,000
Recruiting Specialty: General

Management Search and Consulting

1001 Bishop Street, Suite 2450
Honolulu, HI 96813
(808) 533-4423
Contact: Mr. Peter Glick
Minimum Salary Placed: $35,000
Recruiting Specialty: General

Physician Associates

P.O. Box 75113, Eaton Square
Honolulu, HI 96836
(808) 947-9815
Contact: Ms. Pat Lambrecht
Minimum Salary Placed: $30,000
Recruiting Specialty: Healthcare

Robert Half International

733 Bishop Street, Suite 1750
Honolulu, HI 96813
(808) 531-8056
Contact: Mr. J. Elwood
Minimum Salary Placed: $25,000
Recruiting Specialty: Accounting and finance

Sales Consultants

33 S. King Street, Suite 160-M
Honolulu, HI 96813
(808) 521-7828
Contact: Mr. James Morse
Minimum Salary Placed: $20,000
Recruiting Specialty: Sales

•KAMUELA

Murosky & Associates

HCR Suite 1, P.O. Box 101
Kamuela, HI 96743
(808) 882-4001
Contact: Ms. Joan Murosky
Minimum Salary Placed: $75,000
Recruiting Specialty: General

I D A H O

BOISE

Dunhill of Boise
P.O. Box 9142
Boise, ID 83707
(208) 322-4101
Contact: Ms. Joyce Yungeberg
Minimum Salary Placed: $20,000
Recruiting Specialty: General

Horne-Brown International
101 S. Capital Boulevard, Suite 1200
Boise, ID 83702
(208) 344-9004
Contact: Mr. Gene Horne
Minimum Salary Placed: $35,000
Recruiting Specialty: General

Management Recruiters
290 Bobwhite Court, Suite 220
Boise, ID 83706
(208) 336-6770
Contact: Mr. Craig Alexander
Minimum Salary Placed: $20,000
Recruiting Specialty: Engineering

Sales Consultants
290 Bobwhite Court, Suite 220
Boise, ID 83706
(208) 336-6770
Contact: Mr. Craig Alexander
Minimum Salary Placed: $20,000
Recruiting Specialty: Sales

IDAHO FALLS

Robert William James and Associates
1970 E 17th Street, Suite 116
Idaho Falls, ID 83404
(208) 529-2661
Contact: Ms. S. Brouillette
Minimum Salary Placed: $25,000
Recruiting Specialty: General

KELLOG

Management Recruiters
1 Golf Course Road
Kellog, ID 83837
(912) 232-0132
Contact: Mr. Al Ward
Minimum Salary Placed: $20,000
Recruiting Specialty: General

LEWISTON

Robert William James and Associates
1714 G Street
Lewiston, ID 83501
(208) 743-6507
Contact: Mr. Dennis Murphy
Minimum Salary Placed: $25,000
Recruiting Specialty: General

MOSCOW

Finney and Associates
1329 Tamarack Street
Moscow, ID 83843
(208) 882-3500
Contact: Mr. P. Finney
Minimum Salary Placed: $40,000
Recruiting Specialty: Engineering and
plant manufacturing

I L L I N O I S

ALATINE

Sales Consultants
1540 E. Dundee Road, Suite 245
Alatine, IL 60067
(708) 202-0202
Contact: Mr. Brian Roberts
Minimum Salary Placed: $20,000
Recruiting Specialty: Sales

ALBION

Management Recruiters
129 S. 4th Street
Albion, IL 62806
(618) 445-2333
Contact: Ms. Lois Christensen
Minimum Salary Placed: $20,000
Recruiting Specialty: Foods

ALTON

Availability Inc.
659 E. Broadway
Alton, IL 62002
(618) 462-8831
Contact: Mr. L. Hamel
Recruiting Specialty: General

ARLINGTON HEIGHTS

E. J. Ashton & Associates, Ltd.
3125 N. Wilke Road, Suite A
Arlington Heights, IL 60004
(847) 577-7900
Contact: Mr. Edward Ashton
Minimum Salary Placed: $25,000
Recruiting Specialty: Finance and insurance

Baldwin Group
550 W. Campus Drive
Arlington Heights, IL 60004
(847) 394-4303
Contact: Mr. Keith Baldwin
Minimum Salary Placed: $60,000
Recruiting Specialty: General

Dynamic Search Systems, Inc.
3800 N. Wilke Road, Suite 485
Arlington Heights, IL 60004
(847) 259-3444
Contact: Mr. Michael Brindise
Minimum Salary Placed: $15,000
Recruiting Specialty: Computers and MIS

H.T. Associates Inc.
3030 W. Salt Creek Lane, Suite 121
Arlington Heights, IL 60005
(847) 577-0300
Contact: Mr. R. Tabrosky
Minimum Salary Placed: $35,000
Recruiting Specialty: MIS and engineering

Lytle-Miller and Associates Inc.
3800 N. Wilke Road
Arlington Heights, IL 60004
(847) 632-1600
Contact: Mr. Clyde Lytle
Minimum Salary Placed: $25,000
Recruiting Specialty: General

Management Recruiters
3413 North Kennicott, Suite A
Arlington Heights, IL 60004
(847) 590-8880
Contact: Mr. Steve Briody
Minimum Salary Placed: $20,000
Recruiting Specialty: General

Midwest Consulting Corporation
3800 N. Wilke Road
Arlington Heights, IL 60004
(847) 590-5500
Contact: Mr. G. Miller
Recruiting Specialty: Engineering

The Remington Group
666 Dundee Road, Suite 1603
Arlington Heights, IL 60004
(847) 509-4100
Contact: Mr. Al Tennyson
Minimum Salary Placed: $50,000
Recruiting Specialty: Consumer products
and manufacturing

Sales Consultants
413 N. Kennicott Avenue, Suite A
Arlington Heights, IL 60004
(847) 590-8880
Contact: Mr. Steve Briody
Minimum Salary Placed: $20,000
Recruiting Specialty: Sales

Systems Search
2366 Bradshire Court
Arlington Heights, IL 60004
(847) 577-0595
Contact: Mr. Ed Nathan
Minimum Salary Placed: $25,000
Recruiting Specialty: Data processing

Technical Recruiting Consultants
215 N. Arlington Heights Road,
 Suite 102
Arlington Heights, IL 60004
(847) 394-1101
Contact: Mr. Dick Latimer
Recruiting Specialty: MIS and computers

AURORA

Search Consultants
1070 Rainwood Drive
Aurora, IL 60506
(708) 844-0350
Contact: Mr. B. Smith
Minimum Salary Placed: $25,000
Recruiting Specialty: General

BARRINGTON

Adams & Associates International
463 W. Russell Street, Suite D
Barrington, IL 60010
(847) 304-5300
Contact: Mr. Adam Zak
Minimum Salary Placed: $75,000
Recruiting Specialty: General

Dan B. Brockman
P.O. Box 913
Barrington, IL 60011
(847) 382-6015
Contact: Mr. Dan Brockman
Minimum Salary Placed: $35,000
Recruiting Specialty: Engineering and en-
vironmental

Bryant Associates, Inc.
1390 The Point
Barrington, IL 60010
(312) 346-7445
Contact: Mr. Richard Bryant
Minimum Salary Placed: $25,000
Recruiting Specialty: General

The Garms Group
12 Ferndale Road
Barrington, IL 60010
(847) 382-7200

Contact: Mr. Daniel Garms
Minimum Salary Placed: $75,000
Recruiting Specialty: Sales and manufacturing in high technology

Ronald Hanson and Associates
22 E. Dundee Road
Barrington, IL 60010
(847) 304-8882
Contact: Mr. Ron Hanson
Minimum Salary Placed: $25,000
Recruiting Specialty: Insurance

Howe-Weaver, Inc.
P.O. Box 584
Barrington, IL 60011
(847) 382-7870
Contact: Mr. John Weaver
Minimum Salary Placed: $60,000
Recruiting Specialty: Insurance

Huntington Resource
523 W. Old NW Highway, Suite 301
Barrington, IL 60010
(847) 381-8866
Contact: Ms. R. Cooper
Minimum Salary Placed: $25,000
Recruiting Specialty: General

J.D. Limited
881 Bosworth Field
Barrington, IL 60010
(847) 382-6144
Contact: Mr. John DeGiulio
Minimum Salary Placed: $50,000
Recruiting Specialty: Attorneys

Joslin & Associates, Ltd.
291 Deer Trail Court, Suite C-3
Barrington, IL 60010
(847) 304-1100
Contact: Dr. Robert Joslin
Minimum Salary Placed: $40,000
Recruiting Specialty: Technical disciplines in drugs and pharmaceuticals

The Lumsden Company, Inc.
1300 Grove Avenue, Suite 205
Barrington, IL 60010
(847) 382-8822
Contact: Mr. Roy Lumsden
Minimum Salary Placed: $70,000
Recruiting Specialty: General

Management Recruiters
406 N. Hough Street
Barrington, IL 60010
(847) 382-5544
Contact: Mr. Gary Polvere
Minimum Salary Placed: $25,000
Recruiting Specialty: Construction and high technology, and some general

Spangler-Demarlie and Associates
22 E. Dundee Road
Barrington, IL 60010
(847) 304-8899
Contact: Mr. G. Demarlie
Minimum Salary Placed: $25,000
Recruiting Specialty: Insurance

TSC Management Services Group
P.O. Box 384
Barrington, IL 60011
(847) 381-0167
Contact: Mr. Robert Stanton
Recruiting Specialty: Manufacturing and technical disciplines in manufacturing and fabrication

T. Vincent and Associates
24362 Tanager Court
Barrington, IL 60010
(847) 540-8440
Minimum Salary Placed: $40,000
Recruiting Specialty: Investment securities and brokerages

Ward Howell International, Inc.
1300 S. Grove Avenue, Suite 100
Barrington, IL 60010
(847) 382-2206
Contact: Mr. Laurence Masse
Minimum Salary Placed: $75,000
Recruiting Specialty: General

Wytmar & Company, Inc.
265 Donlea Road
Barrington, IL 60010
(847) 381-7909
Contact: Mr. Richard Wytmar
Minimum Salary Placed: $100,000
Recruiting Specialty: General

BATAVIA

Sales Consultants
150 Houston Street, Suite 305
Batavia, IL 60510
(708) 879-1890
Contact: Mr. John Seebert
Minimum Salary Placed: $20,000
Recruiting Specialty: Sales

BELVIDERE

Manning and Associates
P.O. Box 666
Belvidere, IL 61008
(815) 544-0944
Contact: Mr. John Manning
Minimum Salary Placed: $25,000
Recruiting Specialty: Banking

BLOOMINGTON

James Russell, Inc.
P.O. Box 427
Bloomington, IL 61702
(309) 663-9467
Contact: Mr. Billy Adkisson
Minimum Salary Placed: $50,000
Recruiting Specialty: Healthcare

Sales Consultants
308 N. Main Street, Suite 201
Bloomington, IL 61701
(309) 829-6000
Contact: Mr. Jack Edwards
Minimum Salary Placed: $20,000
Recruiting Specialty: Sales

Snelling Personnel Service
2401 E. Washington Street
Bloomington, IL 61704
(309) 663-0482
Contact: Mr. R. Ogden
Minimum Salary Placed: $25,000
Recruiting Specialty: General

Witzig and Associates
115 W. Jefferson Street
Bloomington IL 61701
(309) 828-5030

Contact: Ms. P. Witzig
Minimum Salary Placed: $30,000
Recruiting Specialty: Advertising

BOLINGBROOK

Craig Hufford and Associates
3 Pembrool Court
Bolingbrook, IL 60440
(847) 378-0005
Contact: Mr. Craig Hufford
Minimum Salary Placed: $25,000
Recruiting Specialty: Voice, data and
wireless communications

BUFFALO GROVE

Earl L. McDermid & Associates
P.O. Box 6202
Buffalo Grove, IL 60089
(847) 541-9066
Contact: Mr. Earl McDermid
Minimum Salary Placed: $25,000
Recruiting Specialty: General

Smith and Partners
1324 Larchmont Drive
Buffalo Grove, IL 60089
(847) 634-2304
Contact: Mr. R. Smith
Minimum Salary Placed: $100,000
Recruiting Specialty: General

BURR RIDGE

Management Recruiters
100 Tower Drive, Suite 224
Burr Ridge, IL 60521
(708) 920-0400

Contact: Mr. Geary Dodendorf
Minimum Salary Placed: $20,000
Recruiting Specialty: General

BUTLER

M. K. and Associates
422 N. Main Street, Suite 2A
Butler, IL 60011
(708) 293-4949
Minimum Salary Placed: $25,000
Recruiting Specialty: Food

CAROL STREAM

C. Berger and Company
327 E. Gundersen Drive
Carol Stream, IL 60188
(630) 653-1115
Contact: Ms. Carol Berger
Minimum Salary Placed: $30,000
Recruiting Specialty: Library institutions

CARY

J.P. Gleason Associates, Inc.
P.O. Box 33
Cary, IL 60013
(847) 516-8900
Contact: Mr. James Gleason
Minimum Salary Placed: $60,000
Recruiting Specialty: General

Raymond Smith and Associates
Cary Oaks Executive
Cary, IL 60013
(847) 639-8250
Contact: Mr. Ray Smith
Minimum Salary Placed: $25,000
Recruiting Specialty: General

CHAMPAIGN

Ady & Associates, Inc.
115 W. Church Street
Champaign, IL 61820
(217) 359-8080
Contact: Mr. John Ady
Minimum Salary Placed: $35,000
Recruiting Specialty: Manufacturing in consumer products, food and metals

Management Recruiters
2110 N. Market Street, Suite 112
Champaign, IL 61821
(217) 398-0050
Contact: Mr. Kenneth Williams
Minimum Salary Placed: $20,000
Recruiting Specialty: General

Snelling Personnel Service
505 S. Neil, Suite 11
Champaign, IL 61820
(217) 352-0074
Contact: Mr. D. Ogden
Minimum Salary Placed: $25,000
Recruiting Specialty: General

CHATHAM

ProTechnology Search Inc.
116 W. Walnut
Chatham, IL 62629
(217) 483-3565
Contact: Sharon
Minimum Salary Placed: $25,000
Recruiting Specialty: Healthcare

CHERRY VALLEY

Management Recruiters
1740 S. Bell School Road, Suite 3
Cherry Valley, IL 61016
(815) 399-1942
Contact: Mr. D. Michael Carter
Minimum Salary Placed: $50,000
Recruiting Specialty: General

CHICAGO

AM&G Certified Public Accountants/Consultants
30 S. Wacker Drive
Chicago, IL 60606
(312) 207-2904
Minimum Salary Placed: $60,000
Recruiting Specialty: Finance and accounting

Abbott Smith Associates
1308 N. Astor Street
Chicago, IL 60610
(312) 664-1976
Contact: Mr. David Dalenberg
Minimum Salary Placed: $25,000
Recruiting Specialty: Human resources

Accountants Center Modern Ltd.
5 N. Wabash Avenue, Suite 1410
Chicago, IL 60602
(312) 782-3960
Contact: Mr. J. Kelly
Minimum Salary Placed: $25,000
Recruiting Specialty: Accounting and finance

Accountants Executive Search
200 N. La Salle Street
Chicago, IL 60601
(312) 782-7711
Contact: Ms. J. Huss
Minimum Salary Placed: $25,000
Recruiting Specialty: Finance and accounting

Accountants On Call
200 N. LaSalle Street, Suite 2830
Chicago, IL 60601
(312) 782-7788
Contact: Ms. Julianne Huss
Recruiting Specialty: Finance and accounting

Accountants Professional Staff
316 N. Michigan Avenue
Chicago, IL 60601
(312) 368-8367
Contact: Mr. K. Ollendorff
Minimum Salary Placed: $25,000
Recruiting Specialty: Accounting and finance

Allerton Heneghan & O'Neill
70 W. Madison Street, Suite 2015
Chicago, IL 60602
(312) 263-1075
Contact: Mr. Donald Allerton
Minimum Salary Placed: $75,000
Recruiting Specialty: General

American Medical Search
555 W. Madison Street
Chicago, IL 60661
(312) 559-7878
Minimum Salary Placed: $25,000
Recruiting Specialty: Medical and healthcare

The Bankers Group
10 S. Riverside Plaza
Chicago, IL 60606
(312) 930-9456
Contact: Mr. Joseph Womak
Minimum Salary Placed: $60,000
Recruiting Specialty: Finance and accounting in banking and securities

Barclay Consultants
155 N. Michigan Avenue
Chicago, IL 60601
(312) 856-1441
Contact: Mr. Darryl Homer
Minimum Salary Placed: $60,000
Recruiting Specialty: Attorneys

Barrett Partners
100 N. La Salle, Suite 1420
Chicago, IL 60602
(312) 443-8877
Contact: Mr. Joseph Thielman
Minimum Salary Placed: $30,000
Recruiting Specialty: Accounting and engineering

Barrington Hart, Inc.
20 N. Wacker Drive, Suite 2710
Chicago, IL 60606
(312) 332-3344
Contact: Ms. Gloria Rosemarin
Recruiting Specialty: General

Martin H. Bauman Associates, Inc.
625 N. Michigan Avenue, Suite 500
Chicago, IL 60611
(312) 751-5407
Contact: Ms. Audrey Hellinger
Minimum Salary Placed: $90,000
Recruiting Specialty: General

Beta Technologies
216 S. Jefferson Street
Chicago, IL 60661
(312) 627-1200
Minimum Salary Placed: $25,000
Recruiting Specialty: Information systems

The Blackman Kallick Search Division
300 S. Riverside Plaza, Suite 660
Chicago, IL 60606
(312) 207-1040
Contact: Mr. Gary Wolfson
Minimum Salary Placed: $60,000
Recruiting Specialty: General

William J. Blender and Associates
1635 N. North Park
Chicago, IL 60614
(312) 642-7400
Contact: Mr. William Blender
Recruiting Specialty: IT and computers

Bloom Gross and Associates
625 N. Michigan Avenue
Chicago, IL 60611
(312) 751-3490
Contact: Ms. Karen Bloom
Minimum Salary Placed: $25,000
Recruiting Specialty: General

Bonner and Stricklin and Associates
8 S. Michigan Avenue
Chicago, IL 60603
(312) 629-9090
Contact: Ms. J. Stricklin
Minimum Salary Placed: $40,000
Recruiting Specialty: Telecommunications

Boulware & Associates Inc.
175 W. Jackson, Suite 1841
Chicago, IL 60604
(312) 322-0088

Contact: Ms. Christine Boulware
Minimum Salary Placed: $50,000
Recruiting Specialty: General

Boyden
180 N. Stetson Avenue, Suite 5050
Chicago, IL 60601
(312) 565-1300
Contact: Mr. Richard McCallister
Minimum Salary Placed: $90,000
Recruiting Specialty: General

Brooke Chase Associates, Inc.
505 N. Lake Shore Drive, Suite 5507
Chicago, IL 60611
(312) 744-0033
Contact: Mr. Joseph McElmeel
Minimum Salary Placed: $30,000
Recruiting Specialty: Manufacturing and
sales in hardware and construction

Burling Group Ltd.
333 W. Wacker Drive
Chicago, IL 60606
(312) 346-0888
Contact: Mr. Ron Deitch
Minimum Salary Placed: $25,000
Recruiting Specialty: General

CMC Consultants
500 N. Michigan Avenue, Suite 1940
Chicago, IL 60611
(312) 670-5300
Contact: Ms. Carol Marcovich
Minimum Salary Placed: $40,000
Recruiting Specialty: General

CRT Chicago Recruiting
9535 South Avenue N., 2 Front
Chicago, IL 60611
(312) 375-2966

Contact: Mr. Frank Carillo
Minimum Salary Placed: $25,000
Recruiting Specialty: Data processing
and engineering

Calkins Group
303 W. Wacker Drive
Chicago, IL 60606
(312) 346-3033
Contact: Mr. Q. Calkins
Minimum Salary Placed: $70,000
Recruiting Specialty: Attorneys

Capital Services Group
10 S. Riverside Plaza
Chicago, IL 60606
(312) 930-1106
Contact: Ms. C. Mulligan
Recruiting Specialty: Stock brokers

Cardwell Enterprises Inc.
P.O. Box 59418
Chicago, IL 60659
(312) 273-5774
Contact: Ms. Jean Cardwell
Recruiting Specialty: Public relations and
communications

The Carlyle Group, Ltd.
401 N. Michigan Avenue, Suite 2500
Chicago, IL 60611
(312) 832-4200
Contact: Mr. Max DeZara
Minimum Salary Placed: $40,000
Recruiting Specialty: Banking and finance

Carpenter Associates Inc.
20 S. Clark, Suite 2210
Chicago, IL 60603
(312) 337-1455
Contact: Ms. J. Carpenter
Minimum Salary Placed: $30,000
Recruiting Specialty: Direct marketing

Carpenter, Shackleton & Company
20 N. Wacker Drive, Suite 3119
Chicago, IL 60606
(312) 236-5700
Contact: Mr. George Shackleton
Recruiting Specialty: General

Carrington and Carrington Ltd.
39 S. La Salle Street
Chicago, IL 60603
(312) 606-0015
Contact: Ms. M. Carrington
Minimum Salary Placed: $35,000
Recruiting Specialty: General

Cemco, Ltd.
20 S. Clark Street, Suite 610
Chicago, IL 60603
(312) 855-1500
Contact: Mr. M. Hale
Minimum Salary Placed: $25,000
Recruiting Specialty: Accounting, finance, MIS and banking

Chicago Financial Search
125 S. Wacker Drive, Suite 300
Chicago, IL 60606
(312) 207-0400
Contact: Mr. M. Kelly
Minimum Salary Placed: $25,000
Recruiting Specialty: Accounting and finance

Chicago Legal Search, Ltd.
770 N. Halsted, Suite 107
Chicago, IL 60622
(312) 243-4964
Contact: Mr. Gary D'Alessio
Minimum Salary Placed: $25,000
Recruiting Specialty: Legal

Joseph Conley & Associates, Inc.
625 N. Michigan Avenue, Suite 500
Chicago, IL 60611
(312) 751-3499
Contact: Mr. Joseph Conley
Minimum Salary Placed: $80,000
Recruiting Specialty: General

Cook Associates Inc.
212 W. Kinzie Street
Chicago, IL 60610
(312) 329-0900
Contact: Mr. A. Kins
Minimum Salary Placed: $25,000
Recruiting Specialty: General

The Corporate Source Group
625 N. Michigan Avenue, 5th Floor
Chicago, IL 60611
(312) 751-4250
Contact: Ms. Barbara McLean
Minimum Salary Placed: $60,000
Recruiting Specialty: General

Credentia Inc.
980 N. Michigan Avenue
Chicago, IL 60611
(312) 649-0522
Contact: Ms. C. Hoppe
Recruiting Specialty: Attorneys

DHR International, Inc.
10 S. Riverside Plaza, Suite 2220
Chicago, IL 60606
(312) 782-1581
Contact: Mr. David Hoffmann
Minimum Salary Placed: $60,000
Recruiting Specialty: General

Data Career Center
225 N. Michigan Avenue, Suite 930
Chicago, IL 60601
(312) 565-1060
Contact: Mr. L. Chaplik
Minimum Salary Placed: $30,000
Recruiting Specialty: Programming, computers and telecommunications

Data Interaction
1647 W. Huron Street
Chicago, IL 60622
(312) 733-2005
Contact: Mr. Don Langor
Minimum Salary Placed: $25,000
Recruiting Specialty: Computers and software

Daubenspeck & Associates, Inc.
225 W. Washington Street, Suite 2200
Chicago, IL 60606
(312) 419-7136
Contact: Mr. Kenneth Daubenspeck
Minimum Salary Placed: $80,000
Recruiting Specialty: MIS and human resources

Dieckmann & Associates, Ltd.
180 N. Stetson Avenue, Suite 5555
Chicago, IL 60601
(312) 819-5900
Contact: Mr. Ralph Dieckmann
Minimum Salary Placed: $65,000
Recruiting Specialty: General

Donahue/Bales Associates
303 W. Madison, Suite 1150
Chicago, IL 60606
(312) 732-0999
Contact: Mr. E.M. Donahue
Minimum Salary Placed: $70,000
Recruiting Specialty: General

Donegan and Associates
444 N. Wells Street
Chicago, IL 60610
(312) 644-6440
Minimum Salary Placed: $25,000
Recruiting Specialty: Accounting and finance

Dunhill of Chicago
68 E. Wacker Place, Suite 1200
Chicago, IL 60601
(312) 346-0933
Contact: Mr. George Baker
Minimum Salary Placed: $30,000
Recruiting Specialty: General

EDMS
P.O. Box 7300
Chicago, IL 60680
(708) 849-3030
Contact: Mr. John Barfield
Minimum Salary Placed: $25,000
Recruiting Specialty: Data processing, MIS and information technology systems

Early, Cochran and Olson, Inc.
55 E. Monroe Street, Suite 4530
Chicago, IL 60603
(312) 595-4200
Contact: Mr. Bert Early
Minimum Salary Placed: $75,000
Recruiting Specialty: Attorneys

Egon Zehnder International Inc.
1 First National Plaza, Suite 3300
Chicago, IL 60603
(312) 782-4500
Contact: Ms. Kai Lindholst
Minimum Salary Placed: $80,000
Recruiting Specialty: General

Execu Search
14 N. Peoria
Chicago, IL 60607
(312) 527-0276
Contact: Mr. Mel Monroe
Minimum Salary Placed: $25,000
Recruiting Specialty: High technology

Executive Referral Services, Inc.
8770 W. Bryn Mawr
Chicago, IL 60631
(312) 693-6622
Contact: Mr. Bruce Freier
Minimum Salary Placed: $25,000
Recruiting Specialty: Hospitality

George Fee Associates, Inc.
345 N. Canal Street, Suite 308
Chicago, IL 60606
(312) 454-1600
Contact: Mr. Richard Quaintance
Minimum Salary Placed: $75,000
Recruiting Specialty: Attorneys

Fergason Associates, Inc.
1350 Lake Shore Drive, Suite 1715
Chicago, IL 60610
(312) 642-6376
Contact: Mr. Loel Hahn
Minimum Salary Placed: $60,000
Recruiting Specialty: General, with some emphasis on senior level manufacturing

First Search
6584 NW Highway, Suite A
Chicago, IL 60631
(312) 774-0001
Minimum Salary Placed: $40,000
Recruiting Specialty: Telecommunications

John Foster and Associates
520 N. Michigan Avenue
Chicago, IL 60611
(312) 644-0030
Contact: Mr. John Foster
Minimum Salary Placed: $25,000
Recruiting Specialty: General

**Friedman Eisenstein Raemer &
Schwartz**
401 N. Michigan Avenue, Suite 2600
Chicago, IL 60611
(312) 245-1708
Contact: Ms. Ilene Hecht Brown
Minimum Salary Placed: $40,000
Recruiting Specialty: General

Gaines & Associates International, Inc.
650 N. Dearborn Street, Suite 450
Chicago, IL 60610
(312) 654-2900
Contact: Ms. Donna Gaines
Minimum Salary Placed: $20,000
Recruiting Specialty: Building, construction and environmental

David Gomez and Associates
20 N. Clark Street, Suite 3535
Chicago, IL 60602
(312) 346-5525
Contact: Mr. David Gomez
Minimum Salary Placed: $25,000
Recruiting Specialty: General

O'Brien and Gordon
676 N. St. Clair Street, Suite 1900
Chicago, IL 60611
(312) 943-2800
Contact: Mr. Dan Gordon
Minimum Salary Placed: $25,000
Recruiting Specialty: General

Hale Associates
1816 N. Sedgwick Street
Chicago, IL 60614
(312) 337-3288
Contact: Ms. Maureen Hale
Minimum Salary Placed: $50,000
Recruiting Specialty: General

Hay & Company
20 S. Clark Street, Suite 2305
Chicago, IL 60603
(312) 782-6510
Contact: Mr. Bill Hay
Minimum Salary Placed: $50,000
Recruiting Specialty: Accounting and finance

Hedlund Corporation
300 N. Wabash Avenue
Chicago, IL 60611
(312) 755-1400
Contact: Mr. David Hedlund
Minimum Salary Placed: $30,000
Recruiting Specialty: General

Heidrick & Struggles, Inc.
125 S. Wacker Drive, Suite 2800
Chicago, IL 60606
(312) 372-8811
Contact: Mr. Robert Hallagan
Minimum Salary Placed: $60,000
Recruiting Specialty: General

The Heidrick Partners, Inc.
20 N. Wacker Drive, Suite 2850
Chicago, IL 60606
(312) 845-9700
Contact: Mr. Robert Heidrick
Minimum Salary Placed: $90,000
Recruiting Specialty: General

W. Warner Hinman and Company
2040 N. Mohawk Street
Chicago, IL 60614
(312) 951-8010
Contact: Mr. Bill Hinman
Minimum Salary Placed: $30,000
Recruiting Specialty: General

Hoglund & Associates, Inc.
303 W. Madison Street, Suite 1150
Chicago, IL 60606
(312) 357-1037
Contact: Mr. Gerald Hoglund
Minimum Salary Placed: $70,000
Recruiting Specialty: General

Holland Rusk & Associates
211 E. Ontario Street, Suite 1100
Chicago, IL 60611
(312) 266-9595
Contact: Ms. Susan Holland
Minimum Salary Placed: $60,000
Recruiting Specialty: General

The Hollins Group, Inc.
225 W. Wacker Drive, Suite 2125
Chicago, IL 60606
(312) 606-8000
Contact: Mr. Lawrence Hollins
Minimum Salary Placed: $60,000
Recruiting Specialty: General

Hunter Resource Group
One North La Salle, Suite 2455
Chicago, IL 60602
(312) 201-0302
Contact: Mr. F. Scarpelli
Minimum Salary Placed: $25,000
Recruiting Specialty: General

IZS Executive Search
20 N. Wacker Drive, Suite 556
Chicago, IL 60606
(312) 346-6300
Contact: Mr. C. Zimmerman
Minimum Salary Placed: $35,000
Recruiting Specialty: Accounting and finance

Jacobson Associates
150 N. Wacker Drive, Suite 1120
Chicago, IL 60606
(312) 726-1578
Contact: Mr. David Jacobson
Minimum Salary Placed: $20,000
Recruiting Specialty: Healthcare and insurance

Jason Dutton Stroden and Associates
20 N. Wacker Drive
Chicago, IL 60606
(312) 368-1730
Contact: Mr. T. Jason
Minimum Salary Placed: $40,000
Recruiting Specialty: Stockbrokers

Jefferson Institute
3942 N. Central Avenue
Chicago, IL 60634
(312) 685-5849
Contact: Mr. G. Noonan
Minimum Salary Placed: $25,000
Recruiting Specialty: General

John H. Johnson & Associates, Inc.
332 S. Michigan Avenue, Suite 1201
Chicago, IL 60604
(312) 663-4257
Contact: Mr. John Johnson
Minimum Salary Placed: $50,000
Recruiting Specialty: General

John Joseph Group Ltd.
332 S. Michigan Avenue, Suite 1201
Chicago, IL 60604
(312) 663-4176
Contact: Mr. Jack Johnson
Minimum Salary Placed: $50,000
Recruiting Specialty: General

A.T. Kearney Executive Search
222 W. Adams Street
Chicago, IL 60606
(312) 648-0111
Contact: Mr. Charles Sweet
Minimum Salary Placed: $60,000
Recruiting Specialty: General

Kennedy & Company
20 N. Wacker Drive, Suite 1745
Chicago, IL 60606
(312) 372-0099
Contact: Mr. Thomas Moran
Minimum Salary Placed: $60,000
Recruiting Specialty: General

Thomas Kennedy and Associates
913 W. Wrightwood Avenue
Chicago, IL 60614
(312) 935-6066
Contact: Mr. Tom Kennedy
Minimum Salary Placed: $25,000
Recruiting Specialty: Accounting

Kenzer Corporation
625 N. Michigan Avenue
Chicago, IL 60611
(312) 266-0976
Contact: Ms. Mary Allgire
Recruiting Specialty: General

Kittleman & Associates
300 S. Wacker Drive, Suite 1710
Chicago, IL 60606
(312) 986-1166
Contact: Mr. James Kittleman
Minimum Salary Placed: $50,000
Recruiting Specialty: Non-profit

Zenner Consulting Group
75 Wacker Drive, Tower Floor 3000
Chicago, IL 60601
(312) 849-3800
Contact: Ms. Teri Zenner Kleiman
Recruiting Specialty: Attorneys

Korn/Ferry International
120 S. Riverside Plaza, Suite 918
Chicago, IL 60606
(312) 726-1841
Contact: Mr. Paul Flask
Minimum Salary Placed: $100,000
Recruiting Specialty: General

Kresin Wingard
333 N. Michigan Avenue, Suite 622
Chicago, IL 60601
(312) 726-8676
Contact: Mr. David Wingard
Minimum Salary Placed: $30,000
Recruiting Specialty: Communications,
publishing, and advertising

Kristophers Consultants
5551 N. Oseola Avenue
Chicago, IL 60656
(312) 594-1301
Minimum Salary Placed: $40,000
Recruiting Specialty: General

Lamalie Amrop International
225 W. Wacker Drive, Suite 2100
Chicago, IL 60606
(312) 782-3113
Contact: Mr. Lawrence Nein
Minimum Salary Placed: $75,000
Recruiting Specialty: General

The Laso Corporation
220 W. Huron, Suite 4001
Chicago, IL 60610
(312) 255-1110
Contact: Ms. Laurie Swanson
Oberhelman
Minimum Salary Placed: $25,000
Recruiting Specialty: MIS

Lauer, Sbarbaro Associates, Inc.
30 N. LaSalle Street, Suite 4030
Chicago, IL 60602
(312) 372-7050
Contact: Mr. Richard Sbarbaro
Minimum Salary Placed: $60,000
Recruiting Specialty: General

Lynch Miller Moore Partners, Inc.
10 S. Wacker Drive, Suite 2935
Chicago, IL 60606
(312) 876-1505
Contact: Mr. Michael Lynch
Minimum Salary Placed: $75,000
Recruiting Specialty: General

Major, Hagen & Africa
35 E. Wacker Drive, Suite 2150
Chicago, IL 60601
(312) 372-1010
Contact: Ms. Laura Hagen
Recruiting Specialty: Attorneys

Management Careers
1300 W. Belmont
Chicago, IL 60657
(312) 880-1319
Contact: Mr. Mike Morawski
Minimum Salary Placed: $25,000
Recruiting Specialty: General

Management Recruiters
2 N. Riverside Plaza, Suite 1815
Chicago, IL 60606
(312) 648-1800
Contact: Mr. David Baranski
Minimum Salary Placed: $20,000
Recruiting Specialty: Accounting and finance

Larry McCullum and Associates
431 S. Dearborn Street
Chicago, IL 60605
(312) 922-3128
Contact: Mr. Larry McCullum
Minimum Salary Placed: $25,000
Recruiting Specialty: General

McFeely Wackerle Shulman
20 N. Wacker Drive, Suite 3110
Chicago, IL 60606
(312) 641-2977
Contact: Mr. Frederick Wackerle
Minimum Salary Placed: $200,000
Recruiting Specialty: General

Mengel & McDonald Ltd.
357 W. Erie, Suite 200
Chicago, IL 60610
(312) 266-0581
Contact: Mr. Thomas McDonald
Minimum Salary Placed: $50,000
Recruiting Specialty: Advertising

Moriarty/Fox, Inc.
20 N. Wacker Drive, Suite 2410
Chicago, IL 60606
(312) 332-4600
Contact: Mr. Philip Moriarty
Minimum Salary Placed: $75,000
Recruiting Specialty: General

Network Consulting Associates
4344 W. 51st Street
Chicago, IL 60632
(312) 582-5465
Contact: Mr. D. Sladek
Minimum Salary Placed: $25,000
Recruiting Specialty: Technical disciplines

Nordeman Grimm, Inc.
150 N. Michigan Avenue
Chicago, IL 60601
(312) 332-0088
Contact: Mr. Ted Martin
Minimum Salary Placed: $100,000
Recruiting Specialty: General

C. J. Noty & Associates
332 S. Michigan Avenue
Chicago, IL 60604
(312) 663-5330
Contact: Mr. Richard Nicholsen
Minimum Salary Placed: $50,000
Recruiting Specialty: General

John R. O'Connor & Associates
111 W. Jackson Boulevard, Suite 1300
Chicago, IL 60604
(312) 939-1392
Contact: Mr. John O'Connor
Minimum Salary Placed: $35,000
Recruiting Specialty: Engineering in construction, utilities and transportation

Onsite Staffing Solutions
53 W. Jackson Boulevard, Suite 1320
Chicago, IL 60604
(312) 939-2208
Contact: Mr. Laddie Polz
Minimum Salary Placed: $20,000
Recruiting Specialty: General

PMA Inc.
8 S. Michigan Avenue
Chicago, IL 60603
(312) 236-9036
Contact: Ms. K. Ruddy
Minimum Salary Placed: $25,000
Recruiting Specialty: Advertising, marketing and communications

Paul Ray Berndtson
10 S. Riverside Plaza, Suite 720
Chicago, IL 60606
(312) 876-0730
Contact: Mr. Andrew Weidener
Minimum Salary Placed: $90,000
Recruiting Specialty: General

Quaintance Associates, Inc.
345 N. Canal Street, Suite 308
Chicago, IL 60606
(312) 454-1234
Contact: Mr. Richard Quaintance
Minimum Salary Placed: $75,000
Recruiting Specialty: Non-profit

Vera L. Rast Partners Inc.
One S. Wacker, Suite 3890
Chicago, IL 60606
(312) 629-0339
Contact: Ms. Vera Rast
Recruiting Specialty: Attorneys

The Registry, Inc.
P.O. Box 81229
Chicago, IL 60681
(708) 748-1115
Contact: Mr. William Kleindorfer
Recruiting Specialty: General

Research Alternatives, Inc.
445 W. Erie, Suite 208
Chicago, IL 60610
(708) 386-0688
Contact: Mr. Robert Kowalski
Minimum Salary Placed: $25,000
Recruiting Specialty: General

Retail Leadership Source
230 N. Michigan Avenue
Chicago, IL 60601
(312) 704-0577
Minimum Salary Placed: $50,000
Recruiting Specialty: Retailing

S. Reyman & Associates, Ltd.
20 N. Michigan Avenue, Suite 520
Chicago, IL 60602
(312) 580-0808
Contact: Ms. Susan Reyman
Minimum Salary Placed: $45,000
Recruiting Specialty: General

Ridenour & Associates
1 E. Wacker Drive, Suite 3500
Chicago, IL 60601
(312) 644-1888
Contact: Ms. Suzanne Ridenour
Minimum Salary Placed: $75,000
Recruiting Specialty: General

Robert Half International
205 N. Michigan Avenue
Chicago, IL 60601
(312) 616-8200

Contact: Mr. F. Getz
Minimum Salary Placed: $25,000
Recruiting Specialty: Accounting and finance

Robertson and Associates
10 S. Riverside Plaza
Chicago, IL 60606
(312) 930-1958
Contact: Mr. George Robertson
Minimum Salary Placed: $80,000
Recruiting Specialty: General

Romac International
20 N. Wacker Drive, Suite 1465
Chicago, IL 60606
(312) 263-0902
Contact: Mr. Richard Cocchiaro
Minimum Salary Placed: $30,000
Recruiting Specialty: Accounting, finance and MIS

Russell Reynolds Associates, Inc.
200 S. Wacker Drive, Suite 3600
Chicago, IL 60606
(312) 993-9696
Contact: Mr. Peter Crist
Minimum Salary Placed: $100,000
Recruiting Specialty: General

SRS Data Search
6 N. Michigan Avenue
Chicago, IL 60602
(312) 346-6383
Contact: Mr. J. Kroe
Minimum Salary Placed: $25,000
Recruiting Specialty: MIS and other technical disciplines

Sales & Management Search, Inc.
10 S. Riverside Plaza
Chicago, IL 60606
(312) 930-1111
Contact: Mr. C.L. Mulligan
Minimum Salary Placed: $50,000
Recruiting Specialty: Manufacturing

Sales Consultants
20 N. Wabash, Suite 201
Chicago, IL 60611
(312) 836-9100
Contact: Mr. Bob Bowes
Minimum Salary Placed: $20,000
Recruiting Specialty: Sales

David Saxner & Associates, Inc.
3 First National Plaza, Suite 1400
Chicago, IL 60602
(312) 201-0964
Contact: Mr. David Saxner
Minimum Salary Placed: $50,000
Recruiting Specialty: Real estate and hospitality

JR Scott and Associates
222 S. Riverside Plaza
Chicago, IL 60606
(312) 648-4630
Contact: Mr. S. Fischer
Minimum Salary Placed: $25,000
Recruiting Specialty: General

Search Dynamics, Inc.
9420 W. Foster Avenue, Suite 200
Chicago, IL 60656
(312) 992-3900
Contact: Mr. George Apostle
Minimum Salary Placed: $30,000
Recruiting Specialty: Engineering and technical disciplines

Search Services
150 S. Wacker Drive, Suite 400
Chicago, IL 60606
(312) 372-1900
Contact: Mr. Larry Stanczak
Recruiting Specialty: Computer software and hardware

Search USA
333 N. Michigan Avenue, Suite 2032
Chicago, IL 60611
(312) 332-5353
Contact: Mr. D. Diotallevi
Minimum Salary Placed: $25,000
Recruiting Specialty: Engineering, data processing, accounting and finance

Sheridan Search
506 N. Clark Street, Suite 4S
Chicago, IL 60610
(312) 822-0232
Contact: Mr. John Sheridan
Minimum Salary Placed: $100,000
Recruiting Specialty: Banking, finance and high technology

John Sibbald Associates, Inc.
8725 Higgins Road
Chicago, IL 60631
(312) 693-0575
Contact: Mr. John Sibbald
Minimum Salary Placed: $60,000
Recruiting Specialty: General

Siegel Associates
330 W. Diversey Parkway, Suite 1109
Chicago, IL 60657
(312) 327-4479
Contact: Mr. Ken Siegel
Minimum Salary Placed: $25,000
Recruiting Specialty: Marketing research

D. W. Simpson & Company
625 N. Michigan Avenue, 12th Floor
Chicago, IL 60611
(312) 654-5220
Contact: Ms. Patricia Jacobsen
Recruiting Specialty: Insurance

Slayton International Inc.
181 W. Madison, Suite 4510
Chicago, IL 60602
(312) 456-0080
Contact: Mr. Richard Slayton
Minimum Salary Placed: $100,000
Recruiting Specialty: General

Smith Hanley Associates
200 W. Madison, Suite 480
Chicago, IL 60606
(312) 629-2400
Contact: Ms. Linda Burtch
Minimum Salary Placed: $40,000
Recruiting Specialty: Marketing and research in finance and consumer products

Specific Recruiting Service
730 N. Franklin Street
Chicago, IL 60610
(312) 649-0304
Contact: Mr. Dave Omlauf
Minimum Salary Placed: $50,000
Recruiting Specialty: Trust and investment

Spencer Stuart
401 N. Michigan Avenue, Suite 3400
Chicago, IL 60611
(312) 822-0080
Contact: Mr. Jim Drury
Minimum Salary Placed: $100,000
Recruiting Specialty: General

Strategic Executives., Inc.
980 N. Michigan Avenue, Suite 1400
Chicago, IL 60611
(312) 988-4821
Minimum Salary Placed: $80,000
Recruiting Specialty: General

Strategic Search Corporation
645 N. Michigan Avenue, Suite 800
Chicago, IL 60611
(312) 944-4000
Contact: Mr. Scott Sargis
Minimum Salary Placed: $50,000
Recruiting Specialty: Manufacturing and production in consumer products

Stern Professional Search, Inc.
680 N. Lake Shore Drive
Chicago, IL 60611
(312) 587-7777
Minimum Salary Placed: $25,000
Recruiting Specialty: Contract furniture and design

Synergistics Associates Ltd.
400 N. State Street, Suite 400
Chicago, IL 60611
(312) 467-5450
Contact: Mr. Alvin Borenstine
Minimum Salary Placed: $70,000
Recruiting Specialty: MIS and computers

Roy Talman and Associates
203 N. Wabash Avenue
Chicago, IL 60601
(312) 630-0130
Contact: Mr. Roy Talman
Minimum Salary Placed: $30,000
Recruiting Specialty: Technical disciplines

Taylor Search Associates, Inc.
5601 Sheridan Road
Chicago, IL 60660
(312) 275-8507
Contact: Mr. M. Kent Taylor
Minimum Salary Placed: $45,000
Recruiting Specialty: High technology

Tesar-Reynes, Inc.
500 N. Michigan Avenue, Suite 1300
Chicago, IL 60611
(312) 661-0700
Contact: Mr. Tony Reynes
Minimum Salary Placed: $40,000
Recruiting Specialty: Advertising and
marketing

Tuft and Associates
1209 N. Astor Street
Chicago, IL 60610
(312) 642-8889
Contact: Ms. Marianne Tuft
Minimum Salary Placed: $25,000
Recruiting Specialty: Non-profit and phil-
anthropic

Universal Executive Search, Inc.
625 N. Michigan Avenue, Suite 500
Chicago, IL 60611
(312) 751-5444
Contact: Ms. Arlene Margolis
Minimum Salary Placed: $60,000
Recruiting Specialty: General

Verdin Associates
25 E. Washington Street, Suite 1600
Chicago, IL 60602
(312) 855-1055
Contact: Mr. Vern Hoffenberg
Minimum Salary Placed: $50,000
Recruiting Specialty: Attorneys

Anne Violante and Associates
770 N. Halsted Street
Chicago, IL 60622
(312) 633-9067
Contact: Ms. Anne Violante
Minimum Salary Placed: $40,000
Recruiting Specialty: Attorneys

Ward Howell International , Inc.
300 S. Wacker Drive, Suite 2940
Chicago, IL 60606
(312) 236-2211
Contact: Mr. Larry Poore
Minimum Salary Placed: $75,000
Recruiting Specialty: General

Lee Weil Associates
2300 Lincoln Park W., Suite 323
Chicago, IL 60614
(312) 880-1944
Contact: Ms. Lee Weil
Minimum Salary Placed: $50,000
Recruiting Specialty: Marketing research
and strategists in consumer products

Westford Group
222 N. La Salle Street
Chicago, IL 60601
(312) 641-5000
Minimum Salary Placed: $25,000
Recruiting Specialty: Accounting, finance, marketing and operations

Wheelless Group
49 E. Elm Street
Chicago, IL 60611
(312) 642-1377
Contact: Ms. Pat Wheelless
Recruiting Specialty: Direct marketing

White, Roberts & Stratton Inc.

444 N. Michigan Avenue, Suite 2940
Chicago, IL 60610
(312) 644-5554
Contact: Mr. Marc P. White
Minimum Salary Placed: $50,000
Recruiting Specialty: General

Ray White Associates

875 N. Michigan Avenue
Chicago, IL 60611
(312) 266-0100
Contact: Mr. Ray White
Minimum Salary Placed: $25,000
Recruiting Specialty: General

Robert Whitfield Associates

155 N. Michigan Avenue
Chicago, IL 60601
(312) 938-9120
Contact: Mr. Bob Whitfield
Minimum Salary Placed: $25,000
Recruiting Specialty: General

Williams, Roth & Krueger, Inc.

20 N. Wacker Drive, Suite 3450
Chicago, IL 60606
(312) 977-0800
Contact: Mr. Robert Roth
Minimum Salary Placed: $85,000
Recruiting Specialty: General

Wilson-Douglas-Jordan

70 W. Madison Street, Suite 1400
Chicago, IL 60602
(312) 782-0286
Contact: Mr. John Wilson
Minimum Salary Placed: $25,000
Recruiting Specialty: General

Winston, Rooney & Green

201 N. Wells, Suite 1410
Chicago, IL 60606
(312) 201-9777
Contact: Mr. David Winston
Minimum Salary Placed: $50,000
Recruiting Specialty: Attorneys

M. Wood Company

10 N. Dearborn Street, Suite 700
Chicago, IL 60602
(312) 368-0633
Contact: Mr. Milton Wood
Minimum Salary Placed: $75,000
Recruiting Specialty: General

Wright-Nelson Enterprises Inc.

770 N. Halsted Street
Chicago, IL 60622
(312) 733-0676
Contact: Ms. N. Wright-Nelson
Minimum Salary Placed: $25,000
Recruiting Specialty: General

Wylie Group Ltd.

345 N. Canal Street
Chicago, IL 60606
(312) 822-0333
Contact: Mr. B. Wylie
Minimum Salary Placed: $30,000
Recruiting Specialty: Sales and marketing
and office furniture

Z. Mas Inc.

P.O. Box 2361
Chicago, IL 60690
(312) 939-5595
Contact: Don
Minimum Salary Placed: $25,000
Recruiting Specialty: MIS

Michael Zwell and Associates Inc.
300 S. Wacker Drive, Suite 650
Chicago, IL 60604
(312) 750-1700
Contact: Mr. Michael Zwell
Minimum Salary Placed: $35,000
Recruiting Specialty: Banking and MIS

COUNTRYSIDE

The Glenwood Group
6428 Joliet Road, Suite 112
Countryside, IL 60525
(708) 482-3750
Contact: Mr. Frank Filippelli
Minimum Salary Placed: $25,000
Recruiting Specialty: General

CRETE

Franchise Recruiters Ltd.
3500 Innsburck
Crete, IL 60417
(708) 757-5595
Contact: Mr. Jerry Wilkerson
Minimum Salary Placed: $40,000
Recruiting Specialty: Franchising

CRYSTAL LAKE

Corporate Environment Ltd.
P.O. Box 798
Crystal Lake, IL 60039
(815) 455-6070
Contact: Mr. Tom McDermott
Minimum Salary Placed: $50,000
Recruiting Specialty: Environmental and
manufacturing

Kinderis & Loercher Group
9510 Turnberry Trail
Crystal Lake, IL 60014
(815) 459-3700
Contact: Mr. Paul Kinderis
Minimum Salary Placed: $20,000
Recruiting Specialty: Insurance

Sales Consultants of Crystal Lake, Inc.
41 Commerce Drive, Suite 101
Crystal Lake, IL 60014
(815) 455-1603
Contact: Mr. Daniel Grant
Minimum Salary Placed: $20,000
Recruiting Specialty: Sales

Thomas MacKenzie and Company
685 Saddle Ridge
Crystal Lake, IL 60012
(815) 459-8550
Minimum Salary Placed: $25,000
Recruiting Specialty: General

DANVILLE

The Halstead Group
417 W. Winter
Danville, IL 61832
(217) 446-2000
Contact: Ms. Jill Salonen
Minimum Salary Placed: $25,000
Recruiting Specialty: Generalist

DEERFIELD

Crosly and Associates
707 Skokie Boulevard, Suite 500
Deerfield, IL 60015
(847) 564-3800
Contact: Mr. Tom Misch
Minimum Salary Placed: $25,000
Recruiting Specialty: General

Diversified Management Resources
1020 N. Milwaukee Avenue
Deerfield, IL 60015
(847) 537-5660
Contact: Mr. Frank Wolowicz
Minimum Salary Placed: $40,000
Recruiting Specialty: General

Higgins Associates, Inc.
108 Wilmot Road
Deerfield, IL 60015
(847) 940-4800
Contact: Mr. John Higgins
Minimum Salary Placed: $75,000
Recruiting Specialty: General

Meder & Associates
111 Pfingsten Road, Suite 312
Deerfield, IL 60015
(847) 564-2422
Contact: Mr. Peter Meder
Minimum Salary Placed: $100,000
Recruiting Specialty: General

Richard Allen Winter Associates Inc.
102 Wilmot Road, Suite 480
Deerfield, IL 60015
(847) 948-8222
Contact: Managing Director
Minimum Salary Placed: $40,000
Recruiting Specialty: General

Ritt-Ritt & Associates, Inc.
424 Swan Boulevard
Deerfield, IL 60015
(847) 520-9999
Contact: Mr. Arthur Ritt
Minimum Salary Placed: $25,000
Recruiting Specialty: Hospitality and food

DES PLAINES

Bowersox & Associates, Inc.
1025 Margret Street
Des Plaines, IL 60016
(847) 699-1150
Contact: Mr. Thomas Bowersox
Minimum Salary Placed: $50,000
Recruiting Specialty: General

Executive Placement Consultants
2700 River Road, Suite 107
Des Plaines, IL 60018
(847) 298-6445
Contact: Mr. Michael Colman
Minimum Salary Placed: $35,000
Recruiting Specialty: Accounting and finance

Financial Search Corporation
2720 Des Plaines Avenue, Suite 106
Des Plaines, IL 60018
(847) 297-4900
Contact: Mr. Robert Collins
Minimum Salary Placed: $20,000
Recruiting Specialty: Finance and accounting

Human Resource Technologies, Inc.
2200 E. Devon Avenue, Suite 183
Des Plaines, IL 60018
(847) 297-8000
Contact: Mr. Rick Sondhi
Minimum Salary Placed: $35,000
Recruiting Specialty: General

Itex Executive Search
2700 S. River Road
Des Plaines, IL 60018
(847) 299-2000

Contact: Mr. M. Skoro
Minimum Salary Placed: $25,000
Recruiting Specialty: Accounting and finance

Lloyd Personnel Consultants
1001 E. Touhy Avenue
Des Plaines, IL 60018
(847) 297-7251
Contact: Mr. C. Graziani
Recruiting Specialty: Office support

Mediquest
2200 E. Devon Avenue
Des Plaines, IL 60018
(847) 297-2504
Contact: Mr. John Winston
Minimum Salary Placed: $35,000
Recruiting Specialty: Medical and healthcare

L.J. Reszotko & Associates
1529 E. Lincoln Avenue
Des Plaines, IL 60018
(847) 803-0888
Contact: Mr. Leonard Reszotko
Minimum Salary Placed: $50,000
Recruiting Specialty: General

DOWNERS GROVE

Susan Alport
3719 Venard Road
Downers Grove, IL 60515
(630) 963-0880
Contact: Ms. Sue Alport
Minimum Salary Placed: $25,000
Recruiting Specialty: General

Evergreene Partners
3051 Oak Grove Road
Downers Grove, IL 60515
(630) 434-9400
Contact: Mr. Mike Greene
Minimum Salary Placed: $30,000
Recruiting Specialty: Technical disciplines in foods

Executive Financial Consultants
6900 Main Street
Downers Grove, IL 60516
(630) 663-9010
Minimum Salary Placed: $25,000
Recruiting Specialty: Finance

Murray, Feldman & Associates
6363 Banburry Road
Downers Grove, IL 60515
(630) 769-1390
Contact: Ms. Jeanette Murray
Minimum Salary Placed: $30,000
Recruiting Specialty: General

Search Centre Inc.
1430 Branding Lane, Suite 119
Downers Grove, IL 60515
(630) 963-3033
Contact: Mr. Scott Rollins
Minimum Salary Placed: $20,000
Recruiting Specialty: Insurance and healthcare

Technical Professional Service
4800 Middaugh Avenue
Downers Grove, IL 60515
(630) 960-4262
Minimum Salary Placed: $35,000
Recruiting Specialty: Technical disciplines

DUNDEE

Norton & Associates
7 Michigan Avenue
Dundee, IL 60118
(847) 428-9255
Contact: Mr. Gregory Norton
Minimum Salary Placed: $35,000
Recruiting Specialty: High technology

EFFINGHAM

Sanford Rose Associates
444 South Willow, Suite 11
Effingham, IL 62401
(217) 342-3911
Contact: Mr. Robert St. Dennis
Minimum Salary Placed: $30,000
Recruiting Specialty: Printing

ELGIN

Creative Staffing Enterprises
10899 S. Airlite Street
Elgin, IL 60123
(847) 888-4691
Contact: Mr. D. Taylor
Minimum Salary Placed: $35,000
Recruiting Specialty: Technical disciplines and marketing in telecommunications

Executive Search Ltd.
2000 Larkin Avenue
Elgin, IL 60123
(847) 697-1170
Contact: Ms. Carol Bonnick
Minimum Salary Placed: $30,000
Recruiting Specialty: General

Management Recruiters
472 North McLean Boulevard, Suite 201
Elgin, IL 60123
(847) 697-2201
Contact: Mr. Ron Reeves
Minimum Salary Placed: $20,000
Recruiting Specialty: Graphic arts and trade show exhibits

Stephen Sellers Associates
805 Augusta Avenue
Elgin, IL 60120
(847) 888-1568
Contact: Mr. Stephen Sellers
Minimum Salary Placed: $25,000
Recruiting Specialty: Technical disciplines in film hybrid microelectronics, SMT and PCBs

Smith Downey and Associates
1038 Center Street
Elgin, IL 60120
(847) 697-4656
Contact: Mr. D. Smith
Minimum Salary Placed: $25,000
Recruiting Specialty: General

Technical Network Search
339 W. River Road
Elgin, IL 60123
(847) 888-0875
Minimum Salary Placed: $40,000
Recruiting Specialty: Technical disciplines in high technology and computers

ELMHURST

Michael Associates
613 Poplar Avenue
Elmhurst, IL 60126
(708) 832-2550
Contact: Mr. Michael Golding
Minimum Salary Placed: $30,000
Recruiting Specialty: Manufacturing

Search Masters
188 Industrial Drive, Suite 108
Elmhurst, IL 60126
(708) 833-7790
Contact: Mr. Glenn Kubat
Recruiting Specialty: General

EVANSTON

Ann Coe & Associates
2033 Sherman Avenue
Evanston, IL 60201
(847) 864-0668
Contact: Ms. Ann Coe
Minimum Salary Placed: $35,000
Recruiting Specialty: MIS

Conway and Associates
1007 Church Street
Evanston, IL 60201
(847) 866-6832
Contact: Ms. M. Conway
Minimum Salary Placed: $25,000
Recruiting Specialty: General

Haydon & Dalebroux Associates
1740 Ridge Avenue
Evanston, IL 60201
(847) 475-4222
Contact: Ms. Meredith Haydon
Recruiting Specialty: Attorneys

Hazlett Associates
2340 Orrington Avenue
Evanston, IL 60201
(847) 866-8382
Contact: Mr. Thomas Hazlett
Minimum Salary Placed: $50,000
Recruiting Specialty: Consumer products, communications and marketing

Richard Marks and Associates
2319 Hartzell
Evanston, IL 60201
(847) 475-7600
Contact: Mr. Rich Marks
Minimum Salary Placed: $25,000
Recruiting Specialty: Sales and system engineers

EVERGREEN PARK

First Attorney Consultants Ltd.
3317-19 W. 95th Street, Suite 5
Evergreen Park, IL 60805
(708) 425-5515
Minimum Salary Placed: $50,000
Recruiting Specialty: Attorneys

FALLON

Kubiak and Associates
P.O. Box 351
Fallon, IL 62269
(618) 632-3308
Contact: Mr. Tom Kubiak
Recruiting Specialty: Physicians

GENESEO

AGRI-Associates
109 S. Center Street
Geneseo, IL 61254
(309) 944-8890
Contact: Mr. Dale Unmisig
Minimum Salary Placed: $25,000
Recruiting Specialty: General

GENEVA

Newport Advisory Group
P.O. Box 164
Geneva, IL 60134
(630) 513-5161
Contact: Mr. Steve Shewalter
Minimum Salary Placed: $25,000
Recruiting Specialty: General

Oberlander & Company, Inc.
223 E. State Street
P.O. Box 789
Geneva, IL 60134
(630) 232-2600
Contact: Mr. Howard Oberlander
Minimum Salary Placed: $60,000
Recruiting Specialty: General

Optima Partners, Inc.
1250 Executive Place, Suite 404
Geneva, IL 60134
(708) 232-7800
Contact: Ms. Leslie Greenley
Minimum Salary Placed: $25,000
Recruiting Specialty: IT

Xagas & Associates
701 E. State Street, Suite 1
Geneva, IL 60134
(630) 232-7044
Contact: Mr. Steve Xagas
Recruiting Specialty: Quality practitioners and operations management

GLEN ELLYN

Masters Associates
799 Roosevelt Road
Glen Ellyn, IL 60137
(630) 790-4545
Contact: Mr. Joe Ross
Minimum Salary Placed: $25,000
Recruiting Specialty: General

Joseph Parker and Associates
799 Roosevelt Road
Glen Ellyn, IL 60137
(630) 858-6221
Contact: Mr. Joe Parker
Minimum Salary Placed: $30,000
Recruiting Specialty: Manufacturing

Parsons Associates Inc.
601 Forest Avenue
Glen Ellyn, IL 60137
(630) 469-7660
Contact: Ms. Sue Parsons
Minimum Salary Placed: $50,000
Recruiting Specialty: General

Philip Daniels Associates, Inc.
551 Roosevelt Road, Suite 139
Glen Ellyn, IL 60137
(630) 665-1114
Contact: Mr. Phil Pollard
Minimum Salary Placed: $40,000
Recruiting Specialty: Sales and general in transportation and information services

Rooney Associates Inc.
501 Pennsylvania Avenue
Glen Ellyn, IL 60137
(630) 469-7102
Contact: Mr. Joe Rooney
Minimum Salary Placed: $25,000
Recruiting Specialty: General

Keith Ross and Associates Inc.
45 S. Park Boulevard
Glen Ellyn, IL 60137
(630) 858-1000
Contact: Mr. Keith Ross
Minimum Salary Placed: $60,000
Recruiting Specialty: Attorneys

Mark Wilcox Associates Ltd.
799 Roosevelt Road
Glen Ellyn, IL 60137
(630) 790-4300
Contact: Mr. Mark Wilcox
Minimum Salary Placed: $35,000
Recruiting Specialty: Pulp and paper,
chemicals and manufacturing

GLENDALE HEIGHTS

Gaffney Management Consultants
35 N. Brandon Drive
Glendale Heights, IL 60139
(630) 307-3380
Contact: Mr. William Gaffney
Minimum Salary Placed: $50,000
Recruiting Specialty: General

GLENVIEW

John C. Boone & Company
1807 Henley Street
Glenview, IL 60025
(847) 998-1905

Contact: Mr. John Boone
Minimum Salary Placed: $40,000
Recruiting Specialty: General

CTH, Ltd.
440 Harlem Avenue
Glenview, IL 60025
(847) 657-0102
Minimum Salary Placed: $40,000
Recruiting Specialty: Telecommunications

Retis Associates
4350 DiPaolo, Suite 1
Glenview, IL 60025
(847) 724-8830
Contact: Ms. Lillian Retis
Recruiting Specialty: Physicians and
healthcare

Spriggs & Company, Inc.
1701 Lake Avenue, Suite 265
Glenview, IL 60025
(847) 657-7181
Contact: Mr. Robert Spriggs
Minimum Salary Placed: $50,000
Recruiting Specialty: General

GRANITE CITY

Search Source, Inc.
2019 B Johnson Road
P.O. Box 1161
Granite City, IL 62040
(618) 876-6060
Contact: Mr. James McKechan
Minimum Salary Placed: $30,000
Recruiting Specialty: Technical disci-
plines in communications and high tech-
nology

GURNEE

H.J. Elliot, Inc.
5136 Eau Claire Court
Gurnee, IL 60031
(708) 249-1091
Contact: Mr. Elliot Hoffenberg
Minimum Salary Placed: $50,000
Recruiting Specialty: MIS and manufacturing

HIGHLAND PARK

LMB Associates
1468 Sunnyside Avenue
Highland Park, IL 60035
(847) 831-5990
Contact: Ms. Lorena Blonsky
Minimum Salary Placed: $30,000
Recruiting Specialty: MIS

HINSDALE

CES Associates
112 S. Grant Street
Hinsdale, IL 60521
(630) 654-2596
Contact: Mr. Jim Baker
Minimum Salary Placed: $35,000
Recruiting Specialty: Insurance, healthcare and manufacturing

Com People Source
17 W. Burr Oak Lane
Hinsdale, IL 60521
(312) 271-5544
Contact: Mr. Jack Hillon
Minimum Salary Placed: $25,000
Recruiting Specialty: Computers

Philip Conway Management
320 Hampton Place
Hinsdale, IL 60521
(630) 655-4566
Contact: Mr. Philip Conway
Minimum Salary Placed: $60,000
Recruiting Specialty: General

Joan Dutton Associates
351 Forest Road
Hinsdale, IL 60521
(630) 325-7774
Contact: Ms. Joan Dutton
Minimum Salary Placed: $25,000
Recruiting Specialty: General

Gnodde Associates
128 N. Lincoln Street
Hinsdale, IL 60521
(630) 887-9510
Contact: Mr. R. Dirk Gnodde
Minimum Salary Placed: $35,000
Recruiting Specialty: Finance and accounting in banking and finance

Hanover, Crown and Associates
P.O. Box 1606
Hinsdale, IL 60522
(630) 834-4250
Contact: Mr. A. Bonilla
Minimum Salary Placed: $25,000
Recruiting Specialty: General

Kolden & Associates, Ltd.
1301 W. 22nd Street
Hinsdale, IL 60521
(630) 986-9110
Contact: Mr. John Kolden
Minimum Salary Placed: $75,000
Recruiting Specialty: General

Kenneth Nicholas and Associates
7 Salt Creek Lane
Hinsdale, IL 60521
(630) 789-0097
Contact: Mr. Kenneth Nicholas
Minimum Salary Placed: $40,000
Recruiting Specialty: Sales and marketing
in medical

Quest Enterprises Ltd.
15 Spinning Wheel Road
Hinsdale, IL 60521
(630) 325-5717
Contact: Mr. R. Honquest
Minimum Salary Placed: $25,000
Recruiting Specialty: Data processing

David Rowe & Associates, Inc.
515 W. Maple Street
Hinsdale, IL 60521
(630) 387-1000
Contact: Mr. David Rowe
Minimum Salary Placed: $80,000
Recruiting Specialty: Healthcare

Target Search Inc.
7545 S. Madison Street
Hinsdale, IL 60521
(630) 654-0800
Minimum Salary Placed: $35,000
Recruiting Specialty: Technical disciplines in computers

HOFFMAN ESTATES

Industrial Recruiting Solutions 3
1566 W. Algonquin Road
Hoffman Estates, IL 60195
(847) 934-7220
Minimum Salary Placed: $35,000
Recruiting Specialty: Technical and
manufacturing

HOMEWOOD

Gregory Laka & Company
17450 S. Halsted Street, Suite 3E
Homewood, IL 60430
(708) 206-2000
Contact: Mr. Gregory Laka
Minimum Salary Placed: $50,000
Recruiting Specialty: MIS

INVERNESS

The Hetzel Group
1601 Colonial Parkway
Inverness, IL 60067
(847) 776-7000
Contact: Mr. William Hetzel
Minimum Salary Placed: $75,000
Recruiting Specialty: General

Les Vaughan
1623 Colonial Parkway, Suite A
Inverness, IL 60067
(847) 705-7100
Contact: Mr. Les Vaughan
Minimum Salary Placed: $35,000
Recruiting Specialty: Finance and occupational physical therapy

ITASCA

BGB Associates, Inc.
P.O. Box 556
Itasca, IL 60143
(708) 250-8993
Contact: Mr. Gregory Burchill
Minimum Salary Placed: $30,000
Recruiting Specialty: General

Technical Search Inc.
450 E. Devon Avenue
Itasca, IL 60143
(630) 775-0700
Minimum Salary Placed: $35,000
Recruiting Specialty: Engineering and software

VanMaldegiam Associates, Inc.
500 Park Boulevard, Suite 800
Itasca, IL 60143
(630) 250-8338
Contact: Mr. Norman VanMaldegiam
Minimum Salary Placed: $60,000
Recruiting Specialty: General

JOLIET

Britt Associates, Inc.
2709 Black Road
Joliet, IL 60435
(815) 744-7200
Contact: Mr. William Lichtenauer
Minimum Salary Placed: $25,000
Recruiting Specialty: Materials and product managers

JES Personnel Consultants
1859 Black Road
Joliet, IL 60435
(815) 741-0440
Contact: Mr. D. Sippel
Recruiting Specialty: General

KENILWORTH

T.A. Davis and Associates
604 Green Bay Road
Kenilworth, IL 60043
(847) 475-8900
Minimum Salary Placed: $25,000
Recruiting Specialty: Hospitality

LA GRANGE

Cast Metals Personnel
512 W. Burlington Avenue
La Grange, IL 60525
(708) 354-0085
Contact: Mr. C. Lundeen
Minimum Salary Placed: $35,000
Recruiting Specialty: Metals and manufacturing

LAKE BLUFF

The PAR Group—Paul A. Reaume, Ltd.
100 N. Waukegan Road, Suite 200
Lake Bluff, IL 60044
(847) 234-0005
Contact: Mr. Paul Reaume
Minimum Salary Placed: $45,000
Recruiting Specialty: Non-profit and government

LAKE FOREST

Kreutz Consulting Group, Inc.
585 N. Bank Lane, Suite 2000
Lake Forest, IL 60045
(847) 234-9115
Contact: Mr. Gary Kreutz
Minimum Salary Placed: $75,000
Recruiting Specialty: General

McDonald Associates International
1290 N. Western Avenue, Suite 209
Lake Forest, IL 60045
(847) 234-6889
Contact: Mr. Stanleigh McDonald
Minimum Salary Placed: $50,000
Recruiting Specialty: General

Wills and Company
222 E. Wisconsin Avenue
Lake Forest, IL 60045
(847) 735-1622
Minimum Salary Placed: $40,000
Recruiting Specialty: Information Sciences

LAKE ZURICH

Nu-Way Search
P.O. Box 494
Lake Zurich, IL 60047
(847) 726-8444
Contact: Mr. Steve Reese
Minimum Salary Placed: $25,000
Recruiting Specialty: General

Premier Search Associates, Inc.
21060 Rand Road, Suite 3
Lake Zurich, IL 60047
(847) 550-1515
Contact: Mr. Dave Melzer
Minimum Salary Placed: $25,000
Recruiting Specialty: General

LIBERTYVILLE

CompuPro
1117 South Milwaukee Avenue
Libertyville, IL 60048
(847) 549-8603
Contact: Mr. Douglas Baniqued
Minimum Salary Placed: $50,000
Recruiting Specialty: Computers

Matthews Professional Employment Specialists
311 E. Park Avenue
Libertyville, IL 60048
(847) 367-1117
Contact: Ms. Jane Ross
Minimum Salary Placed: $20,000
Recruiting Specialty: General

LINCOLN

Agra Placements, Ltd.
2200 N. Kickapoo
Lincoln, IL 62656
(217) 735-4373
Contact: Mr. Perry Schneider
Minimum Salary Placed: $25,000
Recruiting Specialty: Agri-business

LINCOLNSHIRE

Manufacturing Search Company
175 Olde Half Day Road
Lincolnshire, IL 60069
(847) 945-6065
Contact: Mr. R. Nevoral
Minimum Salary Placed: $25,000
Recruiting Specialty: General

Sales Consultants
430 Milwaukee Avenue, Suite 6
Lincolnshire, IL 60069
(708) 634-0300
Contact: Mr. Steve Briody
Minimum Salary Placed: $20,000
Recruiting Specialty: Sales

LINCOLNWOOD

Pre-Search, Inc.
7337 N. Lincoln Avenue, Room 280
Lincolnwood, IL 60646
(847) 679-8080
Contact: Mr. Joel Yaseen
Minimum Salary Placed: $35,000
Recruiting Specialty: General

LISLE

Verkamp-Joyce Associates, Inc.
2443 Warrenville Road, Suite 600
Lisle, IL 60532
(630) 955-3750
Contact: Ms. Sheila Joyce
Minimum Salary Placed: $80,000
Recruiting Specialty: General

LOMBARD

Advanced Search Group Inc.
1910 S. Highland Avenue
Lombard, IL 60148
(630) 620-8778
Contact: Mr. T. Doyle
Minimum Salary Placed: $35,000
Recruiting Specialty: Engineering, operations and general management

Onsite Staffing Solutions
477 E. Butterfield Road
Lombard, IL 60148
(630) 969-7010
Contact: Ms. Noreen Counley
Minimum Salary Placed: $60,000
Recruiting Specialty: General

LOVES PARK

Ned Dickey and Associates, Inc.
1880 Windsor Road
Box 15068
Loves Park, IL 61132
(815) 636-4480
Contact: Mr. Ned Dickey
Minimum Salary Placed: $25,000
Recruiting Specialty: General

MATTESON

Carter Associates
P.O. Box 310
Matteson, IL 60443
(708) 503-5020
Contact: Mr. Chuck Carter
Minimum Salary Placed: $35,000
Recruiting Specialty: General

MATTOON

Management Recruiters
P.O. Box 461
Mattoon, IL 61938
(217) 235-9393
Contact: Mr. David Tolle
Minimum Salary Placed: $20,000
Recruiting Specialty: Flavors and fragrances

MCHENRY

Bratland and Associates
5424 W. Brittany Drive
McHenry, IL 60050
(815) 344-4335
Contact: Mr. A. Bratland
Minimum Salary Placed: $25,000
Recruiting Specialty: General

MOLINE

McGladrey & Pullen
600 35th Avenue
Moline, IL 61265
(309) 762-4040
Contact: Mr. Gary Skarr
Minimum Salary Placed: $30,000
Recruiting Specialty: General

Snelling Personnel Services
2201 5th Avenue, Suite 5
Moline, 61265
(309) 797-1101
Contact: Ms. J. Herrell
Minimum Salary Placed: $25,000
Recruiting Specialty: General

MOUNT PROSPECT

Belson Group
P.O. Box 1414
Mt. Prospect, IL 60056
(847) 342-9730
Contact: Mr. Ted Ferguson
Minimum Salary Placed: $25,000
Recruiting Specialty: Telecommunications, manufacturing and design engineering

Magnum Search
1000 E. Golfhurst Avenue
Mount Prospect, IL 60056
(847) 577-0007
Contact: Mr. Arthur Kristufek
Minimum Salary Placed: $30,000
Recruiting Specialty: Manufacturing

Moran Group
18 W. Busse Avenue
Mount Prospect, IL 60056
(847) 506-1050
Contact: Mr. E. Lysac
Minimum Salary Placed: $25,000
Recruiting Specialty: Leasing and retail

MOUNT VERNON

Technisearch Recruiters, L.L.C.
Mt. Vernon Airport, Route 4, Suite 105
Terminal Building
Mt. Vernon, IL 62864
(618) 242-2460
Contact: Ms. Christine Mueller
Minimum Salary Placed: $25,000
Recruiting Specialty: Technical disciplines in plastics

NAPERVILLE

Joseph Aguglia and Associates
128 W. Webster Place
Naperville, IL 60540
(630) 355-9415
Contact: Mr. Joe Aguglia
Minimum Salary Placed: $70,000
Recruiting Specialty: Physicians

Thomas Baldwin Associates
1335 Creighton Avenue
Naperville, IL 60565
(630) 416-0005
Contact: Mr. Tom Baldwin
Minimum Salary Placed: $25,000
Recruiting Specialty: General

Cumberland Group Inc.
608 S. Washington Street, Suite 101
Naperville, IL 60540
(630) 416-9494
Contact: Mr. Jerry Vogus
Minimum Salary Placed: $30,000
Recruiting Specialty: Sales and marketing in manufacturing

Dalton-Smith & Associates, Inc.
877 Plainfield Road
Naperville, IL 60540
(630) 420-2142
Contact: Mr. Don Smith
Minimum Salary Placed: $20,000
Recruiting Specialty: Computers

Jender & Company
800 W. 5th Avenue, Suite 205B
Naperville, IL 60563
(630) 355-7797
Contact: Mr. Jesse Jender
Minimum Salary Placed: $50,000
Recruiting Specialty: General

LTM Associates
1112 Elizabeth
Naperville, IL 60540
(630) 961-3331
Contact: Ms. Madeleine Ward
Recruiting Specialty: Vehicle leasing

Stephen R. Smith & Company, Inc.
P.O. Box 626
Naperville, IL 60566
(630) 357-4434
Contact: Mr. Stephen Smith
Minimum Salary Placed: $50,000
Recruiting Specialty: General

J.D. Wright & Associates, Inc.
1301 Margate Court
Naperville, IL 60540
(630) 369-1308
Contact: Mr. James Wright
Recruiting Specialty: Data processing, sales and marketing

NILES

Michael Wayne Recruiters
7135 Carol Court
Niles, IL 60714
(847) 966-2227
Contact: Mr. Richard Barnat
Minimum Salary Placed: $25,000
Recruiting Specialty: Consumer products and foods

PolyTechnical Consultants, Inc.
7213 W. Breen
Niles, IL 60714
(847) 470-9000
Contact: Mr. Walt Zimmer
Minimum Salary Placed: $25,000
Recruiting Specialty: Engineering

NORMAL

Heller Kil Associates, Inc.
306 Robert Drive
Normal, IL 61761
(309) 454-7077

Contact: Mr. Larry Shapiro
Minimum Salary Placed: $40,000
Recruiting Specialty: Automotive and
transportation

Management Recruiters
211 Landmark Drive, Suite E-1
Normal, IL 61761
(309) 452-1844
Contact: Mr. Alan Snedden
Minimum Salary Placed: $20,000
Recruiting Specialty: General

NORTHBROOK

Accountants Executive Search
3400 Dundee Road, Suite 260
Northbrook, IL 60062
(847) 205-0808
Contact: Ms. B O'Connell
Minimum Salary Placed: $25,000
Recruiting Specialty: Finance and ac-
counting

Accountants On Call
3400 Dundee Road, Suite 260
Northbrook, IL 60062
(847) 205-0800
Contact: Ms. Bridget O'Connell
Recruiting Specialty: Finance and accounting

K. Carroll & Associates
707 Skokie Boulevard, Suite 600
Northbrook, IL 60062
(847) 291-4310
Contact: Ms. Kathy Carroll
Minimum Salary Placed: $35,000
Recruiting Specialty: MIS and FIS

Clarey & Andrews, Inc.
1200 Shermer Road, Suite 108
Northbrook, IL 60062
(847) 498-2870
Contact: Mr. J. Douglas Andrews
Minimum Salary Placed: $90,000
Recruiting Specialty: General

Diener and Associates
P.O. Box 946
Northbrook, IL 60065
(847) 564-3160
Contact: Mr. Joel Diener
Minimum Salary Placed: $25,000
Recruiting Specialty: General

Eastwood Group
950 Skokie Boulevard
Northbrook, IL 60062
(847) 291-8383
Contact: Ms. B. Miller
Minimum Salary Placed: $30,000
Recruiting Specialty: Marketing and com-
munications

Hersher Associates, Ltd.
3000 Dundee Road, Suite 314
Northbrook, IL 60062
(847) 272-4050
Contact: Ms. Betsy Hersher
Minimum Salary Placed: $50,000
Recruiting Specialty: Healthcare

M.B. Partners
P.O. Box 675
Northbrook, IL 60065
(847) 559-0959
Contact: Ms. Mary Burn
Minimum Salary Placed: $35,000
Recruiting Specialty: Healthcare and
pharmaceuticals

Robert Half International
5 Revere Drive
Northbrook, IL 60062
(847) 480-7995
Contact: Ms. P. Kracke
Minimum Salary Placed: $25,000
Recruiting Specialty: Accounting and finance

Roth Young
3330 W. Dundee Road
Northbrook, IL 60062
(312) 368-8455
Contact: Mr. Steve Friedlander
Minimum Salary Placed: $20,000
Recruiting Specialty: Hospitality

Bonnie Singer and Company
900 Skokie Boulevard
Northbrook, IL 60062
(847) 266-0181
Contact: Ms. Bonnie Singer
Minimum Salary Placed: $25,000
Recruiting Specialty: General

Voigt Associates
601 Skokie Road, Suite 301
Northbrook, IL 60062
(847) 564-4152
Contact: Mr. Raymond Voigt
Minimum Salary Placed: $75,000
Recruiting Specialty: Pharmaceuticals

NORTHFIELD

Financial Executive Search
456 W. Frontage Road
Northfield, IL 60093
(847) 256-2385
Contact: Mr. Chuck Cleave
Minimum Salary Placed: $40,000
Recruiting Specialty: Finance

Ralph Smith & Associates
540 Frontage Road, Suite 3335
Northfield, IL 60093
(847) 441-0900
Contact: Mr. Ralph Smith
Minimum Salary Placed: $50,000
Recruiting Specialty: General

OAK BROOK

Callan Associates, Ltd.
1550 Spring Road
Oak Brook, IL 60521
(630) 574-9300
Contact: Mr. Robert Callan
Minimum Salary Placed: $100,000
Recruiting Specialty: General

Cemco Systems
2015 Spring Road, Suite 250
Oak Brook, IL 60521
(630) 573-5050
Contact: Mr. Dave Gordon
Minimum Salary Placed: $35,000
Recruiting Specialty: MIS

Cizek & Associates
2021 Midwest Road, Suite 200
Oak Brook, IL 60521
(630) 953-8570
Contact: Mr. John Cizek
Minimum Salary Placed: $60,000
Recruiting Specialty: General

Compass Sentrex Inc.
900 Jorie Boulevard
Oak Brook, IL 60521
(630) 990-4888
Contact: Mr. A. Stumbo
Minimum Salary Placed: $25,000
Recruiting Specialty: General

Erwin Associates
2021 Midwest Road, Suite 200
Oak Brook, IL 60521
(630) 953-8519
Contact: Mr. John Cizek
Minimum Salary Placed: $75,000
Recruiting Specialty: Plant and manufacturing

Grossberg & Associates
1100 Jorie Boulevard, Suite 301
Oak Brook, IL 60521
(630) 574-0066
Contact: Mr. Robert Grossberg
Minimum Salary Placed: $45,000
Recruiting Specialty: General

Kunzer Associates, Ltd.
1415 W. 22nd Street
Oak Brook, IL 60521
(630) 574-0010
Contact: Mr. William Kunzer
Minimum Salary Placed: $50,000
Recruiting Specialty: General

Le Beau and Associates
900 Jorie Boulevard
Oak Brook, IL 60521
(630) 990-2233
Contact: Mr. Carl Le Beau
Minimum Salary Placed: $25,000
Recruiting Specialty: General

M/J/A Partners
1100 Jorie Boulevard, Suite 301
Oak Brook, IL 60521
(630) 990-0033
Contact: Mr. Manuel Alves
Minimum Salary Placed: $50,000
Recruiting Specialty: General

Moore Employment Services, Inc.
P.O. Box 3882
Oak Brook, IL 60522
(630) 357-8118
Contact: Ms. Ellie Moore
Minimum Salary Placed: $30,000
Recruiting Specialty: Accounting and finance

Phil Nicholson and Associates
1301 W. 22nd Street
Oak Brook, IL 60521
(630) 574-0555
Contact: Mr. Phil Nicholson
Minimum Salary Placed: $35,000
Recruiting Specialty: Finance and operations

John Paisios Ltd.
2211 York Road
Oak Brook, IL 60521
(630) 571-1080
Contact: Mr. John Paisios
Minimum Salary Placed: $75,000
Recruiting Specialty: General

Jonathan Ross Ltd.
1132 Catherine Avenue
Oak Brook, IL 60521
(630) 305-3030
Minimum Salary Placed: $35,000
Recruiting Specialty: Technical disciplines

Sales Consultants
1100 Jorie Boulevard, Suite 210
Oak Brook, IL 60521
(630) 990-8233
Contact: Mr. Gary Miller
Minimum Salary Placed: $20,000
Recruiting Specialty: Sales

Sanford Rose Associates
2625 Butterfield Road, Suite 107W
Oak Brook, IL 60521
(630) 574-9405
Contact: Mr. James Keogh
Minimum Salary Placed: $30,000
Recruiting Specialty: Manufacturing and banking

Trilogy Enterprises, Inc.
1919 Midwest Road, Suite 108
Oak Brook, IL 60521
(630) 268-0900
Contact: Mr. Eric Schuller
Minimum Salary Placed: $35,000
Recruiting Specialty: General

Witt/Kieffer, Ford, Hadelman & Lloyd
2015 Spring Road, Suite 510
Oak Brook, IL 60521
(630) 990-1370
Contact: Mr. Michael Kieffer
Minimum Salary Placed: $75,000
Recruiting Specialty: Healthcare

OAK PARK

Computer Future Exchange Inc.
1111 Westgate
Oak Park, IL 60301
(708) 445-1494
Contact: Mr. C. Gimbel
Minimum Salary Placed: $35,000
Recruiting Specialty: Computers

Cowell & Associates, Ltd.
906 N. Marion Street
Oak Park, IL 60302
(708) 383-6618

Contact: Mr. Roy Cowell
Minimum Salary Placed: $75,000
Recruiting Specialty: General

Juan Menefee & Associates
503 S. Oak Park Avenue, Suite 206
Oak Park, IL 60304
(708) 848-7722
Contact: Mr. Juan Menefee
Minimum Salary Placed: $25,000
Recruiting Specialty: General; Minorities

O'Toole & Company
1047 Forest Avenue
Oak Park, IL 60302
(708) 848-6200
Contact: Mr. William O'Toole
Minimum Salary Placed: $60,000
Recruiting Specialty: General

OAKBROOK TERRACE

Accountants On Call
1 Lincoln Centre, Suite 1050
Oakbrook Terrace, IL 60181
(708) 261-1300
Contact: Ms. Debbie Bacorn
Recruiting Specialty: Finance and accounting

Compass Group Ltd.
Two Mid America Plaza, Suite 800
Oakbrook Terrace, IL 60181
(708) 954-2255
Contact: Mr. Jerold Lipe
Minimum Salary Placed: $70,000
Recruiting Specialty: General

Fahey Associates, Inc.
17W 755 Butterfield Road
Oakbrook Terrace, IL 60181
(708) 629-6774
Contact: Ms. Barbara Fahey
Minimum Salary Placed: $60,000
Recruiting Specialty: Physicians

Tannura & Associates, Inc.
One Tower Lane, Suite 1700
Oakbrook Terrace, IL 60181
(708) 573-2929
Contact: Mr. Robert Tannura
Minimum Salary Placed: $50,000
Recruiting Specialty: MIS and computers

OLYMPIA FIELDS

Tom McCall Executive Search
20180 Governors Highway
Olympia Fields, IL 60461
(708) 747-5707
Contact: Mr. Tom McCall
Minimum Salary Placed: $25,000
Recruiting Specialty: Bolts, fasteners and screws

ORLAND PARK

Career Placement
Orland Park, IL 60462
(708) 301-3771
Contact: Mr. D. Merkins
Minimum Salary Placed: $35,000
Recruiting Specialty: Metals

Professional Profiles Search
P.O. Box 283
Orland Park, IL 60462
(708) 403-9229

Contact: Mary Beth
Minimum Salary Placed: $25,000
Recruiting Specialty: Equipment leasing

PALATINE

The Robinson Group, D.A., Ltd.
800 E. Northwest Highway, Suite 809
Palatine, IL 60067
(847) 359-0990
Contact: Mr. Donald Alan Robinson
Minimum Salary Placed: $55,000
Recruiting Specialty: Accounting and finance

Youngs Walker and Company
1605 W. Colonial Parkway
Palatine, IL 60067
(847) 991-6900
Contact: Mr. C. Youngs
Minimum Salary Placed: $40,000
Recruiting Specialty: Newspapers

PALOS HEIGHTS

Management Recruiters
7804 W. College Drive
Palos Heights, IL 60463
(708) 361-8778
Contact: Mr. Victor Persico
Minimum Salary Placed: $20,000
Recruiting Specialty: General

Sales Consultants
6420 W. 127th Street, Suite 209
Palos Heights, IL 60463
(708) 371-9677
Contact: Mr. Jack White
Minimum Salary Placed: $20,000
Recruiting Specialty: Sales

PALOS PARK

Twin Oaks Technical, Inc.
12503 S. 90th
Palos Park, IL 60464
(708) 923-6040
Contact: Mr. Rick O'Malley
Minimum Salary Placed: $25,000
Recruiting Specialty: Chemicals

PEORIA

McGladrey & Pullen
401 Main Street, Suite 1200
Peoria, IL 61602
(309) 671-8700
Contact: Ms. Raylana Anderson
Minimum Salary Placed: $30,000
Recruiting Specialty: General

Rush Personnel Service
331 Fulton, 1st Bank Plaza
Peoria, IL 61602
(309) 637-8303
Contact: Mr. R. Rush
Minimum Salary Placed: $25,000
Recruiting Specialty: General

Snelling Personnel Service
331 Fulton Street, Suite 322
Peoria, IL 61602
(309) 676-5581
Contact: Ms. S. Zoller
Minimum Salary Placed: $25,000
Recruiting Specialty: General

RIVERWOODS

Onsite Staffing Solutions
1143 Milwaukee Avenue
Riverwoods, IL 60015
(847) 459-1320
Contact: Ms. Tanya Falk
Minimum Salary Placed: $60,000
Recruiting Specialty: General

ROCKFORD

The Furst Group
1639 N. Alpine Road, Suite 505
Rockford, IL 61107
(815) 229-7800
Contact: Mr. Thomas Furst
Minimum Salary Placed: $50,000
Recruiting Specialty: General

Sanford Rose Associates
416 E. State Street, Suite 205
Rockford, IL 61104
(815) 964-4080
Contact: Mr. Dennis Wallace
Minimum Salary Placed: $30,000
Recruiting Specialty: Technical and engi-
neering in drugs and manufacturing

ROLLING MEADOWS

CGL and Associates
3601 W. Algonquin Road, Suite 440
Rolling Meadows, IL 60008
(847) 394-0661
Contact: Mr. K. Chmeil
Minimum Salary Placed: $25,000
Recruiting Specialty: Data processing

Computer Professionals
3601 Algonquin Road, Suite 129
Rolling Meadows, IL 60008
(847) 577-6266
Contact: Mr. Kevin Hogan
Minimum Salary Placed: $125,000
Recruiting Specialty: Computers

Converge Corporation
5105 Tollview Drive
Rolling Meadows, IL 60008
(847) 705-7272
Contact: Mr. M. Lund
Minimum Salary Placed: $25,000
Recruiting Specialty: General

Dunhill Professional Search
5005 Newport Drive, Suite 201
Rolling Meadows, IL 60008
(847) 398-3400
Contact: Mr. Russ Kunke
Minimum Salary Placed: $25,000
Recruiting Specialty: General

Elsko Executive Search
3601 W. Algonquin Road
Rolling Meadows, IL 60008
(847) 394-2400
Contact: Mr. Dave Speck
Minimum Salary Placed: $25,000
Recruiting Specialty: Accounting and finance

Michael J. Hawkins, Inc.
3601 West Algonquin Road, Suite 300
Rolling Meadows, IL 60008
(847) 705-5400
Contact: Mr. Michael Hawkins
Minimum Salary Placed: $35,000
Recruiting Specialty: Accounting and finance

John Imber Associates, Ltd.
3601 Algonquin Road, Suite 129
Rolling Meadows, IL 60008
(847) 506-1700
Contact: Mr. John Imber
Minimum Salary Placed: $50,000
Recruiting Specialty: General

Mannard & Associates, Inc.
1600 Golf Road, Suite 1200
Rolling Meadows, IL 60008
(847) 981-5170
Contact: Mr. Tom Mannard
Minimum Salary Placed: $60,000
Recruiting Specialty: Manufacturing of plastics and metals

Onsite Staffing Solutions
3315 Algonquin Road
Rolling Meadows, IL 60008
(847) 398-3655
Contact: Ms. Rochelle Sciatti
Minimum Salary Placed: $60,000
Recruiting Specialty: General

Source EDP
3701 Algonquin Road, Suite 380
Rolling Meadows, IL 60008
(847) 392-0244
Contact: Mr. Jerry Lump
Recruiting Specialty: Computer software and hardware

ROSCOE

Effective Search, Inc.
11718 N. Main Street
Roscoe, IL 61073
(815) 654-8505
Contact: Mr. John Cain
Minimum Salary Placed: $40,000
Recruiting Specialty: General

Midwest Management Resources
12303 Legend Lakes Drive
Roscoe, IL 61073
(815) 389-2500
Contact: Mr. E. McCaskey
Minimum Salary Placed: $35,000
Recruiting Specialty: Wholesale and retail
supermarket

ROSELLE

National Restaurant Search, Inc.
910 W. Lake Street, Suite 108
Roselle, IL 60172
(847) 924-1800
Contact: Mr. John Chitvanni
Minimum Salary Placed: $50,000
Recruiting Specialty: Hospitality

M. Rector & Associates, Inc.
40 S. Prospect, Suite 200
Roselle, IL 60172
(847) 894-5060
Contact: Ms. Mona Rector
Minimum Salary Placed: $30,000
Recruiting Specialty: Real estate

ROSEMONT

Bertrand, Ross & Associates, Inc.
6300 N. River Road, Suite 102
Rosemont, IL 60018
(847) 825-5100
Contact: Mr. Thomas Bertrand
Minimum Salary Placed: $50,000
Recruiting Specialty: General

Hodge-Cronin & Associates, Inc.
9575 West Higgins Road, Suite 904
Rosemont, IL 60018
(847) 692-2041

Contact: Ms. Kathleen Cronin
Minimum Salary Placed: $75,000
Recruiting Specialty: General

International Management Services Inc.
6300 N. River Road, Suite 601
Rosemont, IL 60018
(847) 698-2800
Contact: Mr. Carl Johnson
Minimum Salary Placed: $50,000
Recruiting Specialty: General

Sales Search Specialist
9501 W. Devon, Suite 300
Rosemont, IL 60018
(847) 696-1900
Contact: Ms. Darlene Fidlow
Minimum Salary Placed: $40,000
Recruiting Specialty: Sales

SAINT CHARLES

Management Recruiters
10 E. State Avenue, Suite 201
St. Charles, IL 60174
(630) 377-6466
Contact: Mr. Daniel Lasse
Minimum Salary Placed: $25,000
Recruiting Specialty: Manufacturing

SCHAUMBURG

Allen and Associates
1300 E. Woodfield Road, Suite 300
Schaumburg, IL 60173
(847) 517-7792
Contact: Ms. P. Allen
Minimum Salary Placed: $25,000
Recruiting Specialty: General

Executive Concepts Inc.
1000 E. Woodfield Road
Schaumburg, IL 60173
(847) 605-8300
Contact: Mr. T. Werle
Minimum Salary Placed: $25,000
Recruiting Specialty: Data processing

Hays Search
25150 N. Iroquois Court
Schaumburg, IL 60194
(847) 382-5458
Contact: Mr. Carl Hays
Minimum Salary Placed: $25,000
Recruiting Specialty: General

Jim Kay and Associates
1111 Plaza Drive, Suite 480
Schaumburg, IL 60173
(847) 330-9600
Contact: Mr. Jim Kay
Minimum Salary Placed: $75,000
Recruiting Specialty: Software, telecommunications and manufacturing

McCormick Search Inc.
111 Plaza Drive, Suite 520
Schaumburg, IL 60173
(847) 671-0500
Minimum Salary Placed: $25,000
Recruiting Specialty: Data processing

Professional Research Services, Inc.
1101 Perimeter Drive, Suite 725
Schaumburg, IL 60173
(847) 995-8800
Contact: Mr. Tom DeBourcy
Minimum Salary Placed: $35,000
Recruiting Specialty: General

Professional Search Centre, Ltd.
1515 Woodfield Road, Suite 830
Schaumburg, IL 60173
(847) 330-3250

Contact: Mr. Jerry Hirschel
Recruiting Specialty: Computers and MIS

Systems One Ltd.
1100 E. Woodfield Road
Schaumburg, IL 60173
(847) 619-9300
Contact: Mr. John Dahl
Minimum Salary Placed: $50,000
Recruiting Specialty: MIS and computers

United Information Corporation
1051 Perimeter Drive
Schaumburg, IL 60173
(847) 706-1300
Contact: Mr. A. Geller
Minimum Salary Placed: $25,000
Recruiting Specialty: General

Valentine & Associates
One Woodfield Lake, Suite 117
Schaumburg, IL 60173
(847) 605-8090
Contact: Ms. Linda Valentine
Minimum Salary Placed: $25,000
Recruiting Specialty: Manufacturing and plant personnel in the manufacturing environment

SUMNER

Larson & Trent Associates
Box 1
Sumner, IL 62466
(800) 352-6226
Contact: Mr. Wendell Trent
Recruiting Specialty: Physicians

SYCAMORE

Mathey Services
15170 Bethany Road
Sycamore, IL 60178
(815) 895-3846

Contact: Ms. Joyce Mathey
Minimum Salary Placed: $30,000
Recruiting Specialty: Chemical and plastics

TINLEY PARK

Irwin and Wagner Inc.
17720 67th Avenue
Tinley Park, IL 60477
(708) 532-2800
Contact: Ms. Mary Irwin
Minimum Salary Placed: $25,000
Recruiting Specialty: General

Teams, Inc.
17349 70th Avenue
Tinley Park, IL 60477
(708) 532-4585
Contact: Mr. Don Radloff
Minimum Salary Placed: $30,000
Recruiting Specialty: Technical disciplines

VERNON HILLS

Huntington Resource
3 Hawthorne Parkway, Suite 195
Vernon Hills, IL 60061
(847) 367-5777
Minimum Salary Placed: $25,000
Recruiting Specialty: General

VILLA PARK

Hamilton Grey
15280 Summit Avenue, Suite B3
Villa Park, IL 60181
(630) 932-1114

Contact: Mr. F. Baron
Minimum Salary Placed: $35,000
Recruiting Specialty: Information technology

Upp Business Systems
1 Transom Plaza Drive, Suite 430
Villa Park, IL 60181
(630) 932-4300
Contact: Ms. D. Upp
Minimum Salary Placed: $25,000
Recruiting Specialty: General

WARRENVILLE

HCI Corporation
29 W. 585 Batavia Road
Warrenville, IL 60555
(708) 393-6400
Contact: Mr. F. Cianchetti
Minimum Salary Placed: $25,000
Recruiting Specialty: General

WAUKEGAN

Matthews Professional Employment Specialists
321 Grand Avenue
Waukegan, IL 60085
(847) 244-6500
Contact: Mr. Charles Matthews
Minimum Salary Placed: $20,000
Recruiting Specialty: General

WEST DUNDEE

Management Search, Inc.
120 W. Main Street
West Dundee, IL 60118
(847) 551-1200

Contact: Mr. Stefan Levy
Recruiting Specialty: General

WESTCHESTER

CPS Inc.
1 Westbrook Center, Suite 600
Westchester, IL 60154
(708) 531-8370
Contact: Mr. Frank Filippelli
Minimum Salary Placed: $20,000
Recruiting Specialty: Manufacturing in consumer products

The Prairie Group
1 Westbrook Corporation Center,
 Suite 300
Westchester, IL 60154
(708) 449-7710
Contact: Mr. James Kick
Minimum Salary Placed: $50,000
Recruiting Specialty: General

WESTMONT

Networks
101 Cass Avenue
Westmont, IL 60559
(708) 789-3577
Contact: Ms. Joan Bohm
Minimum Salary Placed: $35,000
Recruiting Specialty: Industrial sales and engineering

Nicholaou & Company
56 West Piers Drive
Westmont, IL 60559
(708) 960-2382
Contact: Ms. Jean Nicholaou
Minimum Salary Placed: $50,000
Recruiting Specialty: General

Professional Outlook, Inc.
825 N. Cass Avenue, Suite 111
Westmont, IL 60559
(630) 887-1444
Contact: Ms. Bethany Brevard
Minimum Salary Placed: $25,000
Recruiting Specialty: Engineering, environmental, health/safety and human resources

Search Enterprises, Inc.
160 Quail Ridge Drive
Westmont, IL 60559
(708) 654-2300
Contact: Mr. Frank Polacek
Minimum Salary Placed: $30,000
Recruiting Specialty: General

WHEATON

Ethical Search Professionals, Ltd.
822 W. Arbor Avenue
Wheaton, IL 60187
(630) 668-4009
Contact: Mr. Jim Sullivan
Minimum Salary Placed: $25,000
Recruiting Specialty: Engineering

Krecek and Associates
107 E. Front Street
Wheaton, IL 60187
(630) 653-1300
Contact: Mr. G. Krecek
Minimum Salary Placed: $35,000
Recruiting Specialty: Computer science and data processing

Neal Carden Associates Inc.
620 W. Roosevelt Road
Wheaton, IL 60187
(630) 665-3932

Contact: Mr. Jim Neal
Minimum Salary Placed: $25,000
Recruiting Specialty: General

New Directions, Inc.
1127 Wheaton Oaks Court, P.O. Box 88
Wheaton, IL 60189
(630) 462-1840
Contact: Mr. Dale Frank
Minimum Salary Placed: $50,000
Recruiting Specialty: General

WHEELING

Chatterton and Associates Inc.
135 Wheeling Road
Wheeling, IL 60090
(847) 537-3830
Contact: Mr. T. Chatterton
Minimum Salary Placed: $25,000
Recruiting Specialty: General

Matthews Professional Employment Specialists
505 N. Wolf Road
Wheeling, IL 60090
(847) 215-0183
Contact: Ms. Gail O'Brien
Minimum Salary Placed: $20,000
Recruiting Specialty: General

Select Search
1111 W. Dundee Road
Wheeling, IL 60089
(847) 437-3555
Minimum Salary Placed: $25,000
Recruiting Specialty: General

WILMETTE

Donald F. Dvorak & Company
1000 Skokie Boulevard, Suite 200
Wilmette, IL 60091
(847) 853-8110
Contact: Mr. Donald Dvorak
Minimum Salary Placed: $90,000
Recruiting Specialty: General

Highland Group
1639 Highland Avenue
Wilmette, IL 60091
(847) 251-2900
Contact: Mr. Jim Cadwell
Minimum Salary Placed: $50,000
Recruiting Specialty: Healthcare

Joyce C. Knauff & Associates
P.O. Box 624
Wilmette, IL 60091
(847) 251-7284
Contact: Ms. Joyce Knauff
Minimum Salary Placed: $35,000
Recruiting Specialty: MIS

David White and Associates
809 Ridge Road
Wilmette, IL 60091
(847) 256-8826
Contact: Mr. David White
Minimum Salary Placed: $50,000
Recruiting Specialty: Attorneys

WINFIELD

Waterford Executive Group
1 N. 141 County Farm Road
Winfield, IL 60190
(630) 690-0055

Contact: Mr. P. Atkinson
Minimum Salary Placed: $25,000
Recruiting Specialty: Consultants in compensation

I N D I A N A

ANDERSON

Hudson Associates Inc.
P.O. Box 2502
Anderson, IN 46018
(317) 649-1133
Contact: Mr. George Hudson
Minimum Salary Placed: $25,000
Recruiting Specialty: Insurance, attorneys, marketing and sales

BLOOMINGTON

Curare Group
4001 East 3rd Street
Bloomington, IN 47404
(812) 331-0645
Contact: Mr. Dave Witte
Recruiting Specialty: Physicians

HRS Group
P.O. Box 5931
Bloomington, IN 47407
(812) 331-7633
Contact: Ms. Sheree Demming
Minimum Salary Placed: $25,000
Recruiting Specialty: General

BRAZIL

Hart Line
9670 N. Kennedy Crossing Road
Brazil, IN 47834
(812) 448-3490
Contact: Mr. E. Stearley
Minimum Salary Placed: $25,000
Recruiting Specialty: General

CHESTERTON

Quality Search
1100 S. Calumet Road
Chesterton, IN 46304
(219) 926-8202
Contact: Mr. James Jeselnick
Minimum Salary Placed: $30,000
Recruiting Specialty: Technical disciplines in manufacturing

CLARKSVILLE

Technical and Search Recruiters
P.O. Box 2088
Clarksville, IN 47131
(812) 284-3012
Contact: Mr. Jim Bernola
Minimum Salary Placed: $25,000
Recruiting Specialty: Consumer electronics, human resources, engineering and accounting

COLUMBUS

Gary Hahn and Technical Staffing
4060 25th Street
Columbus, IN 47203
(812) 372-0125

Contact: Mr. Gary Hahn
Minimum Salary Placed: $25,000
Recruiting Specialty: General

Management Recruiters
P.O. Box 2234
Columbus, IN 47202
(812) 372-5500
Contact: Mr. J. Michael Percifield
Minimum Salary Placed: $25,000
Recruiting Specialty: General

Parallel Group International, Inc.
2530 Sandcrest Boulevard, Suite B
Columbus, IN 47203
(812) 379-9510
Contact: Mr. Ken Cohil
Minimum Salary Placed: $25,000
Recruiting Specialty: General

Smith and Syberg Inc.
825 Washington Street, Suite 2A
Columbus, IN 47201
(812) 372-7254
Contact: Mr. K. Syberg
Minimum Salary Placed: $35,000
Recruiting Specialty: General

Tasa International
1428 Franklin Street
Columbus, IN 47202
(812) 376-9061
Contact: Mr. Robert Evans
Minimum Salary Placed: $100,000
Recruiting Specialty: General

DYER

National Recruiting Service
P.O. Box 218
1832 Hart Street
Dyer, IN 46311
(219) 865-2373
Contact: Mr. Stanley Hendricks
Minimum Salary Placed: $35,000
Recruiting Specialty: Metals, plastics and
fabrication

ELKHART

McGladrey & Pullen
121 W. Franklin Street
Elkhart, IN 46515
(219) 522-0410
Minimum Salary Placed: $30,000
Recruiting Specialty: Accounting

Robert Sage Recruiting
127 E. Windsor Avenue
Elkhart, IN 46514
(219) 264-1126
Contact: Mr. Frank Alvey
Minimum Salary Placed: $25,000
Recruiting Specialty: Manufacturing,
transportation and automotive

EVANSVILLE

Career Associates
100 North St. Joseph
Evansville, IN 47712
(812) 423-7263
Contact: Mr. Pat Meehan
Minimum Salary Placed: $25,000
Recruiting Specialty: General

Management Recruiters
101 Court Street, Suite 209
Evansville, IN 47708
(812) 464-9155
Contact: Ms. Marjorie Caldemeyer
Minimum Salary Placed: $25,000
Recruiting Specialty: Industrial manufac-
turing

Sales Consultants
101 Court Street, Suite 207
Evansville, IN 47708
(812) 464-5400
Contact: Mr. Dan Caldemeyer
Minimum Salary Placed: $25,000
Recruiting Specialty: Sales

FISHERS

Q Resources Inc.
10000 Allisonville Road, Suite 150
Fishers, IN 46038
(317) 841-7120
Contact: Ms. S. Breen
Minimum Salary Placed: $25,000
Recruiting Specialty: Healthcare

FORT WAYNE

Alpha Rae Personnel, Inc.
127 West Berry Street, Suite 200
Fort Wayne, IN 46802
(219) 426-8227
Contact: Ms. Rae Pearson
Minimum Salary Placed: $25,000
Recruiting Specialty: General

Dobias Group
130 W. Main Street
Fort Wayne, IN 46802
(219) 436-6570

Contact: Mr. Brian Dobias
Minimum Salary Placed: $25,000
Recruiting Specialty: Hospitality

Dunhill Professional Search
9918 Coldwater Road
Fort Wayne, IN 46825
(219) 489-5966
Contact: Mr. Charlie Davis
Minimum Salary Placed: $25,000
Recruiting Specialty: Healthcare and en-
gineering

Dunhill Professional Search
P.O. Box 25127
Fort Wayne, IN 46825
(219) 486-0905
Contact: Mr. Doug Gillie
Minimum Salary Placed: $25,000
Recruiting Specialty: Healthcare

Mallard Group
3322 Oak Borough
Fort Wayne, IN 46804
(219) 436-3970
Contact: Mr. R. Hoffman
Minimum Salary Placed: $25,000
Recruiting Specialty: Engineering, sales
and marketing

Mayhall Search Group Inc.
3540 Wells Street
Fort Wayne, IN 46808
(219) 484-7770
Contact: Mr. D. Mayhall
Minimum Salary Placed: $25,000
Recruiting Specialty: General

National Corporate Consultants, Inc.
5916 E. State Boulevard
Fort Wayne, IN 46815
(219) 493-4506

Contact: Mr. James Corya
Minimum Salary Placed: $30,000
Recruiting Specialty: General

Roster Inc.
6333 Constitution Drive
Fort Wayne, IN 46804
(219) 436-6330
Contact: Mr. Glenn Johnson
Minimum Salary Placed: $30,000
Recruiting Specialty: General

INDIANAPOLIS

Accountants On Call
111 Monument Circle, Suite 3510
Indianapolis, IN 46204
(317) 686-0001
Contact: Ms. Marge Meyer
Recruiting Specialty: Accounting and finance

The Bennett Group, Inc.
5640 Professional Circle
Indianapolis, IN 46241
(317) 247-1240
Contact: Mr. M. D. Bennett
Minimum Salary Placed: $50,000
Recruiting Specialty: Automotive and electronics

Bindley Associates
10 W. Market Street, Suite 500
Indianapolis, IN 46204
(317) 464-8144
Contact: Mr. Jim Bindley
Minimum Salary Placed: $25,000
Recruiting Specialty: General

Career Consultants Outplacement Intl. Inc.
107 N. Pennsylvania, Suite 400
Indianapolis, IN 46204
(812) 235-8073
Contact: Mr. Richard Abraham
Minimum Salary Placed: $35,000
Recruiting Specialty: Technical disciplines in manufacturing

Dan Lane Personnel
8395 Keystone Crossing, Suite 213
Indianapolis, IN 46240
(317) 255-9632
Contact: Ms. C. Miller
Minimum Salary Placed: $25,000
Recruiting Specialty: General

Data Force
715 N. Park Avenue
Indianapolis, IN 46202
(317) 636-9900
Contact: Mr. S. Miller
Minimum Salary Placed: $25,000
Recruiting Specialty: Data processing

Dunhill Professional Search
11903 Welland Street, Suite I
Indianapolis, IN 46229
(317) 894-8659
Contact: Mr. Paul Miller
Minimum Salary Placed: $25,000
Recruiting Specialty: General

Employment Mart Inc.
7002 N. Graham Road, Suite 100
Indianapolis, IN 46220
(317) 842-8890
Contact: Mr. B. Silcox
Minimum Salary Placed: $35,000
Recruiting Specialty: Engineering and manufacturing support

Gin/Tek Associates
6531 Grant Wood Court
Indianapolis, IN 46256
(317) 842-3831
Contact: Ms. Virginia Trent
Minimum Salary Placed: $25,000
Recruiting Specialty: General

HMO Executive Search
8910 Purdue Road, Suite 200
Indianapolis, IN 46268
(317) 872-1056
Contact: Mr. Richard Carroll
Minimum Salary Placed: $25,000
Recruiting Specialty: Healthcare

Harris Kovacs Alderman
5420 W. Southern Avenue
Indianapolis, IN 46241
(317) 247-7900
Contact: Mr. T. Hart
Recruiting Specialty: Physicians

Insurance People
4755 Kingsway Drive, Suite 300
Indianapolis, IN 46205
(317) 253-2128
Contact: Mr. G. McMath
Minimum Salary Placed: $25,000
Recruiting Specialty: Insurance

JWT Roster Inc.
8041 Knue Road
Indianapolis, IN 46250
(317) 577-4729
Minimum Salary Placed: $25,000
Recruiting Specialty: General

Johnson Brown Associates, Inc.
55 Monument Circle, Suite 1214
Indianapolis, IN 46204
(317) 237-4331

Contact: Mr. Daniel Brown
Minimum Salary Placed: $30,000
Recruiting Specialty: General

Krise Professional Personnel Services
P.O. Box 53136
Indianapolis, IN 46253
(317) 299-3882
Contact: Mr. Randy Krise
Minimum Salary Placed: $25,000
Recruiting Specialty: General

Legal Registry
7 N. Meridian Street, Suite 600
Indianapolis, IN 46204
(317) 634-1200
Contact: Joe
Minimum Salary Placed: $25,000
Recruiting Specialty: Paralegals and attorneys

MacGil-Ross Professionals
5358 Washington Boulevard
Indianapolis, IN 46240
(317) 253-7770
Contact: Mr. Mike MacGil
Minimum Salary Placed: $40,000
Recruiting Specialty: Engineering and science

Management Recruiters
8200 Haverstick Road, Suite 240
Indianapolis, IN 46240
(317) 228-3300
Contact: Ms. Brenda Patterson
Minimum Salary Placed: $25,000
Recruiting Specialty: General

Midwest Medical Consultants
8910 Purdue Road, Suite 200
Indianapolis, IN 46268
(317) 872-1053

Contact: Mr. Richard Carroll
Minimum Salary Placed: $25,000
Recruiting Specialty: In-home healthcare
and physicians assistants

Miller Personnel Consultants
931 E. 86th Street, Suite 103
Indianapolis, IN 46240
(317) 251-5938
Contact: Mr. Mark Miller
Minimum Salary Placed: $35,000
Recruiting Specialty: Engineering and
manufacturing

The Morley Group
8910 Purdue Road, Suite 670
Indianapolis, IN 46268
(317) 879-4770
Contact: Mr. Michael Morley
Minimum Salary Placed: $25,000
Recruiting Specialty: Manufacturing

Robert Half International
135 N. Pennsylvania Street, Suite 2575
Indianapolis, IN 46204
(317) 638-8367
Contact: Mr. Norvis
Minimum Salary Placed: $25,000
Recruiting Specialty: Accounting and finance

Sales Consultants
8200 Haverstick Road, Suite 240
Indianapolis, IN 46240
(317) 257-5411
Contact: Mr. Bill Kuntz
Minimum Salary Placed: $25,000
Recruiting Specialty: Sales

J. Harrington Smith Association
P.O. Box 90065
Indianapolis, IN 46290
(317) 251-0678
Contact: Mr. James Smith
Minimum Salary Placed: $60,000
Recruiting Specialty: General

Source EDP
111 Monument Circle, Suite 3930
Indianapolis, IN 46204
(317) 631-2900
Contact: Mr. Randy Emerson
Minimum Salary Placed: $25,000
Recruiting Specialty: Computer software
and hardware

Strategic Resource Management
8910 Purdue Road, Suite 150
Indianapolis, IN 46268
(317) 872-8900
Contact: Mr. B. Spangler
Minimum Salary Placed: $25,000
Recruiting Specialty: Medical

LA PORTE

P & R Associates
2003 Indiana Avenue
La Porte, IN 46350
(219) 324-5530
Contact: Mr. Paul Rentschler
Minimum Salary Placed: $25,000
Recruiting Specialty: General

MERRILLVILLE

National Executive Consultants, Inc.
2621 W. Lincoln Highway, Suite B
Merrillville, IN 46410
(219) 736-0406

Contact: Mr. Morris Stilley
Minimum Salary Placed: $40,000
Recruiting Specialty: Metals

MICHIGAN CITY

Medical Search
601 Franklin Square, Suite 404
Michigan City, IN 46360
(219) 872-8163
Contact: Mr. Dan Murray
Minimum Salary Placed: $25,000
Recruiting Specialty: Medical and health-care

MIDDLEBURY

Management Services
P.O. Box 830
Middlebury, IN 46540
(219) 294-1646
Contact: Mr. J. Harter
Minimum Salary Placed: $25,000
Recruiting Specialty: General

NASHVILLE

Dunhill Executive Search
P.O. Box 1068
Nashville, IN 47448
(812) 988-1944
Contact: Mr. George Rogers
Minimum Salary Placed: $25,000
Recruiting Specialty: Manufacturing

NOBLESVILLE

Management Recruiters
15209 Herriman Boulevard
Noblesville, IN 46060
(317) 773-4323
Contact: Mr. H. Peter Isenberg
Minimum Salary Placed: $25,000
Recruiting Specialty: Manufacturing

PERU

Agra Placements, Ltd.
16 E. 5th Street
Peru, IN 46970
(317) 472-1988
Contact: Mr. Doug Rice
Minimum Salary Placed: $30,000
Recruiting Specialty: Agriculture and horticulture

RICHMOND

Management Recruiters
2519 E. Main Street, Suite 101
Richmond, IN 47374
(317) 935-3356
Contact: Mr. Rande Martin
Minimum Salary Placed: $25,000
Recruiting Specialty: General

RISING SUN

Monte Denbo Associates Inc.
127 N. Front Street
Rising Sun, IN 47040
(812) 438-2400

Contact: Mr. Rob Russell
Minimum Salary Placed: $30,000
Recruiting Specialty: Engineering and manufacturing, some General

SOUTH BEND

Crowe Chizek and Company
330 E. Jefferson Boulevard
South Bend, IN 46601
(219) 232-3992
Contact: Mr. Carl Bossung
Minimum Salary Placed: $25,000
Recruiting Specialty: General

Executive Search
105 E. Jefferson Boulevard, Suite 800
South Bend, IN 46601
(219) 233-9353
Contact: Mr. Jeff Spicer
Minimum Salary Placed: $30,000
Recruiting Specialty: General

Mfg/Search, Inc.
220 W. Colfax Avenue, Suite 600
South Bend, IN 46601
(219) 282-2547
Contact: Mr. Howard Mueller
Minimum Salary Placed: $30,000
Recruiting Specialty: Manufacturing

Michiana Personnel Service
1441 Northside Boulevard
South Bend, IN 46615
(219) 232-3364
Contact: Ms. Sally Beard
Minimum Salary Placed: $25,000
Recruiting Specialty: General

WABASH

Lange & Associates, Inc.
107 W. Market Street
Wabash, IN 46992
(219) 563-7402
Contact: Mr. Jim Lange
Minimum Salary Placed: $25,000
Recruiting Specialty: Rubber and plastics, metals and electronics

I O W A

BETTENDORF

Management Recruiters
2435 Kimberly Road
Bettendorf, IA 52722
(319) 359-3503
Contact: Mr. Jerry Herrmann
Minimum Salary Placed: $25,000
Recruiting Specialty: General

McKirchy and Company
2535 Technology Drive, Suite 104
Bettendorf, IA 52722
(319) 332-8888
Contact: Ms. K. McKirchy
Minimum Salary Placed: $25,000
Recruiting Specialty: General

CEDAR RAPIDS

Cambridge & Associates, Inc.
100 First Avenue NE, Suite 109
Cedar Rapids, IA 52401
(319) 366-7771
Contact: Mr. Mike Cambridge
Minimum Salary Placed: $20,000
Recruiting Specialty: General

Kaas Employment Services
425 2nd Street SE, Suite 610
Cedar Rapids, IA 52401
(319) 366-1731
Contact: Ms. Linda Kaas
Minimum Salary Placed: $35,000
Recruiting Specialty: Engineering and manufacturing

Management Recruiters
150 First Avenue NE, Suite 400
Cedar Rapids, IA 52401
(319) 366-8441
Contact: Mr. Fritz Weber
Minimum Salary Placed: $20,000
Recruiting Specialty: Technical

McGladrey & Pullen
221 Third Avenue SE, Suite 300
Cedar Rapids, IA 52401
(319) 366-2791
Contact: Mr. Don Rankin
Minimum Salary Placed: $30,000
Recruiting Specialty: General

CLIVE

Management Recruiters
7400 University, Suite D
Clive, IA 50325
(515) 255-1242
Contact: Mr. Mike Vermillion
Minimum Salary Placed: $20,000
Recruiting Specialty: General

DAVENPORT

J.R. Associates
2912 Western Avenue
Davenport, IA 52803
(319) 322-0205

Contact: Ms. JoAnn Roslansky
Minimum Salary Placed: $25,000
Recruiting Specialty: Life insurance

Management Resource Group
400 N. Main Street, Suite 206
Davenport, IA 52801
(319) 323-3333
Contact: Ms. Lynn Gibson
Minimum Salary Placed: $25,000
Recruiting Specialty: General

McGladrey & Pullen
220 N. Main, Suite 900
Davenport, IA 52801
(319) 326-5111
Contact: Mr. Steve Sorensen
Minimum Salary Placed: $30,000
Recruiting Specialty: General

DES MOINES

Corporate Suite, Ltd.
507 Merle Hay Tower
Des Moines, IA 50310
(515) 278-2744
Contact: Ms. Pat Brown
Minimum Salary Placed: $20,000
Recruiting Specialty: Insurance

Spence Ewing and Associates
3612 Ingersoll
Des Moines, IA 50312
(515) 277-2500
Contact: Mr. Spence Ewing
Minimum Salary Placed: $25,000
Recruiting Specialty: General

Executive Resources
3816 Ingersoll Avenue
Des Moines, IA 50312
(515) 287-6880

Contact: Ms. G. Mullane
Minimum Salary Placed: $25,000
Recruiting Specialty: Sales, data processing, insurance and office support

Eyler Associates, Inc.
400 Locust Street, Suite 170
Des Moines, IA 50309
(515) 245-4244
Contact: Mr. Richard Eyler
Minimum Salary Placed: $65,000
Recruiting Specialty: General

Human Resource Group
808 5th Avenue
Des Moines, IA 50309
(515) 243-8855
Contact: Mr. W. Canine
Minimum Salary Placed: $25,000
Recruiting Specialty: General

McGladrey Search Group
400 Locust Street, Suite 640
Des Moines, IA 50309
(515) 284-8660
Contact: Mr. Tom Hamilton
Minimum Salary Placed: $30,000
Recruiting Specialty: General

Personnel Incorporated
604 Locust Street, Suite 516
Des Moines, IA 50309
(515) 243-7687
Contact: Mr. Jack Textor
Minimum Salary Placed: $20,000
Recruiting Specialty: General

Robert Half International
317 6th Avenue, Suite 700
Des Moines, IA 50309
(515) 244-4414

Contact: Mr. A. Palmer
Recruiting Specialty: Accounting and finance

DUBUQUE

Honkamp Kreuger and Company
2345 JFK Road
Dubuque, IA 52002
(319) 556-0123
Contact: Mr. Tom Conry
Minimum Salary Placed: $25,000
Recruiting Specialty: General

Management Recruiters
707 Cycare Plaza
Dubuque, IA 52001
(319) 583-1554
Contact: Mr. Michael Pratt
Minimum Salary Placed: $20,000
Recruiting Specialty: General

FAIRFIELD

Gary Baer Associates
P.O. Box 1364
Fairfield, IA 52556
(515) 472-8589
Contact: Mr. Gary Baer
Minimum Salary Placed: $30,000
Recruiting Specialty: Electronic design automation

Career Resources
101 N. Main Street, Suite 209
Fairfield, IA 52556
(800) 824-2235
Contact: Mr. Tim Eagleson
Minimum Salary Placed: $40,000
Recruiting Specialty: Healthcare

Evergreen Information
406 W. Depot Avenue
Fairfield, IA 52556
(515) 472-9626
Contact: Mr. Al Davis
Minimum Salary Placed: $25,000
Recruiting Specialty: Computers and graphic arts

Management Recruiters
607 W. Broadway, Suite 234
Fairfield, IA 52556
(515) 469-5811
Contact: Mr. Mark Soth
Minimum Salary Placed: $20,000
Recruiting Specialty: General

Small Randall
107 Highland Street
Fairfield, IA 52556
(515) 472-8267
Minimum Salary Placed: $40,000
Recruiting Specialty: Engineering

IOWA CITY

Dunhill Personnel
1233 Gilbert Court, Suite A
Iowa City, IA 52240
(319) 354-1407
Contact: Mr. Lee Stannard
Minimum Salary Placed: $20,000
Recruiting Specialty: General

Management Recruiters
P.O. Box 787
Iowa City, IA 52244
(319) 354-4320
Contact: Mr. John Sims
Minimum Salary Placed: $20,000
Recruiting Specialty: General

MASON CITY

Management Recruiters
1312 Fourth Street SW, Suite 102
Mason City, IA 50401
(515) 424-1680
Contact: Ms. Cheryl Plagge
Minimum Salary Placed: $20,000
Recruiting Specialty: General

MOUNT VERNON

Gallagher & Brei Associates
1145 Linn Ridge Road
Mount Vernon, IA 52314
(319) 895-8042
Contact: Mr. Donald Gallagher
Minimum Salary Placed: $30,000
Recruiting Specialty: Technical disciplines in high technology

SIOUX CITY

Executive Search Associates
P.O. Box 3124
Sioux City, IA 51102
(712) 277-8103
Contact: Mr. Paul Roberts
Minimum Salary Placed: $18,000
Recruiting Specialty: General

SPENCER

Management Recruiters
P.O. Box 3053
Spencer, IA 51301
(712) 262-2701
Contact: Mr. Bradley Dach
Minimum Salary Placed: $20,000
Recruiting Specialty: General

URBANDALE

Career Finders
7517 Douglas Avenue, Suite 7
Urbandale, IA 50322
(515) 278-9467
Contact: Ms. C. Renaud
Recruiting Specialty: Sales and office support

WATERLOO

Byrnes and Rupkey Inc.
3356 Kimball
Waterloo, IA 50701
(319) 234-6201
Contact: Ms. L. Rupkey
Minimum Salary Placed: $25,000
Recruiting Specialty: General

City and National Employment Inc.
221 E. 4th Street
Waterloo, IA 50703
(319) 232-6641
Contact: Mr. P. Martin
Minimum Salary Placed: $25,000
Recruiting Specialty: General

WEST DES MOINES

Agra Placements, Ltd.
4949 Pleasant Street, Suite 1
West Des Moines, IA 50266
(515) 225-6562
Contact: Mr. Gary Follmer
Minimum Salary Placed: $20,000
Recruiting Specialty: Agriculture and horticulture

Carlson and Associates
1601 48th Street
West Des Moines, IA 50266
(515) 225-2525
Contact: Mr. Greg Carlson
Minimum Salary Placed: $25,000
Recruiting Specialty: General

Francis & Associates
6923 Vista Drive
West Des Moines, IA 50266
(515) 221-9800
Contact: Mr. Dwaine Francis
Minimum Salary Placed: $65,000
Recruiting Specialty: General

The Garrison Organization
4090 Westown Parkway, Suite A3
West Des Moines, IA 50309
(515) 223-8755
Contact: Mr. Ed Garrison
Minimum Salary Placed: $50,000
Recruiting Specialty: Insurance

Hedlin Ag Enterprises Inc.
1025 Ashworth Road, Suite 318
West Des Moines, IA 50265
(515) 223-1408
Contact: Mr. L. Hedlin
Minimum Salary Placed: $25,000
Recruiting Specialty: Agriculture and horticulture

Key Employment Services
1001 Office Park Road, Suite 320
West Des Moines, IA 50265
(515) 224-0446
Contact: Mr. Don Jayne
Minimum Salary Placed: $20,000
Recruiting Specialty: General

Reed and Associates
1200 Valley West Drive
West Des Moines, IA 50266
(515) 226-8893
Contact: Ms. Bonnie Reed
Minimum Salary Placed: $25,000
Recruiting Specialty: General

K A N S A S

LAWRENCE

The Human Resource, Inc.
205 W. 8th Street
Lawrence, KS 66044
(913) 841-5934
Contact: Ms. Epsie Shapley
Minimum Salary Placed: $50,000
Recruiting Specialty: Biotechnology,
chemicals and pharmaceuticals

Martin-Smith Personnel
100 E. 9th Street
Lawrence, KS 66044
(913) 842-1515
Contact: Ms. S. Martin-Smith
Recruiting Specialty: General

Winn Group
501 Lawrence Avenue
Lawrence, KS 66049
(913) 842-7111
Contact: Mr. Jim Winn
Recruiting Specialty: Actuaries for the insurance industry

LENEXA

Dunhill Professional Search
9718 Rosehill Road
Lenexa, KS 66215
(913) 599-6270
Contact: Ms. Camilla Marshall
Minimum Salary Placed: $20,000
Recruiting Specialty: General

MISSION

MIS Computers, Inc.
5104 Foxridge Drive, Suite 1A
Mission, KS 66202
(913) 384-3056
Contact: Mr. Norm Capps
Minimum Salary Placed: $25,000
Recruiting Specialty: MIS and data processing

OVERLAND PARK

Bowman & Marshall
P.O. Box 25503
Overland Park, KS 66225
(913) 648-3332
Contact: Mr. Peter Grassl
Minimum Salary Placed: $35,000
Recruiting Specialty: Finance, manufacturing, sales, marketing in foods

Brinkman and Associates
9115 Riggs Lane
Overland Park, KS 66225
(913) 341-8422
Contact: Mr. M. Brinkman
Minimum Salary Placed: $25,000
Recruiting Specialty: General

Dunhill Professional Search
5300 College Boulevard
Overland Park, KS 66210
(913) 451-8333
Contact: Mr. Michael Jones
Minimum Salary Placed: $20,000
Recruiting Specialty: General

EFL Associates
7101 College Boulevard, Suite 550
Overland Park, KS 66210
(913) 451-8866
Contact: Mr. Peter Lemke
Minimum Salary Placed: $50,000
Recruiting Specialty: General

Lee & Burgess Associates, Inc.
6900 College Boulevard, Suite 300
Overland Park, KS 66211
(913) 345-0500
Contact: Mr. Michael Haughton
Minimum Salary Placed: $35,000
Recruiting Specialty: General

Legal Search Associates
6701 W. 64th Street, Suite 304
Overland Park, KS 66202
(913) 722-3500
Contact: Mr. Terry Bashor
Minimum Salary Placed: $40,000
Recruiting Specialty: Attorneys

Management Recruiters
9401 Indian Creek Parkway, Suite 1250
Overland Park, KS 66210
(913) 661-9300
Contact: Mr. Danny Buda
Minimum Salary Placed: $20,000
Recruiting Specialty: General

Midwest Search Group
12904 Richards
Overland Park, KS 66213
(913) 681-8228
Contact: Mr. Bob Handley
Minimum Salary Placed: $20,000
Recruiting Specialty: Accounting and finance

Miller Associates, Inc.
12413 W. 129 Street
Overland Park, KS 66213
(913) 685-2942
Contact: Mr. Richard Miller
Minimum Salary Placed: $20,000
Recruiting Specialty: General

Morgan Hunter Corporation
6800 College Boulevard, Suite 550
Overland Park, KS 66211
(913) 491-3434
Contact: Mr. Jerry Hellebusch
Minimum Salary Placed: $20,000
Recruiting Specialty: General

Network of Excellence Inc.
P.O. 25203
Overland Park, KS 66225
(913) 897-2177
Contact: Henry
Minimum Salary Placed: $40,000
Recruiting Specialty: General

Parr and Associates
6901 W. 63 Street, Suite 211
Overland Park, KS 66202
(913) 677-1555
Contact: Mr. Donald Hunt
Minimum Salary Placed: $20,000
Recruiting Specialty: Technical, manufacturing and science

Robert Half International
10955 Lowell Avenue, Suite 490
Overland Park, KS 66210
(913) 451-7600
Contact: Ms. L. Godwin
Recruiting Specialty: Accounting and finance

Sales Consultants
9401 Indian Creek Parkway, Suite 1250
Overland Park, KS 66210
(913) 661-9200
Contact: Mr. Danny Buda
Minimum Salary Placed: $20,000
Recruiting Specialty: Sales

Sherriff & Associates
10983 Granada Lane, Suite 202
Overland Park, KS 66211
(913) 451-2112
Contact: Mr. William Sherriff
Recruiting Specialty: Healthcare

Michael Shirley Associates Inc.
7300 W. 110th Street, Suite 230
Overland Park, KS 66211
(913) 491-0240
Contact: Mr. Michael Shirley
Minimum Salary Placed: 50,000
Recruiting Specialty: General

Smith Bradley & Associates
Box 25094
Overland Park, KS 66225
(913) 345-2531
Contact: Ms. Renea Bradley
Minimum Salary Placed: $40,000
Recruiting Specialty: Healthcare and
banking

Source EDP
10300 W. 103rd Street, Suite 101
Overland Park, KS 66214
(913) 888-8885
Contact: Mr. Dan Sudeikis
Minimum Salary Placed: $20,000
Recruiting Specialty: Computers

George Waterman Executive Search
7201 W. 129th Street
Overland Park, KS 66213
(913) 451-4448
Contact: Mr. George Waterman
Minimum Salary Placed: $25,000
Recruiting Specialty: Data processing

Wood-Glavin, Inc.
8695 College Boulevard, Suite 260
Overland Park, KS 66210
(913) 451-2015
Contact: Mr. William Wood
Minimum Salary Placed: $50,000
Recruiting Specialty: General

PRAIRIE VALLEY

Huntress Real Estate
5250 W. 94th Terrace
Prairie Valley, KS 66207
(913) 451-0464
Contact: Mr. S. Gadeint
Minimum Salary Placed: $40,000
Recruiting Specialty: Real estate

SHAWNEE MISSION

David Baehr and Associates
6301 W 126th Terrace
Shawnee Mission, KS 66209
(913) 491-4096
Contact: Mr. Dave Baehr
Minimum Salary Placed: $25,000
Recruiting Specialty: General

Brack Hunter Corporation
6333 Long Street
Shawnee Mission, KS 66216
(913) 631-1040

Contact: Mr. John Brack
Minimum Salary Placed: $25,000
Recruiting Specialty: General

Dennis Bryant and Company
7600 W. 110 Street
Shawnee Mission, KS 66210
(913) 345-2806
Contact: Mr. Dennis Bryant
Minimum Salary Placed: $35,000
Recruiting Specialty: Advertising

Continental Business Systems
5845 Horton Street
Shawnee Mission, KS 66202
(913) 677-0200
Contact: Mr. L. McWilliams
Minimum Salary Placed: $25,000
Recruiting Specialty: Data processing

Financial Careers
6405 Metcalf Avenue
Shawnee Mission, KS 66202
(913) 262-8635
Contact: Jennifer
Minimum Salary Placed: $35,000
Recruiting Specialty: Finance and ac-
counting

Bruce Kelly and Associates
9300 Metcalf Avenue
Shawnee Mission, KS 66212
(913) 648-6832
Contact: Mr. Bruce Kelly
Minimum Salary Placed: $25,000
Recruiting Specialty: Healthcare

Medical Search Institute
10901 Lowell Avenue, Suite 285
Shawnee Mission, KS 66210
(913) 451-2117

Contact: Mr. N. Tildon
Minimum Salary Placed: $35,000
Recruiting Specialty: Medical

Michael/Merrill
6600 W. 95th Street
Box 7509
Shawnee Mission, KS 66207
(913) 383-9497
Contact: Mr. Wilson Liggett
Minimum Salary Placed: $20,000
Recruiting Specialty: General

Peterson Group
14351 W. 81st Place
Shawnee Mission, KS 66215
(913) 599-4804
Contact: Mr. Greg Peterson
Minimum Salary Placed: $25,000
Recruiting Specialty: Healthcare

Charles Russ Associates
P.O. Box 6667
Shawnee Mission, KS 66206
(913) 341-2292
Contact: Mr. Charles Russ
Minimum Salary Placed: $40,000
Recruiting Specialty: General

B.E. Smith Associates
10100 Santa Fe Drive
Shawnee Mission, KS 66215
(913) 341-9116
Minimum Salary Placed: $25,000
Recruiting Specialty: Healthcare

Source Finance
10300 W. 103rd Street, Suite 101
Shawnee Mission, KS 66214
(816) 474-3393
Minimum Salary Placed: $25,000
Recruiting Specialty: Finance and accounting

Stoneburner Associates, Inc.
10000 W. 75th Street, Suite 102
Shawnee Mission, KS 66204
(913) 432-0055
Contact: Mr. Dwight Stoneburner
Minimum Salary Placed: $25,000
Recruiting Specialty: Sales

TOPEKA

Dunhill of Topeka, Inc.
3706 SW Topeka Boulevard
Topeka, KS 66609
(913) 267-2773
Contact: Mr. William Pitt
Minimum Salary Placed: $20,000
Recruiting Specialty: General

Management Recruiters
3400 SW Van Buren
Topeka, KS 66611
(913) 267-5430
Contact: Mr. Kirk Hawkins
Minimum Salary Placed: $20,000
Recruiting Specialty: Healthcare, agriculture and finance

Personnel Management Resources
P.O. Box 61513
Topeka, KS 66614
(913) 478-0002
Contact: Mr. Clay Zapletal
Recruiting Specialty: Physicians, nurses and other medical

Western Temporary Service
1031 SW Gage Boulevard
Topeka, KS 66604
(913) 273-3939
Contact: Ms. B. Anderson
Recruiting Specialty: General

WICHITA

Dunhill of Wichita
317 S. Hydraulic
Wichita, KS 67211
(316) 265-9541
Contact: Mr. David Shearer
Minimum Salary Placed: $20,000
Recruiting Specialty: General

Health Search, Inc.
151 Whittier Street, Suite 2100
Wichita, KS 67207
(316) 681-4401
Contact: Ms. Victoria Waller
Minimum Salary Placed: $25,000
Recruiting Specialty: Healthcare

Holden and Associates
2024 N. Woodlawn
Wichita, KS 63393
(316) 689-6868
Minimum Salary Placed: $25,000
Recruiting Specialty: General

Management Recruiters
8100 E. 22nd Street
Wichita, KS 67226
(316) 682-8239
Contact: Mr. Marvin Reimer
Minimum Salary Placed: $20,000
Recruiting Specialty: General

Sales Consultants
8441 E. 32nd Street, N., Suite 100
Wichita, KS 67226
(316) 634-1981
Contact: Mr. Marvin Reimer
Minimum Salary Placed: $20,000
Recruiting Specialty: Sales

K E N T U C K Y

BARDWELL

Preferred Professionals
P.O. Box 654
Bardwell, KY 42023
(502) 628-3727
Contact: Mr. Kevin O'Neill
Minimum Salary Placed: $25,000
Recruiting Specialty: Technical

BOWLING GREEN

Able Recruiting
426 Park Row
Bowling Green, KY 42104
(502) 781-4422
Contact: Mr. M. Barrick
Minimum Salary Placed: $25,000
Recruiting Specialty: General

Management Recruiters
546 Park Street, Suite 300
Bowling Green, KY 42101
(502) 782-3820
Contact: Mr. G.D. Grimes
Recruiting Specialty: Legal

SCS
1711 Ashley Circle, Unit A-6
Bowling Green, KY 42101
(502) 782-9152
Contact: Mr. Bob Toth
Minimum Salary Placed: $20,000
Recruiting Specialty: General

Sales Consultants
1032 College Street, Suite 102
Bowling Green, KY 42101
(502) 843-1325
Contact: Mr. Thomas Ingala
Minimum Salary Placed: $20,000
Recruiting Specialty: Sales

BURGIN

Don Kestler and Associates, Inc.
P.O. Box 659
Burgin, KY 40310
(606) 748-9516
Contact: Mr. Don Kestler
Minimum Salary Placed: $25,000
Recruiting Specialty: General; manufacturing and engineering

CRESTWOOD

Houck Career Consultants Inc.
7404 Old Coach Road
Crestwood, KY 40014
(502) 241-2882
Contact: Mr. D. Houck
Minimum Salary Placed: $25,000
Recruiting Specialty: General

DANVILLE

Management Recruiters
105 Citation Drive, Suite A
Danville, KY 40422
(606) 236-0505
Contact: Mr. Michael Smith
Minimum Salary Placed: $20,000
Recruiting Specialty: General

GEORGETOWN

Barber & Associates
143 Knight Court, Suite 100
Georgetown, KY 40324
(502) 863-5575
Contact: Mr. Bill Barber
Minimum Salary Placed: $20,000
Recruiting Specialty: General

HOPKINSVILLE

Dunhill of Hopkinsville, Inc.
1402 N. Shallow Lake Circle H
Hopkinsville, KY 42240
(502) 885-7535
Contact: Mr. James Posze
Minimum Salary Placed: $20,000
Recruiting Specialty: General

LEXINGTON

Career Management, Inc.
698 Perimeter Drive
Lexington, KY 40517
(606) 266-5000
Contact: Mr. Richard Blanchard
Minimum Salary Placed: $35,000
Recruiting Specialty: Sales

Compton and Associates
2265 Harrodsburg Road, Suite 200.
Lexington, KY 40504
(606) 277-2125
Contact: Mr. Jim Compton
Minimum Salary Placed: $25,000
Recruiting Specialty: General, some restaurant

Dunhill Personnel
2040 Regency Road
Lexington, KY 40503
(606) 278-2525
Contact: Mr. Bill Foley
Minimum Salary Placed: $20,000
Recruiting Specialty: General

Job Guidance of Kentucky Inc.
2365 Harrodsburg Road
Lexington, KY 40504
(606) 223-3000
Contact: Ms. J. Moores
Minimum Salary Placed: $25,000
Recruiting Specialty: General

Management Recruiters
2350 Sterlington Road
Lexington, KY 40502
(606) 273-5665
Contact: Ms. Judy Simpson
Minimum Salary Placed: $20,000
Recruiting Specialty: General

LOUISVILLE

APA
519 E Warnock Street
Louisville, KY 40217
(502) 635-7721
Contact: Mr. Jim Orlee
Minimum Salary Placed: $25,000
Recruiting Specialty: General

The Hindman Company
2000 Warrington Way, Suite 110
Louisville, KY 40222
(502) 426-4040
Contact: Mr. Neil Hindman
Minimum Salary Placed: $50,000
Recruiting Specialty: General

Humphries Personnel Consultants, Inc.
305 West Broadway, Suite 608
Louisville, KY 40202
(502) 584-6265
Contact: Ms. Marie Humphries
Minimum Salary Placed: $25,000
Recruiting Specialty: General

J.C. Malone
1941 Bishop Lane, Suite 100
Louisville, KY 40218
(502) 456-2380
Contact: Mr. J. Malone
Minimum Salary Placed: $25,000
Recruiting Specialty: General

Management Recruiters
1930 Bishop Lane, Suite 426
Louisville, KY 40218
(502) 456-4330
Contact: Mr. Steven Angel
Minimum Salary Placed: $20,000
Recruiting Specialty: General

Management Registry
1256 S 3rd Street
Louisville, KY 40203
(502) 636-5551
Contact: Mr. Dick Jones
Minimum Salary Placed: $35,000
Recruiting Specialty: Engineering, accounting and data processing

Physician Services of America
2000 Warrington Way
Browenton Place, Suite 250
Louisville, KY 40222
(502) 423-9622
Contact: Mr. John Hill
Recruiting Specialty: Physicians

Professional Search Consultants
2500 Meidinger Tower
Louisville, KY 40202
(502) 583-1530
Contact: Ms. Jackie Strange
Minimum Salary Placed: $50,000
Recruiting Specialty: General; attorneys

Resource Factor, Inc.
P.O. Box 740003
Louisville, KY 40201
(502) 580-2626
Contact: Ms. Carolyn Hoge
Minimum Salary Placed: $25,000
Recruiting Specialty: Nursing

Robert Half Accountemps
6200 Dutchmans Lane, Suite 206
Louisville, KY 40205
(502) 456-4253
Contact: Mr. M. Uhls
Recruiting Specialty: Accounting and finance

Sales Consultants
1930 Bishop Lane, Suite 426
Louisville, KY 40218
(502) 456-4330
Contact: Mr. Steve Angel
Minimum Salary Placed: $20,000
Recruiting Specialty: Sales

Source EDP
2850 National City Tower
Louisville, KY 40202
(502) 581-9900
Contact: Ms. Pamela Marlette
Minimum Salary Placed: $20,000
Recruiting Specialty: Computer programming

Tasa International
9300 Shelbyville Road, Suite 1010
Louisville, KY 40222
(502) 426-3500
Contact: Mr. Wayne Jones
Minimum Salary Placed: $120,000
Recruiting Specialty: General

OWNESBORO

Career Counseling
1100 Walnut Street
Owensboro, KY 42301
(502) 686-7766
Contact: Mr. S. Young
Minimum Salary Placed: $25,000
Recruiting Specialty: General

Fortune Personnel Consultants
1035 Frederica Street, Suite 110
Owensboro, KY 42301
(502) 686-7277
Contact: Mr. J. Vance
Minimum Salary Placed: $30,000
Recruiting Specialty: Manufacturing of
plastics and metals

OWENTON

Management Recruiters
P.O. Box 10
Owenton, KY 40359
(502) 484-3545
Contact: Mr. R. Jan Miller
Minimum Salary Placed: $20,000
Recruiting Specialty: General

PROSPECT

Karen Marshall Associates
6304 Deep Creek Drive
Prospect, KY 40059
(502) 228-0800
Contact: Ms. Karen Marshall
Minimum Salary Placed: $30,000
Recruiting Specialty: General; MIS

RICHMOND

Management Recruiters
213 George Street, Suite B
Richmond, KY 40475
(606) 624-3535
Contact: Mr. Ron Lawson
Minimum Salary Placed: $20,000
Recruiting Specialty: General

SAINT MATTHEWS

Gordon Mulvey and Associates
4333 Foeburn Lane
St. Matthews, KY 40207
(502) 897-5371
Contact: Mr. Gordon Mulvey
Minimum Salary Placed: $25,000
Recruiting Specialty: Marketing

Snelling Personnel Service
4010 Dupont Circle, Suite 230
St. Matthews, KY 40207
(502) 895-9494
Contact: Mr. G. Lichtefeld
Minimum Salary Placed: $25,000
Recruiting Specialty: General

WINCHESTER

Technical Recruiting Services
109 Hood Avenue
Winchester, KY 40392
(606) 744-5007
Contact: Mr. Jerald McNutt
Minimum Salary Placed: $20,000
Recruiting Specialty: Technical disciplines

L O U I S I A N A

BATON ROUGE

Advantage Personnel Inc.
11224 Boardwalk, Suite E1-1
Baton Rouge, LA 70816
(504) 292-2356
Contact: Ms. Sherry Freeman
Minimum Salary Placed: $25,000
Recruiting Specialty: General

Ammons Career Center
9622 Airline Highway, Suite C17
Baton Rouge, LA 70815
(504) 926-8378
Contact: Mr. R. Ammon
Recruiting Specialty: Technical disciplines

Coleman Markham and Jones
11832 Newcastle Avenue
Baton Rouge, LA 70816
(504) 292-1289
Contact: Carol
Minimum Salary Placed: $25,000
Recruiting Specialty: General

Dunhill of Baton Rouge, Inc.
5723 Superior Drive, Suite B-4
Baton Rouge, LA 70816
(504) 291-0450
Contact: Mr. Fritz Falcon
Minimum Salary Placed: $20,000
Recruiting Specialty: General

MDR & Associates
11843 Market Place
Baton Rouge, LA 70817
(504) 291-2488
Contact: Mr. Mel Robinson
Minimum Salary Placed: $25,000
Recruiting Specialty: General

Management Recruiters
P.O. Box 3553
Baton Rouge, LA 70821
(504) 383-1234
Contact: Ms. Cecilia Franklin
Minimum Salary Placed: $20,000
Recruiting Specialty: General

Sales Consultants
5551 Corporate Boulevard, Suite 2-H
Baton Rouge, LA 70808
(504) 928-2212
Contact: Mr. Gregory Fell
Minimum Salary Placed: $20,000
Recruiting Specialty: Sales

Snelling Personnel
7809 Jefferson Highway
Baton Rouge, LA 70809
(504) 927-0550
Minimum Salary Placed: $25,000
Recruiting Specialty: General

HARAHAN

Gelpi & Associates
P.O. Box 231187
Harahan, LA 70183
(504) 737-6086
Contact: Ms. Gerry Gelpi
Minimum Salary Placed: $30,000
Recruiting Specialty: Insurance

KENNER

Network Strategies
1101 Veterans Memorial Boulevard
Kenner, LA 70062
(504) 461-5511
Minimum Salary Placed: $25,000
Recruiting Specialty: General

LAFAYETTE

Snelling Search
2014 Pinhook Road
Lafayette, LA 70508
(318) 237-4723
Contact: Ms. Sally Taylor
Minimum Salary Placed: $25,000
Recruiting Specialty: General

LAKE CHARLES

Snelling Personnel Services
1 Lakeshore Drive, Suite 1130
Lake Charles, LA 70629
(318) 433-3033
Contact: Ms. Kim Peshoff
Minimum Salary Placed: $20,000
Recruiting Specialty: General

Southwest Louisiana Human Resource
3417 Ryan Street
Lake Charles, LA 70605
(318) 474-5786
Contact: Mr. Ed Godwin
Minimum Salary Placed: $20,000
Recruiting Specialty: Engineering and accounting

Talley and Associates
1105 W. Prien Lake Road, Suite D
Lake Charles, LA 70601
(318) 474-5627
Contact: Mr. B. Bollotte
Recruiting Specialty: General

MANDEVILLE

Hilbert Company, Inc.
120 Lisa Lane
Mandeville, LA 70448
(504) 626-8908

Contact: Mr. Don Hilbert
Minimum Salary Placed: $20,000
Recruiting Specialty: Refining and petrochemical

METAIRE

Delta Personnel
111 Veterans Memorial Boulevard,
 Suite 1400
Metaire, LA 70005
(504) 833-5200
Contact: Mr. David Lawrence
Minimum Salary Placed: $20,000
Recruiting Specialty: General

Healthcare Recruiters
3500 N. Causeway Boulevard
Metaire, LA 70002
(504) 838-8875
Contact: Mr. V. Palazola
Minimum Salary Placed: $25,000
Recruiting Specialty: Healthcare

Lawrence Personnel Inc.
111 Veterans Memorial, Suite 1400
Metaire, LA 70005
(504) 833-0055
Contact: Mr. Victor Lawrence
Minimum Salary Placed: $25,000
Recruiting Specialty: General

Management Recruiters
P.O. Box 6605
Metaire, LA 70009
(504) 831-7333
Contact: Mr. Edward Ameen
Minimum Salary Placed: $20,000
Recruiting Specialty: General

Sales and Engineering Resources
4405 N. I-10 Service Road W, Suite 302
Metaire, LA 70006
(504) 455-3771
Contact: Ms. Evelyn Hawkins
Minimum Salary Placed: $25,000
Recruiting Specialty: Sales and engineering

MONROE

Management Recruiters
1401 Hudson Lane, Suite 135
Monroe, LA 71201
(318) 324-8060
Contact: Mr. Bruce Hursey
Minimum Salary Placed: $20,000
Recruiting Specialty: Wood products and
capital equipment

Snelling Search
1406 Royal
Monroe, LA 71201
(318) 387-6090
Contact: Mr. Wayne Williamson
Minimum Salary Placed: $25,000
Recruiting Specialty: General

**Snelling Search Medical &
Professional Group**
1500 Louisville Avenue, Suite 102
Monroe, LA 71201
(318) 387-0099
Contact: Mr. Gil Johnson
Minimum Salary Placed: $35,000
Recruiting Specialty: General

NATCHITOCHES

Snelling Personnel Services
116 Highway One South, Suite 105
Natchitoches, LA 71457
(318) 356-9070

Contact: Mr. Larry Mason
Minimum Salary Placed: $35,000
Recruiting Specialty: Poultry processing
and manufacturing

NEW ORLEANS

Accounting and Engineering Personnel
210 Baronne Street, Suite 920
New Orleans, LA 70112
(504) 581-7800
Contact: Mr. David Lucien
Minimum Salary Placed: $30,000
Recruiting Specialty: Engineering and ac-
counting

A.D. Boudreaux and Associates
7701 Sandpiper Drive
New Orleans, LA 70128
(504) 245-1930
Contact: Ms. A. Boudreaux
Minimum Salary Placed: $20,000
Recruiting Specialty: Data processing

Career Personnel Consultants
4640 S. Carrollton Street
New Orleans, LA 70119
(504) 488-6611
Contact: Mr. Bob Adams
Minimum Salary Placed: $25,000
Recruiting Specialty: General

Careers Unlimited
203 Carondelet Street
New Orleans, LA 70130
(504) 525-2861
Minimum Salary Placed: $25,000
Recruiting Specialty: General

Clertech Group Inc.
7029 Canal Boulevard
New Orleans, LA 70130
(504) 486-9733
Contact: Mr. G. Dorko
Minimum Salary Placed: $40,000
Recruiting Specialty: Engineering in utilities and chemicals

Computer Personnel Service
2 Canal Street
New Orleans, LA 70130
(504) 581-2433
Contact: Mr. Phillip Eagner
Minimum Salary Placed: $25,000
Recruiting Specialty: Computers

MSI International
701 Poydras Street
New Orleans, LA 70170
(504) 522-6700
Contact: Ms. Charlotte Haley
Recruiting Specialty: Physicians and healthcare

Romac and Associates
650 Poydras Street, Suite 2523
New Orleans, LA 70130
(504) 522-6611
Contact: Mr. T. Cloudman
Minimum Salary Placed: $25,000
Recruiting Specialty: Accounting, data processing and banking

Shiell Personnel
5400 Jefferson Highway
New Orleans, LA 70123
(504) 734-7986
Contact: Mr. Don Shiell
Minimum Salary Placed: $25,000
Recruiting Specialty: Outside sales

Snelling Personnel
203 Carondelet Street, Suite 530
New Orleans, LA 70130
(504) 529-5781
Contact: Ms. Julie Kent
Minimum Salary Placed: $25,000
Recruiting Specialty: MIS and other technical disciplines

SHREVEPORT

Dunhill of Shreveport, Inc.
2920 Knight Street, Suite 140
Shreveport, LA 71105
(318) 861-3576
Contact: Mr. Don Richards
Minimum Salary Placed: $20,000
Recruiting Specialty: General

Sunbelt Search
910 Pierremont Road, Suite 487
Shreveport, LA 71106
(318) 865-8805
Contact: Mr. John West
Minimum Salary Placed: $25,000
Recruiting Specialty: General

SLIDELL

Blue Chip Personnel
1009 Carnation Street
Slidell, LA 70460
(504) 643-4791
Contact: Ms. A. Starnes
Minimum Salary Placed: $30,000
Recruiting Specialty: General

M A I N E

BRUNSWICK

Ames Personnel Consultants
34 Hennessey Avenue
Brunswick, ME 04011
(207) 729-5158
Contact: Mr. Philip Ames
Minimum Salary Placed: $25,000
Recruiting Specialty: General

CAPE ELIZABETH

Executive Resource Group
29 Oakhurst Road
Cape Elizabeth, ME 04107
(207) 767-1320
Contact: Ms. Sibyl Masquelier
Minimum Salary Placed: $50,000
Recruiting Specialty: General

CUMBERLAND CENTER

Ross Green and Associates
P.O. Box 547
Cumberland Center, ME 04021
(207) 829-6595
Contact: Mr. Ross Green
Minimum Salary Placed: $25,000
Recruiting Specialty: General

GORHAM

Paper Industry Recruitment
36 Main Street
Gorham, ME 04038
(207) 839-2633
Contact: Mr. Maynard Charron
Minimum Salary Placed: $35,000
Recruiting Specialty: Printing and paper

HAMPDEN

Northern Consultants Inc.
17 Western Avenue
Hampden, ME 04444
(207) 862-2323
Contact: Mr. James Brown
Minimum Salary Placed: $50,000
Recruiting Specialty: General

KENNEBUNK

Yake & Associates
9 York Street
P.O. Box 42
Kennebunk, ME 04043
(207) 985-6320
Contact: Mr. Tom Yake
Minimum Salary Placed: $40,000
Recruiting Specialty: Retail

MOUNT VERNON

Management Partners
Belgrade Road
Mount Vernon, ME 04352
(207) 293-3200
Contact: Mr. Charlie Baeder
Minimum Salary Placed: $25,000
Recruiting Specialty: Automotive

PORTLAND

John Jay & Company
44 Exchange Street, Suite 305
Portland, ME 04101
(207) 772-6951
Contact: Mr. Jay Hotchkiss
Minimum Salary Placed: $45,000
Recruiting Specialty: General

Pro Search
100 Middle Street
Portland, ME 04101
(207) 775-7600
Contact: Mr. Steve Strand
Minimum Salary Placed: $20,000
Recruiting Specialty: General

Romac & Associates, Inc.
183 Middle Street
Portland, ME 04112
(800) 341-0263
Contact: Mr. Ralph Struzziero
Recruiting Specialty: General

Sales Consultants
66 Pearl Street, Suite 326
Portland, ME 04101
(207) 775-6565
Contact: Ms. Carla Akalarian
Minimum Salary Placed: $20,000
Recruiting Specialty: Sales

Westbrook Associates
583 Forest Avenue
Portland, ME 04101
(207) 773-1962
Contact: Mr. M. Minkoff
Minimum Salary Placed: $25,000
Recruiting Specialty: General

SACCO

Compusource Inc.
56 Industrial Park Road
Sacco, ME 04072
(207) 284-1188
Contact: Mr. Bill Martin
Minimum Salary Placed: $25,000
Recruiting Specialty: Computers

SOUTH PORTLAND

Executive Search
39 Darling Avenue
South Portland, ME 04106
(207) 772-4677
Contact: Mr. Robert Sloat
Minimum Salary Placed: $20,000
Recruiting Specialty: General

M A R Y L A N D

ANNAPOLIS

The Abbott Group
530 College Parkway, Suite N
Annapolis, MD 21401
(410) 757-4100
Contact: Mr. Peter Darby Abbott
Minimum Salary Placed: $125,000
Recruiting Specialty: General

Ann Bond Associates Inc.
275 West Street, Suite 304
Annapolis, MD 21401
(410) 280-6002
Contact: Ms. Ann Bond
Minimum Salary Placed: $45,000
Recruiting Specialty: Sales and marketing
in food and beverages

Kames & Associates
P.O. Box 3342
Annapolis, MD 21403
(410) 267-0099
Contact: Mr. Robert Kames
Minimum Salary Placed: $35,000
Recruiting Specialty: Technical disci-
plines in high technology

Alan Lerner Associates
P.O. Box 4012
Annapolis, MD 21401
(410) 268-1821
Contact: Mr. Thomas Lamm
Minimum Salary Placed: $20,000
Recruiting Specialty: Retail

Management Recruiters
2083 West Street, Suite 5A
Annapolis, MD 21401
(410) 841-6600
Contact: Mr. John Czajkowski
Minimum Salary Placed: $20,000
Recruiting Specialty: General

BALTIMORE

Accountants On Call
201 N. Charles Street
Baltimore, MD 21202
(410) 685-5700
Contact: Ms. Sharon Hoffman
Recruiting Specialty: Accounting

Alex and Company
10 W. Madison Street
Baltimore, MD 21201
(410) 783-7900
Contact: Ms. E. Alexander
Minimum Salary Placed: $40,000
Recruiting Specialty: Biomedical

Ardent Group
9102 Trannsoms Road
Baltimore, MD 21236
(410) 529-0333
Minimum Salary Placed: $25,000
Recruiting Specialty: General

Attorneys Per Diem, Inc.
16 S. Calvert Street, Suite 501
Baltimore, MD 21202
(410) 385-5350
Contact: Ms. Laura Black
Recruiting Specialty: Legal

D.W. Baird & Associates
10751 Falls Road, Suite 250
Baltimore, MD 21093
(410) 339-7670
Contact: Mr. David Baird
Minimum Salary Placed: $40,000
Recruiting Specialty: Chemicals, pharmaceuticals, environmental and healthcare

Bowie & Associates, Inc.
612 Norhurst Way
Baltimore, MD 21228
(410) 747-1919
Contact: Mr. Andrew Bowie
Minimum Salary Placed: $40,000
Recruiting Specialty: Transportation

Brandjes Associates
16 S. Calvert Street, Suite 500
Baltimore, MD 21202
(410) 547-6887
Contact: Mr. Michael Brandjes
Minimum Salary Placed: $25,000
Recruiting Specialty: Financial Services

A.J. Burton Group, Inc.
120 E. Baltimore Street, Suite 2220
Baltimore, MD 21202
(410) 337-3700
Contact: Mr. Carl Wright
Recruiting Specialty: General

Columbia Consulting Group
20 S. Charles Street, 9th Floor
Baltimore, MD 21201
(410) 385-2525
Contact: Mr. Lawrence Holmes
Minimum Salary Placed: $75,000
Recruiting Specialty: General

Conaway Legal Search
112 Hawthorn Road
Baltimore, MD 21210
(410) 539-1234
Contact: Mr. Howard Conaway
Minimum Salary Placed: $40,000
Recruiting Specialty: Attorneys

Executive Dynamics, Inc.
1107 Kenilworth Drive, Suite 208
Baltimore, MD 21204
(301) 684-3700
Contact: Mr. Thomas Miller
Minimum Salary Placed: $30,000
Recruiting Specialty: Finance and MIS in
banking, finance, insurance and healthcare

Fox-Morris Associates, Inc.
409 Washington Avenue, Suite 1020
Baltimore, MD 21204
(410) 296-4500
Contact: Mr. George Simmons
Minimum Salary Placed: $35,000
Recruiting Specialty: Human resources,
engineering, and manufacturing

Hayden and Associates
100 West Road
Baltimore, MD 21204
(410) 337-7878
Minimum Salary Placed: $50,000
Recruiting Specialty: General

A.T. Kearney Inc.
300 W..Pratt Street
Baltimore, MD 21201
(410) 625-2995
Contact: Mr. Joseph Haberman
Minimum Salary Placed: $80,000
Recruiting Specialty: General

Kostmayer Associates
1 Village Square
Baltimore, MD 21210
(410) 435-2288
Contact: Mr. Roger Kostmayer
Minimum Salary Placed: $40,000
Recruiting Specialty: Financial services

Lordan Associates
300 Northway
Baltimore, MD 21218
(410) 467-1660
Contact: Ms. Susan Lordan
Recruiting Specialty: Sales, marketing,
and management

Management Associates
9735 Magledt Road
Baltimore, MD 21234
(410) 665-6033
Contact: Mr. Walter Sistek
Minimum Salary Placed: $30,000
Recruiting Specialty: General

Marlar International, Inc.
100 E. Pratt Street, Suite 2530
Baltimore, MD 21202
(410) 528-8400
Contact: Mr. H. Edward Muendel
Minimum Salary Placed: $60,000
Recruiting Specialty: General

Sales Consultants
575 S. Charles Street, Suite 401
Baltimore, MD 21201
(410) 727-5750
Contact: Mr. Steven Braun
Minimum Salary Placed: $25,000
Recruiting Specialty: All levels of sales,
marketing, management, and telecommunications

Seek International Inc.
15 Stablemere Court
Baltimore, MD 21209
(410) 653-9680
Contact: Ms. Pamela Mooney
Recruiting Specialty: Computer sales and
sales management

Source EDP
120 E. Baltimore Street, Suite 1950
Baltimore, MD 21202
(410) 727-4050
Minimum Salary Placed: $20,000
Recruiting Specialty: Computer software
and hardware

Williamson Neal Amato
117 Water Street, Suite 401
Baltimore, MD 21202
(410) 547-0062
Contact: Ms. Karen Williamson
Recruiting Specialty: Legal - attorneys,
paralegal, and secretaries

BETHESDA

The Consortium
7315 Wisconsin Avenue, Suite 631N
Bethesda, MD 20814
(301) 986-1412

Contact: Mr. Peter Kaminsky
Recruiting Specialty: Data processing

A.G. Fishkin & Associates, Inc.
P.O. Box 34413
Bethesda, MD 20827
(301) 983-0303
Contact: Ms. Anita Fishkin
Minimum Salary Placed: $40,000
Recruiting Specialty: High technology

Grant/Murphy Associates
7500 Old Georgetown Road, Suite 710
Bethesda, MD 20814
(301) 718-8888
Contact: Mr. Mark Pugrant
Minimum Salary Placed: $40,000
Recruiting Specialty: MIS and finance

MLD Personnel
7200 Wisconsin Avenue
Bethesda, MD 20814
(301) 656-9480
Contact: Ms. Maude Dennis
Recruiting Specialty: General

Quest Systems, Inc.
4701 Sangamore Road, Suite 260N
Bethesda, MD 20816
(301) 229-4200
Contact: Mr. David Samuelson
Recruiting Specialty: Computer and information sciences

Retail Management Associates
7910 Woodmont Avenue
Bethesda, MD 20814
(301) 424-3391
Minimum Salary Placed: $25,000
Recruiting Specialty: Retail

Roberts, Ryan and Bentley
7315 Wisconsin Avenue
Bethesda, MD 20814
(301) 469-3150
Minimum Salary Placed: $50,000
Recruiting Specialty: General

Craig Williamson, Inc.
6550 Rock Spring Drive, Suite 360
Bethesda, MD 20817
(301) 897-9566
Contact: Mr. Craig Williamson
Minimum Salary Placed: $100,000
Recruiting Specialty: High technology

Witt/Kieffer, Ford, Hadelman & Lloyd
4550 Montgomery Avenue, Suite 615N
Bethesda, MD 20814
(301) 654-5070
Contact: Ms. Kathleen Ballein
Minimum Salary Placed: $75,000
Recruiting Specialty: General

CATONSVILLE

Andrew J. Bowie and Associates, Inc.
612 Norhurst Way
Catonsville, MD 21228
(410) 747-1919
Recruiting Specialty: Transportation

CHEVY CHASE

Ames Associates Inc.
6935 Wisconsin Avenue, Suite 300
Chevy Chase, MD 20815
(301) 656-5222

Contact: Mr. Michael Ames
Minimum Salary Placed: $50,000
Recruiting Specialty: Construction and development

Kershner & Company
2 Wisconsin Circle, Suite 700
Chevy Chase, MD 20815
(202) 686-4787
Contact: Mr. Bruce Kershner
Minimum Salary Placed: $50,000
Recruiting Specialty: General

Krauthamer & Associates
5530 Wisconsin Avenue, Suite 1110
Chevy Chase, MD 20815
(301) 654-7533
Contact: Mr. Gary Krauthamer
Minimum Salary Placed: $75,000
Recruiting Specialty: General

COCKEYSVILLE

Fallstaff Search
111 Warren Road, Suite 4B
Cockeysville, MD 21030
(410) 666-1100
Contact: Mr. Robert Chertkof
Recruiting Specialty: Medical and health-care

The Hanover Consulting Group
11707 Hunter's Run Drive
Cockeysville, MD 21030
(410) 785-1912
Contact: Mr. Thomas Graff
Minimum Salary Placed: $45,000
Recruiting Specialty: Technical disciplines in food and banking

COLUMBIA

Concorde Corporation
7181 Rivers Edge Road
Columbia, MD 21044
(410) 988-9400
Contact: Mr. David Trout
Recruiting Specialty: Computer engineering and intelligence

Management Recruiters
5550 Sterrett Place, Suite 314 K & M
Lakefront-N
Columbia, MD 21044
(410) 715-1141
Contact: Mr. Randolph Reyes
Minimum Salary Placed: $20,000
Recruiting Specialty: General

Sales Consultants
10320 Little Patuxent Parkway, Suite 511
Columbia, MD 21044
(410) 992-4900
Contact: Mr. David Rubin
Minimum Salary Placed: $25,000
Recruiting Specialty: Telecommunications, sales, marketing, data processing

Search Consultants
10480 Little Patuxent Parkway
Columbia, MD 21044
(410) 715-0900
Minimum Salary Placed: $35,000
Recruiting Specialty: Computer programming and financial management

Search Group
9405 Hickory Limb
Columbia, MD 21045
(410) 290-8256

Contact: Mr. Thomas Hruska
Recruiting Specialty: Property casualty insurance

C. J. Vincent Associates, Inc.
2000 Century Plaza, Suite 249
Columbia, MD 21044
(410) 997-8590
Contact: Mr. Vincent Cucuzzella
Minimum Salary Placed: $40,000
Recruiting Specialty: Sales and marketing in computers

FREDERICK

Management Recruiters
201 Thomas Johnson Drive, Suite 202
Frederick, MD 21702
(301) 663-0600
Contact: Mr. Richard Bates
Minimum Salary Placed: $20,000
Recruiting Specialty: General

GAITHERSBURG

The Hamilton Group
8118 Exodus Drive
Gaithersburg, MD 20882
(301) 869-2609
Contact: Mr. James Lawrence
Minimum Salary Placed: $100,000
Recruiting Specialty: High technology

Health Search Associates
19632 Club House Road, Suite 525
Gaithersburg, MD 20879
(301) 258-2656
Contact: Mr. Ted Schneider
Minimum Salary Placed: $40,000
Recruiting Specialty: Healthcare

HAGERSTOWN

L.J. Parrish & Associates, Inc.
P.O. Box 2539
Hagerstown, MD 21741
(301) 416-2706
Contact: Ms. Laura Parrish
Recruiting Specialty: Accounting, finance, and banking

HUNT VALLEY

Cross Country Consultants, Inc.
111 Warren Road, Suite 4B
Hunt Valley, MD 21030
(410) 666-1100
Contact: Mr. Sheldon Gottesfeld
Minimum Salary Placed: $30,000
Recruiting Specialty: General

HYATTSVILLE

Sales Consultants
7515 Annapolis Road, Suite 304
Hyattsville, MD 20784
(301) 731-4200
Contact: Mr. Thomas Hummel
Minimum Salary Placed: $25,000
Recruiting Specialty: Sales

LUTHERVILLE

D.W. Baird Associates
10751 Falls Road
Lutherville, MD 21022
(410) 339-7670
Minimum Salary Placed: $40,000
Recruiting Specialty: Technical and engineering

Brindisi Search
10751 Falls Road, Suite 250
Lutherville, MD 21093
(410) 339-7673
Contact: Mr. Thomas Brindisi
Minimum Salary Placed: $50,000
Recruiting Specialty: Human resources

OLNEY

Opportunity Search Inc.
P.O. Box 751
Olney, MD 20830
(301) 924-4741
Contact: Mr. Mark Tappis
Recruiting Specialty: Engineering and computer science in defense intelligence and commercial

OWINGS MILLS

Hotel Executive Placement
10019 Reisterstown Road, Suite 302
Owings Mills, MD 21117
(410) 356-8900
Contact: Mr. Adam Hardie
Recruiting Specialty: Hotel and club management

Telem Adhesive Search Corporation (TASC)
P.O. Box 656
Ownings Mills, MD 21117
(410) 356-6200
Contact: Mr. Peter B. Telem
Recruiting Specialty: Chemicals, technical and marketing functions

Thoroughbred Executive Search
9616 Reisterstown Road, Suite 462
Owings Mills, MD 21117
(410) 581-1124
Contact: Ms. Susan Sellers
Minimum Salary Placed: $30,000
Recruiting Specialty: General; management consulting

ROCKVILLE

Computrade Inc.
51 Monroe Street, Suite 1206
Rockville, MD 20850
(301) 309-6800
Contact: Mr. Michael Jennings
Minimum Salary Placed: $50,000
Recruiting Specialty: Investment and portfolio analysts

The Corporate Source Group
4725 Pommel Drive
Rockville, MD 20850
(301) 251-9500
Contact: Ms. Patricia Carlton
Minimum Salary Placed: $60,000
Recruiting Specialty: General

Dunhill of Rockville
414 Hungerford Drive, Suite 252
Rockville, MD 20850
(301) 424-0450
Contact: Mr. Gordon Powers
Minimum Salary Placed: $20,000
Recruiting Specialty: General

Intell-Search
P.O. Box 1219
Rockville, MD 20849
(301) 424-9599

Contact: Mr. Lorry Clavelli
Recruiting Specialty: Scientists, software engineers, and design and development in defense industry

JDG Associates, Ltd.
1700 Research Boulevard
Rockville, MD 20850
(301) 340-2210
Contact: Mr. Joseph DeGioia
Minimum Salary Placed: $40,000
Recruiting Specialty: Technical disciplines in high technology

MEI/Marks Enterprises Inc.
6001 Montrose Road
Rockville, MD 20852
(301) 231-8150
Contact: Mr. Mark Suss
Minimum Salary Placed: $30,000
Recruiting Specialty: Advertising and public relations

Perry Newton Associates
P.O. Box 1158
Rockville, MD 20849
(301) 340-3360
Contact: Mr. Richard Perry
Recruiting Specialty: Retailing

Rolphco Inc.
4848 Flower Valley Drive
Rockville, MD 20853
(301) 929-1020
Contact: Mr. Robert Philipson
Minimum Salary Placed: $30,000
Recruiting Specialty: Technical disciplines

Sales Consultants
1395 Piccard Drive, Suite 330
Rockville, MD 20850
(301) 417-9100

Contact: Mr. Brian Hoffman
Minimum Salary Placed: $25,000
Recruiting Specialty: Sales, marketing
and high technology

Systems Development International
1350 Piccard Drive, #320
Rockville, MD 20850
(301) 948-6699
Contact: Mr. Vic Viswanath
Recruiting Specialty: Computer and communications industry

Wallach Associates Inc.
6101 Executive Blvd., Suite 380
Rockville, MD 20852
(301) 231-9000
Contact: Mr. Donald Wallach
Recruiting Specialty: Defense electronics,
computer systems, and weapon systems

SALISBURY

Management Recruiters
132 E. Main Street, Suite 300
Salisbury, MD 21801
(410) 548-4473
Contact: Mr. Fred Puente
Minimum Salary Placed: $20,000
Recruiting Specialty: General

SILVER SPRING

Career Byte, Inc.
8604 Second Avenue, Suite 160
Silver Spring, MD 20910
(301) 587-5626
Contact: Mr. Carl Hollenbach
Minimum Salary Placed: $30,000
Recruiting Specialty: MIS

**Management Recruiters of
Washington DC**
1100 Wayne Avenue, Suite 710
Silver Spring, MD 20910
(301) 589-5400
Contact: Mr. Frank S. Black, Jr.
Recruiting Specialty: Management care
industry, tax field, food services management and marketing

Vey Mark Associates Inc.
P.O. Box 3598
Silver Spring, MD 20918
(410) 992-8422
Contact: Mr. Harvey Weisberg
Recruiting Specialty: Hardware and software engineering, contracts administration, and systems analysis

TIMONIUM

BCG Search, Inc.
375 W. Padonia Road, Suite 275
Timonium, MD 21093
(410) 252-1158
Contact: Mr. R. Michael Hornbuckle
Minimum Salary Placed: $75,000
Recruiting Specialty: Non-profit and leisure services

Holland & Associates
2345 York Road
Timonium, MD 21093
(410) 296-6900
Contact: Mr. Ray Holland
Minimum Salary Placed: $50,000
Recruiting Specialty: Accounting and finance

Management Recruiters
9515 Deerco Road, Suite 801
Timonium, MD 21093
(410) 252-6616
Contact: Mr. Kenneth Davis
Minimum Salary Placed: $20,000
Recruiting Specialty: General

Sales Consultants
9515 Deerco Road, Suite 801
Timonium, MD 21093
(410) 252-6616
Contact: Mr. Kenneth Davis
Minimum Salary Placed: $25,000
Recruiting Specialty: Sales

Sanford Rose Associates
57 W. Timonium Road, Suite 310
Timonium, MD 21093
(410) 561-5244
Contact: Mr. Thomas McPoyle
Recruiting Specialty: Technical disciplines in high technology

Sudina Search, Inc.
375 W. Padonia Road, Suite 235
Timonium, MD 21093
(410) 252-6900
Contact: Mr. Chuck Sudina
Minimum Salary Placed: $40,000
Recruiting Specialty: MIS, accounting and telecommunications

Winston Search, Inc.
16 Greenmeadow Drive, Suite 305
Timonium, MD 21093
(410) 560-1111
Contact: Mr. Thomas Winston
Minimum Salary Placed: $50,000
Recruiting Specialty: General

TOWSON

Access Associates Inc.
1107 Kenilworth Drive, Suite 307
Towson, MD 21204
(410) 821-7190
Contact: Ms. Barbara Barrett
Recruiting Specialty: Engineering, information technology, and human resources

Caplan Associates
28 Allegheny Ave., Suite 600
Towson, MD 21204
(410) 821-9351
Contact: Mr. Robert Caplan
Recruiting Specialty: Accounting, finance, data processing, and manufacturing

Computer Management Inc.
809 Gleneagle Court, Suite 205
Towson, MD 21286
(410) 583-0050
Contact: Ms. Janet Miller
Recruiting Specialty: Data processing and software engineers

L. S. Gross & Associates
28 Allegheny Ave., Suite 600
Towson, MD 21204
(401) 821-9351
Contact: Ms. Linda Gross
Recruiting Specialty: Sales, management, and technical

KCS Search Group
809 Gleneagle Court, Suite 205
Towson, MD 21286
(410) 494-9396
Contact: Ms. Kathleen Stone
Recruiting Specialty: Sales, sales support, and marketing in information technology

Sigman & Summerfield
1 Investment Place, Suite 404
Towson, MD 21204
(410) 828-0777
Contact: Ms. Judie Sigman
Recruiting Specialty: Data processing,
sales and marketing, and software engineering

WESTMINSTER

**Healthcare Recruiters of the Mid
Atlantic**
412 Malcolm Drive, Suite 208
Westminster, MD 21157
(410) 876-0300
Contact: Mr. Keith Graham
Recruiting Specialty: Medical and health-
care

John B. Norris & Associates, Inc.
P.O. Box 2068
Westminster, MD 21158
(410) 876-5550
Contact: Mr. John B. Norris
Minimum Salary Placed: $20,000
Recruiting Specialty: Food and dairy in-
dustry

WHEATON

Ken Leiner Associates
11510 George Avenue, Suite 105
Wheaton, MD 20902
(301) 933-8800
Contact: Mr. Ken Leiner
Minimum Salary Placed: $50,000
Recruiting Specialty: Information tech-
nology and software

MASSACHUSETTS

ACCORD

Langlois & Associates
P.O. Box 218
Accord, MA 02018
(617) 740-2781
Contact: Mr. Robert Langlois
Minimum Salary Placed: $40,000
Recruiting Specialty: Healthcare

ACTON

Stimmel Group
460 Main Street
P.O. Box 2258
Acton, MA 01720
(508) 263-1300
Contact: Mr. A. Craig Stimmel
Minimum Salary Placed: $60,000
Recruiting Specialty: General

AMHERST

Allen Davis & Associates
P.O. Box 2007
Amherst, MA 01004
(413) 549-7440
Contact: Mr. Allen Davis
Minimum Salary Placed: $30,000
Recruiting Specialty: MIS and computers

ANDOVER

Kishbaugh Associates International
2 Elm Square, Musgrove Building
Andover, MA 01810
(508) 475-7224

Contact: Mr. Herbert Kishbaugh
Minimum Salary Placed: $75,000
Recruiting Specialty: General

RW Hunter Group
5 George Street
Andover, MA 01810
(508) 470-1411
Contact: Ms. Deborah Richey
Minimum Salary Placed: $60,000
Recruiting Specialty: Medical

ASHBURNAM

Newton Carreiro and Associates
11 Proctor Street
Ashburnam, MA 01430
(508) 827-4711
Minimum Salary Placed: $25,000
Recruiting Specialty: General

ASHLAND

Rafey & Company
148 High Street
Ashland, MA 01721
(508) 881-8312
Contact: Mr. Andrew Rafey
Minimum Salary Placed: $85,000
Recruiting Specialty: General

ATTLEBORO

Tower Group
8 Hunton Circle
Attleboro, MA 02703
(508) 226-6735
Minimum Salary Placed: $25,000
Recruiting Specialty: Medical

AUBURNDALE

Interactive Software Placement
465 Auburn Street
Auburndale, MA 02166
(617) 527-2700
Contact: Mr. S. Leary
Minimum Salary Placed: $25,000
Recruiting Specialty: Computers

Progressive Search Association
465 Auburn Street
Auburndale, MA 02166
(617) 244-1250
Contact: Mr. Dave Abrams
Minimum Salary Placed: $25,000
Recruiting Specialty: Software

BOSTON

ABA Associates Inc.
131 State, Suite 215
Boston, MA 02109
(617) 723-8135
Contact: Ms. Rachel Richard
Recruiting Specialty: Banking and mortgages

Accountants Executive Search
99 Summer Street
Boston, MA 02110
(617) 345-0660
Contact: Ms. B. LeClaire
Minimum Salary Placed: $25,000
Recruiting Specialty: Accounting

Arnold Associates
10 Post Office Square
Boston, MA 02109
(617) 988-0403
Minimum Salary Placed: $50,000
Recruiting Specialty: Financial services

Ashworth Consultants, Inc.
53 Fulton Street
Boston, MA 02109
(617) 720-0350
Contact: Mr. Robert Ash
Minimum Salary Placed: $75,000
Recruiting Specialty: General

Atlantic Search Group, Inc.
1 Liberty Square
Boston, MA 02109
(617) 426-9700
Contact: Mr. John Beckvold
Minimum Salary Placed: $20,000
Recruiting Specialty: Accounting and finance

Aubin International
281 Winter
Boston, MA 02154
(617) 890-1722
Minimum Salary Placed: $75,000
Recruiting Specialty: General

Auerbach Associates, Inc.
30 Winter Street, Suite 1010
Boston, MA 02108
(617) 451-0095
Contact: Ms. Judith Auerbach
Recruiting Specialty: Non-profit, higher education and healthcare

Nathan Barry Associates, Inc.
301 Union Wharf
Boston, MA 02109
(617) 227-6067
Contact: Mr. Nathan Barry
Minimum Salary Placed: $100,000
Recruiting Specialty: Pharmaceutical and healthcare

Bradford Barnes Associates
100 Franklin Street
Boston, MA 02110
(617) 451-1100
Contact: Ms. M. Kilbane
Recruiting Specialty: Healthcare

C.P.S., Inc.
50 Federal Building
Boston, MA 02210
(617) 368-3550
Contact: Ms. Mary O'Connell
Recruiting Specialty: Actuaries and employee benefits

Chaloner Associates
Box 1097, Back Bay Station
Boston, MA 02117
(617) 451-5170
Contact: Mr. Edward Chaloner
Minimum Salary Placed: $35,000
Recruiting Specialty: Advertising and public relations

Charter Associates
50 Congress Street
Boston, MA 02109
(617) 720-4471
Recruiting Specialty: General

M.J. Curran & Associates, Inc.
1 Beacon Street
Boston, MA 02109
(617) 723-7002
Contact: Mr. Martin Curran
Minimum Salary Placed: $75,000
Recruiting Specialty: General

Daley & Company
1 Exeter Place
Boston, MA 02116
(617) 262-2800

Contact: Theresa or Dan
Recruiting Specialty: Office support and restaurants

Diversified Management Resources
10 Post Office Square
Boston, MA 02109
(617) 338-3040
Contact: Mr. Robert Patrick
Minimum Salary Placed: $25,000
Recruiting Specialty: General

The Docker Group, Inc.
53 Commercial Wharf
Boston, MA 02173
(617) 367-0780
Contact: Mr. Angelo Buono
Minimum Salary Placed: $60,000
Recruiting Specialty: General

Excalibur Associates
303 Congress Street
Boston, MA 02210
(617) 261-4936
Contact: Mr. Bryan Mulkern
Minimum Salary Placed: $25,000
Recruiting Specialty: Finance

Execusource
162 Boylston Street, Suite 61
Boston, MA 02116
(617) 859-7737
Contact: Ms. Laura Corcoran
Minimum Salary Placed: $25,000
Recruiting Specialty: General

Fitzwilliam Associates
300 Congress Street
Boston, MA 02210
(617) 482-6862

Contact: Mr. Mike Fitzwilliam
Minimum Salary Placed: $25,000
Recruiting Specialty: General

Gilvar & Associates
29 Concord Square
Boston, MA 02118
(617) 437-0850
Contact: Ms. Barbara Gilvar
Recruiting Specialty: General

Hayden Group, Inc.
One Post Office Square
Boston, MA 02110
(617) 482-2445
Contact: Mr. James Hayden
Minimum Salary Placed: $100,000
Recruiting Specialty: General

Heidrick & Struggles, Inc.
One Post Office Square
Boston, MA 02109
(617) 423-1140
Contact: Mr. George Rossi
Minimum Salary Placed: $60,000
Recruiting Specialty: General

Hospitality Executive Search, Inc.
608 Tremont Street
Boston, MA 02118
(617) 266-7700
Contact: Mr. Jonathan Spatt
Minimum Salary Placed: $75,000
Recruiting Specialty: Food and beverages, hospitality, entertainment and nonprofit

H.I. Hunt
200 High Street
Boston, MA 02110
(617) 261-1611
Contact: Mr. Hunt
Minimum Salary Placed: $25,000
Recruiting Specialty: Financial services

International Search Associates
27 State Street
Boston, MA 02109
(617) 367-0320
Contact: Mr. P. Rabinowitz
Minimum Salary Placed: $25,000
Recruiting Specialty: Healthcare

Isaacson, Miller, Inc.
334 Boylston Street, Suite 500
Boston, MA 02154
(617) 262-6500
Contact: Mr. John Isaacson
Minimum Salary Placed: $50,000
Recruiting Specialty: General

JNB Associates, Inc.
2 Oliver Street, 6th Floor
Boston, MA 02109
(617) 451-0355
Contact: Mr. Joseph Baker
Minimum Salary Placed: $50,000
Recruiting Specialty: Banking and finance

Key Executive Group
1 Winthrop Square
Boston, MA 02110
(617) 737-8626
Contact: Mr. W. Radtke
Minimum Salary Placed: $30,000
Recruiting Specialty: General

Kinlin Company
60 State Street
Boston, MA 02109
(617) 742-7877
Contact: Ms. Ellen Kinlin
Minimum Salary Placed: $100,000
Recruiting Specialty: Financial services

Korn/Ferry International
101 Federal Street, 24th Floor
Boston, MA 02110
(617) 345-0200
Contact: Mr. John Sullivan
Minimum Salary Placed: $100,000
Recruiting Specialty: General

Macpherson and Associates
164 Canal
Boston, MA 02114
(617) 248-8688
Contact: Ms. J. Rossi
Minimum Salary Placed: $40,000
Recruiting Specialty: Legal and finance

Management Recruiters
607 Boylston Street, Suite 700
Boston, MA 02116
(617) 262-5050
Contact: Ms. Meg Piccione
Minimum Salary Placed: $20,000
Recruiting Specialty: General

Mercedes & Company, Inc.
6 Whittier Place
Boston, MA 02114
(617) 227-4277
Contact: Ms. Linda Mercedes Correia
Minimum Salary Placed: $100,000
Recruiting Specialty: Pharmaceuticals

O'Brien Associates
59 Temple Place
Boston, MA 02111
(617) 426-0533
Contact: Mr. Colum O'Brien
Recruiting Specialty: Financial services

Organization Resources Inc.
63 Atlantic Avenue
Boston Harbor
Boston, MA 02110
(617) 742-8970
Contact: Mr. John Kris
Minimum Salary Placed: $90,000
Recruiting Specialty: General

P.A.R. Associates, Inc.
60 State Street
Boston, MA 02109
(617) 367-0320
Contact: Mr. Peter Rabinowitz
Minimum Salary Placed: $90,000
Recruiting Specialty: General

Pendleton James & Associates, Inc.
One International Place, Suite 2350
Boston, MA 02110
(617) 261-9696
Contact: Mr. Durant Hunter
Minimum Salary Placed: $100,000
Recruiting Specialty: General

Placement Company
7 Faneuil Hall Market Place
Boston, MA 02109
(617) 723-9098
Contact: Ms. M. Mitchel
Minimum Salary Placed: $25,000
Recruiting Specialty: Finance and accounting

Prolink Inc.
World Trade Center, Suite 125
Boston, MA 02210
(617) 439-5990
Contact: Mr. Earl Dumas
Minimum Salary Placed: $30,000
Recruiting Specialty: General

Resource Objectives Inc.
185 Devonshire
Boston, MA 02210
(617) 338-5500
Contact: Mr. Don Da Costa
Minimum Salary Placed: $40,000
Recruiting Specialty: Physicians, banking, finance, attorneys and high technology

Robert Half Accountemps
101 Arch Street
Boston, MA 02110
(617) 951-4000
Contact: Mr. W. Mello
Minimum Salary Placed: $20,000
Recruiting Specialty: Accounting and finance

Robsham Associates
4 Faneuil Hall Market Place
Boston, MA 02109
(617) 742-2944
Contact: Ms. B. Robsham
Minimum Salary Placed: $25,000
Recruiting Specialty: General

Romac and Associates
125 Summer Street
Boston, MA 02110
(617) 439-7010
Contact: Mr. B. Cuddy
Minimum Salary Placed: $25,000
Recruiting Specialty: Accounting and finance

Russell Reynolds Associates, Inc.
45 School Street
Boston, MA 02108
(617) 523-1111
Contact: Mr. Jack Vernon
Minimum Salary Placed: $100,000
Recruiting Specialty: General

Russillo/Gardner/Spolsino
1 International Place
Boston, MA 02110
(617) 345-0700
Contact: Mr. Thomas Russillo
Minimum Salary Placed: $50,000
Recruiting Specialty: MIS and insurance

J. Robert Scott
27 State Street
Boston, MA 02109
(617) 720-2770
Contact: Mr. William Holodnak
Minimum Salary Placed: $80,000
Recruiting Specialty: General

Scott-Wayne Associates, Inc.
100 Charles River Plaza, 4th Floor
Boston, MA 02114
(617) 723-7007
Contact: Mr. R. Steven Dow
Minimum Salary Placed: $20,000
Recruiting Specialty: MIS, finance and accounting

Christopher Smallhorn Executive Recruiting
One Boston Place
Boston, MA 02108
(617) 723-8180
Contact: Mr. Christopher Smallhorn
Recruiting Specialty: General

Source EDP
155 Federal Street, Suite 410
Boston, MA 02110
(617) 482-8211
Contact: Mr. David Hayes
Minimum Salary Placed: $20,000
Recruiting Specialty: General

Stone & Youngblood
304 Newbury Street, Suite 210
Boston, MA 02115
(617) 647-0070
Contact: Mr. Stephen Sarkis
Recruiting Specialty: General

BRAINTREE

Hurley Curtis Inc.
100 Grossman Drive
Braintree, MA 02184
(617) 848-1442
Contact: Mr. Hurley Curtis
Minimum Salary Placed: $25,000
Recruiting Specialty: Accounting and finance

Alan Lerner Associates
161 Forbes Road, Suite 104
Braintree, MA 02184
(617) 380-8830
Contact: Mr. Luke Roberts
Minimum Salary Placed: $25,000
Recruiting Specialty: Retail

Management Recruiters
639 Granite Street
Braintree, MA 02184
(617) 848-1666
Contact: Mr. Stephen Morse
Minimum Salary Placed: $20,000
Recruiting Specialty: General

Search Professionals Inc.
150 Wood Road
Braintree, MA 02184
(617) 843-0700
Contact: Mr. R. Barzelay
Minimum Salary Placed: $25,000
Recruiting Specialty: Retail

BROCKTON

Sales Consultants
567 Pleasant Street, Suite 8
Brockton, MA 02401
(508) 587-2030
Contact: Mr. Milton Feinson
Minimum Salary Placed: $20,000
Recruiting Specialty: Sales

Xavier Associates, Inc.
1350 Belmont Street
Brockton, MA 02401
(508) 584-9414
Contact: Mr. Frank McCarthy
Minimum Salary Placed: $25,000
Recruiting Specialty: Minorities and MIS

BROOKLINE

Development Guild DDI
233 Harvard Street
Brookline, MA 02146
(617) 277-2112
Recruiting Specialty: Non-profit

BURLINGTON

Christian & Timbers, Inc.
24 Executive Mall Road
Burlington, MA 01803
(617) 229-9515
Minimum Salary Placed: $75,000
Recruiting Specialty: General

Dinisco Matthews Associates
25 Burlington Mall Road, Suite 300
Burlington, MA 01803
(617) 270-0636
Contact: Mr. Gene Dinisco
Recruiting Specialty: Technical, manufacturing, and engineering

The Elliott Company
5 Burlington Woods Drive
Burlington, MA 01803
(617) 938-6050
Contact: Mr. Roger Elliott
Minimum Salary Placed: $75,000
Recruiting Specialty: General

First National Marketing Group
15 New England Executive Park
Burlington, MA 01803
(617) 273-3541
Contact: Mr. D. Luby
Minimum Salary Placed: $25,000
Recruiting Specialty: Sales, engineering and biotechnology

Pencom Systems Inc.
17 New England Executive Park
Burlington, MA 01803
(617) 229-1111
Contact: Mr. Ralph Hayden
Recruiting Specialty: MIS and computers

Source EDP
20 Mall Road, Suite 305
Burlington, MA 01803
(617) 272-5000
Contact: Ms. Rosemarie Brown
Minimum Salary Placed: $20,000
Recruiting Specialty: Computer hardware and software

Source Services
20 Mall Road, Suite 30
Burlington, MA 01803
(617) 272-5000
Contact: Mr. Jim Twomey
Minimum Salary Placed: $25,000
Recruiting Specialty: Engineering

CAMBRIDGE

Brickerton and Gordon
125 Cambridge Drive
Cambridge, MA 02138
(617) 576-2335
Contact: Mr. Brian Brickerton
Minimum Salary Placed: $60,000
Recruiting Specialty: Attorneys

Dana Associates Inc.
353 Huron Avenue
Cambridge, MA 02138
(617) 661-0779
Contact: Ms. D. Grant
Minimum Salary Placed: $25,000
Recruiting Specialty: Sales and marketing

C. A. Durakis Associates, Inc.
620 Massachusetts Avenue
Cambridge, MA 02138
(617) 497-7769
Contact: Mr. Richard Tufenkjian
Minimum Salary Placed: $80,000
Recruiting Specialty: General

Kingsbury, Wax & Bova
501 Cambridge Street, Suite 101
Cambridge, MA 02141
(617) 868-6166
Contact: Mr. Robert Wax
Minimum Salary Placed: $60,000
Recruiting Specialty: General

Nachman Biomedical
50 Church Street
Cambridge, MA 02138
(617) 492-8911
Contact: Mr. Philip Nachman
Minimum Salary Placed: $50,000
Recruiting Specialty: Pharmaceuticals and biotechnology

CANTON

Alan Levine Associates
275 Turnpike Street, Suite 202
Canton, MA 02021
(617) 821-1131
Contact: Mr. Alan Levine
Minimum Salary Placed: $45,000
Recruiting Specialty: Wholesale and retail and high technology

Stephen M. Sonis Associates
275 Turnpike Street, Suite 202
Canton, MA 02021
(617) 821-0303
Contact: Mr. Stephen Sonis
Minimum Salary Placed: $40,000
Recruiting Specialty: General

CARLISLE

Ford Webb Associates
P.O. Box 645
Carlisle, MA 01741
(508) 371-2484

Contact: Ms. J. Webb
Recruiting Specialty: Government and non-profit

P.N. French Associates, Inc.
126 Noell Farm Road
Carlisle, MA 01741
(508) 369-4569
Contact: Mr. Peter French
Minimum Salary Placed: $60,000
Recruiting Specialty: General

CHELMSFORD

Timothy D. Crowe, Jr.
26 Higate Road, Suite 101
Chelmsford, MA 01824
(508) 256-2008
Contact: Mr. Timothy Crowe
Minimum Salary Placed: $30,000
Recruiting Specialty: General

Marketing Resources
P.O. Box 463, 18 North Road
Chelmsford, MA 01824
(508) 256-8001
Contact: Mr. Joseph Sheedy
Minimum Salary Placed: $50,000
Recruiting Specialty: Sales and marketing in healthcare

CHESTNUT HILL

Scientific Resources
1244 Boylston Street
Chestnut Hill, MA 02167
(617) 449-8760
Contact: Mr. M. Saidell
Minimum Salary Placed: $25,000
Recruiting Specialty: Biotechnology, diagnostics and environmental

CONCORD

Blaney Executive Search
Damon Mill Square
Concord, MA 01742
(508) 371-2192
Contact: Mr. John Blaney
Minimum Salary Placed: $80,000
Recruiting Specialty: High technology

Clayman & Company
30 Monument Square, P.O. Box 488
Concord, MA 01742
(508) 369-1896
Contact: Mr. Steven Clayman
Minimum Salary Placed: $100,000
Recruiting Specialty: High technology

Haddad Associates
P.O. Box 594
Concord, MA 01742
(508) 369-8947
Contact: Mr. Ronald Haddad
Minimum Salary Placed: $50,000
Recruiting Specialty: General

The Human Resource Consulting Group, Inc.
747 Main
Concord, MA 01742
(617) 973-5115
Contact: Mr. Lawrence Stone
Minimum Salary Placed: $50,000
Recruiting Specialty: General

Human Resource Research Inc.
747 Main Street, Suite 222
Concord, MA 01742
(508) 371-2702
Contact: Ms. Claudia Liebesny
Minimum Salary Placed: $60,000
Recruiting Specialty: Pharmaceuticals, finance and high technology

K. Jaeger and Associates
60 Thoreau Street, Suite 300
Concord, MA 01742
(508) 369-3352
Recruiting Specialty: Industrial sales and
marketing

Platt Staunton Associates
97 Lowell Road
Concord, MA 01742
(508) 371-9171
Contact: Mr. P. Staunton
Minimum Salary Placed: $25,000
Recruiting Specialty: Science and engi-
neering

DANVERS

Morency Associates
2 Electronics Avenue
Danvers, MA 01923
(508) 750-4460
Contact: Ms. Marcia Morency
Minimum Salary Placed: $30,000
Recruiting Specialty: General

Sales and Marketing Search Inc.
100 Conifer Hill Drive, Suite 108
Danvers, MA 01923
(508) 777-9997
Contact: Mr. Russ Smith
Minimum Salary Placed: $40,000
Recruiting Specialty: Sales and marketing
in high technology

Sales Consultants
222 Rosewood Drive, Suite 1020
Danvers, MA 01923
(508) 777-5600
Contact: Mr. Robert Stockard
Minimum Salary Placed: $20,000
Recruiting Specialty: Sales

DEDHAM

Gillard Associates Legal Search
850 Providence Highway, Suite 305
Dedham, MA 02026
(617) 329-4731
Contact: Ms. Elizabeth Gillard
Recruiting Specialty: Legal

S.D. Kelly & Associates, Inc.
990 Washington Street, Suite 314 S
Dedham, MA 02026
(617) 326-8038
Contact: Ms. Susan Kelly
Minimum Salary Placed: $60,000
Recruiting Specialty: High technology,
manufacturing and chemicals

Recruiting Specialists
300 VFW Parkway, Suite M-5
Dedham, MA 02027
(617) 329-5850
Contact: Ms. Cindy Laughlin
Minimum Salary Placed: $25,000
Recruiting Specialty: Retailing

DUXBURY

Execuquest
24 Bay Road
Duxbury, MA 02332
(617) 934-9340
Contact: Ms. C. LaDouceur
Minimum Salary Placed: $75,000
Recruiting Specialty: General

S. B. Webster & Associates
30 Tremont Street, Suite 33
Duxbury, MA 02331
(617) 934-6603

Contact: Mr. William Webster
Minimum Salary Placed: $60,000
Recruiting Specialty: General

EAST LONGMEADOW

Sales Consultants
180 Denslow Road, Suite 2
East Longmeadow, MA 01028
(413) 737-7200
Contact: Mr. William Carroll
Minimum Salary Placed: $20,000
Recruiting Specialty: Sales

FALMOUTH

DeLuca and Associates
49 Locust Street
Falmouth, MA 02540
(508) 457-1122
Contact: Mr. David DeLuca
Minimum Salary Placed: $25,000
Recruiting Specialty: Physicians

FRAMINGHAM

Carter/MacKay
111 Speen Street
Framingham, MA 01701
(508) 626-2240
Contact: Mr. Mike Rowell
Recruiting Specialty: Sales in pharmaceuticals and healthcare

Davis and Company
565 Edmands Road
Framingham, MA 01701
(508) 877-2025
Contact: Mr. Al Davis
Minimum Salary Placed: $60,000
Recruiting Specialty: General

Franklin International Search, Inc.
4 Franklin Commons
Framingham, MA 01701
(508) 872-1133
Contact: Mr. Stanley Shindler
Minimum Salary Placed: $50,000
Recruiting Specialty: Technical

H & G Associates
160 Speen Street
Framingham, MA 01701
(508) 820-0048
Contact: Marilyn
Minimum Salary Placed: $50,000
Recruiting Specialty: General

Murphy Associates
1550 Worchester Road, 124 W
Framingham, MA 01702
(508) 879-9934
Contact: Mr. Ed Murphy
Recruiting Specialty: Marketing and sales, management in high technology

Norman Powers Associates, Inc.
P.O. Box 3221
Framingham, MA 01705
(508) 877-2025
Contact: Mr. Norman Powers
Minimum Salary Placed: $25,000
Recruiting Specialty: Technical disciplines in high technology

L. A. Silver Associates, Inc.
463 Worcester Road
Framingham, MA 01701
(508) 879-2603
Contact: Mr. Lee Silver
Minimum Salary Placed: $60,000
Recruiting Specialty: General

GROTON

Groton Planning Group, Inc.
293 Chicopee Row
Groton, MA 01450
(508) 448-3332
Contact: Mr. Stephan Kornacki
Recruiting Specialty: General

HANOVER

Gold Coast Partners
720 Washington Street
Hanover, MA 02339
(617) 826-0317
Contact: Mr. Steve Lomberdo
Minimum Salary Placed: $25,000
Recruiting Specialty: Sales in hospitality
and computer software

HINGHAM

A.K.S. Associates, Ltd.
175 Derby Street, Suite 9
Hingham, MA 02043
(617) 740-1704
Contact: Mr. Alexander Salmela
Minimum Salary Placed: $60,000
Recruiting Specialty: General

Excalibur Associates
1 Pond Park Road
Hingham, MA 02043
(617) 749-6693
Minimum Salary Placed: $25,000
Recruiting Specialty: Finance

Phillips & Associates
62 Derby Street
Hingham, MA 02043
(617) 740-9699
Recruiting Specialty: Healthcare

Search Services Inc.
16 North Street, Suite B
Hingham, MA 02043
(617) 749-2242
Contact: Mr. Neal George
Minimum Salary Placed: $25,000
Recruiting Specialty: General

**Kimball Shaw Associates/KSA
Healthcare**
3 Pleasant Street
Hingham, MA 02043
(617) 749-5574
Contact: Mr. Kimball Shaw
Minimum Salary Placed: $50,000
Recruiting Specialty: General

LEXINGTON

The Corporate Source Group
1 Cranberry Hill
Lexington, MA 02173
(617) 862-1900
Contact: Ms. Dana Willis
Minimum Salary Placed: $70,000
Recruiting Specialty: General

Fenwick Partners
57 Bedford Street, Suite 101
Lexington, MA 02173
(617) 862-3370
Minimum Salary Placed: $90,000
Recruiting Specialty: High technology

Fitzgerald Associates
21 Muzzey Street
Lexington, MA 02173
(617) 863-1945
Contact: Mr. Geoffrey Fitzgerald
Minimum Salary Placed: $60,000
Recruiting Specialty: Healthcare

Hamilton-Chase & Associates, Inc.
20 Maguire Road, Suite 200
Lexington, MA 02173
(617) 863-2811
Contact: Mr. Joseph Russo
Minimum Salary Placed: $60,000
Recruiting Specialty: General

I.T. Resources
3 Wallis Court
Lexington, MA 02173
(617) 863-2661
Contact: Mr. Ken Loomis
Minimum Salary Placed: $25,000
Recruiting Specialty: Information systems

John J. Kennedy Associates, Inc.
35 Bedford Street, Suite 4
Lexington, MA 02173
(617) 863-8860
Contact: Mr. John Kennedy
Minimum Salary Placed: $20,000
Recruiting Specialty: General

The Kleven Group
1 Cranberry Hill, P.O. Box 636
Lexington, MA 02173
(617) 861-1020
Contact: Mr. Robert Kleven
Minimum Salary Placed: $60,000
Recruiting Specialty: High technology

Madison Group
92 Hayden Avenue
Lexington, MA 02173
(617) 862-7717
Minimum Salary Placed: $25,000
Recruiting Specialty: General

Louis Rudzinsky Associates, Inc.
P.O. Box 640
Lexington, MA 02173
(617) 862-6727
Contact: Mr. Louis Rudzinsky
Minimum Salary Placed: $40,000
Recruiting Specialty: Technical disciplines in high technology

Willmott & Associates
922 Waltham Street, Suite 103
Lexington, MA 02173
(617) 863-5400
Contact: Mr. D. Clark Willmott
Minimum Salary Placed: $20,000
Recruiting Specialty: Human resources

LINCOLN

Futures, Inc.
55 Old Bedford Road, Lincoln N.
Lincoln, MA 01773
(617) 259-4500
Contact: Mr. Thomas Colacchio
Minimum Salary Placed: $25,000
Recruiting Specialty: Food

LYNNFIELD

GlobalNet
7 Kimball Lane
Pinewood Office Park A
Lynnfield, MA 01940
(617) 245-3005
Contact: Ms. Bonnie Lappin
Recruiting Specialty: Bilingual recruiting

MANCHESTER BY THE SEA

Gilreath Weatherby Inc.
P.O. Box 1483
Manchester by the Sea, MA 01944
(508) 526-8771
Contact: Mr. James Gilreath
Minimum Salary Placed: $60,000
Recruiting Specialty: General

MANSFIELD

Sales Consultants
272 Chauncy Street
Mansfield, MA 02048
(508) 339-1924
Contact: Mr. Jim Noyes
Minimum Salary Placed: $20,000
Recruiting Specialty: Sales

MARBLEHEAD

New Dimensions in Technology, Inc.
74 Atlantic Avenue, Suite 101
Marblehead, MA 01945
(617) 639-0866
Contact: Ms. Beverly Kahn
Minimum Salary Placed: $55,000
Recruiting Specialty: Computer and high
technology

MARLBOROUGH

Executive Alliance
2 Mount Royal Avenue, Suite 300
Marlborough, MA 01752
(508) 481-7777
Contact: Mr. Don Bateman
Recruiting Specialty: General

Holden Associates, Inc.
33 Boston Post Road W
Marlborough, MA 01752
(508) 485-1870
Recruiting Specialty: General

MARSHFIELD HILLS

Resource Inc.
P.O. Box 620
Marshfield Hills, MA 02051
(617) 837-8113
Contact: Mr. Thomas Healy
Minimum Salary Placed: $50,000
Recruiting Specialty: Food and beverages
and consumer products

MAYNARD

Searchnet
56 A Main Street
Maynard, MA 01754
(508) 897-3855
Recruiting Specialty: General

Steinbach & Company
1 Pleasant Street
Maynard, MA 01754
(508) 897-8661
Contact: Mr. David Steinbach
Minimum Salary Placed: $65,000
Recruiting Specialty: Communications
and high technology

MEDFIELD

Gatti & Associates
266 Main Street, Suite 21
Medfield, MA 02052
(508) 359-4153

Contact: Mr. Robert Gatti
Recruiting Specialty: Human resources

J. S. Lord & Company, Inc.
266 Main Street, Suite 7B
Medfield, MA 02052
(508) 359-5100
Contact: Mr. J. Scott Lord
Minimum Salary Placed: $90,000
Recruiting Specialty: General

Prestonwood Associates
266 Main Street, Suite 9
Medfield, MA 02052
(508) 359-7100
Contact: Ms. Diane Coletti
Minimum Salary Placed: $60,000
Recruiting Specialty: Sales and marketing in high technology and textiles

MENDON

Derek Associates, Inc.
P.O. Box 13
Mendon, MA 01756
(508) 883-2289
Contact: Mr. Joren Fishback
Minimum Salary Placed: $40,000
Recruiting Specialty: Environmental, engineering and hazardous waste

MONSON

Paul Shrenker Associates, Inc.
121 Peck Brothers Road
Monson, MA 01057
(413) 267-4271
Contact: Mr. Paul Shrenker
Recruiting Specialty: Environmental, health and safety professionals

NANTUCKET

Educational Management Network
98 Old South Road
Nantucket, MA 02554
(508) 228-6700
Contact: Ms. Nancy Archer-Martin
Minimum Salary Placed: $50,000
Recruiting Specialty: Non-profit

Yorkshire Group Ltd.
233 W. Central
Nantucket, MA 02554
(508) 653-1222
Contact: Mr. M. Tornesello
Minimum Salary Placed: $25,000
Recruiting Specialty: Insurance

NATICK

McInturff & Associates, Inc.
209 G West Central Street
Natick, MA 01760
(617) 237-0220
Contact: Mr. Robert McInturff
Minimum Salary Placed: $35,000
Recruiting Specialty: Manufacturing and materials management

Weinstein & Company
1 Apple Hill
Natick, MA 01760
(508) 655-3838
Recruiting Specialty: General

The Yorkshire Group, Ltd.
233 W. Central Street
Natick, MA 01760
(508) 653-1222
Contact: Mr. Michael Tornesello
Minimum Salary Placed: $50,000
Recruiting Specialty: General

NEEDHAM

Arancio Associates
542 High Rock Street
Needham, MA 02192
(617) 449-4436
Contact: Mr. N. Joseph Arancio
Minimum Salary Placed: $20,000
Recruiting Specialty: Sales, marketing, chemicals, life science and biotechnology

Ford & Ford
105 Chestnut Street, Suite 34
Needham, MA 02192
(617) 449-8200
Contact: Mr. Bernard Ford
Minimum Salary Placed: $45,000
Recruiting Specialty: General

Glou International, Inc.
687 Highland Avenue
Needham, MA 02194
(617) 449-3310
Contact: Mr. Alan Glou
Minimum Salary Placed: $60,000
Recruiting Specialty: General

Hamilton Wenham Research
105 Chestnut Street
Needham, MA 02192
(617) 449-2714
Contact: Mr. Bernard Ford
Recruiting Specialty: Retail, human resources, marketing & sales, and information technology

J P James Company
105 Chestnut Street, Suite 35
Needham, MA 02192
(617) 449-7520
Recruiting Specialty: Insurance

Trowbridge & Company, Inc.
105 Chestnut Street, Suite 22
Needham, MA 02192
(617) 444-4200
Contact: Mr. Robert Trowbridge
Minimum Salary Placed: $75,000
Recruiting Specialty: General

NEWBURYPORT

Elliot Associates, Inc.
18 Liberty Street
Newburyport, MA 01950
(508) 462-5657
Contact: Mr. Richard Giannino
Minimum Salary Placed: $15,000
Recruiting Specialty: Hospitality

Search International
P.O. Box 81
Newburyport, MA 01950
(508) 465-4000
Recruiting Specialty: Hospitality

NEWTON

Gustin Partners LTD
2276 Washington Street
Newton, MA 02162
(617) 332-0800
Contact: Ms. Vivian Brocard
Recruiting Specialty: Telecommunications, networking and consulting, and systems integration

Interactive Software Placement
465 Auburn Street
Newton, MA 02166
(617) 527-2700
Recruiting Specialty: Executive search, technical

Keane Associates
676 Commonwealth Avenue
Newton, MA 02159
(617) 965-1600
Contact: Mr. Kevin Keane
Minimum Salary Placed: $75,000
Recruiting Specialty: Computers and
high technology

Progressive Search Association
465 Auburn Street
Newton, MA 02166
(617) 244-1250
Recruiting Specialty: Technical

Charles Zabriskie Associates, Inc.
2366 Commonwealth Avenue
Newton, MA 02166
(617) 899-5511
Contact: Mr. Charles Zabriskie
Minimum Salary Placed: $50,000
Recruiting Specialty: Finance and banking

NORTH ANDOVER

Financial Search Group, Inc.
800 Turnpike Street, Suite 300
North Andover, MA 01845
(508) 682-4123
Contact: Mr. Paul Luther
Minimum Salary Placed: $50,000
Recruiting Specialty: Finance

Straube Associates
855 Turnpike Road
North Andover, MA 01845
(508) 687-1993
Contact: Mr. Stan Straube
Minimum Salary Placed: $60,000
Recruiting Specialty: General

NORTH ATTLEBORO

Locke Associates
500 E. Washington Street
North Attleboro, MA 02760
(508) 643-0444
Contact: Mr. John Locke
Recruiting Specialty: Environmental

NORTHBOROUGH

Computer Security Placement Service, Inc.
One Computer Drive, Box 204-D
Northborough, MA 01532
(508) 393-7803
Contact: Mr. Cameron Carey
Minimum Salary Placed: $30,000
Recruiting Specialty: Information security and disaster recovery planning

Kacevich, Lewis & Brown, Inc.
300 W. Main Street, Building B
Northborough, MA 01532
(508) 393-6002
Contact: Mr. Joseph Kacevich
Minimum Salary Placed: $60,000
Recruiting Specialty: Sales in high technology

McCannon Risedorf and Ingalls
300 W. Main Street
Northborough, MA 01532
(508) 393-2234
Contact: Mr. B. Risedorf
Minimum Salary Placed: $25,000
Recruiting Specialty: Telecommunications

NORTH DARTMOUTH

Fontaine Flaherty & D'Aueteuil
859 State Road
North Dartmouth, MA 02747
(508) 991-5446
Recruiting Specialty: General

NORWELL

CEC Associates
52 Accord Park Drive
Norwell, MA 02061
(617) 982-0205
Contact: Ms. C. Connelly
Minimum Salary Placed: $30,000
Recruiting Specialty: Medical

Navin Group
80 Washington Street
Norwell, MA 02061
(617) 871-6770
Contact: Mr. J. Navin
Minimum Salary Placed: $25,000
Recruiting Specialty: Healthcare

NORWOOD

Robert H. Davidson Associates Inc.
1410 Providence Highway
Norwood, MA 02062
(617) 769-8350
Contact: Mr. Robert Davidson
Minimum Salary Placed: $25,000
Recruiting Specialty: Marketing and engineering

A. Greenstein and Company
20 Vernon Street
Norwood, MA 02062
(617) 769-4966
Contact: Ms. Arlene Greenstein
Minimum Salary Placed: $60,000
Recruiting Specialty: General

Heffelfinger Associates, Inc.
470 Washington Street
Norwood, MA 02062
(617) 769-6650
Contact: Mr. Thomas Heffelfinger
Minimum Salary Placed: $80,000
Recruiting Specialty: Computers and communications

OSTERVILLE

The Kinlin Company, Inc.
749 Main Street
Osterville, MA 02655
(508) 420-1165
Contact: Ms. Ellen Kinlin
Minimum Salary Placed: $100,000
Recruiting Specialty: Banking and finance

PITTSFIELD

Berkshire Search & Placement
P.O. Box 562
255 North Street, Suite 4
Pittsfield, MA 01202-0562
(413) 447-7181
Contact: Mr. Donald Munger
Recruiting Specialty: Engineering, design and construction, electrical, mechanical, and environmental

Search and Placement
1st and Fenn Street
Pittsfield, MA 01201
(413) 499-2498
Contact: Ms. C. Welch
Minimum Salary Placed: $25,000
Recruiting Specialty: General

ROCKLAND

Anthony Michael and Company
800 Hingham Street
Rockland, MA 02370
(617) 871-9600
Contact: Mr. M. Kulesza
Minimum Salary Placed: $25,000
Recruiting Specialty: Banking and finance

Executive Search Northeast Inc.
800 Hingham Street
Rockland, MA 02370
(617) 871-6010
Contact: Mr. Michael Arietta
Minimum Salary Placed: $25,000
Recruiting Specialty: Construction

SAGAMORE BEACH

Sales Consultants
P.O. Box 420
Sagamore Beach, MA 02562
(508) 888-8704
Contact: Mr. Edward Cahan
Minimum Salary Placed: $20,000
Recruiting Specialty: Sales

SALEM

American Executive Management, Inc.
30 Federal Street
Salem, MA 01970
(508) 744-5923
Contact: Mr. E. J. Cloutier
Minimum Salary Placed: $70,000
Recruiting Specialty: General

SANDWICH

Dean M. Coe Associates
32 Pine Street
Sandwich, MA 02563
(508) 833-2787
Contact: Mr. Dean Coe
Minimum Salary Placed: $75,000
Recruiting Specialty: Real property

SHARON

Partridge Associates, Inc.
1200 Providence Highway
Sharon, MA 02067
(617) 784-4144
Contact: Mr. Robert Partridge
Minimum Salary Placed: $40,000
Recruiting Specialty: Hospitality

SHERBORN

Greene & Company
5 Powderhouse Lane
P.O. Box 1025
Sherborn, MA 01770
(508) 655-1210
Contact: Mr. Timothy Greene
Recruiting Specialty: Banking

SHREWSBURY

Vanguard Executive Service
512 W. Main Street
Shrewsbury, MA 01545
(508) 842-5600
Contact: Mr. John Matria
Minimum Salary Placed: $25,000
Recruiting Specialty: General

SOMERVILLE

Smallhorn Executive Recruiting
1 Boston Place
Somerville, MA 02144
(617) 723-8180
Contact: Mr. Chris Smallhorn
Minimum Salary Placed: $25,000
Recruiting Specialty: General

SPRINGFIELD

Douglas-Allen, Inc.
1500 Main Street, Suite 2408
Springfield, MA 01115
(413) 739-0900
Contact: Mr. Robert Stevens
Minimum Salary Placed: $50,000
Recruiting Specialty: Finance, banking
and insurance

Dunhill Professional Search
32 Hampden Street
Springfield, MA 01103
(413) 733-7826
Contact: Ms. Eileen Grobard
Recruiting Specialty: General

Management Recruiters
1500 Main Street, Suite 1822
Springfield, MA 01115
(413) 781-1550
Contact: Ms. Irene Garrity
Minimum Salary Placed: $20,000
Recruiting Specialty: General

SUDBURY

L.J. Doherty & Associates
65 Ford Road
Sudbury, MA 01776
(508) 443-9603
Contact: Mr. Leonard Doherty
Minimum Salary Placed: $80,000
Recruiting Specialty: Computers

Travis & Company, Inc.
325 Boston Post Road
Sudbury, MA 01776
(508) 443-4000
Contact: Mr. John Travis
Minimum Salary Placed: $75,000
Recruiting Specialty: General

Joel H. Wilensky Associates, Inc.
P.O. Box 155
Sudbury, MA 01776
(508) 443-5176
Contact: Mr. Joel Wilensky
Minimum Salary Placed: $50,000
Recruiting Specialty: Retail

WALTHAM

Aubin International Inc.
281 Winter Street
Waltham, MA 02154
(617) 890-1722
Contact: Mr. Richard Aubin
Minimum Salary Placed: $90,000
Recruiting Specialty: General

Cibotti Associates, Inc.
611 Trapelo Road
Waltham, MA 02154
(617) 891-0845

Contact: Mr. Thomas Cibotti
Minimum Salary Placed: $40,000
Recruiting Specialty: General

Logix, Inc.
1601 Trapelo Road
Waltham, MA 02154
(617) 890-0500
Contact: Mr. David Zell
Minimum Salary Placed: $40,000
Recruiting Specialty: High technology

George D. Sandel Associates
P.O. Box 588
Waltham, MA 02254
(617) 890-0713
Contact: Mr. Ivan Samuels
Recruiting Specialty: Technical disciplines in high technology, biotechnology and hospitals

Weston Consultants, Inc.
460 Totten Pond Road, Suite 600
Waltham, MA 02154
(617) 890-3750
Contact: Mr. Edmund Walsh
Minimum Salary Placed: $60,000
Recruiting Specialty: General, everything in high technology

WELLESLEY

Michael Anthony Associates
42 Washington Street
Wellesley, MA 02181
(617) 237-4950
Contact: Mr. Mike Anthony
Minimum Salary Placed: $25,000
Recruiting Specialty: Data processing and medical

Dromeshauser Associates
20 William Street
Wellesley, MA 02181
(617) 239-0222
Contact: Mr. Peter Dromeshauser
Minimum Salary Placed: $100,000
Recruiting Specialty: Computers and high technology

Dunhill Personnel
1 Hollis Street, Suite 205
Wellesley, MA 02181
(617) 235-4777
Contact: Mr. Robert Adams
Recruiting Specialty: Nurses

Executive Search International
60 Walnut Street
Wellesley, MA 02181
(617) 239-0303
Contact: Mr. Robert McLeish
Minimum Salary Placed: $50,000
Recruiting Specialty: General

The Marlow Group
149 Benvenue Street
P.O. Box 812707
Wellesley, MA 02181
(617) 237-7012
Contact: Mr. Paul Jones
Minimum Salary Placed: $50,000
Recruiting Specialty: General

Nagler Robins & Poe, Inc.
65 William Street
Wellesley, MA 02181
(617) 431-1330
Contact: Mr. Leon Nagler
Recruiting Specialty: General

The Onstott Group
60 William Street
Wellesley, MA 02181
(617) 235-3050
Contact: Mr. Joe Onstott
Minimum Salary Placed: $80,000
Recruiting Specialty: General

D. P. Parker & Associates, Inc.
372 Washington Street
Wellesley, MA 02181
(617) 237-1220
Contact: Dr. David Parker
Minimum Salary Placed: $60,000
Recruiting Specialty: Technical disciplines in metals, chemicals and biotechnology

Pratt Partners
70 Walnut
Wellesley, MA 02181
(617) 239-8151
Contact: Mr. J. Pratt
Minimum Salary Placed: $25,000
Recruiting Specialty: Information technology

Sales Consultants
245 Washington Street, Suite 202
Wellesley, MA 02181
(617) 235-7700
Contact: Mr. Arthur Durante
Minimum Salary Placed: $20,000
Recruiting Specialty: Sales

Walker Boltons Group Ltd.
60 Walnut
Wellesley, MA 02181
(617) 237-1199
Recruiting Specialty: Voice and data in computers and telecommunications

WELLESLEY HILLS

Alliance Executive Search Inc.
70 Walnut Street
Wellesley Hills, MA 02181
(617) 239-8212
Contact: Mr. Starecheske
Minimum Salary Placed: $75,000
Recruiting Specialty: General

Chestnut Hill Partners, Inc.
20 William Street
Wellesley Hills, MA 02181
(617) 239-1400
Contact: Mr. Steven Garfinkle
Minimum Salary Placed: $80,000
Recruiting Specialty: General

Cyr & Associates, Inc.
177 Worcester Street, Suite 303
Wellesley Hills, MA 02181
(617) 235-5900
Contact: Mr. Maury Cyr
Minimum Salary Placed: $40,000
Recruiting Specialty: General

Henry Elliot & Co. Inc.
70 Walnut Street
Wellesley Hills, MA 02181
(800) 417-7000
Contact: Mr. Ken Wagner
Recruiting Specialty: High technology, information systems

Mazza & Riley, Inc.
255 William Street, Suite 120
Wellesley Hills, MA 02180
(617) 235-7724
Contact: Mr. David Mazza
Minimum Salary Placed: $100,000
Recruiting Specialty: General

Nagler & Company, Inc.
65 William Street
Wellesley Hills, MA 02181
(617) 431-1330
Contact: Mr. Leon Nagler
Minimum Salary Placed: $75,000
Recruiting Specialty: General

WESTBOROUGH

Higley, Hall & Company, Inc.
112 Turnpike Road, Suite 108
Westborough, MA 01581
(508) 836-4292
Contact: Mr. Donald Hall
Minimum Salary Placed: $50,000
Recruiting Specialty: General

Management Recruiters
2000 W. Park Drive
Westborough, MA 01581
(508) 366-9900
Contact: Ms. Irene Garrity
Minimum Salary Placed: $20,000
Recruiting Specialty: General

Source EDP
1500 W. Park Drive
Westborough, MA 01581
(508) 366-2600
Contact: Mr. Gary Zegel
Minimum Salary Placed: $20,000
Recruiting Specialty: Computer hardware and software

Source Services
1500 W. Park Drive
Westborough, MA 01581
(508) 366-2600
Minimum Salary Placed: $25,000
Recruiting Specialty: Engineering, management and marketing

Technology Search International
Box 898
Westborough, MA 01581
(508) 393-8004
Recruiting Specialty: General

WESTFIELD

Pioneer Placement, Inc.
P.O. Box 434
Westfield, MA 01086
(413) 568-2442
Contact: Mr. Nathan Rosenthal
Recruiting Specialty: Insurance

WEST NEWTON

The Bartlett Group
1185 Washington
West Newton, MA 02165
(617) 969-4600
Recruiting Specialty: General

WESTON

F. L. Mannix & Company, Inc.
10 Village Road
Weston, MA 02193
(617) 894-9660
Contact: Mr. Francis Mannix
Minimum Salary Placed: $25,000
Recruiting Specialty: General

Robert T. Morton Associates
35 Fields Pond Road
Weston, MA 02193
(617) 899-4904
Recruiting Specialty: Management consulting

WEST SPRINGFIELD

Hunter Associates
181 Park Avenue
West Springfield, MA 01089
(413) 737-6560
Contact: Mr. D. M. Shooshan
Minimum Salary Placed: $30,000
Recruiting Specialty: High technology

Marlette Personnel Search
380 Union Street, Suite 206
West Springfield, MA 01089
(413) 781-0240
Contact: Mr. Bill Cowie
Recruiting Specialty: Engineering and chemists

Rand Associates
380 Union Street, Suite 200
West Springfield, MA 01089
(413) 781-2121
Recruiting Specialty: General, executive search

WESTWOOD

HRI Services Inc.
1200 East Street
Westwood, MA 02190
(617) 251-9188
Contact: Mr. Paul Tallino
Minimum Salary Placed: $45,000
Recruiting Specialty: Food and beverages and hospitality

WEYMOUTH

Winfield Associates, Inc.
53 Winter Street
Weymouth, MA 02189
(617) 337-1010
Contact: Mr. Carl Siegel
Minimum Salary Placed: $25,000
Recruiting Specialty: Technical, sales and marketing, pharmaceuticals, and medical

WINCHESTER

Therasource, Inc.
8 Winchester Place
Winchester, MA 01890
(617) 721-9700
Contact: Mr. David Robinson
Minimum Salary Placed: $30,000
Recruiting Specialty: Physical, occupational and speech therapists

WOBURN

Harbor Consulting Group
10 State Street
Woburn, MA 01801
(617) 938-6886
Contact: Mr. M. Moore
Minimum Salary Placed: $60,000
Recruiting Specialty: General

Plymouth Associates
8 Cedar Street
Woburn, MA 01801
(617) 938-9070
Minimum Salary Placed: $25,000
Recruiting Specialty: General

Selected Executives, Inc.
76 Winn Street
Woburn, MA 01801
(617) 933-1500
Contact: Mr. Lee Sanborn
Minimum Salary Placed: $30,000
Recruiting Specialty: General

Ward Group
8 Cedar Street
Woburn, MA 01801
(617) 938-4000
Contact: Mr. Jim Ward
Minimum Salary Placed: $25,000
Recruiting Specialty: Marketing and communications

Zurick, Davis & Company, Inc.
10 State Street
Woburn, MA 01801
(617) 938-1975
Contact: Mr. Peter Davis
Minimum Salary Placed: $60,000
Recruiting Specialty: General

WORCESTER

Delores F. George
269 Hamilton Street
Worcester, MA 01604
(508) 754-3451
Contact: Ms. Delores George
Recruiting Specialty: General

M I C H I G A N

ALLEGAN

Acquire Technical Services Inc.
P.O. Box 426
Allegan, MI 49010
(616) 686-0399
Contact: Mr. Ian McGahan
Minimum Salary Placed: $35,000
Recruiting Specialty: Engineering

ALLEN PARK

Job Fair Network of Michigan
10823 Melbourne
Allen Park, MI 48101
(313) 381-0099
Contact: Mr. Chuck Vincent
Recruiting Specialty: Data processing, computers, engineering and other technical

ANN ARBOR

AP International
1000 Victors Way, Suite 300
Ann Arbor, MI 48108
(313) 761-1264
Contact: Mr. Alex Penn
Minimum Salary Placed: $25,000
Recruiting Specialty: General

Charles E. Day & Associates, Inc.
900 Victors Way, Suite 250
Ann Arbor, MI 48104
(313) 769-7407
Contact: Mr. Charles Day
Minimum Salary Placed: $50,000
Recruiting Specialty: Manufacturing and high technology

Clark and Hartman Professional Search Inc.
315 N. Main Street, Suite 400
Ann Arbor, MI 48104
(313) 996-3100
Contact: Mr. Lewis Clark
Minimum Salary Placed: $30,000
Recruiting Specialty: Data processing and telecommunications

Elwell & Associates, Inc.
301 E. Liberty, Suite 535
Ann Arbor, MI 48104
(313) 662-8775
Contact: Mr. Richard Elwell
Minimum Salary Placed: $70,000
Recruiting Specialty: General

George Houchens Associates
5340 Plymouth Road, Suite 101
Ann Arbor, MI 48105
(313) 665-4961
Contact: Mr. George Houchens
Recruiting Specialty: Computers, data processing and marketing/sales

L. J. Johnson & Company
815 Newport Road
Ann Arbor, MI 48103
(313) 663-6446
Contact: Mr. L. J. Johnson
Minimum Salary Placed: $40,000
Recruiting Specialty: General

David Lindemear Associates
117 East Liberty Street, Suite 400
Ann Arbor, MI 48103
(313) 761-3999
Contact: Mr. David Lindemear
Minimum Salary Placed: $25,000
Recruiting Specialty: General

Management Recruiters
2929 Plymouth Road, Suite 209
Ann Arbor, MI 48105
(313) 769-1720
Contact: Mr. Sameer Sarafa
Minimum Salary Placed: $20,000
Recruiting Specialty: General

Open Page Search Service
1354 Ardmoor Avenue
Ann Arbor, MI 48103
(313) 761-3556
Contact: Mr. Fred Page
Minimum Salary Placed: $30,000
Recruiting Specialty: Insurance and securities/investments

Percy Bates and Associates
111 S. Main Street
Ann Arbor, MI 48104
(313) 995-5522
Minimum Salary Placed: $25,000
Recruiting Specialty: General

Personnel Systems
315 E. Eisenhower, Suite 2
Ann Arbor, MI 48108
(313) 761-5252
Contact: Ms. Jeanne Merlanti
Recruiting Specialty: Data processing, computers and engineering

Plante and Moran
350 S. Main, Suite 200
Ann Arbor, MI 48104
(313) 665-9494
Contact: Mr. Bruce Shapiro
Minimum Salary Placed: $25,000
Recruiting Specialty: General

Sales Consultants
2860 Carpenter Road
Sparrow Wood Office, Suite 300
Ann Arbor, MI 48108
(313) 971-4900
Contact: Ms. Barbara Watson
Minimum Salary Placed: $20,000
Recruiting Specialty: Sales

Selective Recruiting
3290 W. N. Territorial Road
Ann Arbor, MI 48105
(313) 994-5632
Contact: Mr. Dave Calhoun
Recruiting Specialty: Sales, engineering
and manufacturing

Software Services Corporation
2850 S. Industrial, Suite 300
Ann Arbor, MI 48104
(313) 971-2300
Contact: Mr. Jack Reinelt
Recruiting Specialty: Data processing,
computers and technical

AUBURN HILLS

Sales Consultants
2701 University, Suite 205
Auburn Hills, MI 48326
(810) 373-7177
Contact: Mr. Bob Embry
Minimum Salary Placed: $20,000
Recruiting Specialty: Sales

BATTLE CREEK

Management Recruiters
500 Country Pine Lane, Suite 1
Battle Creek, MI 49015
(616) 979-3939
Contact: Ms. Mary Barker
Minimum Salary Placed: $20,000
Recruiting Specialty: General

Lou Michaels Associates
1230 E. Columbia Avenue
Battle Creek, MI 49017
(616) 965-1486
Contact: Mr. Lou Michaels
Minimum Salary Placed: $25,000
Recruiting Specialty: Manufacturing, pro-
duction and engineering

Savalli & Associates, Inc.
77 Hickory Lane
Battle Creek, MI 49017
(616) 968-5100
Contact: Mr. Frank Savalli
Minimum Salary Placed: $40,000
Recruiting Specialty: Consumer products

BAY CITY

PA Search
2135 Seventh Street, Suite 100
Bay City, MI 48708
(517) 892-4411
Contact: Mr. Jack Kircher
Recruiting Specialty: Medical

BINGHAM FARMS

Ann Bell Personnel
24044 Bingham Pointe Drive
Bingham Farms, MI 48025
(810) 540-3355
Contact: Ms. Ann Bell
Recruiting Specialty: Insurance

Designers Diversified Services
30200 Telegraph Road, Suite 461
Bingham Farms, MI 48025
(810) 646-4280
Contact: Mr. Stephen Henes
Recruiting Specialty: Data processing,
computers and engineering

Gene Ellefson and Associates Inc.
30100 Telegraph Road, Suite 422
Bingham Farms, MI 48025
(810) 642-3978
Contact: Mr. Gene Ellefson
Recruiting Specialty: Manufacturing, production, marketing and sales

G.A.M. Executive Search, Inc.
30400 Telegraph Road, Suite 358
Bingham Farms, MI 48025
(810) 258-0343
Contact: Ms. Sally August
Minimum Salary Placed: $20,000
Recruiting Specialty: General

Management Recruiters
30300 Telegraph Road, Suite 285
Bingham Farms, MI 48025
(810) 647-2828
Contact: Mr. Fred Bawulski
Minimum Salary Placed: $20,000
Recruiting Specialty: General

BIRMINGHAM

Compass Group Ltd.
401 S. Woodward, Suite 460
Birmingham, MI 48009
(810) 540-9110
Contact: Mr. Paul Czamanske
Minimum Salary Placed: $60,000
Recruiting Specialty: General

Continental Search Associates Inc.
1100 N. Woodward Avenue
Birmingham, MI 48009
(810) 644-4506
Contact: Mr. B. Dewey
Recruiting Specialty: Construction and
building

Crowder & Company
877 S. Adams, Suite 301
Birmingham, MI 48009
(810) 645-0909
Contact: Mr. Edward Crowder
Minimum Salary Placed: $65,000
Recruiting Specialty: General

Executive Interim Management
401 S. Woodward Avenue, Suite 460
Birmingham, MI 48009
(810) 647-4494
Contact: Mr. P. Czamanske
Minimum Salary Placed: $75,000
Recruiting Specialty: General

Executive Search Group
877 S. Adams, Suite 304
Birmingham, MI 48009
(810) 540-4336
Contact: Mr. Gino Canova
Recruiting Specialty: Engineering, manufacturing and production

Rooney Personnel Company
159 Pierce Street, Suite 203
Birmingham, MI 48009
(810) 258-5533
Contact: Mr. Jack Rooney
Minimum Salary Placed: $30,000
Recruiting Specialty: Hospitality and re-
tail

Smith Bridges and Associates
555 S. Woodward, Suite 603
Birmingham, MI 48009
(810) 540-2340
Contact: Mr. Mike Smith
Minimum Salary Placed: $25,000
Recruiting Specialty: Printing

Smith Professional Search
600 S. Adams
Birmingham, MI 48009
(810) 540-8580
Contact: Ms. Sue Smith
Minimum Salary Placed: $25,000
Recruiting Specialty: Accounting, finance
and human resources

Sullivan & Associates
344 N. Woodward, Suite 304
Birmingham, MI 48009
(810) 258-0616
Contact: Mr. Dennis Sullivan
Minimum Salary Placed: $70,000
Recruiting Specialty: General

BLISSFIELD

Management Recruiters
225 W. Adrian Street
P.O. Box 3
Blissfield, MI 49228
(517) 486-2167
Contact: Ms. Mary Snellbaker
Minimum Salary Placed: $20,000
Recruiting Specialty: Manufacturing and
engineering

BLOOMFIELD HILLS

Alden Group, Inc.
74 W. Long Lake Road, Suite 102
Bloomfield Hills, MI 48304
(810) 644-0210
Contact: Mr. John Bell
Minimum Salary Placed: $50,000
Recruiting Specialty: General

Continental Search Associates
1100 Woodward, Suite 224
Bloomfield Hills, MI 49304
(810) 644-0461
Contact: Mr. William Dewey
Recruiting Specialty: Building and construction

S.R. Dunlap & Associates, Inc.
100 W. Long Lake Road, Suite 112
Bloomfield Hills, MI 48304
(810) 540-0315
Contact: Mr. Stanley Dunlap
Minimum Salary Placed: $50,000
Recruiting Specialty: General

Gundersen Partners, Inc.
74 W. Long Lake Road, Suite 102
Bloomfield Hills, MI 48304
(810) 258-3800
Contact: Mr. John Bissell
Minimum Salary Placed: $75,000
Recruiting Specialty: General

D & N Johnston Associates
1684 Keller Lane
Bloomfield Hills, MI 48302
(810) 626-4319
Contact: Mr. David Johnston
Minimum Salary Placed: $50,000
Recruiting Specialty: General

Oakland Consulting Group Ltd.
7 W. Square Lake Road
Bloomfield Hills, MI 48302
(810) 335-0662
Contact: Mr. Ed Wendt
Minimum Salary Placed: $25,000
Recruiting Specialty: Human resources

Professional Search Group, Inc.
473 Kendry
Bloomfield Hills, MI 48302
(810) 332-7411
Contact: Mr. Jim Hurley
Recruiting Specialty: Data processing,
computers and engineering

CALEDONIA

IBA Search
8300 Thornapple River Drive
Caledonia, MI 49316
(616) 891-2160
Contact: Mr. Jim Lakatos
Minimum Salary Placed: $30,000
Recruiting Specialty: Engineering and
manufacturing

CENTER LINE

James Handley and Associates
7341 Bernice Street
Center Line, MI 48015
(810) 755-4544
Contact: Mr. Jim Handley
Minimum Salary Placed: $40,000
Recruiting Specialty: Automotive: vehicle
braking and vehicular electronics

Sharrow & Associates, Inc.
24735 Van Dyke
Center Line, MI 48015
(810) 759-6910
Contact: Mr. Douglas Sharrow
Recruiting Specialty: General

CHELSEA

Holland & Associates, Inc.
P.O. Box 488
Chelsea, MI 48118
(313) 475-3701
Contact: Mr. Daniel O. Holland
Recruiting Specialty: Technical disci-
plines in consumer and commercial prod-
ucts

DEARBORN

Management Recruiters
3 Parklane Boulevard, Suite 1224
Dearborn, MI 48126
(313) 336-6650
Contact: Mr. William Tripp
Minimum Salary Placed: $20,000
Recruiting Specialty: General

Premier Healthcare Recruiters, Inc.
3744 Campbell, Suite B
Dearborn, MI 48124
(313) 277-0821
Contact: Ms. Diana Watson
Minimum Salary Placed: $75,000
Recruiting Specialty: Physicians and
healthcare

DETROIT

B.P.A. Enterprises, Inc.
19967 James Couzens Highway
Detroit, MI 48235
(313) 345-5700
Contact: Mr. Will Atkins
Minimum Salary Placed: $40,000
Recruiting Specialty: Women and minorities; some general

Executive Recruiters International
1150 Griswold Street, Suite 3000
Detroit, MI 48226
(313) 961-6200
Contact: Ms. Kathy Sinclair
Minimum Salary Placed: $35,000
Recruiting Specialty: Engineering and environmental

Management Recruiters
300 River Place, Suite 3000
Detroit, MI 48207
(313) 568-4200
Contact: Ms. Debra Lawson
Minimum Salary Placed: $20,000
Recruiting Specialty: General

EAST LANSING

David Allen Associates
P.O. Box 919
East Lansing, MI 48823
(517) 351-4100
Contact: Mr. David Ritchings
Minimum Salary Placed: $25,000
Recruiting Specialty: General

FARMINGTON HILLS

Ability Search Group
31275 Northwestern Highway, Suite 229
Farmington Hills, MI 48334
(810) 851-3600
Contact: Mr. Uri Katz
Recruiting Specialty: Telecommunications, technical and science

Fortune Personnel Consultants
31800 Northwestern Highway, Suite 200
Farmington Hills, MI 48334
(810) 932-8870
Contact: Mr. Gary Snyder
Recruiting Specialty: General

Joseph Goldring and Associates
31500 W. 13 Mile Road, Suite 200
Farmington Hills, MI 48334
(810) 539-2660
Contact: Mr. Joseph Goldring
Recruiting Specialty: Accounting, finance, data processing, computers and medical

Harper Associates
29870 Middlebelt
Farmington Hills, MI 48334
(810) 932-1170
Contact: Mr. Ben Schwartz
Recruiting Specialty: Finance, healthcare and hospitality

MGM Executive Search
32255 Northwestern Highway, Suite 190
Farmington Hills, MI 48334
(810) 932-9770
Contact: Mr. Stuart Main
Minimum Salary Placed: $40,000
Recruiting Specialty: General

Michigan Search Plus
25882 Orchard Lake Road, Suite 207
Farmington Hills, MI 48336
(810) 471-6110
Contact: Ms. Christy Greeneisen
Recruiting Specialty: General

Robert William James and Associates
38215 West 10 Mile Road
Farmington Hills, MI 48335
(810) 478-0700
Contact: Mr. Thomas Kozler
Minimum Salary Placed: $30,000
Recruiting Specialty: General

Roth Young Personnel
31275 Northwestern Highway, Suite 116
Farmington Hills, MI 48334
(810) 626-6033
Contact: Mr. Samuel Skeegan
Recruiting Specialty: Pharmaceuticals
and healthcare

Sales Consultants
30445 Northwestern Highway, Suite 360
Farmington Hills, MI 48334
(810) 626-6600
Contact: Mr. Harvey Gersin
Minimum Salary Placed: $20,000
Recruiting Specialty: Sales

Selectec Corporation
22000 Springbrook, Suite 106
Farmington Hills, MI 48336
(810) 477-3232
Contact: Ms. Laura Rembisz
Recruiting Specialty: Data processing
and computers

FENTON

Dupuis & Ryden, P.C.
14165 N. Fenton Road, Suite 101
Fenton, MI 48430
(810) 750-6266
Contact: Mr. Kim Virkler
Minimum Salary Placed: $30,000
Recruiting Specialty: General

FLINT

Dupuis & Ryden, P.C.
111 E. Court Street, Suite 1A
Flint, MI 48502
(810) 767-5350
Contact: Ms. Nancy Rosevear
Minimum Salary Placed: $30,000
Recruiting Specialty: General

Management Recruiters
G-5524 S. Saginaw Road
Flint, MI 48507
(810) 695-0120
Contact: Mr. Dave Reed
Minimum Salary Placed: $20,000
Recruiting Specialty: General

FRANKLIN

Braboy and Associates
Box 25013
Franklin, MI 48025
(810) 334-8888
Contact: Mr. Jay Braboy
Minimum Salary Placed: $50,000
Recruiting Specialty: General

GRAND HAVEN

Bob Clark Associates
222 Franklin Street
Grand Haven, MI 49417
(616) 842-8596
Contact: Mr. Bob Clark
Minimum Salary Placed: $30,000
Recruiting Specialty: Plastics, engineering and automotive

Executive Management Search
21 N. Fourth Street
Grand Haven, MI 49417
(616) 846-3051
Contact: Mr. Arthur Schwartz
Minimum Salary Placed: $25,000
Recruiting Specialty: General

Teamwork Services
1120 Robbins Road
Grand Haven, MI 49417
(616) 846-6400
Contact: Mr. J. Meengs
Recruiting Specialty: Manufacturing

GRAND RAPIDS

Account Ability Now
333 Bridge Street NW
Grand Rapids, MI 49504
(616) 235-1149
Contact: Ms. Julie Henderson
Minimum Salary Placed: $25,000
Recruiting Specialty: Accounting and computers

Advanced Executive Resources
4030 Charlevoix Drive
Grand Rapids, MI 49546
(616) 942-4030

Contact: Mr. Michael Harvey
Minimum Salary Placed: $50,000
Recruiting Specialty: General

BDO Seidman
99 Monroe Avenue, N.W
Grand Rapids, MI 49503
(616) 774-7000
Contact: Mr. John Sullivan
Minimum Salary Placed: $70,000
Recruiting Specialty: General

The Clayton Edward Group
146 Monroe Center, Suite 1126
Grand Rapids, MI 49509
(616) 336-8066
Contact: Mr. Ron Meadley
Minimum Salary Placed: $40,000
Recruiting Specialty: Technical disciplines in manufacturing and metal fabrication

Charles Driggers International Inc.
3720 Oak Bluff Drive SE
Grand Rapids, MI 49546
(616) 942-4753
Minimum Salary Placed: $25,000
Recruiting Specialty: General

G.L. Dykstra Associates, Inc.
469 E. Bayberry Point Drive
P.O. Box 141546
Grand Rapids, MI 49514
(616) 791-9651
Contact: Mr. Gene Dykstra
Minimum Salary Placed: $40,000
Recruiting Specialty: General

Execuquest Inc.
2050 Breton Road SE
Grand Rapids, MI 49546
(616) 949-1800

Contact: Pat
Minimum Salary Placed: $60,000
Recruiting Specialty: General

GRS
934 Fulton Street
Grand Rapids, MI 49504
(616) 242-7711
Contact: Mr. Bill Fischer
Minimum Salary Placed: $25,000
Recruiting Specialty: General, some engineering and MIS

Lowery, Cotter, & Associates
2959 SE Lucerne Drive, Suite 104
Grand Rapids, MI 49546
(616) 949-2252
Contact: Ms. Alina Cotter
Minimum Salary Placed: $50,000
Recruiting Specialty: Minorities; General

Robert Half International Inc.
333 Bridge Street NW
Grand Rapids, MI 49504
(616) 454-9444
Contact: Mr. Vern Mathiesen
Minimum Salary Placed: $20,000
Recruiting Specialty: Accounting and finance

Sales Consultants
900 E. Paris Avenue SE, Suite 301
Grand Rapids, MI 49546
(616) 940-3900
Contact: Mr. David Underwood
Minimum Salary Placed: $20,000
Recruiting Specialty: Sales

Source EDP
161 Ottawa NW, Suite 409D
Grand Rapids, MI 49503
(616) 451-2400

Contact: Mr. Tom Combs
Recruiting Specialty: Computer hardware and software

Source Service
161 Ottawa Avenue NW, Suite D409
Grand Rapids, MI 49503
(616) 459-3600
Contact: Mr. M. Trewhella
Minimum Salary Placed: $25,000
Recruiting Specialty: Accounting, finance and data processing

GRANDVILLE

Dacid Alton Associates
2861 Wilson Avenue
Grandville, MI 49418
(616) 667-2969
Contact: Mr. Keith Lambert
Minimum Salary Placed: $30,000
Recruiting Specialty: Technical disciplines

GROSSE POINTE FARMS

Daudlin, De Beaupre & Company, Inc.
18530 Mack Avenue, Suite 315
Grosse Pointe Farms, MI 48236
(810) 771-0029
Contact: Mr. Paul Daudlin
Minimum Salary Placed: $50,000
Recruiting Specialty: Healthcare

Michael W. Parres & Associates
21 Kercheval, Suite 200
Grosse Pointe Farms, MI 48236
(313) 886-8080
Contact: Mr. Mike Parres
Minimum Salary Placed: $60,000
Recruiting Specialty: General

Roberts Ryan & Bentley
245 Dean Lane
Grosse Pointe Farms, MI 48236
(313) 882-9967
Contact: Ms. Sue Ann Whitley
Minimum Salary Placed: $60,000
Recruiting Specialty: General

GROSSE POINTE PARK

Case Executive Search
15008 Kercheval Avenue
Grosse Pointe Park, MI 48230
(313) 331-6095
Contact: Mr. David Case
Minimum Salary Placed: $30,000
Recruiting Specialty: Engineering, manufacturing and production

GROSSE POINTE WOODS

Automotive Careers of Michigan, Inc.
19515 Mack Avenue
Gross Pointe Woods, MI 48236
(313) 886-2424
Contact: Mr. Jerald Henry
Recruiting Specialty: Automotive dealerships management

HASLETT

Premier Recruiting Group
953 Cliffdale Drive
Haslett, MI 48840
(517) 339-9109
Contact: Mr. Rich Krezo
Minimum Salary Placed: $35,000
Recruiting Specialty: General

HOLLAND

Management Recruiters
400 N. 136th Avenue
Suite 6, Building 200
Holland, MI 49424
(616) 396-2620
Contact: Mr. Robert Bakker
Minimum Salary Placed: $20,000
Recruiting Specialty: General

Teamwork Associates
335 E. 16th Street
Holland, MI 49423
(616) 392-1803
Contact: Mr. J. Meengs
Recruiting Specialty: Manufacturing

HOLT

Management Recruiters
2491 Cedar Park Drive
Holt, MI 48842
(517) 694-1153
Contact: Ms. Priscilla Peterson
Minimum Salary Placed: $20,000
Recruiting Specialty: General

JENISON

Alton David Associates
P.O. Box 867
Jenison, MI 49429
(616) 667-2969
Contact: Mr. Keith Lambert
Minimum Salary Placed: $35,000
Recruiting Specialty: Manufacturing and engineering

KALAMAZOO

Circlewood Search Group, Inc.
3307 E. Kilgore Road, Suite 2
Kalamazoo, MI 49002
(616) 383-9530
Contact: Ms. Melissa Webb
Recruiting Specialty: General

Collins and Associates
10188 W. H Avenue
Kalamazoo, MI 49009
(616) 372-3275
Contact: Mr. Philip Collins
Minimum Salary Placed: $25,000
Recruiting Specialty: Computers

Execusource of SW Michigan
4615 W. Main Street
Kalamazoo, MI 49006
(616) 342-5050
Contact: Mr. John Compere
Recruiting Specialty: Engineering, manufacturing and production

Heller Kil Associates, Inc.
4534 Frontier
Kalamazoo, MI 49002
(616) 344-3290
Contact: Mr. Richard Kil
Minimum Salary Placed: $40,000
Recruiting Specialty: Technical disciplines in automotive and transportation

Richard Hudson and Company
275 Radisson Plaza
Kalamazoo, MI 49007
(616) 345-8561
Contact: Mr. Dick Hudson
Minimum Salary Placed: $25,000
Recruiting Specialty: General

R.Z. Kil Associates
4534 Frontier Avenue
Kalamazoo, MI 49002
(616) 344-3290
Contact: Mr. R. Kil
Minimum Salary Placed: $60,000
Recruiting Specialty: Automotive and manufacturing

Management Recruiters
4021 W. Main Street, Suite 200
Kalamazoo, MI 49007
(616) 381-1153
Contact: Dr. M.J. Tessin
Minimum Salary Placed: $20,000
Recruiting Specialty: General

Preferred Resources LLC
4000 Portage Road
Kalamazoo, MI 49001
(616) 344-6893
Contact: Mr. Douglas Scripture
Recruiting Specialty: Accounting, finance, data processing and computers

Professional Career Search Inc.
5464 Holiday Terrace
Kalamazoo, MI 49009
(616) 372-3339
Contact: Ms. Nancy Patterson
Minimum Salary Placed: $25,000
Recruiting Specialty: General

Wise Personnel Service Inc.
200 Admiral Avenue
Kalamazoo, MI 49002
(616) 323-2300
Contact: Mr. Steve Wise
Recruiting Specialty: Engineering, technical and science

KENTWOOD

Professional Career Search Inc.
1680 Viewpond Road
Kentwood, MI 49508
(616) 281-3110
Contact: Ms. N. Barcheski
Minimum Salary Placed: $40,000
Recruiting Specialty: Medical and pharmaceutical sales

LAKEVIEW

Executive Resources
79522 Mile Road
Lakeview, MI 48850
(517) 352-8052
Contact: Ms. Beverly Ives
Minimum Salary Placed: $25,000
Recruiting Specialty: General

LANSING

Dental Medical Services
1375 S. Washington, Suite 200
Lansing, MI 48910
(517) 482-2722
Contact: Ms. Lois Waters
Minimum Salary Placed: $25,000
Recruiting Specialty: Dental and medical

Professional Search Services
6215 W. St. Joseph Highway
Lansing, MI 48917
(517) 323-3443
Contact: Mr. Stephen O'Connor
Recruiting Specialty: Medical

Sales Consultants
6500 Centurion Drive, Suite 265
Lansing, MI 48917
(517) 323-4404
Contact: Mr. Jeffrey Yeager
Minimum Salary Placed: $20,000
Recruiting Specialty: Sales

LAPEER

J. E. Lessner Associates, Inc.
2143 E. Newark Road
Lapeer, MI 48446
(810) 667-9335
Contact: Mr. Jack Lessner
Minimum Salary Placed: $60,000
Recruiting Specialty: General

LASALLE

All States Medical Placement Agency, Inc.
P.O. Box 91
LaSalle, MI 48145
(313) 241-1454
Contact: Mr. Charles Denney
Recruiting Specialty: CRNA, physicians and physician assistants

LIVONIA

Accountants Connection Inc.
32540 Schoolcraft Road, Suite 100
Livonia, MI 48150
(313) 513-7805
Contact: Ms. Deanna Ayers
Recruiting Specialty: Accounting and finance

Acro Service Corporation
17187 N. Laurel Park Drive, Suite 165
Livonia, MI 48152
(313) 591-1100
Contact: Mr. Ron Shahani
Recruiting Specialty: Technical

Barton Group
9914 Cranston Street
Livonia, MI 48150
(313) 458-7555
Contact: Mr. Bart Foster
Minimum Salary Placed: $30,000
Recruiting Specialty: Engineering, technical sales, purchasing and finance

Steven J. Greene and Associates
29200 Vassar, Suite 545
Livonia, MI 48152
(810) 473-7210
Contact: Mr. Steven Greene
Recruiting Specialty: Manufacturing, production and sales

Henry Group
37450 Schoolcraft, Suite 150
Livonia, MI 48150
(313) 462-2330
Contact: Mr. Hugh Spencer
Minimum Salary Placed: $25,000
Recruiting Specialty: General

Management Recruiters
37677 Professional Center Drive,
 Suite 100C
Livonia, MI 48154
(313) 953-9590
Contact: Mr. Don Eden
Minimum Salary Placed: $20,000
Recruiting Specialty: General

Snelling Personnel
17187 N. Laurel Park Drive
Livonia, MI 48152
(313) 464-0909
Contact: Ms. B. Drake
Recruiting Specialty: Engineering, sales, and office support

MARSHALL

National Medsearch
734 Allison Drive
Marshall, MI 49068
(616) 781-9100
Contact: Mr. John Edsall
Minimum Salary Placed: $25,000
Recruiting Specialty: Medical and healthcare

MIDLAND

Management Recruiters
5103 Eastman Place, Suite 101
Midland, MI 48640
(517) 832-5000
Contact: Ms. Vicki Harris
Minimum Salary Placed: $20,000
Recruiting Specialty: General

MONROE

Management Recruiters
1505 Dixie Drive, Suite 2
Monroe, MI 48161
(313) 242-9050
Contact: Mr. Robert Sewell
Minimum Salary Placed: $20,000
Recruiting Specialty: General

MOUNT PLEASANT

Management Recruiters
P.O. Box 423
Mt. Pleasant, MI 48804
(517) 773-2728
Contact: Mr. Patrick Doyle
Minimum Salary Placed: $20,000
Recruiting Specialty: General

Sales Consultants
119 1/2 S. University
Mt. Pleasant, MI 48858
(517) 773-3535
Contact: Mr. Michael Heintz
Minimum Salary Placed: $20,000
Recruiting Specialty: Sales

MUSKEGON

Aucon
3779 Highgate Road
Muskegon, MI 49441
(616) 798-4883
Contact: Mr. Ray Audo
Minimum Salary Placed: $20,000
Recruiting Specialty: Engineering, manu-
facturing and production

Robert Half International
Muskegon, MI 49440
(616) 726-2069
Contact: Mr. Vern Mathiesen
Minimum Salary Placed: $25,000
Recruiting Specialty: Accounting and fi-
nance

Management Recruiters
3145 Henry Street, Suite 203
Muskegon, MI 49441
(616) 755-6486

Contact: Mr. John Mitchell
Minimum Salary Placed: $20,000
Recruiting Specialty: General

NOVI

Aegis Group
23875 Novi Road
Novi, MI 48375
(810) 344-1450
Contact: Mr. T. Ignash
Minimum Salary Placed: $25,000
Recruiting Specialty: Healthcare

Diversified Recruiters Company
27400 Meadowbrook Road
Novi, MI 48377
(810) 344-6700
Contact: Mr. Roger Thomas
Recruiting Specialty: General

NDI Services
43000 W. 9 Mile Road
Novi, MI 48357
(810) 348-8040
Contact: Mr. David Kosteva
Minimum Salary Placed: $45,000
Recruiting Specialty: Human resources

OKEMOS

Management Advisors
2182 Commons Parkway
Okemos, MI 48864
(517) 347-0593
Contact: Mr. Greg Soltysiak
Minimum Salary Placed: $20,000
Recruiting Specialty: General

PETOSKY

PMP Temporary and Permanent Staffing
1483 US 31 N, Suite B
Petosky, MI 49770
(616) 347-9500
Contact: Mr. Gilbert Mosher
Recruiting Specialty: Manufacturing and production

PLYMOUTH

David Franklin and Associates
292 S. Main Street
Plymouth, MI 48170
(313) 459-5966
Contact: Mr. David Germon
Minimum Salary Placed: $25,000
Recruiting Specialty: General

Sales Consultants
340 N. Main, Suite 302
Plymouth, MI 48170
(313) 451-7510
Contact: Ms. Pat Redmond
Minimum Salary Placed: $20,000
Recruiting Specialty: Sales

RICHLAND

Med-Pro
12220 Yorkshire
Richland, MI 49083
(616) 731-4766
Contact: Ms. Sharon Wiley
Recruiting Specialty: Medical and pharmaceuticals

ROCHESTER

Daudlin, De Beaupre & Company, Inc.
145 S. Livernois, Suite 110
Rochester, MI 48307
(810) 693-9240
Contact: Ms. Jill Hodgins Verros
Minimum Salary Placed: $50,000
Recruiting Specialty: Healthcare

Polymer Menschen, Inc.
342 Main Street, Suite 100
Rochester, MI 48307
(810) 650-1112
Contact: Mr. Barry Von Steinen
Recruiting Specialty: Engineering

ROCHESTER HILLS

J. P. Bencik Associates
1332 E. Fairview, Suite 200
Rochester Hills, MI 48306
(810) 651-7426
Contact: Mr. James Bencik
Minimum Salary Placed: $35,000
Recruiting Specialty: General

Health Resource Network, Inc.
2899 S. Rochester Road, Suite 306
Rochester Hills, MI 48307
(810) 844-7160
Contact: Ms. Janet Simon
Recruiting Specialty: Healthcare

Management Recruiters
2530 S. Rochester Road
Rochester Hills, MI 48307
(810) 299-1900
Contact: Mr. Mark Angott
Minimum Salary Placed: $20,000
Recruiting Specialty: General

MedMatch Inc.
441 S. Livernois, Suite 175
Rochester Hills, MI 48307
(810) 651-0652
Contact: Ms. Mary Ann Babcock
Recruiting Specialty: Medical and health-care

SAGINAW

Dunhill Professional Search
4406 Elmhurst
Saginaw, MI 48603
(517) 799-9300
Contact: Mr. Bill Post
Minimum Salary Placed: $25,000
Recruiting Specialty: General

SAINT JOSEPH

Beacon Services Inc.
2611 Niles Avenue
St. Joseph, MI 49085
(616) 983-1330
Contact: Geri
Recruiting Specialty: Office support

Snelling and Snelling
520 Pleasant Street
St. Joseph, MI 49085
(616) 983-7181
Contact: Mr. B. Doehrer
Minimum Salary Placed: $25,000
Recruiting Specialty: Engineering and data processing

Williamson Employment Services, Inc.
3133 Lakeshore Drive
St. Joseph, MI 49805
(616) 983-0142

Contact: Ms. Margaret Williamson
Minimum Salary Placed: $25,000
Recruiting Specialty: Technical

Wood Personnel Services, Inc.
505 Pleasant Street, Suite 305
St. Joseph, MI 49085
(616) 983-6767
Contact: Mr. Douglas Wood
Recruiting Specialty: Office support

SALINE

Metro-Search Associates
7343 Steeple Chase Drive
Saline, MI 48176
(313) 429-0021
Contact: Mr. John Mooradian
Minimum Salary Placed: $25,000
Recruiting Specialty: General

SOUTHFIELD

Accountants One, Inc.
24901 Northwestern Highway, Suite 516
Southfield, MI 48075
(810) 354-2410
Contact: Ms. Betty Gray
Minimum Salary Placed: $25,000
Recruiting Specialty: Accounting and finance

Action Sell Associates
24333 Southfield Road, Suite 201
Southfield, MI 48075
(810) 569-5460
Contact: Mr. S. Sell
Recruiting Specialty: Physicians

Allison Personnel Service, Inc.
3000 Town Center, Suite 770
Southfield, MI 48075
(810) 354-1820
Contact: Mr. Irwin Epstein
Minimum Salary Placed: $40,000
Recruiting Specialty: Insurance

Benford & Associates, Inc.
3000 Town Center, Suite 1333
Southfield, MI 48075
(810) 351-0250
Contact: Mr. Edward Benford
Recruiting Specialty: EEO/minorities
and engineering

Career Associates Inc.
17000 W. 10 Mile Road
Southfield, MI 48075
(810) 552-8532
Contact: Mr. T. Wallace
Minimum Salary Placed: $35,000
Recruiting Specialty: Engineering

Davidson, Laird and Associates
29260 Franklin Road, Suite 110
Southfield, MI 48034
(810) 358-2160
Contact: Ms. Meri Laird
Recruiting Specialty: Engineering, other
technical disciplines

Davis-Smith, Inc.
24725 W. 12 Mile Road, Suite 302
Southfield, MI 48034
(810) 354-4100
Contact: Mr. Charles Corbett
Minimum Salary Placed: $50,000
Recruiting Specialty: Healthcare

Dunhill Personnel System, Inc.
29350 Southfield Road, Suite 1
Southfield, MI 48076
(810) 557-1100
Contact: Mr. Donald Dahlin
Minimum Salary Placed: $30,000
Recruiting Specialty: Engineering and
sales

Dupuis & Ryden, P.C.
26677 W. 12 Mile Road
Southfield, MI 48034
(810) 680-9060
Contact: Mr. Michael Malek
Minimum Salary Placed: $30,000
Recruiting Specialty: General

Executives Personnel Service Inc.
17117 W. Nine Mile Road, Suite 605P
Southfield, MI 48075
(810) 557-9400
Contact: Mr. Frank Cowall
Minimum Salary Placed: $35,000
Recruiting Specialty: General

**Fortune Personnel Consultants of
Detroit**
17515 W. Nine Mile Road, Suite 770
Southfield, MI 48075
(810) 557-7250
Contact: Mr. Mark Schwartz
Recruiting Specialty: Legal

Giacomin Group Inc.
3000 Town Center, Suite 2237
Southfield, MI 48075
(810) 352-1470
Contact: Mr. Joseph Giacomin
Minimum Salary Placed: $25,000
Recruiting Specialty: General

Joe L. Giles & Associates, Inc.
15565 Northland Drive, Suite 608W
Southfield, MI 48075
(810) 569-8660
Contact: Mr. Joe Giles
Minimum Salary Placed: $40,000
Recruiting Specialty: Engineering, data processing and MIS

MGS Services Group
23100 Providence Drive, Suite 151
Southfield, MI 48075
(810) 557-7557
Contact: Mr. Gene Scarpone
Minimum Salary Placed: $25,000
Recruiting Specialty: Accounting, finance, data processing, computers and engineering

Nine to Five Personnel
17348 W. Twelve Mile Road, Suite 201
Southfield, MI 48076
(810) 559-7323
Contact: Ms. Sheri Hill
Minimum Salary Placed: $20,000
Recruiting Specialty: Accounting, legal and office support

Plante and Moran
27400 Northwestern Highway, Suite 307
Southfield, MI 48037
(810) 352-0018
Contact: Ms. Martha Palmer
Minimum Salary Placed: $20,000
Recruiting Specialty: General

Robert Half International Inc.
28588 Northwestern Highway, Suite 250
Southfield, MI 48034
(810) 995-8367

Contact: Mr. Fred Getz
Minimum Salary Placed: $20,000
Recruiting Specialty: Accounting and finance

Sales Consultants
17117 W. Nine Mile Road, Suite 1505
Southfield, MI 48075
(810) 569-8800
Contact: Mr. Thomas Hoy
Minimum Salary Placed: $20,000
Recruiting Specialty: Sales

Source EDP
2000 Town Center, Suite 850
Southfield, MI 48075
(810) 352-6520
Contact: Mr. David Seitz
Recruiting Specialty: Computer hardware and software

Source Finance
2000 Town Center, Suite 350
Southfield, MI 48075
(810) 352-8860
Contact: Mr. W. Swanner
Minimum Salary Placed: $25,000
Recruiting Specialty: Accounting and finance

STERLING HEIGHTS

B. Hans Becker Associates Inc.
2110 15 Mile Road
Sterling Heights, MI 48310
(810) 978-0550
Contact: Mr. Hans Becker
Minimum Salary Placed: $50,000
Recruiting Specialty: Manufacturing and engineering

STEVENSVILLE

Guidarelli Associates, Inc.
5748 James Drive
Stevensville, MI 49127
(616) 429-7001
Contact: Ms. Shelley Guidarelli
Minimum Salary Placed: $50,000
Recruiting Specialty: Sales and marketing in consumer products

TRAVERSE CITY

Icard Group
126 Boardman Avenue, Suite F
Traverse City, MI 49684
(616) 929-2196
Contact: Mr. Robert Icard
Minimum Salary Placed: $20,000
Recruiting Specialty: Automotive, engineering and manufacturing

PLRS/Career Connections
12935 W. Bayshore Drive, Suite 450
Traverse City, MI 49684
(616) 941-5063
Contact: Mr. Daniel White
Minimum Salary Placed: $30,000
Recruiting Specialty: General

TROY

AJM Professional Services
803 W. Big Beaver Road, Suite 357
Troy, MI 48084
(810) 244-2222
Contact: Mr. Charles Muller
Minimum Salary Placed: $30,000
Recruiting Specialty: MIS and computers

Accent on Achievement, Inc.
3190 Rochester Road, Suite 104
Troy, MI 48083
(810) 528-1390
Contact: Ms. Charlene Brown
Minimum Salary Placed: $35,000
Recruiting Specialty: Finance, accounting and human resources

Advantage Group
2690 Crooks Road, Suite 414
Troy, MI 48084
(810) 362-1500
Contact: Mr. Anthony Fontana
Minimum Salary Placed: $50,000
Recruiting Specialty: Finance and accounting

Aim Executive Recruiting and Search
100 West Big Beaver Road, Suite 300
Troy, MI 48084
(810) 689-5055
Contact: Mr. Dave Haggard
Minimum Salary Placed: $20,000
Recruiting Specialty: General

American, SCI, Inc.
888 W. Big Beaver Road, Suite 950
Troy, MI 48084
(810) 269-0448
Contact: Mr. Tom Van Scyoc
Minimum Salary Placed: $25,000
Recruiting Specialty: Data processing, computers and engineering

American Heritage Group
1639 W. Big Beaver
Troy, MI 48084
(810) 816-1400
Contact: Mr. John Holliday
Minimum Salary Placed: $30,000
Recruiting Specialty: Automotive, sales and technical

Bumbales Group
631 E. Big Beaver Road
Troy, MI 48084
(810) 524-9469
Contact: Mr. Ken Bumbales
Minimum Salary Placed: $30,000
Recruiting Specialty: Accounting and finance

CSA Recruiting Group
2820 W. Maple, Suite 245
Troy, MI 48084
(810) 643-0011
Contact: Mr. William MacLood
Recruiting Specialty: General

Contemporary Services, Inc.
2690 Crooks Road, Suite 111
Troy, MI 48083
(810) 362-1212
Contact: Ms. Snadra Wettergren
Minimum Salary Placed: $20,000
Recruiting Specialty: Accounting and finance, some general

DAKO Services
1120 E. Long Lake Road, Suite 200
Troy, MI 48098
(810) 740-3500
Contact: Mr. David Kosuth
Recruiting Specialty: Data processing, computers, engineering and manufacturing

Dickson Associates
3001 W. Big Beaver Road
Troy, MI 48084
(810) 643-9480
Contact: Ms. D. Kyostia
Minimum Salary Placed: $25,000
Recruiting Specialty: Accounting and finance

Dorothy Day Personnel, Inc.
3001 W. Big Beaver Road, Suite 119
Troy, MI 48084
(810) 649-2496
Contact: Ms. Diane York
Minimum Salary Placed: $35,000
Recruiting Specialty: Marketing and sales

Express Personnel Services
1740 W. Big Beaver Road, Suite 220
Troy, MI 48084
(810) 643-8590
Contact: Mr. John Bower
Minimum Salary Placed: $35,000
Recruiting Specialty: Accounting, finance and engineering

Executech Resource Consultants
5700 Crooks Road, Suite 105
Troy, MI 48098
(810) 828-3000
Contact: Mr. David Palma
Minimum Salary Placed: $35,000
Recruiting Specialty: Marketing and sales

Fortune Personnel Consultants of Troy, Inc.
560 Kirts Boulevard, Suite 230
Troy, MI 48084
(810) 244-9646
Contact: Mr. Robert Tell
Minimum Salary Placed: $35,000
Recruiting Specialty: Healthcare and pharmaceuticals

HRC Associates
2820 W. Maple Road, Suite 236
Troy, MI 48084
(810) 643-8520
Contact: Mr. Jim Moore
Minimum Salary Placed: $35,000
Recruiting Specialty: Engineering and plant management

Harvey Hohauser & Associates
5600 New King Street, Suite 355
Troy, MI 48098
(810) 641-1400
Contact: Mr. Harvey Hohauser
Minimum Salary Placed: $60,000
Recruiting Specialty: General

Human Resources Recruiting Services
2899 E. Big Beaver Road, Suite 298
Troy, MI 48083
Contact: Mr. Dennis Kimble
Minimum Salary Placed: $35,000
Recruiting Specialty: Banking

King Personnel
850 Stephenson Highway, Suite 304
Troy, MI 48083
(810) 585 7522
Contact: Ms. Barbara King Hill
Minimum Salary Placed: $25,000
Recruiting Specialty: Legal

Kratec Company
62 Wildwood
Troy, MI 48084
(810) 879-5560
Contact: Mr. B. Krajewski
Minimum Salary Placed: $25,000
Recruiting Specialty: General

Management Recruiters
550 Stephenson Highway, Suite 407
Troy, MI 48083
(810) 585-4200
Contact: Mr. Ed Moeller
Minimum Salary Placed: $20,000
Recruiting Specialty: General

Nationwide Career Network
5445 Corporate Drive, Suite 160
Troy, MI 48098
(810) 641-777
Contact: Ms. Carol Peters
Minimum Salary Placed: $30,000
Recruiting Specialty: Engineering, computers, medical and technical

Profiles, Inc.
801 W. Big Beaver Road, Suite 670
Troy, MI 48084
(810) 244-9444
Contact: Mr. Michael Wilson
Minimum Salary Placed: $40,000
Recruiting Specialty: Engineering

Robert Half International
201 W. Big Beaver Road
Troy, MI 48084
(810) 524-3100
Contact: Mr. Quentin Burchill
Minimum Salary Placed: $25,000
Recruiting Specialty: Accounting and finance

Sales Consultants
550 Stephenson Highway, Suite 407
Troy, MI 48083
(810) 585-4200
Contact: Mr. Edward Muller
Minimum Salary Placed: $20,000
Recruiting Specialty: Sales

Sales Executives, Inc.
755 W. Big Beaver Road, Suite 2107
Troy, MI 48084
(810) 362-1900
Contact: Mr. Dale Statson
Minimum Salary Placed: $25,000
Recruiting Specialty: Sales

Starr Recruiting Inc.
2838 E. Long Lake Road
Troy, MI 48098
(810) 680-9120
Contact: Mr. Mark Motyka
Minimum Salary Placed: $25,000
Recruiting Specialty: General

Sygnetics, Inc.
570 Kirts Boulevard, Suite 237
Troy, MI 48084
(810) 244-9595
Contact: Mr. Tony Tarkowski
Minimum Salary Placed: $25,000
Recruiting Specialty: General

Duane Wilson and Associates
3133 Myddleton Drive
Troy, MI 48084
(810) 647-3234
Contact: Mr. Duane Wilson
Minimum Salary Placed: $40,000
Recruiting Specialty: General

Wing Tips & Pumps, Inc.
P.O. Box 99580
Troy, MI 48099
(810) 641-0980
Contact: Mr. Verba Lee Edwards
Minimum Salary Placed: $20,000
Recruiting Specialty: General

UNION LAKE

Classic Personnel Consultants, Inc.
P.O. Box 550
Union Lake, MI 48387
(810) 682-4570
Contact: Mr. T.E. Smith
Minimum Salary Placed: $25,000
Recruiting Specialty: Engineering

UNION PIER

Thomas & Associates
16283 Red Arrow Highway
P.O. Box 366
Union Pier, MI 49129
(616) 469-5760
Contact: Mr. Thomas Zonka
Minimum Salary Placed: $30,000
Recruiting Specialty: General

WALLED LAKE

Wildman Personnel Division
P.O. Box 27
Walled Lake, MI 48390
(810) 960-3786
Contact: Ms. Lori Widman
Minimum Salary Placed: $20,000
Recruiting Specialty: Building and construction, insurance and office support

WEST BLOOMFIELD

Allen Mirsky Associates
7142 Pebble Park Drive
West Bloomfield, MI 48322
(810) 855-4000
Minimum Salary Placed: $50,000
Recruiting Specialty: General

Aquarian Resources Inc.
7316 Creekview Court
West Bloomfield, MI 48322
(810) 851-0409
Minimum Salary Placed: $25,000
Recruiting Specialty: General

WHITE LAKE

Sales Consultants
9467 Marina Drive
White Lake, MI 48386
(810) 553-6800
Contact: Ms. Mary Walsh
Minimum Salary Placed: $20,000
Recruiting Specialty: Sales

WYOMING

Management Recruiters
1849 R. West Berends Drive SW
Wyoming, MI 49509
(616) 336-8484
Contact: Mr. Ron Meadley
Minimum Salary Placed: $20,000
Recruiting Specialty: General

YPSILANTI

Technical Engineering Consultants
391 Airport Industrial Drive
Ypsilanti, MI 48198
(313) 485-3900
Minimum Salary Placed: $30,000
Recruiting Specialty: Computer vision,
autocad and unigraphics

ZEELAND

Manpower Technical and Professional
400 South State Street, Suite 150
Zeeland, MI 49464
(616) 748-2100
Contact: Ms. Elizabeth Militello
Minimum Salary Placed: $30,000
Recruiting Specialty: Engineering and
telecommunications

MINNESOTA

APPLE VALLEY

Altnow and Associates
P.O. Box 24431
Apple Valley, MN 55124
(612) 432-3308
Minimum Salary Placed: $25,000
Recruiting Specialty: Finance

BLOOMINGTON

Accountemps
5001 W. 80th Street, Suite 701
Bloomington, MN 55437
(612) 893-9585
Contact: Mr. S. Kenney
Recruiting Specialty: Accounting

Bradley & Associates
5341 River Bluff Curve, Suite 116
Bloomington, MN 55437
(612) 884-2607
Contact: Mr. T. John Bradley
Minimum Salary Placed: $35,000
Recruiting Specialty: Technical disciplines in food and beverages and chemicals

Burrel-Laurent
1550 E. 79th Street, Suite 680
Bloomington, MN 55425
(612) 854-8486
Contact: Mr. Cy Laurent
Minimum Salary Placed: $75,000
Recruiting Specialty: General

Dennhardt & Associates, Inc.
7900 Xerxes Avenue South, Suite 718
Bloomington, MN 55431
(612) 835-4333
Contact: Ms. Char Dennhardt
Recruiting Specialty: Office support

Firstaff, Inc.
Northland Plaza, 8300 West 80th Street,
  Suite 870
Bloomington, MN 55431-4426
(612) 896-3999
Contact: Ms. Jan Lavin
Recruiting Specialty: Office support

Fogarty and Associates
3880 W 89th Street
Bloomington, MN 55431
(612) 831-2828
Contact: Ms. C. Fogarty
Minimum Salary Placed: $25,000
Recruiting Specialty: Healthcare

The Furst Group/MPI
One Appletree Square, Suite 1300
Bloomington, MN 55420
(612) 851-9213
Contact: Mr. Thomas Heaney
Minimum Salary Placed: $50,000
Recruiting Specialty: Medical, healthcare,
and insurance

Helleren and Associates
8300 Norman Center Drive, Suite 510
Bloomington, MN 55437
(612) 835-2677
Contact: Mr. Christopher Ward
Minimum Salary Placed: $25,000
Recruiting Specialty: Medical

John Ho & Associates, Inc.
10374 Rich Road
Bloomington, MN 55437
(612) 897-0359
Contact: Mr. John Ho
Recruiting Specialty: Medical

Kroefsky & Associates
8400 Normandale Lake Boulevard,
  Suite 938
Bloomington, MN 55437
(612) 921-8820
Contact: Mr. Dean Kroefsky
Recruiting Specialty: Computer-sales and
software, hardware, and service

Lee Marsh and Associates
1 Appletree Square, Suite 202N
Bloomington, MN 55425
(612) 854-6811
Contact: Mr. Lee Marsh
Minimum Salary Placed: $25,000
Recruiting Specialty: Computer

Metro Hospitality Consultants
9448 Lyndale Avenue South, Suite 223
Bloomington, MN 55420
(612) 884-4299
Contact: Ms. Debra Kiefat
Recruiting Specialty: Hospitality, hotel
and restaurant

The Sapphire Company
4000 West 100th Street
Bloomington, MN 55437
(612) 893-9309
Contact: Mr. Dean Barthel
Recruiting Specialty: Insurance

Security Resource Network, Inc.
2901 Washburn Place
Bloomington, MN 55431
(612) 888-7324

Contact: Mr. David Stauffer
Recruiting Specialty: Electric security

Source EDP
8400 Normandale Lake Boulevard
Bloomington, MN 55437
(612) 835-5100
Contact: Mr. Chuck Lodge
Minimum Salary Placed: $25,000
Recruiting Specialty: Computers and MIS

BURNSVILLE

Jackley Search Consultants
14581 Grand Avenue South
Burnsville, MN 55306
(612) 831-2344
Contact: Mr. Brian Jackley
Minimum Salary Placed: $40,000
Recruiting Specialty: Engineering

CENTER CITY

Pioneer Search, Inc.
31594 Oasis Road
Center City, MN 55012
(612) 257-3957
Contact: Mr. Nate Vitalis
Recruiting Specialty: Computer, hardware, software, and service

COLUMBIA HEIGHTS

Twin City Search
3989 Central Avenue, NE
Columbia Heights, MN 55421
(612) 789-4537
Minimum Salary Placed: $25,000
Recruiting Specialty: General

DULUTH

AAA Employment of Duluth
2631 W. Superior Street, Suite 102
Duluth, MN 55806
(218) 727-8810
Contact: Mr. David McVean
Recruiting Specialty: General

McGladrey & Pullen
700 Missabe Building
Duluth, MN 55802
(218) 727-5025
Contact: Mr. Ken Buck
Minimum Salary Placed: $30,000
Recruiting Specialty: General

EDEN PRARIE

FM Industries
10125 Crosstown Circle, Suite 300
Eden Prarie, MN 55344
(612) 941-0966
Contact: Mr. Larry Alter
Minimum Salary Placed: $25,000
Recruiting Specialty: General

Healthcare Recruiters
6442 City West Parkway, Suite 100
Eden Prarie, MN 55344
(612) 942-5424
Contact: Mr. S. Yunger
Minimum Salary Placed: $25,000
Recruiting Specialty: Healthcare

Squire Search Consulting
9593 Anderson Lakes Parkway, Suite 169
Eden Prarie, MN 55344
(612) 473-8994
Contact: Ms. Jane Squire
Minimum Salary Placed: $25,000
Recruiting Specialty: General

Wyatt and Jaffe
9900 Bren Road, East, Suite 550
Eden Prarie, MN 55343
(612) 945-0099
Contact: Mr. J. Wyatt
Minimum Salary Placed: $25,000
Recruiting Specialty: Healthcare and high technology

Sales Search, Inc.
8100 Mitchell Road
Eden Prairie, MN 55344-2231
(612) 937-5429
Contact: Mr. Richard Nelles
Recruiting Specialty: Marketing and sales

EDINA

Agri Search/Compu Search Inc.
7550 France Avenue S., Suite 180
Edina, MN 55435
(612) 830-1569
Minimum Salary Placed: $25,000
Recruiting Specialty: Agriculture

Apple Personnel, Inc.
4532 France Avenue South
Edina, MN 55410
(612) 921-3044
Contact: Ms. Jane Bygness
Recruiting Specialty: Office administration

Arthur-Erspamer Associates
7300 France Avenue S
Edina, MN 55435
(612) 831-5564
Contact: Mr. Roy Erspamer
Minimum Salary Placed: $25,000
Recruiting Specialty: General

Brink International Associates
5780 Lincoln Drive, Suite 110
Edina, MN 55436
(612) 931-9622
Contact: Ms. P. Brink-Juster
Minimum Salary Placed: $25,000
Recruiting Specialty: Hospitality

Arlene Clapp Ltd.
6600 France Avenue S, Suite 460
Edina, MN 55435
(612) 922-6181
Contact: Ms. Arlene Clapp
Minimum Salary Placed: $25,000
Recruiting Specialty: Real estate and healthcare

Computer Employment
5151 Edina Industrial Boulevard
Edina, MN 55439
(612) 831-4566
Contact: Mr. M. Koepp
Minimum Salary Placed: $25,000
Recruiting Specialty: Computer

Gleason Dale Keene & Associates, Inc.
7401 Metro Boulevard, Suite 460
Edina, MN 55439
(612) 844-0121
Contact: Mr. Bill Gleason
Minimum Salary Placed: $25,000
Recruiting Specialty: Manufacturing and production

MedSearch Corporation
6545 France Avenue South
Edina, MN 55435
(612) 926-6584
Contact: Ms. Shirley Baker
Recruiting Specialty: Medical

Mefford Knutson
4940 Viking Drive
Edina, MN 55435
(612) 897-0010
Minimum Salary Placed: $35,000
Recruiting Specialty: Home healthcare

Nycor Search, Inc.
4930 West 77th Street, Suite 300
Edina, MN 55435
(612) 831-6444
Contact: Mr. Paul Nymark
Recruiting Specialty: Engineering

Pro Staff IT Consulting
5151 Edina Industrial Boulevard
Edina, MN 55439
(612) 832-9922
Contact: Mr. Scott Groven
Recruiting Specialty: Computer consulting

Rauenhorst Recruiting Company
7600 Parklawn Avenue, Suite 215
Edina, MN 55435
(612) 897-1420
Contact: Mr. C. Rauenhorst
Recruiting Specialty: General

Triad International Corp.
7200 France Avenue South, Suite 212
Edina, MN 55435
(612) 832-574
Contact: Mr. Daniel Fischer
Recruiting Specialty: General

FINLAYSON

Underwriters Search Inc.
2204 Finland Avenue
Finlayson, MN 55735
(612) 233-6622
Minimum Salary Placed: $35,000
Recruiting Specialty: Insurance

FRIDLEY

Agro Quality Search Inc.
7260 University Avenue NE, Suite 305
Fridley, MN 55432
(612) 572-3737
Contact: Mr. J. Olson
Minimum Salary Placed: $25,000
Recruiting Specialty: Agriculture and horticulture

Total Search
1590 60th Avenue NE
Fridley, MN 55432
(612) 571-0247
Contact: Mr. Tom Harrington
Minimum Salary Placed: $25,000
Recruiting Specialty: General

GOLDEN VALLEY

Advance Resource Consultants
715 Florida Avenue S, Suite 206
Golden Valley, MN 55426
(612) 546-6779
Contact: Mr. Larry Happe
Minimum Salary Placed: $25,000
Recruiting Specialty: General

Diversified Employment
4825 Olson Memorial Highway,
 Suite 101
Golden Valley, MN 55422
(612) 546-8255
Contact: Mr. Michael J. Duthoy
Recruiting Specialty: Manufacturing and
production

Johnston and Associates
715 Florida Avenue S, Suite 406
Golden Valley, MN 55426
(612) 544-0212
Contact: Ms. A. Johnston
Minimum Salary Placed: $25,000
Recruiting Specialty: General

HAMEL

Mary L. Mayer, Ltd.
P.O. Box 250
Hamel, MN 55340
(612) 473-7700
Contact: Ms. Mary L. Mayer
Minimum Salary Placed: $40,000
Recruiting Specialty: Insurance

HOPKINS

Brimeyer Group
904 Main Street, Suite 205
Hopkins, MN 55343
(612) 945-0246
Contact: Mr. James Brimeyer
Minimum Salary Placed: $45,000
Recruiting Specialty: General; public sector

HUTCHINSON

Delacore Resources
101 Park Place, Suite 206
Hutchinson, MN 55350
(612) 587-4420
Contact: Mr. Verne Meyer
Minimum Salary Placed: $30,000
Recruiting Specialty: Physicians and
healthcare

LAKEVILLE

Agri-Business Services, Inc.
20950 Holyoke Avenue
Lakeville, MN 55044
(612) 469-6767
Recruiting Specialty: Food and agriculture, production, processing, research &
development, and engineering

Professional Recruiters Inc.
17641 Kettering Trail
Lakeville, MN 55044
(612) 894-5650
Contact: Mr. Robert Reinitz
Minimum Salary Placed: $40,000
Recruiting Specialty: High technology
and industrial sales

R. L. Rystrom & Associates, Inc.
11325 - 172nd Street West
Lakeville, MN 55402
(612) 898-3140
Contact: Mr. Bob Rystrom
Recruiting Specialty: Computers

MAPLE GROVE

Gwen Popelka Search
6264 Magda Drive, Suite A
Maple Grove, MN 55369
(612) 537-2660
Contact: Ms. Gwen Popelka
Minimum Salary Placed: $25,000
Recruiting Specialty: Insurance

Hamborg & Associates
P.O. Box 1444
Maple Grove, MN 55311
(612) 424-6486
Contact: Mr. Steve Hamborg
Minimum Salary Placed: $60,000
Recruiting Specialty: General

MAPLE PLAINS

Palesch and Associates Inc.
530 Kristen Lane
Maple Plains, MN 55359
(612) 955-3390
Contact: Mr. Tom Palesch
Minimum Salary Placed: $25,000
Recruiting Specialty: General

MINNEAPOLIS

Accountants On Call / Accountants Executive Search
45 S. 7th Street, Suite 2312
Minneapolis, MN 55402
(612) 341-9900
Contact: Ms. Jan Kruchoski
Recruiting Specialty: Accounting

ADIA Personnel Services
900 Second Avenue South, Suite 270
Minneapolis, MN 55402
(612) 339-1153
Contact: Mr. Todd D. Schuler
Recruiting Specialty: Office support

Agro Quality Search, Inc.
7260 University Avenue N.E., Suite 305
Minneapolis, MN 55432
(612) 572-3737
Contact: Mr. Jerry Olson
Recruiting Specialty: Agricultural

Bright Search
8120 Penn Avenue S, Suite 167
Minneapolis, MN 55431
(612) 884-8111
Contact: Mr. Leo Bright
Minimum Salary Placed: $35,000
Recruiting Specialty: Sales, marketing and engineering

Lyn Calder Search
6317 Parnell Avenue South
Minneapolis, MN 55435
(612) 922-8286
Contact: Ms. Lyn Calder
Recruiting Specialty: Insurance, actuarial search

Robert Connelly & Associates, Inc.
3500 W 80th Street
Minneapolis, MN 55431
(612) 925-3039
Contact: Mr. Robert Olsen
Minimum Salary Placed: $40,000
Recruiting Specialty: General

Construct Management Services
3030 Harbor Lane, Suite 200F
Minneapolis, MN 55447
(612) 551-1675
Contact: Mr. Robert Lyngen
Minimum Salary Placed: $40,000
Recruiting Specialty: Technical disciplines in construction and manufacturing

Corporate Resources Professional Placement
4205 Lancaster Lane N., Suite 108
Minneapolis, MN 55441
(612) 550-9222
Contact: Mr. Bill Lanctot
Minimum Salary Placed: $40,000
Recruiting Specialty: Electronics, mechanical and biomedical engineering

Charles Dahl Associates
77 13th Avenue NE
Minneapolis, MN 55413
(612) 379-5311
Contact: Mr. Charles Dahl
Minimum Salary Placed: $30,000
Recruiting Specialty: Legal, research and development, high technology and biotechnology

Lake Calhoun Executive Suites
3033 Excelsior Boulevard
Minneapolis, MN 55416
(612) 924-2366
Minimum Salary Placed: $30,000
Recruiting Specialty: General

Electronic Systems Personnel
701 4th Avenue S, Suite 1800
Minneapolis, MN 55415
(612) 337-3000

Contact: Mr. B. Hildreth
Minimum Salary Placed: $25,000
Recruiting Specialty: General and computers

Ells Personnel Systems Inc.
9900 Bren Road, Suite 105
Minneapolis, MN 55343
(612) 932-9933
Contact: Mr. Don Stevenson
Minimum Salary Placed: $75,000
Recruiting Specialty: Construction, engineering, and medical administrative

Mary R. Erickson & Associates
8300 Norman Center Drive, Suite 545
Minneapolis, MN 55437
(612) 893-1010
Contact: Ms. Mary R. Erickson
Minimum Salary Placed: $80,000
Recruiting Specialty: General

Esquire Search, Ltd.
430 First Avenue, W., Suite 630
Minneapolis, MN 55401
(612) 340-9068
Contact: Ms. Patricia Comeford
Minimum Salary Placed: $40,000
Recruiting Specialty: Attorneys

Executive Search Inc.
5401 Gamble Drive, Suite 275
Minneapolis, MN 55416
(612) 541-9153
Contact: Mr. James Gresham
Minimum Salary Placed: $50,000
Recruiting Specialty: General

Falls Medical Search
34 Forestdale Road
Minneapolis, MN 55410
(612) 922-0207
Minimum Salary Placed: $25,000
Recruiting Specialty: Healthcare

Gerdes Singer and Associates Inc.
120 S. 6th Street, Suite 1007
Minneapolis, MN 55402
(612) 335-3553
Contact: Mr. D. Gerdes
Minimum Salary Placed: $25,000
Recruiting Specialty: Art directors and
copy writers

Focus Executive Search
431 S. 7th Street
Minneapolis, MN 55415
(612) 334-5858
Recruiting Specialty: General

Furst Group
Riverview Office Tower
8009 34th Avenue, Suite 1450
Minneapolis, MN 55425
(612) 851-9213
Recruiting Specialty: Healthcare

Robert Half International
90 S. 7th Street, Suite 2800
Minneapolis, MN 55402
(612) 339-9001
Contact: Mr. A. Giesen
Minimum Salary Placed: $25,000
Recruiting Specialty: Accounting and fi-
nance

Hayden & Associates, Inc.
7825 Washington Avenue S, Suite 120
Minneapolis, MN 55439
(612) 941-6300

Contact: Mr. Steve Benedict
Minimum Salary Placed: $30,000
Recruiting Specialty: General

Hayden Group
100 N. 6th Street, Suite 307C
Minneapolis, MN 55403
(612) 338-3933
Contact: Mr. Mike Hayden
Minimum Salary Placed: $25,000
Recruiting Specialty: General

Heinze and Associates Inc.
3033 Excelsior Boulevard
Minneapolis, MN 55416
(612) 924-2389
Minimum Salary Placed: $25,000
Recruiting Specialty: General

T.H. Hunter Inc.
526 Nicollet Mall, Suite 310
Minneapolis, MN 55402
(612) 339-0530
Contact: Debra
Minimum Salary Placed: $25,000
Recruiting Specialty: General

JFK Search
10 S. 5th Street, Suite 700
Minneapolis, MN 55402
(612) 332-8082
Contact: Mr. J. Kessler
Minimum Salary Placed: $25,000
Recruiting Specialty: Advertising and
public relations

Johnston & Associates
715 Florida Avenue South, Suite 406E
Minneapolis, MN 55426
(612) 5544-0212
Contact: Ms. Ann Johnston
Recruiting Specialty: Food manufacturing and processing

A.T. Kearney Executive Search
8500 Normandale Lake Boulevard,
 Suite 1630
Minneapolis, MN 55437
(612) 921-8436
Contact: Mr. Don Hykes
Minimum Salary Placed: $60,000
Recruiting Specialty: General

Eric Kercheval and Associates
100 Washington Avenue S
Minneapolis, MN 55401
(612) 338-7944
Contact: Mr. Eric Kercheval
Minimum Salary Placed: $25,000
Recruiting Specialty: Advertising, communications and hospitality

Korn/Ferry Int'l.
2508 IDS Center, 80 S. 8th Street
Minneapolis, MN 55402
(612) 333-1834
Contact: Mr. Allan Raymond
Minimum Salary Placed: $100,000
Recruiting Specialty: General

Lane Dunham Company
80 S. 8th Street, Suite 2306
Minneapolis, MN 55402
(612) 338-6462
Contact: Mr. Larry Dunham
Minimum Salary Placed: $25,000
Recruiting Specialty: General

Lieberman and Associates
311 1st Avenue N, Suite 503
Minneapolis, MN 55401
(612) 338-2432
Contact: Mr. Howard Lieberman
Minimum Salary Placed: $45,000
Recruiting Specialty: Attorneys

Management Recruiters
7625 Metro Boulevard
Minneapolis, MN 55439
(612) 835-4466
Contact: Mr. Robert Hammer
Minimum Salary Placed: $20,000
Recruiting Specialty: General

McGladrey & Pullen
800 Marquette Avenue
1300 Midwest Plaza E.
Minneapolis, MN 55402
(612) 332-4300
Contact: Mr. Paul Annett
Minimum Salary Placed: $40,000
Recruiting Specialty: General

Ness Group Inc.
762 Pillsbury Court
200 South 6th Street
Minneapolis, MN 55406
(612) 344-1100
Contact: Ms. M. Ness
Minimum Salary Placed: $50,000
Recruiting Specialty: General

NYCOR Search, Inc.
4930 W. 77th Street, Suite 300
Minneapolis, MN 55435
(612) 831-6444
Contact: Mr. Mark Cline
Minimum Salary Placed: $40,000
Recruiting Specialty: Healthcare

Northland Recruiting Inc.
10801 Wayzata Boulevard, Suite 325
Minneapolis, MN 55426
(612) 541-1060
Contact: Mr. David Gavin
Minimum Salary Placed: $35,000
Recruiting Specialty: Manufacturing,
banking and biotechnology

O'Leary and Grant
800 Nicollet Mall
Minneapolis, MN 55402
(612) 349-3778
Contact: Ms. Betty Grant
Minimum Salary Placed: $25,000
Recruiting Specialty: General

Personnel Directions, Inc.
625 Fourth Avenue South, Suite 1200
Minneapolis, MN 55415
(612) 339-1636
Contact: Ms. Jeanne Birkeland
Recruiting Specialty: Office support

Polson & Company, Inc.
15 S. Fifth Street, Suite 1104
Minneapolis, MN 55402
(612) 332-6607
Contact: Ms. Shirley Norman
Minimum Salary Placed: $60,000
Recruiting Specialty: General

Professional Alternatives, Inc.
601 Lakeshore Parkway, Suite 1050
Minneapolis, MN 55305
(612) 975-9200
Contact: Ms. Vickey Kent
Recruiting Specialty: Temporary and permanent executive search

Rauenhorst Recruiting Company
7600 Parklawn Avenue, Suite 215
Minneapolis, MN 55435
(612) 897-1420
Contact: Mr. Charles Rauenhorst
Minimum Salary Placed: $80,000
Recruiting Specialty: General

Recruiting Group
5354 Parkdale Drive, Suite 104
Minneapolis, MN 55416
(612) 544-8550
Contact: Mr. Jack Jones
Recruiting Specialty: Accounting, engineering, operations and office support

Russell Reynolds Associates, Inc.
3050 Norwest Center
90 S. Seventh Street
Minneapolis, MN 55402
(612) 332-6966
Contact: Mr. Stephen Parker
Minimum Salary Placed: $100,000
Recruiting Specialty: General

Romac & Associates, Inc.
120 South Sixth Street, Suite 2500
Minneapolis, MN 55402
(612) 334-5990
Contact: Mr. Keith Johnson
Minimum Salary Placed: $20,000
Recruiting Specialty: General

**Roth Young Personnel Executive
Recruiters**
4620 W. 77th Street, Suite 290
Minneapolis, MN 55435
(612) 831-6655
Contact: Dorrie
Minimum Salary Placed: $35,000
Recruiting Specialty: General

Sales Consultants
7550 France Avenue S, Suite 180
Minneapolis, MN 55435
(612) 830-1420
Contact: Mr. Robert Hammer
Minimum Salary Placed: $25,000
Recruiting Specialty: Sales

Sathe & Associates, Inc.
5821 Cedar Lake Road
Minneapolis, MN 55416
(612) 546-2100
Contact: Mr. Mark Sathe
Minimum Salary Placed: $50,000
Recruiting Specialty: General

Schalekamp & Associates, Inc.
2608 West 102nd Street
Minneapolis, MN 55431
(612) 948-1948
Contact: Mr. Paul Schalekamp
Minimum Salary Placed: $30,000
Recruiting Specialty: Insurance

Schall Executive Search
821 Marquette Avenue, Suite 2100
Minneapolis, MN 55402
(612) 338-3119
Contact: Mr. David Schall
Minimum Salary Placed: $50,000
Recruiting Specialty: General

Search Consultants
13801 Utica Avenue South
Minneapolis, MN 55348
(612) 707-9293
Contact: Mr. Scott Hedberg
Recruiting Specialty: Accounting and finance

Searchtek
4900 North Hwy 169
Minneapolis, MN 55428
(612) 531-0766
Contact: Mr. Gerald Otten
Recruiting Specialty: Engineering and manufacturing

Source EDP
80 South 8th Street, Suite 4696
Minneapolis, MN 55402
(612) 332-6460
Contact: Mr. Steven Wolf
Minimum Salary Placed: $25,000
Recruiting Specialty: Computers and MIS, engineering, manufacturing, and marketing

Stewart, Stein & Scott, Ltd.
1000 Shelard Pkwy., Suite 606
Minneapolis, MN 55426
(612) 545-8151
Contact: Mr. Terry Stein
Minimum Salary Placed: $60,000
Recruiting Specialty: General

Stone, Murphy & Olson
5500 Wayzata Boulevard, Suite 1020
Minneapolis, MN 55416
(612) 591-2300
Contact: Mr. Toni Barnum
Minimum Salary Placed: $50,000
Recruiting Specialty: Human resources and finance

Richard Thompson Associates
701 4th Avenue S
Minneapolis, MN 55415
(612) 339-6060
Contact: Mr. Rich Thompson
Minimum Salary Placed: $75,000
Recruiting Specialty: General

Walker Group, Inc.
2600 Fernbrook Lane, Suite 106
Minneapolis, MN 55447
(612) 553-1356
Contact: Mr. Walter Walker
Minimum Salary Placed: $50,000
Recruiting Specialty: Retail and healthcare

Whitbeck & Associates
701 Fourth Avenue S, Suite 500
Minneapolis, MN 55415
(612) 337-9568
Contact: Ms. Elizabeth Whitbeck
Minimum Salary Placed: $50,000
Recruiting Specialty: Attorneys

Whitney and Associates Inc.
920 2nd Avenue South, Suite 625
Minneapolis, MN 55402
(612) 338-5600
Contact: Mr. David Whitney
Minimum Salary Placed: $25,000
Recruiting Specialty: Accounting and finance

Williams Executive Search, Inc.
4200 Norwest Center
90 S. Seventh Street
Minneapolis, MN 55402
(612) 339-2900
Contact: Mr. Bill Dubbs
Minimum Salary Placed: $100,000
Recruiting Specialty: General

Wood, Franchot Inc.
1550 Utica Avenue S, Suite 425
Minneapolis, MN 55416
(612) 546-6997
Contact: Mr. Michael Wood
Minimum Salary Placed: $60,000
Recruiting Specialty: General

Steven Yungerberg Associates, Inc.
80 South 8th Street, Suite 1022
Minneapolis, MN 55402
(612) 332-5313
Contact: Mr. Steven Yungerberg
Minimum Salary Placed: $50,000
Recruiting Specialty: General

MINNETONKA

Bartz Rogers & Partners
12800 Whitewater Drive, Suite 110
Minnetonka, MN 55343
(612) 936-0657
Contact: Mr. Douglas Bartz
Minimum Salary Placed: $35,000
Recruiting Specialty: Information technology, MIS

Emerging Technology Services
5517 Highland Road
Minnetonka, MN 55345
(612) 937-2200
Contact: Mr. K. Kapaun
Recruiting Specialty: Information, engineers

S. G. Mossberg & Associates
3670 Robinwood Terrace
Minnetonka, MN 55305
(612) 935-2584
Contact: Mr. Steven Mossberg
Recruiting Specialty: Marketing and sales

Northland Recruiting, Inc.
10801 Wayzata Boulevard, Suite 325
Minnetonka, MN 55305
(612) 541-1060
Contact: Mr. R. Skip Black
Recruiting Specialty: Mechanical, engineering, and computer

Professional Alternatives Inc.
601 Lakeshore Parkway, Suite 1050
Minnetonka, MN 55305
(612) 975-9200
Contact: Ms. Vicki Kent
Recruiting Specialty: Human resources,
finance, and marketing

ProPlace, Inc.
P.O. Box 1089
Minnetonka, MN 55345
(612) 934-0292
Contact: Mr. Jeffrey Dolan
Recruiting Specialty: General

NEW BRIGHTEN

Preferred Temps & Placements, Inc.
888 North County Road D, Suite 210
New Brighten, MN 55112
(612) 639-1403
Contact: Mr. Craig Prescott
Recruiting Specialty: Manufacturing and
production

NEW ULM

Agra Placements, Ltd
710 North Broadway
New Ulm, MN 56031
(507) 354-4900
Contact: Mr. Dennis Sjorgren
Recruiting Specialty: Agricultural

NORTHFIELD

Management Resource Group
106 East Third Street, Suite 106
Northfield, MN 55057
(507) 645-9869

Contact: Mr. Michael Northrop
Recruiting Specialty: Sales, software, and
telecommunications

ORONO

Search Specialists
2655 North Shore Drive
Orono, MN 55391
(612) 449-8990
Contact: Mr. Craig Lindell
Recruiting Specialty: Data processing
and engineering

OWATONNA

Bernhart Associates
2068 Greenwood Drive
Owatonna, MN 55060
(507) 451-4270
Contact: Mr. Jerry Bernhart
Recruiting Specialty: Marketing

RWJ & Associates
812 South Elm Street
Owatonna, MN 55060
(507) 455-3002
Contact: Ms. Betsy Lindgren
Recruiting Specialty: General

PLYMOUTH

Corporate Resources
420 Lancaster Lane, North Suite 108
Plymouth, MN 55441
(612) 550-9222
Recruiting Specialty: Engineering

Custom Search Inc.
9800 Shelard Parkway, Suite 104
Plymouth, MN 55441
(612) 591-6111
Contact: Mr. K. Anderson
Minimum Salary Placed: $35,000
Recruiting Specialty: MIS and engineering

Executive Lines
Box 4581
Plymouth, MN 55441
(612) 550-1905
Contact: Mr. Leo Ohnstad
Minimum Salary Placed: $25,000
Recruiting Specialty: Manufacturing, engineering, sales, and marketing

Fairfax Management
First Star Bank Building
13605 27th Avenue N.
Plymouth, MN 55441
(612) 553-1033
Contact: Mr. D. Campbell
Minimum Salary Placed: $25,000
Recruiting Specialty: General

First Technical Search
13895 Industrial Park Boulevard
Plymouth, MN 55441
(612) 551-2535
Contact: Mr. K. Garmaker
Minimum Salary Placed: $25,000
Recruiting Specialty: Food and beverages and consumer products

Personnel Assistance Corporation
3030 Harbor Lane North
Plymouth, MN 55441
(612) 577-0555

Contact: Mr. Don Pearson
Minimum Salary Placed: $25,000
Recruiting Specialty: Manufacturing and engineering

Quest Resources
2915 Garland Lane N
Plymouth, MN 55447
(612) 473-3248
Contact: Mr. Andy Labowitch
Minimum Salary Placed: $40,000
Recruiting Specialty: LAN interconnect and client server

Robert Half International
605 Highway 169 N
Plymouth, MN 55441
(612) 545-0911
Contact: Mr. A. Giesen
Minimum Salary Placed: $25,000
Recruiting Specialty: Accounting and finance

ROCHESTER

Express Personnel Services
2360 North Broadway
Rochester, MN 55906
(507) 285-9270
Contact: Ms. Sheryl Tasler
Recruiting Specialty: Manufacturing and information technology

Management Recruiters
1903 South Broadway
Rochester, MN 55904
(507) 282-2400
Contact: Mr. Robert Vierkant
Minimum Salary Placed: $20,000
Recruiting Specialty: Data processing

Robert William James and Associates
2360 N. Broadway Street
Rochester MN 55904
(507) 285-9270
Contact: Mr. M. Tasler
Minimum Salary Placed: $25,000
Recruiting Specialty: General

ROCKFORD

HR Service
Box 564
Rockford, MN 55373
(612) 559-8841
Contact: Mr. Dan Frump
Minimum Salary Placed: $25,000
Recruiting Specialty: Manufacturing (industrial), technical, and general

ROSEVILLE

Accountants Exchange Inc.
2233 Hamline Avenue N., Suite 509
Roseville, MN 55113
(612) 636-5490
Contact: Mr. C. McBride
Minimum Salary Placed: $25,000
Recruiting Specialty: Accounting

Alpha Omega Employment, Inc.
1315 West Larpenteur Avenue, Suite K
Roseville, MN 55113
(612) 645-7799
Contact: Ms. Mary K. Kahnke
Recruiting Specialty: Manufacturing and production

Rolle Schmidt & Associates
1711 West County Road B, Suite 300N
Roseville, MN 55113
(612) 639-0789
Contact: Ms. Peggy Rolle Schmidt
Recruiting Specialty: Human resources

Snelling Search
2685 Long Lake Road
Roseville, MN 55113
(612) 631-3040
Contact: Mr. Andrew Haak
Recruiting Specialty: Engineering

SAINT CLOUD

Express Personnel Service
606 25th Avenue South, Suite 104
Saint Cloud, MN 56301
(616) 251-1038
Contact: Mr. Tom Fillenworth
Recruiting Specialty: General

Terry Kurash & Associates
P.O. Box 231, Suite 107
Saint Cloud, MN 56302
(612) 251-4071
Contact: Ms. Terry Kurash
Recruiting Specialty: Sales

SAINT LOUIS PARK

Best and Associates
1660 Highway 100 S
Saint Louis Park, MN 55416
(612) 591-9106
Contact: Ms. Barbara Best
Minimum Salary Placed: $25,000
Recruiting Specialty: Consumer packaged goods

Brad Martin and Associates
5353 Wayzata Boulevard
Saint Louis Park, MN 55416
(612) 544-4130
Contact: Mr. B. Olson
Minimum Salary Placed: $50,000
Recruiting Specialty: Engineering and manufacturing

Carlson Research Group
3821 Inglewood Avenue S
Saint Louis Park, MN 55416
(612) 929-7112
Contact: Mr. Bob Carlson
Minimum Salary Placed: $25,000
Recruiting Specialty: General

Ices Ltd.
5354 Parkdale Drive
Saint Louis Park, MN 55416
(612) 542-0028
Contact: Mr. Joe Carroll
Minimum Salary Placed: $40,000
Recruiting Specialty: Computer programming

North American Recruiters
1660 Highway 1005, Suite 519
Saint Louis Park, MN 55416
(612) 591-1951
Contact: Mr. Dave Knutson
Minimum Salary Placed: $60,000
Recruiting Specialty: General

Resource Search
1660 Highway 100 S, Suite 122
Saint Louis Park, MN 55416
(612) 546-0099
Contact: Mr. John Breczinski
Minimum Salary Placed: $30,000
Recruiting Specialty: Sales, marketing and advertising

TRA Inc.
7035 Wayzata Boulevard, Suite 220
Saint Louis Park, MN 55426
(612) 593-9696
Contact: Mr. T. Richards
Minimum Salary Placed: $25,000
Recruiting Specialty: General

SAINT PAUL

A & B Personnel, Inc.
101 East Fifth Street, Suite 2206
Saint Paul, MN 55101
(612) 292-8519
Contact: Ms. Denise Reuss
Recruiting Specialty: General

Business Talent
1419 Osceola Avenue
Saint Paul, MN 55104
(612) 690-0695
Contact: Mr. Bob Salisbury
Recruiting Specialty: Marketing and sales and general

Robert Connelly and Associates
46 4th Street E
Saint Paul, MN 55101
(612) 292-8733
Contact: Mr. Larry Clausen
Minimum Salary Placed: $40,000
Recruiting Specialty: Engineering and architecture

Development Search Specialists
W 3072 First National Bank Building
Saint Paul, MN 55101
(612) 224-3750
Contact: Mr. Fred Lauerman
Minimum Salary Placed: $50,000
Recruiting Specialty: Non-profit

Employment Counselors Inc.
1624 Rosewood Lane S.
Saint Paul, MN 55113
(612) 642-1756
Contact: Mr. Barry Evans
Recruiting Specialty: Engineering and professionals in manufacturing

Friedman Group, Inc.
332 Minnesota Street, Suite W 1272
Saint Paul, MN 55101
(612) 222-4420
Contact: Chris
Recruiting Specialty: General

Robert Half International
840 Piper Jaffray Plaza
Saint Paul, MN 55101
(612) 227-6531
Contact: Mr. P. Bees
Minimum Salary Placed: $25,000
Recruiting Specialty: Accounting and finance

Medsource
357 Kellogg Boulevard E
Saint Paul, MN 55101
(612) 292-1530
Contact: Mr. J. Zeller
Minimum Salary Placed: $25,000
Recruiting Specialty: Healthcare

Preston & Manthey Associates
2550 University Avenue West,
 Suite 315 N
Saint Paul, MN 55114
(800) 279-2345
Minimum Salary Placed: $60,000
Recruiting Specialty: Healthcare

Search Resources .
4756 Banning Avenue
Saint Paul, MN 55110
(612) 429-3576
Contact: Mr. R. Campbell
Minimum Salary Placed: $25,000
Recruiting Specialty: Welding and factory

Sedona Staffing Services
1992-A Suburban Ave., Suite 146
Saint Paul, MN 55119
(612) 578-7290
Contact: Ms. Dee Heeschen
Recruiting Specialty: Computers and engineering

Viking Personnel
Court International
2550 University W., Suite 140 N.
Saint Paul, MN 55114
(612) 623-8353
Contact: Mr. Don Brown
Minimum Salary Placed: $40,000
Recruiting Specialty: General

Wells, Bradley & Associates
7582 Currell Boulevard, Suite 207
Saint Paul, MN 55125
(612) 731-9202
Contact: Mr. Sandy Bradley
Minimum Salary Placed: $30,000
Recruiting Specialty: Banking, savings and loan and investment

Whiteford and Associates
46 4th Street E, Suite 410
Saint Paul, MN 55101
(612) 227-7977
Contact: Mr. Jim Whiteford
Minimum Salary Placed: $50,000
Recruiting Specialty: General

WAYZATA

Andcor Human Resources
539 E Lake Street
Wayzata, MN 55391
(612) 404-8060
Contact: Mr. Dennis Anderson
Recruiting Specialty: General

James Bangert & Associates, Inc.
15500 Wayzata Boulevard, Suite 1022
Wayzata, MN 55391
(612) 475-3454
Contact: Mr. James Bangert
Minimum Salary Placed: $50,000
Recruiting Specialty: General

Gateway Search
604 12 Oaks Center, Suite 262
Wayzata, MN 55391
(612) 473-3137
Contact: Jim
Minimum Salary Placed: $25,000
Recruiting Specialty: General

Inter Search Inc.
15813 White Pine Drive
Wayzata, MN 55391
(612) 449-0801
Contact: Ms. Diana Peterson
Minimum Salary Placed: $25,000
Recruiting Specialty: General

Johnson Executive Search
288 Wayzata Boulevard
Wayzata, MN 55391
(612) 475-2134
Contact: Ms. Kathryn Johnson
Minimum Salary Placed: $25,000
Recruiting Specialty: General

The Mazzitelli Group, Ltd.
603 E. Lake Street, Suite 200
Wayzata, MN 55391
(612) 449-9490
Contact: Ms. Teresa Mazzitelli
Minimum Salary Placed: $40,000
Recruiting Specialty: General

C A Moore and Associates, Inc.
15500 Wayzata Boulevard
Wayzata, MN 55391
(612) 473-0990
Contact: Ms. Connie Moore
Minimum Salary Placed: $35,000
Recruiting Specialty: General

Peter Van Leer & Associates
15500 Wayzata Boulevard, Suite 1022
Wayzata, MN 55391
(612) 473-3793
Contact: Mr. Peter Van Leer
Minimum Salary Placed: $50,000
Recruiting Specialty: Insurance

WEST SAINT PAUL

Selective Search Inc.
60 Marie Avenue E
West Saint Paul, MN 55118
(612) 450-7718
Contact: Mr. Art Anderson
Minimum Salary Placed: $25,000
Recruiting Specialty: General

WHITE BEAR LAKE

Messicci & Associates
3724 Auger Avenue
White Bear Lake, MN 55110
(612) 429-7756
Contact: Mr. Joseph A. Messicci
Minimum Salary Placed: $50,000
Recruiting Specialty: Service, education,
insurance, healthcare and non-profit

Pivotal Decision
4281 Oakmead Lane
White Bear Lake, MN 55110
(612) 653-9392
Contact: Ms. M. Ann Buck
Minimum Salary Placed: $50,000
Recruiting Specialty: General

WOODBURY

Professional Service Consultants
1811 Weir Drive, Suite 190
Woodbury, MN 55125
(612) 738-8561
Contact: Terry Petra
Minimum Salary Placed: $50,000
Recruiting Specialty: General

M I S S I S S I P P I

EDWARDS

Buzhardt Associates
1385 Narrow Gauge Road
Edwards, MS 39066
(601) 852-8042
Contact: Mr. J.F. Buzhardt
Minimum Salary Placed: $50,000
Recruiting Specialty: General

JACKSON

Dunhill Professional Search
13 Northtown Drive, Suite 220
Jackson, MS 39211
(601) 956-1060
Contact: Mr. Ronnie Fulton
Minimum Salary Placed: $20,000
Recruiting Specialty: General

Management Recruiters
2506 Lakeland Drive, Suite 408
Jackson, MS 39208
(601) 936-7900
Contact: Mr. Mike Van Wick
Minimum Salary Placed: $20,000
Recruiting Specialty: General

Management Recruiters
1755 Lelia Drive, Suite 102
Jackson, MS 39216
(601) 366-4488
Contact: Mr. J.W. Gardner
Minimum Salary Placed: $20,000
Recruiting Specialty: General

Snelling Personnel Services
840 East River Place, #507
Jackson, MS 39202
(601) 949-3333
Contact: Ms. Alison Johnson
Recruiting Specialty: Engineering, food
service management and accounting

Jim Woodson & Associates, Inc.
1080 River Oaks Drive, Suite B-102
Jackson, MS 39208
(601) 936-4037
Contact: Mr. Jim Woodson
Recruiting Specialty: Technical in engineering and manufacturing

MADISON

Dunhill of Madison
PO Box 1218
Madison, MS 39130
(601) 856-4095
Contact: Ms. Pat Bruce
Minimum Salary Placed: $20,000
Recruiting Specialty: General

MERIDIAN

Blakely Associates
7753 Stae Boulevard Extension
Meridian, MS 39305
(601) 693-5185
Contact: Mr. Larry Blakely
Minimum Salary Placed: $20,000
Recruiting Specialty: Audio/music and
entertainment technology

PASCAGOULA

Bird and Associates
P.O. Box 2208
Pascagoula, MS 39569
(601) 762-7928
Contact: Mr. Conrad Bird
Minimum Salary Placed: $20,000
Recruiting Specialty: General

VICKSBURG

Snelling Personnel Services
2480 Frontage Road South, Suite C
Vicksburg, MS 39180-5281
(601) 630-9011
Contact: Mr. Danny Perrett
Recruiting Specialty: Gaming industry

M I S S O U R I

BALLWIN

Burke Group
119 Hill Avenue
Ballwin, MO 63011
(314) 230-8100
Recruiting Specialty: Engineering

J. J. Conover
300 Ozark Trail Drive, Suite 208
Ballwin, MO 63011
(314) 256-0303
Contact: Mr. J. Gibbons
Minimum Salary Placed: $25,000
Recruiting Specialty: Plastics, manufactur-
ing and engineering

Estes Management Group
P.O. Box 739
Ballwin, MO 63011
(314) 861-2080
Contact: Mr. David Estes
Minimum Salary Placed: $25,000
Recruiting Specialty: General

Haskell Associates, Inc.
180 S. Neidman Road
Ballwin, MO 63021
(314) 230-0108
Contact: Mr. Jerry Haskell
Recruiting Specialty: General

Huey Enterprises, Inc.
273 Clarkson Executive Park
Ballwin, MO 63011
(314) 394-9393
Recruiting Specialty: Real estate, marketing, and accounting

J. M. Group
P.O. Box 1128
Ballwin, MO 63022
(314) 227-3838
Contact: Mr. J. Milovich
Minimum Salary Placed: $35,000
Recruiting Specialty: Real Estate, con-
struction, engineering and architecture

R. Adrian McBride & Co.
1823 Sullivan Point Drive
Ballwin, MO 63011
(314) 458-8551
Recruiting Specialty: General

BRIDGETON

Raiche and Associates
11021 Natural Bridge Road
Bridgeton, MO 63044
(314) 895-4554
Contact: Mr. Don Raiche
Minimum Salary Placed: $30,000
Recruiting Specialty: Mid-range and PC
systems

CAMDENTON

Management Recruiters
P.O. Box 1197
Camdenton, MO 65020
(573) 346-4833
Contact: Ms. Judy Hodgson
Minimum Salary Placed: $25,000
Recruiting Specialty: Physicians and phy-
sician assistants, nurses, and computers
technicians

CHESTERFIELD

Davis & James, Inc.
14377 Woodlake Drive, Suite 312
Chesterfield, MO 63017
(314) 205-1234
Contact: Jerry
Recruiting Specialty: Financial institutions, engineering, and technical

Gateway Consultants
14258 Dinsmoor Drive
Chesterfield, MO 63017
(314) 576-3550
Recruiting Specialty: General

Healthcare Recruiters International
15400 S. Outer 40
Chesterfield, MO 63017
(314) 530-1031
Contact: Dan
Recruiting Specialty: Medical sales and
sales management

J. B. Linde Associates
16100 Chesterfield Parkway
Chesterfield, MO 63017
(314) 532-8040
Contact: J.B. Linde
Minimum Salary Placed: $35,000
Recruiting Specialty: Manufacturing,
management

Charles Luntz & Associates, Inc.
14323 S. Outer Forty, Suite 400 S.
Chesterfield, MO 63017
(314) 275-7992
Contact: Mr. Charles Luntz
Minimum Salary Placed: $50,000
Recruiting Specialty: General

J.L. Paetzhold
14377 Woodlake Drive, Suite 312
Chesterfield, MO 63017
(314) 205-1228
Contact: Mr. Jerry Paetzhold
Minimum Salary Placed: $40,000
Recruiting Specialty: Banking and finan-
cial services

River Bend Group
36 Seasons 4 Shopping Center, Suite 315
Chesterfield, MO 63017
(314) 579-9729
Contact: Mr. John Sroka
Minimum Salary Placed: $25,000
Recruiting Specialty: Computers and
data processing

COLUMBIA

Management Recruiters
1310 Business 63 S., Suite 1
Columbia, MO 65201
(314) 874-5698
Contact: Mr. David Dunn
Minimum Salary Placed: $25,000
Recruiting Specialty: General

CREVE COEUR

Arwood & Associates
12400 Olive Boulevard
Creve Coeur, MO 63141
(314) 434-7770
Recruiting Specialty: Banking and finance

Bankers Resource
745 Craig Road, Suite 218
Creve Coeur, MO 63141
(314) 994-1984
Minimum Salary Placed: $25,000
Recruiting Specialty: Banking

John & Powers, Inc.
12935 N. Outer 40
Creve Coeur, MO 63141
(314) 453-0080
Recruiting Specialty: General

EARTH CITY

Compu Search
3301 S. Rider Trail
Earth City, MO 63045
(314) 344-0922
Contact: Mr. Jack Evans
Minimum Salary Placed: $25,000
Recruiting Specialty: General

ELLISVILLE

Huey Enterprises, Inc.
273 Clarkson Executive Park
Ellisville, MO 63011
(314) 394-9393
Contact: Mr. Arthur Huey
Minimum Salary Placed: $50,000
Recruiting Specialty: General and real estate

G.M. Snyder and Associates
300 Ozark Trail
Ellisville, MO 63011
(314) 256-3870
Contact: Mr. G. Snyder
Minimum Salary Placed: $25,000
Recruiting Specialty: Manufacturing

FENTON

Management Recruiters
200 Fabricator Drive
Fenton, MO 63026
(314) 349-4455
Contact: Mr. Edward Travis
Minimum Salary Placed: $25,000
Recruiting Specialty: General

FLORISSANT

Dunhill Personnel of Brentwood, Inc.
11220 W. Florissant, Suite 238
Florissant, MO 63033
(314) 298-1617
Contact: Ms. Lynn Smith
Minimum Salary Placed: $25,000
Recruiting Specialty: General

Roberta Weller and Associates
1130 Elder Drive
Florissant, MO 63033
(314) 921-2302
Contact: Ms. Roberta Weller
Minimum Salary Placed: $25,000
Recruiting Specialty: General

GREENWOOD

Erickson and Associates
338 N. Winnebago Drive
Greenwood, MO 64034
(816) 537-6767
Contact: Ms. Pat Erickson
Minimum Salary Placed: $25,000
Recruiting Specialty: Healthcare

INDEPENDENCE

American Consultants
14400 E 42nd Street South
Independence, MO 64055
(816) 373-2222
Contact: Ms. M. Witkowski
Minimum Salary Placed: $25,000
Recruiting Specialty: Medical and insurance

Management Recruiters
14825 E. 42nd Street, Suite 250
Independence, MO 64055
(816) 478-3131
Contact: Mr. Brian Howard
Minimum Salary Placed: $25,000
Recruiting Specialty: General

Management Science Associates
4721 Cliff Avenue, Suite 105
Independence, MO 64055
(816) 373-9988
Contact: Mrs. Jane Groves
Minimum Salary Placed: $25,000
Recruiting Specialty: Healthcare

KANSAS CITY

Accountants On Call
911 Main Street, Suite 620
Kansas City, MO 64105
(816) 421-7774
Contact: Ms. Brenda Hunzeker
Recruiting Specialty: Accounting

Agri-Associates
500 Nichols Road
Kansas City, MO 64112
(816) 531-7980
Contact: Mr. Glenn Person
Minimum Salary Placed: $25,000
Recruiting Specialty: Agriculture and horticulture

Agri-Technology Personnel, Inc.
3113 NE 69th Street
Kansas City, MO 64119
(816) 453-7200
Contact: Mr. Dale Pickering
Minimum Salary Placed: $20,000
Recruiting Specialty: Agriculture and horticulture

Austin Nichols Technical Search
1100 Main Street, Suite 1560
Kansas City, MO 64105
(816) 471-5575

Contact: Mr. D. McDowell
Minimum Salary Placed: $35,000
Recruiting Specialty: Technical disciplines

Ron Ball & Associates
P.O. Box 480391
Kansas City, MO 64148
(816) 322-2727
Contact: Mr. Ronald Ball
Minimum Salary Placed: $35,000
Recruiting Specialty: Industrial sales

The Christopher Group
P.O. Box 30085
Kansas City, MO 64112
(913) 722-2777
Contact: Mr. R. Andrew Sprehe
Minimum Salary Placed: $35,000
Recruiting Specialty: Finance, banking,
and real estate

DHR International, Inc.
500 Nichols Road, Suite 430
Kansas City, MO 64112
(816) 756-2965
Contact: Mr. Jerry Lunn
Minimum Salary Placed: $45,000
Recruiting Specialty: General

Dunhill Personnel
400 E. Red Bridge Road, Suite 203
Kansas City, MO 64131
(816) 942-8620
Contact: Mr. Don Phillips
Minimum Salary Placed: $25,000
Recruiting Specialty: General

JRL Executive Recruiters
2700 Rock Creek Parkway
Kansas City, MO 64117
(816) 471-4022
Contact: Mr. L. Eason
Minimum Salary Placed: $35,000
Recruiting Specialty: Manufacturing and
engineering

Kennison & Associates
3101 Broadway
Kansas City, MO 64111
(816) 753-4401
Contact: Mr. Gary Fawkes
Recruiting Specialty: General; data processing and electrical engineering

Kirdonne Group
106 West 11th Street, Suite 1250
Kansas City, MO 64105
(816) 474-0700
Recruiting Specialty: General

Management Recruiters
2300 Main Street, Suite 1020
Kansas City, MO 64108
(816) 221-2377
Contact: Mr. Stephen Orr
Minimum Salary Placed: $25,000
Recruiting Specialty: General

Robert Half International
127 W. 10th Street, Suite 956
Kansas City, MO 64152
(816) 474-4583
Contact: Mr. M. Hersh
Minimum Salary Placed: $25,000
Recruiting Specialty: Accounting and fi-
nance

Smith Brown and Jones
800 W. 47th Street
Kansas City, MO 64112
(531)-4770
Contact: Mr. Don Smith
Minimum Salary Placed: $25,000
Recruiting Specialty: Food, agri-business
and equipment manufacturing

Software Synergy
1200 E. 104th Street
Kansas City, MO 64131
(816) 941-7444
Contact: Ms. Kathy Smith
Minimum Salary Placed: $35,000
Recruiting Specialty: Computer programming and software engineering

Personnel Connection
1111 Main Street
Kansas City, MO 64152
(816) 471-8280
Minimum Salary Placed: $25,000
Recruiting Specialty: General

KIRKWOOD

Crider and Associates
699 W. Woodbine Avenue
Kirkwood, MO 63122
(314) 965-6665
Contact: Mr. P. Crider
Minimum Salary Placed: $25,000
Recruiting Specialty: Metals and manufacturing

Trouveer Associates Inc.
10097 Manchester Road
Kirkwood, MO 63122
(314) 822-9900
Recruiting Specialty: Physicians

LAKE OZARK

Whitehead & Associates, Inc.
330 Palisades Drive
Lake Ozark, MO 65049
(573) 365-2112
Contact: Mr. Robert Whitehead
Minimum Salary Placed: $25,000
Recruiting Specialty: Engineering and manufacturing

MANCHESTER

The Burke Group
119 Hill Avenue
Manchester, MO 63011
(800) 737-8100
Contact: Mr. George Burke
Minimum Salary Placed: $35,000
Recruiting Specialty: Metals and plastics manufacturing

MARYLAND HEIGHTS

Christopher and Long
15 Worthington Access Drive
Maryland Heights, MO 63043
(314) 576-6300 or (800) 800-5664
Contact: Mr. K. Long
Minimum Salary Placed: $50,000
Recruiting Specialty: Physicians, engineering in manufacturing, apparel, and automotive

MOUNTAIN VIEW

Rowlett and Associates
6500 US Highway 60
Mountain View, MO 65548
(417) 934-6188
Contact: Mr. Chuck Rowlett
Minimum Salary Placed: $25,000
Recruiting Specialty: General

OVERLAND PARK

JAG and Associates Attorney Search
7299 West 98th Terrace
Overland Park, MO 66212
(816) 221-1555
Minimum Salary Placed: $35,000
Recruiting Specialty: Attorneys

SAINT JOSEPH

Robert William James and Associates
3919 Sherman Road
Saint Joseph, MO 64507
(816) 364-5775
Recruiting Specialty: General

SAINT LOUIS

Aaron Consulting, Inc.
415 DeBaliviere Avenue, Suite 200
Saint Louis, MO 63112
(314) 367-2627
Contact: Mr. Aaron Williams
Minimum Salary Placed: $50,000
Recruiting Specialty: Attorneys

Accountants On Call
515 N. 6th Street, Suite 2002
Saint Louis, MO 63101
(314) 436-0500
Contact: Ms. Deborah Cotten
Recruiting Specialty: Accounting

Barney Oldfield Group
1807 Park 270 Drive
Saint Louis, MO 63146
(314) 579-9755
Minimum Salary Placed: $35,000
Recruiting Specialty: Engineering

J. B. Boyd and Associates
9 Hortus Court
Saint Louis, MO 63110
(314) 664-1300
Contact: Ms. J. Boyd
Minimum Salary Placed: $50,000
Recruiting Specialty: Attorneys

Bradford & Galt, Inc.
12400 Olive Boulevard, Suite 430
Saint Louis, MO 63111
(314) 434-9200
Contact: Mr. Bradford Layton
Recruiting Specialty: General

Broeker and Associates Inc.
655 Craig Road, P.O. Box 411246
Saint Louis, MO 63141
(314) 576-4440
Contact: Ms. Barbara Broeker
Minimum Salary Placed: $40,000
Recruiting Specialty: General

Cejka & Company
222 S. Central, Suite 400
Saint Louis, MO 63105
(314) 726-1603
Contact: Ms. Susan Cejka
Minimum Salary Placed: $60,000
Recruiting Specialty: Healthcare

Corbin Packaging Professionals
11729 Casa Grande Drive
Saint Louis, MO 63146
(314) 993-1419
Contact: Mr. Earl Corbin
Minimum Salary Placed: $35,000
Recruiting Specialty: Packaging and
manufacturing

Corporate Search
727 N. 1st Street
Saint Louis, MO 63102
(314) 231-6662
Contact: Mr. K. Gehling
Minimum Salary Placed: $30,000
Recruiting Specialty: Technical disciplines in sales

Debbon Recruiting Group
P.O. Box 510323
Saint Louis, MO 63151
(314) 846-9101
Contact: Mr. John Zipfel
Minimum Salary Placed: $30,000
Recruiting Specialty: Pharmaceuticals,
food and manufacturing

James L. Fisk & Associates
1921 Buckington Drive
Saint Louis, MO 63017
(314) 394-5381
Contact: Mr. Jim Fisk
Minimum Salary Placed: $25,000
Recruiting Specialty: Healthcare and
management consulting

Grant Cooper & Associates, Inc.
795 Office Pkwy., Suite 117
Saint Louis, MO 63141
(314) 567-4690
Contact: Mr. Stephen Loeb
Minimum Salary Placed: $40,000
Recruiting Specialty: Manufacturing

Robert Half Accountemps
1 Metropolitan Square
Saint Louis, MO 63102
(314) 621-8367
Recruiting Specialty: Accounting and finance

Robert Half Accountemps
10733 Sunset Office Drive, Suite 255
Saint Louis, MO 63127
(314) 966-0669
Recruiting Specialty: Accounting and finance

Robert Half International
12655 Olive Boulevard, Suite 315
Saint Louis, MO 63141
(314) 878-9975
Contact: Ms. C. Breth
Recruiting Specialty: Accounting and finance

Healthcare Recruiters
111 Westport Plaza, Suite 600
Saint Louis, MO 63146
(314) 530-1030
Contact: Mr. Dan Bemus
Minimum Salary Placed: $25,000
Recruiting Specialty: Healthcare

Healthline Management Inc.
3115 S. Grand Boulevard, Suite 600
Saint Louis, MO 63118
(314) 776-3900
Contact: Mr. F. Siano
Minimum Salary Placed: $25,000
Recruiting Specialty: Healthcare

Hitchens & Foster, Inc.
Pines Office Ctr., 1 Pine Court
Saint Louis, MO 63141
(314) 453-0800
Contact: Mr. Rex Hermsmeyer
Recruiting Specialty: Physicians and gen-
eral

Holohan Group, Ltd.
755 S. New Ballas Road, Suite 260
Saint Louis, MO 63141
(314) 997-8981
Contact: Mr. Barth Holohan
Minimum Salary Placed: $50,000
Recruiting Specialty: General

Irvin-Edwards & Associates
12300 Olive, Suite 302
Saint Louis, MO 63141
(314) 453-0200
Contact: Mr. Dan Donnelly
Minimum Salary Placed: $25,000
Recruiting Specialty: Sales and marketing

John & Powers, Inc.
12935 N. Forty Drive, Suite 214
Saint Louis, MO 63141
(314) 453-0080
Contact: Mr. Harold John
Minimum Salary Placed: $60,000
Recruiting Specialty: General

Keldon Company
12239 Manchester Road
Saint Louis, MO 63131
(314) 965-9600
Minimum Salary Placed: $25,000
Recruiting Specialty: General

Kendall & Davis Company, Inc.
11325 Concord Village Avenue
Saint Louis, MO 63123
(314) 843-8838
Contact: Mr. James Kendall
Recruiting Specialty: Physicians

Lab Market Specialists
1515 N. Warson Road, Suite 257
Saint Louis, MO 63132
(314) 432-0381

Contact: Ms. Karen Mendrala
Recruiting Specialty: Technical disciplines in a lab environment

L'Ange Group
2129 Barrett Station Road
Saint Louis, MO 63131
(314) 227-3383
Contact: Mr. Terry L'Ange
Recruiting Specialty: Sales

Michael Latas & Associates, Inc.
1311 Lindbergh Plaza Center
Saint Louis, MO 63132
(314) 993-6500
Contact: Mr. Michael Latas
Minimum Salary Placed: $40,000
Recruiting Specialty: Construction, architectural and construction engineering

The Logan Group, Inc.
7710 Carondelet, Suite 402
Saint Louis, MO 63105
(314) 862-2828
Contact: Mr. Brian Ryan
Minimum Salary Placed: $25,000
Recruiting Specialty: General

Lynco Limited
655 Craig Road
Saint Louis, MO 63141
(314) 993-9931
Contact: Ms. L. Sher
Recruiting Specialty: Physicians

Management Recruiters
3301 Rider Trail S., Suite 100
Saint Louis, MO 63045
(314) 344-0959
Contact: Mr. Robert Keymer
Minimum Salary Placed: $25,000
Recruiting Specialty: General

Management Recruiters

11701 Borman Drive, Suite 250
Saint Louis, MO 63146
(314) 991-4355
Contact: Mr. Phil Bertsch
Minimum Salary Placed: $25,000
Recruiting Specialty: General

R. F. Mulvaney & Associates, Inc.

8220 Delmar Boulevard, Suite 210
Saint Louis, MO 63124
(314) 993-3222
Contact: Mr. Ron Mulvaney
Minimum Salary Placed: $50,000
Recruiting Specialty: General

Romac & Associates, Inc.

1001 Craig Road, Suite 260
Saint Louis, MO 63146
(314) 569-9898
Contact: Ms. Mel Weinberg
Recruiting Specialty: Accounting, finance
and data processing

S.J. Associates

5865 Hampton Avenue
Saint Louis, MO 63109
(314) 481-2715
Contact: Mr. Steve Doss
Minimum Salary Placed: $35,000
Recruiting Specialty: Sales in computers

Sales Consultants

3301 Rider Trail S., Suite 100
Saint Louis, MO 63045
(314) 344-0900
Contact: Mr. Bob Keymer
Minimum Salary Placed: $25,000
Recruiting Specialty: Sales

Source EDP

1 City Place, Suite 170
Saint Louis, MO 63141
(314) 997-2001
Contact: Ms. Nancy Riehl
Minimum Salary Placed: $25,000
Recruiting Specialty: Information systems and computers

Source Finance

1 City Place Drive, Suite 170
Saint Louis, MO 63141
(314) 432-0333
Contact: Mr. Marvin Smiley
Minimum Salary Placed: $25,000
Recruiting Specialty: Finance and accounting

Toberson Group

1034 S. Brentwood Boulevard
Saint Louis, MO 63117
(314) 726-6038
Contact: Mr. J. Anderson
Recruiting Specialty: Physicians and
nurse practitioners

Woodbridge Associates

12025 Manchester Road
Saint Louis, MO 63131
(314) 965-0413
Contact: Mr. R. Jones
Minimum Salary Placed: $40,000
Recruiting Specialty: Human resource development and some general

SHAWNEE MISSION

Lawrence-Leiter & Company
4400 Shawnee Mission Parkway
Shawnee Mission, MO 66205
(816) 474-8340
Contact: Mr. William Beeson
Minimum Salary Placed: $40,000
Recruiting Specialty: General

SPRINGFIELD

Christiansen Group
2101 N. Chesterfield Boulevard,
 Suite B202
Springfield, MO 65807
(417) 889-9696
Contact: Mr. Scott Christiansen
Minimum Salary Placed: $25,000
Recruiting Specialty: Food and beverage
industry in engineering and manufactur-
ing

Jim Crumpley & Associates
1200 E. Woodhurst Drive, B-400
Springfield, MO 65804
(417) 882-7555
Contact: Mr. Jim Crumpley
Minimum Salary Placed: $60,000
Recruiting Specialty: Pharmaceuticals
and biotechnology

Fortune Personnel Consultants
1736 E. Sunshine, Suite 707
Springfield, MO 65804
(417) 887-6737
Contact: Mr. Bill Belle Isle
Minimum Salary Placed: $25,000
Recruiting Specialty: Manufacturing

Gibson and Associates
2345 E. Grand Street
Springfield, MO 65804
(417) 886-3534
Contact: Mr. Gary Gibson
Minimum Salary Placed: $25,000
Recruiting Specialty: General

Management Recruiters
1807 E. Edgewood, Suite B
Springfield, MO 65804
(417) 882-6220
Contact: Ms. Arlyn Rudolph
Minimum Salary Placed: $25,000
Recruiting Specialty: General

Don Schooler and Associates
4810 East Farm Road, Road 132
Springfield, MO 65804
(417) 831-0004
Contact: Mr. Don Schooler
Minimum Salary Placed: $25,000
Recruiting Specialty: Banking

M O N T A N A

BILLINGS

Pater Search
561 Pinon Drive
Billings, MT 59105
(406) 252-6789
Contact: Ms. K. Ostermiller
Minimum Salary Placed: $25,000
Recruiting Specialty: General

BOZEMAN

Fortune Personnel
104 E. Main Street
Bozeman, MT 59715
(406) 585-1332
Contact: Mr. R. Regan
Minimum Salary Placed: $25,000
Recruiting Specialty: General

KALISPELL

Labor Contractors
275 Corporate Drive
Kalispell, MT 59901
(406) 752-0191
Contact: Mr. R. Brown
Minimum Salary Placed: $25,000
Recruiting Specialty: General

Management Recruiters
275 Corporate Avenue, Suite 400
Kalispell, MT 59901
(406) 755-3360
Contact: Mr. Clyde Stearns
Minimum Salary Placed: $20,000
Recruiting Specialty: General

MISSOULA

W. Robert Knapp and Associates
4290 Wild Fox Road, Suite 200
Missoula, MT 59802
(406) 721-2221
Contact: Mr. Bob Knapp
Minimum Salary Placed: $30,000
Recruiting Specialty: Transportation planning, civil engineering and environmental

N E B R A S K A

BELLEVUE

Apex Systems Inc.
1820 Hillcrest Drive, Suite F
Bellevue, NE 68005
(402) 291-1200
Contact: Mr. G. Delahoussaye
Minimum Salary Placed: $25,000
Recruiting Specialty: Data processing

LINCOLN

Blau Kaptain Schroeder
800 First Tier Bank Building
Lincoln, NE 65808
(402) 434-1494
Contact: Mr. Lee Schroeder
Minimum Salary Placed: $75,000
Recruiting Specialty: Biotechnology and
pharmaceuticals

William J. Elam & Associates
210 Gateway Mall, Suite 434
Lincoln, NE 68505
(402) 467-5638
Contact: Mr. William Elam
Minimum Salary Placed: $75,000
Recruiting Specialty: Biotechnology and
pharmaceuticals

Lincoln Group Inc.
Box 5208
Lincoln, NE 68505
(402) 434-5919
Contact: Mr. Jack Mosow
Minimum Salary Placed: $25,000
Recruiting Specialty: Technical for food,
pharmaceutical, and consumer package
goods

Management Recruiters
210 Gateway, Suite 434
Lincoln, NE 68505
(402) 467-5534
Contact: Mr. Bill Elam
Minimum Salary Placed: $20,000
Recruiting Specialty: General

Professional Personnel Service
3201 Pioneers Boulevard, Suite 222
Lincoln, NE 68502
(402) 483-7821
Contact: Mr. B. Beuthe
Minimum Salary Placed: $25,000
Recruiting Specialty: General

OMAHA

Adams Inc.
13906 Gold Circle, Suite 101
Omaha, NE 68144
(402) 333-3009
Contact: Mr. J. Adams
Minimum Salary Placed: $40,000
Recruiting Specialty: Financial institu-
tions and banking

Aureus Medical
8744 Frederick Street
Omaha, NE 68124
(402) 397-2980
Contact: Ms. Barb Sundeen
Recruiting Specialty: Full search medical
except physicians

Dunhill Professional Search
P.O. Box 37287
Omaha, NE 68144
(402) 334-1233
Contact: Mr. Kenneth Jaspersen
Minimum Salary Placed: $20,000
Recruiting Specialty: General

Dunhill Professional Search

5809 South 105th Street
Omaha, NE 68127
(402) 331-1644
Contact: Mr. Gary Durbin
Minimum Salary Placed: $20,000
Recruiting Specialty: General

Eggers Consulting Company

11272 Elm Street
Omaha, NE 68144
(402) 333-3480
Contact: Mr. J. Eggers
Minimum Salary Placed: $25,000
Recruiting Specialty: General

Harrison Moore Inc.

7638 Pierce Street
Omaha, NE 68124
(402) 391-5494
Contact: Mr. Curt McLey
Recruiting Specialty: Technical disciplines in manufacturing, metals, fabrication and plastics (foundry industry)

Management Recruiters

7171 W. Mercy Road, Suite 252
Omaha, NE 68106
(402) 397-8320
Contact: Mr. Les Zanotti
Minimum Salary Placed: $20,000
Recruiting Specialty: General

Odyssey Group

7602 Pacific Street, Suite 100
Omaha, NE 68114
(402) 391-2065
Contact: Ms. J. Malone
Minimum Salary Placed: $25,000
Recruiting Specialty: General

Reb and Associates

256 N 115th Street
Omaha, NE 68154
(402) 333-1794
Contact: Mr. R. Brixius
Minimum Salary Placed: $35,000
Recruiting Specialty: Banking

Recruiters International Inc.

11330 Q Street, Suite 218
Omaha, NE 68137
(402) 339-9839
Contact: Mr. Ken Mertins
Minimum Salary Placed: $25,000
Recruiting Specialty: General

The Regency Group, Ltd.

256 N. 115th Street, Suite 1
Omaha, NE 68154
(402) 334-7255
Contact: Mr. Dan J. Barrow
Minimum Salary Placed: $30,000
Recruiting Specialty: MIS in high technology

Tele Electronics Company

206 S 19th Street, Suite 204
Omaha, NE 68102
(402) 346-3421
Minimum Salary Placed: $30,000
Recruiting Specialty: Technical disciplines

Value Based Leadership

1716 S 153rd Avenue Circle
Omaha, NE 68144
(402) 333-2648
Contact: Mr. Glen Trembley
Minimum Salary Placed: $25,000
Recruiting Specialty: Healthcare

N E V A D A

LAS VEGAS

Executive Management Resources
3885 S. Decatur, Suite 3000
Las Vegas, NV 89118
(702) 220-3000
Contact: Mr. K. Powers
Minimum Salary Placed: $50,000
Recruiting Specialty: Gaming

Beth Isabelle and Associates Inc.
6655 W. Sahara, Suite B200
Las Vegas, NV 89102
(702) 247-1756
Contact: Ms. Beth Isabelle
Minimum Salary Placed: $40,000
Recruiting Specialty: Senior management
in Mexico

Management Recruiters
6875 W. Charleston Boulevard, Suite B
Las Vegas, NV 89117
(702) 254-4558
Contact: Ms. Margaret Brown
Minimum Salary Placed: $20,000
Recruiting Specialty: General

Matrix Group
501 S. Rancho Drive, Suite H53
Las Vegas, NV 89106
(702) 598-0070
Contact: Ms. D. Karn
Recruiting Specialty: Mortgage banking,
medical and clerical

McGladrey & Pullen
300 S. 4th Street, Suite 900
P.O. Box 16044
Las Vegas, NV 89101
(702) 386-5800
Contact: Mr. Bob Geile
Minimum Salary Placed: $30,000
Recruiting Specialty: General

Resource Network
2001 E. Flamingo Road
Las Vegas, NV 89119
(702) 796-0111
Contact: Ms. Gloria Crockett
Minimum Salary Placed: $25,000
Recruiting Specialty: General

RENO

Management Recruiters
1025 Ridgeview Drive, Suite 100
Reno, NV 89509
(702) 826-5243
Contact: Mr. Ed Trapp
Minimum Salary Placed: $20,000
Recruiting Specialty: General

Robert Half International
50 W. Liberty Street
Reno, NV 89501
(702) 786-3338
Contact: Ms. S. Day
Recruiting Specialty: Accounting and finance

Snelling and Snelling
1755 E. Plumb Lane, Suite 264
Reno, NV 89502
(702) 329-1366
Contact: Mr. D. Loffswold
Recruiting Specialty: General

NEW HAMPSHIRE

AMHERST

Shawn Alexander Associates
103 Ponemah Road
Amherst, NH 03031
(603) 672-6116
Contact: Ms. Shawn Alexander
Minimum Salary Placed: $80,000
Recruiting Specialty: General

ATKINSON

Multi Processing, Inc.
20 Crown Hill Road
Atkinson, NH 03811
(617) 861-6300
Contact: Mr. Joseph Vito
Minimum Salary Placed: $40,000
Recruiting Specialty: MIS and computers

BEDFORD

Availability Personnel Consultants
169 S. River Road
Bedford, NH 03110
(603) 669-4440
Contact: Mr. Walter Kilian
Minimum Salary Placed: $30,000
Recruiting Specialty: General

Barclay Temporaries
1 Executive Park Drive
Bedford, NH 03110
(603) 669-2011
Contact: Ms. D. Kennedy
Recruiting Specialty: General

Emerald Legal Search
22 Eastman Avenue
Bedford, NH 03110
(603) 623-5300
Contact: Ms. Judy Mulligan
Minimum Salary Placed: $40,000
Recruiting Specialty: Attorneys

Management Recruiters
116-C South River Road
Bedford, NH 03110
(603) 669-9800
Contact: Mr. John Murray
Minimum Salary Placed: $20,000
Recruiting Specialty: General

Sprout/Standish, Inc.
82 Palomino Lane, Suite 503
Bedford, NH 03110
(603) 622-0700
Contact: Mr. Joseph Hunt
Recruiting Specialty: Consumer products

CENTER HARBOR

Barger & Sargeant, Inc.
22 Windermere Road, Suite B
P.O. Box 1420
Center Harbor, NH 03226
(603) 253-4700
Contact: Mr. H. Carter Barger
Minimum Salary Placed: $80,000
Recruiting Specialty: General

DOVER

Individual Employment Services
P.O. Box 917
Dover, NH 03820
(603) 742-5616
Contact: Ms. Anita Labell
Recruiting Specialty: General

DUBLIN

Anthony Executive Search
P.O. Box 320
Dublin, NH 03444
(603) 563-8222
Contact: Mr. Tony Anthony
Minimum Salary Placed: $60,000
Recruiting Specialty: General

EXETER

Bartholdi & Company
14 Douglas Way
Exeter, NH 03833
(603) 772-4228
Contact: Mr. Theodore Bartholdi
Minimum Salary Placed: $70,000
Recruiting Specialty: General but mainly
high technology

HAMPSTEAD

Mullaney Management Resources
61 Picadilly Road
Hampstead, NH 03841
(603) 329-4900
Minimum Salary Placed: $25,000
Recruiting Specialty: Healthcare, some
general

Power Search
472 State Route 111, Unit B
Hampstead, NH 03841
(603) 329-1144
Contact: Mr. Ed Murphy
Recruiting Specialty: Power generation

HAMPTON

Exeter 2100
Computers Park, P.O. Box 2120
Hampton, NH 03842
(603) 926-6712
Contact: Mr. Bruce Montville
Minimum Salary Placed: $50,000
Recruiting Specialty: MIS and computer
networking

HOOKSET

Sales Consultants
1106 Hookset Road
Hookset, NH 03106
(603) 626-8400
Contact: Mr. John Cote
Minimum Salary Placed: $20,000
Recruiting Specialty: Sales

HOPKINTON

Pamela L. Mulligan, Inc.
56 Hopkins Green Road
Hopkinton, NH 03229
(603) 226-2262
Contact: Ms. Pamela Mulligan
Minimum Salary Placed: $50,000
Recruiting Specialty: Healthcare and in-
surance

KEENE

Networking Unlimited of NH, Inc.
67 W. Surry Road, P.O. Box 802
Keene, NH 03431
(603) 357-1918
Contact: Mr. Denis Dubois
Minimum Salary Placed: $50,000
Recruiting Specialty: Healthcare

Gal Friday, Inc.
30 Main Street
Keene, NH 03431
(603) 357-3116
Contact: Ms. Susan Breen
Minimum Salary Placed: $20,000
Recruiting Specialty: Administrative support

MANCHESTER

Access Data Personnel, Inc.
503 Beech Street
Manchester, NH 03104
(603) 641-6300
Contact: Mr. Glen Axne
Minimum Salary Placed: $20,000
Recruiting Specialty: Data processing, MIS, accounting, finance and communications

Baeder Kalinski International Group
45 Bay Street
Manchester, NH 03104
(603) 669-1570
Contact: Dr. Kaliski
Minimum Salary Placed: $50,000
Recruiting Specialty: General

Clayman Management Service
500 N. Commercial Street
Manchester, NH 03101
(603) 644-7800
Contact: Mr. Stan Clayman
Minimum Salary Placed: $25,000
Recruiting Specialty: Sporting goods, footwear, and healthcare

Dunhill of Manchester Inc.
814 Elm Street, Beacon Building
Manchester, NH 03101
(603) 645-6330

Contact: Mr. Jack Schoenfeld
Recruiting Specialty: Finance, banking, insurance and healthcare

Furst Group / MPI
15 Constitution Drive
Bedrod, NY 03110
(603) 472-5100
Recruiting Specialty: General

Zymac & EDA Plus
500 Harvey Road
Manchester, NH 03103
(603) 625-4411
Contact: Mr. B. Maclead
Minimum Salary Placed: $35,000
Recruiting Specialty: EDA and semi-conductors

MERRIMACK

Lloyd Consultants
7 Medallion Center
Merrimack, NH 06054
(603) 424-0020
Contact: Mr. P. Smith
Minimum Salary Placed: $35,000
Recruiting Specialty: High technology, sales and marketing

Sales Consultants
6 Medallion Center, Greeley Street & Route 3
Merrimack, NH 03054
(603) 424-3282
Contact: Mr. Sheldon Baron
Minimum Salary Placed: $20,000
Recruiting Specialty: Sales

NASHUA

Source EDP
71 Spit Brook Road, Suite 205
Nashua, NH 03060
(603) 888-7650
Recruiting Specialty: Computer hardware and software

Source Engineering
71 Spit Brook Road, Suite 305
Nashua, NH 03060
(603) 888-3931
Contact: Mr. Brent Byersi
Recruiting Specialty: Engineering

NEW LONDON

Chaucer Group
40 Acres Road
New London, NH 03257
(603) 526-4299
Contact: Paul
Minimum Salary Placed: $25,000
Recruiting Specialty: General

Linford Stiles Associates
P.O. Box 2577
New London, NH 03257
(603) 735-5330
Contact: Mr. Linford Stiles
Minimum Salary Placed: $60,000
Recruiting Specialty: General

SALEM

High Tech Opportunities, Inc.
264 B North Broadway, Suite 206
Salem, NH 03079
(603) 893-9486
Contact: Mr. Ron Cooper
Minimum Salary Placed: $30,000
Recruiting Specialty: Electronic design automation, semi-conductor and satellite communications

PORTSMOUTH

Career Profiles
44 Market Street, P.O. Box 4430
Portsmouth, NH 03802
(603) 433-3355
Contact: Ms. Leanne Gray
Recruiting Specialty: Sales and marketing in pharmaceuticals and healthcare

RGT Associates Inc.
507 State Street
Portsmouth, NH 03801
(603) 431-9500
Contact: Mr. R. Thiboutot
Minimum Salary Placed: $40,000
Recruiting Specialty: General

Snowden Associates
400 The Hill, Suite 101
Portsmouth, NH 03801
(603) 431-1553
Contact: Mr. G. Vanderveer
Minimum Salary Placed: $75,000
Recruiting Specialty: Healthcare and engineering

N E W J E R S E Y

ABERDEEN

Adel-Lawrence Associates, Inc.
300 Highway 34, Suite 18
Aberdeen, NJ 07747
(908) 566-4914
Contact: Mr. Larry Radzely
Recruiting Specialty: General

ANDOVER

Carris, Jackowitz Associates
Box 54
Andover, NJ 07821
(201) 786-5884
Contact: Mr. Ronald Jackowitz
Minimum Salary Placed: $70,000
Recruiting Specialty: General

AUDUBON

Howard Clark Associates
231 S. White Horse Pike
Audubon, NJ 08106
(609) 467-3725
Contact: Mr. Howard Clark
Minimum Salary Placed: $30,000
Recruiting Specialty: MIS and taxation

Insearch Inc.
231 S. White Horse Pike
Audubon, NJ 08106
(609) 546-6500
Contact: Mr. C. Marcantonio
Minimum Salary Placed: $25,000
Recruiting Specialty: Insurance and hospitality

James F. Robinson
231 S. White Horse Pike
Audubon, NJ 08106
(609) 547-5800
Contact: Mr. Jim Robinson
Minimum Salary Placed: $25,000
Recruiting Specialty: General

AUGUSTA

Accelerated Data Decision, Inc.
P.O. Box 152
Augusta, NJ 07822
(201) 875-8375
Contact: Mr. Walter M. Sullivan
Minimum Salary Placed: $25,000
Recruiting Specialty: Consumer Products

BASKING RIDGE

Oldwick Enterprises, Inc.
P.O. Box 22
Basking Ridge, NJ 07920
(908) 647-4774
Contact: Mr. Eugene Kenny
Minimum Salary Placed: $55,000
Recruiting Specialty: Planning and engineering in construction

BEACH HAVEN

Maschal/Connors Inc.
P.O. Box 1301
Beach Haven, NJ 08008
(609) 492-3400
Contact: Mr. Chuck Maschal
Minimum Salary Placed: $100,000
Recruiting Specialty: Manufacturing

BELVEDERE

Gilbert & Van Campen International
393 Lake Shore Drive
Belvedere, NJ 07823
(908) 475-2222
Contact: Ms. Suzanne Miller
Minimum Salary Placed: $100,000
Recruiting Specialty: General

BERNARDSVILLE

Management Recruiters
10 Anderson Road, Suite 7
Bernardsville, NJ 07924
(908) 204-0070
Contact: Mr. Marlon O'Brien
Minimum Salary Placed: $30,000
Recruiting Specialty: General

Northern Communications Association
36 Orchard Hill Road
Bernardsville, NJ 07924
(908) 766-5600
Recruiting Specialty: General

BLACKWOOD

Kiley-Owen Associates, Inc.
P.O. Box 68
Blackwood, NJ 08012
(609) 227-5332
Contact: Ms. Sheila McGovern
Minimum Salary Placed: $25,000
Recruiting Specialty: General

BOONTON

Price Baker Search
139 Oxford Avenue
Boonton, NJ 07005
(201) 316-8877
Contact: Mr. L. Baker
Minimum Salary Placed: $25,000
Recruiting Specialty: Credit and collections

BORDENTOWN

Management Recruiters
163 Route 130, Building 2—Suite R
Bordentown, NJ 08505
(609) 298-6969
Contact: Mr. Randy Ruschak
Minimum Salary Placed: $35,000
Recruiting Specialty: Insurance risk in environmental and waste operations

BOUND BROOK

Gardner, Savage Associates
Box 430
Bound Brook, NJ 08805
(908) 457-9070
Contact: Mr. Jack Gardner
Minimum Salary Placed: $30,000
Recruiting Specialty: Sales and marketing in diagnostics and medical devices

BRIDGEWATER

T. J. Koellhoffer & Associates
250 Route 28, Suite 206
Bridgewater, NJ 08807
(908) 526-6880
Contact: Mr. Thomas Koellhoffer
Minimum Salary Placed: $50,000
Recruiting Specialty: General

Lakeland Personnel Inc.
1303 Prince Rogers Avenue
Bridgewater, NJ 08807
(908) 685-0303
Contact: Mr. D. Marotto
Recruiting Specialty: General

Sales Consultants Bridgewater, Inc.
1120 Route 22 E.
Bridgewater, NJ 08807
(908) 725-2595
Contact: Mr. David Campeas
Minimum Salary Placed: $20,000
Recruiting Specialty: Sales

BRIELLE

Barclay Consultants, Inc.
201 Union Lane
Brielle, NJ 08730
(908) 223-1131
Contact: Mr. Jules Silverman
Minimum Salary Placed: $30,000
Recruiting Specialty: Computer and high
technology

The Yaiser Group
904 Riverview Drive
Brielle, NJ 08730
(908) 528-0443
Contact: Mr. Richard Yaiser
Minimum Salary Placed: $40,000
Recruiting Specialty: Consumer products
and pharmaceuticals

BUDD LAKE

The Consortium
Village Green, 100 Route 46
Budd Lake, NJ 07828
(201) 347-2747
Contact: Mr. Scott Ream
Minimum Salary Placed: $30,000
Recruiting Specialty: General

CALDWELL

McMahon Associates
26 Westover Avenue
Caldwell, NJ 07006
(201) 226-3888
Contact: Mr. B. McMahon
Minimum Salary Placed: $35,000
Recruiting Specialty: Engineering

CALIFON

Management Recruiters
440 County Road, Suite 513
Califon, NJ 07830
(908) 832-6455
Contact: Ms. Sarah Rodgers
Minimum Salary Placed: $30,000
Recruiting Specialty: General

CEDAR GROVE

Ruderfer & Company
908 Pompton Avenue
Cedar Grove, NJ 07009
(201) 857-2400
Recruiting Specialty: Pharmaceuticals

CEDAR KNOLLS

Paul Falcone Associates, Inc.
14 Ridgedale Avenue, Suite 207
Cedar Knolls, NJ 07927
(201) 984-1010
Contact: Mr. Paul Falcone
Minimum Salary Placed: $50,000
Recruiting Specialty: Sales, marketing
and manufacturing in consumer products

Hayes Associates, Inc.
218 Ridgedale Avenue
Cedar Knolls, NJ 07927
(201) 285-0550
Contact: Mr. J. Robert McCrystal
Minimum Salary Placed: $50,000
Recruiting Specialty: General

Pennmor Group
14 Ridgedale Avenue
Cedar Knolls, NJ 07927
(201) 455-1300
Contact: Mr. R. Jewell
Minimum Salary Placed: $25,000
Recruiting Specialty: General

CHATHAM

Christenson & Hutchison
466 Southern Blvd.
Chatham, NJ 07928
(201) 966-1600

Contact: Mr. H. Alan Christenson
Minimum Salary Placed: $80,000
Recruiting Specialty: General

McCulloch Associates
346 Main Street, P.O. Box 210
Chatham, NJ 07928
(201) 635-6868
Contact: Mr. John Donovan
Minimum Salary Placed: $40,000
Recruiting Specialty: High technology

Scott Executive Search, Inc.
88 Westminster Road, Suite 100
Chatham, NJ 07928
(201) 701-0100
Contact: Ms. E. Ann Scott
Minimum Salary Placed: $60,000
Recruiting Specialty: Consumer prod-
ucts, hospitality and healthcare

Technology Vision Company
30 Stonewyck, Suite 1100
Chatham, NJ 07928
(201) 635-4555
Contact: Mr. Robert Molnar
Minimum Salary Placed: $60,000
Recruiting Specialty: General

CHERRY HILL

Access Resources
1060 Kings Highway North, Suite 653
Cherry Hill, NJ 08034
(609) 779-9077
Recruiting Specialty: Accountants

Accountemps
1950 Route 70 East
Cherry Hill, NJ 08003
(609) 751-8400

Recruiting Specialty: Accounting and finance

ACSYS Resources Inc.
1060 Kings Highway North
Cherry Hill, NJ 08034
(609) 779-9077
Recruiting Specialty: Accounting

The Currier-Winn Company, Inc.
P.O. Box 902
Cherry Hill, NJ 08003
(609) 429-0710
Contact: Mr. Ed Bauzenberger
Minimum Salary Placed: $35,000
Recruiting Specialty: Plastics

Dunhill of Cherry Hill, Inc.
1040 Kings Hwy. N, Suite 400
Cherry Hill, NJ 08034
(609) 667-9180
Contact: Mr. William Emerson
Minimum Salary Placed: $30,000
Recruiting Specialty: General

Executive Healthcare Placement Inc.
1500 N. Kings Highway, Suite 206
Cherry Hill, NJ 08034
(609) 795-4930
Contact: Mr. Steven Rudin
Recruiting Specialty: Healthcare

Dorothy W. Farnath & Associates
5 Pawtucket Drive
Cherry Hill, NJ 08003
(609) 751-1993
Contact: Ms. Dorothy Farnath
Recruiting Specialty: Clinical research

Grant-Franks & Associates
929 N. Kings Highway North
Cherry Hill, NJ 08034
(609) 779-8844
Contact: Ms. Lee Grant
Minimum Salary Placed: $30,000
Recruiting Specialty: General

Ramming & Associates, Inc.
3 Thackery Lane
Cherry Hill, NJ 08003
(609) 428-7172
Contact: Mr. George Ramming
Minimum Salary Placed: $50,000
Recruiting Specialty: General

Romeo-Hudgins & Associates Ltd.
200 Lake Drive E., Suite 206
Cherry Hill, NJ 08002
(609) 482-7840
Contact: Mr. Paul Romeo
Minimum Salary Placed: $60,000
Recruiting Specialty: MIS and human resources in pharmaceuticals

S-H-S International of Cherry Hill
929 N. Kings Highway
Cherry Hill, NJ 08034
(609) 779-9030
Contact: Mr. Lee Grant
Minimum Salary Placed: $20,000
Recruiting Specialty: General

Sales Consultants
800 Kings Highway N., Suite 402
Cherry Hill, NJ 08034
(609) 779-9100
Contact: Mr. Jere Chambers
Minimum Salary Placed: $20,000
Recruiting Specialty: Sales

Worlco Computer Resources, Inc.
901 Route 38
Cherry Hill, NJ 08002
(609) 665-4700
Contact: Mr. Frank Parisi
Minimum Salary Placed: $25,000
Recruiting Specialty: MIS and computers

CINNAMINSON

Careers First Inc.
305 Route 130 N.
Cinnaminson, NJ 08077
(609) 786-0004
Minimum Salary Placed: $25,000
Recruiting Specialty: Computers

CEO Services, Inc.
305 Route 130 North
Cinnaminson, NJ 08077
(609) 786-3334
Contact: Ms. Gail Duncan
Recruiting Specialty: Technical and computers

CLARK

HRD Consultants, Inc.
60 Walnut Avenue
Clark, NJ 07066
(908) 815-7825
Contact: Ms. Marcia Glatman
Minimum Salary Placed: $90,000
Recruiting Specialty: Human resources

Jeff Rich Associates
67 Walnut Avenue, Suite 303
Clark, NJ 07066
(908) 574-3888

Contact: Mr. Richard Thunberg
Minimum Salary Placed: $30,000
Recruiting Specialty: Accounting and finance

ProStaff Personnel
60 Walnut Avenue, Suite 100
Clark, NJ 07066
(908) 815-7839
Contact: Mr. Elliot Jagoda
Minimum Salary Placed: $20,000
Recruiting Specialty: Restaurants

Sales Consultants
181 Westfield Avenue, Suite 2
Clark, NJ 07066
(908) 396-8282
Contact: Mr. Mark Daly
Minimum Salary Placed: $20,000
Recruiting Specialty: Sales

Sherbrooke Associates
727 Raritan Road, Suite 202B
Clark, NJ 07066
(908) 382-5505
Contact: Mr. Jim Scanlon
Minimum Salary Placed: $30,000
Recruiting Specialty: General

CLIFFSIDE PARK

BR & Associates
300 Winston Drive, Suite 3123
Cliffside Park, NJ 07010
(201) 886-2721
Contact: Mr. Dan Andrews
Minimum Salary Placed: $40,000
Recruiting Specialty: MIS in computers and retail

CLIFTON

Data Professionals Unlimited
1634 Main Avenue
Clifton, NJ 07011
(201) 478-9718
Minimum Salary Placed: $25,000
Recruiting Specialty: Data processing

COLONIA

Sherbrooke Associates, Inc.
430 Lake Avenue
Colonia, NJ 07067
(908) 382-5505
Contact: Mr. William Levy
Minimum Salary Placed: $40,000
Recruiting Specialty: General

CONVENT STATION

Binary Search, Inc.
P.O. Box 130
Convent Station, NJ 07961
(201) 993-9270
Contact: Mr. Roy Madsen
Minimum Salary Placed: $40,000
Recruiting Specialty: Information systems and software

CRANBURY

Metanoic Consultants Inc.
37 Main Street
Cranbury, NJ 08512
(609) 395-7617
Minimum Salary Placed: $35,000
Recruiting Specialty: Software systems

Princeton Executive Search
P.O. Box 3
Cranbury, NJ 08512
(609) 655-5070
Contact: Mr. G. Haley
Minimum Salary Placed: $25,000
Recruiting Specialty: General

CRANFORD

G.A. Teachers Agency
524 South Avenue East
Cranford, NJ 07016-3209
(908) 272-2080
Contact: Mr. Randy F. Ring
Minimum Salary Placed: $25,000
Recruiting Specialty: Teaching and education

McCullough Associates
6 Commerce Drive, Suite 2000
Cranford, NJ 07016
(908) 276-2444
Contact: Mr. Kenneth McCullough
Minimum Salary Placed: $50,000
Recruiting Specialty: General

DAYTON

Softrix, Inc.
P.O. Box 937
Dayton, NJ 08810
(908) 274-0073
Contact: Amritha Raj
Minimum Salary Placed: $30,000
Recruiting Specialty: Technical and high technology

DENVILLE

E&K Group
3 McDermott Pass
Denville, NJ 07834
(201) 627-9312
Minimum Salary Placed: $25,000
Recruiting Specialty: General

EAST BRUNSWICK

Blair/Technology Recruiters, Inc.
77 Milltown Road
East Brunswick, NJ 08816
(908) 390-5550
Contact: Mr. Kenneth Rathborne
Minimum Salary Placed: $30,000
Recruiting Specialty: Engineering and science

Career Management
197 State Route 18, Suite 102
East Brunswick, NJ 08816
(908) 937-4800
Contact: Mr. Lloyd Lippman
Minimum Salary Placed: $30,000
Recruiting Specialty: Retail, catalogs and direct mail

Diedre Moire Corporation
579 Cranbury Road
East Brunswick, NJ 08816
(908) 390-8181
Recruiting Specialty: General

Elias Associates, Inc.
P.O. Box 396
East Brunswick, NJ 08816
(908) 390-4600
Contact: Mr. Bill Elias
Recruiting Specialty: General

Royce Ashland Group, Inc.
197 Route 18, Suite 3000
East Brunswick, NJ 08816
(908) 214-2618
Contact: Mr. Ron Cali
Minimum Salary Placed: $30,000
Recruiting Specialty: Printing, publishing, and sales

Vista Associates, Inc.
214 Highway 18
East Brunswick, NJ 08816
(908) 937-6788
Contact: Mr. Bob Jones
Recruiting Specialty: General

Williamsburg Group Inc.
37 Brunswick Woods
East Brunswick, NJ 08816
(908) 651-0404
Contact: Ms. Eileen Levine
Recruiting Specialty: Technical

EAST HANOVER

Arc Medical & Professional Personnel, Inc.
36 Route 10
East Hanover, NJ 07936
(201) 428-0101
Contact: Ms. Tanya Tabak
Minimum Salary Placed: $30,000
Recruiting Specialty: Medical and pharmaceutical research

EAST ORANGE

The Carter-Bingham International Group
44 Glenwood Avenue, Suite 301
East Orange, NJ 07017
(201) 673-6080
Contact: Ms. Marjorie Lee
Minimum Salary Placed: $75,000
Recruiting Specialty: Environmental and utilities

EAST WINDSOR

Personnel Alliance Group
221 Probasco Road
East Windsor, NJ 08520
(609) 443-5761
Contact: Mr. Alan Brown
Minimum Salary Placed: $30,000
Recruiting Specialty: Finance, accounting and environmental disciplines in environmental and hazardous waste

EATONTOWN

Snelling Personnel Service
142 Highway 35, Suite 202
Eatontown, NJ 07724
(908) 389-0300
Contact: Mr. F. Wyckoff
Minimum Salary Placed: $25,000
Recruiting Specialty: General

EDISON

Accountants On Call/Accountants Executive Search
379 Thornall Street
Edison, NJ 08837
(908) 906-1100
Contact: Ms. A. Cannon
Minimum Salary Placed: $25,000
Recruiting Specialty: Accounting

The Altco Group
100 Menlo Park
Edison, NJ 08839
(908) 549-6100
Contact: Mr. Ken Altreuter
Minimum Salary Placed: $35,000
Recruiting Specialty: Consumer packaged goods and medical device

The Cittone Group
1697 Oak Tree Road
Edison, NJ 08820-2896
(908) 548-9810
Contact: Ms. Laura Friedman
Recruiting Specialty: General

A. Davis Grant & Company
295 Pierson Avenue
Edison, NJ 08837
(908) 636-1300
Recruiting Specialty: MIS and high technology

Fortune of Menlo Park
100 Menlo Park, Suite 206
Edison, NJ 08837
(908) 494-6266
Contact: Mr. P. Provda
Minimum Salary Placed: $25,000
Recruiting Specialty: Engineering, data processing, pharmaceuticals and chemicals

Joan Leslie Personnel Inc.
100 Menlo Park, Suite 314
Edison, NJ 08837
(908) 494-6650
Contact: Ms. Barbara Falk
Minimum Salary Placed: $25,000
Recruiting Specialty: General

Martin Personnel Services, Inc.
858 US Highway 1
Edison, NJ 08817
(908) 287-3311
Recruiting Specialty: Accounting and finance

Metro Plus Executive Search
85 State Route 27
Edison, NJ 08820
(908) 321-9300
Recruiting Specialty: Medical

Northeastern Financial Inc.
1163 Inman Avenue
Edison, NJ 08820
(908) 321-4007
Contact: Ms. Terry Michaels
Minimum Salary Placed: $25,000
Recruiting Specialty: Finance and banking

Shifrin-Fischer Group/Healthcare
379 Thornall Street
Edison, NJ 08837
(908) 548-9600
Contact: Mr. M. Fischer
Minimum Salary Placed: $25,000
Recruiting Specialty: General

Source EDP
379 Thornall Street, 3rd Floor
Edison, NJ 08837
(908) 494-2800
Recruiting Specialty: Computers

Source Finance
379 Thornall Street, 3rd Floor
Edison, NJ 08837
(908) 494-2060
Contact: Mr. Ramon Menendez
Minimum Salary Placed: $25,000
Recruiting Specialty: Finance and accounting

Tenax, Inc.
250 Carter Drive
Edison, NJ 08817
(908) 248-8334
Contact: Bill
Minimum Salary Placed: $25,000
Recruiting Specialty: Environmental, computer and electronics, office support

EMERSON

Bryant Research
466 Old Hook Road, Suite 32
Emerson, NJ 07630
(201) 599-0590
Contact: Mr. Tom Bryant
Minimum Salary Placed: $50,000
Recruiting Specialty: Technical disciplines in pharmaceuticals and healthcare

ENGLEWOOD

Anderson Wright Associates
50 E. Palisade Avenue
Englewood, NJ 07631
(201) 567-8080
Contact: Mr. Donald Anderson
Minimum Salary Placed: $30,000
Recruiting Specialty: Banking, pharmaceuticals and finance

ENGLEWOOD CLIFFS

Phyllis Solomon Executive Search, Inc.
120 Sylvan Avenue
Englewood Cliffs, NJ 07632
(201) 947-8600
Contact: Ms. Phyllis Solomon
Minimum Salary Placed: $40,000
Recruiting Specialty: Pharmaceutical

SkuppSearch, Inc.
580 Sylvan Avenue
Englewood Cliffs, NJ 07024
(201) 894-1824
Contact: Ms. Holly Skupp
Minimum Salary Placed: $40,000
Recruiting Specialty: Technical communications

The Stevenson Group, Inc.
560 Sylvan Avenue
Englewood Cliffs, NJ 07632
(201) 568-1900
Contact: Mr. Stephen Steiman
Minimum Salary Placed: $70,000
Recruiting Specialty: General

ENGLISHTOWN

Stewart/Laurence Associates, Inc.
P.O. Box 1156
Englishtown, NJ 07726
(908) 972-8000
Contact: Mr. Mel Stewart
Minimum Salary Placed: $60,000
Recruiting Specialty: General

FAIR LAWN

Harris Executive Search
18-00 Fair Lawn Avenue
Fair Lawn, NJ 07410
(201) 703-1414
Contact: Mr. Harris Tokayer
Minimum Salary Placed: $40,000
Recruiting Specialty: Engineering and manufacturing

FAIRFIELD

The Consortium
277 Fairfield Road
Fairfield, NJ 07004
(201) 882-7725
Contact: Mr. Barry Meyers
Minimum Salary Placed: $30,000
Recruiting Specialty: General

Eagle Research, Inc.
30 Two Bridges Road, Suite 330
Fairfield, NJ 07004
(201) 244-0992
Contact: Ms. Annette Baron
Recruiting Specialty: Physicians for pharmaceutical industry

Phoenix Bio Search, Inc.
202 Fairfield Road
Fairfield, NJ 07004
(201) 812-2666
Recruiting Specialty: Biotechnology

Razzino-Claymore Associates
277 Fairfield Road, Suite 332
Fairfield, NJ 07004
(201) 882-3388

Contact: Ms. Janelle Razzino
Minimum Salary Placed: $35,000
Recruiting Specialty: Financial

Retail Pacesetters, Inc.
271 Route 46 W., Suite D105
Fairfield, NJ 07004
(201) 882-0303
Contact: Ms. Mindy Bell
Minimum Salary Placed: $15,000
Recruiting Specialty: Retail

Sales Consultants
271 Route 46 W., Suite 205, Building A
Fairfield, NJ 07006
(201) 227-8292
Contact: Mr. Charles Seminerio
Minimum Salary Placed: $20,000
Recruiting Specialty: Sales

FANWOOD

Engineering & Scientific Search Associates
P.O. Box 14
Fanwood, NJ 07023
(908) 889-7828
Contact: Mr. Steve Skaar
Minimum Salary Placed: $25,000
Recruiting Specialty: Technical and manufacturing in drugs, chemicals, materials and consumer products

Peeney Associates, Inc.
141 South Avenue
Fanwood, NJ 07023
(908) 322-2324
Contact: Mr. James Peeney
Minimum Salary Placed: $50,000
Recruiting Specialty: General

FAR HILLS

Intelegra, Inc.
P.O. Box 505
Far Hills, NJ 07931
(908) 876-5900
Contact: Mr. John Palmer
Minimum Salary Placed: $40,000
Recruiting Specialty: Technical disciplines and marketing in MIS and computers

FLANDERS

The Comwell Company, Inc.
227 Route 206
Flanders, NJ 07836
(201) 927-9400
Contact: Mr. John Sobecki
Minimum Salary Placed: $75,000
Recruiting Specialty: General

Permian International, Inc.
227 Route 206, 3rd Floor, Building One
Flanders, NJ 07836
(201) 927-7373
Contact: Mr. Don Marletta
Minimum Salary Placed: $40,000
Recruiting Specialty: Outplacement and marketing

FLORHAM PARK

Frank E. Allen & Associates
15 James Street
Florham Park, NJ 07932
(201) 966-1606
Contact: Mr. Frank Allen
Minimum Salary Placed: $45,000
Recruiting Specialty: Human resources

The Corporate Advisory Group, Inc.
256 Columbia Turnpike, Suite 101
Florham Park, NJ 07932
(201) 377-2466
Contact: Mr. Roy Nunn
Minimum Salary Placed: $100,000
Recruiting Specialty: General

The Foster McKay Group
30 Vreeland Road
Florham Park, NJ 07932
(201) 966-0909
Contact: Mr. Daniel Jarvis
Recruiting Specialty: Accounting and finance

Hadley Associates
147 Columbia Turnpike, Suite 104
Florham Park, NJ 07932
(201) 377-9177
Contact: Mr. Thomas Hadley
Recruiting Specialty: Pharmaceuticals and biotechnology

FORDS

Cella Associates Inc.
720 King Georges Post Road, Suite 1A
Fords, NJ 08863
(908) 738-8989
Contact: Mr. G. Sassone
Minimum Salary Placed: $25,000
Recruiting Specialty: General

Datamatics Management Services, Inc.
330 New Brunswick Avenue
Fords, NJ 08863
(908) 738-9600
Contact: Mr. Norman Heinle
Minimum Salary Placed: $20,000
Recruiting Specialty: General

FORT LEE

Career Works
520 Main Street, Suite 203
Fort Lee, NJ 07024
(201) 592-1460
Minimum Salary Placed: $25,000
Recruiting Specialty: General

Brooks Executive Personnel, Inc.
2337 Lemoine Avenue
Fort Lee, NJ 07024
(201) 585-7200
Contact: Mr. Marty Kay
Recruiting Specialty: General

Donna Davis Associates
530 Main Street, Suite 4
Fort Lee, NJ 07024
(201) 592-6000
Contact: Ms. Donna Davis
Minimum Salary Placed: $40,000
Recruiting Specialty: Human resources and marketing

Devin Scott Associates
2125 Center Avenue, Suite 402
Fort Lee, NJ 07024
(201) 346-0331
Contact: Mr. Rocco Fedele
Minimum Salary Placed: $50,000
Recruiting Specialty: Hospitality and retail

Haley Stuart, Inc.
1605 John Street
Fort Lee, NJ 07024
(201) 944-7777
Contact: Ms. Cindi Crepea
Minimum Salary Placed: $20,000
Recruiting Specialty: Legal

FREEHOLD

Donaldson
4400 US Highway 9
Freehold, NJ 07728
(908) 308-1005
Contact: Mr. Sol Donaldson
Recruiting Specialty: Cosmetics, pharmaceuticals in cosmetics, chemicals

Dunhill of Freehold, Inc.
303 W. Main Street
Freehold, NJ 07728
(908) 431-2700
Contact: Mr. Gary Livingston
Minimum Salary Placed: $30,000
Recruiting Specialty: General

GIBBSBORO

Cox, Darrow and Owens Inc.
6 Clementon Road East
Gibbsboro, NJ 08026
(609) 782-1300
Contact: Mr. Bill Cox
Minimum Salary Placed: $25,000
Recruiting Specialty: General

Fab Associates
146 Lakeview Drive South
Gibbsboro, NJ 08026
(609) 783-7361
Minimum Salary Placed: $25,000
Recruiting Specialty: Insurance and computer

Alan Lerner Associates
400 Lakeview Commons, Suite 400
Gibbsboro, NJ 08026
(609) 435-1600
Contact: Mr. Jeff Senges
Minimum Salary Placed: $20,000
Recruiting Specialty: Retail

GLEN ROCK

Gary S. Bell Associates, Inc.
55 Harristown Road
Glen Rock, NJ 07452
(201) 670-4900
Contact: Mr. Gary Bell
Minimum Salary Placed: $50,000
Recruiting Specialty: Manufacturing in consumer products

Brunkmeyer Group
190 South Highwood Avenue
Glen Rock, NJ 07452
(201) 670-4640
Contact: Ms. Jan Meyer
Minimum Salary Placed: $50,000
Recruiting Specialty: General

Healthcare Recruiters
55 Harristown Road
Glen Rock, NJ 07452
(201) 670-9800
Contact: Mr. H. Conant
Minimum Salary Placed: $25,000
Recruiting Specialty: Healthcare

Sales Consultants of Northern Jersey, Inc.
139 Harristown Road
Glen Rock, NJ 07452
(201) 444-9400
Contact: Mr. William Soodsma
Minimum Salary Placed: $20,000
Recruiting Specialty: Sales

GREEN BROOK

Personnel Associates, Inc.
239 Route 22 East
Green Brook, NJ 08812
(908) 968-8866
Contact: Mr. Thomas Wood
Minimum Salary Placed: $35,000
Recruiting Specialty: Computers

Trac One
239 Route 22 E.
Green Brook, NJ 08812
(908) 968-1600
Contact: Mr. Thomas Wood
Minimum Salary Placed: $50,000
Recruiting Specialty: MIS

HACKENSACK

ABC Employment Inc.
241 Main Street
Hackensack, NJ 07601
(201) 487-5515
Contact: Ms. Kelly Jones
Minimum Salary Placed: $25,000
Recruiting Specialty: General

Career Center, Inc.
194 Passaic Street
Hackensack, NJ 07601
(201) 342-1777
Contact: Mr. Barry Franzino, Jr.
Minimum Salary Placed: $20,000
Recruiting Specialty: General

Robert Drexler Associates, Inc.
210 River Street
Hackensack, NJ 07601
(201) 342-0200
Contact: Mr. Robert Drexler
Minimum Salary Placed: $50,000
Recruiting Specialty: Technical disciplines

Garden State Personnel
540 Hudson Street
Hackensack, NJ 07607
(201) 440-6400
Contact: Ms. Marie Laine
Minimum Salary Placed: $30,000
Recruiting Specialty: Healthcare

HADDONFIELD

David Allen Associates
Box 56
Haddonfield, NJ 08033
(609) 795-6470
Contact: Mr. David Ritching
Minimum Salary Placed: $50,000
Recruiting Specialty: General

Management Recruiters
19 Tanner Street
Haddonfield, NJ 08033
(609) 428-2233
Contact: Mr. Roy Kelly
Minimum Salary Placed: $30,000
Recruiting Specialty: General

HARRINGTON PARK

Seco & Zetto Associates, Inc.
P.O. Box 225
Harrington Park, NJ 07640
(201) 784-0674
Contact: Mr. William Seco
Minimum Salary Placed: $75,000
Recruiting Specialty: Information technology

HASBROUCK HEIGHTS

Carter/MacKay
777 Terrace Avenue
Hasbrouck Heights, NJ 07604
(201) 288-5100
Contact: Mr. Bruce Green
Recruiting Specialty: Sales in healthcare

JSP Personnel, Inc.
500 Route 17 South
Hasbrouck Heights, NJ 07604
(201) 393-9800
Contact: Ms. Jill A. Petrozzini
Recruiting Specialty: General

HAZLET

Norm Sanders Associates, Inc.
2 Village Court
Hazlet, NJ 07730
(908) 264-3700
Contact: Mr. Norman Sanders
Minimum Salary Placed: $25,000
Recruiting Specialty: MIS and FIS

HIGH BRIDGE

J.M. Joseph Associates
P.O. Box 104
High Bridge, NJ 08829
(908) 638-6877
Contact: Mr. C. Russell Ditzel
Minimum Salary Placed: $40,000
Recruiting Specialty: Data processing

HIGHTSTOWN

Personnel Alliance Group
221 Probasco Road
Hightstown, NJ 08520
(609) 443-5761
Contact: Mr. Alan Brown
Minimum Salary Placed: $30,000
Recruiting Specialty: Environmental

Simon Associates Inc.
897 U.S. Highway 130 North
Hightstown, NJ 08520
(609) 426-4370
Contact: Mr. J. Simon
Minimum Salary Placed: $25,000
Recruiting Specialty: MIS

HILLSDALE

Performance Professionals
P.O. Box 301
Hillside, NJ 07205
(908) 351-2653
Contact: Mr. Caesar Ferrara
Minimum Salary Placed: $35,000
Recruiting Specialty: General

HOBOKEN

Florence Pape Legal Search, Inc.
1208 Washington Street
Hoboken, NJ 07030
(201) 798-0200
Contact: Ms. Florence Pape
Minimum Salary Placed: $50,000
Recruiting Specialty: Attorneys

Sales Consultants
2 Hudson Place, Baker Building
Hoboken, NJ 07030
(201) 659-5205
Contact: Mr. Richard Sinay
Minimum Salary Placed: $20,000
Recruiting Specialty: Sales

HOPE

Management Recruiters of North Warren Inc.
Route 519 American House Annex
Box 244
Hope, NJ 07844
(908) 459-5798
Contact: Mr. Henry Magnusen
Minimum Salary Placed: $25,000
Recruiting Specialty: Human Resources

HOPEWELL

Capital Management Consulting, Inc.
114 Hopewell-Lambertville Road
Hopewell, NJ 08525
(609) 466-2822
Contact: Mr. Joseph Kowalski
Minimum Salary Placed: $30,000
Recruiting Specialty: General

HOWELL TOWNSHIP

William Bell Associates
605 Candlewood Commons
Howell Township, NJ 07731
(908) 901-6000
Recruiting Specialty: Pharmaceuticals in cosmetics and cosmetics

D.M. Rein & Company, Inc.
4599 Highway Nine, N.
Howell Township, NJ 07731
(908) 367-3300
Contact: Mr. David Rein
Minimum Salary Placed: $75,000
Recruiting Specialty: General

ISELIN

Allen Associates, Inc. of N.J.
33 Wood Avenue South, Suite 600
Iselin, NJ 08830
(908) 549-7555
Contact: Ms. Amy Regan
Recruiting Specialty: General

Battalia Winston International, Inc.
120 Wood Avenue S, Suite 300
Iselin, NJ 08830
(908) 549-2002
Contact: Mr. Terence Gallagher
Minimum Salary Placed: $75,000
Recruiting Specialty: General

Clark Davis Associates
120 Wood Avenue S.
Iselin, NJ 08830
(908) 548-1127
Minimum Salary Placed: $25,000
Recruiting Specialty: Accounting, engineering and data processing

The Fourbes Group, Inc.
1030 Saint George Avenue, Suite 300
Iselin, NJ 08830
(908) 855-7722
Contact: Ms. Suzanne Burgey
Recruiting Specialty: General

Arlene Gold Associates
120 Wood Avenue South, Suite 300
Iselin, NJ 08830
(908) 906-6685
Contact: Ms. Arlene Gold
Minimum Salary Placed: $25,000
Recruiting Specialty: MIS

The Kleinstein Group, Inc.
33 Wood Avenue, S.
Iselin, NJ 08830
(908) 494-7500
Contact: Mr. Jonah Kleinstein
Minimum Salary Placed: $60,000
Recruiting Specialty: General

Sales Consultants
458A Route 1 South
Iselin, NJ 08830
(908) 750-9696
Contact: Mr. Harris Cohen
Minimum Salary Placed: $20,000
Recruiting Specialty: Sales

JERSEY CITY

Aries Group
89 Mercer Street
Jersey City, NJ 07302
(201) 333-0320
Contact: Ms. Mia Scanga
Recruiting Specialty: Accounting and finance

Dalton Management Consultants, Ltd.
327 Grove Street, Suite 279
Jersey City, NJ 07302
(201) 309-2351
Contact: Ms. Evonne Dalton
Minimum Salary Placed: $50,000
Recruiting Specialty: Human resources

Questar Corporation
247 Montgomery Street
Jersey City, NJ 07302
(201) 451-8376
Minimum Salary Placed: $25,000
Recruiting Specialty: Data processing, engineering and computers

KINNELON

Brentwood Group, Inc.
170 Kinnelon Road, Suite 29B
Kinnelon, NJ 07405
(201) 283-1000
Contact: Ms. Doris Osenni
Recruiting Specialty: General

LAFAYETTE

Management Recruiters
Box 54, Olde Lafayette Village
Lafayette, NJ 07848
(201) 579-7688
Contact: Mr. Gary Chiusano
Minimum Salary Placed: $30,000
Recruiting Specialty: General

LANDING

George Cromwell & Company
143 Lake Side Boulevard
Landing, NJ 07850
(201) 398-2700
Contact: Mr. Dick Shafer
Recruiting Specialty: Pharmaceuticals

LAWRENCEVILLE

Carnegie Group
2 Carnegie Road
Lawrenceville, NJ 08648
(609) 883-5100
Contact: Mr. W. Hogan
Minimum Salary Placed: $25,000
Recruiting Specialty: Pharmaceuticals
and computer sales

Pat Lipton and Associates
993 Lexox Drive, Suite 101
Lawrenceville, NJ 08648
(609) 452-0049
Contact: Ms. Pat Lipton
Minimum Salary Placed: $25,000
Recruiting Specialty: Marketing, sales
and advertising

Woldoff Associates, Ltd.
3371 Route One, Suite 214
Lawrenceville, NJ 08648
(609) 452-1117
Contact: Mr. William Woldof
Recruiting Specialty: Finance and accounting

LITTLE SILVER

Allen Thomas Associates
518 Prospect Avenue
Little Silver, NJ 07739
(908) 219-5353
Contact: Mr. T. Benoit
Minimum Salary Placed: $25,000
Recruiting Specialty: Healthcare

Graham & Company
34 Sycamore Avenue, Building 2E
Little Silver, NJ 07739
(908) 747-8000
Contact: Mr. Harold Scott
Minimum Salary Placed: $50,000
Recruiting Specialty: General

LIVINGSTON

Accountants Executive Search
354 Eisenhower Parkway
Livingston, NJ 07039
(201) 992-6900
Contact: Mr. Stuart Libes
Minimum Salary Placed: $25,000
Recruiting Specialty: Accounting

Accountants On Call
354 Eisenhower Parkway
Livingston, NJ 07039
(201) 533-0600
Contact: Ms. Rita Silverstein
Recruiting Specialty: Accounting

Law Pros Legal Placement Services, Inc.
107 E. Mt. Pleasant Avenue, Suite 105
Livingston, NJ 07039
(201) 535-8446
Contact: Beth Fleischer
Minimum Salary Placed: $20,000
Recruiting Specialty: Paralegals

Management Recruiters
7 Regent Street, Suite 708
Livingston, NJ 07039
(201) 994-9300
Contact: Ms. Joanne Jamison
Minimum Salary Placed: $30,000
Recruiting Specialty: General

LONG VALLEY

Bonner Group
59 East Mill Road
Long Valley, NJ 17853
(908) 876-5200
Contact: Mr. Bernard Bonner
Minimum Salary Placed: $35,000
Recruiting Specialty: Pharmaceuticals

Technitrac Inc.
16 Coleman Road
Long Valley, NJ 07853
(908) 876-3000
Recruiting Specialty: Heavy rotating
equipment and technical

MADISON

Joseph R. Burns & Associates, Inc.
2 Shunpike Road
Madison, NJ 07940
(201) 377-1350
Contact: Mr. Joseph Burns
Minimum Salary Placed: $70,000
Recruiting Specialty: General

Karras Personnel, Inc.
2 Central Avenue
Madison, NJ 07940
(201) 966-6800
Contact: Mr. Bill Karras
Minimum Salary Placed: $20,000
Recruiting Specialty: Human resources

Parker Clark Data Processing, Inc.
14 Main Street
Madison, NJ 07940
(201) 822-2657

Contact: Mr. Ralph Clark
Minimum Salary Placed: $30,000
Recruiting Specialty: Data processing
and MIS

MAHWAH

Butterfass, Pepe & MacCallan Inc.
P.O. Box 721
Mahwah, NJ 07430
(201) 512-3330
Contact: Mr. Stanley Butterfass
Minimum Salary Placed: $50,000
Recruiting Specialty: Financial Services

MANALAPAN

The Garret Group
P.O. Box 661
Manalapan, NJ 07726
(908) 972-0792
Contact: Mr. James Finn
Minimum Salary Placed: $50,000
Recruiting Specialty: Engineering and
product development in consumer prod-
ucts

MANASQUAN

R. W. Apple & Associates
200 Atlantic Avenue, Box 200
Manasquan, NJ 08736
(908) 223-4305
Contact: Mr. Richard Apple
Minimum Salary Placed: $30,000
Recruiting Specialty: Engineering in envi-
ronmental

Carr Consultants
2517 Highway 35, Building F, Suite 101
Manasquan, NJ 08736
(908) 223-4044
Contact: Ms. Lois S. Carr
Minimum Salary Placed: $30,000
Recruiting Specialty: Medical and electronics

Executive Exchange Corporation
2517 Hwy. 35 G-103
Manasquan, NJ 08736
(908) 223-6655
Contact: Ms. Elizabeth Glosser
Recruiting Specialty: Data processing, MIS and computer

The Mulshine Company, Inc.
2517 Route 35, Suite D-201
Manasquan, NJ 08736
(908) 528-8585
Contact: Mr. Michael Mulshine
Minimum Salary Placed: $50,000
Recruiting Specialty: General

MARLTON

Accountants On Call
1 Eves Dr., Suite 101
Marlton, NJ 08053
(609) 596-9200
Contact: Mr. Mark Libes
Recruiting Specialty: Accounting

Agnew and Gravatt Inc.
8000 Lincoln Drive East
Marlton, NJ 08053
(609) 985-7400
Contact: Mr. John Agnew
Minimum Salary Placed: $40,000
Recruiting Specialty: Banking

Bonifield Associates
3003E Lincoln Drive West
Marlton, NJ 08053
(609) 596-3300
Contact: Mr. Len Bonifield
Minimum Salary Placed: $50,000
Recruiting Specialty: Banking and insurance

DVA
P.O. Box 549
Marlton, NJ 08053
(609) 985-1018
Contact: Ms. Helen DiVincenzo
Minimum Salary Placed: $25,000
Recruiting Specialty: Food manufacturing

Healthcare Recruiters International
3 Eves Drive
Marlton, NJ 08053
(609) 596-7179
Contact: Mr. Frank Osamelia
Recruiting Specialty: Healthcare

Management Recruiters
108-D Centre Blvd.
Marlton, NJ 08053
(609) 983-7070
Contact: Mr. Fred Hollander
Minimum Salary Placed: $30,000
Recruiting Specialty: General

Mid-Atlantic Management Group
309 N. Route 73
Marlton, NJ 08053
(609) 234-8725
Minimum Salary Placed: $25,000
Recruiting Specialty: General

Perry Temps
525 Route 73 South, Suite 201
Marlton, NJ 08053
(609) 596-9400
Contact: Mr. R. Spadaro
Recruiting Specialty: General

MATAWAN

E & A Associates
1070-E Highway 34, Suite 194
Matawan, NJ 07747
(908) 739-6222
Contact: Mr. Allan Adelson
Minimum Salary Placed: $35,000
Recruiting Specialty: Technical and engineering

N. Willner & Company, Inc.
P.O. Box 746
Matawan, NJ 07747
(908) 566-8882
Contact: Mr. Nathaniel Willner
Minimum Salary Placed: $50,000
Recruiting Specialty: Sales, marketing and advertising

MAYWOOD

Able Careers
240 W. Passaic Street
Maywood, NJ 07607
(201) 845-7771
Contact: Fran and Leib
Recruiting Specialty: General

The DataFinders Group, Inc.
25 Spring Valley Avenue
Maywood, NJ 07607
(201) 845-7700

Contact: Mr. Thomas Credidio
Minimum Salary Placed: $25,000
Recruiting Specialty: MIS and computers in high technology

Randt Associates
19 E. Forest Avenue
Maywood, NJ 07607
(201) 843-8008
Minimum Salary Placed: $25,000
Recruiting Specialty: General

The Zaccaria Group, Inc.
25 East Spring Valley Avenue
Maywood, NJ 07607
(201) 712-0070
Contact: Ms. Frances Zaccaria
Minimum Salary Placed: $40,000
Recruiting Specialty: Retailing and marketing

MEDFORD

The Addison Consulting Group
12 Strafford Circle Road
Medford, NJ 08055
(609) 953-7650
Contact: Mr. Sandy Korkuch
Minimum Salary Placed: $50,000
Recruiting Specialty: Pharmaceuticals and biotechnology

Associated Business Consultants
43 North Main Street
Medford, NJ 08055
(609) 953-8600
Minimum Salary Placed: $50,000
Recruiting Specialty: Pharmaceuticals and medical

Best Resources
30 Jackson Road
Medford, NJ 08055
(609) 654-1166
Contact: Mr. Joe Silverstein
Minimum Salary Placed: $25,000
Recruiting Specialty: General

Dunhill Search
520 Stokes Road, Suite B-11
Medford, NJ 08055
(609) 953-1515
Contact: Mr. Karl Fischer
Minimum Salary Placed: $30,000
Recruiting Specialty: General

Jenkins Associates Ltd.
22 South Lakeside Drive West
Medford, NJ 08055
(609) 953-3900
Minimum Salary Placed: $25,000
Recruiting Specialty: General

Management Recruiters
520 Stokes Road, Building A
Medford, NJ 08055
(609) 654-9109
Contact: Mr. Norman Talbot
Recruiting Specialty: Consumer products

METUCHEN

PROsource, Inc.
P.O. Box 4708
Metuchen, NJ 08840
(908) 549-2511
Contact: Toni Sowinski
Minimum Salary Placed: $30,000
Recruiting Specialty: Technical and science

MILFORD

A.L.S. Group
104 Mt. Joy Road
Milford, NJ 08848
(908) 995-9500
Contact: Mr. Scott Lysenko
Minimum Salary Placed: $35,000
Recruiting Specialty: General

MILLBURN

Marra/Pizzi Associates, Inc.
Millburn Esplanade
Millburn, NJ 07041
(201) 376-8999
Contact: Mr. John Marra
Minimum Salary Placed: $70,000
Recruiting Specialty: General

MILLTOWN

LRB Associates Inc.
440 S. Main Street
Milltown, NJ 08850
(908) 238-4610
Contact: Mr. L. Barbato
Minimum Salary Placed: $40,000
Recruiting Specialty: Engineering

MONMOUTH BEACH

Hartman & Barnette
P.O. Box 190
Monmouth, NJ 07750
(908) 870-3232
Contact: Mr. Fred Barnette
Minimum Salary Placed: $70,000
Recruiting Specialty: Pharmaceuticals

MONTCLAIR

DHR International, Inc.
560 Valley Road
Montclair, NJ 07043
(201) 746-2100
Recruiting Specialty: General

Drew Associates International
77 Park Street
Montclair, NJ 07042
(201) 746-8877
Contact: Mr. Robert Detore
Minimum Salary Placed: 60,000
Recruiting Specialty: Healthcare

Foster Associates
209 Cooper Avenue
Montclair, NJ 07043
(201) 746-2800
Contact: Mr. Donald Foster
Recruiting Specialty: General

MONTVILLE

Search EDP
150 River Road, Building C, Suite 3
Montville, NJ 07045
(201) 335-6600
Contact: Mr. J. Hauser
Minimum Salary Placed: $25,000
Recruiting Specialty: Telecommunications

J. Vincent Associates
150 River Road, Building C, Suite 4A
Montville, NJ 07045
(201) 334-5900
Contact: Mr. D. Caporusso
Minimum Salary Placed: $25,000
Recruiting Specialty: Accounting and finance

MOORESTOWN

Lawrence Glaser Associates Inc.
505 S. Lenola Road
Moorestown, NJ 08057
(609) 778-9500
Contact: Mr. Lawrence Glaser
Minimum Salary Placed: $25,000
Recruiting Specialty: Sales and marketing, and general

Recruitment Alternatives Inc.
214 W. Main Street
Moorestown, NJ 08057
(609) 273-1066
Minimum Salary Placed: $35,000
Recruiting Specialty: Human resources

MORGANVILLE

LAS Management Consulting Group, Inc.
23 Kilmer Drive, Suite G, Building 1
Morganville, NJ 07751
(908) 972-8800
Contact: Mr. Philip Salvatore
Minimum Salary Placed: $40,000
Recruiting Specialty: Information systems, audit, and security

MORRIS PLAINS

Access Systems
101 Gibraltar Drive, Suite 2C
Morris Plains, NJ 07950
(201) 984-7960
Contact: Ms. J. Palzer
Minimum Salary Placed: $25,000
Recruiting Specialty: General

Ballos & Company, Inc.
45 Fieldstone Drive
Morris Plains, NJ 07950
(201) 538-4609
Contact: Ms. Constantine J. Ballos
Minimum Salary Placed: $80,000
Recruiting Specialty: General

Martin F. Hass & Associates
30 Pondview Road
Morris Plains, NJ 07950
(201) 540-8729
Contact: Mr. Martin Hass
Minimum Salary Placed: $60,000
Recruiting Specialty: General

McDermott Resources, Inc.
74 South Powder Mill Road
Morris Plains, NJ 07950
(201) 285-0066
Contact: Ms. Maureen McDermott
Minimum Salary Placed: $20,000
Recruiting Specialty: Banking

MORRISTOWN

Boyden
55 Madison Avenue, Suite 400
Morristown, NJ 07960
(201) 267-0980
Contact: Mr. Peter Schmidt
Minimum Salary Placed: $90,000
Recruiting Specialty: General

Kate Carter Employment Services, Inc.
55 Madison Avenue, Suite 200
Morristown, NJ 07960
(201) 267-6776

Contact: Ms. Kate Carter
Minimum Salary Placed: $35,000
Recruiting Specialty: Consumer product
sales and marketing in supermarket industry

Corporate Search
35 Airport Road
Morristown, NJ 07960
(201) 540-0850
Recruiting Specialty: Data processing
and MIS

Executive Search Inc.
48 Headquarters Plaza
Morristown, NJ 07960
(908) 906-8000
Contact: Ms. Debbie Baseil
Minimum Salary Placed: $25,000
Recruiting Specialty: General

Foley/Proctor Associates
1 Cattano Avenue
Morristown, NJ 07960
(201) 605-1000
Contact: Mr. Thomas J. Foley
Minimum Salary Placed: $50,000
Recruiting Specialty: Healthcare

I.E. Associates, Inc.
60 Washington Street
Morristown, NJ 07960
(201) 538-1900
Contact: Ms. Irene Eisgrau Goldstoff
Minimum Salary Placed: $50,000
Recruiting Specialty: Biopharmaceutical

Joseph Lynder
55 Madison Avenue
Morristown, NJ 07960
(201) 829-1011

Minimum Salary Placed: $25,000
Recruiting Specialty: Medical and health-care

Management Recruiters
42 Court Street
Morristown, NJ 07960
(201) 984-0700
Contact: Ms. Susan Young
Minimum Salary Placed: $30,000
Recruiting Specialty: General

Skott/Edwards Consultants
1776 On The Green
Morristown, NJ 07960
(201) 935-8000
Contact: Mr. Skott Burkland
Minimum Salary Placed: $75,000
Recruiting Specialty: Pharmaceuticals
and biotechnology

Trout Associates Inc.
31 South Street
Morristown, NJ 07960
(201) 984-9030
Minimum Salary Placed: $25,000
Recruiting Specialty: General

MOUNT LAUREL

ASL and Associates
3111 Route 38, Suite 202
Mount Laurel, NJ 08054
(609) 231-1400
Contact: Mr. R. Jibboni
Minimum Salary Placed: $40,000
Recruiting Specialty: Engineering and
systems in high technology

Scientific Search, Inc.
560 Fellowship Road, Suite 309
Mount Laurel, NJ 08054
(609) 866-0200
Recruiting Specialty: Data processing
and medical

MOUNTAIN LAKES

Besen Associates Inc.
115 Route 46 W., Building C-21
Mountain Lakes, NJ 07046
(201) 334-5533
Contact: Mr. Douglas Besen
Minimum Salary Placed: $45,000
Recruiting Specialty: Consumer prod-
ucts, pharmaceuticals, and OTC

Managing Partners Inc.
43 W. Shore Road
Mountain Lakes, NJ 07046
(201) 263-1038
Contact: Mr. C. Ahlemeyer
Minimum Salary Placed: $25,000
Recruiting Specialty: Data processing

Orion Consulting, Inc.
115 Route 46, Building B, Suite 13/14
Mountain Lakes, NJ 07046
(201) 402-8866
Contact: Mr. James Dromsky
Minimum Salary Placed: $45,000
Recruiting Specialty: General

Stevens MB
420 Boulevard
Mountain Lakes, NJ 07046
(201) 316-0218
Minimum Salary Placed: $25,000
Recruiting Specialty: General

MOUNTAINSIDE

Management Recruiters
1104 Springfield Avenue
Mountainside, NJ 07092
(908) 789-9400
Contact: Mr. Jim Malfetti
Minimum Salary Placed: $30,000
Recruiting Specialty: General

Office Mates 5
1100 Springfield, Avenue
Mountainside, NJ 07092
(908) 789-8805
Minimum Salary Placed: $20,000
Recruiting Specialty: Office support

Professional Recruiting & Placement
P.O. Box 1216
Mountainside, NJ 07092
(908) 756-8467
Contact: Mr. Jack Saunier
Minimum Salary Placed: $25,000
Recruiting Specialty: Consumer products, healthcare and environmental

Jack Saunier, CPC Professional Recruiter
P.O. Box 1216
Mountainside, NJ 07092
(908) 756-8467
Contact: Mr. Jack Saunier
Minimum Salary Placed: $20,000
Recruiting Specialty: General

NEW BRUNSWICK

Place Mart Personnel Service
5 Elm Row
New Brunswick, NJ 08901
(908) 247-8844

Contact: Mr. William Kuhl
Minimum Salary Placed: $20,000
Recruiting Specialty: Technical disciplines

Sonlight Personnel
356 George Street
New Brunswick, NJ 08901
(908) 937-4646
Contact: Ms. Y. Albanese
Minimum Salary Placed: $20,000
Recruiting Specialty: General

NEW PROVIDENCE

Management Recruiters
76 Floral Avenue
New Providence, NJ 07974
(908) 771-0600
Contact: Mr. Andrew Miller
Minimum Salary Placed: $40,000
Recruiting Specialty: Environmental, healthcare and high technology

Page Consulting Group Inc.
139 South Street
New Providence, NJ 07974
(908) 771-0500
Minimum Salary Placed: $25,000
Recruiting Specialty: Accounting

NEWARK

Excorp Management Systems
Gateway 1 Lower Lobby
Newark, NJ 07102
(201) 642-0400
Contact: Mr. T. Jennings
Minimum Salary Placed: $25,000
Recruiting Specialty: General

L. J. Gonzer Associates
1225 Raymond Blvd.
Newark, NJ 07102
(201) 624-5600
Contact: Mr. Arthur Frank
Minimum Salary Placed: $25,000
Recruiting Specialty: General

NORTH ARLINGTON

Globe Employment Agency
42 Ridge Road
North Arlington, NJ 07031
(201) 997-4251
Contact: Ms. M. Ruvo
Minimum Salary Placed: $25,000
Recruiting Specialty: General

Universal Personnel Services
42 Ridge Road
North Arlington, NJ 07031
(201) 997-2299
Contact: Mr. Matthew S. Buonomo
Minimum Salary Placed: $30,000
Recruiting Specialty: Engineering, production, and technical

NORTH BERGEN

Allan Karson Associates, Inc.
8200 Blvd. East
North Bergen, NJ 07047
(201) 868-4344
Contact: Mr. Allan Karson
Minimum Salary Placed: $100,000
Recruiting Specialty: High technology

NORTH BRUNSWICK

Hreshko Cavaliere and Associates
850 U.S. Highway 1
North Brunswick, NJ 08902
(908) 545-9000
Contact: Mr. F. Hreshko
Minimum Salary Placed: $25,000
Recruiting Specialty: General

JLM Professional Resources
1950 Route 27
North Brunswick, NJ 08902
(908) 940-3100
Contact: Mr. Lou Cavaliere
Minimum Salary Placed: $35,000
Recruiting Specialty: MIS

Key Employment
1014 Livingston Avenue
North Brunswick, NJ 08902
(908) 249-2454
Contact: Mr. Gary Silberger
Minimum Salary Placed: $30,000
Recruiting Specialty: Chemicals, energy and construction

Management Recruiters of North Brunswick, Inc.
669 Nassau Street, Suite 5
North Brunswick, NJ 08902
(908) 545-1900
Contact: Mr. Raymond Sadow
Minimum Salary Placed: $30,000
Recruiting Specialty: General

Miller Resources International Inc.
720 US Highway 1
North Brunswick, NJ 08902
(908) 247-5600
Contact: Mr. S. Miller
Minimum Salary Placed: $25,000
Recruiting Specialty: General

NORTH CALDWELL

Eastern Executive Associates
45 Hamilton Drive E.
North Caldwell, NJ 07006
(201) 226-7341
Contact: Ms. Madeline Jones
Recruiting Specialty: General

K. L. Whitney & Company, Inc.
6 Aspen Drive
North Caldwell, NJ 07006
(212) 725-0780
Contact: Mr. Kenneth Whitney
Minimum Salary Placed: $75,000
Recruiting Specialty: Sales, finance and accounting in finance

OAKLAND

Dunhill Professional Search
393 State Route 202
Oakland, NJ 07436
(201) 337-2200
Contact: Mr. Roger Lippincott
Minimum Salary Placed: $30,000
Recruiting Specialty: General

OCEAN CITY

Huff Associates
500 Bay Avenue N., Suite B
Ocean City, NJ 08226
(609) 399-2867
Contact: Mr. William Huff
Minimum Salary Placed: $40,000
Recruiting Specialty: General

OCEANPORT

Career Search Associates
284 E. Main Street
Oceanport, NJ 07757
(908) 222-5333
Contact: Mr. Bruce Rovinsky
Recruiting Specialty: Retail

ORADELL

Legal Briefs Inc.
327 Merritt Drive
Oradell, NJ 07649
(201) 967-7073
Contact: Mr. L. Samet
Recruiting Specialty: Legal

Management Decisions Systems
466 Kinderkamack Road
Oradell, NJ 07649
(201) 986-1200
Minimum Salary Placed: $25,000
Recruiting Specialty: Computer sales

PALISADES PARK

Capital Finance Recruiters Inc.
321 Commercial Avenue
Palisades Park, NJ 07650
(201) 585-8444
Contact: Mr. B. Patel
Minimum Salary Placed: $25,000
Recruiting Specialty: Auditing

PARAMUS

AES Search
1 Kalisa Way, Suite 109
Paramus, NJ 07675
(201) 261-1600
Contact: Mr. Michael Goldstein
Recruiting Specialty: General

Accountant Source Temps
15 Essex Road
Paramus, NJ 07652
(201) 843-2020
Contact: Mr. Les Ward
Minimum Salary Placed: $20,000
Recruiting Specialty: Accounting and finance

Accountants On Call/Accountants Executive Search
80 E. State Road 4, Suite 230
Paramus, NJ 07652
(201) 348-4333
Minimum Salary Placed: $25,000
Recruiting Specialty: Accounting

Berman & Larson Associates Ltd.
140 Rte. 17 N., Suite 204
Paramus, NJ 07652
(201) 262-9200
Contact: Mr. Robert Larson
Minimum Salary Placed: $30,000
Recruiting Specialty: MIS and computers

Career Path Inc.
502 Marion Lane
Paramus, NJ 07652
(201) 265-6665
Contact: Mr. G. Mettler
Minimum Salary Placed: $25,000
Recruiting Specialty: Data processing

David Anthony Personnel Associates
64 E. Ridgewood Avenue
Paramus, NJ 07652
(201) 262-6100
Contact: Mr. D. Ferrara
Minimum Salary Placed: $20,000
Recruiting Specialty: General

Douglas Personnel Associates Inc.
12 N. State Road 17
Paramus, NJ 07652
(201) 368-3300
Contact: Ms. T. Klein
Minimum Salary Placed: $25,000
Recruiting Specialty: Retail

Robert Half International
210 E. State Road 4
Paramus, NJ 07652
(201) 843-3799
Contact: Mr. P. McDonald
Minimum Salary Placed: $25,000
Recruiting Specialty: Finance and accounting

Gale Harris Company
140 N. State Road 17, Suite 210
Paramus, NJ 07652
(201) 265-9660
Contact: Ms. Gale Harris
Minimum Salary Placed: $25,000
Recruiting Specialty: R & D, cosmetics and technical disciplines in chemicals

Hunter Stone Inc.
28 Fairview Terrace
Paramus, NJ 07652
(201) 845-0610
Contact: Ms. B. Berger
Minimum Salary Placed: $25,000
Recruiting Specialty: Marketing and marketing research

Joseph Keyes Associates
275 Forest Avenue, Suite 206
Paramus, NJ 07653
(201) 261-7400
Contact: Mr. Joseph Keyes
Minimum Salary Placed: $30,000
Recruiting Specialty: General

Norrell Staffing Services
120 Route 17 North
Paramus, NJ 07652
(201) 261-2500
Contact: Ms. Bonnie O'Brien
Recruiting Specialty: Technical support

Prime IV Service
140 N. State Road 17, Suite 210
Paramus, NJ 07652
(201) 265-8921
Contact: Mr. M. Mancusco
Minimum Salary Placed: $25,000
Recruiting Specialty: Data processing

Search Consultants
1 East Ridgewood Avenue
Paramus , NJ 07652
(201) 444-1770
Contact: Mr. Walter Perog
Minimum Salary Placed: $30,000
Recruiting Specialty: General

Source EDP
15 Essex Road, Suite 201
Paramus, NJ 07652
(201) 845-3900
Contact: Mr. Tom Peressini
Recruiting Specialty: Computers

Source Finance
15 Essex Road, Suite 201
Paramus, NJ 07652
(201) 843-2777

Contact: Mr. Matthew Burgay
Minimum Salary Placed: $25,000
Recruiting Specialty: Finance and accounting

PARLIN

Management Recruiters
984 Route 9, Suite 5
Parlin, NJ 08859
(908) 727-8300
Contact: Mr. Herbert Hardbrod
Minimum Salary Placed: $30,000
Recruiting Specialty: Healthcare, advertising, and marketing

PARSIPPANY

Baker Scott & Company
1259 Route 46
Parsippany, NJ 07054
(201) 263-3355
Contact: Ms. Judy Bouer
Minimum Salary Placed: $40,000
Recruiting Specialty: Communications

Bosland Gray Associates
2001 Route 46, Suite 310
Parsippany, NJ 07054
(201) 402-4964
Contact: Mr. Andrew Gray
Minimum Salary Placed: $60,000
Recruiting Specialty: General

Clark Davis Associates
7 Century Drive
Parsippany, NJ 07054
(201) 267-5511
Contact: Mr. F. Luzzie
Minimum Salary Placed: $25,000
Recruiting Specialty: MIS, accounting, engineering and data processing

Eliob & Carr Group, Inc.
50 Cherry Hill Road
Parsippany, NJ 07054
(201) 402-8844
Minimum Salary Placed: $40,000
Recruiting Specialty: Chemical and plastics

The Goodrich & Sherwood Company
6 Century Drive
Parsippany, NJ 07054
(201) 455-7100
Contact: Mr. Frank Palma
Minimum Salary Placed: $60,000
Recruiting Specialty: General

The Haran Management Group, Inc.
1055 Parsippany Boulevard, Suite 313
Parsippany, NJ 07054
(201) 884-1987
Contact: Mr. Richard Arends
Minimum Salary Placed: $40,000
Recruiting Specialty: General

Hartshorn Group
8 Woodhollow Road
Parsippany, NJ 07054
(201) 884-1010
Contact: Mr. Leonard Hartshorn
Recruiting Specialty: Office support and
PC technical support

Jonathan Lawrence Associates
2001 US Highway 46
Parsippany, NJ 07054
(201) 285-1988
Contact: Mr. John Singel
Minimum Salary Placed: $25,000
Recruiting Specialty: Information systems

Lloyd Creative Staffing
1719 State Route 10, Suite 114
Parsippany, NJ 07054
(201) 984-8000
Contact: Mr. Frank T. Masi
Minimum Salary Placed: $25,000
Recruiting Specialty: General

Moore International Inc.
362 Parsippany Road
Parsippany, NJ 07054
(201) 503-9400
Contact: Mr. M. Krantz
Minimum Salary Placed: $35,000
Recruiting Specialty: Finance

Normann Staffing Services
3621 Hill Road
Parsippany, NJ 07054
(201) 299-1950
Contact: Mr. Bill Allison
Minimum Salary Placed: $25,000
Recruiting Specialty: General

Orion Consulting, Inc.
115 US Highway 46
Parsippany, NJ 07054
(201) 402-8866
Recruiting Specialty: General

Prime Time Personnel, Inc.
129 Littleton Road
Parsippany, NJ 07054
(201) 334-9600
Contact: Ms. Laura DeRose
Minimum Salary Placed: $25,000
Recruiting Specialty: General

Professionals Unlimited, Inc.
2001 Route 46, Suite 310
Parsippany, NJ 07054
(908) 766-0100

Contact: Ms. Nancy Calabrese
Recruiting Specialty: Insurance

Sales Consultants of Morris County, Inc.

364 Parsippany Road, Suite 8B
Parsippany, NJ 07054
(201) 887-3838
Contact: Mr. Ernest Bivona
Minimum Salary Placed: $20,000
Recruiting Specialty: Sales, chemical, consumer, industrial, healthcare, and telecommunication

Source EDP

One Gatehall Drive, Suite 250
Parsippany, NJ 07054
(201) 267-3222
Contact: Mr. Joe Eiseman
Recruiting Specialty: Computers

Source Finance

1 Gatehall Drive, Suite 250
Parsippany, NJ 07054
(201) 267-3222
Contact: Mr. M. Lowenbraun
Minimum Salary Placed: $25,000
Recruiting Specialty: Finance and accounting

Tri-Tech Associates

40 Baldwin Road
Parsippany, NJ 07054
(201) 299-0055
Contact: Ms. Marlene Levitt
Minimum Salary Placed: $35,000
Recruiting Specialty: Technology and engineering

PENNINGTON

Palmer Associates

54 West Shore Drive
Pennington, NJ 08534
(609) 737-2237
Contact: Mr. Jack Palmer
Minimum Salary Placed: $25,000
Recruiting Specialty: General

Pennington Consulting Group

65 S. Main Street, Building B
Pennington, NJ 08534
(609) 737-8500
Contact: Mr. Robert White
Recruiting Specialty: Telecommunications

Princeton BioTechnology Inc.

54 West Shore Drive
Pennington, NJ 08534
(609) 737-2799
Contact: Mr. Jack Palmer
Minimum Salary Placed: $25,000
Recruiting Specialty: Technical disciplines in biotechnology and medical

PLAINSBORO

Future Resource Systems

503 Plainsboro Road
Plainsboro, NJ 08536
(609) 734-9108
Contact: Ms. B. Dye
Minimum Salary Placed: $25,000
Recruiting Specialty: General

POINT PLEASANT BEACH

Industrial Recruiting Service
201 Arnold Avenue
Pt. Pleasant Beach, NJ 08742
(908) 295-8444
Contact: Mr. Rober Smith
Minimum Salary Placed: $30,000
Recruiting Specialty: Engineering

POMPTON LAKES

Inter Regional Executive Search, Inc.
191 Hamburg Turnpike, Suite 4B
Pompton Lakes, NJ 07442
(201) 616-8800
Contact: Mr. Frank Risalvato
Minimum Salary Placed: $40,000
Recruiting Specialty: General

Management Recruiters
750 Hamburg Turnpike, Suite 203
Pompton Lakes, NJ 07442
(201) 831-7778
Contact: Mr. David Zawicki
Minimum Salary Placed: $30,000
Recruiting Specialty: Computer sales

PRINCETON

Accountants Executive Search
138 Washington Road
Princeton, NJ 08540
(609) 452-7117
Contact: Ms. Sandra Wujack
Minimum Salary Placed: $25,000
Recruiting Specialty: Accounting

Barone-O'Hara Associates, Inc.
29 Emmons Drive, Building 5
Princeton, NJ 08540
(609) 452-1980
Contact: Ms. Marialice Barone
Minimum Salary Placed: $45,000
Recruiting Specialty: Manufacturing in healthcare and medical devices

Blau Kaptain Schroeder
12 Roszel Road, Suite C-101
Princeton, NJ 08540
(609) 520-8400
Contact: Mr. John Kaptain
Minimum Salary Placed: $75,000
Recruiting Specialty: Healthcare

Burke, O'Brien & Bishop Associates, Inc.
1000 Herrontown Road
Princeton, NJ 08540
(609) 921-3510
Contact: Mr. James Bishop
Minimum Salary Placed: $100,000
Recruiting Specialty: General

Campbell Sacchetti & Associates
Mount Lucas Road
Princeton, NJ 08540
(609) 924-4747
Contact: Ms. Andrea Sacchetti
Recruiting Specialty: General

China Human Resources Group
29 Airpark Road
Princeton, NJ 08540
(609) 683-4521
Contact: Ms. Christine Casati
Minimum Salary Placed: $30,000
Recruiting Specialty: General

Churchhill & Harriman
601 Ewing Street, Suite B7
Princeton, NJ 08540
(609) 921-3551
Recruiting Specialty: Data processing

Dunhill Personnel System, Inc.
105 College Road, E.
Princeton, NJ 08540
(609) 452-1222
Contact: Mr. Joseph Marino
Minimum Salary Placed: $30,000
Recruiting Specialty: General

Force II Associates, Inc.
13 Roszel Road, Suite 104
Princeton, NJ 08540
(609) 987-8818
Contact: Ms. Renee Dale
Minimum Salary Placed: $25,000
Recruiting Specialty: General

The Goodrich & Sherwood Company
1 Independence Way
Princeton, NJ 08540
(609) 452-0202
Contact: Mr. David Kostka
Minimum Salary Placed: $60,000
Recruiting Specialty: General

Hollander Horizon International
16 Wall Street
Princeton, NJ 08540
(609) 924-7577
Minimum Salary Placed: $25,000
Recruiting Specialty: Technical disciplines in consumer products

Korn/Ferry International
1 Palmer Square
Princeton, NJ 08542
(908) 647-4131
Contact: Mr. Kenneth Clark
Minimum Salary Placed: $100,000
Recruiting Specialty: General

Management Advisors
301 N. Harrison Street, Suite 483
Princeton, NJ 08540
(609) 921-3622
Contact: Mr. A. Currier
Minimum Salary Placed: $25,000
Recruiting Specialty: General

Management Recruiters
707 State Road, Suite 220
Princeton, NJ 08540
(609) 252-0506
Contact: Mr. Warren Schorr
Minimum Salary Placed: $30,000
Recruiting Specialty: General

Merrill Adams Association
125 Village Boulevard, Suite 303
Princeton, NJ 08540
(609) 951-9333
Minimum Salary Placed: $50,000
Recruiting Specialty: General

Neil Mason Executive Search
301 N. Harrison Street, Suite 179
Princeton, NJ 08540
(609) 895-1400
Contact: Mr. Neil Mason
Minimum Salary Placed: $35,000
Recruiting Specialty: Direct marketing

PR Management Consultants
601 Ewing Street
Princeton, NJ 08540
(609) 921-6565
Minimum Salary Placed: $40,000
Recruiting Specialty: Pharmaceuticals
and the biomedical; consumer products

Princeton Executive Search
P.O. Box 7373
Princeton, NJ 08543
(609) 584-1100
Contact: Mr. Andrew Barkocy
Minimum Salary Placed: $50,000
Recruiting Specialty: Executive search

Raymond Karsan Associates
348 Wall Street
Princeton, NJ 08540
(609) 252-0999
Contact: Ms. Natalie Brooks
Recruiting Specialty: General

Source EDP
5 Independence Way
Princeton, NJ 08540
(609) 452-7277
Contact: Ms. Martha Murphy
Recruiting Specialty: Computers

Source Finance
5 Independence Way
Princeton, NJ 08540
(609) 452-7277
Contact: Ms. Martha Murphy
Minimum Salary Placed: $25,000
Recruiting Specialty: Accounting and finance

Tucker Associates
1015 Mercer Road
Princeton, NJ 08540
(609) 921-0800
Contact: Mr. John Tucker
Minimum Salary Placed: $75,000
Recruiting Specialty: General

Wadsworth & Associates, Inc.
212 Carnegie Court
Princeton, NJ 08540
(609) 987-0010
Recruiting Specialty: Executives for mutual fund positions

Michael D. Zinn & Associates, Inc.
601 Ewing Street, Suite C-9
Princeton, NJ 08540
(609) 921-8755
Contact: Mr. Michael Zinn
Minimum Salary Placed: $75,000
Recruiting Specialty: General

PRINCETON JUNCTION

Morgan Mercedes Human Resources Group
34 Washington Road
Princeton Junction, NJ 08550
(609) 987-1122
Contact: Ms. P. Dempsey
Minimum Salary Placed: $20,000
Recruiting Specialty: Office support

Quality Associates
186 Princeton Hightstown Road
Princeton Junction, NJ 08550
(609) 799-7755
Contact: Mr. Bill Williams
Minimum Salary Placed: $25,000
Recruiting Specialty: General

RAMSEY

Dreier Consulting
P.O. Box 356, 10 S. Franklin Turnpike
Ramsey, NJ 07446
(201) 327-1113
Contact: Mr. John Dreier
Minimum Salary Placed: $40,000
Recruiting Specialty: High technology

Major Search
500 No. Franklin Turnpike, Suite 17
Ramsey, NJ 07446
(201) 934-9666
Contact: Mr. Lou Ordini
Minimum Salary Placed: $25,000
Recruiting Specialty: General

Merlin International Inc.
P.O. Box 313
Ramsey, NJ 07446
(201) 825-7220
Contact: Mr. V. James Cinquina
Minimum Salary Placed: $50,000
Recruiting Specialty: Pharmaceuticals
and biotechnology

RANDOLPH

Paul Kull & Company
18 Meadow Brook Road
Randolph, NJ 07869
(201) 361-7440
Contact: Mr. Paul Kull
Minimum Salary Placed: $40,000
Recruiting Specialty: General

RED BANK

Broad Waverly & Associates
200 Broad Street, P.O. Box 741
Red Bank, NJ 07701
(908) 747-4400
Contact: Mr. Bill Saloukas
Minimum Salary Placed: $25,000
Recruiting Specialty: Insurance in finance
and insurance

Deuel and Egan Management
90 Maple Avenue
Red Bank, NJ 07701
(908) 842-8885
Minimum Salary Placed: $25,000
Recruiting Specialty: Data communications

Hartley Personnel, Inc.
P.O. Box 194
Red Bank, NJ 07701
(908) 741-6117 or (800) 349-4449
Contact: Teri Hartley
Minimum Salary Placed: $40,000
Recruiting Specialty: General

Management Recruiters
225 Highway 35 North
Red Bank, NJ 07701
(908) 295-9340
Contact: Ms. Terri Sabados
Minimum Salary Placed: $30,000
Recruiting Specialty: General

The Resource Group
P.O. Box 331
Red Bank, NJ 07701
(908) 842-6555
Contact: Mr. Timothy Howe
Minimum Salary Placed: $50,000
Recruiting Specialty: General

Rochester Systems, Inc.
227 E. Bergen Place
Red Bank, NJ 07701
(908) 747-7474
Minimum Salary Placed: $25,000
Recruiting Specialty: General

Sales Consultants
210 W. Front Street, Suite 102
Red Bank, NJ 07701
(908) 530-0600
Contact: Mr. Mike Unger
Minimum Salary Placed: $20,000
Recruiting Specialty: Sales

RIDGEWOOD

Management Recruiters
1172 E. Ridgewood, Suite 7
Ridgewood, NJ 07450
(201) 445-9600
Contact: Mr. Jack Osher
Minimum Salary Placed: $30,000
Recruiting Specialty: General

McCooe & Associates, Inc.
615 Franklin Turnpike
Ridgewood, NJ 07450
(201) 445-3161
Contact: Mr. John McCooe
Recruiting Specialty: General

RIVER EDGE

TeleQuest Communications, Inc.
P.O. Box 4232
River Edge, NJ 07661
(914) 357-2212
Contact: Mr. Tom Bartchak
Recruiting Specialty: Telecommunications

RIVER VALE

Dr. H. Tschudin Associates
215 Riverdale Road
River Vale, NJ 07675
(201) 666-3456
Contact: Dr. Hugo Tschudin
Minimum Salary Placed: $100,000
Recruiting Specialty: General; European
companies

RIVERDALE

The Garret Group
20 Hamburg Turnpike
Riverdale, NJ 07457
(201) 835-4443
Contact: Mr. Bernd Stecker
Minimum Salary Placed: $50,000
Recruiting Specialty: Engineering and
product development in consumer products

Weinpel Search, Inc.
P.O. Box 248, 20 Hamburg Turnpike
Riverdale, NJ 07457
(201) 839-4207
Contact: Mr. Charles Weinpel
Recruiting Specialty: High technology

ROCHELLE PARK

Corporate One Inc.
350 W. Passaic Street
Rochelle Park, NJ 07662
(201) 368-0088
Contact: Mr. R. Coleman
Minimum Salary Placed: $25,000
Recruiting Specialty: General

Fortune Personnel Consultants
350 W. Passaic Street
Rochelle Park, NJ 07662
(201) 843-2100
Contact: Mr. H. Klein
Minimum Salary Placed: $25,000
Recruiting Specialty: Pharmaceutical and medical

The Normyle/Erstling Health Search Group
350 W. Passaic Street
Rochelle Park, NJ 07662
(201) 843-6009
Contact: Mr. Charles Kreps
Minimum Salary Placed: $30,000
Recruiting Specialty: Sales in healthcare

Ultimate Solutions, Inc.
151 W. Passaic Street
Rochelle Park, NJ 07662
(201) 909-3717
Contact: Mr. Walter A. Casola
Minimum Salary Placed: $25,000
Recruiting Specialty: MIS and data processing

ROCKAWAY

Besen Associates, Inc.
115 US Highway 46
Rockaway, NJ 07866
(201) 334-5533
Recruiting Specialty: OTC and nutrition

R-1 Consultants
179 Route 46, Suite 335
Rockaway, NJ 07866
(201) 586-4500
Contact: Mr. Frank Masi
Recruiting Specialty: MIS

ROSELAND

The Ascher Group
7 Becker Farm Road
Roseland, NJ 07068
(201) 597-1900
Contact: Ms. Susan Asche
Minimum Salary Placed: $50,000
Recruiting Specialty: General

The Partnership Group
7 Becker Farm Road
Roseland, NJ 07068
(201) 535-8566
Contact: Mr. Peter Maher
Minimum Salary Placed: $60,000
Recruiting Specialty: General

RUTHERFORD

Corporate Information Search
71 Union Avenue
Rutherford, NJ 07070
(201) 896-0600
Contact: Mr. T. Ryder
Minimum Salary Placed: $25,000
Recruiting Specialty: MIS and data processing

Financial Search Consultants, Inc.
301 Rte. 17 N., Suite 800
Rutherford, NJ 07070
(201) 939-6777
Contact: Ms. Linda Kase
Minimum Salary Placed: $30,000
Recruiting Specialty: Banking

Fox-Morris Associates, Inc.
201 Route 17 N.
Rutherford, NJ 07070
(201) 933-8900

Contact: Mr. Tom Hughes
Minimum Salary Placed: $35,000
Recruiting Specialty: General

Interstate Personnel, Inc.
301 Route 17 North, Suite 800
Rutherford, NJ 07070
(201) 896-1300
Contact: Mr. Michael Topper
Recruiting Specialty: Apparels

The Macdonald Group, Inc.
301 Route 17, Suite 800
Rutherford, NJ 07070
(201) 939-2312
Contact: Mr. G. William Macdonald
Recruiting Specialty: General but mainly
high technology and healthcare

Park Avenue Personnel
41 Park Avenue/2 Sylvan Street
Rutherford, NJ 07075
(201) 939-1911
Contact: Ms. Mary Falzarano
Recruiting Specialty: General

Snelling and Snelling
8 Station Square
Rutherford, NJ 07070
(201) 935-5700
Contact: Mr. R. Camp
Minimum Salary Placed: $25,000
Recruiting Specialty: General

SADDLE BROOK

Accountants On Call
Park 80 West Plaza 11, 9th Floor
Saddle Brook, NJ 07662
(201) 843-0006
Contact: Mr. Stewart Libes
Recruiting Specialty: Accounting

SCOTCH PLAINS

Atlantic Management Resources
1812 Front Street
Scotch Plains, NJ 07076
(908) 322-2252
Contact: Mr. Lloyd Mandel
Recruiting Specialty: Sales in pharmaceuticals and medical

Petruzzi Associates
P.O. Box 141
Scotch Plains, NJ 07076
(908) 754-1940
Contact: Mr. Vincent Petruzzi
Minimum Salary Placed: $40,000
Recruiting Specialty: Healthcare, plastics
and chemicals

Pomerantz Personnel
1913 Westfield Avenue
Scotch Plains, NJ 07076
(908) 322-7300
Contact: Mr. G. Gusciora
Minimum Salary Placed: $20,000
Recruiting Specialty: General

SECAUCUS

Management Recruiters
1325 Paterson Plank Road
Secaucus, NJ 07094
(201) 864-3100
Contact: Mr. Ted Prehodka
Minimum Salary Placed: $30,000
Recruiting Specialty: General

MIS Search
450 Harmon Meadow Boulevard
Secaucus, NJ 07094
(201) 330-0080

Contact: Mr. B. Violette
Minimum Salary Placed: $25,000
Recruiting Specialty: MIS

Reinecke & Associates
P.O. Box 1141
Secaucus, NJ 07094
(201) 865-5935
Contact: Mr. Robert Schumann
Minimum Salary Placed: $35,000
Recruiting Specialty: Transportation

SHIP BOTTOM

Management Catalysts
P.O. Box 70
Ship Bottom, NJ 08008
(609) 597-0079
Contact: Mr. J. R. Stockton
Recruiting Specialty: Science and engineering in consumer products

SHREWSBURY

Dunhill Professional Search of Red Bank, Inc.
621 Shrewsbury Avenue
Shrewsbury, NJ 07702
(908) 219-1605
Contact: Mr. Martin Dowd
Minimum Salary Placed: $30,000
Recruiting Specialty: General

SKILLMAN

Management Recruiters
118 Tamarack Circle
Skillman, NJ 08558
(609) 497-9300
Contact: Ms. Julia Neri
Minimum Salary Placed: $30,000
Recruiting Specialty: General

SOMERSET

Delta Personnel Services
100 Franklin Square Drive
Somerset, NJ 08873
(908) 560-9000
Contact: Ms. Rose Liccardi
Minimum Salary Placed: $35,000
Recruiting Specialty: General

SOMERVILLE

Dean-Wharton Associates
166 West End Avenue, P.O. Box 279
Somerville, NJ 08876
(908) 231-1818
Contact: Mr. James Dean
Minimum Salary Placed: $35,000
Recruiting Specialty: Human resources

H.P. Job Shop Professionals
281 East Main Street
Somerville, NJ 08876
(908) 231-9543
Contact: Mr. Edward M. Hughes
Minimum Salary Placed: $30,000
Recruiting Specialty: Engineering

**Hughes & Podesla Personnel,
Associates**
281 East Main Street
Somerville, NJ 08876
(908) 231-0880
Contact: Mr. Edward M. Hughes
Minimum Salary Placed: $50,000
Recruiting Specialty: Pharmaceuticals
and medical devices

Lancaster Associates, Inc.
94 Grove Street
Somerville, NJ 08876
(908) 526-5440
Contact: Ms. Barbara Swan
Minimum Salary Placed: $40,000
Recruiting Specialty: MIS and high tech-
nology in consumer products

Janet Stoakes Associates
150 West End Avenue
Somerville, NJ 08876
(908) 722-3636
Contact: Ms. Janet Stoakes
Minimum Salary Placed: $30,000
Recruiting Specialty: Pharmaceuticals
and healthcare

SOUTH PLAINFIELD

Allen Associates
128 Elliott Place
South Plainfield, NJ 07080
(908) 753-3751
Recruiting Specialty: Marketing

Stelton Group Inc.
904 Oak Tree Road
South Plainfield, NJ 07080
(908) 757-9888

Contact: Betty
Minimum Salary Placed: $40,000
Recruiting Specialty: Plastics, engineering, medical devices, scientific, manufacturing, and human resources

SPARTA

Management Recruiters
191 Woodport Road, Suite 201
Sparta, NJ 07871
(201) 729-1888
Contact: Mr. Lance Incitti
Minimum Salary Placed: $30,000
Recruiting Specialty: Retail

Sales Consultants
376 Route 15, Suite 109
Sparta, NJ 07871
(201) 579-5555
Contact: Mr. Harvey Bass
Minimum Salary Placed: $20,000
Recruiting Specialty: Sales

SPOTSWOOD

Globe Placement, Inc.
P.O. Box 61
Spotswood, NJ 08884
(908) 238-6834
Contact: Mr. Barry L. Fine
Minimum Salary Placed: $40,000
Recruiting Specialty: Technical, materi-
als, and science

SPRINGFIELD

D. S. Allen Associates
823 S. Springfield Avenue
Springfield, NJ 07081
(201) 376-4800
Contact: Mr. Don Allen
Minimum Salary Placed: $40,000
Recruiting Specialty: High technology

Jaral LTD Consultants
P.O. Box 498
Springfield, NJ 07081
(201) 564-9236
Contact: Mr. Joseph Morgan
Minimum Salary Placed: $75,000
Recruiting Specialty: Fashion

Tarnow International
150 Morris Avenue
Springfield, NJ 07081
(201) 376-3900
Contact: Mr. Emil Vogel
Minimum Salary Placed: $70,000
Recruiting Specialty: General

STANHOPE

Management Recruiters
4 Waterloo Road
Stanhope, NJ 07874
(201) 691-2020
Contact: Mr. Arthur Young
Minimum Salary Placed: $25,000
Recruiting Specialty: Technical, MIS and
computers

Sales Consultants
4 Waterloo Road
Stanhope, NJ 07874
(201) 347-8400

Contact: Mr. Robert Ceresi
Minimum Salary Placed: $20,000
Recruiting Specialty: Sales in electrical

STIRLING

The Garret Group
P.O. Box 53
Stirling, NJ 07980
(908) 580-0810
Contact: Mr. John Wharton
Minimum Salary Placed: $50,000
Recruiting Specialty: Engineering and
product development in consumer prod-
ucts

SUCCASUNNA

MSI Consulting Group Inc.
7 Norman Lane
Succasunna, NJ 07876
(201) 927-5550
Contact: Mr. A. Chanes
Minimum Salary Placed: $25,000
Recruiting Specialty: Accounting

SUMMIT

Sales Consultants
18 Bank Street, Suite 201
Summit, NJ 07901
(908) 522-0700
Contact: Mr. Remus Klimaski
Minimum Salary Placed: $20,000
Recruiting Specialty: Sales

Search Associates, Inc.
18 Bank Street
Summit, NJ 07901
(908) 277-1400

Contact: Ms. Trina Lawson
Recruiting Specialty: General

TEANECK

Careers, Inc.
814 Perry Lane
Teaneck, NJ 07666
(201) 837-6567
Contact: Ms. Barbara Kane
Minimum Salary Placed: $35,000
Recruiting Specialty: Package goods and market research and sales

TENAFLY

Careers on Track
150 County Road
Tenafly, NJ 07670
(201) 894-0600
Contact: Mr. Gary Tabor
Recruiting Specialty: General and consumer products

Phillips Associates
P.O. Box 747
Tenafly, NJ 07670
(201) 569-5033
Contact: Ms. Veronica Phillips
Minimum Salary Placed: $20,000
Recruiting Specialty: Advertising, human resources and environmental sciences

Zwicker Associates
140 County Road
Tenafly, NJ 07670
(201) 567-8734
Contact: Mr. A. Zwicker
Minimum Salary Placed: $25,000
Recruiting Specialty: Technical disciplines in foods

TOTOWA

Global Search, Inc.
41 Vreeland Avenue
Totowa, NJ 07512
(201) 890-1025
Contact: Mr. Barry Rosen
Minimum Salary Placed: $35,000
Recruiting Specialty: MIS

Kane Associates
41 Vreeland Avenue
Totowa, NJ 07512
(201) 890-9110
Contact: Ms. R. Kane
Minimum Salary Placed: $25,000
Recruiting Specialty: General

MJE Recruiters, Inc.
12 Furler Street
Totowa, NJ 07512
(201) 785-0885
Contact: Mr. Barry Emen
Minimum Salary Placed: $30,000
Recruiting Specialty: Finance

RT Associates, Inc.
12 Furler Street
Totowa, NJ 07512
(201) 785-4040
Contact: Mr. Robert Turano
Minimum Salary Placed: $25,000
Recruiting Specialty: Accounting and finance

Raymond Alexander Associates
420 Minnisink Road
Totowa, NJ 07512
(201) 256-1000

Contact: Mr. Raymond Jezierski
Minimum Salary Placed: $30,000
Recruiting Specialty: Accounting and finance

Paula Stagno Personnel
41 Vreeland Avenue
Totowa, NJ 07512
(201) 890-1969
Contact: Ms. Paula Stagno
Minimum Salary Placed: $25,000
Recruiting Specialty: General

TRENTON

Aade Associates
1968 Klockner Road
Trenton, NJ 08619
(609) 584-8300
Contact: Mr. A. Angeledes
Minimum Salary Placed: $25,000
Recruiting Specialty: Pharmaceuticals

Princeton Executive Search
2667 Nottingham Way
Trenton, NJ 08619
(609) 584-1100
Contact: Mr. Andrew Barkocy
Minimum Salary Placed: $25,000
Recruiting Specialty: General

UNION

Brett Personnel Specialists
2184 Morris Avenue
Union, NJ 07083
(908) 687-7772
Contact: Mr. Gene Reight
Minimum Salary Placed: $25,000
Recruiting Specialty: Manufacturing in consumer products

S.K. Associates
1767 Morris Avenue
Union, NJ 07083
(908) 687-7350
Contact: Mr. J. Goldberg
Minimum Salary Placed: $25,000
Recruiting Specialty: Retail

Search East Technical
1600 US Highway 22 E.
Union, NJ 07083
(908) 687-6336
Minimum Salary Placed: $25,000
Recruiting Specialty: High technology and electronics

UPPER MONTCLAIR

DHR International, Inc.
248 Lorraine Avenue
Upper Montclair, NJ 07043
(201) 746-2100
Contact: Mr. David Richardson
Minimum Salary Placed: $50,000
Recruiting Specialty: General

Foster Associates
209 Cooper Avenue
Upper Montclair, NJ 07043
(201) 746-2800
Contact: Mr. Donald Foster
Minimum Salary Placed: $60,000
Recruiting Specialty: General

UPPER SADDLE RIVER

META/MAT, Ltd.
2 Parkway Route 175
Upper Saddle River, NJ 07458
(201) 818-0101

Contact: Mr. Fred Kopff
Minimum Salary Placed: $75,000
Recruiting Specialty: General

VOORHEES

Legal-Medical Staffing Services, Inc.
Plaza 1000 Building, Main St., Suite 202
Voorhees, NJ 08043
(609)751-7999
Contact: Ms. Cheryl Keenan
Minimum Salary Placed: $20,000
Recruiting Specialty: Healthcare

J. White & Company
1307 Whitehorse Road, Suite 601
Voorhees, NJ 08043
(609) 784-7777
Recruiting Specialty: Insurance

WALDWICK

Personnel Service
24 Wyckoff Avenue
Waldwick, NJ 07463
(201) 444-6643
Minimum Salary Placed: $20,000
Recruiting Specialty: Office support

WARREN

Kurtz Pro-Search, Inc.
P.O. Box 4263
Warren, NJ 07059
(908) 647-7789
Contact: Mr. Sheldon Kurtz
Minimum Salary Placed: $35,000
Recruiting Specialty: Sales and marketing
in computers and communications

Pharma Design Inc.
30 Technology Drive
Warren, NJ 07059
(908) 769-1234
Contact: Mr. F. Pether
Minimum Salary Placed: $25,000
Recruiting Specialty: Pharmaceuticals
and advertising

WAYNE

Dow-Tech Associates
1700 State Route 23 North, Suite 330
Wayne, NJ 07470
(201) 696-8000
Contact: Ms. Monica Ryan
Minimum Salary Placed: $35,000
Recruiting Specialty: Technical, sales,
and engineering

Normann Staffing Services
155 Willowbrook Blvd.
Wayne, NJ 07470
(201) 785-4064
Contact: Mr. Bill Allison
Recruiting Specialty: General

Salem Associates
1501 Paterson Hamburg Turnpike,
 Suite 414
Wayne, NJ 07470
(201) 305-6667
Contact: Mr. Joe Salem
Minimum Salary Placed: $25,000
Recruiting Specialty: General

Robert K. Stryker
600 Valley Road
Wayne, NJ 07470
(201) 628-9585

Contact: Mr. Bob Stryker
Minimum Salary Placed: $25,000
Recruiting Specialty: General

Trans-Technology Associates
1700 State Route 23
Wayne, NJ 07470
(201) 696-4022
Contact: Mr. C. Dowling
Minimum Salary Placed: $25,000
Recruiting Specialty: Sales and marketing
in high technology

WorkSource 2000, Inc.
P.O. Box 163
Wayne, NJ 07474
(201) 628-2951
Contact: Ms. Diane M. Rothong
Minimum Salary Placed: $40,000
Recruiting Specialty: Physicians, medical
and pharmaceuticals

WEEHAWKEN

Balcor Associates
700 Boulevard East
Weehawken, NJ 07087
(201) 866-1150
Minimum Salary Placed: $50,000
Recruiting Specialty: Finance, accounting, and human resources

WEST CALDWELL

Key Ingredient Consultants
1140 Bloomfield Avenue
West Caldwell, NJ 07006
(201) 227-5797
Contact: Mr. Edward Rubenstein
Recruiting Specialty: Chemists, scientists,
engineer, technical sales and marketing in
all research areas

Phoenix BioSearch, Inc.
P.O. Box 6157
West Caldwell, NJ 07007
(201) 812-2666
Contact: Ms. E. A. Stephenson
Minimum Salary Placed: $50,000
Recruiting Specialty: Technical disci-
plines in pharmaceuticals and biotechnol-
ogy

Triad Consultants, Inc.
P.O. Box 717
West Caldwell, NJ 07007
(201) 890-1655
Contact: Mr. Jack Daudt
Minimum Salary Placed: $50,000
Recruiting Specialty: Human resources

WEST ORANGE

Carter McKenzie, Inc.
200 Executive Drive, Suite 350
West Orange, NJ 07052
(201) 736-7100
Contact: Mr. Richard Kilcoyne
Minimum Salary Placed: $25,000
Recruiting Specialty: MIS

Gilbert Tweed Associates, Inc.
155 Prospect Avenue
West Orange, NJ 07052
(201) 731-3033
Contact: Ms. Stephanie Pinson
Minimum Salary Placed: $70,000
Recruiting Specialty: General

Topaz International, Inc.
383 Northfield Avenue
West Orange, NJ 07052
(201) 669-7300

Contact: Ms. Ronni Gaines
Minimum Salary Placed: $50,000
Recruiting Specialty: Attorneys and paralegals

WEST TRENTON

Management Recruiters
1230 Parkway Avenue, Suite 102
West Trenton, NJ 08628
(609) 882-8388
Contact: Ms. Beverly Bodnar
Minimum Salary Placed: $30,000
Recruiting Specialty: General

Sales Consultants
1230 Parkway Avenue, Suite 102
West Trenton, NJ 08628
(609) 882-8388
Contact: Mr. Robert Bodnar
Minimum Salary Placed: $20,000
Recruiting Specialty: Sales in electrical

WESTFIELD

W.N. Garbarini & Associates
961 Cherokee Court
Westfield, NJ 07090
(908) 232-2737
Contact: Mr. William Garbarini
Minimum Salary Placed: $70,000
Recruiting Specialty: General

Healthcare Career Consultants
215 North Avenue West Suite 237
Westfield, NJ 07090
(908) 232-8181
Contact: Ms. Annette Farley
Minimum Salary Placed: $40,000
Recruiting Specialty: Physicians, physical therapists, and healthcare

Hill Associates
189 Elm Street
Westfield, NJ 07090
(908) 233-7917
Contact: Mr. Lou DeMatthews
Minimum Salary Placed: $25,000
Recruiting Specialty: General

Tate & Associates, Inc.
1020 Springfield Avenue, Suite 201
Westfield, NJ 07090
(908) 232-2443
Contact: Mr. Gene Tate
Minimum Salary Placed: $40,000
Recruiting Specialty: General

WOODBRIDGE

Barone Associates
57 Green Street
Woodbridge, NJ 07095
(908) 634-4300
Contact: Mr. L. Donald Rizzo
Minimum Salary Placed: $30,000
Recruiting Specialty: Manufacturing, healthcare and chemicals

GSP International
90 Woodbridge Center Drive
Woodbridge, NJ 07095
(908) 602-0300
Contact: Mr. J. Sicilia
Minimum Salary Placed: $25,000
Recruiting Specialty: Accounting and finance

WOODCLIFF LAKE

Stuart, Wood Inc.
188 Broadway, P.O. Box 8675
Woodcliff Lake, NJ 07675
(201) 666-2441
Contact: Mr. Wallace Schneider
Minimum Salary Placed: $75,000
Recruiting Specialty: General

WYCKOFF

Naomi Levine and Associates
400 W. Main Street
Wyckoff, NJ 07481
(201) 848-1600
Contact: Ms. Naomi Levine
Minimum Salary Placed: $25,000
Recruiting Specialty: Computer programming

N E W   M E X I C O

ALBUQUERQUE

ACC Consultants, Inc.
P.O. Box 91240
Albuquerque, NM 87199
(505) 298-9177
Contact: Mr. Jerry Berger
Recruiting Specialty: Technical disciplines in energy, environmental and healthcare

The Agency
3240 Juan Tabo Boulevard NE
Albuquerque, NM 87111
(505) 837-2024

Contact: Ms. S. Herndon
Minimum Salary Placed: $25,000
Recruiting Specialty: Banking

Tom Allison Associates
625 Stagecoach Road SE
Albuquerque, NM 87124
(505) 275-7771
Contact: Mr. Tom Allison
Minimum Salary Placed: $25,000
Recruiting Specialty: Food and consumer products

Culver Group
P.O. Box 3645
Albuquerque, NM 87110
(505) 255-8973
Contact: Ms. Vivian Leslie
Minimum Salary Placed: $50,000
Recruiting Specialty: Healthcare

Dolan Tech Search
1208 San Pedro NE
Albuquerque, NM 87110
(505) 255-4440
Contact: Mr. Jack Dolan
Minimum Salary Placed: $35,000
Recruiting Specialty: Technical, mining, electronics and environmental

Dunhill Professional Search
2425 San Pedro NE, Suite C
Albuquerque, NM 87110
(505) 883-9393
Contact: Ms. Peggy Cave
Minimum Salary Placed: $20,000
Recruiting Specialty: General

Executive Search
8100 Mountain Road NE, Suite 110
Albuquerque, NM 87110
(505) 268-3100

Contact: Mr. S. Dunlap
Minimum Salary Placed: $25,000
Recruiting Specialty: General

Management Resource Consulting
11200 Montgomery Boulevard NE,
 Suite 8
Albuquerque, NM 87111
(505) 275-1234
Contact: Mr. R. Schultz
Minimum Salary Placed: $25,000
Recruiting Specialty: Mining and human
resources

Roadrunner Personnel
4015 Carlisle Boulevard NE, Suite C
Albuquerque, NM 87107
(505) 881-1994
Contact: Mr. D. Elliott
Minimum Salary Placed: $25,000
Recruiting Specialty: Sales and marketing

Snelling Personnel Service
2601 Wyoming Boulevard NE
Albuquerque, NM 87112
(505) 293-7800
Contact: Ms. Sue Lane
Minimum Salary Placed: $25,000
Recruiting Specialty: General

Trambley the Recruiter
5325 Wyoming Boulevard NE
Albuquerque, NM 87109
(505) 821-5440
Contact: Mr. Brian Trambley
Minimum Salary Placed: $35,000
Recruiting Specialty: Engineering and
manufacturing

CORRALES

Western Healthcare Search
Corrales, NM 87048
(505) 897-1201
Minimum Salary Placed: $25,000
Recruiting Specialty: Healthcare

SANTA FE

Marcia Owen Associates
660 Granada Street
Santa Fe, NM 87501
(505) 983-7775
Contact: Ms. Marcia Owen
Minimum Salary Placed: $25,000
Recruiting Specialty: General

Radin Associates
2373 Brother Abdon Way
Santa Fe, NM 87505
(505) 983-2243
Contact: Mr. Bill Radin
Minimum Salary Placed: $50,000
Recruiting Specialty: High technology

Santa Fe Service
142 Lincoln Avenue, Suite 205
Santa Fe, NM 87501
(505) 984-8511
Contact: Mr. D. Woodin
Recruiting Specialty: Office and legal support

James Ticer Associates
268 El Diane Court
Santa Fe, NM 87501
(505) 982-5252
Contact: Mr. James Ticer
Minimum Salary Placed: $25,000
Recruiting Specialty: General

N E W   Y O R K

ALBANY

Capital Career Consultants Inc.
1 Steuban Place
Albany, NY 12207
(518) 463-6726
Contact: Mr. W. Losasso
Minimum Salary Placed: $25,000
Recruiting Specialty: Accounting, finance
and administration

De Matteo Associates
P.O. Box 13955
Albany, NY 12212
(518) 356-3900
Contact: Robena De Matteo
Minimum Salary Placed: $20,000
Recruiting Specialty: General

Management Recruiters
One Executive Park Drive
Albany, NY 12203
(518) 438-7722
Contact: Mr. Bob Mulcahey
Minimum Salary Placed: $20,000
Recruiting Specialty: General

Management Recruiters
435 New Karner Road
Albany, NY 12205
(518) 464-1461
Contact: Mr. Bob Kayajian
Minimum Salary Placed: $20,000
Recruiting Specialty: Packaged goods
marketing

Personnel Professionals Inc.
4 Computer Drive West
Albany, NY 12205
(518) 437-9095
Contact: Mr. Joseph Burke
Minimum Salary Placed: $25,000
Recruiting Specialty: General

Ritta Associates
6 Automation Lane
Albany, NY 12205
(518) 458-7340
Contact: Mr. Arthur Hansen
Minimum Salary Placed: $40,000
Recruiting Specialty: Engineering and
marketing in defense, power generation
and wireless communications

Lake Associates
125 Wolf Road
Albany, NY 12205
(518) 877-3071
Contact: Mr. Ralph Bohlke
Minimum Salary Placed: $25,000
Recruiting Specialty: Pharmaceutical,
chemical, electronics and environmental

Technical Staffing Association
12 Corporate Woods Boulevard
Albany, NY 12211
(518) 463-4598
Contact: Mr. Donald Munger
Recruiting Specialty: Environmental,
chemical and pharmaceuticals

AMAGANSETT

Executive Search Services
P.O. Box 2759
Amagansett, NY 11930
(516) 267-3730

Contact: Ms. Martha Ward
Minimum Salary Placed: $50,000
Recruiting Specialty: Sales and marketing
in consumer products and finance

AMHERST

Allen and Speth of Buffalo, Inc.
3131 Sheridan Drive
Amherst, NY 14226
(716) 836-5070
Contact: Mr. S. Silverman
Minimum Salary Placed: $30,000
Recruiting Specialty: Engineering, data
processing, sales and marketing

Database Search, Inc.
146 Lamarck Drive
Amherst, NY 14226
(716) 839-1958
Contact: Ms. Collen Switala
Recruiting Specialty: Data architects,
data modelers, database administrators

Robert Half International
4053 Maple Road
Amherst, NY 14226
(716) 833-5322
Contact: Mr. J. Creuz
Minimum Salary Placed: $25,000
Recruiting Specialty: Accounting and fi-
nance

G.R. Walker & Associate
170 Parkledge Drive
Amherst, NY 14226
(716) 839-9132
Contact: Gary Walker
Minimum Salary Placed: $35,000
Recruiting Specialty: Sales and market-
ing, manufacturing

ARMONK

E.G. Todd Physician Search Inc.
1 Byram Brook Place
Armonk, NY 10504
(914) 273-5666
Contact: Mr. R. Glehan
Minimum Salary Placed: $40,000
Recruiting Specialty: Healthcare and phy-
sicians

AUBURN

Management Recruiters
120 Genesee Street, Suite 602
Auburn, NY 13021
(315) 638-7475
Contact: Mr. Ed Dunn
Minimum Salary Placed: $20,000
Recruiting Specialty: General

AVALON

Inside Management Associates
P.O. Box 370
Avalon, NY 11072
(212) 683-7200
Contact: Mr. Paul Steinberg
Minimum Salary Placed: $60,000
Recruiting Specialty: General

BABYLON

Inside Management Associates
106 Peninsula Drive
Babylon, NY 11702
(516) 587-4525
Contact: Mr. Paul Steinberg
Minimum Salary Placed: $60,000
Recruiting Specialty: General

BALDWIN

Ahrens Agency / Frontrunner Search, LTD.
P.O. Box 349
Baldwin, NY 11520
(516) 223-5627
Contact: Mr. Daniel Ahrens
Minimum Salary Placed: $40,000
Recruiting Specialty: Banking and mortgages

BAY SHORE

Eltra Search
1047 Carll Drive
Bay Shore, NY 11706
(516) 665-3408
Contact: Ms. L. Bashe
Minimum Salary Placed: $25,000
Recruiting Specialty: General

BEDFORD HILLS

HLR Consulting, Inc.
2 South Beechwood Road, 1st Floor
Bedford Hills, NY 10507
(914) 242-7300
Contact: Mr. Harvey Zuckerman
Minimum Salary Placed: $25,000
Recruiting Specialty: Healthcare

BINGHAMTON

Richard D. Holbrook Associates
107 Court Street, Suite 440
Binghamton, NY 13901
(607) 723-3096
Contact: Mr. Richard Holbrook
Minimum Salary Placed: $75,000
Recruiting Specialty: General

BREWSTER

Resource National
Route 22
Brewster, NY 10509
(914) 279-8827
Contact: Ms. Connie Grewan
Minimum Salary Placed: $25,000
Recruiting Specialty: General

Roberts Executive Recruitment
Colonial Square, Route 22
Brewster, NY 10509
(914) 279-5575
Contact: Mr. Bob Roberts
Recruiting Specialty: Pulp and paper, converting, chemical, human resources, plastics, and engineering

Westport Tax Management Inc.
Colonial Square Office Park, Route 22
Brewster, NY 10509
(914) 278-8100
Minimum Salary Placed: $30,000
Recruiting Specialty: Taxation

BRONX

Charles J. McBride and Associates
76 Chatfield Road
Bronxville, NY 10708
(914) 779-0014
Contact: Mr. Charles McBride
Minimum Salary Placed: $25,000
Recruiting Specialty: General

BROOKLYN

Hutchinson Resources International
573 76th Street
Brooklyn, NY 11209
(718) 748-5056

Contact: Ms. Loretta Hutchinson
Minimum Salary Placed: $50,000
Recruiting Specialty: General

PSP Agency
188 Montague Street
Brooklyn, NY 11201
(718) 596-3786
Contact: Ms. Iris Nunez
Minimum Salary Placed: $40,000
Recruiting Specialty: Telecommunications and engineering

BUFFALO

Beishline Executive Research
3527 Harlem Road
Buffalo, NY 14225
(716) 836-7650
Contact: Mr. J. Beishline
Minimum Salary Placed: $45,000
Recruiting Specialty: Engineering and marketing in manufacturing and high technology

C-R Associates
1231 Delaware Avenue
Buffalo, NY 14209
(716) 884-1734
Contact: Mr. P. Cramer
Minimum Salary Placed: $25,000
Recruiting Specialty: Finance and banking

Dunhill of Buffalo Agency, Ltd.
584 Delaware Avenue
Buffalo, NY 14202
(716) 885-3576
Contact: Mrs. Lupe Breen
Minimum Salary Placed: $25,000
Recruiting Specialty: General

Alan Fenster Associates
3178 Delaware Avenue
Buffalo, NY 14217
(716) 873-4615
Contact: Mr. Alan Fenster
Minimum Salary Placed: $35,000
Recruiting Specialty: Attorneys, accounting and finance

Physician International
4 Vermont Street
Buffalo, NY 14213
(800) 846-0220
Contact: Mr. Charles Cimasi
Minimum Salary Placed: $100,000
Recruiting Specialty: Physicians

CAMILLUS

R. P. Clarke Associates, Inc.
100 Main Street
Camillus, NY 13031
(315) 488-1911
Contact: Mr. Peter Clark
Recruiting Specialty: General

Dapexs Consultants Inc.
5320 West Genesee Street
Camillus, NY 13031
(315) 484-9300
Contact: Mr. Peter Leofsky
Minimum Salary Placed: $50,000
Recruiting Specialty: Computers, finance and engineering, MIS, FIS

CARLE PLACE

Cowin Association
1 Old Country Road
Carle Place, NY 11514
(516) 741-3020

Contact: Mr. David Cowin
Minimum Salary Placed: $60,000
Recruiting Specialty: High technology

CENTRAL SQUARE

C.F. Holm and Associates
Fulton Road
Central Square, NY 13036
(315) 676-7955
Contact: Mr. Chris Holm
Minimum Salary Placed: $25,000
Recruiting Specialty: Pharmaceuticals
and process industry

CHAPPAQUA

HRP Consulting Corporation
31 Mayberry Road
Chappaqua, NY 10514
(914) 241-3022
Minimum Salary Placed: $25,000
Recruiting Specialty: Computer

CHATHAM

Global Recruiting Inc.
George Road
Chatham, NY 12037
(518) 392-2429
Recruiting Specialty: Paper and chemical
field

CLARENCE

Kozlin Associates, Inc.
9070 Main Street
Clarence, NY 14031
(716) 634-5955

Contact: Mr. Jeffrey Kozlin
Minimum Salary Placed: $50,000
Recruiting Specialty: Manufacturing and
textiles, and general

CLIFTON PARK

Lake Associates
453 Kinns Road
Clifton Park, NY 12065
(518) 877-3071
Contact: Mr. Ernest Steinmann
Recruiting Specialty: Management and
technical personnel, biotech, pharmaceutical, and electronics

CORTLAND

Hospitality International
181 Port Watson Street
Cortland, NY 13045
(607) 756-8550
Contact: Ms. Susan Stafford
Minimum Salary Placed: $25,000
Recruiting Specialty: Hospitality

CROTON-ON-HUDSON

Laguzza Associates, Ltd.
McGuire Lane
Croton-on-Hudson, NY 10520
(914) 271-4002
Contact: Mr. John Laguzza
Minimum Salary Placed: $75,000
Recruiting Specialty: Finance mainly and
insurance occasionally

DELMAR

Nortech Resources
321 Delaware Avenue
Delmar, NY 12054
(518) 475-9700
Recruiting Specialty: General

John Wales Associates
3 Normanskill Boulevard
Delmar, NY 12054
(518) 439-8615
Contact: Dr. John Wales
Recruiting Specialty: Physicians in health-care and education

DEWITT

Sales Consultants of Syracuse Inc.
5730 Commons Park, P.O. Box 727
Dewitt, NY 13214
(315) 449-0244
Contact: Mr. Roderick Seabrook
Minimum Salary Placed: $20,000
Recruiting Specialty: Sales

EAST NORTHPORT

Shupack & Michaels, Inc.
27 Monmouth Drive, Suite 277
East Northport, NY 11731-1332
(516) 757-4559
Contact: Mr. Joseph Shupack
Recruiting Specialty: HVAC and mechanical, electrical, civil, sanitary, transportation, and structural

EAST WILLISTON

Peter R. Taylor Associates, Inc.
43 Orchard Drive
East Williston, NY 11596
(516) 742-9292
Contact: Mr. Peter Taylor
Minimum Salary Placed: $40,000
Recruiting Specialty: Retail and real estate

ELMONT

Vincent Lee Associates
91 Fallon Avenue
Elmont, NY 11003
(516) 775-8551
Contact: Mr. Vincent Lee
Minimum Salary Placed: $25,000
Recruiting Specialty: Accounting, finance and insurance

ENDICOTT

Career Management Services
112 Nanticoke Avenue
Endicott, NY 13760
(607) 785-2551
Recruiting Specialty: Technical

FAIRPORT

Good Associates
54 West Avenue
Fairport, NY 14450
(716) 223-8826
Recruiting Specialty: General

FISHKILL

Management Recruiters of Poughkeepsie, Inc.
2 Summit Court, Suite 302
Fishkill, NY 12524
(914) 897-2055
Contact: Mr. Michael Gionta
Minimum Salary Placed: $30,000
Recruiting Specialty: Sales in computers healthcare

FLUSHING

Adams Personnel Agency
3915 Main Street, Suite 301
Flushing, NY 11354
(718) 359-0800
Contact: Mr. T. Khan
Minimum Salary Placed: $25,000
Recruiting Specialty: General

CareerPower Inc.
10015 34th Avenue
Flushing, NY 11368
(718) 478-0322
Recruiting Specialty: General

Viva Personnel Agency
11821 Queens Boulevard, Suite 600
Flushing, NY 11375
(516) 621-5500
Contact: Ms. Viva Labrella
Minimum Salary Placed: $25,000
Recruiting Specialty: General

FORT PLAIN

T.J. Koellhoffer & Associates
ROAD 1
Ft. Plain, NY 13339
(315) 823-1077
Contact: Mr. Robert Ritz
Minimum Salary Placed: $50,000
Recruiting Specialty: High technology

FREEPORT

CFI Resources Inc.
68 West 1st Street
Freeport, NY 11520
(516) 623-4563
Contact: Mr. Chuck Winick
Minimum Salary Placed: $25,000
Recruiting Specialty: High technology and sales and marketing

GARDEN CITY

R.O.I. Associates Inc.
401 Franklin Avenue, Suite 102
Garden City, NY 11530-5943
(516) 746-4842
Contact: Mr. Peter Portanova
Recruiting Specialty: Materials management, manufacturing and manufacturing consultants

Franklin Allen Consultants Ltd.
401 Franklin Ave., Suite 102
Garden City, NY 11530
(516) 248-4511
Contact: Mr. H. Roher
Minimum Salary Placed: $40,000
Recruiting Specialty: Healthcare

John Mulligan Associates
647 Franklin Avenue
Garden City, NY 11530
(516) 742-7100
Contact: Mr. John Mulligan
Minimum Salary Placed: $50,000
Recruiting Specialty: Pension planning

P. G. Prager Search Associates, Ltd.
1461 Franklin Avenue
Garden City, NY 11530
(516) 294-4400
Contact: Mr. Paul Gershon Prager
Recruiting Specialty: General

GLEN COVE

Heyman Associates Inc.
20 Marietta Road
Glen Cove, NY 11542
(516) 759-9076
Contact: Ms. L. Ryan
Minimum Salary Placed: $25,000
Recruiting Specialty: Public relations

GOLDENS BRIDGE

Pat Allen Associates
23 Indian Hill Road
Goldens Bridge, NY 10526
(914) 232-1545
Contact: Mr. Pat Allen
Minimum Salary Placed: $25,000
Recruiting Specialty: Insurance and safety

GRAND ISLAND

Anne P. Dyet
P.O. Box 1222
Grand Island, NY 14072
(716) 773-0151
Contact: Ms. Anne Dyet
Recruiting Specialty: Medical, production development and marketing

GREAT NECK

APR Executive Search
17 Barstow Road
Great Neck, NY 11021
(516) 466-4120
Contact: Mr. S. Berkowitz
Minimum Salary Placed: $25,000
Recruiting Specialty: General

Carter/MacKay
111 Great Neck Road
Great Neck, NY 11021
(516) 829-9250
Contact: Mr. Larry Orbach
Minimum Salary Placed: $40,000
Recruiting Specialty: Sales in drugs and pharmaceuticals

CFI Resources Inc.
7 Clover Drive
Great Neck, NY 11021
(516) 466-1221
Contact: Mr. Leo Cohen
Minimum Salary Placed: $25,000
Recruiting Specialty: High technology, sales and marketing in engineering, semiconductor and electronics

A.E. Feldman Association
445 Northern Boulevard
Great Neck, NY 11021
(516) 466-4708
Contact: Mr. Abe Feldman
Minimum Salary Placed: $40,000
Recruiting Specialty: General

N. Steven Fells & Company, Inc.
11 Grace Avenue, Suite 200
Great Neck, NY 11021
(516) 829-9200
Contact: Mr. Norman Fells
Minimum Salary Placed: $40,000
Recruiting Specialty: Computer and
equipment leasing

Barry Nathanson Associates
40 Cutter Mill Road
Great Neck, NY 11021
(516) 482-7222
Contact: Mr. Barry Nathanson
Minimum Salary Placed: $100,000
Recruiting Specialty: General

Travel Executive Search
5 Rose Avenue
Great Neck, NY 11021
(516) 829-8829
Contact: Ms. Karen Rubin
Minimum Salary Placed: $30,000
Recruiting Specialty: Travel

H. N. Wasserman & Company, Inc.
P.O. Box 188
Great Neck, NY 11022
(516) 829-3800
Contact: Mr. Hilton Wasserman
Minimum Salary Placed: $40,000
Recruiting Specialty: General

GREENWOOD

**Management Recruiters of Orange
County, Inc.**
P.O. Box 1530
Greenwood Lake, NY 10925
(914) 477-9509
Contact: Ms. Carolyn Chermak
Recruiting Specialty: General

HARTSDALE

Olaf S. Meyer & Company, Ltd.
250 E. Hartsdale Avenue, Suite 31
Hartsdale, NY 10530
(914) 723-3777
Contact: Mr. Olaf Meyer
Minimum Salary Placed: $75,000
Recruiting Specialty: Finance and banking

Newport Management
100 E. Hartsdale Avenue
Hartsdale, NY 10530
(914) 725-5244
Contact: Mr. Kenneth Zeif
Minimum Salary Placed: $25,000
Recruiting Specialty: Sales and marketing
in computers and communications and
technical support

HAUPPAUGE

Ames-O'Neill Associates, Inc.
330 Vanderbilt Motor Pkwy.
Hauppauge, NY 11788
(516) 582-4800
Contact: Mr. Chet Ames
Minimum Salary Placed: $35,000
Recruiting Specialty: Engineering, high
technology and some general

Eastbourne Associates, Inc.
330 Motor Parkway
Hauppauge, NY 11788
(516) 231-2555
Contact: Ms. Rosemary Kissel
Recruiting Specialty: General

HAWTHORNE

Boyden
364 Elwood Avenue
Hawthorne, NY 10532
(914) 747-0093
Contact: Mr. Richard Foy
Minimum Salary Placed: $90,000
Recruiting Specialty: General

**Sales Consultants of
Westchester-South, Inc.**
Nine Skyline Drive
Hawthorne, NY 10532
(914) 592-1290
Contact: Mr. Robert Penney
Minimum Salary Placed: $30,000
Recruiting Specialty: Sales

HEWLETT

Fred Koffler Associates
1344 Broadway, Suite 300
Hewlett, NY 11557
(516) 569-6582
Contact: Mr. Fred Koffler
Minimum Salary Placed: $60,000
Recruiting Specialty: General

HICKSVILLE

Amherst Personnel Group Inc.
550 Old Country Road
Hicksville, NY 11801
(516) 433-7610
Contact: Mr. Charles Eibeler
Minimum Salary Placed: $30,000
Recruiting Specialty: Sales and marketing
in retail

Arrow Employment Agency Inc.
320 North Broadway
Hicksville, NY 11801
(516) 931-4200
Contact: Mr. N. Sharp
Minimum Salary Placed: $25,000
Recruiting Specialty: General

Zachary & Sanders, Inc.
82 N. Broadway, Suite 102
Hicksville, NY 11801
(516) 931-6103
Contact: Ms. Jasmine Andrews
Minimum Salary Placed: $45,000
Recruiting Specialty: General

HUNTINGTON

Joseph Associates
31 Hollywood Place
Huntington, NY 11743
(516) 351-5805
Contact: Mr. J. Nakelski
Minimum Salary Placed: $25,000
Recruiting Specialty: Data processing
and statistical programming

M.A. Pelle Associates, Inc.
P.O. Box 476
Huntington, NY 11743
(516) 385-8925
Contact: Mr. Michael Pelle
Minimum Salary Placed: $50,000
Recruiting Specialty: General

Weber Executive Search
205 E. Main Street, Suite 2-3A
Huntington, NY 11743
(516) 673-4700
Contact: Mr. Ronald Weber
Minimum Salary Placed: $75,000
Recruiting Specialty: Food and beverage

HUNTINGTON STATION

BPCG International
175 A East Second Street
Huntington Station, NY 11746
(516) 271-0800
Contact: Mr. Justin Thompson
Minimum Salary Placed: $85,000
Recruiting Specialty: International trade

Management Recruiters
33 Walt Whitman Road, Suite 208
Huntington Station, NY 11746
(516) 385-0633
Contact: Mr. Bob Levitt
Minimum Salary Placed: $30,000
Recruiting Specialty: High technology,
and computer hardware and software general

Sales Consultants
33 Walt Whitman Road, Suite 208
Huntington Station, NY 11746
(516) 385-0633
Contact: Mr. Bob Levitt
Minimum Salary Placed: $20,000
Recruiting Specialty: Sales

JERICHO

Accountants On Call
500 N. Broadway
Jericho, NY 11753
(516) 935-0050
Contact: Mr. Andy Targovnik
Recruiting Specialty: Accounting and
bookkeeping

Bartl & Evins
The Penthouse, 333 N. Broadway
Jericho, NY 11753
(516) 433-3333
Contact: Ms. Susan Evins
Minimum Salary Placed: $35,000
Recruiting Specialty: Finance and accounting

Bruml Associates Inc.
306 Birchwood Park Drive
Jericho, NY 11753
(516) 822-7940
Contact: Mr. Mike Bruml
Minimum Salary Placed: $25,000
Recruiting Specialty: Electronics

Mogul Consultants, Inc.
380 N. Broadway
Jericho, NY 11753
(516) 822-4363
Contact: Mr. Gene Mogul
Minimum Salary Placed: $40,000
Recruiting Specialty: High technology

The P & L Group
366 N. Broadway, Suite 228
Jericho, NY 11753
(516) 938-7337
Contact: Mr. Hyman Livingston
Minimum Salary Placed: $35,000
Recruiting Specialty: Manufacturing and purchasing

Roth Young
333 North Broadway Street
Jericho, NY 11753
(516) 822-6000
Contact: Mr. Anthony Capece
Minimum Salary Placed: $25,000
Recruiting Specialty: Accounting, finance, and healthcare

TMC Management Consultants
333 Jericho Turnpike
Jericho, NY 11753
(516) 681-0000
Recruiting Specialty: General

Woodbury Personnel Associates Inc.
375 North Broadway, Suite 103
Jericho, NY 11753
(516) 938-7910
Minimum Salary Placed: $25,000
Recruiting Specialty: General

KENMORE

Todd Arro Inc.
3024 Delaware Avenue
Kenmore, NY 14217
(716) 871-0993
Contact: Mr. Todd Arro
Minimum Salary Placed: $25,000
Recruiting Specialty: Outside sales

LARCHMONT

E.J. Michaels, Ltd.
1865 Palmer Avenue, Suite 101
Larchmont, NY 10538
(914) 833-1700
Contact: Mr. Phillip Jacobs
Recruiting Specialty: Physicians

Dennis P. O'Toole & Associates Inc.
1865 Palmer Avenue, Suite 210
Larchmont, NY 10538
(914) 833-3712
Contact: Mr. Dennis O'Toole
Minimum Salary Placed: $70,000
Recruiting Specialty: Hospitality

LATHAM

Ethan Allen Medical Search
404 Troy-Schenectady Road
Latham, NY 12110
(518) 785-7555
Contact: Mr. Harris Metzner
Minimum Salary Placed: $35,000
Recruiting Specialty: Healthcare and clinical search

People Seekers
8 Stanley Circle
Latham, NY 12110
(518) 786-0785
Contact: Mr. P. Cerutti
Minimum Salary Placed: $25,000
Recruiting Specialty: General

LEVITTOWN

Mar-El Employment Agency Inc.
3000 Hempstead Turnpike
Levittown, NY 11756
(516) 579-7777
Contact: Mr. A. Mogul
Minimum Salary Placed: $25,000
Recruiting Specialty: General

LITTLE NECK

Robert Bennett Associates
P.O. Box 261
Little Neck, NY 11363
(718) 428-5455
Contact: Mr. Robert Bennett
Minimum Salary Placed: $40,000
Recruiting Specialty: Attorneys

LIVERPOOL

Norris INC.
P.O. Box 2460
Liverpool, NY 13089
(315) 695-4999
Contact: Mr. Don Norris
Recruiting Specialty: Engineering, human resources, manufacturing, automation, purchasing and materials

MADRID

Management Recruiters
P.O. Box 218
Madrid, NY 13660
(315) 322-0222
Contact: Mr. James Infantino
Minimum Salary Placed: $20,000
Recruiting Specialty: General

MALVERNE

Sales Consultants
363 Hempstead Avenue
Malverne, NY 11565
(516) 599-5824
Contact: Mr. James Jacobs
Minimum Salary Placed: $20,000
Recruiting Specialty: Sales

MAMARONECK

Perry Jacobs Partner Search
14 Marbourne Drive
Mamaroneck, NY 10543
(914) 381-7272
Contact: Mr. Perry Jacobs
Minimum Salary Placed: $75,000
Recruiting Specialty: Attorneys

Spanusa Inc.
135 Beach Avenue
Mamaroneck, NY 10543
(914) 381-5555
Contact: Mr. Manuel Boado
Minimum Salary Placed: $50,000
Recruiting Specialty: General; spanish-speaking professionals

MANHASSET

P. Burton Associates Inc.
1615 Northern Boulevard
Manhasset, NY 11030
(516) 365-6060
Contact: Ms. Priscilla Friedman
Minimum Salary Placed: $25,000
Recruiting Specialty: General

MANLIUS

D.D. Chunka Associates Inc.
4530 Waltham Circle
Manlius, NY 13104
(315) 682-2221
Contact: Mr. D. Chunka
Minimum Salary Placed: $30,000
Recruiting Specialty: Manufacturing

Healthcare Recruiters of New York
8195 Cazenovia Road
Manlius, NY 13104
(315) 682-5550
Minimum Salary Placed: $25,000
Recruiting Specialty: Healthcare

MASSAPEQUA

AAA Consultant
175 Veterans Boulevard
Massapequa, NY 11758
(516) 795-7670
Minimum Salary Placed: $25,000
Recruiting Specialty: Biotech and medical

C.T. Group
264 North Elm Street
Massapequa, NY 11758
(516) 797-3642
Contact: Ms. Camille Coppola
Minimum Salary Placed: $25,000
Recruiting Specialty: In-home healthcare

Dunhill Professional Search
12 Carmans Road
Massapequa, NY 11758
(516) 797-1000
Contact: Mr. Philip Missirlian
Minimum Salary Placed: $25,000
Recruiting Specialty: General

Image Associates, Inc.
5254 Merrick Road
Massapequa, NY 11758
(516) 798-3993
Contact: Ms. Pearl Martin
Recruiting Specialty: Electronics, aerospace, MIS, pharmaceutical, and chemical

Morgan/Webber
5510 Merrick Road
Massapequa, NY 11758
(516) 798-0100
Contact: Mr. Steven Lavender
Minimum Salary Placed: $50,000
Recruiting Specialty: General

MELVILLE

Audit Data Search Ltd.
535 Broadhollow Road, Suite 413
Melville, NY 11747
(516) 454-6666
Contact: Mr. A. Harris
Minimum Salary Placed: $25,000
Recruiting Specialty: Information systems auditing

Lloyd Personnel Consultants, Inc.
445 Broadhollow Road, Suite 120
Melville, NY 11747
(516) 777-7600
Contact: Mr. Merrill Banks
Minimum Salary Placed: $50,000
Recruiting Specialty: General

Sigma Search Inc.
535 Broadhollow Road, Suite A3
Melville, NY 11747
(516) 694-7707
Contact: Ms. Thea Linker
Recruiting Specialty: Office support

MILLBROOK

Abbott Smith Associates, Inc.
P.O. Box 318, Franklin Avenue
Millbrook, NY 12545
(914) 677-5300
Contact: Mr. David Brinkerhoff
Minimum Salary Placed: $60,000
Recruiting Specialty: General

MILLWOOD

Allen Barry & Company, Inc.
358 Saw Mill River Road
Millwood, NY 10546
(914) 923-3500
Contact: Mr. Allen Ancowitz
Minimum Salary Placed: $50,000
Recruiting Specialty: Consumer products, biotech, and research and development

MINEOLA

Dorst Information Service
250 Old Country Road, Suite 505
Mineola, NY 11501
(516) 294-0884
Contact: Ms. G. Grillo
Minimum Salary Placed: $25,000
Recruiting Specialty: Telecommunications, sales, marketing and computers

HVS Executive Search
372 Willis Avenue
Mineola, NY 11501
(516) 248-8828
Contact: Mr. Keith Kefgen
Minimum Salary Placed: $50,000
Recruiting Specialty: Hospitality

NESCONSET

Romano McAvoy Associates, Inc.
872 Jericho Turnpike
Nesconset, NY 11767
(516) 265-7878
Contact: Mr. J. Romano
Minimum Salary Placed: $25,000
Recruiting Specialty: Computers and communications

NEW HARTFORD

Carlile Personnel Agency Inc.
3 Ellinwood Court, Suite 202
New Hartford, NY 13413
(315) 736-3083
Contact: Mr. A. Douglas Manning
Recruiting Specialty: Manufacturing and engineering, design, manufacturing management and purchasing

NEW CITY

Joan Alpert Associates, Inc.
20 Squadron Boulevard
New City, NY 10956
(914) 634-0000
Contact: Ms. Joan Alpert
Minimum Salary Placed: $25,000
Recruiting Specialty: General

Information Systems Search
490 Route 304
New City, NY 10956
(914) 634-1772
Contact: Ms. N. Rubin
Minimum Salary Placed: $25,000
Recruiting Specialty: Computers and telecommunication

Jakobs & Associates, International
79 Burda Avenue
New City, NY 10956
(914) 638-9432
Contact: Ms. Nancy Jakobs
Minimum Salary Placed: $75,000
Recruiting Specialty: General

Logistics Management Resources, Inc.
P.O. Box 2204
New City, NY 10956
(914) 638-4224
Contact: Ms. Marjorie Slater
Minimum Salary Placed: $45,000
Recruiting Specialty: Logistics

Professional Resources
44 Omni Court
New City, NY 10956
(914) 638-4296
Contact: Mr. Irwin Feigenbaum
Minimum Salary Placed: $40,000
Recruiting Specialty: Retail and banking

Shapiro Associates
10 Esquire Road, Suite 10
New City, NY 10956
(914) 634-0803
Contact: Mr. Martin Shapiro
Minimum Salary Placed: $40,000
Recruiting Specialty: General

Solo Management Inc.
20 Squadron Boulevard
New City, NY 10956
(914) 634-2600 or (212) 432-6300

Contact: Mr. P. Solomon
Minimum Salary Placed: $50,000
Recruiting Specialty: Investment bankers
and brokers

NEW HYDE PARK

Richard Farber Associates
P.O. Box 3556
New Hyde Park, NY 11040
(516) 627-6090
Contact: Mr. Richard Farber
Minimum Salary Placed: $25,000
Recruiting Specialty: General

NEW ROCHELLE

Newell Associates
89 Devonshire Road
New Rochelle, NY 10804
(914) 636-3254
Contact: Mr. Donald Pierce Newell
Minimum Salary Placed: $50,000
Recruiting Specialty: Stockbrokers; general

Daniel F. Reilly and Associates
2241 Palmer Avenue
New Rochelle, NY 10801
(914) 633-3898
Contact: Mr. Dan Reilly
Minimum Salary Placed: $40,000
Recruiting Specialty: Software industry
(inventors of software)

NEW YORK

A-K-A (Anita Kaufmann Associates)
1301 Avenue of the Americas, 41st Floor
New York, NY 10019
(212) 581-8166
Contact: Ms. Anita Kaufmann
Minimum Salary Placed: $50,000
Recruiting Specialty: Attorneys

A-L Associates Inc.
355 Lexington Avenue, Suite 10
New York, NY 10017
(212) 878-9000
Contact: Mr. E. Orchant
Minimum Salary Placed: $35,000
Recruiting Specialty: Attorneys, accounting and finance

Able Personnel Inc.
280 Madison Avenue
New York, NY 10016
(212) 689-5500
Contact: Ms. Laura Hill
Minimum Salary Placed: $60,000
Recruiting Specialty: New media and interactive

Absolutely Professional Staffing
7 Dey Street
New York, NY 10007
(212) 608-1444
Contact: Mr. Jack Talabisco
Recruiting Specialty: Office support

The Accord Group, Johnson, Smith & Knisely
100 Park Avenue, 15th Floor
New York, NY 10169
(212) 885-9100
Contact: Mr. Gary Knisely
Recruiting Specialty: Financial, fashion and retail, media and entertainment, and healthcare

Accountants Executive Search
535 5th Avenue, Suite 1200
New York, NY 10017
(212) 682-5900
Contact: Mr. Bernard Simon
Minimum Salary Placed: $25,000
Recruiting Specialty: Accounting and finance

Accountant's Choice Personnel
230 Park Avenue, Suite 1000
New York, NY 10169
(212) 643-4400
Contact: Mr. Michael Thomas
Recruiting Specialty: Accounting

Accounting Resources International, Inc.
One Battery Park Plaza
New York, NY 10004
(212) 269-0556
Contact: Mr. Bob Kaufmann
Minimum Salary Placed: $30,000
Recruiting Specialty: Accounting and finance

Affirmative Action Associates
443 West 50th Street
New York, NY 10019
(212) 688-5177
Contact: Mr. Melvyn Black
Minimum Salary Placed: $25,000
Recruiting Specialty: General; minorities and disabled professionals

Helen Akullian Agency, Inc.
280 Madison Avenue, Suite 604
New York, NY 10016
(212) 532-3210
Contact: Ms. Helen Akullian
Recruiting Specialty: Corporate communications

Alexander Ross Inc.
280 Madison Avenue
New York, NY 10016
(212) 889-9333
Contact: Mr. Ben Lichtenstein
Minimum Salary Placed: $80,000
Recruiting Specialty: Human resources and general

The Alfus Group
353 Lexington Avenue, Sutie 600
New York, NY 10016
(212) 599-1000
Contact: Mr. Phillip Alfus
Minimum Salary Placed: $70,000
Recruiting Specialty: Hospitality

Allard Associates
150 Broadway, 23rd Floor
New York, NY 10038
(212) 741-0045
Contact: Mr. Lou Giacalone
Minimum Salary Placed: $50,000
Recruiting Specialty: Consumer banking and finance

Allen Evans Associates
157 E. 57th Street
New York, NY 10022
(212) 486-6626
Contact: Mr. Robert Klein
Minimum Salary Placed: $60,000
Recruiting Specialty: Communications and technical publishing

American Group Practice, Inc.
420 Madison Avenue, 7th Floor
New York, NY 10017
(212) 371-3091
Contact: Mr. Ralph Herz
Minimum Salary Placed: $60,000
Recruiting Specialty: Healthcare and physicians

Analysts Resources Inc.
75 Maiden Lane
New York, NY 10038
(212) 755-2777
Contact: Ms. Monica Smith
Minimum Salary Placed: $60,000
Recruiting Specialty: Financial services

Analytic Recruiting, Inc.
21 E. 40 Street, Suite 500
New York, NY 10016
(212) 545-8511
Contact: Mr. Daniel Raz
Minimum Salary Placed: $40,000
Recruiting Specialty: General

Alexander, Thompson and Company Ltd.
521 5th Avenue, 17th Floor
New York, NY 10175
(212) 599-2055
Contact: Ms. T. Lee
Minimum Salary Placed: $35,000
Recruiting Specialty: MIS, finance and accounting

Alfus Group
353 Lexington Avenue
New York, NY 10016
(212) 599-1000
Minimum Salary Placed: $25,000
Recruiting Specialty: General

Altschular Harb and Associates
118 East 25th Street
New York, NY 10010
(212) 505-2630
Minimum Salary Placed: $35,000
Recruiting Specialty: Advertising

Anapol Enterprises Inc.
192 Lexington Avenue, Suite 902
New York, NY 10016
(212) 481-0944
Contact: Ms. J. Anapol
Minimum Salary Placed: $60,000
Recruiting Specialty: Physicians

Anderson and Schwab Inc.
444 Madison Avenue
New York, NY 10022
(212) 758-6800
Contact: Mr. F. Schwab
Minimum Salary Placed: $50,000
Recruiting Specialty: Mining and natural
resources

Arnold Huberman Associates Inc.
51 East 25th Street, Suite 501
New York, NY 10010
(212) 545-9033
Contact: Mr. Arnold Huberman
Minimum Salary Placed: $25,000
Recruiting Specialty: General

Aronow Associates, Inc.
1 Pennsylvania Plaza, Suite 2131
New York, NY 10119
(212) 947-3777
Contact: Mr. Lawrence Aronow
Minimum Salary Placed: $40,000
Recruiting Specialty: Financial services

Arton Perez Consultants
350 Lexington Avenue
New York, NY 10016
(212) 986-1630
Contact: Ms. Maria Perez
Minimum Salary Placed: $40,000
Recruiting Specialty: Higher education

Aster Search Group
555 Madison Avenue
New York, NY 10022
(212) 888-6182
Minimum Salary Placed: $70,000
Recruiting Specialty: General

Avery Crafts Associates, Ltd.
116 John Street, Suite 820
New York, NY 10038
(212) 285-1074
Contact: Mr. Norman Crafts
Minimum Salary Placed: $70,000
Recruiting Specialty: Insurance and finan-
cial institutions

Avalon Health
245 E. 54th Street
New York, NY 10022
(212) 758-5243
Recruiting Specialty: Managed care

The Ayers Group, Inc.
370 Lexington Avenue, 24th Floor
New York, NY 10017
(212) 599-5656
Contact: Mr. William Ayers
Minimum Salary Placed: $50,000
Recruiting Specialty: MIS

BLB Consulting
535 Fifth Avenue, Suite 1004
New York, NY 10017
(212) 808-0577

Contact: Ms. Barbara Bartell
Recruiting Specialty: Human resources

The BMW Group, Inc.
40 Exchange Place, Suite 700
New York, NY 10005
(212) 943-8800
Contact: Mr. Alan Burke
Minimum Salary Placed: $40,000
Recruiting Specialty: MIS and computers

D. Bacal and Associates
10 E. 39th Street, Suite 1106
New York, NY 10165
(212) 953-7200
Contact: Ms. D. Bacal
Minimum Salary Placed: $30,000
Recruiting Specialty: Legal support and
computers

Bader Research Corporation
6 E. 45th Street, Suite 901
New York, NY 10017
(212) 682-4750
Contact: Mr. Sam Bader
Minimum Salary Placed: $50,000
Recruiting Specialty: Attorneys

The Bankers Register
500 Fifth Avenue, Suite 414
New York, NY 10110
(212) 840-0800
Contact: Mr. James Bogart
Recruiting Specialty: Banking

The Barack Group, Inc.
885 Third Avenue
New York, NY 10022
(212) 230-3280
Contact: Ms. Brianne Barack
Minimum Salary Placed: $75,000
Recruiting Specialty: Consumer goods
and services

Barr Associates
521 Fifth Avenue, 17th Floor
New York, NY 10017
(212) 867-3215
Contact: Mr. Jamie Barr
Minimum Salary Placed: $40,000
Recruiting Specialty: Investment and
commercial banking and insurance

Battalia Winston
300 Park Avenue
New York, NY 10022
(212) 308-8080
Contact: Mr. O. William Battalia
Minimum Salary Placed: $100,000
Recruiting Specialty: General

Baum Stevens Inc.
950 3rd Avenue
New York, NY 10022
(212) 755-2500
Contact: Ms. Catherine Baum
Minimum Salary Placed: $60,000
Recruiting Specialty: Attorneys

Martin H. Bauman Associates, Inc.
375 Park Avenue, Suite 2002
New York, NY 10152
(212) 752-6580
Contact: Mr. Martin Bauman
Minimum Salary Placed: $90,000
Recruiting Specialty: General

The Beam Group
600 Third Street
New York, NY 10016
(914) 694-1130
Contact: Mr. Rick Evans
Minimum Salary Placed: $60,000
Recruiting Specialty: General

Cherie Becker Associates Ltd.
60 East 42nd Street
New York, NY 10165
(212) 818-0400
Contact: Ms. Cherie Becker
Minimum Salary Placed: $25,000
Recruiting Specialty: Travel

Marcia Beilin, Inc.
230 Park Avenue, Suite 1530
New York, NY 10169
(212) 370-4330
Contact: Ms. Marcia Beilin
Minimum Salary Placed: $60,000
Recruiting Specialty: Attorneys

Nelson Bell and Partners
280 Park Avenue
New York, NY 10017
(212) 949-6666
Contact: Mr. Nelson Bell
Minimum Salary Placed: $40,000
Recruiting Specialty: Finance

Bell Wishingrad Partners Inc.
230 Park Avenue, Suite 1000
New York, NY 10017
(212) 949-6666
Contact: Mr. Nelson Bell
Minimum Salary Placed: $150,000
Recruiting Specialty: Financial services
and management consultants

Benson Associates
280 Madison Avenue
New York, NY 10016
(212) 683-5962
Contact: Mr. Lawrence Rutkowski
Minimum Salary Placed: $50,000
Recruiting Specialty: Public accounting,
marketing, sales and taxation

Bialecki Inc.
780 Third Avenue, Suite 4203
New York, NY 10017
(212) 755-1090
Contact: Ms. Linda Bialecki
Minimum Salary Placed: $50,000
Recruiting Specialty: General

Bishop Partners, Ltd.
708 Third Avenue, Suite 2200
New York, NY 10017
(212) 986-3419
Contact: Ms. Susan Bishop
Minimum Salary Placed: $75,000
Recruiting Specialty: Communications
and entertainment

Blake, Hansen & Nye, Ltd.
151 West 74th Street, Suite 3A
New York, NY 10023
(212) 874-4933
Contact: Ms. Jeri Schmidt
Minimum Salary Placed: $65,000
Recruiting Specialty: General

Michael Blitzer Associates Inc.
59th & 5th Avenue
New York, NY 10022
(212) 935-9177
Contact: Mr. Mike Blitzer
Minimum Salary Placed: $50,000
Recruiting Specialty: General

Nadine Bocelli & Company Inc.
420 Madison Avenue, Suite 401
New York, NY 10017
(212) 644-8181
Contact: Ms. Nadine Bocelli
Recruiting Specialty: Legal

Bodner Inc.
372 Fifth Avenue, Suite 9K
New York, NY 10018
(212) 714-0371
Contact: Ms. Marilyn Bodner
Minimum Salary Placed: $25,000
Recruiting Specialty: Accounting and finance

Bornholdt Shivas & Friends
295 Madison Avenue, Suite 1206
New York, NY 10017
(212) 557-5252
Contact: Mr. John Bornholdt
Minimum Salary Placed: $60,000
Recruiting Specialty: General

Botal Associates, Inc.
7 Dey Street
New York, NY 10007
(212) 227-7370
Contact: Mr. Steve Collins
Recruiting Specialty: Office support

Boyden
375 Park Avenue, Suite 1008
New York, NY 10152
(212) 980-6480
Contact: Mr. William Goodman
Minimum Salary Placed: $90,000
Recruiting Specialty: General

Bradley Group Ltd.
300 E. 51st Street, Suite 900
New York, NY 10022
(212) 683-3500
Contact: Ms. Sue Bradley
Minimum Salary Placed: $50,000
Recruiting Specialty: International

Brady Associates International, Inc.
310 Madison Avenue, Suite 423
New York, NY 10017
(212) 599-1120
Contact: Mr. Robert Brady
Minimum Salary Placed: $50,000
Recruiting Specialty: Banking and utilities

Branthover Associates
51 East 42nd Street, Suite 500
New York, NY 10017
(212) 949-9400
Contact: Ms. Barbara Howe
Minimum Salary Placed: $40,000
Recruiting Specialty: Financial services
and management operations

Bremar Associates
420 Lexington Avenue, Suite 2060
New York, NY 10170
(212) 661-0909
Contact: Mr. Edwin Bremar
Recruiting Specialty: Accounting, finance, and banking

The British Connection
120 E 56th Street
New York, NY 10022
(212) 223-2510
Contact: Ms. Sally Dwek
Recruiting Specialty: Office support and
administrative assistants

Arthur B. Britten Associates Ltd.
605 Park Avenue
New York, NY 10021
(212) 535-5703
Contact: Mr. Arthur Britten
Minimum Salary Placed: $75,000
Recruiting Specialty: Fashion and cosmetics

David Brooke Associates
1120 Avenue of the Americas, 21th Floor
New York, NY 10036
(212) 997-1870
Contact: Mr. C. Richards
Minimum Salary Placed: $40,000
Recruiting Specialty: General

Brookman Associates
21 E. 40th Street, Suite 501
New York, NY 10016
(212) 213-5666
Contact: Mr. Geoffrey Brookman
Minimum Salary Placed: $50,000
Recruiting Specialty: General

Charles Buck & Associates, Inc.
400 E 59th
New York, NY 10019
(212) 759-2356
Contact: Mr. Charles Buck
Minimum Salary Placed: $100,000
Recruiting Specialty: General

C.C. Burke, LTD
60 E. 42nd Street, Suite 911
New York, NY 10165
(212) 286-0092
Contact: Ms. Charlene Burke
Minimum Salary Placed: $25,000
Recruiting Specialty: General

CAS Comsearch Inc.
501 Madison Avenue, Suite 406
New York, NY 10022
(212) 593-0861
Contact: Ms. Gail Kleinberg Koch
Minimum Salary Placed: $40,000
Recruiting Specialty: Marketing and telecommunications in high technology and
financial services

Callaghan Associates
119 W 57th Street
New York, NY 10019
(212) 265-9200
Contact: Catherine Callaghan
Recruiting Specialty: General

Cameron Associates Executive
123 E, 54th Street
New York, NY 10022
(212) 826-1001
Contact: Mr. H. Hirsh
Minimum Salary Placed: $35,000
Recruiting Specialty: Advertising

Canny, Bowen Inc.
200 Park Avenue
New York, NY 10166
(212) 949-6611
Contact: Mr. Carl Menk
Minimum Salary Placed: $100,000
Recruiting Specialty: General

J.P. Canon Association
225 Broadway, Suite 3602
New York, NY 10007
(212) 233-3131
Contact: Mr. James Rohan
Minimum Salary Placed: $35,000
Recruiting Specialty: Manufacturing and
materials

The Cantor Concern, Inc.
330 W. 58th Street, Suite 216
New York, NY 10019
(212) 333-3000
Contact: Mr. Bill Cantor
Minimum Salary Placed: $45,000
Recruiting Specialty: Public relations

Cardiff Group Inc.
226 West 26th Street
New York, NY 10001
(212) 924-4377
Contact: Mr. J. Surdoval
Minimum Salary Placed: $25,000
Recruiting Specialty: General

Career Blazers
590 Fifth Avenue
New York, NY 10036
(212) 719-3232
Contact: Ms. Kathy Klein
Recruiting Specialty: Office support and
administrative assistant

Career Concepts, Inc.
25 W. 43rd Street, Suite 708
New York, NY 10036
(212) 790-2600
Contact: Mr. Steven A. Sandler
Recruiting Specialty: Accounting and financial, banking, human resources, and
some general

Career Management Inc.
21 West 38th Street
New York, NY 10018
(212) 997-0044
Contact: Mr. L. Lipman
Minimum Salary Placed: $40,000
Recruiting Specialty: Retail

Careers for Women
80 5th Avenue, Suite 1104
New York, NY 10011
(212) 807-7633
Contact: Mr. D. King
Minimum Salary Placed: $35,000
Recruiting Specialty: Marketing, sales, ad-
vertising and public relations

Strategic Executives
One Dag Hammarskjold Plaza, 7th Floor
New York, NY 10017
(212) 207-9866
Contact: Mr. Harlan Halper
Minimum Salary Placed: $40,000
Recruiting Specialty: Management con-
sulting

Carris, Jackowitz Associates
201 E. 79th Street
New York, NY 10021
(212) 879-5482
Contact: Mr. S. Joseph Carris
Minimum Salary Placed: $70,000
Recruiting Specialty: General

Carson Associates Inc.
61 Broadway, Suite 2525
New York, NY 10006
(212) 668-1170
Contact: Mr. Carl Carson
Minimum Salary Placed: $25,000
Recruiting Specialty: General

Carmichael Associates Inc.
521 5th Avenue
New York, NY 10175
(212) 808-9005
Contact: Ms. J. Pinto
Minimum Salary Placed: $25,000
Recruiting Specialty: General

Cassell and Kaye
102 East 30th Avenue
New York, NY 10016
(212) 545-8800
Contact: Ms. S. Kaye
Minimum Salary Placed: $25,000
Recruiting Specialty: General

Catalyx Group, Inc.
One Harkness Plaza, Suite 300
61 W. 62nd Street
New York, NY 10023
(212) 956-3525
Contact: Mr. Lawrence Poster
Minimum Salary Placed: $85,000
Recruiting Specialty: Manufacturing,
drugs and high technology

Malin Cederquist, Esquire
240 Central Park S., Suite 11 H
New York, NY 10019
(212) 586-9206
Contact: Ms. Malin Cederquist
Minimum Salary Placed: $25,000
Recruiting Specialty: Legal

Chanko-Ward, Ltd.
2 West 45th Street
New York, NY 10036
(212) 869-4040
Contact: Mr. Jim Chanko
Minimum Salary Placed: $60,000
Recruiting Specialty: Finance, account-
ing, MIS and FIS

Christiana Company
420 Lexington Avenue
New York, NY 10170
(212) 687-2344
Contact: Mr. Nicholas Crispi
Minimum Salary Placed: $100,000
Recruiting Specialty: Investment

Toby Clark Associates, Inc.
405 E. 54th Street
New York, NY 10022
(212) 752-5670
Contact: Ms. Toby Clark
Minimum Salary Placed: $30,000
Recruiting Specialty: Advertising, market-
ing and public relations

Richard Clarke Associates, Inc.
9 West 95th Street, Suite C-1
New York, NY 10025
(212) 222-5600
Contact: Mr. Richard Clarke
Minimum Salary Placed: $40,000
Recruiting Specialty: General; minorities

Clement Myerson
575 Madison Avenue, 10th Floor
New York, NY 10022
(212) 605-0177
Contact: Ms. M. Myerson
Minimum Salary Placed: $75,000
Recruiting Specialty: General

Ellen Colton Associates Inc.
11 E. 44th Street, Suite 808
New York, NY 10017
(212) 687-3033
Contact: Ms. Ellen Colton
Minimum Salary Placed: $30,000
Recruiting Specialty: General

The Colton Partnership, Inc.
63 Wall Street
New York, NY 10005
(212) 509-1800
Contact: Mr. W. Hoyt Colton
Minimum Salary Placed: $75,000
Recruiting Specialty: Financial

Columbia Consulting Group
230 Park Avenue, Suite 456
New York, NY 10169
(212) 983-2525
Contact: Mr. Gregory Ohman
Minimum Salary Placed: $75,000
Recruiting Specialty: General

Computer Resources Corporation
25 W 43rd Street, Suite 1502
New York, NY 10036
(212) 575-0817
Contact: Mr. Tony Pico
Recruiting Specialty: Computers

Concepts in Staffing Inc.
9 East 37th Street
New York, NY 10016
(212) 725-0300
Contact: Mr. Norman Wasserman
Minimum Salary Placed: $20,000
Recruiting Specialty: Computers, accounting, finance and administration

Concorde Group
10 E 40th Street, Suite 3205
New York, NY 10116
(212) 779-4200
Minimum Salary Placed: $50,000
Recruiting Specialty: Financial industry and systems and technology

Conex Inc.
919 Third Avenue, 18th Floor
New York, NY 10022
(212) 371-3737
Contact: Mr. Fred Siegel
Minimum Salary Placed: $60,000
Recruiting Specialty: General

Confidential Search Inc.
226 East 68th Street
New York, NY 10021
(212) 734-0584
Contact: Mr. M. Cantor
Minimum Salary Placed: $25,000
Recruiting Specialty: General

Connolly Associates
160 Broadway, Suite 607
New York, NY 10038
(212) 406-1215
Contact: Mr. Bernard Connolly
Minimum Salary Placed: $60,000
Recruiting Specialty: Investment management

The Consortium
1156 Avenue of the Americas, 4th floor
New York, NY 10036
(212) 221-1544
Contact: Mr. Martin Blaire
Minimum Salary Placed: $30,000
Recruiting Specialty: Legal, banking and finance, sales and data processing

Consultants Period
9 N Moore Street
New York, NY 10013
(212) 966-7540
Contact: Mr. Norman Gershman
Recruiting Specialty: General

The Consulting Group Ltd.
501 Madison Avenue, 26th Floor
New York, NY 10022
(212) 751-8484
Contact: Mr. Michael Mitchell
Minimum Salary Placed: $75,000
Recruiting Specialty: Banking and finance

Contact Corporation
515 Madison, Suite 1201
New York, NY 10022
(212) 371-8111
Contact: Ms. V. Mirzy
Minimum Salary Placed: $25,000
Recruiting Specialty: General

Cooper Stevens Inc.
111 Fulton Street
New York, NY 10038
(212) 374-1150
Contact: Mr. Mark Cooper
Minimum Salary Placed: $30,000
Recruiting Specialty: Medical

David P. Cordell Associates
82 Wall Street, Suite 1105
New York, NY 10005
(212) 285-0634
Contact: Mr. David Cordell
Minimum Salary Placed: $40,000
Recruiting Specialty: Economists

The Corporate Source Group
90 Park Avenue, 16th Floor
New York, NY 10016
(212) 984-0738
Contact: Ms. Carolyn Culbreth
Minimum Salary Placed: $60,000
Recruiting Specialty: General

Leonard Corwen Associates
P.O. Box 350453
New York, NY 11235
(718) 646-7581
Contact: Mr. Leonard Corwen
Minimum Salary Placed: $30,000
Recruiting Specialty: General

Crandall Associates Inc.
114 East 32nd Street
New York, NY 10016
(212) 213-1700
Minimum Salary Placed: $25,000
Recruiting Specialty: Direct marketing

Creative Management Strategies, Ltd.
305 Madison Avenue, Suite 2033
New York, NY 10165
(212) 697-7207
Contact: Mr. John Prufeta
Minimum Salary Placed: $60,000
Recruiting Specialty: Healthcare

The Cris Group, Inc.
501 Madison Avenue, Suite 1105
New York, NY 10022
(212) 752-2838
Contact: Ms. Jan Cris
Minimum Salary Placed: $75,000
Recruiting Specialty: General

Crispi, Wagner & Company, Inc.
420 Lexington Avenue, Suite 400
New York, NY 10170
(212) 687-2340
Contact: Mr. Nicholas Crispi
Minimum Salary Placed: $100,000
Recruiting Specialty: Senior investment
professionals

Cromwell Partners Inc.
441 Lexington Avenue
New York, NY 10017
(212) 953-3220
Minimum Salary Placed: $40,000
Recruiting Specialty: Finance and banking

Peter Cusack & Partners, Inc.
575 Madison Avenue, Suite 1006
New York, NY 10022
(212) 605-0440
Contact: Mr. Peter Cusack
Minimum Salary Placed: $100,000
Recruiting Specialty: General and man-
agement consulting

DHR International Inc.
80 Park Avenue, Suite 2M
New York, NY 10016
(212) 573-6111
Contact: Mr. Dave Richardson
Minimum Salary Placed: $30,000
Recruiting Specialty: General

D.K. Personnel, Inc.
59 E. 42nd Street
New York, NY 10017-5405
(212) 370-0221
Contact: Ms. Dena Kaufman
Minimum Salary Placed: $30,000
Recruiting Specialty: Legal staffing

DLB Associates
271 Madison Avenue, Suite 1406
New York, NY 10016
(212) 953-6460
Contact: Mr. Lawrence Brolin
Minimum Salary Placed: $50,000
Recruiting Specialty: Advertising, sales
and marketing

D.P. Placement Power Inc.
38 W 32nd Street, Suite 1503
New York, NY 10001
(212) 967-2944
Contact: Ms. G. Rosen
Minimum Salary Placed: $25,000
Recruiting Specialty: General

D'Andrea Associates
170 Broadway, 10th Floor
New York, NY 10038
(212) 964-9001
Contact: Mr. N. D'Andrea
Minimum Salary Placed: $25,000
Recruiting Specialty: International banking

Vivian Darrow Associates
151 E. 38th Street
New York, NY 10016
(212) 683-8466
Minimum Salary Placed: $30,000
Recruiting Specialty: Garments

The Dartmouth Group
1200 Broadway, 7D-8D
New York, NY 10001
(212) 689-2713
Contact: Mr. Herbert Storfer
Minimum Salary Placed: $50,000
Recruiting Specialty: Cosmetics, pharmaceuticals, healthcare, and packaging

Dataco Search, Inc.
139 Fulton Street, Suite 801
New York, NY 10038
(212) 608-2670
Contact: Ms. Madeline York
Recruiting Specialty: Management consulting

Datamark Associates Inc.
145 W 45th
New York, NY 10018
(212) 354-7800
Minimum Salary Placed: $25,000
Recruiting Specialty: Data processing

Daudlin, De Beaupre and Company, Inc.
545 8th Avenue, Suite 401
New York, NY 10018
(212) 560-7376
Contact: Ms. Mary Ann De Beaupre
Minimum Salary Placed: $50,000
Recruiting Specialty: Healthcare

**Bert Davis Publishing Placement
Consultants**
425 Madison Avenue, Suite 14A
New York, NY 10017
(212) 838-4000
Contact: Ms. Sally Dougan
Minimum Salary Placed: $25,000
Recruiting Specialty: Publishing and
communications

John J. Davis & Associates, Inc.
521 Fifth Avenue, Suite 1740
New York, NY 10175
(212) 286-9489
Contact: Mr. John Davis
Minimum Salary Placed: $95,000
Recruiting Specialty: MIS and communi-
cations

Joseph A. Davis Consultants, Inc.
104 E. 40th Street, Suite 203
New York, NY 10016
(212) 682-4006
Contact: Mr. Joseph Davis
Minimum Salary Placed: $30,000
Recruiting Specialty: General, minorities

DeLalla - Fried Associates
201 E. 69th Street, Suite 4K
New York, NY 10021
(212) 879-9100
Contact: Ms. Barbara DeLalla
Minimum Salary Placed: $45,000
Recruiting Specialty: Marketing

Denison Group
122 E. 42nd Street, 46th Floor
New York, NY 10168
(212) 949-6594
Contact: Mr. Robert Long
Minimum Salary Placed: $30,000
Recruiting Specialty: General

Thorndike Deland Association
275 Madison Avenue, 13th Floor
New York, NY 10016
(212) 661-6200
Contact: Mr. Howard Bratches
Minimum Salary Placed: $75,000
Recruiting Specialty: Consumer products

Development Resource Group
104 E. 40th Street, Room 806
New York, NY 10016
(212) 983-1600
Contact: Mr. David Edell
Recruiting Specialty: Non-profit

Diamond Tax Recruiting
2 Pennsylvania Plaza, Suite 1500
New York, NY 10121
(212) 695-4220
Contact: Mr. Steven Hunter
Minimum Salary Placed: $35,000
Recruiting Specialty: Taxation

Donahue and Moore Associates Ltd.
295 Madison Avenue
New York, NY 10017
(212) 683-8255
Minimum Salary Placed: $30,000
Recruiting Specialty: Computers and
data processing

J P Donnelly Associates, Inc.
420 Lexington Avenue
New York, NY 10017
(212) 297-6127
Contact: Mr. John Donnelly
Minimum Salary Placed: $40,000
Recruiting Specialty: MIS and human re-
sources in finance

Dotson & Associates
412 E. 55th Street, Suite 8A
New York, NY 10022
(212) 593-4274
Contact: Ms. M. Ileen Dotson
Minimum Salary Placed: $40,000
Recruiting Specialty: Sales and marketing
in banking and finance

Drummond Associates, Inc.
50 Broadway, Suite 1201
New York, NY 10004
(212) 248-1120
Contact: Mr. Chester Fienberg
Minimum Salary Placed: $35,000
Recruiting Specialty: Finance, general

Dryden Cross and Company
25 W. 43rd Street, Suite 920
New York, NY 10036
(212) 869-2660
Contact: Mr. N. Tessler
Minimum Salary Placed: $30,000
Recruiting Specialty: Banking

Duncan Group Inc.
341 Madison Avenue
New York, NY 10017
(212) 697-3737
Contact: Ms. M. Duncan
Minimum Salary Placed: $25,000
Recruiting Specialty: Administrative assis-
tants

E.J. Associates of New York Ltd.
295 Madison Avenue, Suite 1028
New York, NY 10017
(212) 953-3663
Contact: Mr. E. Levine
Minimum Salary Placed: $30,000
Recruiting Specialty: Retail

E.S. Vee EDP Placement Agency
421 7th Avenue, Suite 1205
New York, NY 10001
(212) 947-7730
Contact: Mr. Steven Vanchel
Minimum Salary Placed: $35,000
Recruiting Specialty: Data processing
and computers

Earley Kielty & Associates, Inc.
2 Pennsylvania Plaza
New York, NY 10121
(212) 736-5626
Contact: Mr. John Kielty
Minimum Salary Placed: $60,000
Recruiting Specialty: General

David M. Ellner Association
2 Penn Plaza, Suite 1500
New York, NY 10121
(212) 279-0665
Contact: Mr. David Ellner
Minimum Salary Placed: $50,000
Recruiting Specialty: General

Mark Elzweig Company Ltd.
101 5th Avenue, Suite 10A
New York, NY 10012
(212) 274-8264
Contact: Mr. Mark Elzweig
Minimum Salary Placed: $35,000
Recruiting Specialty: Sales in securities
and commodities trading, portfolio and
money managers

W.H. Eolis International Inc.
200 Central Park South
New York, NY 10019
(212) 779-9000
Minimum Salary Placed: $50,000
Recruiting Specialty: Attorneys

**Enwood Personnel & Temporary
Services, Inc.**
6 E. 45th Street
New York, NY 10017
(212) 682-4080
Contact: Mr. Isaac Assael
Recruiting Specialty: Office personnel

Equate Executive Search Inc.
12 West 37th Street
New York, NY 10018
(212) 736-0606
Contact: Mr. Harry Miller
Minimum Salary Placed: $40,000
Recruiting Specialty: Systems and finance
professionals

ETC Search, Inc.
226 E. 54th Street, Sutie 308
New York, NY 10022
(212) 371-3880
Contact: Ms. Marlene Eskenazie
Recruiting Specialty: Information services

Execu-Reps Inc.
515 Madison Avenue
New York, NY 10022
(212) 826-4082
Contact: Ms. Meryl Bladgette
Minimum Salary Placed: $35,000
Recruiting Specialty: General

Execu-Search
675 Third Avenue
New York, NY 10017
(212) 922-1001
Contact: Mr. Edward Fleischman
Minimum Salary Placed: $30,000
Recruiting Specialty: Accounting, finance
and taxation

Executive Directions Inc.
2 Penn Plaza, Suite 1185
New York, NY 10121
(212) 594-5775
Contact: Mr. G. Oakes
Minimum Salary Placed: $35,000
Recruiting Specialty: Data processing,
technical and sales

Executive Exchange LTD
450 7th Avenue
New York, NY 10123
(212) 736-2350
Recruiting Specialty: Telecommunications

Executive Image Inc.
330 3rd Avenue
New York, NY 10022
(212) 532-8565
Contact: Ms. C. Feingold
Minimum Salary Placed: $35,000
Recruiting Specialty: Finance and ac-
counting

Executive Link
15 Penn Plaza, Office 2
New York, NY 10001
(212) 760-0176
Contact: Ms. Diane Lieberman
Minimum Salary Placed: $35,000
Recruiting Specialty: Hospitality

Executive Resources LTD
200 E 66th Street
New York, NY 10021
(212) 593-2819
Recruiting Specialty: Financial services

Executive Search Associates, Inc.
51 E 42nd Street, Suite 1804
New York, NY 10017
(212) 697-2045
Recruiting Specialty: Financial services
and marketing

**Executive Search Consultants
International Ltd.**
350 5th Avenue
New York, NY 10022
(212) 330 -1900
Contact: Mr. V. Elliot
Minimum Salary Placed: $35,000
Recruiting Specialty: General

Executive Search Group
116 W 32nd Street
New York, NY 10034
(212) 594-1448
Contact: Mr. J. Incendio
Minimum Salary Placed: $50,000
Recruiting Specialty: Securities and fi-
nance

Fabian Associates, Inc.
521 Fifth Avenue, 17th Floor
New York, NY 10017
(212) 697-9460
Contact: Ms. Jeanne Fabian
Recruiting Specialty: Financial, marketing, and systems analysis

Fanning Personnel Agency, Inc.
507 Fifth Avenue, Suite 800
New York, NY 10017
(212) 867-1725
Contact: Mr. Ron Morgan
Recruiting Specialty: Support staff, tron-
ics (computer web site)

Fergus Legal Search & Consulting, Inc.
350 Fifth Avenue, Suite 5809
New York, NY 10118
(212) 947-1775
Contact: Mr. Colin Fergus
Minimum Salary Placed: $80,000
Recruiting Specialty: Attorneys

Jerry Fields Associates
353 Lexington Avenue, 11th Floor
New York, NY 10016
(212) 661-6644
Contact: Mr. Jerry Fields
Minimum Salary Placed: $20,000
Recruiting Specialty: Advertising and
publishing

Fisher-Todd Associates
535 Fifth Avenue, Suite 710
New York, NY 10017
(212) 986-9052
Contact: Mr. Ronald Franz
Minimum Salary Placed: $25,000
Recruiting Specialty: Office support and
medical personnel

M Franklin Associates Inc.
329 East 63rd Street
New York, NY 10021
(212) 308-5560
Minimum Salary Placed: $35,000
Recruiting Specialty: Taxation

Focus & Focus Capital Markets
71 Vanderbilt Ave., Suite 200
New York, NY 10169
(212) 986-3344
Recruiting Specialty: Computer technology

Forray Associates, Inc.
950 3rd Avenue
New York, NY 10122
(212) 279-0404
Contact: Ms. Karen Forray
Minimum Salary Placed: $80,000
Recruiting Specialty: Finance and accounting

Fortune Personnel Consultants of NYC, Inc.
505 Fifth Avenue, Suite 1100
New York, NY 10017
(212) 557-1000
Contact: Mr. H.R. Brakel
Minimum Salary Placed: $35,000
Recruiting Specialty: Manufacturing and technical

Forum Personnel
342 Madison Avenue, Suite 509
New York, NY 10017
(212) 687-4050
Contact: Mr. Steve Goldstein
Minimum Salary Placed: $50,000
Recruiting Specialty: General

Foster McKay International
535 Fifth Avenue, 32nd Floor
New York, NY 10017
(212) 953-0200
Contact: Mr. Rolfe Kopelan
Minimum Salary Placed: $75,000
Recruiting Specialty: Finance and accounting

Foy, Schneid & Daniel, Inc.
555 Madison Avenue, 12th Floor
New York, NY 10022
(212) 980-2525
Contact: Mr. James Foy
Minimum Salary Placed: $50,000
Recruiting Specialty: MIS, marketing, and logistics

Francis Ryan Associates Inc.
488 Madison, Suite 1100
New York, NY 10107
(212) 980-8818
Contact: Ms. Donna Ryan
Minimum Salary Placed: $30,000
Recruiting Specialty: Real estate

Gerald Frisch Associates, Inc.
181 E. 73rd Street
New York, NY 10021
(212) 737-4810
Contact: Mr. Gerald Frisch
Minimum Salary Placed: $70,000
Recruiting Specialty: General

The Fry Group, Inc.
18 E. 41st Street
New York, NY 10017
(212) 532-8100
Contact: Mr. John Fry
Minimum Salary Placed: $25,000
Recruiting Specialty: Marketing and advertising

Jay Gaines & Company, Inc.
450 Park Avenue
New York, NY 10022
(212) 308-9222
Contact: Mr. Jay Gaines
Minimum Salary Placed: $125,000
Recruiting Specialty: Finance and banking

Galaxy Management Group, Inc.
2 Penn Plaza, Suite 1535
New York, NY 11021
(212) 843-3530
Contact: Mr. Jim Sullivan
Recruiting Specialty: Computer professionals

Sylvia Ganser and Associates
80 Park Avenue, Suite 18N
New York, NY 10016
(212) 867-7111
Contact: Ms. Sylvia Ganser
Minimum Salary Placed: $30,000
Recruiting Specialty: Advertising

Gardiner International
101 East 52nd Street
New York, NY 10022
(212) 838-0707
Contact: Mr. Nicholas Gardiner
Minimum Salary Placed: $50,000
Recruiting Specialty: General

Gardner-Ross Association, Inc.
300 Madison Avenue
New York, NY 10017
(212) 687-6616
Contact: Mr. Marvin Gardner
Minimum Salary Placed: $75,000
Recruiting Specialty: General

Dick Garland Consultants
31 E. 32nd Street,
New York, NY 10016
(212) 481-8484
Contact: Mr. Dick Garland
Minimum Salary Placed: $75,000
Recruiting Specialty: General

Gateway Search, Inc.
1120 Avenue of the Americas
New York, NY 10036
(212) 626-6714
Recruiting Specialty: Technical computer

Gilbert & Van Campen International
420 Lexington Avenue, Suite 1624-27
New York, NY 10170
(212) 661-2122
Contact: Mr. Jerry Gilbert
Minimum Salary Placed: $100,000
Recruiting Specialty: General

Gilbert Tweed Associates, Inc.
415 Madison Avenue
New York, NY 10017
(212) 758-3000
Contact: Ms. Janet Tweed
Minimum Salary Placed: $70,000
Recruiting Specialty: General

Liz Glatzer and Associates
420 Lexington Avenue
New York, NY 10170
(212) 297-6160
Contact: Ms. Liz Glatzer
Minimum Salary Placed: $35,000
Recruiting Specialty: Advertising account management

Global Investment Search, Inc.
FDR Station
New York, NY 10150
(212) 734-9700
Contact: Ms. Roberta Dindial
Minimum Salary Placed: $80,000
Recruiting Specialty: General

Global Research
444 East 82nd Street
New York, NY 10028
(212) 980-3800
Contact: Mr. Rick Wolf
Minimum Salary Placed: $35,000
Recruiting Specialty: General

The Goldman Group Inc.
183 Madison Avenue, Suite 1105
New York, NY 10016
(212) 685-9311
Contact: Ms. Elaine Goldman
Minimum Salary Placed: $40,000
Recruiting Specialty: Marketing and communications

Goodman Resources Inc.
370 Lexington Avenue
New York, NY 10017
(212) 697-7100
Minimum Salary Placed: $35,000
Recruiting Specialty: General

The Goodrich & Sherwood Company
521 Fifth Avenue
New York, NY 10175
(212) 697-4131
Contact: Mr. Andrew Sherwood
Minimum Salary Placed: $60,000
Recruiting Specialty: Manufacturing, finance and insurance

Gossage Regan Association
25 W. 43rd Street, Suite 812
New York, NY 10036
(212) 869-3348
Contact: Mr. Wayne Gossage
Minimum Salary Placed: $40,000
Recruiting Specialty: Museum and library non-profit

Gould & McCoy, Inc.
300 Park Avenue
New York, NY 10022
(212) 688-8671
Contact: Mr. William Gould
Minimum Salary Placed: $100,000
Recruiting Specialty: General

Gumbinner/Haubenstock, Inc.
509 Madison Avenue, Suite 708
New York, NY 10022
(212) 688-0129
Contact: Mr. Paul Gumbinner
Minimum Salary Placed: $50,000
Recruiting Specialty: Advertising

Gundersen Partners, Inc.
137 Fifth Avenue, 5th Floor
New York, NY 10010
(212) 529-5400
Contact: Mr. Steven Gundersen
Minimum Salary Placed: $75,000
Recruiting Specialty: Marketing in consumer products

HBC Group
370 Lexington Avenue, Suite 2200
New York, NY 10017
(212) 661-8300
Contact: Mr. Norman Gershgorn
Minimum Salary Placed: $50,000
Recruiting Specialty: Banking

Hadley Lockwood, Inc.
17 State Street, 38th Floor
New York, NY 10004
(212) 785-4405
Minimum Salary Placed: $100,000
Recruiting Specialty: Finance and banking

Stan Hamlet Associates Inc.
274 Madison Avenue, Suite 1801
New York, NY 10016
(212) 685-4884
Contact: Ms. Stan Hamlet
Minimum Salary Placed: $30,000
Recruiting Specialty: Accounting, finance
and data processing

Handy HRM
250 Park Avenue
New York, NY 10177
(212) 557-0400
Contact: Mr. J. Gerald Simmons
Minimum Salary Placed: $100,000
Recruiting Specialty: General

Hanzel & Company, Inc.
60 E. 42nd Street, Suite 1146
New York, NY 10165
(212) 972-1832
Contact: Mr. Bruce Hanzel
Minimum Salary Placed: $80,000
Recruiting Specialty: Financial services
and banking

Hass Associates
443 W. 24th Street, Suite C
New York, NY 10011
(212) 741-2457
Contact: Ms. Margaret Hass
Minimum Salary Placed: $50,000
Recruiting Specialty: General: Far East
and Japan

Hawkes Peers
805 3rd Avenue, 28th Floor
New York, NY 10022
(212) 593-3131

Contact: Mr. T. King
Minimum Salary Placed: $50,000
Recruiting Specialty: Corporate business
development and marketing

Hayward Simone Associates, Inc.
1 Wall Street Court
New York, NY 10005
(212) 785-3550
Contact: Ms. Judy Karpel
Minimum Salary Placed: $35,000
Recruiting Specialty: Technical staffing
and contract consulting

F.P. Healy & Company, Inc.
230 Park Avenue, Suite 232
New York, NY 10169
(212) 661-0366
Contact: Mr. Frank Healy
Minimum Salary Placed: $50,000
Recruiting Specialty: General

Heath/Norton Associates, Inc.
545 Eighth Avenue
New York, NY 10018
(212) 695-3600
Contact: Mr. Richard Stoller
Minimum Salary Placed: $65,000
Recruiting Specialty: General

Heidrick & Struggles, Inc.
245 Park Avenue, Suite 4300
New York, NY 10167
(212) 867-9876
Contact: Ms. Brenda Ruello
Minimum Salary Placed: $60,000
Recruiting Specialty: General

Jay Heino Company
7 Penn Plaza, Suite 830
New York, NY 10001
(212) 279-6780
Contact: Mr. Jay Heino
Minimum Salary Placed: $35,000
Recruiting Specialty: Taxation

Henry and Company
1285 6th Avenue, 36th Floor
New York, NY 10036
(212) 921-5600
Contact: Ms. Jane Henry
Minimum Salary Placed: $60,000
Recruiting Specialty: Investment Banking

Adel Herman Inc.
369 Lexington Ave.
New York, NY 10017
(212) 490-8640
Recruiting Specialty: General

Robert Herman Inc.
28 East 22nd Street, 2nd Floor
New York, NY 10010
(212) 979-0400
Contact: Mr. Robert Herman
Minimum Salary Placed: $35,000
Recruiting Specialty: Advertising

Hessel Association, Inc.
420 Lexington Avenue, Suite 300
New York, NY 10170
(212) 297-6105
Contact: Mr. Jeffrey J. Hessel
Minimum Salary Placed: $50,000
Recruiting Specialty: Accounting and finance

Heyman Associates Inc.
341 Madison Avenue, 12th Floor
New York, NY 10017
(212) 681-7818
Contact: Mr. William Heyman
Minimum Salary Placed: $45,000
Recruiting Specialty: Public relations

Higdon Prince
230 Park Avenue, Suite 1455
New York, NY 10169
(212) 986-4662
Contact: Mr. Henry Higdon
Minimum Salary Placed: $150,000
Recruiting Specialty: General

Hiring Line
10 East 23rd Street and FDR Drive
New York, NY 10010
(212) 460-8000
Minimum Salary Placed: $35,000
Recruiting Specialty: Public relations

Holden Partners
32 Broadway
New York, NY 10004
(212) 635-0200
Contact: Mr. B. Hawks
Minimum Salary Placed: $40,000
Recruiting Specialty: Finance

Holt Pearson & Caldwell, Inc.
250 Park Avenue, 11th Floor
New York, NY 10169
(212) 983-5850
Contact: Ms. Paula Whitton
Minimum Salary Placed: $100,000
Recruiting Specialty: Financial services

J.B. Homer Associates, Inc.
420 Lexington Avenue, Suite 2328
New York, NY 10170
(212) 697-3300
Contact: Ms. Judy Homer
Minimum Salary Placed: $80,000
Recruiting Specialty: Information technology

Horton International, Inc.
666 Fifth Avenue, 37th Floor
New York, NY 10103
(212) 541-3900
Contact: Mr. Edward Schneider
Minimum Salary Placed: $100,000
Recruiting Specialty: General

Hospitality International
23 West 73, Suite 100
New York, NY 10023
(212) 769-8800
Contact: Mr. Joseph Radice
Minimum Salary Placed: $25,000
Recruiting Specialty: Hospitality

Howard-Sloan Associates
353 Lexington Avenue
New York, NY 10016
(212) 661-5250
Contact: Mr. Edward Koller
Minimum Salary Placed: $50,000
Recruiting Specialty: Publishing and media communications

Howe-Lewis International, Inc.
521 Fifth Avenue, 36th Floor
New York, NY 10017
(212) 697-5000
Contact: Ms. Anita Howe
Minimum Salary Placed: $80,000
Recruiting Specialty: Biotechnology and healthcare

Arnold Huberman Associates, Inc.
51 E. 25th Street, Suite 501
New York, NY 10010
(212) 545-9033
Contact: Mr. Arnold Huberman
Minimum Salary Placed: $35,000
Recruiting Specialty: Public relations

E. A. Hughes & Company, Inc.
146 E. 37th Street
New York, NY 10016
(212) 689-4600
Contact: Ms. Elaine Hughes
Minimum Salary Placed: $50,000
Recruiting Specialty: General

The Hunt Company
274 Madison Avenue
New York, NY 10016
(212) 889-2020
Contact: Mr. Bridgford Hunt
Minimum Salary Placed: $80,000
Recruiting Specialty: General

Hunt Ltd.
21 W. 38th Street
New York, NY 10018
(212) 997-2299
Contact: Mr. Alex Metz
Minimum Salary Placed: $30,000
Recruiting Specialty: Distribution and transportation

Huss Viseltear and Associates Inc.
800 3rd Avenue
New York, NY 10022
(212) 486-9270 or 866-6648
Contact: Ms. G. Viseltear
Minimum Salary Placed: $35,000
Recruiting Specialty: General

IMCOR, Inc.
475 Park Avenue S., 33rd Floor
New York, NY 10016
(212) 213-3600
Contact: Mr. John Thompson
Minimum Salary Placed: $75,000
Recruiting Specialty: General

Ingram & Aydelotte, Inc.
430 Park Avenue
New York, NY 10022
(212) 319-7777
Contact: Mr. D. John Ingram
Minimum Salary Placed: $100,000
Recruiting Specialty: General

Innkeeper's Management Corporation
14 E. 60th Street, Suite 1210
New York, NY 10022
(212) 838-9535
Contact: Mr. Herbert Regehly
Minimum Salary Placed: $60,000
Recruiting Specialty: Hospitality

Integrated Management Solutions
32 Broadway, Suite 1200
New York, NY 10004
(212) 509-7800
Contact: Mr. Howard Spindel
Recruiting Specialty: Finance and accounting in banking and finance

Interlangue International
509 Park Avenue
New York, NY 10017
(212) 687-5050
Contact: Mr. Bill Hamilton
Minimum Salary Placed: $35,000
Recruiting Specialty: Foreign bank

International Management Advisors, Inc.
516 Fifth Avenue
New York, NY 10036
(212) 768-4121
Contact: Ms. Constance Klages
Minimum Salary Placed: $60,000
Recruiting Specialty: General

Interquest, Inc.
747 Third Avenue, 19th Floor
New York, NY 10017
(212) 319-0790
Contact: Mr. Meyer Haberman
Minimum Salary Placed: $80,000
Recruiting Specialty: Attorneys

Interspace Interactive Inc.
50 E. 42nd Street
New York, NY 10017
(212) 867-6661
Contact: Mr. Bill Ellis
Recruiting Specialty: Sales and account executives

Joan Isbister Consultants
350 W. 20th Street, Suite D
New York, NY 10011
(212) 243-8733
Contact: Ms. Joan Isbister
Minimum Salary Placed: $25,000
Recruiting Specialty: Printing

Ann Israel & Associates, Inc.
730 Fifth Avenue, Suite 900
New York, NY 10019
(212) 333-8730
Contact: Ms. Ann Israel
Recruiting Specialty: Legal

JH Associates
370 Lexington Avenue
New York, NY 10017
(212) 682-8700
Minimum Salary Placed: $40,000
Recruiting Specialty: Finance and accounting

Jacobs Associates
950 3rd Avenue
New York, NY 10022
(212) 935-3520
Contact: Ms. Ellen Jacobs
Minimum Salary Placed: $75,000
Recruiting Specialty: Attorneys

Pendleton James & Associates, Inc.
200 Park Avenue, Suite 4520
New York, NY 10166
(212) 557-1599
Contact: Mr. E. Pendleton James
Minimum Salary Placed: $100,000
Recruiting Specialty: General

R.I. James, Inc.
325 Riverside Drive., Suite 54
New York, NY 10025
(212) 662-0203
Contact: Ms. Rhoda Isaacs
Minimum Salary Placed: $40,000
Recruiting Specialty: General

Janou Pakter Associates
5 W 19th Street, 6th Floor
New York, NY 10011
(212) 989-1288
Contact: Mr. J. Tavin
Minimum Salary Placed: $35,000
Recruiting Specialty: Sales, marketing, graphic design and multi-media

The Johnson Group, Inc.
1 World Trade Center, Suite 4517
New York, NY 10048
(212) 775-0036
Contact: Ms. Priscilla Johnson
Minimum Salary Placed: $50,000
Recruiting Specialty: General

KPA Assoc., Inc.
150 Broadway, Suite 1802
New York, NY 10038
(212) 964-3640
Contact: Mr. Len Adams
Minimum Salary Placed: $25,000
Recruiting Specialty: Finance and banking

Lisa Kalus & Associates, Inc.
26 Broadway, Suite 400
New York, NY 10004
(212) 837-7889
Contact: Ms. Lisa Kalus
Recruiting Specialty: Construction and management

Kanarek and Shaw
301 East 53rd Street
New York, NY 10022
(212) 371-0967
Contact: Ms. J. Shaw
Minimum Salary Placed: $35,000
Recruiting Specialty: General

Kane Ford & Associates
777 Third Avenue
New York, NY 10017
(212) 838-6565
Contact: Mr. Richard Kane
Minimum Salary Placed: $80,000
Recruiting Specialty: Lawyers

Martin Kartin & Company, Inc.
211 E. 70th Street
New York, NY 10021
(212) 628-7676
Contact: Mr. Martin Kartin
Minimum Salary Placed: $50,000
Recruiting Specialty: Consumer products

Kauffman and Company
1 Battery Park Plaza
New York, NY 10004
(212) 269-0572
Contact: Mr. Robert Kauffman
Minimum Salary Placed: $35,000
Recruiting Specialty: General

Kaufman and Swan
450 7th Avenue, Suite 913
New York, NY 10123
(212) 643-643-0625
Contact: Mr. Gene Kaufman
Minimum Salary Placed: $35,000
Recruiting Specialty: General

Leslie Kavanugh Associates, Inc.
505 5th Avenue, Suite 1300
New York, NY 10017
(212) 661-0670
Contact: Mr. F. Marcus
Minimum Salary Placed: $35,000
Recruiting Specialty: Human resources,
MIS and manufacturing

The Kaye Group of 5th Avenue
350 Fifth Avenue, Suite 2205
New York, NY 10118
(212) 947-3131
Contact: Mr. Joseph Kay
Minimum Salary Placed: $40,000
Recruiting Specialty: Accounting, advertising, publishing, and industrial sales

A.T. Kearney Executive Search
153 E. 53rd Street
New York, NY 10022
(212) 751-7040
Contact: Ms. Elizabeth Ortiz
Minimum Salary Placed: $60,000
Recruiting Specialty: General

Kenny, Kindler, Hunt & Howe
1 Dag Hammarskjold Plaza, 34th Floor
New York, NY 10017
(212) 355-5560
Contact: Mr. James Hunt
Minimum Salary Placed: $100,000
Recruiting Specialty: General

Kenzer Corporation
777 Third Avenue
New York, NY 10017
(212) 308-4300
Contact: Mr. Robert Kenzer
Recruiting Specialty: Finance and accounting

Barbara Kerner Consultants
230 Park Avenue, Suite 315
New York, NY 10169
(212) 682-1100
Contact: Ms. Barbara Kerner
Minimum Salary Placed: $50,000
Recruiting Specialty: Attorneys

Michael King and Associates
366 Madison Avenue
New York, NY 10017
(212) 687-5490
Contact: Mr. Michael King
Minimum Salary Placed: $45,000
Recruiting Specialty: Retail account executives

Kingsbury, Wax & Bova
230 Park Avenue, Suite 1000
New York, NY 10170
(212) 297-0300
Contact: Mr. Barry Bova
Minimum Salary Placed: $60,000
Recruiting Specialty: Manufacturing and finance

Kinser & Associates
919 Third Avenue, 10th Floor
New York, NY 10022
(212) 735-2740
Contact: Mr. Richard Kinser
Minimum Salary Placed: $75,000
Recruiting Specialty: General

Kline Consulting, Inc.
9 E. 37th Street, 9th Floor
New York, NY 10016
(212) 685-0400
Contact: Ms. Ellen Couch
Minimum Salary Placed: $75,000
Recruiting Specialty: General

Koltnow & Company
1120 Avenue of the Americas, 4th Floor
New York, NY 10036
(212) 626-6606
Contact: Ms. Emily Koltnow
Minimum Salary Placed: $50,000
Recruiting Specialty: Sales and marketing in textiles and apparel

Korn/Ferry International
237 Park Avenue, 11th Floor
New York, NY 10017
(212) 687-1834
Contact: Mr. Richard Ferry
Minimum Salary Placed: $100,000
Recruiting Specialty: General

Kramer Executive Resources, Inc.
110 E 59th Street, Suite 251
New York, NY 10022
(212) 832-1122
Contact: Mr. Alan Kramer
Minimum Salary Placed: $50,000
Recruiting Specialty: Accounting, finance and taxation

Evie Kreisler Associates, Inc.
1460 Broadway
New York, NY 10036
(212) 921-8999
Contact: Ms. Kathy Gross
Minimum Salary Placed: $25,000
Recruiting Specialty: Manufacturing and distribution of consumer products

Ktech Systems Group
150 Broadway, Suite 515
New York, NY 10038
(212) 227-0800
Contact: Mr. Dick Lewis
Recruiting Specialty: Information systems

LCP Group
355 Lexington Avenue, 14th Floor
New York, NY 10017
(212) 986-4983
Contact: Mr. R. Rosking
Minimum Salary Placed: $50,000
Recruiting Specialty: Commercial real estate

Laguzza Associates, Ltd.
810 Seventh Avenue
New York, NY 10019
(212) 247-8190
Contact: Mr. John Laguzza
Minimum Salary Placed: $75,000
Recruiting Specialty: Finance and insurance

Lamalie Amrop International
200 Park Avenue, Suite 100
New York, NY 10066
(212) 953-7900
Contact: Mr. John Johnson
Minimum Salary Placed: $75,000
Recruiting Specialty: General

E.J. Lance Management Associates, Inc.
261 Madison Avenue, 2nd Floor
New York, NY 10016
(212) 490-9600
Contact: Ms. Elizabeth Kay
Minimum Salary Placed: $40,000
Recruiting Specialty: Finance

Lawrence L. Lapham, Inc.
80 Park Avenue, Suite 3K
New York, NY 10016
(212) 599-0644
Contact: Mr. Lawrence
Minimum Salary Placed: $75,000
Recruiting Specialty: General

Lease Labau & Wolf, Inc.
275 Madison Avenue
New York, NY 10016
(212) 922-3535
Contact: Ms. Linda Lease
Recruiting Specialty: Legal

Ledbetter, Davidson International
101 Park Avenue
New York, NY 10178
(212) 687-6600
Contact: Ms. Charlene Ledbetter
Recruiting Specialty: Biotechnology,
pharmaceuticals and healthcare

Legal Search Associates, Inc.
725 Fifth Avenue, Trump Tower
New York, NY 10022
(212) 758-3600
Contact: Mr. Ross Miller
Minimum Salary Placed: $50,000
Recruiting Specialty: Attorneys

Debra Levey and Associates
112 East 19th Street
New York, NY 10003
(212) 674-8301
Contact: Ms. Debra Levey
Minimum Salary Placed: $30,000
Recruiting Specialty: General

Lewin-Koblin Associates, Inc.
30 E. 42nd Street
New York, NY 10017
(212) 687-6100
Contact: Ms. Barbara Koblin
Recruiting Specialty: General

Barry Lipter Associates Inc.
292 Madison Avenue, 17th Floor
New York, NY 10017
(212) 725-3344
Contact: Mr. Barry Lipter
Minimum Salary Placed: $25,000
Recruiting Specialty: General

Lloyd Creative Staffing
310 Madison Avenue
New York, NY 10017
(212) 687-7500
Contact: Mr. Keith Banks
Recruiting Specialty: General

J.P. Logan & Company, Inc.
144 E. 44th Street, 6th Floor
New York, NY 10017
(212) 832-1800
Contact: Mr. James Logan
Minimum Salary Placed: $100,000
Recruiting Specialty: General

Logic Associates, Inc.
170 Broadway, Suite 814
New York, NY 10038
(212) 227-8000
Contact: Mr. Bill Perry
Minimum Salary Placed: $50,000
Recruiting Specialty: Finance and insurance

London & Company
360 Lexington Avenue, Suite 1902
New York, NY 10017
(212) 599-2200
Contact: Mr. Anne London
Minimum Salary Placed: $60,000
Recruiting Specialty: Attorneys

H. M. Long International, Ltd.
237 Park Avenue
New York, NY 10017
(212) 725-5150
Contact: Ms. Helga Long
Minimum Salary Placed: $125,000
Recruiting Specialty: General

William K. Long Associates Inc.
11 John Street, Suite 300
New York, NY 10038
(212) 571-0960
Contact: Ms. M. Cahill
Minimum Salary Placed: $30,000
Recruiting Specialty: Insurance

Lucas Tama Ltd.
150 W. End Avenue
New York, NY 10023
(212) 922-9010
Contact: Ms. Phylis Tama
Minimum Salary Placed: $35,000
Recruiting Specialty: General

William Lucas/Philip Cole
324 E. 50th Street
New York, NY 10022
(212) 571-0960
Contact: Mr. Philip Cole
Minimum Salary Placed: $30,000
Recruiting Specialty: Advertising

The John Lucht Consultancy Inc.
641 Fifth Avenue
New York, NY 10022
(212) 935-4660
Contact: Mr. John Lucht
Minimum Salary Placed: $20,000
Recruiting Specialty: General

Lynne Palmer Inc.
14 E. 60th Street, Suite 311
New York, NY 10022
(212) 759-2942
Contact: Ms. L. Polpon
Minimum Salary Placed: $35,000
Recruiting Specialty: Publishing

Lyons Pruitt, International
40 Wall Street, 32nd Floor
New York, NY 10005
(212) 797-8888
Contact: Mr. Scott Lyons
Recruiting Specialty: Finance, information technology, sales and marketing and some general

MB Inc.
505 Fifth Avenue
New York, NY 10017
(212) 661-4937
Contact: Mr. Alan Levine
Minimum Salary Placed: $40,000
Recruiting Specialty: Consumer products
and finance

META/MAT, Ltd.
237 Park Avenue, 21st Floor
New York, NY 10017
(212) 551-1472
Contact: Mr. Andrew Borkin
Minimum Salary Placed: $75,000
Recruiting Specialty: General

MVP Group
150 Broadway, Suite 2100
New York, NY 10038
(212) 571-1830
Contact: Mr. L. Romer
Minimum Salary Placed: $50,000
Recruiting Specialty: Finance

Macinnis, Ward and Associates Inc.
551 5th Avenue
New York, NY 10176
(212) 808-8080
Contact: Ms. Mary Ward
Minimum Salary Placed: $40,000
Recruiting Specialty: Commercial real es-
tate

The Madison Group
342 Madison Avenue, Suite 1060
New York, NY 10173
(212) 599-0032
Contact: Mr. David Soloway
Minimum Salary Placed: $75,000
Recruiting Specialty: General

Major, Hagen & Africa
900 Third Avenue, 16th Floor
New York, NY 10022
(212) 421-1011
Contact: Ms. June Eichbaum
Recruiting Specialty: Attorneys

Maloney and Associates
51 E 42nd Street, Suite 1508
New York, NY 10006
(212) 425-6290
Contact: Barbara
Minimum Salary Placed: $35,000
Recruiting Specialty: Banking and broker-
ages

Management Recruiters
370 Lexington Avenue, Suite 1412
New York, NY 10017
(212) 972-7300
Contact: Mr. Jeffrey Heath
Minimum Salary Placed: $25,000
Recruiting Specialty: High technology
and personal computers

**Management Recruiters of Gramercy,
Inc.**
200 Park Avenue S., Suite 1510
New York, NY 10003
(212) 505-5530
Contact: Mr. Stephen Schwartz
Recruiting Specialty: Publishing

Management Resource Group, Inc.
77 Bleecker Street, Suite 124
New York, NY 10012
(212) 475-5327
Contact: Mr. Matthew DeLuca
Minimum Salary Placed: $40,000
Recruiting Specialty: Banking and finance

Management Resources International
160 E. 88th Street, Suite 12G
New York, NY 10028
(212) 722-4885
Contact: Mr. F. J. Rotundo
Minimum Salary Placed: $20,000
Recruiting Specialty: General

Margolin Consultants, Inc.
350 5th Avenue, Suite 2819
New York, NY 10018
(212) 268-1940
Contact: Mr. Efraim Margolin
Minimum Salary Placed: $35,000
Recruiting Specialty: General

Mariaschin and Company
747 3rd Avenue
New York, NY 10017
(212) 308-6500
Contact: Mr. Mark Mariaschin
Minimum Salary Placed: $50,000
Recruiting Specialty: Financial services
and commercial banking

Marketing Research Pros Inc.
555 5th Avenue
New York, NY 10017
(212) 972-0300
Contact: Ms. Cindy Asen
Minimum Salary Placed: $35,000
Recruiting Specialty: Marketing research

Marshall-Alan Assoc., Inc.
5 W. 37th Street
New York, NY 10018
(212) 382-2440
Contact: Mr. Alan Massarsky
Minimum Salary Placed: $35,000
Recruiting Specialty: Hospitality

Marshall Consultants, Inc.
360 E. 65th Street
New York, NY 10021
(212) 628-8400
Contact: Mr. Larry Marshall
Minimum Salary Placed: $25,000
Recruiting Specialty: Advertising, public
relations, corporate communications and
advertising

Maximum Management Corp.
60 E. 42nd Street, Suite 2226
New York, NY 10165
(212) 867-4646
Contact: Ms. Melissa Brophy
Recruiting Specialty: General

Maxwell Group
10 East 40th Street, 26th Floor
New York, NY 10016
(212) 725-7400
Contact: Mr. R. Turano
Minimum Salary Placed: $50,000
Recruiting Specialty: Finance and ac-
counting

The McConnell Group
500 Fifth Avenue, Suite 4815
New York, NY 10126
(212) 997-0112
Contact: Ms. Christine McConnell
Minimum Salary Placed: $25,000
Recruiting Specialty: General

John McLellan Associates, Inc.
521 5th Avenue
New York, NY 10175
(212) 292--4240
Contact: Mr. John McLellan
Minimum Salary Placed: $50,000
Recruiting Specialty: Municipal finance

McManners Associates, Inc.
245 E. 63rd Street, Suite 225
New York, NY 10021
(212) 980-7140
Contact: Mr. Donald McManners
Minimum Salary Placed: $100,000
Recruiting Specialty: General

Medical Action Agency
18 W. 45th Street, Suite 409
New York, NY 10036
(212) 354-1204
Contact: Mr. M. Pass
Minimum Salary Placed: $35,000
Recruiting Specialty: Medical

Medical Directions
101 Fifth Avenue, 9th Floor
New York, NY 10003-1008
(212) 255-1001
Contact: Mr. David J. Kapiloff
Recruiting Specialty: Physicians and social workers

Martin H. Meisel Associates, Inc.
55 E. 87th Street
New York, NY 10128
(212) 369-4300
Contact: Mr. Martin Meisel
Minimum Salary Placed: $75,000
Recruiting Specialty: Medical

Meridian Legal Search
25 W. 43rd Street, Suite 700
New York, NY 10036
(212) 354-9300
Contact: Mr. Joel Berger
Minimum Salary Placed: $50,000
Recruiting Specialty: Attorneys

Milo Research
60 E. 42nd Street, Suite 1762
New York, NY 10165
(212) 972-2780
Contact: Mr. Lance Goulbourne
Minimum Salary Placed: $35,000
Recruiting Specialty: General; women and minorities

Herbert Mines Associates, Inc.
399 Park Avenue, 27th Floor
New York, NY 10022
(212) 355-0909
Contact: Mr. Herbert Mines
Minimum Salary Placed: $75,000
Recruiting Specialty: Retail and marketing of consumer products

Mitchell / Martin, Inc.
80 Wall Street, Suite 1215
New York, NY 10005
(212) 943-1404
Recruiting Specialty: Information technology

Morgan Research Inc.
521 5th Avenue, Suite 1723
New York, NY 10175
(212) 557-7977
Contact: Mr. W. Cirincione
Minimum Salary Placed: $35,000
Recruiting Specialty: General

Morgan Stampfl, Inc.
6 W. 32nd Street, Suite 909
New York, NY 10001
(212) 643-7165
Contact: Mr. David Morgan
Minimum Salary Placed: $50,000
Recruiting Specialty: Investment banking

Mruk & Partners
675 Third Avenue, Suite 1805
New York, NY 10017
(212) 983-7676
Contact: Mr. Edwin Mruk
Minimum Salary Placed: $100,000
Recruiting Specialty: General

Much & Company
237 Park Avenue
New York, NY 10017
(212) 551-3578
Contact: Mr. Isaac Much
Minimum Salary Placed: $200,000
Recruiting Specialty: Investment banking

National Recruiting Advisors
90 West Street
New York, NY 10006
(212) 488-8834
Contact: Mr. J. Neudorfer
Minimum Salary Placed: $60,000
Recruiting Specialty: Retail stockbrokers

The Neil Michael Group, Inc.
305 Madison Avenue, Suite 902
New York, NY 10165
(212) 986-3790
Contact: Dr. Neil Solomon
Minimum Salary Placed: $70,000
Recruiting Specialty: Healthcare, biotechnology and pharmaceuticals

William Nelson and Company
295 Madison Avenue
New York, NY 10017
(212) 986-5000
Contact: Mr. William Nelson
Minimum Salary Placed: $40,000
Recruiting Specialty: Taxation

Network Dynamics
200 W 57th Street, Suite 1103
New York, NY 10019
(212) 258-2600
Contact: Mr. Mark O'Brien
Minimum Salary Placed: $30,000
Recruiting Specialty: High technology

Steve Newman Associates
500 5th Avenue
New York, NY 10110
(212) 768-3535
Contact: Mr. Steve Newman
Minimum Salary Placed: $30,000
Recruiting Specialty: General

New York-New York
170 Broadway
New York, NY 10038
(212) 267-3500
Contact: Ms. Marsha Sommers
Recruiting Specialty: Office support, administrative assistants, accounting, and banking

Marc Nichols Associates, Inc.
271 Madison Avenue, 15th Floor
New York, NY 10016
(212) 725-1750
Contact: Mr. Marc Nichols
Minimum Salary Placed: $40,000
Recruiting Specialty: General

Noble & Associates, Inc.
420 Madison Avenue, Suite 803
New York, NY 10017
(212) 838-7020
Contact: Mr. Donald Noble
Minimum Salary Placed: $50,000
Recruiting Specialty: Marketing and advertising

Nordeman Grimm, Inc.
717 Fifth Avenue
New York, NY 10022
(212) 935-1000
Contact: Mr. Peter Grimm
Minimum Salary Placed: $100,000
Recruiting Specialty: General; MBA
graduates

Norden and Associates
1 Haven Plaza
New York, NY 10009
(212) 995-2300
Contact: Mr. Arthur Norden
Minimum Salary Placed: $35,000
Recruiting Specialty: General

Norman Broadbent International, Inc.
200 Park Avenue
New York, NY 10166
(212) 953-6990
Contact: Research Department
Minimum Salary Placed: $100,000
Recruiting Specialty: General

NorthStar Technologies, Inc.
15 Maiden Lane, Suite 803
New York, NY 10038
(212) 267-4100
Contact: Mr. Harry Plastik
Recruiting Specialty: Management consulting, re-engineering and technology

The Ogdon Partnership
375 Park Avenue
New York, NY 10152
(212) 308-1600
Contact: Mr. Thomas Ogdon
Minimum Salary Placed: $75,000
Recruiting Specialty: General

O'Hare & Associates
369 Lexington Avenue
New York, NY 10017
(212) 286-9555
Contact: Mr. Kurt O'Hare
Recruiting Specialty: Advertising

Oliver & Rozner Associates, Inc.
598 Madison Avenue
New York, NY 10022
(212) 688-1850
Contact: Mr. Burton Rozner
Minimum Salary Placed: $100,000
Recruiting Specialty: General

Oppedisano & Company, Inc.
370 Lexington Avenue, Suite 1200
New York, NY 10017
(212) 696-0144
Contact: Mr. Edward Oppedisano
Recruiting Specialty: Finance

Kitty Ossow & Associates
160 E. 48th Street
New York, NY 10017
(212) 753-5873
Contact: Ms. Kitty Ossow
Minimum Salary Placed: $50,000
Recruiting Specialty: Advertising and
marketing in consumer products

P.N. Consultants
45 John Street
New York, NY 10038
(212) 619-0740
Contact: Ms. P. Nicholson
Minimum Salary Placed: $45,000
Recruiting Specialty: Insurance

Janou Pakter, Inc.
5 W 19th Avenue, 6th Floor
New York, NY 10003
(212) 989-1288
Contact: Ms. Janou Pakter
Minimum Salary Placed: $20,000
Recruiting Specialty: Advertising and
publishing

Kirk Palmer & Assoc., Inc.
6 E. 43rd Street, Suite 2004
New York, NY 10017
(212) 983-6477
Contact: Mr. Kirk Palmer
Minimum Salary Placed: $50,000
Recruiting Specialty: Retail and apparel

R. Parker & Associates, Inc.
551 5th Avenue, Suite 222
New York, NY 10176
(212) 661-8074
Contact: Ms. Roberta Parker
Minimum Salary Placed: $50,000
Recruiting Specialty: Consumer products

Parker Clark Data Processing, Inc.
535 Fifth Avenue, Suite 1004
New York, NY 10017
(212) 983-5630
Contact: Mr. Ralph Clark
Recruiting Specialty: Data processing

Parker Clark Executive
370 Lexington Avenue, Suite 1804
New York, NY 10016
(212) 983-5950
Contact: Mr. H. Parker
Minimum Salary Placed: $35,000
Recruiting Specialty: Accounting and fi-
nance

V.A. Parr Associates
171 Madison Avenue, Suite 204
New York, NY 10016
(212) 889-4810
Contact: Ms. V. Parr
Minimum Salary Placed: $30,000
Recruiting Specialty: Public relations
writers

Pathway Executive Search, Inc.
60 E. 42nd Street, Suite 405
New York, NY 10165
(212) 557-2650
Contact: Mr. Jay Berger
Recruiting Specialty: Information systems and computers

Joel H. Paul & Associates, Inc.
352 Seventh Avenue
New York, NY 10001
(212) 564-6500
Contact: Mr. Joel Paul
Recruiting Specialty: Non-profit

Paul Ray Berndtson
101 Park Avenue
New York, NY 10178
(212) 370-1316
Contact: Mr. William Weed
Minimum Salary Placed: $90,000
Recruiting Specialty: General

Peak Search, Inc.
25 W. 31st Street
New York, NY 10001
(212) 947-6600
Contact: Mr. Richard Eichenberg
Recruiting Specialty: Auditing, accounting and finance and attorneys

The Peck Consultancy
17 West 54th Street
New York, NY 10019
(212) 757-2688
Contact: Mr. David Peck
Minimum Salary Placed: $75,000
Recruiting Specialty: Non-profit

Pencom Systems Inc.
150 Broadway, Suite 600
New York, NY 10038
(212) 513-7777
Contact: Mr. Stephen Markman
Minimum Salary Placed: $30,000
Recruiting Specialty: MIS and computer
support

People Inc.
350 5th Avenue, Suite 3304
New York, NY 10118
(212) 753-7933
Contact: Mr. Tony Warren
Minimum Salary Placed: $35,000
Recruiting Specialty: General

Personnel Services Center
10 East 39th Street
New York, NY 10016
(212) 447-9173
Minimum Salary Placed: $35,000
Recruiting Specialty: General

Alec Peters Associates Inc.
342 Madison Avenue
New York, NY 10173
(212) 661-0202
Contact: Mr. Alec Peters
Minimum Salary Placed: $35,000
Recruiting Specialty: Finance

Pharmaceutical Recruiters Inc.
271 Madison Avenue
New York, NY 10016
(212) 557-5627
Contact: Ms. Linda Weiss
Minimum Salary Placed: $60,000
Recruiting Specialty: Pharmaceuticals

Picard International, Ltd.
125 E 38th Street
New York, NY 10116
(212) 972-5310
Contact: Mr. Daniel Picard
Recruiting Specialty: General

The Pinnacle Group
130 Water Street, Suite 12C
New York, NY 10005
(212) 968-1200
Contact: Mr. Stephen Flynn
Minimum Salary Placed: $50,000
Recruiting Specialty: Finance, investment
banking and real estate

Placement Associates, Inc.
136 E 57th Street
New York, NY 10022
(212) 620-7620
Contact: Mr. Len Daniels
Minimum Salary Placed: $50,000
Recruiting Specialty: Public relations

Rene Plessner Associates, Inc.
375 Park Avenue
New York, NY 10152
(212) 421-3490
Contact: Mr. Rene Plessner
Minimum Salary Placed: $75,000
Recruiting Specialty: Consumer products

Preston Associates, Inc.
20 E. 46th Street, Suite 600
New York, NY 10017
(212) 661-1950
Contact: Mr. Ron Sussman
Recruiting Specialty: Office support, publishing, and computer programming

Quantex Association, Inc.
545 Madison Avenue, Suite 2
New York, NY 10022
(212) 661-5450
Contact: Mr. Robert Hechkoff
Minimum Salary Placed: $30,000
Recruiting Specialty: Information systems in communications

The Quest Organization
11 Penn Plaza, Suite 935
New York, NY 10001
(212) 971-0033
Contact: Mr. Michael F. Rosenblatt
Recruiting Specialty: Financial

L. J. Quinn & Association, Inc.
90 Park Avenue, Suite 1600
New York, NY 10016
(212) 687-7798
Contact: Mr. L. J. Quinn
Minimum Salary Placed: $60,000
Recruiting Specialty: General

R.L. Executive Search
305 Madison Avenue, Suite 440
New York, NY 10017
(212) 682-9600
Contact: Mr. H. Krzeninski
Minimum Salary Placed: $45,000
Recruiting Specialty: Tax and audit professionals

Raines International, Inc.
1120 Avenue of the Americas, 21st Floor
New York, NY 10036
(212) 997-1100
Contact: Mr. Bruce Raines
Minimum Salary Placed: $50,000
Recruiting Specialty: General

Rand Thompson Consultants
261 Madison Avenue, 27th Floor
New York, NY 10016
(212) 972-0090
Contact: Mr. J. Kelly
Minimum Salary Placed: $35,000
Recruiting Specialty: Accounting and finance

Randell-Heiken, Inc.
60 E. 42nd Street, 21st Floor
New York, NY 10165
(212) 490-1313
Contact: Mr. James Randell
Minimum Salary Placed: $60,000
Recruiting Specialty: Human resources and marketing

Rasch and Associates
235 W. 75th Street, Suite 10-F
New York, NY 10023
(212) 799-7134
Contact: Ms. Judith Fredericks
Minimum Salary Placed: $50,000
Recruiting Specialty: Financial services

Recruiter International
630 Fifth Avenue, Suite 240
New York, NY 10111
(212) 332-8020
Contact: Ms. Linda Liebman
Minimum Salary Placed: $40,000
Recruiting Specialty: Healthcare

Redwood Partners
152 Madison Avenue, 22nd Floor
New York, NY 10016
(212) 843-8585
Contact: Ms. Marcelo Wainberg
Minimum Salary Placed: $50,000
Recruiting Specialty: Marketing, multi-media and outside sales

Sally Reich Associates
232 East 50th Street
New York, NY 10022
(212) 308-3276
Contact: Ms. Sally Reich
Minimum Salary Placed: $30,000
Recruiting Specialty: Direct marketing

Rem Resources
507 5th Avenue
New York, NY 10017
(212) 661-0090
Contact: Ms. G. Rem
Minimum Salary Placed: $35,000
Recruiting Specialty: General

Retail Recruiters Inc.
225 West 34th Street, Suite 1616
New York, NY 10122
(212) 714-0313
Contact: Mr. R. Harmann
Minimum Salary Placed: $35,000
Recruiting Specialty: Retail

Rex Associates, Inc.
157 E. 57th Street
New York, NY 10022
(212) 935-0100
Contact: Mr. David Hochberg
Minimum Salary Placed: $40,000
Recruiting Specialty: Advertising and marketing in finance and healthcare

Reynolds Partners
380 Madison Avenue, 7th Floor
New York, NY 10017
(212) 856-4466
Contact: Ms. Sydney Reynolds
Minimum Salary Placed: $35,000
Recruiting Specialty: Manufacturing in high technology

Eric Robert Associates, Inc.
350 Seventh Avenue, 7th Floor
New York, NY 10001
(212) 695-5900
Contact: Mr. Eric Silverman
Recruiting Specialty: Computers

Russell Reynolds Associates, Inc.
200 Park Avenue
New York, NY 10166
(212) 351-2000
Contact: Mr. Hobson Brown
Minimum Salary Placed: $100,000
Recruiting Specialty: General

E.J. Rhodes Associates
555 5th Avenue
New York, NY 10017
(212) 983-2000
Contact: Mr. Stephen Littman
Minimum Salary Placed: $75,000
Recruiting Specialty: General

Ribolow Associates
230 Park Avenue, Suite 222
New York, NY 10169
(212) 808-0580
Contact: Ms. Adele Ribolow
Recruiting Specialty: Market search, publishing, strategic planning in advertising

Riotto - Jones Association, Inc.
600 Third Avenue, 20th Floor
New York, NY 10016
(212) 697-4575
Contact: Mr. Anthony Riotto
Minimum Salary Placed: $60,000
Recruiting Specialty: Banking and finance

Ritech Management Inc.
2 Penn Plaza, Suite 1500
New York, NY 10121
(212) 268-7778
Contact: Mr. Ben Michaels
Minimum Salary Placed: $35,000
Recruiting Specialty: Personal computer programming

Alan Roberts and Associates Inc.
767 3rd Avenue
New York, NY 10017
(212) 688-3080
Contact: Mr. Alan Roberts
Minimum Salary Placed: $50,000
Recruiting Specialty: Attorneys

Roberts-Lund Associates, Ltd.
366 Madison Avenue
New York, NY 10017
(212) 490-3300
Contact: Mr. Michael Iserson
Minimum Salary Placed: $75,000
Recruiting Specialty: Banking and finance

Rockwood Associates
1202 Lexington, Suite 153
New York, NY 10028
(212) 744-0905
Contact: Mr. Charles Bamford
Minimum Salary Placed: $40,000
Recruiting Specialty: Utility, energy and finance

W. R. Rosato & Associates, Inc.
71 Broadway, 16th Floor
New York, NY 10006
(212) 509-5700
Contact: Mr. William Rosato
Minimum Salary Placed: $100,000
Recruiting Specialty: Investment banking

Cheryl Roshak Associates, Inc.
141 5th Avenue, 4th Floor
New York, NY 10010
(212) 228-5050
Contact: Ms. Cheryl Roshak
Minimum Salary Placed: $25,000
Recruiting Specialty: Technical disciplines in graphic arts and new media technology

J.D. Ross International
375 Park Avenue, Suite 3101
New York, NY 10152
(212) 644-9100
Contact: Mr. Don Ross
Minimum Salary Placed: $100,000
Recruiting Specialty: Consumer products

Alex Roth Management
360 Lexington Avenue, 21st Floor
New York, NY 10017
(212) 972-3100
Contact: Mr. Alex Roth
Minimum Salary Placed: $35,000
Recruiting Specialty: Data processing and MIS

Francis Ryan Associates
488 Madison Avenue
New York, NY 10022
(212) 980-8818
Contact: Ms. Ann Ryan
Minimum Salary Placed: $50,000
Recruiting Specialty: Attorneys

SKB Enterprises
1 World Trade Center, Suite 4517
New York, NY 10048
Contact: Ms. Sandra Booth
Minimum Salary Placed: $30,000
Recruiting Specialty: General

Safian Associates Ltd.
55 East 80th Street
New York, NY 10021
(212) 439-6990
Contact: Ms. Dorothy Safian
Minimum Salary Placed: $50,000
Recruiting Specialty: Investment banking

Santangelo Consultants Inc.
60 E. 42nd Street
New York, NY 10165
(212) 867-6664
Contact: Mr. Richard Santangelo
Minimum Salary Placed: $60,000
Recruiting Specialty: General

Allan Sarn Associates, Inc.
230 Park Avenue, Suite 1522
New York, NY 10169
(212) 687-0600
Contact: Mr. Allan Sarn
Minimum Salary Placed: $80,000
Recruiting Specialty: Human resources,
personnel, and industrial relations

Savitt & Company
317 Madison Avenue, Suite 2315
New York, NY 10017
(212) 661-4100
Contact: Ms. Mimi Savitt
Recruiting Specialty: Office support for
legal and financial

Schildgen & Ross Associates
65 Broadway
New York, NY 10006
Contact: Ms. Carol Schildgen
Minimum Salary Placed: $40,000
Recruiting Specialty: Analysts

Michael Scott Associates
810 7th Avenue
New York, NY 10019
(212) 307-1030
Contact: Mr. Victor Caleo
Minimum Salary Placed: $35,000
Recruiting Specialty: Insurance

Seiden Krieger Associates, Inc.
375 Park Avenue
New York, NY 10152
(212) 688-8383
Contact: Mr. Steven Seiden
Minimum Salary Placed: $75,000
Recruiting Specialty: General

Seitchik, Corwin & Seitchik Inc.
330 E. 38th Street, Suite 5P
New York, NY 10016
(212) 245-1162
Contact: Mr. William Seitchik
Recruiting Specialty: Fashion and cloth-
ing, textiles, and footware

Setford-Shaw-Najarian Associates, Ltd.
111 Broadway, 10th Floor
New York, NY 10006
(212) 962-1500
Contact: Mr. Jeffrey Najarian
Minimum Salary Placed: $40,000
Recruiting Specialty: Data processing

Simpson Associates
106 Central Park S., Suite 3B
New York, NY 10019
(212) 767-0006
Contact: Ms. Terre Simpson
Minimum Salary Placed: $65,000
Recruiting Specialty: Retail manufacturing

Marina Sirras and Associates
420 Lexington Avenue
New York, NY 10170
(212) 490-0333
Contact: Ms. Marina Sirras
Recruiting Specialty: Legal

Ruth Sklar Associates, Inc.
475 Park Avenue S., 8th Floor
New York, NY 10016
(212) 213-2929
Contact: Ms. Ruth Sklar
Minimum Salary Placed: $50,000
Recruiting Specialty: Consumer products

Skott/Edwards Consultants
500 Fifth Avenue
New York, NY 10110
(212) 382-1166
Minimum Salary Placed: $75,000
Recruiting Specialty: Consumer products and finance

Sloan Staffing Services
317 Madison Avenue at 42nd
New York, NY 10017
(212) 949-7200
Contact: Ms. Arlene Covney
Recruiting Specialty: Office support

Smith Hanley Associates, Inc.
99 Park Avenue
New York, NY 10016
(212) 687-9696
Contact: Mr. Thomas Hanley
Minimum Salary Placed: $40,000
Recruiting Specialty: Market research and finance in consumer products

Judy Smith Associates
420 Lexington Avenue
New York, NY 10170
(212) 867-9203
Minimum Salary Placed: $65,000
Recruiting Specialty: Legal

Smith, Roth & Squires
237 Park Avenue, 21st Floor
New York, NY 10175
(516) 767-9480
Contact: Mr. Steven Smith
Minimum Salary Placed: $60,000
Recruiting Specialty: General

Smith's Fifth Avenue Agency, Inc.
17 E. 45th Street
New York, NY 10017
(212) 682-5300
Contact: Mr. Arthur Teicher
Minimum Salary Placed: $30,000
Recruiting Specialty: Market research

Smyth Associates
630 3rd Avenue, 18th Floor
New York, NY 10017
(212) 682-9300
Contact: Ms. S. Smyth
Minimum Salary Placed: $40,000
Recruiting Specialty: Finance

Smythe Masterson & Judd, Inc.
380 Lexington Avenue, Suite 3908
New York, NY 10168
(212) 286-0003
Contact: Mr. Mark Henley
Minimum Salary Placed: $75,000
Recruiting Specialty: Legal and finance

Smyth Executive Search Inc.
630 3rd Avenue
New York, NY 10017
(212) 682-9300
Minimum Salary Placed: $75,000
Recruiting Specialty: Finance

Soloman-Page Healthcare Group
1140 Avenue of the Americas, 9th Floor
New York, NY 10036
(212) 764-9200
Contact: Mr. Marc Gouran
Minimum Salary Placed: $50,000
Recruiting Specialty: Healthcare

Source EDP
2 Penn Plaza, Suite 1176
New York, NY 10121
(212) 760-2200
Contact: Mr. Stephen Licota
Minimum Salary Placed: $20,000
Recruiting Specialty: Computers

Source Finance
2 Penn Plaza, Suite 1176
New York, NY 10121
(516) 868-5100
Contact: Mr. Phillip Bank
Minimum Salary Placed: $30,000
Recruiting Specialty: Finance

Spencer Stuart
277 Park Avenue, 29th Floor
New York, NY 10172
(212) 366-0200
Contact: Mr. Robert Damon
Minimum Salary Placed: $100,000
Recruiting Specialty: General

Toby Spitz
110 E 59th Street, 6th floor
New York, NY 10022
(212) 867-7750
Contact: Ms. Toby Spitz
Minimum Salary Placed: $45,000
Recruiting Specialty: Attorneys

Spring Associates, Inc.
10 East 23rd Street
New York, NY 10010
(212) 473-0013
Contact: Mr. Dennis Spring
Minimum Salary Placed: $30,000
Recruiting Specialty: Public relations,
corporate communications, and marketing

Staffing by Manning Ltd.
38 E. 57th Street
New York, NY 10022
(212) 753-8080
Contact: Ms. R. Manning
Minimum Salary Placed: $20,000
Recruiting Specialty: Administrative assistants

Staub, Warmbold & Associates, Inc.
575 Madison Avenue
New York, NY 10022
(212) 605-0554
Contact: Mr. Robert Staub
Minimum Salary Placed: $90,000
Recruiting Specialty: General

Stentiford and Beradi Associates
1140 6th Avenue, 9th floor
New York, NY 10036
(212) 382-1616
Contact: Ms. Loretta Beradi
Recruiting Specialty: Publishing and new media technology

G.Z. Stephens Inc.
1 World Trade Center, Suite 4749
New York, NY 10048
(212) 321-3040
Contact: Mr. H. Gabler
Minimum Salary Placed: $50,000
Recruiting Specialty: Investment banking

Storfer & Associates
1200 Broadway, Suite 7D
New York, NY 10001
(212) 689-2713
Contact: Mr. Herbert Storfer
Minimum Salary Placed: $30,000
Recruiting Specialty: Consumer products and healthcare

W. R. Strathmann Associates
150 Fifth Avenue
New York, NY 10011
(212) 243-8660
Contact: Mr. Winfried Strathmann
Minimum Salary Placed: $90,000
Recruiting Specialty: International organizations operating domestically

Stricker & Zagor
342 Madison Avenue, 4th Floor
New York, NY 10173
(212) 983-0388
Contact: Mr. Sidney Stricker
Minimum Salary Placed: $90,000
Recruiting Specialty: Consumer products

Michelle Stuhl and Associates
51 East 25th Street
New York, NY 10010
(212) 545-1234
Contact: Ms. Michelle Stuhl
Minimum Salary Placed: $35,000
Recruiting Specialty: Graphic arts, architecture and Interior design

Sullivan & Company
20 Exchange Place, 50th Floor
New York, NY 10005
(212) 422-3000
Contact: Mr. Brian Sullivan
Minimum Salary Placed: $100,000
Recruiting Specialty: Investment banking, securities and capital markets

John Sutton Associates
1501 Broadway
New York, NY 10036
(212) 730-8000
Contact: Mr. M. Bruce
Minimum Salary Placed: $50,000
Recruiting Specialty: General

TTS Personnel
420 Lexington Avenue
New York, NY 10170
(212) 687-9001
Contact: Mr. J. Loureiro
Minimum Salary Placed: $30,000
Recruiting Specialty: Accounting, finance, and data processing

TASA, Inc.
750 Lexington Avenue, Suite 1800
New York, NY 10022
(212) 486-1490
Contact: Mr. Klaus Jacobs
Minimum Salary Placed: $120,000
Recruiting Specialty: General

Tallman Cohen Associates
230 Park Avenue
New York, NY 10169
(212) 972-1544
Contact: Ms. A. Tallman
Minimum Salary Placed: $45,000
Recruiting Specialty: Advertising and
marketing

Tama Lucas Ltd.
150 West End Avenue
New York, NY 10023
(212) 922-9010
Contact: Ms. Phyllis Tama
Minimum Salary Placed: $75,000
Recruiting Specialty: Wholesale and retail
trade

Tax Network Resources, Inc.
60 East 42nd Street, Room 746
New York, NY 10165
(212) 983-3030
Contact: Mr. Howard Kutcher
Minimum Salary Placed: $25,000
Recruiting Specialty: Tax, accounting
and internal auditing

Taylor Grey
516 Fifth Avenue, Suite 701
New York, NY 10036
(212) 398-6400
Contact: Ms. Jodi Fournier
Recruiting Specialty: General

Taylor Hodson, Inc.
40 Wateside Plaza, Level C
New York, NY 10010
(212) 725-6722
Contact: Ms. Minerva Taylor
Recruiting Specialty: Administrative assistants

Tech Options Inc.
300 East 71st Street, 15th Floor
New York, NY 10021
(212) 988-3067
Contact: Ms. S. Goldin
Minimum Salary Placed: $30,000
Recruiting Specialty: Mini-microcom-
puter

Technet Systems
45 W. 34th Street, Suite 1104
New York, NY 10001
(212) 967-4260
Contact: Ms. M. Pigano
Minimum Salary Placed: $35,000
Recruiting Specialty: Technical disciplines

Techno-Trac Systems, Inc.
251 Central Park West
New York, NY 10024
(212) 769-8722
Contact: Mr. Mort Trachtenberg
Minimum Salary Placed: $25,000
Recruiting Specialty: Computer and data
processing

Thorndike Deland Associates
275 Madison Avenue, Suite 1300
New York, NY 10016
(212) 661-6200
Contact: Ms. M. Percheski
Minimum Salary Placed: $30,000
Recruiting Specialty: General

Thorne, Brieger Associates, Inc.
11 E. 44th Street
New York, NY 10017
(212) 682-5424
Contact: Mr. Steven Brieger
Minimum Salary Placed: $90,000
Recruiting Specialty: General

McCann & Choi, Inc.
590 Madison Avenue, 26th Floor
New York, NY 10022
(212) 755-7051
Contact: Mr. McCann or Mr. Choi
Minimum Salary Placed: $150,000
Recruiting Specialty: General

Travaglini Associates
340 East 63rd Street
New York, NY 10021
(212) 832-9115
Contact: Mr. Nick Travaglini
Minimum Salary Placed: $50,000
Recruiting Specialty: General

Trebor Weldon Lawrence
342 Madison, Suite 1522
New York, NY 10022
(212) 867-0066
Contact: Mr. Lawrence Levine
Minimum Salary Placed: $45,000
Recruiting Specialty: Sales and marketing
in consumer products

Karen Tripi Associates
60 East 42nd Street, Suite 2140
New York, NY 10165
(212) 972-5258
Contact: Ms. Karen Tripi
Minimum Salary Placed: $35,000
Recruiting Specialty: Advertising and
marketing

Gayle Tudisco Associates Inc.
866 3rd Avenue, 30th Floor
New York, NY 10022
(212) 980-1411
Contact: Ms. Gayle Tudisco
Minimum Salary Placed: $35,000
Recruiting Specialty: General

The Viscusi Group, Inc.
Box 261
New York, NY 10023
(212) 595-3811
Contact: Mr. Stephen Viscusi
Minimum Salary Placed: $75,000
Recruiting Specialty: Marketing and sales
in textiles and interior design

WTW Associates, Inc.
675 Third Avenue, Suite 2808
New York, NY 10017
(212) 972-6990
Contact: Mr. Warren Wasp
Minimum Salary Placed: $75,000
Recruiting Specialty: General; entertain-
ment, banking and publishing

Don Waldron and Associates
450 7th Avenue, Suite 507A
New York, NY 10123
(212) 239-9110
Contact: Mr. Don Waldron
Minimum Salary Placed: $50,000
Recruiting Specialty: Physicians and sales

Walker Associates, Inc.
507 Fifth Avenue, Room 700
New York, NY 10017
(212) 661-6767
Contact: Mr. Michael Walker
Recruiting Specialty: General

Robert D. Walsh
25 Tudor City Place, Suite 1315
New York, NY 10017
(212) 661-0959
Contact: Mr. Bob Walsh
Recruiting Specialty: Internal and external communications, public relations, etc.

Ward Howell International, Inc.
99 Park Avenue, Suite 2000
New York, NY 10016
(212) 697-3730
Contact: Mr. Dave Witte
Minimum Salary Placed: $75,000
Recruiting Specialty: General

Wayne Group Ltd.
84 Williams Street
New York, NY 10038
(212) 668-1414
Contact: Mr. Samuel Schwimmer
Minimum Salary Placed: $40,000
Recruiting Specialty: Data processing

Webb, Johnson Associates
280 Park Avenue
New York, NY 10017
(212) 661-3700
Contact: Mr. George Webb
Minimum Salary Placed: $100,000
Recruiting Specialty: General

Dina Wehn Associates
71 Vanderbilt
New York, NY 10017
(212) 675-3224
Contact: Ms. Dina Wehn
Minimum Salary Placed: $30,000
Recruiting Specialty: Computers

C. Weiss Associates, Inc.
60 W. 57th Street
New York, NY 10019
(212) 581-4040
Contact: Ms. Cathy Weiss
Minimum Salary Placed: $40,000
Recruiting Specialty: Consumer financial services

Werbin Associates Executive Search, Inc.
521 Fifth Avenue, Suite 1749
New York, NY 10175
(212) 953-0909
Contact: Ms. Susan Werbin
Recruiting Specialty: Computer and research

David Werner International
420 Lexington Avenue, Suite 2811
New York, NY 10170
(212) 682-8888
Contact: Mr. David Werner
Minimum Salary Placed: $50,000
Recruiting Specialty: General

Wesley Brown & Bartle Company, Inc.
152 Madison Avenue
New York, NY 10016
(212) 684-6900
Contact: Mr. Wesley Poriotis
Minimum Salary Placed: $50,000
Recruiting Specialty: General; minorities

S.J. Wexler Associates, Inc.
1120 Avenue of the Americas
New York, NY 10036
(212) 626-6599
Contact: Ms. Suzanne Wexler
Minimum Salary Placed: $65,000
Recruiting Specialty: Human resources, information systems and finance

White Marine Associates Inc.
36 West 44th Street, Suite 1111
New York, NY 10036
(212) 354-7878
Contact: Mr. A. Marine
Minimum Salary Placed: $45,000
Recruiting Specialty: Technical disciplines in banking and finance

K. L. Whitney & Company, Inc.
7 East 35th Street
New York, NY 10016
(212) 725-0780
Contact: Mr. Kenneth Whitney
Minimum Salary Placed: $75,000
Recruiting Specialty: Finance and banking

Winmar Personnel Agency, Inc.
535 Fifth Avenue, Suite 1008
New York, NY 10017
(212) 687-8977
Contact: Ms. Susan Winters
Recruiting Specialty: Human resources and office support

Winston Personnel, Inc.
535 Fifth Avenue, Suite 701
New York, NY 10017
(212) 557-5000
Contact: Mr. Gregg Kaye
Recruiting Specialty: Hospitality, healthcare, computers

D.S. Wolf Associates, Inc.
516 Fifth Avenue, 14th Floor
New York, NY 10036
(212) 719-0101
Contact: Mr. David Wolf
Minimum Salary Placed: $60,000
Recruiting Specialty: Investment banking

S. R. Wolman Associates, Inc.
133 E. 35th Street
New York, NY 10016
(212) 685-2692
Contact: Mr. Steve Wolman
Minimum Salary Placed: $50,000
Recruiting Specialty: Consumer products

Worth Group
295 Madison Avenue, Suite 1028
New York, NY 10017
(212) 986-9630
Contact: Mr. Al Rosenbaum
Minimum Salary Placed: $60,000
Recruiting Specialty: General

X Cel Consulting Inc.
17 Battery Place
New York, NY 10004
(212) 376-6010
Recruiting Specialty: General

Egon Zehnder International, Inc.
55 E. 59th Street, 14th Floor
New York, NY 10022
(212) 838-9199
Contact: Mr. A. Daniel Meiland
Minimum Salary Placed: $80,000
Recruiting Specialty: General

Chuck Zimering Advertising Recruitment
170 W. End Avenue, Suite 11G
New York, NY 10023
(212) 724-7904
Contact: Mr. Chuck Zimering
Minimum Salary Placed: $25,000
Recruiting Specialty: Advertising

NEWBURGH

Career Directions
180 N Plank Road
Newburgh, NY 12550
(914) 565-8861
Contact: Suzanne Gould
Recruiting Specialty: General

Cornell Group
180 N. Plank Road
Newburgh, NY 12550
(914) 565-8905
Contact: Ms. D. Cornell
Minimum Salary Placed: $45,000
Recruiting Specialty: Finance and banking

NORTH SALEM

Robert M. Flanagan & Associates, Ltd.
39 Fields Lane, JMKB Building
North Salem, NY 10560
(914) 277-7210
Contact: Mr. Robert Flanagan
Minimum Salary Placed: $100,000
Recruiting Specialty: General

NORTHPORT

Global Data Services, Inc.
694 Ft. Salonga Road
Northport, NY 11768
(516) 754-0771
Contact: Mr. Garry Silivanch
Minimum Salary Placed: $60,000
Recruiting Specialty: High technology
and pharmaceuticals

Management Recruiters
225 Main Street, Suite 204
Northport, NY 11768
(516) 261-0400
Contact: Mr. Sebastian Livolsi
Minimum Salary Placed: $20,000
Recruiting Specialty: Engineering and
high-technology capital equipment

Resin Resources Ltd.
P.O. Box 186
Northport, NY 11768
(516) 757-4010
Contact: Mr. Malcolm Scar
Minimum Salary Placed: $50,000
Recruiting Specialty: Materials manufacturing

NYACK

Sales Search Ltd.
48 Burd Street
Nyack, NY 10960
(914) 353-2040
Contact: Mr. J. Ratcliff
Minimum Salary Placed: $30,000
Recruiting Specialty: Sales in industrial
and consumer

Tix Travel
48 Burd Street
Nyack, NY 10960
(914) 358-1007
Contact: Mr. Bud Tix
Recruiting Specialty: Travel

ORCHARD PARK

Walter Meyer & Associates
P.O. Box 133
Orchard Park, NY 14127
(716) 662-0427
Contact: Mr. Walter Meyer
Minimum Salary Placed: $50,000
Recruiting Specialty: General

Eileen K. Ward and Associates
4098 N Buffalo Road
Orchard Park, NY 14227
(716) 667-0045
Contact: John
Minimum Salary Placed: $25,000
Recruiting Specialty: General and human resource

OSSINING

Ramsey/Beirne Association, Inc.
500 Executive Boulevard
Ossining, NY 10562
(914) 762-2012
Contact: Mr. David Beirne
Minimum Salary Placed: $20,000
Recruiting Specialty: High technology

OYSTER BAY

TFP Managers Search
115 South Street
Oyster Bay, NY 11771
(516) 921-2803
Contact: Mr. T. Person
Minimum Salary Placed: $30,000
Recruiting Specialty: Life insurance

PATCHOGUE

The Executive Consulting Group
215 N. Ocean Avenue
Patchogue, NY 11772
(516) 447-1118
Contact: Mr. David Glaser
Minimum Salary Placed: $35,000
Recruiting Specialty: Tax and financial planning

PEARL RIVER

Management Recruiters
P.O. Box 1603
Pearl River, NY 10965
(914) 735-7015
Contact: Mr. Tom Malone
Minimum Salary Placed: $20,000
Recruiting Specialty: General

PEEKSKILL

NDS Associates, LTD
8 John Walsh Boulevard, Suite 302
Peekskill, NY 10566
(914) 736-3666
Recruiting Specialty: Printed circuit, manufacturers and related supplier companies

PENFIELD

A-Tec Personnel
1777 Penfield Road
Penfield, NY 14526
(716) 586-9024
Contact: Mr. T. Amann
Minimum Salary Placed: $20,000
Recruiting Specialty: General

PINE BUSH

North Coast Meridian
P.O. Box 640, Main Street
Pine Bush, NY 12566
(914) 744-3061
Contact: Mr. Charlie Thomaschek
Minimum Salary Placed: $40,000
Recruiting Specialty: Manufacturing and engineering

PITTSFORD

Brucks Technical Search
Tobey Park
Pittsford, NY 14534
(716) 248-9090
Contact: Mr. Murray Brandes
Minimum Salary Placed: $35,000
Recruiting Specialty: Technical disciplines in the science and engineering related industries

Christopher C. Carey Associates
35 Burr Oak Drive
Pittsford, NY 14534
(716) 248-5246
Contact: Mr. Christopher Carey
Minimum Salary Placed: $25,000
Recruiting Specialty: General

Dunhill of Rochester
P.O. Box 528
Pittsford, NY 14534
(716) 586-9690
Contact: Mr. Jack Tanner
Minimum Salary Placed: $25,000
Recruiting Specialty: General

Parsons, Anderson & Gee
642 Kreag Road
Pittsford, NY 14534
(716) 586-8679
Contact: Mr. William Parsons
Minimum Salary Placed: $75,000
Recruiting Specialty: General

Traynor Confidential, Ltd.
P.O. Box 189
Pittsford, NY 14534
(716) 387-0383
Contact: Mr. Tom Traynor
Minimum Salary Placed: $20,000
Recruiting Specialty: Accounting, finance and MIS

PLAINVIEW

Amherst Personnel Group Inc.
550 Old Country Road
Plainview, NY 11803
(516) 433-7610
Recruiting Specialty: Retail sales

Transcriptions Limited
1 Dupont Street
Plainview, NY 11803
(516) 576-3355
Contact: Mr. Stu Sheridan
Minimum Salary Placed: $25,000
Recruiting Specialty: Medical transcriptions

PLEASANTVILLE

Redden & McGrath Association, Inc.
427 Bedford Road
Pleasantville, NY 10570
(914) 747-3900

Contact: Ms. Mary Redden
Minimum Salary Placed: $50,000
Recruiting Specialty: Marketing research

W.F. Richer Associates, Inc.
50 Deerfield Lane S.
Pleasantville, NY 10570
(212) 682-4000
Contact: Mr. William Richer
Minimum Salary Placed: $75,000
Recruiting Specialty: Information technology, distributed computing, client serve technology, global communications

POMONA

Saxon Morse Associates
Burning Brush Court
Pomona, NY 10970
(914) 361-1300
Recruiting Specialty: Consumer electronics

PORT CHESTER

Professional Placement Association
14 Rye Ridge Plaza
Port Chester, NY 11050
(914) 939-1195
Contact: Ms. Laura Schacter
Minimum Salary Placed: $30,000
Recruiting Specialty: Medical

PORT WASHINGTON

Carlyle Association
33 Main Street
Port Washington, NY 11050
(516) 767-3030

Contact: Mr. Laurence Janis
Minimum Salary Placed: $75,000
Recruiting Specialty: General

Dunhill Personnel
P.O. Box 1347
Port Washington, NY 11050
(516) 883-1172
Contact: Mr. Neville Newby
Minimum Salary Placed: $25,000
Recruiting Specialty: General

Spector Executive Search Inc.
34 Marlin Lane
Port Washington, NY 11050
(516) 944-8500
Contact: Mr. Marvin Spector
Recruiting Specialty: Attorneys

Tecmark Associates, Inc.
P.O. Box 545
Port Washington, NY 11050
(516) 883-6336
Contact: Mr. Donald Valentine
Minimum Salary Placed: $40,000
Recruiting Specialty: High technology and computers

POUGHKEEPSIE

Ethan Allen Personnel Group
59 Academy Street
Poughkeepsie. NY 12601
(914) 471-9700
Contact: Ms. Fran Domenico
Minimum Salary Placed: $25,000
Recruiting Specialty: General

QUEENSBURY

The Mulshine Company, Ltd.
48 Helen Drive
Queensbury, NY 12804
(518) 743-9301
Contact: Mr. Michael Mulshine
Minimum Salary Placed: $50,000
Recruiting Specialty: Consumer products, research and development in packaging food, pharmaceuticals

RED HOOK

Circuit Search
7 Moul Drive, P.O. Box 218
Red Hook, NY 12571
(914) 758-1979
Contact: Mr. Kevin Stack
Minimum Salary Placed: $35,000
Recruiting Specialty: Electronics and chemical engineering

ROCHESTER

Allinger Personnel Inc.
820 Temple Building
Rochester, NY 14604
(716) 232-1593
Contact: Mr. D. Allinger
Recruiting Specialty: General

Bailey Personnel Consultants Inc.
130 Allens Creek Road
Rochester, NY 14618
(716) 473-9610
Contact: Mr. Hal Levy
Minimum Salary Placed: $20,000
Recruiting Specialty: Engineering, MIS, advertising and general administration

Cochran, Cochran, & Yale, Inc.
955 E. Henrietta Road
Rochester, NY 14623
(716) 424-6060
Contact: Mr. Gary Baker
Minimum Salary Placed: $30,000
Recruiting Specialty: General

Compu Search
16 W Main
Rochester, NY 14614
(716) 325-1660
Recruiting Specialty: Data processing, sales, and engineering

Exek Recruiters 3
5 Flatt Road
Rochester, NY 14623
(716) 292-0550
Contact: Mr. A. Ploscowe
Minimum Salary Placed: $20,000
Recruiting Specialty: Technical disciplines in manufacturing and computers; attorneys

Robert Half International
2 State Street, Suite 910
Rochester, NY 14614
(716) 232-6055
Contact: Mr. M. McDonald
Minimum Salary Placed: $20,000
Recruiting Specialty: Accounting and finance

Management Recruiters
47 S. Fitzhugh Street
Rochester, NY 14614
(716) 454-2440
Contact: Mr. Jerry Annesi
Minimum Salary Placed: $20,000
Recruiting Specialty: Engineering, data processing, and outside sales

Professional Support Inc.
500 Helendale Road, Suite 190
Rochester, NY 14609
(716) 654-7800
Contact: Mr. Ed Sandersky
Minimum Salary Placed: $30,000
Recruiting Specialty: Accounting and
computer programming

Sales Careers
925 Midtown Tower
Rochester, NY 14604
(716) 546-4620
Contact: Mr. T. Quinn
Minimum Salary Placed: $20,000
Recruiting Specialty: Sales

Sales Consultants
47 S. Fitzhugh Street
Rochester, NY 14614
(716) 454-6650
Contact: Mr. Jerry Annesi
Minimum Salary Placed: $20,000
Recruiting Specialty: Sales

Weterrings & Agnew, Inc.
925 Midtown Tower
Rochester, NY 14604
(716) 454-3888
Contact: Mr. Thomas Quinn
Minimum Salary Placed: $30,000
Recruiting Specialty: General

ROCKVILLE CENTRE

ESP Management Services, Inc.
P.O. Box 14
Rockville Centre, NY 11571
(516) 766-0661
Contact: Mr. John Foehl
Minimum Salary Placed: $60,000
Recruiting Specialty: Financial services

Management Recruiters of Nassau, Inc.
77 N. Centre Avenue, Suite 211
Rockville Centre, NY 11570
(516) 536-3111
Contact: Mr. Thomas Wieder
Recruiting Specialty: Engineering, accounting, bankers, and investment people

Val Personnel
100 Merrick Road, Suite 302
Rockville Centre, NY 11570
(516) 764-9000
Contact: Mr. T. Talumbo
Minimum Salary Placed: $20,000
Recruiting Specialty: Banking and insur-
ance

ROME

Management Recruiters
1721 Black River Boulevard, Suite 205
Rome, NY 13440
(315) 339-6342
Contact: Mr. Carl Tardugno
Minimum Salary Placed: $20,000
Recruiting Specialty: Healthcare

ROSLYN

Park-Sloan Associates Inc.
83 The Intervale
Roslyn, NY 11576
(516) 625-8899
Contact: Mr. David Foss
Minimum Salary Placed: $20,000
Recruiting Specialty: Technology

Harold L. Rapp Associates
80 Hemlock Drive
Roslyn, NY 11576
(516) 625-4341

Contact: Mr. Harold Rapp
Minimum Salary Placed: $35,000
Recruiting Specialty: Jewelry

ROSYLN HEIGHTS

Search America Inc.
99 Powerhouse Road, Suite 204
Roslyn Heights, NY 11577
(516) 484-6006
Contact: Mr. J. Messer
Minimum Salary Placed: $30,000
Recruiting Specialty: Retail, stock broker-age, investment banking

RYE

Conspectus Inc.
222 Purchase Street
Rye, NY 10580
(914) 698-8300
Minimum Salary Placed: $50,000
Recruiting Specialty: Investment banking and finance

RYE BROOK

Dunhill Personnel Search
41 Mohegan Lane
Rye Brook, NY 10573
(914) 934-0801
Contact: Mr. Robert Morris
Minimum Salary Placed: $40,000
Recruiting Specialty: Sales and informa-tion systems in high technology

Professional Placement Associates, Inc.
14 Rye Ridge Plaza
Rye Brook, NY 10573
(914) 251-1000

Contact: Ms. Laura Schachter
Recruiting Specialty: Healthcare

SAINT JAMES

Romano McAvoy Associates, Inc.
872 Jericho Turnpike
St. James, NY 11780
(516) 265-7878
Contact: Mr. Joseph Romano
Minimum Salary Placed: $20,000
Recruiting Specialty: Finance and high technology

SARATOGA SPRINGS

NaTek Corporation
9 Maple Avenue, 2nd Floor
Saratoga Springs, NY 12866
(518) 583-0456
Contact: Mr. Mark Dillon
Minimum Salary Placed: $40,000
Recruiting Specialty: Technical disci-plines in high technology

SCARSDALE

Adept Tech Recruiting. Inc.
219 Glendale Road
Scarsdale, NY 10583
(212) 517-8110
Contact: Mr. Frederick Press
Minimum Salary Placed: $25,000
Recruiting Specialty: Information sys-tems in healthcare, analysts for securities

Aqua-Vize Inc.
4 Fountain Terrace
Scarsdale, NY 10583
(914) 271-1300

Minimum Salary Placed: $20,000
Recruiting Specialty: General

Frank Cuomo & Associates, Inc.
111 Brook Street
Scarsdale, NY 10583
(914) 723-8001
Contact: Mr. Frank Cuomo
Minimum Salary Placed: $30,000
Recruiting Specialty: Manufacturing and service

McDonald, Long & Associates, Inc.
670 White Plains Road
Scarsdale, NY 10583
(914) 723-5400
Contact: Mr. William Long
Minimum Salary Placed: $75,000
Recruiting Specialty: Finance and accounting

Mitchell Group
8 Archer Lane
Scarsdale, NY 10583
(914) 472-4500
Contact: Mr. Kenneth Mitchell
Minimum Salary Placed: $20,000
Recruiting Specialty: Actuaries in insurance

Promotion Recruiters, Inc.
11 Rectory Lane
Scarsdale, NY 10583
(914) 723-2657
Contact: Mr. Howard Burkat
Minimum Salary Placed: $30,000
Recruiting Specialty: Media communications

SCOTTSVILLE

R.R. Columbus Executive Search
P.O. Box 37
Scottsville, NY 14546
(716) 889-5364
Contact: Mr. Robert Columbus
Minimum Salary Placed: $50,000
Recruiting Specialty: General

SEA CLIFF

Franchise Search, Inc.
431 Carpenter Avenue
Sea Cliff, NY 11579
(516) 671-6447
Contact: Mr. Douglas Kushell
Minimum Salary Placed: $30,000
Recruiting Specialty: Franchising

SOMERS

Stanley Herz & Company
Mill Pond Office Complex, Suite 103
Somers, NY 10589
(914) 277-7500
Contact: Mr. Stanley Herz
Minimum Salary Placed: $90,000
Recruiting Specialty: Manufacturing

Techsearch Services Inc.
Suite 6 Hachliah Brown Drive
Somers, NY 10589
(212) 302-7010
Contact: Mr. David Taft
Minimum Salary Placed: $40,000
Recruiting Specialty: MIS, banking and finance

SOUTHHOLD

Joe Sullivan & Associates, Inc.
44210 County Road 48, P.O. Box 612
Southold, NY 11971
(516) 765-5050
Contact: Mr. Joseph Sullivan
Minimum Salary Placed: $70,000
Recruiting Specialty: Broadcast industry

SPRINGWATER

Kingsley Quinn/USA
7032 County Road 37
Springwater, NY 14560
(716) 669-2120
Contact: Mr. William Doyle
Minimum Salary Placed: $75,000
Recruiting Specialty: Pharmaceuticals,
consumer products and high technology

STATEN ISLAND

Gerri G. Inc.
604 Forest Avenue
Staten Island, NY 10310
(718) 981-9100
Contact: Ms. Geraldine Gibney
Recruiting Specialty: General

STONE RIDGE

Management Recruiters
P.O. Box 386
Stone Ridge, NY 12484
(914) 339-1300
Contact: Mr. Robert Mackenzie
Minimum Salary Placed: $30,000
Recruiting Specialty: Chemical, sales, and
marketing international

SUFFERN

Federal Placement Services
35 Park Avenue, Suite 6M
Suffern, NY 10901
(914) 357-4577
Contact: Ms. Joan Bialkin
Minimum Salary Placed: $20,000
Recruiting Specialty: Finance and banking

SYOSSET

Corporate Search Inc.
6800 Jericho Turnpike, Suite 203W
Syosset, NY 11791
(516) 496-3200
Minimum Salary Placed: $20,000
Recruiting Specialty: Accounting and finance

SYRACUSE

Accounting & Computer Personnel
200 Salina Meadows Parkway, Suite 180
Syracuse, NY 13212
(315) 457-8000
Contact: Mr. William Winnewisser
Minimum Salary Placed: $20,000
Recruiting Specialty: Accounting and
computers

Personnel Associates Inc.
731 James Street, Suite 209
Syracuse, NY 13203
(315) 422-0070
Contact: Mr. Peter Baskin
Minimum Salary Placed: $25,000
Recruiting Specialty: Insurance

St. Lawrence International, Inc.
112 DeWitt
Syracuse, NY 13203
(315) 432-4588

Contact: Ms. Kathi Rodgers
Minimum Salary Placed: $30,000
Recruiting Specialty: General

Willard Associates
327 W. Fayette Street
Syracuse, NY 13202
(315) 479-8367
Contact: Ms. Priscilla Pryor
Minimum Salary Placed: $20,000
Recruiting Specialty: Office support

TAPPAN

Liz Peters Associates
6 Pinetree Lane
Tappan, NY 10983
(914) 376-6100
Contact: Ms. Liz Peters
Minimum Salary Placed: $25,000
Recruiting Specialty: Real estate

TARRYTOWN

SRI LTD
660 White Plains Road
Tarrytown, NY 10591
(212) 319-6255
Recruiting Specialty: Consumer products, telecommunications, industrial and commericial flooring

Elliot Associates, Inc.
104 S. Broadway
Tarrytown, NY 10591
(914) 631-4904
Contact: Ms. Alice Elliot
Minimum Salary Placed: $15,000
Recruiting Specialty: Hospitality

Management Recruiters of Westchester, Inc.
220 White Plains Road
Tarrytown, NY 10591
(914) 524-9400
Contact: Mr. R.P. Neuffer
Minimum Salary Placed: $50,000
Recruiting Specialty: Consumer products

Preston Robert & Associates–Health Care Division
220 White Plains Road
Tarrytown, NY 10591
(914) 524-9410
Contact: Mr. Robert Neuffer
Minimum Salary Placed: $75,000
Recruiting Specialty: Consumer products

Sales Recruiters International Ltd.
660 White Plains Road
Tarrytown, NY 10591
(914) 631-0090
Contact: Mr. R. Harris
Minimum Salary Placed: $20,000
Recruiting Specialty: Sales

TONAWANDA

Pedersen, Kolb & Associates, Inc.
2504 Niagara Falls Boulevard
Tonawanda, NY 14150
(716) 695-8500
Contact: Richard J. Pedersen
Recruiting Specialty: Engineering, technical, manufacturing, and human resources

TROY

Executech
120 DeFreest Drive
Troy, NY 12180
(518) 283-8300
Contact: Ms. Amy Johnson
Minimum Salary Placed: $50,000
Recruiting Specialty: Technical disciplines in manufacturing; paper and chemicals, college and university directors

UNIONDALE

Accountants Choice Personnel
50 Charles Lindbergh, Suite 400
Uniondale, NY 11553
(516) 229-2371
Contact: Mr. Peter Kasnicki
Minimum Salary Placed: $20,000
Recruiting Specialty: Accounting

VALHALLA

Hintz Associates
Box 442
Valhalla, NY 10595
(914) 761-4227
Contact: Mr. George Hintz
Minimum Salary Placed: $25,000
Recruiting Specialty: Industrial, engineering, methods improvement consultants, and some general

WEST AMHERST

Professional Support Inc.
501 John James Audubon Parkway,
  Suite 400
West Amherst, NY 14228
(716) 688-0235
Contact: Mr. Paul Eastmer
Minimum Salary Placed: $30,000
Recruiting Specialty: Accounting and computer programming

WEST SYOSSET

Ads Search Consultants Inc.
6800 Jericho Turnpike, Suite 203
West Syosset, NY 11791
(516) 364-0010
Contact: Ms. Judy Brothers
Minimum Salary Placed: $30,000
Recruiting Specialty: Technical, programming and accounting

WESTBURY

Sharp Placement Professionals
55 Post Avenue, Suite 202
Westbury, NY 11590
(516) 876-9222
Contact: Mr. Miles Weiss
Minimum Salary Placed: $25,000
Recruiting Specialty: RF, communications, sales and marketing of electronics

WHITE PLAINS

APA Search, Inc.
1 Water Street
White Plains, NY 10601
(914) 949-5500
Contact: Mr. Howard Kesten
Recruiting Specialty: Automotive

Accountants On Call/Accountants Executive Search
50 Main Street, 10th Floor
White Plains, NY 10606
(914) 968-1100
Contact: Mr. Marvin Sternlicht
Recruiting Specialty: Accounting and bookkeeping

Concorde Search Association
1 N. Broadway, Suite 410
White Plains, NY 10601
(914) 428-0700
Contact: Mr. Richard Greenwald
Minimum Salary Placed: $25,000
Recruiting Specialty: Banking and finance

Carolyn Davis Associates, Inc.
701 Westchester Avenue, Suite 317W
White Plains, NY 10604
(914) 682-7040
Contact: Ms. Carolyn Davis
Recruiting Specialty: Insurance

Robert Half International
701 Westchester, Suite 1A1
White Plains, NY 10604
(914) 682-8842
Contact: Mr. R. Preis
Minimum Salary Placed: $20,000
Recruiting Specialty: Accounting and finance

Koren, Rogers Associates
701 Westchester Avenue, Suite 317W
White Plains, NY 10604
(914) 686-5800
Contact: Mr. Michael Koren
Minimum Salary Placed: $60,000
Recruiting Specialty: Finance and accounting

Leitner Search Consultants Ltd.
170 Woodbrook Road
White Plains, NY 10605
(914) 682-4000
Contact: Mr. Danny Sarch
Minimum Salary Placed: $20,000
Recruiting Specialty: General

George J. Mollo Associates
50 Main Street, Suite 1000
White Plains, NY 10606
(914) 328-0076
Contact: Mr. George Mollo
Minimum Salary Placed: $30,000
Recruiting Specialty: Accounting and finance

Arthur Pann Associates
188 E. Post Road, Suite 401
White Plains, NY 10601
(914) 686-0700
Contact: Mr. Arthur Pann
Minimum Salary Placed: $40,000
Recruiting Specialty: General

Paxton Resources Inc.
50 Main Street, Suite 1000
White Plains, NY 10606
(914) 946-1300
Contact: Ms. B. Paxton
Minimum Salary Placed: $25,000
Recruiting Specialty: Human resources and public relations

R.J. Associates
188 E. Post Road
White Plains, NY 10601
(914) 946-0278
Contact: Mr. Richard Birnbaum
Minimum Salary Placed: $60,000
Recruiting Specialty: General

Redstone Affiliates
50 Main Street
White Plains, NY 10604
(914) 945-0735
Minimum Salary Placed: $50,000
Recruiting Specialty: General

Wilbur M. Sachtjen Associates, Inc.
50 Main Street, Suite 1047
White Plains, NY 10606
(914) 682-2047
Contact: Mr. Wilbur Sachtjen
Minimum Salary Placed: $100,000
Recruiting Specialty: General

Source Finance / Source EDP
925 Westchester Avenue, Suite 309
White Plains, NY 10604
(914) 428-9100
Contact: Mr. Vince Rios
Recruiting Specialty: Finance

Westfield Staffing Services
1 North Broadway
White Plains, NY 10601
(914) 761-4333
Contact: Ms. Joanne Fiala
Minimum Salary Placed: $30,000
Recruiting Specialty: General

WILLIAMSVILLE

Corporate Movers, Inc.
P.O. Box 1638
Williamsville, NY 14231
(716) 633-0234
Recruiting Specialty: Sales and marketing

DeBellis and Catherine Associates
5830 Main Street, Suite 201
Williamsville, NY 14221
(716) 632-1500
Contact: Mr. J. Catherine
Minimum Salary Placed: $20,000
Recruiting Specialty: General

Sales Consultants
8560 Main Street
Williamsville, NY 14221
(716) 631-3100
Contact: Mr. Robert Artis
Minimum Salary Placed: $20,000
Recruiting Specialty: Sales

WILSON

TSL Associates
2771 Daniels Road
Wilson, NY 14172
(716) 751-6344
Contact: Mr. Todd Lyon
Recruiting Specialty: High tech HW,
semi, video, wireless, audio, and multimedia

WOODBURY

Management Recruiters of Woodbury Inc.
100 Crossways Park W.
Woodbury, NY 11797
(516) 364-9290
Contact: Mr. William Jose
Minimum Salary Placed: $35,000
Recruiting Specialty: Pharmaceuticals,
medical device, data processing, banking
and finance

Personnel Consulting Associates
7600 Jericho Turnpike, Suite LL1
Woodbury, NY 11797
(516) 364-1460 or (212) 269-8508
Contact: Mr. J. Slater
Minimum Salary Placed: $40,000
Recruiting Specialty: Banking and investment banking

Resource Services, Inc.
20 Crossways Park N.
Woodbury, NY 11797
(516) 496-4100
Contact: Mr. Joseph Trainor
Minimum Salary Placed: $35,000
Recruiting Specialty: Software in areas of accounting, finance and communications

WOODMERE

Fred Koffler Associates
942 Greenfield Road
Woodmere, NY 11598
(516) 569-6582
Recruiting Specialty: General

WOODSTOCK

London August, Inc.
146 Spencer Road
Woodstock, NY 12498
(914) 657-8300
Contact: Mr. Joe August
Recruiting Specialty: General; women and minorities

Sloane, Sloane & Mayne
41 Glasco Turnpike
Woodstock, NY 12498
(914) 679-8788
Contact: Mr. William Sloane
Minimum Salary Placed: $60,000
Recruiting Specialty: General

YONKERS

Anderson Associates
225 Murray Avenue, Suite 44
Yonkers, NY 10704
(914) 376-8724
Minimum Salary Placed: $30,000
Recruiting Specialty: Sales and technical in telecommunications, entertainment and media

YORKTOWN HEIGHTS

Marcus & Associates
345 Kear Street
Yorktown Heights, NY 10598
(914) 962-7600
Contact: Mr. Alvin Marcus
Minimum Salary Placed: $40,000
Recruiting Specialty: Technical disciplines in consumer products

NORTH CAROLINA

ASHEBORO

Marketing Recruiters, Inc.
P.O. Box 4098
Asheboro, NC 27204
(910) 626-4009
Contact: Mr. Rass Bagley
Minimum Salary Placed: $35,000
Recruiting Specialty: Sales in pharmaceuticals

ASHEVILLE

Branch Associates, Inc.
Box 18105
Asheville, NC 28814
(704) 586-8137
Contact: Ms. Minnie Branch
Minimum Salary Placed: $45,000
Recruiting Specialty: Sales and technical
in telecommunications

Kimmel & Associates
25 Page Avenue
Asheville, NC 28801
(704) 251-9900
Contact: Mr. Joe Kimmel
Minimum Salary Placed: $50,000
Recruiting Specialty: Real property and
development

Management Recruiters
22 S. Pack Square, Suite 302
Asheville, NC 28801
(704) 258-9646
Contact: Mr. Paul Rumson
Minimum Salary Placed: $20,000
Recruiting Specialty: Manufacturing and
hospitality

Moffit International
1316 A Patton Avenue
Asheville, NC 28806
(704) 251-4550
Contact: Mr. T. Moffit
Minimum Salary Placed: $25,000
Recruiting Specialty: General

Weatherby Health Care
225 Governors View Road
Asheville, NC 28805
(704) 299-0260

Contact: Mr. M. Stewart
Minimum Salary Placed: $25,000
Recruiting Specialty: Healthcare

Wilson Personnel, Inc.
134 Montford Avenue
Asheville, NC 28801
(704) 258-3900
Contact: Mr. Charles Wilson
Minimum Salary Placed: $30,000
Recruiting Specialty: Engineering

BETHLEHEM

Management Recruiters
PO Box 6077
Bethlehem, NC 28603
(704) 495-8233
Contact: Mr. J.D. Liles
Minimum Salary Placed: $20,000
Recruiting Specialty: General

BURLINGTON

Management Recruiters
336 Holy Hill Lane
Burlington, NC 27215
(910) 584-1444
Contact: Mr. Dick Pike
Minimum Salary Placed: $20,000
Recruiting Specialty: General

CARY

ARJay & Associates
875 Walnut Street, Suite 150
Cary, NC 27511
(919) 469-5540

Contact: Mr. Ronald Jones
Minimum Salary Placed: $30,000
Recruiting Specialty: Electrical, automotive, construction and environmental science

Carter/MacKay
1135 Kildaire Farm Road, Suite 200
Cary, NC 27511
(910) 380-1200
Contact: Mr. Al Hertz
Recruiting Specialty: Sales in pharmaceuticals

Dunhill Professional Search
975 Walnut Street, Suite 260
Cary, NC 27511
(919) 460-9988
Contact: Mr. Jay Babson
Minimum Salary Placed: $25,000
Recruiting Specialty: General

Rothrock Associates, Inc.
P.O. Box 698
Cary, NC 27512
(919) 460-0070
Contact: Mr. T. Hardy Rothrock
Minimum Salary Placed: $30,000
Recruiting Specialty: Manufacturing and high technology

Sales Consultants
113 Edinburgh South, Suite 203
Cary, NC 27511
(919) 460-9595
Contact: Mr. David Bunce
Minimum Salary Placed: $20,000
Recruiting Specialty: Sales

Trevor Randolph Associates Inc.
1135 Kildaire Farm Road
Cary, NC 27511
(919) 460-1444
Contact: Mr. Gary Hayden
Minimum Salary Placed: $25,000
Recruiting Specialty: General

CEDAR MOUNTAIN

Management Recruiters
P.O. Box 399
Cedar Mountain, NC 28718
(704) 884-4118
Contact: Mr. Frank Schoff
Minimum Salary Placed: $20,000
Recruiting Specialty: General

CHAPEL HILL

Atlantic West International
1201 Raleigh Road, Suite F-101
Chapel Hill, NC 27514
(919) 942-3080
Contact: Mr. Richard Valenti
Minimum Salary Placed: $50,000
Recruiting Specialty: Pharmaceuticals

CHARLOTTE

Accountants On Call
227 W. Trade Street, Suite 1908
Charlotte, NC 28202
(704) 376-0006
Contact: Ms. Beth Herman
Recruiting Specialty: Accounting

Bennett Allen and Associates
7422 Carmel Executive Park Drive
Charlotte, NC 28226
(704) 541-5891
Contact: Mr. Bennet Allen
Minimum Salary Placed: $40,000
Recruiting Specialty: Engineering

Anderson & Associates
112 S. Tryon Street, Suite 540
Charlotte, NC 28284
(704) 347-0090
Contact: Mr. Douglas Anderson
Minimum Salary Placed: $50,000
Recruiting Specialty: General

Andrews and Associates
6100 Fairview Road
Charlotte, NC 28210
(704) 556-0088
Contact: Mr. D. Andrews
Minimum Salary Placed: $25,000
Recruiting Specialty: Accounting

Jim Beatty and Associates
6525 Morrison Boulevard
Charlotte, NC 28211
(704) 366-6525
Contact: Mr. Jim Beatty
Minimum Salary Placed: $25,000
Recruiting Specialty: General; foreign
and domestic

Carnegie Resources Inc.
1100 S. Mint Street
Charlotte, NC 28203
(704) 375-7701
Recruiting Specialty: Engineering and
manufacturing

Coleman Lew & Associates, Inc.
326 W. Tenth Street
Charlotte, NC 28202
(704) 377-0362
Contact: Mr. Charles Lew
Recruiting Specialty: General

S L Collins Associates
P.O. Box 472181
Charlotte, NC 28247
(704) 365-9889
Contact: Mr. Steve Collins
Minimum Salary Placed: $40,000
Recruiting Specialty: Pharmaceuticals

Continental Management Consultant
1515 Mockingbird Lane
Charlotte, NC 28209
(704) 527-9701
Contact: Ms. M. Hogue
Minimum Salary Placed: $25,000
Recruiting Specialty: General

Direct Marketing Resources
4401 Colwick Road
Charlotte, NC 28211
(704) 365-5890
Contact: Mr. Dan Sullivan
Minimum Salary Placed: $25,000
Recruiting Specialty: Marketing

Don Richard Associates
2650 Two First Union Building
Charlotte, NC 28282
(704) 377-6447
Contact: Mr. E. Turner
Minimum Salary Placed: $20,000
Recruiting Specialty: Banking, account-
ing and office support

Executive Recruitment Specialists
6407 Idlewild Road
Charlotte, NC 28212
(704) 536-8830
Contact: Mr. Jim Rosenburger
Minimum Salary Placed: $50,000
Recruiting Specialty: General

Fox-Morris Associates, Inc.
9140 Arrowpoint Boulevard, Suite 380
Charlotte, NC 28273
(704) 522-8244
Minimum Salary Placed: $45,000
Recruiting Specialty: General

Glovier and Associates
4732 Lebanon Road
Charlotte, NC 28227
(704) 545-0877
Contact: Mr. Jim Glovier
Minimum Salary Placed: $25,000
Recruiting Specialty: Furniture

Guaranteed Personnel Service
4801 E. Independence Boulevard
Charlotte, NC 28212
(704) 568-7750
Contact: Ms. W. Cottier
Minimum Salary Placed: $25,000
Recruiting Specialty: General

The Halyburton Company, Inc.
6201 Fairview Road, Suite 200
Charlotte, NC 28210
(704) 556-9892
Contact: Mr. Robert Halyburton
Minimum Salary Placed: $50,000
Recruiting Specialty: General

Heller Associates
2915 Providence Road, Suite 410
Charlotte, NC 28211
(704) 365-0293
Contact: Ms. Carol Heller
Minimum Salary Placed: $50,000
Recruiting Specialty: Healthcare

Hunkler Medical Associates
6701 Carmel Road
Charlotte, NC 28226
(704) 542-6691
Contact: Mr. P. Hunkler
Minimum Salary Placed: $25,000
Recruiting Specialty: Medical and health-care

Kapp and Associates
223 E. Boulevard
Charlotte, NC 28281
(704) 338-9985
Contact: Mr. D. Kapp
Minimum Salary Placed: $40,000
Recruiting Specialty: General

D.E. Kilgo and Company
8318 Pineville Matthews Road
Charlotte, NC 28226
(704) 544-0342
Contact: Mr. Don Kilgore
Minimum Salary Placed: $35,000
Recruiting Specialty: Sales and general
management in computers

The Linden Group
6407 Idlewild Road, Suite 3107
Charlotte, NC 28212
(704) 567-0073
Contact: Mr. Bruce Lindal
Minimum Salary Placed: $30,000
Recruiting Specialty: Technical disci-
plines in consumer products

Locke & Associates
101 S. Tryon Street
Charlotte, NC 28280
(704) 372-6600
Contact: Mr. M. Fred Locke
Minimum Salary Placed: $50,000
Recruiting Specialty: General

R.E. Lowe Associates
7621 Little Avenue, Suite 212
Charlotte, NC 28226
(704) 543-1111
Contact: Mr. Patrick Perkins
Minimum Salary Placed: $30,000
Recruiting Specialty: General

MSI International
Suite 408, 4801 Independence Boulevard
Charlotte, NC 28212
(704) 535-6610
Contact: Mr. Emery Hill
Minimum Salary Placed: $25,000
Recruiting Specialty: Healthcare

Management Advisors International, Inc.
4600 Park Road, Suite 400
Charlotte, NC 28209
(704) 521-9595
Contact: Ms. Gina Polyzos
Recruiting Specialty: Finance and real estate

Mark III Personnel, Inc.
4801 E. Independence Boulevard,
  Suite 604
Charlotte, NC 28212
(704) 535-5883
Contact: Mr. Lindsay Allen
Minimum Salary Placed: $40,000
Recruiting Specialty: General

McGladrey & Pullen
6805 Morrison Boulevard, Suite 200
Charlotte, NC 28211
(704) 367-6250
Contact: Mr. Bob Wilson
Minimum Salary Placed: $30,000
Recruiting Specialty: General

Nuance Personnel Search, Inc.
P.O. Box 13113
Charlotte, NC 28270
(704) 364-8413
Contact: Ms. Lynn Green
Minimum Salary Placed: $30,000
Recruiting Specialty: Insurance

Patton/Perry Associates, Inc.
112 S. Tryon Street, Suite 500
Charlotte, NC 28202
(704) 376-4292
Contact: Mr. Mitchell Patton
Minimum Salary Placed: $60,000
Recruiting Specialty: General

Robert Half International
201 S. College Street, Suite 1710
Charlotte, NC 28244
(704) 339-0550
Contact: Ms. M. McGuire
Minimum Salary Placed: $25,000
Recruiting Specialty: Accounting and finance

Jay D. Robinson and Associates Inc.
4801 E. Independence Boulevard
Charlotte, NC 28212
(704) 567-8886
Recruiting Specialty: Poultry

Robison & Associates
1350 First Citizens Plaza
128 S. Tryon Street
Charlotte, NC 28202
(704) 376-0059
Contact: Ms. Sue Hunter
Minimum Salary Placed: $50,000
Recruiting Specialty: General

Sales Consultants
5815 Westpark Drive, Suite 106
Charlotte, NC 28217
(704) 525-9270
Contact: Mr. Bob Brown
Minimum Salary Placed: $20,000
Recruiting Specialty: Sales

Sanford Rose Associates
233 S. Sharon Amity Road
Charlotte, NC 28211
(704) 366-0730
Contact: Mr. James Downs
Minimum Salary Placed: $35,000
Recruiting Specialty: MIS, finance, sales
and insurance

Schwab-Carrese Associates
128 S. Tyron Street
Charlotte, NC 28202
(704) 331-0006
Contact: Mr. J. Schwab
Minimum Salary Placed: $50,000
Recruiting Specialty: General

Search Consultants Worldwide
6401 Carmel Road, Suite 206
Charlotte, NC 28226
(704) 544-0344
Minimum Salary Placed: $50,000
Recruiting Specialty: General

Select Executive Search, Inc.
7508 E. Independence Boulevard,
  Suite 160
Charlotte, NC 28227
(704) 532-2599
Contact: Mr. Gregg Whitt
Minimum Salary Placed: $30,000
Recruiting Specialty: General

Ron Snead Associates
6701 Carmel Road
Charlotte, NC 28226
(704) 541-8844
Contact: Mr. Ron Snead
Minimum Salary Placed: $25,000
Recruiting Specialty: General

Sockwell & Associates
227 W. Trade Street, Suite 1930
Charlotte, NC 28202
(704) 372-1865
Contact: Mr. J. Edgar Sockwell
Minimum Salary Placed: $60,000
Recruiting Specialty: General

Source EDP
100 N. Tryon Street, Suite 3130
Charlotte, NC 28202
(704) 333-8311
Recruiting Specialty: Finance, healthcare,
engineering and manufacturing

Waddy R. Thompson and Associates
233 S. Sharon Amity Road, Suite 106
Charlotte, NC 28211
(704) 366-1956
Minimum Salary Placed: $25,000
Recruiting Specialty: Environmental
safety and industrial hygiene

Winston Personnel Agency Inc.
Box 32695
Charlotte, NC 28284
(704) 376-4456
Contact: Mr. Jerry Morris
Minimum Salary Placed: $20,000
Recruiting Specialty: General

CONCORD

Sales Consultants
254 Church Street, NE
Concord, NC 28025
(704) 786-0700
Contact: Ms. Anna Lee Pearson
Minimum Salary Placed: $20,000
Recruiting Specialty: Sales

CORNELIUS

Parenica and Company
19250 Stableford Lane
Cornelius, NC 28031
(704) 869-0060
Contact: Mr. Jim Parenica
Minimum Salary Placed: $35,000
Recruiting Specialty: Information technology

DAVIDSON

AmeriPro Search, Inc.
20468 Chartwell Centre Drive, Suite A
Davidson, NC 28036
(704) 896-8991
Contact: Ms. Elaine Brauninger
Minimum Salary Placed: $40,000
Recruiting Specialty: General

DURHAM

Accountemps
3101 Petty Road, Suite 500
Durham, NC 27707
(919) 682-3944
Contact: Mr. M. Gregory
Recruiting Specialty: Accounting

Careers Unlimited Inc.
1911 Hillandale Road, Suite 120
Durham, NC 27705
(919) 383-7431
Contact: Ms. Phyliss Carswell
Recruiting Specialty: General

Bruce Edwards & Associates, Inc.
2200 W. Main Street, Suite 910
Durham, NC 27705
(919) 286-5885
Contact: Mr. S. Bruce Edwards
Minimum Salary Placed: $75,000
Recruiting Specialty: General

Management Recruiters
5102 Chapel Hill-Durham Boulevard,
 Suite 112
Durham, NC 27707
(919) 489-6521
Contact: Mr. Neil McNulty
Recruiting Specialty: General

ENFIELD

Management Recruiters
111 NW Railroad Street
Enfield, NC 27823
(919) 445-4251
Contact: Ms. Maria Snook
Minimum Salary Placed: $20,000
Recruiting Specialty: General

FAYETTEVILLE

Management Recruiters
951 S. McPherson Church Road,
  Suite 105
Fayetteville, NC 28303
(910) 483-2555
Contact: Mr. John Semmes
Minimum Salary Placed: $20,000
Recruiting Specialty: General

Professional Careers, Inc.
P.O. Box 53629
Fayetteville, NC 28305
(910) 323-3987
Contact: Ms. Vicki Hayes
Minimum Salary Placed: $25,000
Recruiting Specialty: MIS and engineering

GASTONIA

Management Recruiters
438 E. Garrison Boulevard
Gastonia, NC 28054
(704) 868-8080
Contact: Mr. Chuck Deal
Recruiting Specialty: Manufacturing,
waste and environmental

SRA-Gastonia
3816 S. New Hope Road, Suite 21
Gastonia, NC 28056
(704) 824-0895
Contact: Mr. F. Halek
Minimum Salary Placed: $25,000
Recruiting Specialty: Construction, engineering in metals and plastics

Sales Consultants
438 E. Garrison Boulevard, Suite B
Gastonia, NC 28054
(704) 868-8080
Contact: Mr. Chuck Deal
Minimum Salary Placed: $20,000
Recruiting Specialty: Sales

GREENSBORO

Accountants On Call
1801 Stanley Road
Greensboro, NC 27407
(910) 292-3800
Recruiting Specialty: Accounting

Adkins and Associates
119 E. Lewis Street
Greensboro, NC 27406
(910) 378-1261
Contact: Mr. K. Adkins
Minimum Salary Placed: $25,000
Recruiting Specialty: Apparel and textiles

Advanced Personnel Resources
20 Oak Branch Drive, Suite D
Greensboro, NC 27407
(910) 855-6664
Contact: Ms. Dana Foster
Minimum Salary Placed: $25,000
Recruiting Specialty: General

Ariail & Associates
210 W. Friendly Avenue, Suite 200
Greensboro, NC 27401
(910) 275-2906
Contact: Mr. Randolph Ariail
Minimum Salary Placed: $80,000
Recruiting Specialty: Wood furnishings

Atchison and Associates
612 Pasteur Drive, Suite 106
Greensboro, NC 27403
(910) 855-5943
Contact: Mr. Bill Atchison
Minimum Salary Placed: $40,000
Recruiting Specialty: Manufacturing

Bryant Bureau
108 State Street, Suite 101
Greensboro, NC 27408
(910) 272-1433
Recruiting Specialty: Manufacturing management in engineering

Data Masters
338 N. Elm Street, Suite H
Greensboro, NC 27401
(910) 373-1461
Contact: Ms. Paula White
Minimum Salary Placed: $25,000
Recruiting Specialty: Information systems and data processing

Financial Recruiters of NC
P.O. Box 7902
Greensboro, NC 27417
(910) 218-0333
Contact: Ms. S. McKay
Minimum Salary Placed: $25,000
Recruiting Specialty: Finance and accounting

Fortune Personnel Consultants
304 Ponoma Drive, Suite B
Greensboro, NC 27407
(910) 852-4455
Contact: Mr. B. Martin
Minimum Salary Placed: $25,000
Recruiting Specialty: Manufacturing

Highlander Search
210 W. Friendly Avenue, Suite 200
Greensboro, NC 27401
(910) 333-9886
Recruiting Specialty: In-home furnishings

Management Recruiters
324 W. Wendover, Suite 230
Greensboro, NC 27408
(910) 378-1818
Contact: Mr. Mitch Oakley
Minimum Salary Placed: $20,000
Recruiting Specialty: General

Tom Plihcik
3200 Northlin Avenue, Suite 524
Greensboro, NC 27408
(910) 852-9159
Contact: Mr. Tom Plihcik
Minimum Salary Placed: $25,000
Recruiting Specialty: Accounting, some general

Robert Half International
300 N. Greene Street, Suite 275
Greensboro, NC 27401
(910) 274-4253
Contact: Ms. M. McGuire
Minimum Salary Placed: $25,000
Recruiting Specialty: Accounting and finance

Sain-Wade Corporation
400 W. Market Street
Greensboro, NC 27401
(910) 274-3336
Contact: Ms. Mary Wade
Minimum Salary Placed: $25,000
Recruiting Specialty: General

Sales Consultants
P.O. Box 35254
Greensboro, NC 27425
(910) 665-9698

Contact: Mr. Wally Adams
Minimum Salary Placed: $20,000
Recruiting Specialty: Sales

Sickenberger Associates
612 Pasteur Drive, Suite 300
Greensboro, NC 27403
(910) 852-4220
Contact: Mr. R. Sickenberger
Minimum Salary Placed: $25,000
Recruiting Specialty: Textiles and manu-
facturing

John R. Williams & Associates, Inc.
2102 N. Elm Street, Suite H-6
Greensboro, NC 27408
(910) 279-8800
Contact: Mr. John Williams
Minimum Salary Placed: $40,000
Recruiting Specialty: Manufacturing, tex-
tiles, chemicals

HENDERSONVILLE

S.N. Jones and Associates
424 Woodbyne Avenue
Hendersonville, NC 28739
(704) 692-3546
Contact: Ms. Sandra Jones
Minimum Salary Placed: $25,000
Recruiting Specialty: General

HICKORY

**Management Advisors International,
Inc.**
P.O. Box 3708
Hickory, NC 28603
(704) 324-5772
Contact: Mr. William Castell
Recruiting Specialty: Mortgage banking

Management Recruiters
835 SE Highland Avenue
Hickory, NC 28602
(704) 324-2020
Contact: Mr. Scott Volz
Minimum Salary Placed: $20,000
Recruiting Specialty: General

HIGH POINT

Management Recruiters
110 Scott
High Point, NC 27262
(910) 869-1200
Contact: Mr. Steve Smith
Minimum Salary Placed: $20,000
Recruiting Specialty: General

Metals and Wood Agency
P.O. Box 5354
High Point, NC 27262
(910) 869-3867
Contact: Mr. G. Lloyd
Minimum Salary Placed: $25,000
Recruiting Specialty: Metal and wood
fabrication and manufacturing

Sales Consultants
2411 Penny Road, Suite 101
High Point, NC 27265
(910) 883-4433
Contact: Mr. Tom Bunton
Minimum Salary Placed: $20,000
Recruiting Specialty: Sales

HUNTERSVILLE

Myers and Associates
13420 Reese Boulevard W
Huntersville, NC 28078
(704) 875-8300

Contact: Mr. Joe Myers
Minimum Salary Placed: $25,000
Recruiting Specialty: General

Systems Search Group
9801 Kincey Avenue, Suite 135
Huntersville, NC 28078
(704) 948-9480
Contact: Ms. Eileen Brady
Recruiting Specialty: MIS and computer

KANNAPOLIS

Management Recruiters
907 Centergrove Road
Kannapolis, NC 28081
(704) 938-6144
Contact: Mr. Tom Whitley
Minimum Salary Placed: $20,000
Recruiting Specialty: Data processing

KERNERSVILLE

Dunhill Professional Search
108 S. Main Street
Kernersville, NC 27284
(910) 996-2286
Contact: Mr. Bob Martineau
Minimum Salary Placed: $25,000
Recruiting Specialty: General

KINSTON

Management Recruiters
1 Village Square, Highway 258 North
P.O. Box 219
Kinston, NC 28502
(910) 527-9191

Contact: Mr. Bill Thomas
Minimum Salary Placed: $30,000
Recruiting Specialty: Paper, chemicals
and manufacturing

LOUISBURG

Management Recruiters
P.O. Box 8
Louisburg, NC 27549
(919) 496-2153
Contact: Mr. Darrell Perry
Minimum Salary Placed: $20,000
Recruiting Specialty: Engineering and
manufacturing

LUMBERTON

Compton Group Inc.
26 Trinity Drive
Lumberton, NC 28358
(910) 739-7077
Contact: Mr. Compton
Minimum Salary Placed: $25,000
Recruiting Specialty: General

MATTHEWS

Management Recruiters
624 Matthews-Mint Hill Road, Suite 224
Matthews, NC 28105
(704) 841-8850
Contact: Mr. David Camp
Minimum Salary Placed: $20,000
Recruiting Specialty: Sales and engineer-
ing in high technology

MONROE

Management Recruiters
2605 West Roosevelt Boulevard
Monroe, NC 28110
(704) 283-1500
Contact: Mr. Drew Chaplin
Minimum Salary Placed: $20,000
Recruiting Specialty: General

MOORESVILLE

Hallmark Recruiters
194 Wood Duck Loop
Mooresville, NC 28115
(704) 664-9800
Contact: Ms. Linda Beckham
Recruiting Specialty: Manufacturing

Management Recruiters
322 East Center Avenue
Mooresville, NC 28115
(704) 664-4997
Contact: Mr. Hugh Sykes
Minimum Salary Placed: $20,000
Recruiting Specialty: General

Sales Consultants
322 E. Center Avenue
Mooresville, NC 28115
(704) 664-4997
Contact: Mr. Hugh Sykes
Minimum Salary Placed: $20,000
Recruiting Specialty: Sales

NEW BERN

Management Recruiters
1319 S. Glenburnie Road
New Bern, NC 28562
(919) 633-1900

Contact: Mr. Fred Eatman
Minimum Salary Placed: $20,000
Recruiting Specialty: General

PINEHURST

C.D. Fayling Associates Inc.
5 Market Square
Pinehurst, NC 28374
(910) 295-4901
Contact: Mr. Chuck Fayling
Minimum Salary Placed: $25,000
Recruiting Specialty: General

PLEASANT GARDEN

Stewart Greene and Company
504 Stonebridge Road
Pleasant Garden, NC 27313
(910) 674-5345
Recruiting Specialty: Home furnishings
and wood products

RALEIGH

The Christopher Group
400 Oberlin Road
Raleigh, NC 27605
(919) 863-5650
Contact: Mr. J. Christopher Sprehe
Minimum Salary Placed: $40,000
Recruiting Specialty: Real estate

Cline Jobe and Associates
812 Salem Woods Drive, Suite 201
Raleigh, NC 27609
(919) 870-9333
Contact: Mr. Gerry Cline
Minimum Salary Placed: $25,000
Recruiting Specialty: General

ESA, North Carolina Office
6200 Falls of Neuse Road, Suite 200
Raleigh, NC 27609
(919) 878-0670
Contact: Mr. A. Daniel Pigott
Minimum Salary Placed: $40,000
Recruiting Specialty: Technical disciplines in high technology

Fortune Personnel Consultants
800 Salem Woods Drive, Suite 201
Raleigh, NC 27615
(919) 848-9929
Contact: Ms. S. Deckelbaum
Minimum Salary Placed: $25,000
Recruiting Specialty: General

Paul Goldram Search Research
1017 Hunting Ridge Road, Suite E
Raleigh, NC 27615
(919) 846-2721
Contact: Mr. Paul Goldram
Minimum Salary Placed: $60,000
Recruiting Specialty: Pharmaceuticals, healthcare and biotechnology

Information Systems Professionals
5904 Castlebrook Drive
Raleigh, NC 27604
(919) 954-9100
Contact: Mr. Brad Moses
Recruiting Specialty: MIS

Kirby and Harwood Inc.
4601 Six Forks Road
Raleigh, NC 27609
(919) 571-7727
Contact: Mr. D. Kirby
Minimum Salary Placed: $25,000
Recruiting Specialty: Financial

Long Group
5604 Departure Drive
Raleigh, NC 27604
(919) 872-2167
Contact: Ms. P. Long
Minimum Salary Placed: $25,000
Recruiting Specialty: General

Management Recruiters
5509 Creedmoor Road, Suite 206
Raleigh, NC 27612
(919) 781-0400
Contact: Mr. Wade Stanley
Minimum Salary Placed: $20,000
Recruiting Specialty: General

National Recruiters
1025 Dresser Court
Raleigh, NC 27609
(919) 872-2400
Contact: Mr. Richard Adams
Minimum Salary Placed: $25,000
Recruiting Specialty: General

National Search, Inc.
P.O. Box 36099
Raleigh, NC 27606
(919) 460-9000
Contact: Mr. Marshall Molliver
Minimum Salary Placed: $70,000
Recruiting Specialty: General

Pronet, Inc.
3200 Glen Royal Road, Suite 100
Raleigh, NC 27612
(919) 782-2760
Contact: Mr. Dick Starling
Minimum Salary Placed: $25,000
Recruiting Specialty: MIS

Robert Half International Inc.
3700 National Drive
Raleigh, NC 27612
(919) 787-8226
Contact: Ms. Terri Arom
Minimum Salary Placed: $20,000
Recruiting Specialty: Accounting and finance

Rodzik and Associates
8601 Six Forks Road, Suite 703
Raleigh, NC 27615
(919) 847-3450
Contact: Mr. Gerald Rodzik
Minimum Salary Placed: $50,000
Recruiting Specialty: General

Romac & Associates, Inc.
3200 Beechleaf Court, Suite 409
Raleigh, NC 27625
(919) 878-4454
Contact: Mr. Randy Bye
Minimum Salary Placed: $20,000
Recruiting Specialty: General

Snelling Search
5838 Faringdon Place, Suite 1
Raleigh, NC 27609
(919) 876-0660
Contact: Mr. R. Helfenbein
Minimum Salary Placed: $50,000
Recruiting Specialty: General

Sports Group International
804 Salem Woods Drive, Suite 203
Raleigh, NC 27615
(919) 846-1860
Contact: Mr. Joseph White
Minimum Salary Placed: $40,000
Recruiting Specialty: Sales and promotional in sports and recreation

Sutphin and Associates
8601 Six Forks Road, Suite 703
Raleigh, NC 27615
(919) 676-5284
Contact: Mr. Kem Sutphin
Minimum Salary Placed: $25,000
Recruiting Specialty: General

Underwood Group
2840 Plaza Place
Raleigh, NC 27609
(919) 782-3024
Contact: Mr. Mark Underwood
Minimum Salary Placed: $35,000
Recruiting Specialty: Data processing and software engineering

David Weinfeld Group
6512 Six Forks Road, Suite 603B
Raleigh, NC 27615
(919) 676-7828
Contact: Mr. David Weinfeld
Recruiting Specialty: Sales and technical disciplines in telecommunications and computers

ROCKY MOUNT

Management Recruiters
P.O. Box 1186
Rocky Mount, NC 27802
(919) 442-8000
Contact: Mr. Robert Manning
Minimum Salary Placed: $20,000
Recruiting Specialty: General

ProLink
5040 Netherwood Road
Rocky Mount, NC 27803
(919) 443-2259

Contact: Mr. Don Gladwell
Minimum Salary Placed: $25,000
Recruiting Specialty: MIS

SKYLAND

Bell Professional Placement
P.O. Box 1429
Skyland, NC 28776
(704) 684-7302
Contact: Mr. James Bell
Minimum Salary Placed: $30,000
Recruiting Specialty: Textiles and chemicals

STATESVILLE

Management Recruiters
211 South Center, Suite 305
Statesville, NC 28677
(704) 871-9890
Contact: Mr. Neil Coleman
Minimum Salary Placed: $20,000
Recruiting Specialty: General

SWANNANOA

Nayland Associates
106 Lady Slipper Trail
Swannanoa, NC 28778
(704) 686-7777
Contact: Mr. Mark Tokay
Minimum Salary Placed: $30,000
Recruiting Specialty: MIS and computers

WILMINGTON

A&B Personnel Service Inc.
1201 South 16th Street
Wilmington, NC 28401
(910) 251-0505
Contact: Ms. Nancy Allen
Recruiting Specialty: General

Allman & Company, Inc.
P.O. Box 4573
Wilmington, NC 28406
(910) 395-5219
Contact: Mr. Steven Allman
Minimum Salary Placed: $40,000
Recruiting Specialty: Trust and banking

Eastern Search Group
1201 Floral Parkway
Wilmington, NC 28403
(910) 799-7700
Contact: Mr. F. Wells
Minimum Salary Placed: $25,000
Recruiting Specialty: Engineering and data processing

Phil Ellis Associates Inc.
2030 Eastwood Road, Suite 5
Wilmington, NC 28403
(910) 256-9810
Contact: Mr. Phil Ellis
Recruiting Specialty: Healthcare products

Management Consultant Service
6800 Wrightsville Avenue
Wilmington, NC 28403
(910) 256-8006
Contact: Ms. M. Wilcox
Minimum Salary Placed: $40,000
Recruiting Specialty: Engineering

Management Recruiters
4006 Oleander Drive, Suite 4-B
Wilmington, NC 28403
(910) 791-2999
Contact: Mr. Harry Bargholz
Minimum Salary Placed: $20,000
Recruiting Specialty: General

Moley and Associates Inc.
530 Causeway Drive
Wilmington, NC 28403
(910) 256-3826
Contact: Mr. David Moley
Minimum Salary Placed: $25,000
Recruiting Specialty: Food services

Nagel Executive Search Inc.
376 John S. Mosby Drive
Wilmington, NC 28412
(910) 392-0797
Contact: Mr. Conrad Nagel
Minimum Salary Placed: $25,000
Recruiting Specialty: Textiles

WINSTON SALEM

Accounting Personnel
4400 Silas Creek Parkway, Suite 200
Winston Salem, NC 27104
(910) 768-8188
Contact: Mr. D. Nesbitt
Minimum Salary Placed: $20,000
Recruiting Specialty: Accounting and finance

Bryant and Company
846 W. 4th Street
Winston Salem, NC 27101
(910) 723-7077

Contact: Mr. David Bryant
Minimum Salary Placed: $25,000
Recruiting Specialty: General

Fox-Morris Associates, Inc.
119 Brookstown Avenue, Suite 305
Winston Salem, NC 27101
(910) 722-6792
Contact: Mr. Jeff Owens
Minimum Salary Placed: $35,000
Recruiting Specialty: General

Management Recruiters
P.O. Box 17054
Winston Salem, NC 27116
(910) 723-0484
Contact: Mr. Mike Jones
Minimum Salary Placed: $20,000
Recruiting Specialty: General

LaVallee & Associates
4176 Sulgrave Court
Winston Salem, NC 27105
(910) 760-1911
Contact: Mr. Michael LaVallee
Minimum Salary Placed: $35,000
Recruiting Specialty: Computer

Sales Consultants
112 Cambridge Plaza, Suite A
Winston Salem, NC 27104
(910) 659-1777
Contact: Mr. Donald Hicks
Minimum Salary Placed: $20,000
Recruiting Specialty: Sales

Unique Personnel Inc.
3500 Vest Mill Road
Winston Salem, NC 27103
(910) 768-1390
Contact: Ms. U. Doub
Recruiting Specialty: General

Winston Placement Inc.
253 Executive Park Boulevard
Winston Salem, NC 27103
(910) 768-4040
Contact: Ms. S. Shouse
Recruiting Specialty: General

WRIGHTSVILLE BEACH

John M. Horton, Inc.
P.O. Box 891
Wrightsville Beach, NC 28480
(910) 256-5150
Contact: Mr. John Horton
Minimum Salary Placed: $45,000
Recruiting Specialty: Sales and marketing
in pharmaceuticals

Matrix Consultants, Inc.
P.O. Box 986
Wrightsville Beach, NC 28480
(910) 256-8080
Contact: Mr. O. J. Womble
Minimum Salary Placed: $50,000
Recruiting Specialty: Food and beverages

NORTH DAKOTA

BISMARK

Olsten Temporary Service
101 W. Main Street
Bismark, ND 58504
(701) 258-4121
Contact: Mr. A. Kramer
Recruiting Specialty: General

FARGO

Dunhill Personnel Service
109½ Broadway
Fargo, ND 58102
(701) 235-3719
Contact: Mr. Albert Raney
Minimum Salary Placed: $20,000
Recruiting Specialty: Healthcare and engineering

O'Leary and Company
807 Black Building
Fargo, ND 58102
(701) 235-2404
Contact: Mr. M. O'Leary
Minimum Salary Placed: $25,000
Recruiting Specialty: Banking

Professional Management Consultants
109½ Broadway
Fargo, ND 58102
(701) 237-9262
Contact: Ms. N. Raney
Recruiting Specialty: General

Snelling Personnel Services
609½ 1st Avenue N
Fargo, ND 58102
(701) 237-0600
Contact: Ms. D. Almeida
Minimum Salary Placed: $25,000
Recruiting Specialty: General

O H I O

AKRON

A.M.C.R., Inc.
55 South Miller Road, Suite 202
Akron, OH 44333
(330) 869-0777
Contact: Mr. Harvey Lipton
Minimum Salary Placed: $30,000
Recruiting Specialty: General

Callos Personnel Services
150 Springside Drive, Suite B250
Akron, OH 44333
(330) 665-4400
Contact: Mr. Daniel Wismas
Recruiting Specialty: General

Elite Resources Group
71 Baker Boulevard
Akron, OH 44333
(330) 867-9412
Recruiting Specialty: Trucking and transportation

Robert Half International
76 S. Main Street, Suite 1704
Akron, OH 44308
(216) 253-8367
Contact: Mr. G. Jacob
Minimum Salary Placed: $25,000
Recruiting Specialty: Accounting and finance

Management Recruiters
66 S. Miller Road
Akron, OH 44333
(330) 867-2900
Contact: Mr. Tom Gerst
Minimum Salary Placed: $20,000
Recruiting Specialty: Plastics and rubber

Metrix, Inc.
3810 Ridgewood Road
Akron, OH 44321
(330) 666-6150
Contact: Mr. Karl Rohrer
Recruiting Specialty: Computer science, engineering, and manufacturing

Professional Dynamics Inc.
1700 Akron Peninsula Road, Suite 311
Akron, OH 44313
(330) 922-4244
Contact: Mr. D. Hirsch
Minimum Salary Placed: $40,000
Recruiting Specialty: Technical disciplines in engineering and plant management

Sanford Rose Associates
265 South Main Street, Suite 200
Akron, OH 44308
(330) 762-6211
Contact: Mr. Sanford Rose
Recruiting Specialty: General

ALLIANCE

Ryan Callos and Associates
131 W. State Street
Alliance, OH 44601
(216) 823-6536
Contact: Mr. J. Callos
Recruiting Specialty: General

ASHLAND

Management Recruiters
1114 Rook Drive, Suite 200
Ashland, OH 44805
(419) 281-0595

Contact: Mr. Edward Houska
Minimum Salary Placed: $20,000
Recruiting Specialty: General

AURORA

Western Reserve Search Associates
P.O. Box 606
Aurora, OH 44206
(216) 562-4811
Contact: Mr. Darrell Robertson
Minimum Salary Placed: $75,000
Recruiting Specialty: Products manufacturing and finance

AVON

Advancement Recruiting Services
P.O. Box 209
Avon, OH 44011
(216) 937-9910
Contact: Mr. Rudy Socha
Minimum Salary Placed: $30,000
Recruiting Specialty: General

BATH

The Revere Associates, Inc.
1947 Cleveland-Massillon Road
P.O. Box 498
Bath, OH 44210
(216) 666-6442
Contact: Mr. Michael Fremon
Minimum Salary Placed: $50,000
Recruiting Specialty: Plastics and packaging

BEACHWOOD

D.S. Allen Associates
24200 Chagrin Boulevard, Suite 222
Beachwood, OH 44122
(216) 831-1701
Contact: Mr. John Falk
Minimum Salary Placed: $40,000
Recruiting Specialty: Consumer products and high technology

Cencor Services
25700 Science Park, Suite 300
Beachwood, OH 44122
(216) 464-9000
Contact: Ms. Nancy Taber
Recruiting Specialty: Accounting and finance, banking, human resources, and legal

Cornerstone Recruiters
24200 Chagrin Boulevard, Suite 324
Beachwood, OH 44122
(216) 591-1744
Contact: Mr. Bernard Katz
Recruiting Specialty: Computer science, distribution, manufacturing, and sales

R.J. Evans & Assoc., Inc.
26949 Chagrin Blvd., Suite 300
Beachwood, OH 44122
(216) 464-5100
Contact: Mr. Bob Evans
Recruiting Specialty: General

Howard Gilmore & Associates
15 Chelsea Court
Beachwood, OH 44122
(216) 831-6248
Contact: Mr. Howard Gilmore
Minimum Salary Placed: $25,000
Recruiting Specialty: Manufacturing

Sales Consultants
23518 E. Baintree Road
Beachwood, OH 44122
(216) 867-7494
Contact: Mr. Sidney Kaufman
Minimum Salary Placed: $20,000
Recruiting Specialty: Sales

BEREA

Effective Search Inc.
398 W. Bagley Road
Berea, OH 44017
(216) 234-2205
Contact: Mr. Craig Toedman
Minimum Salary Placed: $25,000
Recruiting Specialty: Manufacturing and industrial

Jaeger Plus
2 Berea Commons, Suite 205
Berea, OH 44017
(216) 243-0010
Contact: Mr. Donald Auble
Recruiting Specialty: Advertising

Richard Kader & Associates
343 W. Bagley Road, Suite 209
Berea, OH 44017
(216) 891-1700
Contact: Mr. Richard Kader
Minimum Salary Placed: $40,000
Recruiting Specialty: General

BOARDMAN

Management Recruiters
8090 Market Street, Suite 2
Boardman, OH 44512
(216) 726-6656

Contact: Mr. Robert Lutsky
Minimum Salary Placed: $20,000
Recruiting Specialty: General

BRECKSVILLE

Executive Connection
8221 Brecksville Road
Building 3, Suite 2
Brecksville, OH 44141
(216) 838-5657
Contact: Mr. Steven Brandvold
Minimum Salary Placed: $30,000
Recruiting Specialty: Manufacturing in consumer products

Professional Support Inc.
8221 Brecksville Road, 3-107
Brecksville, OH 44141
(216) 526-7650
Contact: Mr. Richard Beldon
Minimum Salary Placed: $30,000
Recruiting Specialty: Computer consulting and support

BROOKLYN

Midland Consultants
4311 Ridge Road
Brooklyn, OH 44144
(216) 398-9330
Contact: Mr. David Sgro
Recruiting Specialty: Rubber, plastics and chemicals

BRUNSWICK

Management Recruiters
P.O. Box 178
Brunswick, OH 44212
(216) 273-4300
Contact: Mr. Robert Boal
Minimum Salary Placed: $20,000
Recruiting Specialty: General

CANFIELD

Hindman Company
123 Lakhani Lane
Canfield, OH 44406
(330) 533-5450
Minimum Salary Placed: $50,000
Recruiting Specialty: General

Sanford Rose Associates
545 N. Broad Street, Suite 2
Canfield, OH 44406
(216) 533-9270
Contact: Mr. Richard Ellison
Minimum Salary Placed: $30,000
Recruiting Specialty: MIS and telecommunications

CANTON

Executive Directions
4919 Spruce Hill Drive NW
Canton, OH 44718
(330) 499-1001
Contact: Mr. Paul Richards
Minimum Salary Placed: $45,000
Recruiting Specialty: Plastics and packaging in automotive

Reed Recruiting
4450 Belden Village Street NW
Canton, OH 44718
(330) 492-2577
Contact: Ms. Betty Reed
Minimum Salary Placed: $25,000
Recruiting Specialty: General

CENTERVILLE

Russ Hadick and Associates
7100 Corporate Way, Suite B
Centerville, OH 45459
(513) 439-7700
Contact: Mr. Russ Hadick
Minimum Salary Placed: $25,000
Recruiting Specialty: General

CHAGRIN FALLS

Roger Glander
100 N. Main Street
Chagrin Falls, OH 44022
(216) 247-4030
Contact: Mr. Roger Glander
Minimum Salary Placed: $25,000
Recruiting Specialty: Rubber and plastics manufacturing

CHESTERLAND

The Hanna Group
8437 Mayfield Road, Unit 102
Chesterland, OH 44026
(216) 729-1255
Contact: Mr. Jack Hanna
Recruiting Specialty: Heavy capital equipment

CINCINNATI

Accountants Executive Search
250 E. 5th Street
Cincinnati, OH 45202
(513) 381-4545
Contact: Mr. S. Libes
Minimum Salary Placed: $25,000
Recruiting Specialty: Accounting and finance

Accountants On Call
250 E. Fifth Street, Suite 1630
Cincinnati, OH 45202
(513) 381-4545
Contact: Mr. Gary Merrifield
Recruiting Specialty: Accounting

Accountemps
255 E. 5th Street
Cincinnati, OH 45202
(513) 621-7711
Recruiting Specialty: Accounting

Allen/Associates
4555 Lake Forest Drive
Cincinnati, OH 45242
(513) 563-3040
Contact: Mr. Michael Allen
Minimum Salary Placed: $100,000
Recruiting Specialty: Retail

American Business Personnel Services, Inc.
11499 Chester Road, Suite 2610
Cincinnati, Oh 45246
(513) 772-1200
Contact: Mr. James E. Wilson
Recruiting Specialty: Sales and hospitality

The Angus Group, Inc.
2337 Victory Parkway
Cincinnati, OH 45206
(513) 961-5575
Contact: Mr. Thomas Angus
Minimum Salary Placed: $25,000
Recruiting Specialty: General

Automation Search Company
2812 Queen City Avenue
Cincinnati, OH 45238
(513) 661-4009
Minimum Salary Placed: $35,000
Recruiting Specialty: Technical disciplines

Baldwin & Associates
3975 Erie Avenue
Cincinnati, OH 45208
(513) 272-2400
Contact: Mr. W. Keith Baldwin
Minimum Salary Placed: $25,000
Recruiting Specialty: General

Barkalow Executive Search
21 Allen Avenue
Cincinnati, OH 45215
(513) 821-9400
Contact: Mr. Lee Barkalow
Minimum Salary Placed: $25,000
Recruiting Specialty: General

Bason Associates, Inc.
11311 Carmel Park Drive, Suite 200
Cincinnati, OH 45242
(513) 469-9881
Contact: Mr. Maurice Bason
Minimum Salary Placed: $40,000
Recruiting Specialty: General

CBS Personnel Service
435 Elm Street, Suite 700
Cincinnati, OH 45238
(513) 651-1111
Contact: Mr. Robert Brown
Recruiting Specialty: General

Career Center
4600 Vine St.
Cincinnati, OH 45217
(513) 641-0900
Contact: Mr. Bob Wick
Recruiting Specialty: Engineering, manufacturing technical

Centennial Inc.
1014 Vine Street, 23rd Floor
Cincinnati, OH 45202
(513) 381-4411
Contact: Mr. M. Sipple
Minimum Salary Placed: $25,000
Recruiting Specialty: General

W.J. Comer Associates Inc.
4248 W. 8th Street
Cincinnati, OH 45205
(513) 251-8432
Contact: Mr. W. Comer
Minimum Salary Placed: $45,000
Recruiting Specialty: General

Communications Resources, Inc.
P.O. Box 141397
Cincinnati, OH 45250
(606) 491-5410
Minimum Salary Placed: $40,000
Recruiting Specialty: Telecommunications

Cova Recruiting Services
P.O. Box 428708
Cincinnati, OH 45242
(513) 791-7607
Contact: Mr. Ken Cova
Minimum Salary Placed: $30,000
Recruiting Specialty: Engineering

Drayton and Associates
120 W. 5th Street, Suite 902
Cincinnati, OH 45202
(513) 621-4018
Contact: Mr. Brad Drayton
Minimum Salary Placed: $35,000
Recruiting Specialty: General

Executech Consultants Inc.
3915 Reading Road
Cincinnati, OH 45229
(513) 281-6416
Contact: Mr. Howard Bond
Minimum Salary Placed: $25,000
Recruiting Specialty: General

Executive Search, Ltd.
4830 Interstate Drive
Cincinnati, OH 45246
(513) 874-6901
Contact: Mr. James Cimino
Minimum Salary Placed: $40,000
Recruiting Specialty: General

Fortune Personnel Consultants
8170 Corporate Park Drive, Suite 304
Cincinnati, OH 45242
(513) 469-0808
Contact: Mr. Rick Davis
Minimum Salary Placed: $25,000
Recruiting Specialty: General

Genesis Personnel Service, Inc.
10921 Reed Hartman Highway,
 Suite 226
Cincinnati, OH 45242
(513) 891-4433
Contact: Ms. Delora Bennett
Minimum Salary Placed: $20,000
Recruiting Specialty: General; Minorities

I.S.C. of Cincinnati, Inc.
130 Tri County Parkway
Cincinnati, OH 45246
(513) 771-4484
Contact: Mr. Bill Drier
Minimum Salary Placed: $25,000
Recruiting Specialty: General

Management Recruiters
4050 Executive Park Drive, Suite 125
Cincinnati, OH 45241
(513) 769-4747
Contact: Mr. William O'Reilly
Minimum Salary Placed: $20,000
Recruiting Specialty: General

Management Recruiters
36 E. 4th Street, Suite 800
Cincinnati, OH 45202
(513) 651-5500
Contact: Mr. Joe McCullough
Minimum Salary Placed: $20,000
Recruiting Specialty: General

Million & Associates, Inc.
441 Vine Street, Suite 1831
Cincinnati, OH 45202
(513) 579-8770
Contact: Mr. Ken Million
Minimum Salary Placed: $40,000
Recruiting Specialty: General

The C. B. Mueller Company, Inc.
550 E. 4th Street
Cincinnati, OH 45202
(513) 651-4700
Contact: Mr. Clifford Mueller
Minimum Salary Placed: $55,000
Recruiting Specialty: General

Professions, Inc.
4665 Cornell Road, Suite 160
Cincinnati, OH 45241
(513) 530-0909
Contact: Ms. Karen Kranak
Minimum Salary Placed: $25,000
Recruiting Specialty: Metal and paper
production, fabrication and manufacturing

Sales Consultants
11311 Cornell Park Drive, Suite 404
Cincinnati, OH 45242
(513) 247-0707
Contact: Mr. Jerry Kuper
Minimum Salary Placed: $20,000
Recruiting Specialty: Sales

Source EDP
525 Vine Street, Suite 2250
Cincinnati, OH 45202
(513) 651-3303
Contact: Mr. Greg Johnson
Recruiting Specialty: Computers, healthcare, finance and manufacturing

Speer and Associates
9624 Cincinnati Columbus, Suite 312
Cincinnati, OH 45241
(513) 777-0200
Contact: Ms. B. Speer
Minimum Salary Placed: $40,000
Recruiting Specialty: Transportation

S. K. Stewart & Associates
560 Brunner Avenue
Box 40110
Cincinnati, OH 45240
(513) 851-7060
Contact: Mr. Stephen Stewart
Minimum Salary Placed: $75,000
Recruiting Specialty: General

CLEVELAND

Action Management Service
6100 Rockside Woods Boulevard
Cleveland, OH 44131
(216) 642-8777
Contact: Mr. D. Chorba
Minimum Salary Placed: $25,000
Recruiting Specialty: Accounting, finance
and tax

Anders & Company, Inc.
P.O. Box 20429
Cleveland, OH 44120
(216) 561-4460
Contact: Mr. Kenneth Anderson
Minimum Salary Placed: $60,000
Recruiting Specialty: General

Artgo, Inc.
1422 Euclid Avenue, Suite 545
Cleveland, OH 44115
(216) 241-1548
Contact: Mr. Arthur Baldwin
Minimum Salary Placed: $50,000
Recruiting Specialty: General

Richard Bencin and Associates
8553 Timber Trail
Cleveland, OH 44141
(216) 526-6726

Contact: Mr. R. Bencin
Minimum Salary Placed: $25,000
Recruiting Specialty: General

Bowden & Company, Inc.
5000 Rockside Road, Suite 550
Cleveland, OH 44131
(216) 447-1800
Contact: Mr. Otis Bowden
Minimum Salary Placed: $80,000
Recruiting Specialty: General

Bryan & Louis Research Associates
6263 Mayfield Road, Suite 226
Cleveland, OH 44124
(216) 442-8744
Contact: Mr. Robert Terlizzi
Minimum Salary Placed: $25,000
Recruiting Specialty: Technical manufac-
turing and production

Cardwell Group
1991 Crocker Road
Cleveland, OH 44145
(216) 892-1410
Contact: Mr. J. Cardwell
Minimum Salary Placed: $25,000
Recruiting Specialty: Healthcare and
credit unions

N.S. Charney and Associates
14650 Detroit Avenue
Cleveland, OH 44107
(216) 228-1199
Recruiting Specialty: Medical sales and
engineering

Christian & Timbers, Inc.
25825 Science Park Drive, Suite 400
Cleveland, OH 44122
(216) 464-8710

Contact: Mr. Adam Kohn
Minimum Salary Placed: $75,000
Recruiting Specialty: General

Christopher-Patrick & Associates
24800 Chagrin Boulevard, Suite 103
Cleveland, OH 44122
(216) 321-1429
Contact: Mr. John Donnelly
Minimum Salary Placed: $50,000
Recruiting Specialty: General

Cleveland Business Consultants
1148 Euclid Avenue, Suite 416
Cleveland, OH 44115
(216) 781-5300
Recruiting Specialty: Engineering

Combined Resources Inc.
14701 Detroit Avenue
Cleveland, OH 44107
(216) 221-1161
Recruiting Specialty: Technical

Daniel Davis and Associates Inc.
24100 Chagrin Boulevard
Cleveland, OH 44122
(216) 831-7760
Contact: Mr. Dan Davis
Minimum Salary Placed: $25,000
Recruiting Specialty: General

Direct Recruiters Inc.
24100 Chagrin Boulevard, Suite 450
Cleveland, OH 44122
(216) 464-5570
Contact: Mr. S. Myeroff
Minimum Salary Placed: $25,000
Recruiting Specialty: Computer sales

Driscol and Associates Inc.
75 Windrush Drive
Cleveland, OH 44122
(216) 247-8568
Contact: Ms. Barbara Driscol
Recruiting Specialty: Physicians

Davis Law Group
700 W. St. Clair, Hoyt Building
Cleveland, OH 44113
(216) 241-4544
Contact: Mr. Davis
Minimum Salary Placed: $40,000
Recruiting Specialty: Attorneys

R.J. Evans and Associates
26949 Chagrin Boulevard, Suite 300
Cleveland, OH 44122
(216) 464-5100
Contact: Mr. Robert Allen
Minimum Salary Placed: $25,000
Recruiting Specialty: Accounting and finance

Executive Work Search
15300 Pearl Road
Cleveland, OH 44136
(216) 238-9789
Contact: Mr. Mike Wagner
Minimum Salary Placed: $25,000
Recruiting Specialty: Technical, some general

FWC Recruiters
1300 E. Granger Road,
Cleveland, OH 44131
(216) 351-3930
Recruiting Specialty: General

Ferrari Search Group
16781 Chagrin Boulevard, Suite 164
Cleveland, OH 44120
(216) 491-1122
Contact: Mr. S. Jay Ferrari
Minimum Salary Placed: $60,000
Recruiting Specialty: Finance

Fox-Morris Associates, Inc.
4700 Rockside Road, Suite 640
Cleveland, OH 44131
(216) 524-6565
Contact: Mr. Bill York
Minimum Salary Placed: $35,000
Recruiting Specialty: General

Gayhart and Associates
1250 Old River Road, Suite 2
Cleveland, OH 44113
(216) 861-7010
Minimum Salary Placed: $50,000
Recruiting Specialty: General

George Gum and Associates
24400 Highland Road
Cleveland, OH 44143
(216) 531-1888
Contact: Ms. Robin Rizzo
Minimum Salary Placed: $25,000
Recruiting Specialty: Retail

Robert Half International
1300 E. 9th Street
Cleveland, OH 44114
(216) 621-4253
Contact: Mr. A. Geisen
Minimum Salary Placed: $25,000
Recruiting Specialty: Accounting and finance

Heidrick & Struggles, Inc.
600 Superior Avenue East
Cleveland, OH 44114
(216) 241-7410
Contact: Mr. Charles Wallace
Minimum Salary Placed: $60,000
Recruiting Specialty: General

Gretchen S. Herbuck
3161 Coleridge Road
Cleveland, OH 44118
(216) 371-9982
Recruiting Specialty: Healthcare

Herron and Company
20325 Center Ridge Road
Cleveland, OH 44116
(216) 356-6250
Contact: Ms. Nan Herron
Minimum Salary Placed: $25,000
Recruiting Specialty: General

Hite Executive Search
Box 43217
Cleveland, OH 44143
(216) 461-1600
Contact: Mr. William Hite
Minimum Salary Placed: $75,000
Recruiting Specialty: General

The Human Resource Group, Inc.
8221 Brecksville Road
Building 1, Suite 103
Cleveland, OH 44141
(216) 838-5818
Contact: Mr. Michael Coman
Minimum Salary Placed: $75,000
Recruiting Specialty: General

Human Resource Recruiters
Box 18007
Cleveland, OH 44118
(216) 932-1592
Contact: Mr. John Goldthwaite
Recruiting Specialty: Human resources

I.S.C. of Cleveland, Inc.
22700 Shore Center Drive
Cleveland, OH 44123
(216) 261-7400
Contact: Mr. Scott Carpenter
Minimum Salary Placed: $30,000
Recruiting Specialty: Technical disciplines in chemicals, electrical, mechanical and healthcare

A.T. Kearney Executive Search
600 Superior Avenue East
1200 Bank One Center
Cleveland, OH 44114
(216) 241-6880
Contact: Mr. Lewis Lenkaitis
Minimum Salary Placed: $60,000
Recruiting Specialty: General

Knight and Associates
20325 Center Ridge Road
Cleveland, OH 44116
(216) 356-0330
Contact: Ms. Paula Knight
Minimum Salary Placed: $25,000
Recruiting Specialty: General

Michael Kosmetos and Associates
333 Babbitt Road, Suite 300
Cleveland, OH 44123
(216) 261-1950
Contact: Mr. Michael Kosmetos
Minimum Salary Placed: $30,000
Recruiting Specialty: Retail

Krance Search Corporation
6213 N. Woodlane Drive
Cleveland, OH 44143
(216) 943-3333
Contact: Mr. Jim Krancvic
Minimum Salary Placed: $25,000
Recruiting Specialty: General

Lamalie Amrop International
Key Tower Suite 4110, 127 Public Square
Cleveland, OH 44114
(216) 694-3000
Contact: Mr. John Johnson
Minimum Salary Placed: $75,000
Recruiting Specialty: General

M & M Personnel/ProPlacement Recruiting Services
812 Huron Road, Suite 760
Cleveland, OH 44115
(216) 436-2436
Contact: Mr. Gary Gardiner
Recruiting Specialty: Engineers, telecommunications, auto and aerospace

Management Recruiters
20600 Chagrin Boulevard, Suite 703
Cleveland, OH 44122
(216) 561-6776
Contact: Mr. Robert Gandee
Minimum Salary Placed: $20,000
Recruiting Specialty: General

Management Recruiters
26250 Euclid Avenue, Suite 811
Cleveland, OH 44132
(216) 261-7696
Contact: Mr. Terry Wesley
Minimum Salary Placed: $20,000
Recruiting Specialty: General

Management Recruiters
9700 Rockside Road, Suite 490
Cleveland, OH 44125
(216) 642-5788
Contact: Mr. Paul Montigny
Minimum Salary Placed: $20,000
Recruiting Specialty: General

Management Recruiters
7550 Lucerne Drive
Cleveland, OH 44130
(216) 243-5151
Contact: Mr. Jeff DiPaolo
Minimum Salary Placed: $20,000
Recruiting Specialty: General

Martin, Marshall and Associates
Box 21745
Cleveland, OH 44118
(216) 321-1200
Contact: Mr. W. Marshall
Minimum Salary Placed: $25,000
Recruiting Specialty: Environmental

Marvel Consultants Inc.
28601 Chagrin Boulevard, Suite 470
Cleveland, OH 44122
(216) 292-2855
Contact: Mr. Marvin Basil
Minimum Salary Placed: $25,000
Recruiting Specialty: General

Louis Thomas Masterson & Company
1375 E. 9th Street, Suite 1950
Cleveland, OH 44114
(216) 621-2112

Contact: Mr. Louis Thomas Masterson
Minimum Salary Placed: $75,000
Recruiting Specialty: General

McCrea and Company
1701 E. 12th Street
Cleveland, OH 44114
(216) 696-1090
Contact: Mr. J. MacArther
Minimum Salary Placed: $35,000
Recruiting Specialty: General

McRoberts & Associates
27683 Remington Drive
Cleveland, OH 44145
(216) 892-0210
Contact: Mr. C.F. McRoberts
Minimum Salary Placed: $40,000
Recruiting Specialty: General

Midwest Search, Inc.
14650 Detroit Avenue, Suite 120
Cleveland, OH 44107
(216) 226-1900
Contact: Mr. Robert Reusser
Recruiting Specialty: General

Laurie Mitchell & Company
25018 Hazelmere Road
Cleveland, OH 44122
(216) 292-6001
Contact: Ms. Laurie Mitchell
Minimum Salary Placed: $40,000
Recruiting Specialty: Advertising, public
relations and consumer marketing

E.W. Nishnic and Associates
7650 Chippewa Road
Cleveland, OH 44141
(216) 838-5008
Contact: Mr. Ed Nishnic
Minimum Salary Placed: $25,000
Recruiting Specialty: General

Northcoast Personnel
1250 Old River Road
Cleveland, OH 44113
(216) 861-2200
Contact: Mr. Richard Albertini
Minimum Salary Placed: $25,000
Recruiting Specialty: General

O'Brien & Company, Inc.
812 Huron Road, Suite 535
Cleveland, OH 44115
(216) 575-1212
Contact: Mr. Tim O'Brien
Minimum Salary Placed: $75,000
Recruiting Specialty: Manufacturing,
healthcare and retail

ProResource, Inc.
715 Ohio Savings Plaza
1801 East Ninth Street
Cleveland, OH 44114
(216) 579-1515
Recruiting Specialty: General

Questry Associates
5001 Mayfield Road, Suite 115
Cleveland, OH 44124
(216) 381-4799
Contact: Mr. Dan Landau
Minimum Salary Placed: $25,000
Recruiting Specialty: General

Recruiting Professionals
11351 Pearl Road
Cleveland, OH 44136
(216) 572-1800
Contact: Mr. Joe Raabe
Minimum Salary Placed: $25,000
Recruiting Specialty: Insurance

Romac & Associates, Inc.
956 Hanna Building
Cleveland, OH 44115
(216) 771-6822
Contact: Mr. Norman Benke
Minimum Salary Placed: $20,000
Recruiting Specialty: General

Roth Young Personnel Service
5311 Northfield Road
Cleveland, OH 44146
(216) 663-4700
Contact: Mr. M. Kushkin
Minimum Salary Placed: $25,000
Recruiting Specialty: Retail, hospitality
and building

SJR and Associates
24300 Chagrin Boulevard
Cleveland, OH 44122
(216) 831-5228
Contact: Mr. Scott Riffle
Minimum Salary Placed: $30,000
Recruiting Specialty: Engineering

Sales Consultants
1127 Euclid Avenue, Suite 1400
Cleveland, OH 44115
(216) 696-1122
Contact: Mr. Alan Schonberg
Minimum Salary Placed: $20,000
Recruiting Specialty: Sales

Sales Consultants
20600 Chagrin Boulevard, Suite 703
Cleveland, OH 44122
(216) 561-6676
Contact: Mr. Bob Gandee
Minimum Salary Placed: $20,000
Recruiting Specialty: Sales

Search Masters
1148 Euclid Avenue, Suite 509
Cleveland, OH 44115
(216) 781-5311
Recruiting Specialty: Technical disciplines in manufacturing

H.C. Smith Ltd.
20600 Chagrin Boulevard
Cleveland, OH 44122
(216) 752-9966
Minimum Salary Placed: $20,000
Recruiting Specialty: General

Charles Snider and Associates Inc.
6929 West 130th Street, Suite 401
Cleveland, OH 44130
(216) 884-1656
Contact: Mr. Charles Snider
Minimum Salary Placed: $20,000
Recruiting Specialty: Paralegals and attorneys

Technical Search Consultants
1127 Euclid Avenue, Suite 1130
Cleveland, OH 44115
(216) 348-0404
Contact: Mr. John Romah
Minimum Salary Placed: $35,000
Recruiting Specialty: Manufacturing, engineering, and automotive

Thomas-Shade and Associates
15110 Foltz Industrial Parkway
Cleveland, OH 44136
(216) 846-0011
Contact: Ms. Dani Shade
Minimum Salary Placed: $25,000
Recruiting Specialty: Security, fire and safety and engineering

Tupa Slack and Associates
24803 Detroit Road
Cleveland, OH 44145
(216) 835-2848
Contact: Mr. Gary Tupa
Minimum Salary Placed: $25,000
Recruiting Specialty: General

T. M. Vaughn Company
24601 Center Ridge Road, Suite 200
Cleveland, OH 44145
(216) 892-4800
Contact: Mr. Terry Vaughn
Minimum Salary Placed: $40,000
Recruiting Specialty: General

Ty Blake Ltd.
2143 Fairhill Road
Cleveland, OH 44106
(216) 791-1245
Minimum Salary Placed: $75,000
Recruiting Specialty: General

J.P. Walton and Associates
9601 Dorothy Avenue
Cleveland, OH 44125
(216) 883-4141
Contact: Mr. John Walton
Minimum Salary Placed: $25,000
Recruiting Specialty: Corrugated container and folding cartons

COLUMBUS

Accountants On Call
700 Ackerman Road
Columbus, OH 43202
(614) 267-7200
Contact: Mr. John Marshall
Recruiting Specialty: Accounting

Accountemps
355 E. Campus View Boulevard,
 Suite 115
Columbus, OH 43235
(614) 433-7200
Contact: Mr. A. Denka
Recruiting Specialty: Accounting

Adams and Associates
100 E. Campus View Boulevard
Columbus, OH 43235
(614) 438-2617
Recruiting Specialty: Computers

Blackwood and Sach
1335 Dublin Road
Columbus, OH 43215
(614) 481-3506
Recruiting Specialty: General

BenchMark Resources
2487 Powell Avenue
Columbus, OH 43209-1748
(614) 231-3133
Contact: Ms. Deborah Krantz
Recruiting Specialty: Health insurance
and managed care

Buckman-Enochs and Associates Inc.
1625 Bethel Road
Columbus, OH 43220
(614) 457-7807

Contact: Mr. Steve Enochs
Minimum Salary Placed: $25,000
Recruiting Specialty: Sales in medical,
healthcare, consumer products and packaging

Career Insights, Inc.
1 East Campus View Boulevard,
 Suite 345
Columbus, OH 43235
(614) 888-0008
Contact: Mr. Pat DiNunzio
Recruiting Specialty: General

J.D. Cotter Search
2999 E. Dublin-Granville Road,
 Suite 103
Columbus, OH 43231
Contact: Mr. Joe Cotter
Minimum Salary Placed: $40,000
Recruiting Specialty: Computer science,
engineering, and manufacturing

Delta Medical Search Associates
615 Rome-Hilliard Road, Suite 107
Columbus, OH 43228
(614) 878-0550
Contact: Ms. Marilyn Wallace
Minimum Salary Placed: $30,000
Recruiting Specialty: Healthcare

Dillard Executive Search
1617 Hawthorne Park
Columbus, OH 43203
(614) 252-5848
Contact: Mr. Tom Dillard
Minimum Salary Placed: $30,000
Recruiting Specialty: General; Minorities

Dunhill Professional Search Inc.
1166 E. Goodale Street
Columbus, OH 43215
(614) 421-0111
Contact: Mr. Leo Salzman
Minimum Salary Placed: $25,000
Recruiting Specialty: Technical disciplines

Fament, Inc.
17 Aldrich Road, Suite B
Columbus, OH 43214
(614) 261-0552
Contact: Mr. Marty Shuherk
Minimum Salary Placed: $35,000
Recruiting Specialty: Insurance

General Employment Enterprises, Inc.
88 E. Broad Street, Suite 1450
Columbus, OH 43215
(614) 228-5192
Contact: Mr. Tim Schwenk
Recruiting Specialty: Accounting, electronics, engineering, and IT

Grover and Associates
7870 Olentangy River Road
Columbus, OH 43235
(614) 885-8917
Contact: Mr. Jim Grover
Minimum Salary Placed: $25,000
Recruiting Specialty: Manufacturing

G.W. Henn & Company
42 E. Gay Street, Suite 1312
Columbus, OH 43215
(614) 469-9666
Contact: Mr. George Henn
Minimum Salary Placed: $100,000
Recruiting Specialty: General

J. D. Hersey & Associates
1685 Old Henderson Road
Columbus, OH 43220
(614) 459-4555
Contact: Mr. Jeffrey Hersey
Minimum Salary Placed: $30,000
Recruiting Specialty: General

Insurance Recruiting Specialists
6100 Channingway Boulevard, Suite 506
Columbus, OH 43232
(614) 864-2324
Contact: Mr. Steve Barker
Minimum Salary Placed: $25,000
Recruiting Specialty: Insurance

Ives and Associates
471 E. Broad Street, Suite 2010
Columbus, OH 43215
(614) 228-0202
Contact: Ms. Dina Diveto
Minimum Salary Placed: $25,000
Recruiting Specialty: General

Jaeger International
4889 Sinclair Road, Suite 112
Columbus, OH 43229
(614) 885-0364
Minimum Salary Placed: $25,000
Recruiting Specialty: General

January Management Group
513 E. Rich Street, Suite 302
Columbus, OH 43215
(614) 462-2703
Contact: Mr. Bruce Bastoky
Minimum Salary Placed: $60,000
Recruiting Specialty: General

Management Recruiters
800 East Broad Street
Columbus, OH 43205
(614) 252-6200
Contact: Mr. David Oberting
Minimum Salary Placed: $20,000
Recruiting Specialty: General

Management Recruiters
1900 E. Dublin-Granville Road,
  Suite 110B
Columbus, OH 43229
(614) 794-3200
Contact: Mr. Robert Stultz
Minimum Salary Placed: $20,000
Recruiting Specialty: General

Midwest Search Consultants
471 E. Broad Street, Suite 1201
Columbus, OH 43215
(614) 224-3600
Minimum Salary Placed: $60,000
Recruiting Specialty: General

National Register Inc.
2700 E. Dublin Granville Road
Columbus, OH 43231
(614) 890-1200
Contact: Mr. David Molnar
Minimum Salary Placed: $45,000
Recruiting Specialty: Sales and marketing

The O'Brien & Roof Company
6812 Caine Road
Columbus, OH 43235
(614) 766-8500
Contact: Ms. Lindy O'Brien
Minimum Salary Placed: $30,000
Recruiting Specialty: General

Robert Half International
88 E. Broad Street
Columbus, OH 43215
(614) 866-6300
Contact: Mr. A. Denka
Minimum Salary Placed: $25,000
Recruiting Specialty: Accounting and finance

Sales Consultants
800 E. Broad Street
Columbus, OH 43205
(614) 252-6200
Contact: Mr. David Oberting
Minimum Salary Placed: $20,000
Recruiting Specialty: Sales

Sales Consultants
7650 Rivers Edge Drive, Suite 130
Columbus, OH 43235
(614) 785-0111
Contact: Mr. Mark Brubach
Minimum Salary Placed: $20,000
Recruiting Specialty: Sales

Sell and Associates
94 Northwoods Boulevard
Columbus, OH 43235
(614) 888-4188
Contact: Mr. Mark Sell
Recruiting Specialty: Finance, MIS and computers

Source EDP
1105 Schrock Road, Suite 510
Columbus, OH 43229
(614) 846-3311
Contact: Mr. Timothy Mogan
Recruiting Specialty: Computers

Stephens Associates Ltd., Inc.
88 N. 5th Street
P.O. Box 151114
Columbus, OH 43215
(614) 469-9990
Contact: Mr. Stephen Martinez
Minimum Salary Placed: $75,000
Recruiting Specialty: General

Technical Management Advisors
P.O. Box 307110
Columbus, OH 43230
(614) 863-0673
Contact: Mr. Gerald Brown
Recruiting Specialty: Pharmaceutical,
quality control, engineering, and technical

Technical Recruiting Services
6100 Channingway Boulevard, Suite 506
Columbus, OH 43232
(614) 864-2270
Contact: Mr. Nick Lang
Minimum Salary Placed: $35,000
Recruiting Specialty: General

Tully Woodmansee and Associates
7720 Rivers Edge Drive, Suite 101
Columbus, OH 43235
(614) 844-5480
Minimum Salary Placed: $50,000
Recruiting Specialty: General

Wells Inc.
4200 Dublin Road
Columbus, OH 43221
(614) 876-0651
Contact: Mr. M. Wells
Minimum Salary Placed: $75,000
Recruiting Specialty: General

CUYAHOGA FALLS

Dunhill of Greater Akron, Inc.
P.O. Box 67048
Cuyahoga Falls, OH 44222
(216) 929-7110
Contact: Mr. Charles Woodward
Minimum Salary Placed: $25,000
Recruiting Specialty: Technical disciplines

Providence Personal Consultants
2404 4th Street
Cuyahoga Falls, OH 44221
(330) 929-6431
Contact: Ms. D. Early
Minimum Salary Placed: $25,000
Recruiting Specialty: General

DAYTON

R.L. Brown and Associates
130 W. 2nd Street
Dayton, OH 45402
(513) 222-2525
Contact: Mr. R. Brown
Minimum Salary Placed: $25,000
Recruiting Specialty: General

Executive Resources Inc.
2036 Rustic Road
Dayton, OH 45405
(513) 274-4500
Contact: Mr. Vaughn
Recruiting Specialty: Food and pharmaceuticals

Executive Search Consultants
5609 N. Dixie Drive
Dayton, OH 45414
(513) 898-8872

Contact: Mr. Chuck Beatrice
Minimum Salary Placed: $40,000
Recruiting Specialty: General

H. L. Goehring & Associates, Inc.
3200 Wrenford Street
Dayton, OH 45409
(513) 294-8854
Contact: Mr. Hal Goehring
Minimum Salary Placed: $40,000
Recruiting Specialty: General

Russ Hadick and Associates
7100 Corporate Way, Suite B
Dayton, OH 45459
(513) 439-7700
Contact: Mr. Russ Hadick
Recruiting Specialty: General

Hahn & Associates, Inc.
7026 Corporate Way, Suite 212
Dayton, OH 45459
(513) 436-3141
Contact: Mr. Kenneth Hahn
Recruiting Specialty: General

Kaiser Nationwide
P.O. Box 41297
Dayton, OH 45441
(513) 885-4105
Contact: Mr. Hermann Kaiser
Recruiting Specialty: Engineering and
technical, MIS and IT

MAS Resources
1476 Miamisburg Centerville Road
Dayton, OH 45402
(513) 433-1223
Minimum Salary Placed: $35,000
Recruiting Specialty: Accounting and
data processing

Management Recruiters
40 W. 4th Street, Suite 1222
Dayton, OH 45402
(513) 228-8271
Contact: Mr. Jeff Noble
Minimum Salary Placed: $20,000
Recruiting Specialty: General

Robert Half International
1 Citizens Federal Center
Dayton, OH 45402
(513) 898-8367
Contact: Mr. B. Lane
Minimum Salary Placed: $25,000
Recruiting Specialty: Accounting and fi-
nance

Romac & Associates, Inc.
111 W. First Street, Suite 420
Dayton, OH 45402
(513) 461-1373
Contact: Mr. Alan Scothon
Minimum Salary Placed: $15,000
Recruiting Specialty: Accounting and
MIS in finance and banking

Sales Consultants
3490 S. Dixie Highway
Dayton, OH 45439
(513) 298-3300
Contact: Mr. C.E. Ford
Minimum Salary Placed: $20,000
Recruiting Specialty: Sales

Source EDP
One South Main Street, Suite 1440
Dayton, OH 45402
(513) 461-4660
Contact: Mr. Bruce Rockwell
Recruiting Specialty: General

Sterling Executive Search
7031 Corporate Way, Suite 201
Dayton, OH 45459
(513) 435-3585
Contact: Ms. I. Bond
Recruiting Specialty: General

Teknon Employment Resources, Inc.
17 S. Saint Clair Street, Suite 300
Dayton, OH 45402
(513) 222-5300
Contact: Mr. Raymond Gooch
Recruiting Specialty: Hospitality, sales
and marketing, telecommunications, bar
coding, and software

World Search
4130 Linden Avenue, Suite 105
Dayton, OH 45432
(513) 254-9071
Contact: Mr. Robert Rushbrook
Minimum Salary Placed: $40,000
Recruiting Specialty: Manufacturing and
production

DELPHOS

The Career Specialists
P.O. Box 371
Delphos, OH 45833
(419) 695-1234
Contact: Mr. Jerry Backus
Recruiting Specialty: Manufacturing and
engineering

DUBLIN

Melvin Kent and Associates
6477 Quarry Lane
Dublin, OH 43017
(614) 798-9501

Contact: Mr. Mel Kent
Minimum Salary Placed: $25,000
Recruiting Specialty: General

Lewis and Associates
425 Metro Place North
Dublin, OH 43017
(614) 766-0712
Contact: Ms. P. Lewis
Minimum Salary Placed: $25,000
Recruiting Specialty: Data processing

McIntyre Company
6221 Riverside Drive, Suite 1
Dublin, OH 43017
(614) 889-6000
Contact: Ms. A. McIntyre
Minimum Salary Placed: $25,000
Recruiting Specialty: General

R. Wegesin and Associates
7236 Fitzwilliam Drive
Dublin, OH 43017
(614) 798-0431
Contact: Mr. Ron Wegesin
Minimum Salary Placed: $25,000
Recruiting Specialty: Manufacturing

EUCLID

Sanford Rose Associates
26250 Euclid Avenue, Suite 11
Euclid, OH 44132
(216) 731-0005
Contact: Mr. Ralph Orkin
Recruiting Specialty: MIS

FAIRLAWN

Elite Resources Group
71 Baker Boulevard, Suite 204
Fairlawn, OH 44333
(330) 867-9412
Contact: Mr. Gary Suhay
Minimum Salary Placed: $30,000
Recruiting Specialty: General

George Mild Group
3221 Bancroft Road
Fairlawn, OH 44333
(330) 836-9191
Contact: Mr. George Mild
Minimum Salary Placed: $30,000
Recruiting Specialty: Technical disciplines in plastics and rubber

GALENA

Lowry Personnel Services
13545 Center Village Road
Galena, OH 43021
(614) 965-2220
Contact: Mr. Ken Lowry
Recruiting Specialty: Manufacturing and engineering

HIGHLAND HEIGHTS

Central Executive Search, Inc.
6151 Wilson Mills Road, Suite 240
Highland Heights, OH 44143
(216) 461-5400
Contact: Mr. Gary Giallombardo
Recruiting Specialty: Paper, printing, chemicals and packaging

HUDSON

Career Enterprises Inc.
5 East Main
Hudson, OH 44236
(216) 656-1700
Contact: Mr. S. Taylor
Minimum Salary Placed: $25,000
Recruiting Specialty: General

Sanford Rose Associates
P.O. Box 6093
Hudson, OH 44236
(216) 653-3325
Contact: Mr. Harry Cummings
Minimum Salary Placed: $50,000
Recruiting Specialty: Engineering and human resources

The Zammataro Company
P.O. Box 339
Hudson, OH 44236
(216) 656-1055
Contact: Mr. Frank Zammataro
Minimum Salary Placed: $70,000
Recruiting Specialty: Technical and manufactured products

INDEPENDENCE

Source EDP
3 Summit Park Drive, Suite 550
Independence, OH 44131
(216) 328-5900
Contact: Mr. Albert Rubino
Recruiting Specialty: Computers, marketing, finance, healthcare and manufacturing

IRONTON

Fenzel Milar Associates
602 Quincy Street
Ironton, OH 45638
(614) 532-6409
Contact: Mr. John Milar
Minimum Salary Placed: $30,000
Recruiting Specialty: Engineering, data processing and heavy industries

KENT

Cascade Group
136 E, Main Street
Kent, OH 44240
(330) 677-1118
Contact: Mr. R. King
Minimum Salary Placed: $25,000
Recruiting Specialty: General

Higgins and Associates
121 E. Main Street
Kent, OH 44240
(330) 673-2245
Contact: Mr. L. Higgins
Minimum Salary Placed: $25,000
Recruiting Specialty: General

LAKEWOOD

Combined Resources Inc.
14701 Detroit Avenue, Suite 750
Lakewood, OH 44107
(216) 221-1161
Contact: Mr. Gilbert Sherman
Recruiting Specialty: Consumer products

Quality Source Inc.
14650 Detroit
Lakewood Center West, Suite 325
Lakewood, OH 44107
(216) 529-9911
Contact: Ms. Debra L. Stitt
Recruiting Specialty: General

LIMA

R.M. Schulte and Associates
309 W. High Street
Lima, OH 45801
(419) 224-0106
Minimum Salary Placed: $35,000
Recruiting Specialty: Engineering

LOVELAND

Nationwide Personnel Placement, Inc.
P.O. Box 206
Loveland, OH 45140
(513) 677-1998
Contact: Mr. K. Michael Gowetski
Minimum Salary Placed: $20,000
Recruiting Specialty: General

MARIETTA

Fred C. Tippel and Associates
105 Shawnee Drive
Marietta, OH 45750
(614) 374-3288
Contact: Mr. Fred Tippel
Minimum Salary Placed: $35,000
Recruiting Specialty: Technical disciplines in various materials and manufacturing

MARYSVILLE

MRG International
19370 Northwest Parkway
Marysville, OH 45150
(513) 246-5903
Contact: Norm
Recruiting Specialty: General

MASON

Messina Management Systems
4770 Duke Drive, Suite 140
Mason, OH 45040
(513) 398-3331
Contact: Mr. Vincent Messina
Recruiting Specialty: Accounting and finance, computer science, engineering and manufacturing

MAUMEE

AIM Executive Recruiting
1760 Manley Raod
Maumee, OH 43537
(419) 893-2400
Contact: Mr. Jeffrey DePerro
Recruiting Specialty: Accounting and finance, engineering and human resources

Flowers & Associates
1446 S. Reynolds, Suite 112
Maumee, OH 43537
(419) 893-4816
Contact: Mr. William Ross
Minimum Salary Placed: $35,000
Recruiting Specialty: General

MEDINA

Cross-Jordan Corporation
4986 Gateway Drive
Medina, OH 44256
(330) 723-7203
Contact: Mr. Al Ferris
Minimum Salary Placed: $25,000
Recruiting Specialty: Technical disciplines in engineering and plant management

MENTOR

Downing & Downing
6988 Spinach Avenue
Mentor, OH 44060
(216) 255-1177
Contact: Mr. Gus Downing
Minimum Salary Placed: $25,000
Recruiting Specialty: Retailing

Maze Recruiters & Associates USA
7547 Mentor Avenue, Suite 104
Mentor, OH 44060
(216) 269-8511
Contact: Mr. Jim Gunn
Recruiting Specialty: Engineering, manufacturing, and human resources

Personalized Career Service
5970 Heisley Road, Suite 150
Mentor, OH 44060
(216) 352-7937
Contact: Ms. R. Hentemann
Minimum Salary Placed: $45,000
Recruiting Specialty: Computer science and engineering

Quality Search
P.O. Box 215
Mentor, OH 44061
(216) 428-4556
Contact: Mr. Robert Johnson
Minimum Salary Placed: $30,000
Recruiting Specialty: Technical disciplines in manufacturing and high technology

MIAMISBURG

Aim Executive Consulting Services
445 Byers
Miamisburg, OH 45430
(513) 859-1717
Contact: Mr. Wayne Voris
Minimum Salary Placed: $70,000
Recruiting Specialty: General

MIDDLETOWN

Aegis Associates
4826 Carlow
Middletown, OH 45042
(513) 424-8502
Contact: Mr. Don Henry
Recruiting Specialty: Technical in paper, steel and plastics

MILFORD

Newcomb-Desmond & Associates
73 Powhatton Drive
Milford, OH 45150
(513) 831-9522
Contact: Mr. Mike Desmond
Minimum Salary Placed: $40,000
Recruiting Specialty: General

MILLERSBURG

Patterson Personal Associates
156 West Jackson Street
Millersburg, OH 44654
(330) 674-4040
Contact: Ms. B. Patterson
Minimum Salary Placed: $40,000
Recruiting Specialty: Engineering and technical disciplines in manufacturing

MONROE FALLS

Heartland Personnel
253 Steeplechase Lane
Monroe Falls, OH 44262
(330) 633-6773
Contact: Ms. Theresa Wilson
Minimum Salary Placed: $30,000
Recruiting Specialty: Food and beverages

NEWARK

Dennis C. McKnew & Company
815 Mount Vernon Road
Newark, OH 43055
(614) 366-6338
Contact: Mr. Dennis McKnew
Recruiting Specialty: Engineering

NILES

G.E. Hassell Associates
P.O. Box 471
Niles, OH 44446
(330) 652-5871
Contact: Mr. Gordon Hassell
Recruiting Specialty: Engineering, manufacturing and quality control

NORTH OLMSTED

Lear Group
Clock Tower Office Suite 1, 660 Dover
North Olmsted, OH 44141
(216) 892-9828
Contact: Mr. Larry Gregg
Minimum Salary Placed: $25,000
Recruiting Specialty: Engineering, marketing and sales

NORTH RIDGEVILLE

Management Recruiters
34100 Center Ridge Road, Suite 110
North Ridgeville, OH 44039
(216) 327-2800
Contact: Mr. James Spellacy
Minimum Salary Placed: $20,000
Recruiting Specialty: General

NORTHFIELD

Griffiths and Associates
386 Apple Hill Drive
Northfield, OH 44067
(216) 467-3131
Contact: Mr. B. Griffiths
Minimum Salary Placed: $40,000
Recruiting Specialty: Manufacturing

OSTRANDER

Deffet Group Inc.
7801 Marysville Road
Ostrander, OH 43061
(614) 666-7600
Contact: Mr. D. Deffet
Minimum Salary Placed: $25,000
Recruiting Specialty: Healthcare

PATASKALA

Icon Management
621 W. Broad Street, Suite 2B
Pataskala, OH 43062
(614) 927-4404
Contact: Mr. Bob Bremer
Minimum Salary Placed: $30,000
Recruiting Specialty: MIS

PERRYSBURG

Renhill Group
27511 Holiday Lane
Perrysburg, OH 43551
(419) 874-2203
Recruiting Specialty: General

POWELL

Don Gopp and Associates
1595 Wren Lane
Powell, OH 43065
(614) 848-8280
Contact: Mr. Don Gopp
Minimum Salary Placed: $35,000
Recruiting Specialty: Computer programming and engineering

REYNOLDSBURG

J.W. Barleycorn & Associates
1614 Lancaster Avenue
Reynoldsburg, OH 43068
(614) 861-4400
Contact: Mr. James Barleycorn
Minimum Salary Placed: $50,000
Recruiting Specialty: General

ROCKY RIVER

Technical Search Associates
20325 Center Ridge Road, Suite 622
Rocky River, OH 44116
(216) 356-0880
Contact: Mr. John Brunschwig
Minimum Salary Placed: $40,000
Recruiting Specialty: Electrical, mechanical and manufacturing

SHAKER HEIGHTS

Dise & Company
20600 Chagrin Boulevard
Shaker Heights, OH 44122
(216) 752-1700
Contact: Mr. Ralph A. Dise, Jr.
Recruiting Specialty: Accounting and finance, banking, and manufacturing

H.C. Smith Ltd.
20600 Chagrin Boulevard, Suite 200
Shaker Heights, OH 44122
(216) 752-9966
Contact: Mr. Herbert Smith
Minimum Salary Placed: $70,000
Recruiting Specialty: General

SIDNEY

Pete DeLuke and Assoc., Inc.
113 N. Ohio Ave., Suite 204
Sidney, OH 45365
(513) 497-1515
Contact: Mr. Pete DeLuke
Recruiting Specialty: Manufacturing, human resources, and engineering

Sutton Associates
1200 Stephens Road
Sidney, OH 45365
(513) 497-1700
Contact: Mr. T. Sutton
Minimum Salary Placed: $25,000
Recruiting Specialty: General

SOLON

Management Recruiters
P.O. Box 39361
Solon, OH 44139
(216) 248-7300
Contact: Ms. Kim Barnett
Minimum Salary Placed: $20,000
Recruiting Specialty: General

SPRINGFIELD

F.L.A.G.
625 E. County Line Road
Springfield, OH 45502
(513) 342-0200
Contact: Mr. Tom Warren
Minimum Salary Placed: $40,000
Recruiting Specialty: Sales and R&D in chemicals and fuel products

STOW

J. Joseph and Associates
3809 Darrow Road
Stow, OH 44224
(216) 688-2101
Minimum Salary Placed: $25,000
Recruiting Specialty: Outside sales

SYLVANIA

Eagle Group
5800 Monroe Street
Sylvania, OH 43560
(419) 882-8006
Contact: Mr. Dave Kleeberger
Minimum Salary Placed: $25,000
Recruiting Specialty: Manufacturing and materials

TERRACE PARK

Tyler Scott Inc.
313 Rugby Avenue
Terrace Park, OH 45174
(513) 831-7603
Minimum Salary Placed: $40,000
Recruiting Specialty: Chemical engineering

TOLEDO

Avca-Tech Service Inc.
2735 N. Holland Sylvania, Suite B3
Toledo, OH 43615
(419) 534-6400
Contact: Mr. K. Wenninger
Minimum Salary Placed: $40,000
Recruiting Specialty: Technical disciplines in mechanical and industrial structures

Corporate Research
3540 Secor Road
Toledo, OH 43606
(419) 535-1941
Contact: Mr. B. Macraury
Recruiting Specialty: General

Counsel Search Company
124 N. Summit Street, Suite 305
Toledo, OH 43604
(419) 242-8696
Contact: Mr. William Falvey
Minimum Salary Placed: $60,000
Recruiting Specialty: Legal and human resources

R. Green & Associates, Inc.
3454 Oak Alley Court, Suite 507
Toledo, OH 43606
(419) 534-2800
Contact: Ms. Rita Green
Minimum Salary Placed: $40,000
Recruiting Specialty: General

The Human Resources Group, LTD.
1995 Tremainsville Road
Toledo, OH 43613
(419) 474-0536
Contact: Mr. Mark Craver
Recruiting Specialty: MIS and IT

Interconnect Technical Services
911 Madison Avenue
Toledo, OH 43624
(419) 259-3656
Contact: Mr. Roger Radeloff
Recruiting Specialty: Computer science, engineering, human resources, and manufacturing

Management Recruiters
350 S. Reynolds Road
Toledo, OH 43615
(419) 537-1100
Contact: Mr. Gary Fruchtman
Minimum Salary Placed: $40,000
Recruiting Specialty: General

TROY

Granger, Counts & Associates
728 Trade Square West
Troy, OH 45373
(513) 339-1119
Contact: Mr. Robert Counts
Minimum Salary Placed: $30,000
Recruiting Specialty: General

Schafer Jones Associates
1001 S. Dorset Road
Troy, OH 45373
(513) 335-1885
Contact: Mr. Paul Jones
Minimum Salary Placed: $25,000
Recruiting Specialty: General

WESTERVILLE

Five Star Temps, Inc.
133 S. State
Westerville, OH 43081
(614) 794-3101
Contact: Mr. Joe Lang
Recruiting Specialty: General

Guthoff & Associates
575 Copeland Mill Road, Suite 1B
Westerville, OH 43081
(614) 794-9950
Contact: Mr. Pete Guthoff
Minimum Salary Placed: $35,000
Recruiting Specialty: Manufacturing, distribution and telecommunications

Management Recruiters
676 Enterprise Drive, Suite B
Westerville, OH 43081
(614) 785-1400

Contact: Mr. Richard Harkins
Minimum Salary Placed: $20,000
Recruiting Specialty: General

R M Associates
403 Venture Drive
Westerville, OH 43081
(614) 764-1587
Contact: Mr. Richard Marling
Minimum Salary Placed: $50,000
Recruiting Specialty: General

Selective Search Inc.
659 Park Meadow Road, Suite 2
Westerville, OH 43081
(614) 899-0575
Contact: Mr. Tom Madine
Minimum Salary Placed: $25,000
Recruiting Specialty: General

Warner & Associates, Inc.
101 E. College Avenue
Westerville, OH 43081
(614) 891-9003
Contact: Mr. Thomas Warner
Minimum Salary Placed: $40,000
Recruiting Specialty: Manufacturing

WESTLAKE

Quality Executive Search
24549 Detroit Road
Westlake, OH 44012
(216) 899-5070
Contact: Mr. Joe Drapcho
Minimum Salary Placed: $30,000
Recruiting Specialty: Raw materials, electronics and technical

WICKLIFFE

Management Recruiters
30432 Euclid Avenue, Suite 205
Wickliffe, OH 44092
(216) 946-2355
Contact: Mr. Ronald Sterling
Recruiting Specialty: Banking

WILLOUGHBY HILLS

Aim Executive Inc.
35000 Chardon Road
Willoughby Hills, OH 44094
(216) 975-0444
Contact: Mr. Thomas Beers
Minimum Salary Placed: $25,000
Recruiting Specialty: Manufacturing,
plastics and plant management

Benchmark Systems Group
P.O. Box 281
Willoughby Hills, OH 44094
(216) 975-1400
Contact: Mr. Brian McCollum
Recruiting Specialty: Engineering and
manufacturing

ProSearch, Inc.
2550 SOM Center Road
Willoughby Hills, OH 44094
(216) 585-9099
Contact: Mr. Cary Wayne
Minimum Salary Placed: $40,000
Recruiting Specialty: General

Terry Richards, CPC
36 Public Square
Willoughby Hills, OH 44094
(216) 918-1800
Contact: Mr. Terry Richards
Recruiting Specialty: Distribution and
manufacturing

WORTHINGTON

Arthur Adams & Associates
1046 Ravine Ridge Drive, Suite 200
Worthington, OH 43055
(614) 846-5075
Contact: Mr. Arthur Adams
Minimum Salary Placed: $40,000
Recruiting Specialty: Sales and system en-
gineering in computer networking

Gammill Group
500 W. Wilson Bridge Road, Suite 316
Worthington, OH 43285
(614) 848-7726
Contact: Mr. R. Gammill
Minimum Salary Placed: $25,000
Recruiting Specialty: Healthcare

Grover & Associates
1310 Hickory Ridge
Worthington, OH 43235
(614) 885-8917
Contact: Mr. James Grover
Minimum Salary Placed: $70,000
Recruiting Specialty: General

R.E. Lowe Associates, Inc.
3080 Ravines Edge Court
Worthington, OH 43235
(614) 436-6650
Contact: Mr. Richard Lowe
Minimum Salary Placed: $40,000
Recruiting Specialty: Healthcare, financial services, manufacturing and distribution

Michael Thomas Inc.
100 Old Wilson Bridge Road, Suite 207
Worthington, OH 43085
(614) 846-0926
Contact: Mr. M. Becaert
Minimum Salary Placed: $25,000
Recruiting Specialty: Data processing,
MIS and accounting

Quicksearch
893 High Street
Worthington, OH 43085
(614) 847-0356
Minimum Salary Placed: $25,000
Recruiting Specialty: General

YOUNGSTOWN

Callos Personnel Services
5083 Market Street
Youngstown, OH 44512
(330) 788-4001
Contact: Mr. Eric Sutton
Recruiting Specialty: General

Central Employment Service
70 McKinley Way W., Suite 20
Youngstown, OH 44514
(330) 757-0096
Contact: Ms. Eleanore Semancik
Recruiting Specialty: General

KBK Management Associates
5500 Market Street, Suite 92
Youngstown, OH 44512
(330) 788-6508
Contact: Ms. Debbie Taylor
Recruiting Specialty: Metals and data
processing

Michael Latas & Associates, Inc.
P.O. Box 4503
Youngstown, OH 44515
(330) 799-9445
Contact: Mr. Samuel Rusnov
Minimum Salary Placed: $40,000
Recruiting Specialty: Material handling

Fran Scott Technical Personnel
6960 Market Street, Suite 111
Youngstown, OH 44512
(330) 629-8333
Contact: Ms. Fran Scott
Minimum Salary Placed: $35,000
Recruiting Specialty: Technical disciplines

O K L A H O M A

ARDMORE

Dunhill Personnel
1500 West Broadway
Ardmore, OK 73401
(405) 226-6710
Contact: Mr. Larry Kalesnik
Minimum Salary Placed: $25,000
Recruiting Specialty: General

DEL CITY

Healthcare Resources Group
3945 SE 15th Street, Suite 101
Del City, OK 73115
(405) 677-7872
Contact: Mr. Dan Smith
Recruiting Specialty: Healthcare and
biotechnology

EDMOND

Dalton Boggs and Associates
P.O. Box 2288
Edmond, OK 73083
(405) 348-1654
Contact: Mr. Dalton Boggs
Minimum Salary Placed: $25,000
Recruiting Specialty: Managed healthcare

Health Specialties
Box 7081
Edmond, OK 73013
(405) 943-1231
Contact: Mr. Kenny Bryant
Minimum Salary Placed: $75,000
Recruiting Specialty: Physicians

NORMAN

Banker Personnel Service
2211 Westpark Drive
Norman, OK 73069
(405) 364-4322
Contact: Mr. L. Bentley
Minimum Salary Placed: $80,000
Recruiting Specialty: Banking and finance

OKLAHOMA CITY

Dunhill Professional Search
5500 N. Western, Suite 278
Oklahoma City, OK 73118
(405) 330-0590
Contact: Mr. Michael Dore
Minimum Salary Placed: $25,000
Recruiting Specialty: General

Executive Resources Group Inc.
6051 N Brookline Avenue
Oklahoma City, OK 73112
(405) 843-8344
Contact: Mr. George Orr
Minimum Salary Placed: $25,000
Recruiting Specialty: General

Express Temporary Service
5909 NW Expressway Street, Suite 150
Oklahoma City, OK 73132
(405) 720-4606
Contact: Mr. R. Funk
Recruiting Specialty: General

James Farris Associates
4900 Richmond Square, Suite 201
Oklahoma City, OK 73118
(405) 848-0535
Contact: Mr. James Farris
Minimum Salary Placed: $40,000
Recruiting Specialty: General

Genie Personnel Service
351 N Air Depot Boulevard, Suite Q
Oklahoma City, OK 73110
(405) 947-2222
Contact: Ms. J. Mercer
Minimum Salary Placed: $25,000
Recruiting Specialty: General

Management Recruiters
3441 W. Memorial Road, Suite 4
Oklahoma City, OK 73134
(405) 752-8848
Contact: Mr. Gary Roy
Minimum Salary Placed: $20,000
Recruiting Specialty: General

Management Search, Inc.
6051 N. Brookline, Suite 125
Oklahoma City, OK 73116
(405) 842-3173
Contact: Mr. David Orwig
Minimum Salary Placed: $25,000
Recruiting Specialty: Agriculture

Robert Half International
119 N Robinson Avenue, Suite 350
Oklahoma City, OK 73102
(405) 236-0880
Contact: MS. D. Moore
Recruiting Specialty: Accounting and finance

Eddie Robertson and Associates
2525 NW Expressway Street, Suite 102
Oklahoma City, OK 73112
(405) 840-1991
Contact: Ms. E. Robertson
Minimum Salary Placed: $20,000
Recruiting Specialty: Data processing

Sales Careers
5929 N. May Avenue
Oklahoma City, OK 73112
(405) 848-6858
Contact: Mr. L. Toth
Minimum Salary Placed: $25,000
Recruiting Specialty: Sales

Sales Consultants
6525 N. Meridian, Suite 212
Oklahoma City, OK 73116
(405) 721-6400
Contact: Ms. Darla Emig
Minimum Salary Placed: $20,000
Recruiting Specialty: Sales

TULSA

Andrews and Associates Inc.
45000 S. Garnette Street
Tulsa, OK 74146
(918) 664-3537
Contact: Mr. J. Andrews
Minimum Salary Placed: $25,000
Recruiting Specialty: State and local taxation

Bank Search
5731 E 72nd Place
Tulsa, OK 74136
(918) 496-9477
Contact: Mr. D. Cunningham
Minimum Salary Placed: $25,000
Recruiting Specialty: Banking

Joy Reed Belt & Associates, Inc.
P.O. Box 700688
Tulsa, OK 74170
(405) 748-8844
Contact: Ms. Deborah Hughes
Minimum Salary Placed: $40,000
Recruiting Specialty: General

Bullock and Company
5800 E. Skelly Drive, Suite 712
Tulsa, OK 74135
(918) 665-0735
Contact: Ms. Janet Bullock
Minimum Salary Placed: $25,000
Recruiting Specialty: Accounting, finance, data processing and computers

Clawson and Company
5840 S. Memorial Drive, Suite 3005
Tulsa, OK 74145
(918) 664-4203

Contact: Mr. Dan Clawson
Minimum Salary Placed: $25,000
Recruiting Specialty: General

DP Select Personnel Inc.
9717 E. 42nd Street
Tulsa, OK 74146
(918) 663-3847
Minimum Salary Placed: $20,000
Recruiting Specialty: Data processing

Dunhill Personnel
10159 E. 11th Street, Suite 370
Tulsa, OK 74128
(918) 832-8857
Contact: Ms. Joy M. Porrello
Minimum Salary Placed: $40,000
Recruiting Specialty: Credit card services

J. Gifford, Inc.
5310 E. 31st Street, Suite 514
Tulsa, OK 74135
(918) 665-2626
Contact: Mr. James Gifford
Minimum Salary Placed: $30,000
Recruiting Specialty: Engineering

Hunt Patton & Brazeal, Inc.
2250 East 73rd Street, Suite 120
Tulsa, OK 74136
(918) 492-6910
Contact: Mr. Michael Patton
Minimum Salary Placed: $20,000
Recruiting Specialty: General

International Search
9717 E. 42nd Street, Suite 210
Tulsa, OK 74146
(918) 627-9070
Contact: Mr. W. Smith
Minimum Salary Placed: $30,000
Recruiting Specialty: Engineering and
other technical disciplines

Management Recruiters
5801 E. 41st, Suite 440
Tulsa, OK 74135
(918) 663-6744
Contact: Mr. Tony Wolters
Minimum Salary Placed: $20,000
Recruiting Specialty: General

Overland Management Corporation
7666 W. 61st Street
Tulsa, OK 74131
(918) 254-5444
Contact: Mr. John Engdahl
Minimum Salary Placed: $25,000
Recruiting Specialty: General

Polston Company
4500 S. Garnett Road, Suite 205
Tulsa, OK 74146
(918) 628-1311
Contact: Ms. Carolyn Polston
Minimum Salary Placed: $25,000
Recruiting Specialty: Technical

The Reality Group, Inc.
5555 E. 71st Street, Suite 6300
Tulsa, OK 74135
(918) 622-0228
Contact: Mr. Larry Sims
Recruiting Specialty: Environmental and
hazardous waste

**A. Lloyd Richards Personnel Services,
Inc.**
507 S. Main Street, Suite 502
Tulsa, OK 74103
(918) 582-5251
Contact: Mr. Lloyd Richards
Minimum Salary Placed: $25,000
Recruiting Specialty: General

Robert Half International
1 W 3rd Street, Suite 1120
Tulsa, OK 74103
(918) 585-1700
Contact: Mr. D. Rowland
Recruiting Specialty: Accounting and finance

Sales Consultants
5801 E. 41st Street, Suite 440
Tulsa, OK 74135
(918) 663-6744
Contact: Mr. Tony Wolters
Minimum Salary Placed: $20,000
Recruiting Specialty: Sales

Snelling Personnel Services, Inc.
7633 East 63rd Place, Suite 160
Tulsa, OK 74133
(918) 453-0802
Contact: Mr. Lewis Jones
Recruiting Specialty: Engineering and computers

Sumner Ray Technical Resources
4775 S. Harvard, #D
Tulsa, OK 74135
(918) 742-9760
Contact: Ms. D. Ray
Minimum Salary Placed: $35,000
Recruiting Specialty: Engineering and drafting

Tax Search Inc.
6102 S. Memorial Drive
Tulsa, OK 74133
(918) 252-3100
Contact: Mr. Anthony Santiago
Recruiting Specialty: Taxation

U.S. Gas Search
5215 E 71st Street
Tulsa, OK 74136
(918) 492-6668
Contact: Mr. K. Louderback
Minimum Salary Placed: $30,000
Recruiting Specialty: Petro and natural gas

Villareal & Associates, Inc.
427 S. Boston, Suite 215
Tulsa, OK 74103
(918) 584-0808
Contact: Mr. Morey Villareal
Minimum Salary Placed: $40,000
Recruiting Specialty: General

John Wylie Associates, Inc.
1727 E. 71st Street
Tulsa, OK 74136
(918) 496-2100
Contact: Mr. John Wylie
Minimum Salary Placed: $25,000
Recruiting Specialty: General

O R E G O N

BEAVERTON

John M. Clarke & Associates
11855 SW Ridgecrest Drive, Suite 205
Beaverton, OR 97005
(503) 627-0820
Contact: Mr. John Clarke
Minimum Salary Placed: $40,000
Recruiting Specialty: Banking

John T. Cole and Associates
4800 SW Griffith Drive
Beaverton, OR 97005
(503) 645-8647
Contact: Mr. John Cole
Minimum Salary Placed: $25,000
Recruiting Specialty: Forestry

Computer Recruiters Corporation
6700 SW 105th Avenue
Beaverton, OR 97005
(503) 643-2464
Contact: Mr. C. Conner
Minimum Salary Placed: $25,000
Recruiting Specialty: Computers

Hackenschmidt Weaver and Fox
13747 SW Farmington Road
Beaverton, OR 97005
(503) 644-7744
Contact: Mr. Bob Weaver
Minimum Salary Placed: $35,000
Recruiting Specialty: Technical disciplines in the processing of metals, pulp and paper

Curt Sands Recruiting
Box 25365
Beaverton, OR 97005
(503) 643-0193
Contact: Mr. Curt Sands
Minimum Salary Placed: $25,000
Recruiting Specialty: General

BEND

Ardent Group Inc.
1883 NW Wall Street, Suite D
Bend, OR 97701
(541) 383-0973

Contact: Mr. Peter May
Recruiting Specialty: Communications and computers

Executives Worldwide
P.O. Box 145
Bend, OR 97709
(503) 385-5405
Contact: Mr. Cotter Ray Gould
Recruiting Specialty: Environmental, law and biotechnology

The O'Kane Group
25 NW Minnesota Avenue, Suite 4
Bend, OR 97701
(503) 389-5127
Contact: Ms. Barbara Stoefen
Recruiting Specialty: Physicians

CLACKAMAS

Search Northwest Associates
10117 SE Sunnyside Road, Suite F727
Clackamas, OR 97015
(503) 654-1487
Contact: Mr. Douglas Jansen
Minimum Salary Placed: $30,000
Recruiting Specialty: Technical disciplines in chemicals, manufacturing, environmental and high technology

CORVALLIS

Dunhill Professional Search
P.O. Box 1436
Corvallis, OR 97333
(503) 757-3014
Contact: Mr. Michael Riley
Minimum Salary Placed: $25,000
Recruiting Specialty: General

Heartbeat Medical Executive Search
425 Madison Avenue, Suite M
Corvallis, OR 97333
(541) 752-5557
Minimum Salary Placed: $25,000
Recruiting Specialty: Medical device

EUGENE

Management Recruiters
927 Country Club Road, Suite 175
Eugene, OR 97401
(503) 345-4211
Contact: Mr. Tom Hirsch
Recruiting Specialty: Product development, engineering in high technology

Pacific Coast Recruiters
Box 7080, Suite 144
Eugene, OR 97401
(503) 345-6866
Contact: Mr. Dave Watson
Recruiting Specialty: Insurance

Robert William James & Associates
977 Garfield Street
Eugene, OR 97402
(541) 686-0003
Contact: Mr. Dennis Murphy
Minimum Salary Placed: $25,000
Recruiting Specialty: General

HILLSBORO

Furlong Search, Inc.
634 E. Main Street
Hillsboro, OR 97123
(503) 640-3221
Contact: Mr. James Furlong
Minimum Salary Placed: $60,000
Recruiting Specialty: Electronics

MRD Group
21960 NW Quatama Road
Hillsboro, OR 97124
(503) 693-7666
Contact: Mr. Edward Doran
Minimum Salary Placed: $25,000
Recruiting Specialty: IT

Process Automation Personnel
16435 SW Hillsboro Highway
Hillsboro, OR 97123
(503) 628-2703
Minimum Salary Placed: $25,000
Recruiting Specialty: Real time process control

JUNCTION CITY

RBW Associates
30352 Lassen Lane
Junction City, OR 97448
(541) 688-9212
Contact: Mr. Ray Wheeler
Minimum Salary Placed: $25,000
Recruiting Specialty: Pulp and paper and related industries

LAKE OSWEGO

Brentwood Group Ltd.
9 Monroe Parkway
Lake Oswego, OR 97035
(503) 697-8136
Contact: Ms. K. Blackney
Minimum Salary Placed: $25,000
Recruiting Specialty: High technology, healthcare and insurance

Dunnahoe and Associates
15800 Boones Ferry Road, Suite C202
Lake Oswego, OR 97035
(503) 699-1611
Contact: Mr. Dick Dunnahoe
Minimum Salary Placed: $40,000
Recruiting Specialty: General

Murphy, Symonds & Stowell Search, Inc.
1 Centerpointe Drive, Suite 570
Lake Oswego, OR 97035
(503) 524-8101
Contact: Ms. Linda Kozlowski
Minimum Salary Placed: $50,000
Recruiting Specialty: General

Terry Associates
16016 SW Boones Ferry Road
Lake Oswego, OR 97035
(503) 636-5054
Contact: Ms. M. Terry
Minimum Salary Placed: $25,000
Recruiting Specialty: General

MEDFORD

Best Agency Personnel Service
820 Crater Avenue, Suite 208
Medford, OR 97504
(503) 734-2013
Contact: Mr. G. Canape
Minimum Salary Placed: $25,000
Recruiting Specialty: General

PORTLAND

Adams and Associates
121 SW Morrison Street, Suite 430
Portland, OR 97204
(503) 224-5870

Contact: Ms. M. Fallon
Recruiting Specialty: Office and accounting support

Auguston and Associates Inc.
510 SW 3rd Avenue, Suite 400
Portland, OR 97204
(503) 299-6298
Contact: Ms. Gina Auguston
Minimum Salary Placed: $25,000
Recruiting Specialty: Medical devices

D. Brown & Associates, Inc.
610 SW Alder, Suite 1111
Portland, OR 97205
(503) 224-6860
Contact: Mr. Dennis Brown
Minimum Salary Placed: $30,000
Recruiting Specialty: Engineering, MIS, data processing and accounting

Corporate Builders, Inc.
812 SW Washington, Suite 660
Portland, OR 97205
(503) 223-4344
Contact: Mr. William Meysing
Recruiting Specialty: Construction

Corporate Finance Search
614 SW 11th Avenue
Portland, OR 97205
(503) 224-4525
Contact: Ms. Carol Burke
Minimum Salary Placed: $25,000
Recruiting Specialty: Finance and accounting

ETSI
13500 SW 72nd Street
Portland, OR 97229
(503) 684-9100

Contact: Mr. Gary Nashif
Minimum Salary Placed: $25,000
Recruiting Specialty: General

Forum Associates
4520 SW Water Avenue, Suite 201
Portland, OR 97201
(503) 220-4075
Contact: Mr. Chris Rickford
Minimum Salary Placed: $50,000
Recruiting Specialty: High technology

GPSA
9135 SW 57th Avenue
Portland, OR 97219
(503) 244-8762
Contact: Mr. Tom Martin
Minimum Salary Placed: $40,000
Recruiting Specialty: Engineering, science and technical

Hale Musat and Associates Ltd.
506 SW 6th Avenue
Portland, OR 97204
(503) 223-9190
Contact: Mr. Dominique Masut
Minimum Salary Placed: $25,000
Recruiting Specialty: General

Lee Koehn Associates, Inc.
4380 SW Macadam Avenue, Suite 185
Portland, OR 97201
(503) 224-9067
Contact: Mr. Lee Koehn
Minimum Salary Placed: $60,000
Recruiting Specialty: General

Management Recruiters
2020 Lloyd Center
Portland, OR 97232
(503) 287-8701

Contact: Mr. Larry Engelgau
Minimum Salary Placed: $30,000
Recruiting Specialty: Technical

Northwest Legal Search
2701 NW Vaughn, Suite 1910
Portland, OR 97210
(503) 224-9601
Contact: Mr. L. Green
Minimum Salary Placed: $50,000
Recruiting Specialty: Attorneys

Prior Martech Associates
707 SW Washington Street, Suite 1000
Portland, OR 97205
(503) 226-4985
Contact: Mr. Donald Walker
Minimum Salary Placed: $50,000
Recruiting Specialty: General

Douglas Reiter Company
1221 SW Yamhill, Suite 301A
Portland, OR 97204
(503) 228-6916
Contact: Mr. Douglas Reiter
Minimum Salary Placed: $50,000
Recruiting Specialty: General

Robert William James & Associates
621 SW Morrison, Suite 500
Portland, OR 97205
(503) 224-5505
Contact: Ms. Deborah LeBer
Recruiting Specialty: General

Sales Consultants
5100 SW Macadam Avenue, Suite 270
Portland, OR 97201
(503) 241-1230
Contact: Mr. Paul Maduell
Minimum Salary Placed: $20,000
Recruiting Specialty: Sales

Sanford Rose Associates
10200 SW Eastridge, Suite 200
Portland, OR 97225
(503) 297-9191
Contact: Mr. Jack Stiles
Minimum Salary Placed: $40,000
Recruiting Specialty: Manufacturing,
food, computer and semiconductors

Search North America, Inc.
620 SW Fifth, Suite 925
Portland, OR 97204
(503) 222-6461
Contact: Mr. Carl Jansen
Minimum Salary Placed: $35,000
Recruiting Specialty: Wood products,
pulp and paper

Source EDP
10220 SW Greensburg Road, Suite 625
Portland, OR 97223
(503) 768-4546
Minimum Salary Placed: $20,000
Recruiting Specialty: Computers

Source Engineering
10220 SW Greensburg Road, Suite 625
Portland, OR 97223
(503) 768-4546
Contact: Mr. George Bartosh
Recruiting Specialty: Engineering

Summit Staffing
149 SE 3rd Avenue, Suite 100
Portland, OR 97123
(503) 640-4288
Contact: Mr. Brent Weide
Minimum Salary Placed: $25,000
Recruiting Specialty: Civil engineering
support

Technical Solutions, Inc.
12990 NW Sue Street
Portland, OR 97219
(503) 626-4739
Contact: Mr. Jeff Yang
Minimum Salary Placed: $25,000
Recruiting Specialty: High technology
and software

Wolf Environmental Group
909 SW Saint Clair Avenue
Portland, OR 97205
(503) 241-0881
Contact: Ms. Judy Stockton
Minimum Salary Placed: $40,000
Recruiting Specialty: Engineering and environmental

Woodworth International Group
620 SW Fifth Avenue, Suite 1225
Portland, OR 97204
(503) 225-5000
Contact: Ms. Gail Martwick
Minimum Salary Placed: $40,000
Recruiting Specialty: General

SALEM

Advance Personnel Agency
441 Union Street NE
Salem, OR 97301
(503) 581-8906
Contact: Phil
Minimum Salary Placed: $20,000
Recruiting Specialty: General

PENNSYLVANIA

ALLENTOWN

Premier Placement Inc.
P.O. Box 3436
Allentown, PA 18106
(610) 395-9123
Contact: Ms. Laura Schmieder
Minimum Salary Placed: $35,000
Recruiting Specialty: Marketing and engineering

S-H-S of Allentown
1401 N. Cedar Crest Boulevard, Suite 56
Allentown, PA 18104
(610) 437-5551
Contact: Mr. Donald Hall
Minimum Salary Placed: $25,000
Recruiting Specialty: Mineral, construction, chemicals and printing

Lyons-Pruitt, International
2020 Downey Flake Lane
Allentown, PA 18103
(610) 791-0110
Contact: Mr. Jim Pruitt
Minimum Salary Placed: $25,000
Recruiting Specialty: General

ALLISON PARK

Becker, Norton & Company
4088 Alpha Drive
Allison Park, PA 15101
(412) 486-5553
Contact: Mr. Robert Becker
Minimum Salary Placed: $60,000
Recruiting Specialty: General

ARDMORE

Molloy Associates
700 Pont Reading Road
Ardmore, PA 19003
(610) 649-7112
Contact: Mr. G. Parrotto
Minimum Salary Placed: $25,000
Recruiting Specialty: Equipment leasing and finance

BALA CYNWYD

Fernow Associates
191 Presidential Boulevard, Suite BN13
Bala Cynwyd, PA 19004
(215) 664-2281
Contact: Mr. Charles Fernow
Minimum Salary Placed: $35,000
Recruiting Specialty: General

Management Resources
P.O. Box 243
Bala Cynwyd, PA 19004
(215) 449-4730
Contact: Mr. Harry Dunlavy
Minimum Salary Placed: $40,000
Recruiting Specialty: R&D in chemicals and environmental

Retail Recruiters/Spectrum Consultants, Inc.
111 Presidential Boulevard, Suite 211
Bala Cynwyd, PA 19004
(215) 667-6565
Contact: Ms. Shirlee Berman
Recruiting Specialty: Retail and healthcare

The Robinson Group, Ltd.
725 Conshohocken State Road
Bala Cynwyd, PA 19004
(215) 668-9311
Minimum Salary Placed: $30,000
Recruiting Specialty: MIS and high technology

BEAVER

Robert McClure and Associates
P.O. Box 497
Beaver, PA 15009
(412) 922-6936
Contact: Mr. Robert McClure
Recruiting Specialty: General

BENSALEM

Professional Placement Specialists, Inc.
3070 Bristol Pike, Building II, Suite 209
Bensalem, PA 19020
(215) 638-9777
Contact: Dr. Kenneth Cohen
Minimum Salary Placed: $45,000
Recruiting Specialty: Pharmaceuticals and healthcare

Select Personnel Inc.
3070 Bristol Pike, Suite 205
Bensalem, PA 19020
(215) 245-4800
Recruiting Specialty: General

BERWYN

Empire International
1147 Lancaster Avenue
Berwyn, PA 19312
(215) 647-7976

Contact: Mr. Charles Combe
Minimum Salary Placed: $50,000
Recruiting Specialty: Technical disciplines

BETHLEHEM

J-Rand Search
2 Bethlehem Plaza
Bethlehem, PA 18018
(610) 867-4649
Contact: Mr. Michael Watts
Minimum Salary Placed: $25,000
Recruiting Specialty: Finance, human resources, and operations management

J. Kauffman Resources
1056 Jeter Avenue
Bethlehem, PA 18015
(610) 867-5997
Contact: Ms. Jane Kauffman
Minimum Salary Placed: $30,000
Recruiting Specialty: Healthcare and environmental

Kelly Associates
510 E. Fourth Street, Suite 100
Bethlehem, PA 18015
(610) 868-6831
Contact: Mr. Richard Kelly
Minimum Salary Placed: $40,000
Recruiting Specialty: General

Management Recruiters
1414 Millard Street, Suite 102
Bethlehem, PA 18018
(610) 974-9770
Contact: Mr. Fred Meyer
Minimum Salary Placed: $20,000
Recruiting Specialty: General

BIRCHRUNVILLE

Lee Calhoon & Company, Inc.
P.O. Box 201, 1621 Birchrun Road
Birchrunville, PA 19421
(610) 469-9000
Contact: Mr. Lee Calhoon
Minimum Salary Placed: $75,000
Recruiting Specialty: Healthcare

BROOMALL

John McKenna Associates
6 Elm Circle
Broomall, PA 19008
(610) 353-1660
Contact: Mr. John McKenna
Minimum Salary Placed: $25,000
Recruiting Specialty: General

BRYN MAWR

Conrad Associates
740 E. Haverford Road
Bryn Mawr, PA 19010
(610) 526-9773
Contact: Mr. Herb Conrad
Minimum Salary Placed: $35,000
Recruiting Specialty: Pharmaceuticals

McMahon Company
1084 E. Lancaster Avenue
Bryn Mawr, PA 19010
(610) 527-5757
Minimum Salary Placed: $25,000
Recruiting Specialty: General

BUTLER

Robert Hoffman and Associates
6216 Old Route 8
Butler, PA 16001
(412) 586-7324
Contact: Mr. Robert Hoffman
Minimum Salary Placed: $25,000
Recruiting Specialty: General

M.K. & Associates
422 N. Main Street, Suite 2A
Butler, PA 16001
(412) 285-7474
Contact: Mr. John Mossman
Recruiting Specialty: Food and beverages

CAMP HILL

The Byrnes Group
395 Saint John's Church Road
Camp Hill, PA 17011
(717) 761-0713
Contact: Ms. Pat Burns
Minimum Salary Placed: $18,000
Recruiting Specialty: Clerical and office
support

Sales Consultants
702 Lisburn Road
Camp Hill, PA 17011
(717) 731-8550
Contact: Mr. Thomas Waite
Minimum Salary Placed: $25,000
Recruiting Specialty: Sales

CANONSBURG

N.R. Affinito and Associates
125 Technology Drive
Canonsburg, PA 15317
(412) 746-5810
Minimum Salary Placed: $35,000
Recruiting Specialty: Technology and systems integration

CARLISLE

Carlisle Executive Search
325 South Hanover Street
Carlisle, PA 17013
(717) 243-0135
Contact: Mr. Mark Howell
Minimum Salary Placed: $30,000
Recruiting Specialty: General

Ruderfer and Company
1309 Georgetown Center
Carlisle, PA 17013
(717) 240-0248
Contact: Dr. Louise Greenberg
Minimum Salary Placed: $25,000
Recruiting Specialty: Pharmaceuticals and healthcare

CARNEGIE

Pro Search Personnel
Kings Highway and Baldwin Road
Carnegie, PA 15106
(412) 276-4200
Minimum Salary Placed: $25,000
Recruiting Specialty: General

CENTER SQUARE

Alexander Enterprises, Inc.
P.O. Box 148
Center Square, PA 19422
(610) 279-0100
Contact: Ms. Florence Young
Minimum Salary Placed: $25,000
Recruiting Specialty: Pharmaceuticals and human resources

CHADDS FORD

Aitken & Associates
P.O. Box 317
Chadds Ford, PA 19317
(610) 388-0587
Contact: Ms. Carol Aitken
Minimum Salary Placed: $50,000
Recruiting Specialty: MIS - AS 400 only

CHESTER SPRINGS

Travaglini Associates
Green Lane
Chester Springs, PA 19425
(610) 469-6518
Contact: Mr. N. Travaglini
Minimum Salary Placed: $100,000
Recruiting Specialty: General

CLARKS SUMMIT

Courtright & Associates
P.O. Box 503
Clarks Summit, PA 18411
(717) 586-0735
Contact: Mr. Robert Courtright
Minimum Salary Placed: $40,000
Recruiting Specialty: Biotechnology and high technology

COLMAR

Questor Consultants, Inc.
2515 N. Broad Street
Colmar, PA 18915
(215) 997-9262
Contact: Mr. Sal Bevivino
Minimum Salary Placed: $20,000
Recruiting Specialty: Insurance

COOPERSBURG

The Rodman Group
6366 Robin Lane
Coopersburg, PA 18036
(610) 282-0665
Contact: Mr. John Tekowitz
Recruiting Specialty: General

CONSHOHOCKEN

D. A. K. Associates, Inc.
1100 E. Hector Street, Suite 388 R
Conshohocken, PA 19428
(610) 834-1100
Contact: Mr. Daniel Kreuter
Minimum Salary Placed: $50,000
Recruiting Specialty: Finance and insurance

CORAOPOLIS

W.G. Baird and Associates
600 Commerce Drive, Suite 602
Coraopolis, PA 15108
(412) 262-0842
Contact: Mr. Frank Mattison
Recruiting Specialty: Manufacturing

L.A. Neal and Associates
114 Vanita Drive
Coraopolis, PA 15108
(412) 264-0660
Contact: Mr. H. Vogel
Minimum Salary Placed: $25,000
Recruiting Specialty: General

DANVILLE

The Leading Edge
132 Mill Street
Danville, PA 17821
(717) 275-4460
Contact: Mr. Mike Singleton
Minimum Salary Placed: $20,000
Recruiting Specialty: Environmental, agriculture and hazardous waste

DEVON

Hamson Ginn Associates Inc.
1 Devon Square
Devon, PA 19333
(610) 293-9110
Recruiting Specialty: Computers

DOYLESTOWN

Corporate Staffing Group
4268 Fell Road
Doylestown, PA 18901
(215) 345-1100
Contact: Mr. Charles Baker
Minimum Salary Placed: $50,000
Recruiting Specialty: Telecommunications

George R. Martin
P.O. Box 673
Doylestown, PA 18901
(215) 348-8146

Contact: Mr. George Martin
Minimum Salary Placed: $50,000
Recruiting Specialty: Manufacturing and
biotechnology

DREXEL HILL

Search America, Inc.
678 Burmont Road
Drexel Hill, PA 19008
(610) 356-2100
Contact: Mr. Thomas Giacoponello
Minimum Salary Placed: $50,000
Recruiting Specialty: General

EAST PITTSBURGH

Career Management Group
824 E. Pittsburgh Mall
East Pittsburgh, PA 15112
(412) 829-2670
Contact: Mr. R. Croushore
Minimum Salary Placed: $25,000
Recruiting Specialty: General

EASTON

Cassie & Associates
2906 Wm. Penn Highway
Easton, PA 18042
(610) 250-7010
Contact: Mr. Ronald Cassie
Minimum Salary Placed: $50,000
Recruiting Specialty: Healthcare

Lacrosse Associates, Inc.
P.O. Box 3596
Easton, PA 18043
(610) 258-5712

Contact: Mr. Anthony Badway
Minimum Salary Placed: $50,000
Recruiting Specialty: General

EPHRATA

Robert Harkins Associates, Inc.
P.O. Box 236
Ephrata, PA 17522
(717) 733-9664
Contact: Mr. Robert Harkins
Minimum Salary Placed: $25,000
Recruiting Specialty: General

ERIE

Career Concepts Staffing Services, Inc.
4504 Peach Street
Erie, PA 16509
(814) 868-2333
Contact: Mr. Charles Campagne
Recruiting Specialty: Plastics

Consearch
911 Poplar Street
Erie, PA 16502
(814) 459-5588
Minimum Salary Placed: $40,000
Recruiting Specialty: General

Blair Kershaw Associates, Inc.
1903 W. 8th Street, Box 302
Erie, PA 16501
(814) 454-5872
Contact: Mr. Blair Kershaw
Minimum Salary Placed: $40,000
Recruiting Specialty: Manufacturing

Jack B. Larsen & Associates
334 West 8th Street
Erie, PA 16502
(814) 459-3725
Contact: Mr. Jack Larsen
Minimum Salary Placed: $35,000
Recruiting Specialty: General

National Computerized Employment Service, Inc.
2014 W. 8th Street
Erie, PA 16505
(814) 454-3874
Contact: Mr. Joseph Beck
Recruiting Specialty: Plastics

FAIRVIEW VILLAGE

E. F. Humay Associates
P.O. Box 173 R
Fairview Village, PA 19409
(610) 275-1559
Contact: Mr. Gene Humay
Minimum Salary Placed: $35,000
Recruiting Specialty: Construction equipment

FEASTERVILLE

Dunhill Professional Search
801 W. Street Road, 2nd Floor
Feasterville, PA 19053
(215) 357-6590
Contact: Mr. David Bontempo
Minimum Salary Placed: $25,000
Recruiting Specialty: General

FEASTERVILLE TRAVEL

Scott Kane Associates Inc.
221 W. Street Road
Feasterville Travel, PA 19053
(215) 355-6440
Contact: Mr. Scott Kane
Minimum Salary Placed: $25,000
Recruiting Specialty: Food management and grocery

FORT WASHINGTON

Corporate Recruiters Inc.
275 Commerce Drive, Suite 310
Ft. Washington, PA 19034
(215) 540-0454
Contact: Mr. Stephen Berlin
Minimum Salary Placed: $100,000
Recruiting Specialty: R&D and scientific disciplines in pharmaceuticals

Fortune Personnel
455 Pennsylvania Avenue, Suite 105
Fort Washington, PA 19034
(215) 542-9800
Contact: Ms. S. Richards
Minimum Salary Placed: $40,000
Recruiting Specialty: Attorneys

GETTYSBURG

Scan Management Inc.
Drawer 4835
Gettysburg, PA 17325
(717) 359-7473
Contact: Ms. Diana Hallberg
Minimum Salary Placed: $100,000
Recruiting Specialty: Commodities and futures

GREENSBURG

Dunn Associates
229 Limberline Drive
Greensburg, PA 15601
(412) 832-9822
Recruiting Specialty: General

The Edge Resource Group
P.O. Box 457
Greensburg, PA 15601
(412) 523-4795
Contact: Ms. Diane Schoff
Recruiting Specialty: General

General Placement Services
521 Plymouth Street, Suite 2
Greensburg, PA 15601
(412) 836-2300
Contact: Mr. Charles Vecchiola
Recruiting Specialty: Insurance

HANOVER

Studwell Associates
P.O. Box 760
Hanover, PA 17331
(717) 637-1722
Contact: Mr. John Huskin
Minimum Salary Placed: $50,000
Recruiting Specialty: General

HARRISBURG

Laura Good Associates
2017 Verona Drive
Harrisburg, PA 17110
(717) 671-0812
Contact: Ms. Laura Good
Minimum Salary Placed: $40,000
Recruiting Specialty: Attorneys

HOLICONG

Wells and Associates
Box 108
Holicong, PA 18928
(215) 794-8888
Contact: Mr. Gary Wells
Minimum Salary Placed: $25,000
Recruiting Specialty: General

HOLLAND

Technical Employment Consultants
40 Penn Circle
Holland, PA 18966
(215) 968-4858
Contact: Mr. Carl Richards
Minimum Salary Placed: $25,000
Recruiting Specialty: General

HUNTINGDON VALLEY

Vogel Associates
P.O. Box 269R
Huntingdon Valley, PA 19006
(215) 938-1700
Contact: Mr. Michael Vogel
Minimum Salary Placed: $30,000
Recruiting Specialty: Human resources

INDIANA

Cornerstone Health Services
39 N 7th Street, Suite D
Indiana, PA 15701
(800) 473-5551
Contact: Mr. Floyd Garrett
Minimum Salary Placed: $35,000
Recruiting Specialty: Healthcare

JENKINTOWN

Innovative Search Inc.
201 Old York Road
Jenkintown, PA 19046
(215) 654-1911
Contact: Ms. M Goodman
Minimum Salary Placed: $35,000
Recruiting Specialty: Computers

S.H. Jacobs and Associates
The Pavilion
Jenkintown, PA 19046
(215) 886-2700
Contact: Mr. S. Jacobs
Minimum Salary Placed: $25,000
Recruiting Specialty: Advertising and
marketing

Jordon & Jordon, Inc.
101 Greenwood Avenue, Suite LC-10
Jenkintown, PA 19046
(215) 885-1644
Contact: Mr. Bud Jordon
Minimum Salary Placed: $40,000
Recruiting Specialty: Retail

Michael Laksin Associates
100 West Avenue
Jenkintown, PA 19046
(215) 576-1410
Contact: Mr. Michael Laskin
Recruiting Specialty: Non-profit, universities and MIS

Sanders Associates
Benson E, Suite 114
Jenkintown, PA 19046
(215) 576-0426
Contact: Ms. Marilyn Sanders
Minimum Salary Placed: $25,000
Recruiting Specialty: General

KING OF PRUSSIA

ACA Drew Technical Service Company
2000 Valley Forge Towers
King Of Prussia, PA 19406
(610) 783-5900
Contact: Mr. R. Green
Minimum Salary Placed: $35,000
Recruiting Specialty: Technical disci-
plines in science and chemicals

Accountants On Call
1150 First Avenue, Suite 1005
King of Prussia, PA 19406
(610) 337-8500
Contact: Mr. Mark Libes
Recruiting Specialty: Accounting

The Andre Group, Inc.
500 N. Gulph Road, Suite 210
King of Prussia, PA 19406
(610) 337-0600
Contact: Mr. Richard Andre
Minimum Salary Placed: $50,000
Recruiting Specialty: Human resources

Probe Technology
P.O. Box 60521
King of Prussia, PA 19406
(610) 337-8544
Contact: Mr. Thomas Belletieri
Minimum Salary Placed: $40,000
Recruiting Specialty: General

Source EDP
150 S. Warner Road, Suite 238
King of Prussia, PA 19406
(610) 341-1960
Contact: Mr. Timothy Kessler
Recruiting Specialty: Computer hardware and software, and finance

LANCASTER

The Byrnes Group
1380 A Harrisburg Pike
Lancaster, PA 17601
(717) 291-4487
Contact: Mr. Bill Traum
Minimum Salary Placed: $25,000
Recruiting Specialty: General

C & H Personnel
126 White Oak Drive
Lancaster, PA 17601
(717)) 581-1380
Contact: Mr. Jon Singer
Recruiting Specialty: General

Paul S. Pelland, P.C.
1134 Helen Avenue
Lancaster, PA 17601
(717) 393-9711
Contact: Mr. Paul Pelland
Minimum Salary Placed: $40,000
Recruiting Specialty: Manufacturing of
metals

Sales Consultants
8 N. Queen Street, Penn Square
Lancaster, PA 17603
(717) 397-7799
Contact: Mr. James Landis
Minimum Salary Placed: $25,000
Recruiting Specialty: Sales

Stewart Associates
245 Butler Avenue
Lancaster, PA 17601
(717) 299-9242
Contact: Mr. Walter S.Poyck
Minimum Salary Placed: $35,000
Recruiting Specialty: Manufacturing

Charles Stickler Associates
P.O. Box 5312C
Lancaster, PA 17606
(717) 569-2881
Contact: Mr. Charles Stickler
Minimum Salary Placed: $50,000
Recruiting Specialty: Metals

LANGHORNE

Tell/Com Recruiters
306 Corporate Drive East
Langhorne, PA 19047
(215) 860-4100
Contact: Mr. Dennis Young
Recruiting Specialty: Telecommunications

LANSDOWNE

Balfour Associates
P.O. Box 173
Lansdowne, PA 19050
(610) 259-3314
Contact: Mr. John Flowers
Minimum Salary Placed: $20,000
Recruiting Specialty: Graphic arts and
printing

LIGONIER

Fagan & Company
Robb Road, P.O. Box 611
Ligonier, PA 15658
(412) 238-9571
Contact: Ms. Stephanie Bronder
Minimum Salary Placed: $75,000
Recruiting Specialty: General

MALVERN

Brandywine Consulting Group
5 Great Valley Parkway, Suite 262
Malvern, PA 19355
(610) 648-3900
Contact: Mr. Richard Beatty
Minimum Salary Placed: $70,000
Recruiting Specialty: General

KRB Associates, Inc.
274 W. Lancaster Ave., Suite 101
Malvern, PA 19355
(610) 296-2200
Contact: Mr. Gene Nussbaum
Recruiting Specialty: Chemicals, engineering and manufacturing, and insurance

Northstar Management Recruiting
10 James Thomas Road
Malvern, PA 19355
(610) 889-0693
Recruiting Specialty: Actuaries

Professional Search Associates, Inc.
312 Great Valley Center
Malvern, PA 19355
(610) 993-0540
Contact: Mr. Edwin Thomas
Minimum Salary Placed: $35,000
Recruiting Specialty: Insurance and high technology

Target Search, Inc.
288 Lancaster Avenue, Suite 15
Malvern, PA 19355
(610) 889-2000
Contact: Mr. Paul Berry
Minimum Salary Placed: $30,000
Recruiting Specialty: Healthcare and hospitality

Young International Group
7 Great Valley Parkway, Suite 220
Malvern, PA 19355
(610) 251-6860
Contact: Mr. James Young
Minimum Salary Placed: $90,000
Recruiting Specialty: Healthcare

MAPLE GLEN

Innovative Search Inc.
1 Shalimar Lane
Maple Glen, PA 19002
(215) 654-1911
Contact: Ms. Mindy Wexler
Minimum Salary Placed: $30,000
Recruiting Specialty: MIS

MCMURRAY

Management Recruiters
115 Hidden Valley Road
McMurray, PA 15317
(412) 942-4100
Contact: Mr. Mike Fosnot
Minimum Salary Placed: $20,000
Recruiting Specialty: Chemicals

MEDIA

R. Christine Associates
Front & Orange Streets
Media, PA 19063
(610) 565-3310
Contact: Mr. Rich Christine
Minimum Salary Placed: $25,000
Recruiting Specialty: Engineering, manufacturing and sales

Fitz Gibbon Associates
11 E. State Street
Media, PA 19063
(610) 565-7566
Contact: Mr. Mike Fitz Gibbon
Minimum Salary Placed: $60,000
Recruiting Specialty: Retail, direct mail
and telecommunications

The Kennett Group, Inc.
15 W. Third Street
Media, PA 19063
(610) 565-8080
Contact: Mr. Patrick Sweeney
Minimum Salary Placed: $35,000
Recruiting Specialty: MIS

Schneider, Hill & Spangler, Inc.
P.O. Box 70
Media, PA 19063
(610) 566-9550
Contact: Mr. Steven Schneider
Minimum Salary Placed: $75,000
Recruiting Specialty: General

System Personnel Inc.
115 W. State Street
Media, PA 19063
(610) 565-8880
Contact: Mr. J. Doherty
Minimum Salary Placed: $25,000
Recruiting Specialty: Computers

Gordon Wahls Company
610 E. Baltimore Pike
Media, PA 19063
(610) 565-0800
Contact: Mr. Gordon Wahls
Minimum Salary Placed: $25,000
Recruiting Specialty: Printing, packaging
and newspaper

MONROEVILLE

Clifton Johnson Associates Inc.
1 Monroeville Center, Suite 450
Monroeville, PA 15146
(412) 856-8000
Contact: Mr. Clifton Johnson
Minimum Salary Placed: $30,000
Recruiting Specialty: Engineering and
technical disciplines

Raymond Carson and Associates
2500 Mosside Boulevard
Monroeville, PA 15146
(412) 373-5433
Recruiting Specialty: Insurance

MURRYSVILLE

Management Recruiters
3925 Reed Boulevard, Suite 200
Murrysville, PA 15668
(412) 325-4011
Contact: Mr. Frank Williamson
Minimum Salary Placed: $30,000
Recruiting Specialty: Healthcare

Roth Young of Pittsburgh
3087 Carson Street
Murrysville, PA 15668
(412) 733-5900
Contact: Mr. Len Di Naples
Minimum Salary Placed: $25,000
Recruiting Specialty: Healthcare, super-
markets and hospitality

NEW CASTLE

Frederick and Associates
125 East North Street
New Castle, PA 16101
(412) 658-4005
Contact: Mr. Fred Scarnati
Minimum Salary Placed: $40,000
Recruiting Specialty: Banking

NEWTOWN

Sales Consultants
252 S. State Street
Newtown, PA 18940
(215) 579-2450
Contact: Mr. James Plappert
Minimum Salary Placed: $25,000
Recruiting Specialty: Sales

Albert J. Walsh & Associates
P.O. Box 301
Newtown, PA 18940
(215) 968-0707
Contact: Mr. Albert Walsh
Minimum Salary Placed: $60,000
Recruiting Specialty: General

NEWTOWN SQUARE

Graphic Search Associates Inc.
P.O. Box 373
Newtown Square, PA 19073
(215) 359-1234
Contact: Mr. Roger Linde
Minimum Salary Placed: $25,000
Recruiting Specialty: Graphic arts in the
printing industry

Management Recruiters
90 S. Newtown Street, Suite 9
Newtown Square, PA 19073
(215) 356-8360
Contact: Mr. M.A. Bishop
Minimum Salary Placed: $20,000
Recruiting Specialty: General

NORRISTOWN

High Mark Associates
1400 W. Main Street
Norristown, PA 19403
(610) 279-3440
Minimum Salary Placed: $35,000
Recruiting Specialty: Pharmaceuticals
and healthcare

ORELAND

Bomark Industries Inc.
324 Twining Road
Oreland, PA 19075
(215) 884-5711
Contact: Mr. Dean Kristiniak
Recruiting Specialty: Sales, process engineers from paper, and technical service

PAOLI

Eden & Associates, Inc.
794 N. Valley Road
Paoli, PA 19301
(610) 889-9993
Contact: Mr. Brooks Eden
Minimum Salary Placed: $50,000
Recruiting Specialty: Food and drug re-
tailing

PERKIOMENVILLE

M.D. Mattes & Associates
1204 Snyder Road
Perkiomenville, PA 18074
(610) 754-9764
Contact: Mr. Mike Mattes
Recruiting Specialty: Automation, human resources, and manufacturing

PHILADELPHIA

ACSYS Resources Inc.
1700 Market Street, Suite 2702
Philadelphia, PA 19103
(215) 568-6810
Recruiting Specialty: Financial services, accounting, marketing and consulting

Cathy Abelson Legal Search
1601 Market Street, Suite 300
Philadelphia, PA 19103
(215) 561-3010
Contact: Ms. Cathy Abelson
Recruiting Specialty: Attorneys

Access Resources
1700 Market Street, Suite 2702
Philadelphia, PA 19103
(215) 568-6810
Contact: Mr. Harry Sauer
Minimum Salary Placed: $15,000
Recruiting Specialty: Banking, accounting and data processing

Accountants On Call
2005 Market Street, Suite 520
Philadelphia, PA 19103
(215) 568-5600
Contact: Mr. Mark Libes
Recruiting Specialty: Accounting

The Beam Group
11 Penn Center Plaza, Suite 502
Philadelphia, PA 19103
(215) 988-2100
Contact: Mr. Russell Glicksman
Minimum Salary Placed: $70,000
Recruiting Specialty: General

Bettinger Company
42 S. 15th Street
Philadelphia, PA 19102
(215) 564-0700
Contact: Mr. E. Bettinger
Recruiting Specialty: Accounting

Bio-scientific Search Consultants
3346 Friendship Street
Philadelphia, PA 19149
(215) 338-5192
Contact: Ms. J. Arcangelo
Minimum Salary Placed: $35,000
Recruiting Specialty: Science and biotechnology

Cole, Warren & Long, Inc.
2 Penn Center Plaza, Suite 312
Philadelphia, PA 19102
(215) 563-0701
Contact: Mr. Ronald Cole
Minimum Salary Placed: $70,000
Recruiting Specialty: General

Coleman Legal Search Consultants
1435 Walnut Street
Philadelphia, PA 19102
(215) 864-2700
Contact: Mr. Michael Coleman
Recruiting Specialty: Legal

Diversified Health Search
2005 Market Street, Suite 3300
Philadelphia, PA 19103
(215) 732-6666
Contact: Ms. Judith von Seldeneck
Minimum Salary Placed: $75,000
Recruiting Specialty: Healthcare

Everly Associates
2903 Southampton Road
Philadelphia, PA 19115
(215) 671-0181
Contact: Ms. Penelope Smith
Minimum Salary Placed: $25,000
Recruiting Specialty: General

Howard Fischer Associates Inc.
1800 Kennedy Boulevard, 7th Floor
Philadelphia, PA 19103
(215) 568-8363
Contact: Mr. Howard Fischer
Minimum Salary Placed: $75,000
Recruiting Specialty: General

Jack Stuart Fisher Associates
328 Poplar Street
Philadelphia, PA 19123
(215) 925-9859
Contact: Mr. Jack Stuart Fisher
Minimum Salary Placed: $45,000
Recruiting Specialty: General

Fox-Morris Associates, Inc.
1617 JFK Boulevard, Suite 210
Philadelphia, PA 19103
(215) 561-6300
Contact: Mr. Thomas Glynn
Minimum Salary Placed: $35,000
Recruiting Specialty: General

Genesis Consulting Service
306 S. Philip Street
Philadelphia, PA 19106
(215) 627-3350
Minimum Salary Placed: $25,000
Recruiting Specialty: Pharmaceuticals
and biochemical engineering

J.H. Glass and Associates
7200 Brentwood Road
Philadelphia, PA 19151
(215) 877-0101
Contact: Mr. Jay Glass
Minimum Salary Placed: $25,000
Recruiting Specialty: General

Gordon/Tyler
2220 Brandywine Street
Philadelphia, PA 19130
(215) 569-2344
Contact: Dr. Fern Polaski
Minimum Salary Placed: $60,000
Recruiting Specialty: R&D and engineering in consumer products

Jefferson-Ross Associates Inc.
2 Penn Center Plaza, Suite 312
Philadelphia, PA 19102
(215) 564-5322
Contact: Mr. Craig Zander
Minimum Salary Placed: $25,000
Recruiting Specialty: General

KBLC Associates
4203 Houghton Street
Philadelphia, PA 19128
(215) 487-3606
Contact: Mr. K. Olney
Minimum Salary Placed: $25,000
Recruiting Specialty: Healthcare

The Koehler Group
P.O. Box 18156
Philadelphia, PA 19116
(215) 673-8315
Contact: Mr. Frank Koehler
Minimum Salary Placed: $45,000
Recruiting Specialty: General

Legal Pool Inc.
2 Penn Center Plaza
Philadelphia, PA 19102
(215) 561-1515
Contact: Mr. S. Harris
Minimum Salary Placed: $20,000
Recruiting Specialty: Paralegals

Madsen Associates
2135 Walnut Street, Suite 202
Philadelphia, PA 19103
(215) 665-0805
Contact: Mr. John Madsen
Minimum Salary Placed: $40,000
Recruiting Specialty: Banking

Management Recruiters
100 N. 17th Street
Philadelphia, PA 19103
(215) 665-9430
Contact: Mr. Thomas Lucas
Minimum Salary Placed: $20,000
Recruiting Specialty: General

Management Recruiters
1835 Market Street, Suite 1717
11 Penn Center
Philadelphia, PA 19103
(215) 567-1448
Contact: Mr. Allen Salikof
Minimum Salary Placed: $20,000
Recruiting Specialty: General

Management Recruiters
4419 Main Street
Philadelphia, PA 19127
(215) 482-6881
Contact: Mr. Scott Quitel
Minimum Salary Placed: $20,000
Recruiting Specialty: General

McNichol Associates
620 Chestnut Street, Suite 1031
Philadelphia, PA 19106
(215) 922-4142
Contact: Mr. John McNichol
Minimum Salary Placed: $60,000
Recruiting Specialty: General

Ann Moran Associates Inc.
1524 E. Willow Grove Avenue
Philadelphia, PA 19118
(215) 233-4060
Contact: Ms. Ann Moran
Minimum Salary Placed: $40,000
Recruiting Specialty: Attorneys

Nuessle, Kurdziel & Weiss, Inc.
1601 Market Street
5 Penn Center Plaza
Philadelphia, PA 19103
(215) 561-3700
Contact: Mr. John Kurdziel
Minimum Salary Placed: $50,000
Recruiting Specialty: General

LaMonte Owens, Inc.
805 E. Willow Grove Avenue, Suite 2C
Philadelphia, PA 19118
(215) 248-0500
Contact: Mr. LaMonte Owens
Minimum Salary Placed: $40,000
Recruiting Specialty: General

Penn Associates
210 Penn Center Plaza
Philadelphia, PA 19102
(215) 854-6336
Contact: Mr. Joseph Dickerson
Minimum Salary Placed: $60,000
Recruiting Specialty: Human resources

The Penn Partners, Inc.
117 South 17th Street
Philadelphia, PA 19103
(215) 568-9285
Contact: Ms. Kathleen Shea
Minimum Salary Placed: $50,000
Recruiting Specialty: General

Personnel Resources Organization
121 Broad Street, Suite 1030
Philadelphia, PA 19107
(215) 735-7500
Contact: Mr. Lawrence Cesare
Minimum Salary Placed: $75,000
Recruiting Specialty: Attorneys

Pratt Placement Services, Inc.
P.O. Box 42704
Philadelphia, PA 19101
(610) 461-3503
Contact: Mr. Joseph P. Egan
Recruiting Specialty: Manufacturing management and engineers

J.P. Roddy Consultants
258 South Third Street, Suite 101
Philadelphia, PA 19106
(215) 923-6770
Contact: Mr. Jack Roddy
Recruiting Specialty: Automotive and plastics industry

Selective Management Services, Inc.
319 S. Sixteenth Street
Philadelphia, PA 19102
(215) 545-7111
Contact: Mr. Alan Schwartz
Minimum Salary Placed: $25,000
Recruiting Specialty: Packaging, paper and insurance

Source EDP
1800 JFK Boulevard
Philadelphia, PA 19103
(215) 665-1717
Contact: Mr. Rich Strimel
Recruiting Specialty: Computer hardware and software

Source Finance
1800 JFK Boulevard, Suite F
Philadelphia, PA 19103
(215) 569-3900
Contact: Mr. Timothy Kessler
Minimum Salary Placed: $25,000
Recruiting Specialty: Accounting and finance

Spencer Stuart
2005 Market Street, Suite 2350
Philadelphia, PA 19103
(215) 851-6200
Contact: Mr. Dennis Carey
Minimum Salary Placed: $75,000
Recruiting Specialty: General

University City Human Resources
3901 Market Street
Philadelphia, PA 19103
(215) 387-5911
Contact: Mr. David Rayon
Minimum Salary Placed: $50,000
Recruiting Specialty: Physicians and healthcare

Wellington Management Group
117 S. 17th Street, Suite 1625
Philadelphia, PA 19103
(215) 569-8900
Contact: Mr. Walter Romanchek
Minimum Salary Placed: $70,000
Recruiting Specialty: High technology,
pharmaceuticals, chemicals and healthcare

PITTSBURGH

Accountants On Call
437 Grant Street
Pittsburgh, PA 15219
(412) 391-0900
Recruiting Specialty: Accounting and finance

Accounting Personnel Associates
2100 Wharton Street, Suite 710
Pittsburgh, PA 15203
(412) 481-6015
Contact: Mr. Dennis Papciak
Recruiting Specialty: Finance, accounting
and banking

Basilone-Oliver Executive Search
2987 Babcock Boulevard
Pittsburgh, PA 15237
(412) 931-9501
Recruiting Specialty: Finance and accounting

Bendel-Spear Associates, Inc.
651 Holiday Drive, Suite 300
Pittsburgh, PA 15220
(412) 928-3290
Contact: Mr. Kenneth Spear
Minimum Salary Placed: $30,000
Recruiting Specialty: General

Boyden
625 Stanwix Street, Suite 2405
Pittsburgh, PA 15222
(412) 391-3020
Contact: Mr. E. Wade Close
Minimum Salary Placed: $90,000
Recruiting Specialty: General

Brackin and Sayers Associates
1000 McKnight Park Drive
Pittsburgh, PA 15237
(412) 367-4644
Contact: Mr. J. Brackin
Minimum Salary Placed: $25,000
Recruiting Specialty: Accounting, finance
and human resources

C.G. & Associates
Box 11160
Pittsburgh, PA 15237
(412) 935-1288
Contact: Mr. Charles Groom
Minimum Salary Placed: $40,000
Recruiting Specialty: Real property

Corporate Management Services
P.O. Box 16271
Pittsburgh, PA 15220
(412) 279-1180
Contact: Mr. Robert Bushee
Minimum Salary Placed: $30,000
Recruiting Specialty: Plastics and metals

DMS & Associates
245 Cedar Boulevard, Suite 100
Pittsburgh, PA 15228
(412) 343-4892
Contact: Mr. David Stobbe
Minimum Salary Placed: $40,000
Recruiting Specialty: General

Emrick Associates
29 Rhodes Ave.
Pittsburgh, PA 15220
(412) 722-4927
Contact: Mr. Ron Emrick
Recruiting Specialty: Metals industry

Susan Fletcher Attorney Employment Services
501 Grant Street
475 Union Trust Building
Pittsburgh, PA 15219
(412) 281-6609
Contact: Ms. Susan Fletcher
Recruiting Specialty: General

Fox-Morris Associates, Inc.
One Gateway Center, 18th Floor
North Wing
Pittsburgh, PA 15222
(412) 232-0410
Contact: Mr. Murray Leety
Minimum Salary Placed: $35,000
Recruiting Specialty: General

W.T. Glover and Associates Inc.
2 Gateway Center, 18th Floor
Pittsburgh, PA 15222
(412) 642-4400
Contact: Mr. W. Glover
Minimum Salary Placed: $40,000
Recruiting Specialty: General

HRS Inc.
4405 Steubenville Pike, P.O. Box 4499
Pittsburgh, PA 15205
(412) 922-0900
Contact: Mr. David Smith
Minimum Salary Placed: $50,000
Recruiting Specialty: General

Robert Lohrke Associates
239 4th Avenue, Room 307
Pittsburgh, PA 15222
(412) 261-2601
Contact: Mr. Dan Buckley
Recruiting Specialty: Engineering and manufacturing, steel and aluminum

McAnney, Esposito and Kraybill
104 Alleyne
Pittsburgh, PA 15212
(412) 882-8480
Contact: Ms. Susan Kraybill
Recruiting Specialty: Legal

Management Recruiters
4840 McKnight Road
Pittsburgh, PA 15237
(412) 364-0282
Contact: Ms. Patricia Holupka
Minimum Salary Placed: $20,000
Recruiting Specialty: Windows, building products, ceramics, plastics and metals

Management Recruiters
300 Weyman Plaza, Suite 140
Pittsburgh, PA 15236
(412) 885-5222
Contact: Mr. Andy Hallam
Minimum Salary Placed: $20,000
Recruiting Specialty: Data processing

K. Maxin & Associates
Allegheny Center, Building 10, Suite 421
Pittsburgh, PA 15212
(412) 322-2595
Contact: Mr. Keith Maxin
Minimum Salary Placed: $50,000
Recruiting Specialty: Construction and real estate

R.P. McKinley Inc.
1000 RIDC Plaza, Suite 102
Pittsburgh, PA 15238
(412) 963-5946
Contact: Mr. R. McKinley
Minimum Salary Placed: $25,000
Recruiting Specialty: General

Roy Morris Associates
4550 McKnight Road
Pittsburgh, PA 15237
(412) 931-0353
Contact: Mr. Roy Morris
Minimum Salary Placed: $40,000
Recruiting Specialty: General

O'Connor, O'Connor, Lordi, Ltd.
707 Grant Street, Suite 2727
Pittsburgh, PA 15219
(412) 261-4020
Contact: Mr. Thomas O'Connor
Minimum Salary Placed: $70,000
Recruiting Specialty: General

Orion Delta Group Ltd.
1200 Reedsdale Street
Pittsburgh, PA 15233
(412) 231-2414
Recruiting Specialty: General

Resources for Management
221 7th Street, Suite 302
Pittsburgh, PA 15228
(412) 820-7559
Contact: Mr. Thomas Flannery
Minimum Salary Placed: $40,000
Recruiting Specialty: General

Robert Half Accountemps
603 Stanwix Street, 6th Floor
Pittsburgh, PA 15222
(412) 471-5946

Contact: Mr. D. Prince
Recruiting Specialty: Accounting

Sales Consultants
125 Seventh Street
Pittsburgh, PA 15222
(412) 281-6900
Contact: Mr. Douglas Cain
Minimum Salary Placed: $25,000
Recruiting Specialty: Sales

Source EDP
Foster Plaza Building VI
681 Andersen Drive, 2nd Floor
Pittsburgh, PA 15220
(412) 928-8300
Recruiting Specialty: Computer hardware and software

Specialty Consultants, Inc.
Gateway Towers, Suite 2710
Pittsburgh, PA 15222
(412) 355-8200
Contact: Mr. Charles Abbott
Minimum Salary Placed: $40,000
Recruiting Specialty: Real estate and con-
struction

Daniel Stern & Associates
211 N. Whitfield Street, Suite 240
Pittsburgh, PA 15206
(412) 363-9700
Contact: Mr. Daniel Stern
Minimum Salary Placed: $75,000
Recruiting Specialty: Physicians

Strauss Personnel Service
239 4th Avenue, Suite 1105
Pittsburgh, PA 15222
(412) 281-8235

Contact: Mr. Jay Jarrell
Recruiting Specialty: Manufacturing, finance and human resources

Suber and Meeks Executive Search
875 Greentree Road, Suite 200
Pittsburgh, PA 15220
(412) 922-3336
Contact: Mr. J. Suber
Minimum Salary Placed: $35,000
Recruiting Specialty: Engineering and manufacturing

Thornton Resources
100 4th Avenue
Pittsburgh, PA 15222
(412) 364-2111
Contact: Mr. John Thornton
Minimum Salary Placed: $30,000
Recruiting Specialty: Finance and banking

PLYMOUTH MEETING

ProSearch, Inc.
610 W. Germantown Pike
Plymouth Meeting, PA 19462
(610) 834-8260
Contact: Ms. Suzanne Fairlie
Minimum Salary Placed: $35,000
Recruiting Specialty: Software, hardware and MIS

QUAKERTOWN

Barr Associates
93 S. West End Boulevard, Suite 105B
Quakertown, PA 18951
(215) 538-9411
Contact: Ms. Sharon Barr
Recruiting Specialty: Semiconductors

RADNOR

Howe, Lawlor & Associates
5 Radnor Corporation Center, Suite 448
Radnor, PA 19087
(610) 975-9124
Contact: Mr. Edward Howe
Minimum Salary Placed: $70,000
Recruiting Specialty: General

Soltis Management Services
876 Brower Road
Radnor, PA 19087
(610) 687-4200
Contact: Mr. Charles Soltis
Minimum Salary Placed: $70,000
Recruiting Specialty: General

READING

Beard and Company
P.O. Box 311
Reading, PA 19603
(610) 376-2833
Contact: Mr. Bob Gibble
Minimum Salary Placed: $35,000
Recruiting Specialty: Accounting and auditing

Synergistic Resources
1413 N. 12th Street
Reading, PA 19604
(610) 373-5446
Contact: Mr. George Naughton
Recruiting specialty: General

ROSEMONT

The Morris Group
919 Conestoga
Rosemont, PA 19010
(610) 520-0100
Contact: Mr. Paul Morris
Minimum Salary Placed: $30,000
Recruiting Specialty: Pharmaceuticals

SAINT PETERS

Lee Calhoon & Company, Inc.
P.O. Box 399
St. Peters, PA 19470
(610) 469-6900
Contact: Ms. Abby Mayes
Minimum Salary Placed: $75,000
Recruiting Specialty: Healthcare

SEWICKLEY

Management Recruiters
435 Broad Street
P.O. Box 69
Sewickley, PA 15143
(412) 741-5805
Contact: Mr. Richard Lampl
Minimum Salary Placed: $20,000
Recruiting Specialty: General

SOUTHAMPTON

M.A. Churchill & Associates, Inc.
1111 Street Road
Southampton, PA 18966
(215) 953-0300
Contact: Mr. Lawrence Sher
Minimum Salary Placed: $50,000
Recruiting Specialty: Finance and securities

Technical Employment Consultants
308 Lakeside Drive
Southampton, PA 18966
(215) 396-1500
Contact: Mr. Carl Richards
Recruiting Specialty: Military and commercial electronics

SPRINGFIELD

Ahrensdorf and Associates
1489 Baltimore Pike
Springfield, PA 19064
(610) 543-7888
Contact: Mr. Lee Ahrensdorf
Minimum Salary Placed: $60,000
Recruiting Specialty: General

System Search Consultants
130 S. State Road
Springfield, PA 19064
(610) 544-8690
Contact: Mr. John Grant
Minimum Salary Placed: $25,000
Recruiting Specialty: Communications

STATE COLLEGE

J.N. Adams & Associates
301 South Allen St., Suite 103A
State College, PA 16801
(814) 234-0670
Contact: Mr. Eric M. Berg
Recruiting Specialty: Quality assurance and manufacturing

Fox-Morris Associates, Inc.
P.O. Box 10087
Calder Square, Suite 405
State College, PA 16805
(814) 237-2218

Contact: Mr. Dick Wilson
Minimum Salary Placed: $35,000
Recruiting Specialty: Human resources

Sterling Systems
2515 Green Tech Drive, Suite B
State College, PA 16803
(814) 234-1747
Contact: Mr. J. Evans
Minimum Salary Placed: $25,000
Recruiting Specialty: MIS

VALLEY FORGE

Hospitality International
Davis Road, Box 906
Valley Forge, PA 19481
(610) 783-5200
Contact: Mrs. Ralda Adams
Minimum Salary Placed: $25,000
Recruiting Specialty: Hospitality

Sales Consultants
P.O. Box 827
Valley Forge, PA 19481
(610) 783-5904
Contact: Mr. Doug Mitchell
Minimum Salary Placed: $25,000
Recruiting Specialty: Sales

VILLANOVA

Eisenbud and Associates Inc.
757 Panarama Road
Villanova, PA 19085
(610) 527-6300
Contact: Ms. B. Eisenbud
Minimum Salary Placed: $25,000
Recruiting Specialty: Healthcare

Tower Consultants Limited
771 East Lancaster Avenue, 2nd Floor
Villanova, PA 19085
(610) 519-1700
Contact: Ms. Donna Friedman
Minimum Salary Placed: $30,000
Recruiting Specialty: Human resources

WALLINGFORD

CEO Resources Inc.
3 Blackhorn Road
Wallingford, PA 19086
(610) 565-9767
Contact: Ms. Linda Resnick
Minimum Salary Placed: $75,000
Recruiting Specialty: General

WARMINSTER

Cawley Associates
670 Louis Drive
Warminster, PA 18974
(215) 957-9162
Contact: Mr. Patrick Cawley
Recruiting Specialty: Packaging

Intercontinental Executive Group
P.O. Box 2642
Warminster, PA 18966
(215) 957-9012
Contact: Mr. David Weir
Minimum Salary Placed: $70,000
Recruiting Specialty: Technical in energy
and utilities

WARRINGTON

Triangle Associates
P.O. Box 506
Warrington, PA 18976
(215) 343-3702
Contact: Mr. Stephen Ostroff
Minimum Salary Placed: $30,000
Recruiting Specialty: Technical disciplines in consumer products, pharmaceuticals and raw materials

WASHINGTON

Colonial Park Search
2155 Park Avenue
Washington, PA 15301
(412) 229-9250
Contact: Mr. Mark Holtkamp
Recruiting Specialty: Mechanical and manufacturing

WAYNE

Access Resources
530 E. Swedesford Road, Suite 202
Wayne, PA 19087
(610) 687-6107
Contact: Ms. Mary Kay Hamm
Minimum Salary Placed: $15,000
Recruiting Specialty: Banking, accounting and data processing

Caliber Associates
125 Strafford Avenue
Wayne, PA 19087
(610) 971-1880
Contact: Mr. Steven Hochberg
Minimum Salary Placed: $40,000
Recruiting Specialty: Technical disciplines in pharmaceuticals and biotechnology

Devon Consulting
950 West Valley Road, Suite 2602
Wayne, PA 19087-1898
(610) 964-2700
Recruiting Specialty: Data processing

Hamson-Ginn Associates Inc.
Devon Square, Suite 206
Wayne, PA 19087
(610) 293-9110
Contact: Mr. M. Hamson
Minimum Salary Placed: $25,000
Recruiting Specialty: Data processing

Howe and Associates
100 Matsonford Road, Suite 448
Wayne, PA 19087
(610) 975-9124
Contact: Mr. E. Howe
Minimum Salary Placed: $25,000
Recruiting Specialty: General

JM & Company
P.O. Box 285
Wayne, PA 19087
(215) 964-0200
Contact: Mr. John Marshall
Minimum Salary Placed: $60,000
Recruiting Specialty: Technical and production

Patriot Associates
125 Strafford Avenue, Suite 300
Wayne, PA 19087
(610) 687-7770
Contact: Mr. Thomas Meltser
Minimum Salary Placed: $25,000
Recruiting Specialty: Pharmaceuticals and healthcare

Raymond Karsan Associates
989 Old Eagle School Road, Suite 814
Wayne, PA 19087
(610) 971-9171
Contact: Mr. Barry Raymond
Recruiting Specialty: General

Yannelli, Randolph & Company
997 Old Eagle School Road, Suite 202
Wayne, PA 19087
(610) 964-1616
Contact: Mr. Albert Yannelli
Minimum Salary Placed: $75,000
Recruiting Specialty: Physicians

WEST CHESTER

CMIS
24 Haggerty Boulevard
West Chester, PA 19382
(610) 430-0013
Minimum Salary Placed: $25,000
Recruiting Specialty: Computer systems

William J. Christopher Associates, Inc.
307 N. Walnut Street
West Chester, PA 19380
(610) 696-4397
Contact: Mr. John Jeffrey Bole
Minimum Salary Placed: $30,000
Recruiting Specialty: Paper products, publishing and printing

Management Recruiters
129 Willowbrook Lane
West Chester, PA 19382
(610) 436-6556
Contact: Mr. Robert Meitz
Minimum Salary Placed: $40,000
Recruiting Specialty: General

Whittlesey & Associates, Inc.
300 S. High Street
West Chester, PA 19382
(610) 436-6500
Contact: Mr. James Hogg
Minimum Salary Placed: $40,000
Recruiting Specialty: General

WEST READING

Management Recruiters
529 Reading Avenue, Suite J
West Reading, PA 19611
(215) 372-4756
Contact: Mr. Robert O'Hayer
Minimum Salary Placed: $20,000
Recruiting Specialty: General

WEXFORD

Reese Associates
10475 Perry Highway
Wexford, PA 15090
(412) 935-8644
Contact: Mr. Charles Reese
Minimum Salary Placed: $50,000
Recruiting Specialty: Metal fabrication and manufacturing

WILKES BARRE

Andy Check Associates Inc.
22 E. Union Street
Wilkes Barre, PA 19704
(717) 829-5066
Contact: Mr. Andy Check
Minimum Salary Placed: $25,000
Recruiting Specialty: General

Dunhill Search
15 Public Square, Suite 212
Wilkes Barre, PA 18701
(717) 826-8953
Contact: Mr. Anthony Desiderio
Minimum Salary Placed: $25,000
Recruiting Specialty: General

Tierney Associates, Inc.
51 Downing Street
Wilkes Barre, PA 18702
(717) 825-9500
Contact: Mr. George Tierney
Minimum Salary Placed: $40,000
Recruiting Specialty: Manufacturing

WILLOW GROVE

Management Recruiters
2500 Maryland Road, Suite 612
Willow Grove, PA 19090
(215) 657-6250
Contact: Mr. Rowland Norris
Minimum Salary Placed: $20,000
Recruiting Specialty: General

YARDLEY

Sales Consultants
301 Oxford Valley Road, Suite 204
Yardley, PA 19067
(215) 321-4100
Contact: Mr. Jeff Cohen
Minimum Salary Placed: $25,000
Recruiting Specialty: Sales

YORK

The Byrnes Group
155 W. Market Street, 3rd Floor
York, PA 17401
(717) 846-5656
Contact: Mr. Randy Byrnes
Minimum Salary Placed: $25,000
Recruiting Specialty: General

RHODE ISLAND

BARRINGTON

Bay Search Group
12 Barton Avenue
Barrington, RI 02806
(401) 751-2870
Contact: Mr. F. Sayre
Minimum Salary Placed: $25,000
Recruiting Specialty: MIS

CHARLESTOWN

Marshall Rice Associates
40 Boulder Avenue
P.O. Box 1485
Charlestown, RI 02813
(401) 322-1993
Contact: Mr. Marshall Rice
Minimum Salary Placed: $50,000
Recruiting Specialty: Non-profit, academia and hospitals

CRANSTON

Greene Personnel Consultants
1925 Broad Street
Cranston, RI 02905
(401) 461-9700
Contact: Ms. Dorcas Greene
Minimum Salary Placed: $40,000
Recruiting Specialty: General

Networks Professional Placement
400 Reservoir Avenue
Cranston, RI 02907
(401) 785-1717
Contact: Ms. Leslie Milner
Recruiting Specialty: Engineering

EAST GREENWICH

Creative Input Inc.
45 Water Street
East Greenwich, RI 02818
(401) 885-3254
Minimum Salary Placed: $25,000
Recruiting Specialty: General

The Greenwich Group
P.O. Box 734
East Greenwich, RI 02818
(401) 781-5021
Contact: Mr. Fred Raisner
Recruiting Specialty: Electronics, software, MIS, and semiconductor

The Greenwich Group
P.O. Box 734
East Greenwich, RI 02818
(401) 885-7007
Contact: Ms. Pam Weisgerber
Recruiting Specialty: General

Sylvestro Associates
5586 Post Road, Suite 208
East Greenwich, RI 02818
(401) 885-0855
Recruiting Specialty: Engineering and data processing

EAST PROVIDENCE

Capital Personnel
P.O. Box 14524
East Providence, RI 02914
(401) 438-6067
Contact: Ms. JoAnn Wheeler
Minimum Salary Placed: $25,000
Recruiting Specialty: General

HOPE VALLEY

Tech International
P.O. Box 297
Hope Valley, RI 02832
(401) 539-7925
Contact: Mr. Howard A. Smith
Minimum Salary Placed: $30,000
Recruiting Specialty: Technical and scientific disciplines

JAMESTOWN

W.S. Berman Associates
Box 425
Jamestown, RI 02835
(401) 423-3600
Contact: Mr. W.S. Berman
Minimum Salary Placed: $25,000
Recruiting Specialty: General

KINGSTON

Furlong Professional Employment
P.O. Box 300
Kingston, RI 02881
(401) 539-9011
Contact: Mr. David Furlong
Recruiting Specialty: MIS

LITTLE COMPTON

Bedford Group
154 Quicksand Pond Road
Little Compton, RI 02837
(401) 635-4646
Contact: Mr. Jack Edwards
Minimum Salary Placed: $25,000
Recruiting Specialty: General

NEWPORT

Lybrook Associates, Inc.
P.O. Box 572
Newport, RI 02840
(401) 683-6990
Contact: Ms. Karen Lybrook
Minimum Salary Placed: $25,000
Recruiting Specialty: Technical disciplines in scientific industries

Spectrum Business Associates Ltd.
17 McCormick Road
Newport, RI 02840
(401) 849-6560
Contact: Mr. Bob Sleiertin
Minimum Salary Placed: $25,000
Recruiting Specialty: Maritime

NORTH KINGSTOWN

Schattle and Driquette
1130 Ten Rod Road, B-207
North Kingstown, RI 02852
(401) 739-0500
Contact: Mr. Donald Schattle
Minimum Salary Placed: $40,000
Recruiting Specialty: MIS

PAWTUCKET

Alan Price Associates, Inc.
300 Front Street, Suite 207
Pawtucket, RI 02861
(401) 728-8499
Contact: Mr. Alan J. Price
Recruiting Specialty: Technical, software & hardware designs, advertising, financial, and manufacturing

PROVIDENCE

Career Consultants
1 Jackson Walkway
Providence, RI 02903
(401) 273-8910
Recruiting Specialty: General

Darra Search Inc.
One Richmond Square, Suite 317
Providence, RI 02906
(401) 453-1555
Contact: Ms. Bethany Gold-Croll
Recruiting Specialty: MIS

Employment USA
705 Westminister Street
Providence, RI 02903
(401) 351-5590
Contact: Mr. Mike Cooney
Recruiting Specialty: Office support and
industrial

Executive Resources, Inc.
155 Westminster Street, Suite 1100
Providence, RI 02903
(401) 861-8620
Contact: Mr. Maurice Paradis
Minimum Salary Placed: $75,000
Recruiting Specialty: General

Executive Silent Partner
400 Reservoir Avenue, Suite 3J
Providence, RI 02907
(401) 461-5170
Contact: Mr. E. Lemire
Minimum Salary Placed: $25,000
Recruiting Specialty: Jewelry manufacturing

Robert Half Accountemps
1313 Turks Head Building
Providence, RI 02903
(401) 274-8700
Contact: Mr. D. DeBolt
Recruiting Specialty: Accounting and finance

Human Resources Inc.
203 S. Main
Providence, RI 02903
(401) 861-2550
Contact: Mr. A. Richard
Minimum Salary Placed: $25,000
Recruiting Specialty: Computers

Johnson & Tregar Associates
321 Turks Head Bldg.
Providence, RI 02903
(401) 831-5550
Contact: Mr. Jack Tregar
Recruiting Specialty: Manufacturing, engineering, human resources, and technical sales & marketing

Management Recruiters
101 Dyer Street, Suite 5-A
Providence, RI 02903
(401) 274-2810
Contact: Mr. Stephen Morse
Minimum Salary Placed: $20,000
Recruiting Specialty: General

Management Search Inc.
One State Street
Providence, RI 02908
(401) 273-5511
Contact: Mr. James Meyer
Recruiting Specialty: General

Stanelun Associates, Inc.
Two Richmond Square
Providence, RI 02906
(401) 331-0245
Contact: Ms. Kay Stanelun
Recruiting Specialty: Legal

Technical Opportunity
10 Dorrance Street
Providence, RI 02903
(401) 751-6642
Contact: Mr. Larry O'Brien
Recruiting Specialty: Engineering

Westminster Group
40 Westminster Street
Providence, RI 02903
(401) 270-9300
Contact: Mr. Robert Graham
Minimum Salary Placed: $85,000
Recruiting Specialty: General

RUMFORD

Albert G. Lee Associates
106 Greenwood Avenue
Rumford, RI 02916
(401) 434-7614
Contact: Mr. Albert Lee
Minimum Salary Placed: $50,000
Recruiting Specialty: General

WARWICK

Careers Unlimited
560 Jefferson Blvd., Suite 205
Warwick, RI 02886
(401) 736-8880
Contact: Ms. Arlette Dumais
Recruiting Specialty: Insurance

Dunhill Executive Search
1545 Bald Park Court
Warwick, RI 02886
(401) 828-7000
Contact: Mr. Robert DaCosta
Minimum Salary Placed: $20,000
Recruiting Specialty: Healthcare

Pro Search
3960 Post Road
Warwick, RI 02886
(401) 885-9595
Contact: Ms. Janet Morgan
Recruiting Specialty: Banking and administrative

Sales Consultants
Office Commons 95
349 Centerville Road
Warwick, RI 02886
(401) 737-3200
Contact: Mr. Peter Cotton
Minimum Salary Placed: $20,000
Recruiting Specialty: Sales

Sullivan & Cogliano
100 Jefferson Boulevard
Warwick, RI 02888
(401) 463-3811
Contact: Mr. Ron Wnek
Recruiting Specialty: MIS

WEST GREENWICH

Carter, Lavoie Associates
773 Victory Highway
West Greenwich, RI 02817
(401) 392-1250
Contact: Mr. Leo Lavoie
Minimum Salary Placed: $30,000
Recruiting Specialty: General

SOUTH CAROLINA

AIKEN

Apple and Associates
P.O. Box 57777
Aiken, SC 29804
(803) 648-5777
Contact: Ms. Debbie Apple
Recruiting Specialty: Engineering, environmental and mental safety

Job Search Personnel
950 Millbrook Avenue, Suite B
Aiken, SC 29803
(803) 649-3436
Minimum Salary Placed: $20,000
Recruiting Specialty: General

Management Recruiters
P.O. Box 730
Aiken, SC 29802
(803) 648-1361
Contact: Mr. Michael Hardwick
Minimum Salary Placed: $25,000
Recruiting Specialty: General

Southern Recruiters & Consultants, Inc.
P.O. Box 2745
Aiken, SC 29802
(803) 648-7834
Contact: Mr. Ray Fehrenbach
Minimum Salary Placed: $25,000
Recruiting Specialty: General

ANDERSON

Management Recruiters
P.O. Box 2874
Anderson, SC 29622
(864) 225-1258
Contact: Mr. Vernon Pagan
Minimum Salary Placed: $25,000
Recruiting Specialty: General

BAMBERG

Carter and Associates
P.O. Box 1007
Bamberg, SC 29003
(803) 245-5651
Contact: Mr. D. Wayne Carter
Recruiting Specialty: Logistics

BEAUFORT

Exsource
920 Bay Street
Beaufort, SC 29901
(803) 525-0333
Contact: Mr. Sam Domby
Minimum Salary Placed: $25,000
Recruiting Specialty: Banking, data processing and telecommunications

CHARLESTON

Foodstaff
7 Charlotte Street
Charleston, SC 29403
(803) 577-7770
Contact: Mr. Bailey Bolen
Recruiting Specialty: Food and beverages and hospitality

Management Recruiters
4 Carriage Lane, Suite 301
Charleston, SC 29407
(803) 556-6461
Contact: Mr. Robert Bean
Minimum Salary Placed: $25,000
Recruiting Specialty: Manufacturing and
insurance

Synergy Search
1350 Ashley River Road, Suite F
Charleston, SC 29407
(803) 769-4445
Contact: Mr. W. Smith
Minimum Salary Placed: $25,000
Recruiting Specialty: MIS, accounting
and finance

COLUMBIA

Campbell Associates
136 Village Farm Road
Columbia, SC 29223
(803) 736-6475
Contact: Mr. Bill Campbell
Minimum Salary Placed: $25,000
Recruiting Specialty: Food manufacturing

Crutchfield Associates
1000 St. Andrews Road, Suite D
Columbia, SC 29210
(803) 772-6152
Contact: Mr. Bob Crutchfield
Minimum Salary Placed: $40,000
Recruiting Specialty: Sales and marketing

DOT, Inc.
3506 Medical Drive
Columbia, SC 29203
(803) 779-3061

Contact: Mr. William Clowney
Recruiting Specialty: Sales, marketing
and technical

Dunhill of St. Andrews
16 Berry Hill Road, Suite 120
Columbia, SC 29210
(803) 772-6751
Contact: Mr. Richard Bramblett
Minimum Salary Placed: $25,000
Recruiting Specialty: General

Evers Personnel Service
1345 Garner Lane, Suite 103A
Columbia, SC 29210
(803) 772-0451
Contact: Mr. Jim Evers
Minimum Salary Placed: $30,000
Recruiting Specialty: Sales

Fortune Personnel
108 Columbia NE Drive, Suite H
Columbia, SC 29223
(803) 788-8877
Contact: Ms. Jill Felts
Recruiting Specialty: General

Gallman Personnel, Inc.
201 Executive Center Drive, Suite 101
Columbia, SC 29120
(803) 750-4878
Contact: Ms. Stephanie Berry
Recruiting Specialty: Accounting, engineering, and some general

Howett Personnel Associates
2711 Middlesburg Drive, Suite 103
Columbia, SC 29204
(803) 254-6100
Contact: Ms. S. Howett
Minimum Salary Placed: $25,000
Recruiting Specialty: Technical disci-
plines in manufacturing

Keshlear Associates, Inc.
128 Charles Towne Court
Columbia, SC 29209
(803) 783-9466
Contact: Mr. Joe Keshlear
Recruiting Specialty: Data processing
and telecommunication

Management Recruiters
P.O. Box 50785
Columbia, SC 29250
(803) 254-1334
Contact: Mr. Robert Keen
Minimum Salary Placed: $25,000
Recruiting Specialty: Nursing executives
and MIS

The Personnel Network, Inc.
1246 Lake Murray Boulevard
P.O. Box 1426
Columbia, SC 29212
(803) 781-2087
Contact: Mr. Charles Larsen
Minimum Salary Placed: $25,000
Recruiting Specialty: General

Rona Russ & Associates, Inc.
2516 Two Notch Road
Columbia, SC 29204
(803) 256-0600
Contact: Ms. Rona Russ
Recruiting Specialty: Medical therapists

Sales Consultants
1310 Lady Street, Suite 1010
Columbia, SC 29201
(803) 779-7333
Contact: Mr. Harry Grohman
Minimum Salary Placed: $25,000
Recruiting Specialty: Sales

John Shell Associates, Inc.
115 Atrium Way, Suite 122
Columbia, SC 29224
(803) 788-6619
Contact: Mr. John Shell
Minimum Salary Placed: $25,000
Recruiting Specialty: Accounting and fi-
nance

**Snelling Personnel Services of
Columbia**
P.O. Box 8839
Columbia, SC 29202-8839
(803) 252-8888
Contact: Ms. Pam Adams
Recruiting Specialty: General

FLORENCE

Management Recruiters
1224 W. Evans Street, Suite B
Florence, SC 29501
(803) 664-1112
Contact: Mr. Richard Harrington
Minimum Salary Placed: $25,000
Recruiting Specialty: General

FORT MILL

R. Baker & Associates
P.O. Box 3529
Ft. Mill, SC 29715
(803) 548-3101
Contact: Mr. Reed Baker
Recruiting Specialty: Human resources,
manufacturing, engineering, quality, fi-
nance and accounting

Phillips Resource Group
2031-B Carolina Place
Fort Mill, SC 29715
(803) 548-6918
Contact: Mr. Joel McIntyre
Minimum Salary Placed: $25,000
Recruiting Specialty: General

FRIPP ISLAND

The Personnel Shop, Inc.
6 Royal Tern Cove
Fripp Island, SC 29920
(803) 838-4770
Contact: Mr. Michael Ryan
Recruiting Specialty: General

GREENVILLE

AIDE, Inc. Design Services
P.O. Box 6746
Greenville, SC 29606
(864) 244-6123
Contact: Mr. Jim Delaney
Recruiting Specialty: General

Careers Unlimited Group
84 Villa Road, Suite 720
Greenville, SC 29606
(864) 233-1947
Contact: Mr. Thomas Ninan
Minimum Salary Placed: $25,000
Recruiting Specialty: General

Contemporary Management Services, Inc.
60 Pointe Circle, Box A, Suite 226
Greenville, SC 29615
(864) 235-5271

Contact: Mr. Charles Pitts
Minimum Salary Placed: $30,000
Recruiting Specialty: Engineering, technical, manufacturing and production

Dunhill of Greenville
96 Villa Road
Greenville, SC 29615
(864) 271-7180
Contact: Mr. Duke Haynie
Minimum Salary Placed: $25,000
Recruiting Specialty: General

Edmonds Personnel
P.O. Box 26313
Greenville, SC 29616-1313
(864) 288-4848
Contact: Mr. Dave Edmonds
Recruiting Specialty: Engineering and technology

Enterprise Personnel
P.O. Box 4889
Greenville, SC 29608
(864) 246-1200
Contact: Ms. Sue Strange
Recruiting Specialty: Engineers

Financial Search Associates
33 Villa Road
Greenville, SC 29615
(864) 370-9872
Contact: Ms. N. Gladden
Minimum Salary Placed: $25,000
Recruiting Specialty: Accounting, finance and data processing

Fortune Personnel Consultants
25 Woodslake Road
Greenville, SC 29607
(864) 241-7700
Recruiting Specialty: Pharmaceuticals

Godshall and Godshall Personnel
27 Cleveland Street
Greenville, SC 29601
(864) 242-3491
Contact: Mr. Wayne Godshall
Minimum Salary Placed: $25,000
Recruiting Specialty: General

Healthcare Search Associates
P.O. Box 17334
Greenville, SC 29606
(864) 272-1999
Contact: Mr. Dave Gahan
Minimum Salary Placed: $50,000
Recruiting Specialty: Healthcare

Lee Resources, Inc.
P.O. Box 16711
Greenville, SC 29606
(864) 232-5264
Contact: Mr. Jim Hershey
Recruiting Specialty: Sales and marketing, textiles, building materials and business forms

Management Recruiters
330 Pelham Road, Suite 109-B
Greenville, SC 29615
(864) 370-1341
Contact: Mr. R. C. Brennecke
Minimum Salary Placed: $35,000
Recruiting Specialty: General

Jennifer Munro & Partners, Inc.
33 Normandy Road
Greenville, SC 29615
(864) 268-6482
Contact: Ms. Jennifer Munro
Minimum Salary Placed: $70,000
Recruiting Specialty: General

Nase Associates
210 W. Stone Avenue
Greenville, SC 29609
(864) 241-0986
Contact: Mr. Mike Nase
Minimum Salary Placed: $25,000
Recruiting Specialty: Technical disciplines

Phelps Personnel Associates, Inc.
P.O. Box 4177
Greenville, SC 29608
(864) 232-8139
Contact: Mr. Ron Phelps
Recruiting Specialty: Engineering and technical, metalworking, chemical, and film

Phillips Resource Group
Box 5664
Greenville, SC 29607
(864) 271-6350
Contact: Mr. Sam Phillips
Minimum Salary Placed: $20,000
Recruiting Specialty: General

Sales Consultants
330 Pelham Road, Suite 109-B
Greenville, SC 29615
(864) 370-1341
Contact: Mr. R. C. Brennecke
Minimum Salary Placed: $25,000
Recruiting Specialty: Sales

GREENWOOD

Dunhill Personnel
231 F Hampton Street, 6 Village Square
Greenwood, SC 29646
(803) 229-5251
Contact: Mr. Hal Freese
Minimum Salary Placed: $25,000
Recruiting Specialty: General

GREER

HRC Inc.
3 Century Place
Greer, SC 29651
(803) 879-0104
Contact: Ms. Wanda Kneece
Minimum Salary Placed: $18,000
Recruiting Specialty: General

Paragon Placement Services, Inc.
810 West Wade Hampton Boulevard
Greer, SC 29650
(864) 879-8166
Contact: Ms. Judy Brigman
Recruiting Specialty: General

HILTON HEAD ISLAND

Executive Placement
P.O. Box 5663
Hilton Head Island, SC 29938
(803) 785-3705
Contact: Mr. Norm Glick
Recruiting Specialty: Healthcare and
some general

Gold Coast Partners
3 Cardinal Court, Suite 239
Hilton Head Island, SC 29926
(803) 757-5771
Contact: Mr. William Slaughter
Minimum Salary Placed: $25,000
Recruiting Specialty: Sales in computers

The Lawson Group
P.O. Box 7491
Hilton Head Island, SC 29938
(803) 842-4949
Contact: Mr. Jim Lawson
Recruiting Specialty: Printing, pulp and
paper

Tempo Personnel Service
Box 22448
Hilton Head Island, SC 29925
(803) 681-9066
Contact: Mr. Mark Heles
Minimum Salary Placed: $25,000
Recruiting Specialty: General

WDI International
79 Lighthouse Road, Suite 220
Hilton Head Island, SC 29928
(803) 363-2088
Contact: Mr. Jack Cumming
Minimum Salary Placed: $75,000
Recruiting Specialty: Pharmaceuticals
and healthcare

ISLE OF PALMS

Engineer One of South Carolina
103 Palm Blvd., Suite 2B, P.O. Box 441
Isle of Palms, SC 29451
(803) 886-8982
Contact: Kerry Anderson
Recruiting Specialty: Manufacturing,
data processing, design and project engineers and quality engineers

LEXINGTON

Howett Personnel Associates
P.O. Box 9010
Lexington, SC 29071
(803) 957-6929
Contact: Ms. Susan Howett
Recruiting Specialty: Engineering

Snelling Personnel Services
114 Haygood Avenue
Lexington, SC 29072
(803) 359-7644

Contact: Ms. Gina Robbins-McCuen
Recruiting Specialty: General

MARION

Tem-Per, Inc.
204 W. Dozier Street
Marion, SC 29571
(803) 423-7540
Contact: Mr. Alan Heaton
Recruiting Specialty: Manufacturing and production, technology and textiles

MOUNT PLEASANT

James Dooley and Associates
1051 B. Johnnie Dodd Boulevard
Mt. Pleasant, SC 29464
(803) 856-0544
Contact: Mr. James Dooley
Minimum Salary Placed: $25,000
Recruiting Specialty: Healthcare and automotive industrial engineering

Thomas J. Dougherty & Associates Inc.
1470 Ben Sawyer Boulevard
Mt. Pleasant, SC 29451
(803) 881-9898
Contact: Mr. Tom Dougherty
Recruiting Specialty: Engineering, I.E., manufacturing, quality, and purchasing

McClain Group
941 Houston Northcutt, Suite 203
Mt. Pleasant, SC 29464
(803) 881-2840
Contact: Mr. Mark Davis
Recruiting Specialty: Home healthcare

The Rand Company
890 Johnnie Dodds Boulevard, Suite 2-C
Mt. Pleasant, SC 29464
(803) 849-1980
Contact: Mr. Ken Poole
Recruiting Specialty: Engineering

Sales Consultants
454 Coleman Boulevard
Mt. Pleasant, SC 29465
(803) 849-8080
Contact: Mr. Joe Rigter
Minimum Salary Placed: $25,000
Recruiting Specialty: Sales

MYRTLE BEACH

Ford & Associates, Inc.
P.O. Box 3648
Myrtle Beach, SC 29578
(803) 497-5350
Contact: Mr. Travis Ford
Minimum Salary Placed: $25,000
Recruiting Specialty: Textile and chemicals

NORTH CHARLESTON

Charles Foster Staffing
7301 Rivers Avenue, Suite 240
North Charleston, SC 29406
(803) 572-8100
Contact: Ms. Dottie Karst
Recruiting Specialty: General

Power Services
8731 Northpark Boulevard
North Charleston, SC 29406-9264
(803) 572-3000
Contact: Mr. Dan Heagerty
Recruiting Specialty: Engineering

Sales Consultants
3251 Landmark Drive, Suite 141
North Charleston, SC 29418
(803) 767-9300
Contact: Mr. John Dick
Minimum Salary Placed: $25,000
Recruiting Specialty: Sales

Search & Recruit International
2501 Northforest Drive
North Charleston, SC 29420
(803) 572-4040
Contact: Mr. Les Callahan
Minimum Salary Placed: $25,000
Recruiting Specialty: Technical disciplines in high technology

ORANGEBURG

Management Recruiters
2037 St. Matthews Road
Orangeburg, SC 29115
(803) 531-4101
Contact: Mr. Dick Crawford
Minimum Salary Placed: $25,000
Recruiting Specialty: Engineering

Sales Consultants
117 Doyle Street NE
Orangeburg, SC 29116
(803) 536-4601
Contact: Mr. Rick Jackson
Minimum Salary Placed: $25,000
Recruiting Specialty: Sales

PAWLEYS ISLAND

Penn Hill Associates
P.O. Box 1367
Pawleys Island, SC 29585
(803) 237-8988

Contact: Mr. Conrad Kohler
Minimum Salary Placed: $25,000
Recruiting Specialty: Credit finance

ROCK HILL

Management Recruiters
1925 Ebenezer Road
Rock Hill, SC 29732
(803) 324-5181
Contact: Mr. Herman Smith
Minimum Salary Placed: $25,000
Recruiting Specialty: General

Staff Resources, Inc.
P.O. Box 4557
Rock Hill, SC 29732
(803) 366-0500
Contact: Mr. Dick Jordan
Recruiting Specialty: Manufacturing and engineering, also textiles and food

SENECA

Cooper Management Associates
12 Boardwalk Place
Seneca, SC 29678
(864) 885-6100
Contact: Mr. Mike Cooper
Minimum Salary Placed: $25,000
Recruiting Specialty: Textiles

SIMPSONVILLE

Corporate Solutions
Box 1974
Simpsonville, SC 29681
(864) 297-5888
Contact: Mr. James Webb
Minimum Salary Placed: $25,000
Recruiting Specialty: General

SPARTANBURG

AAA Employment
145 North Church Street, Suite 27
Spartanburg, SC 29306
(864) 591-4201
Contact: Mr. Les Koivula
Recruiting Specialty: General

Atlantic Recruiters
10 Metro Drive
Spartanburg, SC 29303
(864) 573-7800
Minimum Salary Placed: $25,000
Recruiting Specialty: Textiles

Atlas Personnel Inc.
465 Kennedy Street, P.O. Box 3261
Spartanburg, SC 29304
(864) 585-8161
Contact: Ms. Thelma Bridgeman
Recruiting Specialty: Engineering and
data processing

Harvey Personnel, Inc.
P.O. Box 1931
Spartanburg, SC 29304
(864) 582-5616
Contact: Mr. Howard Harvey
Recruiting Specialty: General

The Hiring Link
P.O. Box 5399
Spartanburg, SC 29304
(864) 573-9575
Contact: Ms. Francis Lee
Recruiting Specialty: Industrial and clerical

Kersey and Associates
600 Oak Forest Road
Spartanburg, SC 29301
(864) 574-6724
Minimum Salary Placed: $35,000
Recruiting Specialty: Data processing

Quest
141½ W Main Street
Spartanburg, SC 29306
(864) 573-7337
Minimum Salary Placed: $40,000
Recruiting Specialty: Manufacturing in
textiles

SUMTER

Dunhill Professional Search
345 Mallard Drive
Sumter, SC 29150
(803) 469-9951
Contact: Ms. Brenda Skelton
Recruiting Specialty: General

People Resources, Inc.
P.O. Box 846
Sumter, SC 29150
(803) 773-6600
Contact: Mr. Ben Griffith
Recruiting Specialty: Office administration and industrial

TAYLORS

Management Search Associates
7 Bridgewood Avenue
Taylors, SC 29687
(864) 292-5888
Contact: Mr. Donald V. Brown
Recruiting Specialty: General

TRAVELERS REST

Management Recruiters
907 N. Main Street
Travelers Rest, SC 29690
(864) 834-0643
Contact: Mr. Guy Carter
Minimum Salary Placed: $25,000
Recruiting Specialty: Manufacturing in textiles

UNION

Advanced Professional
P.O. Box 1162
Union, SC 29379
(864) 427-3623
Contact: Mr. Jerry Dorsey
Recruiting Specialty: General

John Carwile Personnel Consultants
P.O. Box 401
Union, SC 29379
(864) 427-1227
Contact: Mr. Brooks Carwile
Recruiting Specialty: Textiles

Wades Employment Agency, Inc.
204 South Gadberry Street
Union, SC 29379
(864) 427-1212
Contact: Mr. Darrell Wade
Recruiting Specialty: General

SOUTH DAKOTA

PIERRE

McGladrey & Pullen
711 Wells Avenue
Pierre, SD 59501
(605) 224-8826
Recruiting Specialty: General

RAPID CITY

McGladrey & Pullen
529 Kansas City Street
P.O. Box 2654
Rapid City, SD 57709
(605) 342-9345
Contact: Mr. Jim Books
Minimum Salary Placed: $30,000
Recruiting Specialty: General

SIOUX FALLS

Management Recruiters
2600 S. Minnesota Avenue, Suite 202
Sioux Falls, SD 57105
(605) 334-9291
Contact: Mr. Bob Good
Minimum Salary Placed: $20,000
Recruiting Specialty: General

McGladrey & Pullen
100 S. Phillips Avenue, Suite 404
Sioux Falls, SD 57102
(605) 336-0753
Contact: Mr. Mike Shull
Minimum Salary Placed: $30,000
Recruiting Specialty: General

T E N N E S S E E

ARDMORE

First Search
P.O. Box 85
Ardmore, TN 38449
(615) 427-8800
Contact: Mr. Jim Fowler
Minimum Salary Placed: $25,000
Recruiting Specialty: Animal and agri-business

BRENTWOOD

Reid Group
7000 Executive Center Drive, Suite 125
Brentwood, TN 37027
(615) 371-1689
Contact: Ms. Linda Reid
Recruiting Specialty: Life insurance

Bain Personnel Inc.
5110 Maryland Way, Suite 290
Brentwood, TN 37027
(615) 371-1400
Contact: Mr. Tom Bain
Minimum Salary Placed: $25,000
Recruiting Specialty: General

Cook Associates
700 Chadwick Drive
Brentwood, TN 37027
(615) 373-8263
Contact: Mr. P. Gene Cook
Minimum Salary Placed: $25,000
Recruiting Specialty: General

Gros Executive Search
7003 Chadwick Drive
Brentwood, TN 37027
(615) 661-4568
Contact: Mr. Dennis Gros
Minimum Salary Placed: $25,000
Recruiting Specialty: General

Ingold Group
5115 Maryland Way
Brentwood, TN 37027
(615) 377-1940
Contact: Mr. Bill Ingold
Minimum Salary Placed: $25,000
Recruiting Specialty: General

Koerner & Associates, Inc.
750 Old Hickory Boulevard, Suite 150
Brentwood, TN 37027
(615) 371-6162
Contact: Ms. Pam Koerner
Minimum Salary Placed: $50,000
Recruiting Specialty: Attorneys

Questar Partners Inc.
100 Winners Circle, Suite 160
Brentwood, TN 37027
(615) 371-8800
Contact: Mr. R. Petty
Minimum Salary Placed: $35,000
Recruiting Specialty: General

Rick Robertson / Drew Foster Sales Consultants of Brentwood
7003 Chadwick Drive, Suite 331
Brentwood, TN 37027
(615) 373-1111
Recruiting Specialty: General

Russell, Montgomery & Associates
101 Continental Place, Suite 105
Brentwood, TN 37027
(615) 377-9603
Contact: Mr. Dennis Russell
Minimum Salary Placed: $30,000
Recruiting Specialty: General

Sales Consultants
7003 Chadwick Drive, Suite 331
Brentwood, TN 37027
(615) 373-1111
Contact: Mr. Drew Foster
Minimum Salary Placed: $20,000
Recruiting Specialty: Sales

Shiloh Careers International, Inc.
P.O. Box 831
Brentwood, TN 37024
(615) 373-3090
Contact: Ms. Mary Ann Webber
Minimum Salary Placed: $25,000
Recruiting Specialty: Insurance

BUTLER

The Haley Enterprises
P.O. Box 90
Butler, TN 37640
(423) 768-2183
Contact: Ms. Trula Haley
Recruiting Specialty: Engineering, manu-
facturing, and nuclear generalist

CHATTANOOGA

Bowman and Associates Inc.
5700 Brainer Road
Uptain Building, Suite 522
Chattanooga, TN 37411
(423) 894-9552
Contact: Ms. Jean Bowman
Minimum Salary Placed: $25,000
Recruiting Specialty: General

Corporate Staffing Resources
5700 Brainerd Road, Suite 5800
Chattanooga, TN 37411
(423) 499-0692

Contact: Mr. A. Gay
Recruiting Specialty: General

Dougherty & Associates
2345 Ashford Drive
Chattanooga, TN 37421
(615) 899-1060
Contact: Mr. Robert Dougherty
Minimum Salary Placed: $35,000
Recruiting Specialty: Chemicals, water
treatment and energy/environmental

Fortune Personnel Consultants
202 Franklin Building
Chattanooga, TN 97411
(423) 855-0444
Contact: Mr. Dave Dickson
Minimum Salary Placed: $25,000
Recruiting Specialty: General

Grant and Associates Inc.
2 Northgate Park
Chattanooga, TN 67415
(423) 877-4561
Contact: Mr. Mike Grant
Minimum Salary Placed: $25,000
Recruiting Specialty: General

Management Recruiters
7405 Shallowford Road, Suite 520
Chattanooga, TN 37421
(423) 894-5500
Contact: Mr. Bill Cooper
Minimum Salary Placed: $25,000
Recruiting Specialty: General

Management Recruiters
5211 Highway 153, Suite H
Plaza 153 Building
Chattanooga, TN 37343
(423) 877-4040

Contact: Mr. Chub Ensimger
Minimum Salary Placed: $25,000
Recruiting Specialty: General

Notetics
118 Le Parkway Drive, Suite 302
Chattanooga, TN 37421
(423) 954-1866
Contact: Mr. Scott Nash
Recruiting Specialty: MIS and electrical
engineers

Phoenix Consulting Group Inc.
118 Lee Parkway Drive
Chattanooga, TN 37421
(423) 892-3897
Contact: Mr. Don Holly
Minimum Salary Placed: $25,000
Recruiting Specialty: Rubber, metals and
computers

Sales Consultants
7405 Shallowford Road, Suite 520
Chattanooga, TN 37421
(423) 894-5500
Contact: Mr. Bill Cooper
Minimum Salary Placed: $20,000
Recruiting Specialty: Sales

CLEVELAND

Dunhill Personnel
301 King Den Drive NW
Cleveland, TN 37312
(423) 339-0177
Contact: Ms. Brenda Skelton
Minimum Salary Placed: $25,000
Recruiting Specialty: Engineering

COLLEGE GROVE

Dunhill Professional Search
6805 Arno-Allisons Road
College Grove, TN 37046
(615) 368-7979
Contact: Mr. Ray O'Steen
Minimum Salary Placed: $25,000
Recruiting Specialty: General

COLLIERVILLE

Healthcare Recruiters
155 North Main, 103 A
Collierville, TN 38017
(901) 853-0900
Contact: Mr. Jeb Blanchard
Recruiting Specialty: Healthcare

The Pitman Group
347 Harpers Ferry
Collierville, TN 38017
(901) 854-6828
Contact: Ms. Melinda Pittman
Recruiting Specialty: Information systems and technical

CORDOVA

Austin - Allen Company
8127 Walnut Grove Road
Cordova, TN 38018
(901) 756-0900
Contact: Ms. Charlotte Cupp
Minimum Salary Placed: $30,000
Recruiting Specialty: Manufacturing and
engineering

Fortune Personnel Consultants
52 Timber Creek Drive
Cordova, TN 38018
(901) 757-5031
Contact: Mr. Fred O'Connor
Minimum Salary Placed: $25,000
Recruiting Specialty: Raw materials and technical disciplines

Howard Randall and Associates, Inc.
320 S. Walnut Bend Road
Cordova, TN 38018
(901) 754-3333
Recruiting Specialty: General

DANDRIDGE

Academy Graduates Career
1764 Doc Terry Road
Dandridge, TN 37725
(423) 397-3300
Contact: Mr. T. Carpick
Minimum Salary Placed: $25,000
Recruiting Specialty: Technical and engineering

EAST RIDGE

Advantage Personnel
4159 Ringgold Road
East Ridge, TN 37412
(423) 697-0774
Minimum Salary Placed: $25,000
Recruiting Specialty: General

FRANKLIN

Management Recruiters
236 Public Square, Suite 201
Franklin, TN 37064
(615) 791-4391

Contact: Mr. Roger Marriott
Minimum Salary Placed: $25,000
Recruiting Specialty: Printing

Gene Murphy and Associates
1102 Murray Creek Lane
Franklin, TN 37064
(615) 790-6955
Contact: Mr. Gene Murphy
Minimum Salary Placed: $25,000
Recruiting Specialty: Data processing

Physician Placement Service
906 Loggers Run
Franklin, TN 37069
(615) 662-5435
Contact: Mr. Dennis Bottomley
Recruiting Specialty: Physicians

GOODLETTSVILLE

Darrell Walker Personnel
515 Two Mile Parkway
Goodlettsville, TN 37072
(615) 859-1153
Contact: Ms. Myra Hunter
Recruiting Specialty: Restaurant, management, and general

HENDERSONVILLE

Baker & Baker Employment Services
1191 W. Main Street
Hendersonville, TN 37075
(615) 824-5253
Recruiting Specialty: General

Quest International
123 Lake Haven Lane
Hendersonville, TN 37075
(615) 824-8900

Contact: Mr. B. Griffin
Minimum Salary Placed: $25,000
Recruiting Specialty: Hospitality

Technical Resource Associates
313 E. Main Street, Suite 12
Hendersonville, TN 37075
(615) 824-1444
Contact: Mr. Richard Holtz
Minimum Salary Placed: $25,000
Recruiting Specialty: Technical disciplines

HUNTINGDON

Walt Montgomery Associates
385 Northwood Drive
Huntingdon, TN 38344
(901) 986-8328
Contact: Mr. Walt Montgomery
Minimum Salary Placed: $50,000
Recruiting Specialty: Agri-food

JOHNSON CITY

Fortune Personnel Consultants
2700 S. Roan Street, Suite 206
Johnson City, TN 37601
(423) 926-1123
Contact: Mr. Walter Engel
Minimum Salary Placed: $30,000
Recruiting Specialty: Manufacturing

KINGSPORT

Rasmussen & Associates, Inc.
P.O. Box 5037
Kingsport, TN 37663
(423) 239-6664
Contact: Mr. Bill Rasmussen
Recruiting Specialty: Manufacturing
(plant managers, office support, no sales)

KNOXVILLE

Engineer One Incorporated
P.O. Box 23037
Knoxville, TN 37933
(423) 675-1221
Contact: Mr. George Chaney
Recruiting Specialty: Engineering

Management Recruiters
9050 Executive Park Drive, Suite 6
Knoxville, TN 37923
(423) 694-1628
Contact: Mr. James Kline
Minimum Salary Placed: $25,000
Recruiting Specialty: General

Phillips & Phillips Associates, Inc.
8839 Ashton Court
Knoxville, TN 37923
Contact: Ms. Cathy Phillips
Recruiting Specialty: General

Russell, Montgomery & Associates
301 Gallaher View Road, Suite 111
Knoxville, TN 37919
(423) 691-4733
Contact: Mr. Richard Bowling
Minimum Salary Placed: $30,000
Recruiting Specialty: General

Snelling Personnel
408 North Cedar Bluff Road
Knoxville, TN 37923
(615) 693-6620
Contact: Ms. Marcia Dobbin
Minimum Salary Placed: $20,000
Recruiting Specialty: General

LENOIR CITY

Management Recruiters
603 Highway 321 North, Suite 202
Lenoir City, TN 37771
(423) 986-3000
Contact: Mr. Ray Strobo
Minimum Salary Placed: $25,000
Recruiting Specialty: General

LEWISBURG

B.S.D. & Associates
P.O. Box 1063
Lewisburg, TN 37091
(615) 270-5939
Contact: Ronnie Dalton
Recruiting Specialty: Manufacturing

LOUDON

Sillman & Associates
3503 Marble Bluff Rd.
Loudon, TN 37774
(423) 458-9888
Contact: Mr. Roy R. Sillman
Recruiting Specialty: General

MADISON

Technisearch
104 Cude Lane, Suite 122
Madison, TN 37115
(615) 865-8004
Contact: Mr. Sam Gee
Recruiting Specialty: Machine designers,
surface mount techs, project engineers

MARTIN

The Hamilton-Ryker Co.
P.O. Box 1068
Martin, TN 38237
(901) 587-3161
Contact: Mr. Johnny Nanney
Recruiting Specialty: General

MEMPHIS

AAA Employment
5336 Estate Office Park, Suite 2
Memphis, TN 38119
(901) 763-0999
Contact: Ms. Marylee Galloney
Recruiting Specialty: General

Adia Personnel Services
5100 Poplar, Suite 500
Memphis, TN 38137
(901) 683-2342
Contact: Ms. Joni Richardson
Recruiting Specialty: Office support

American National Recruiters
6263 Poplar Avenue, Suite 940
Memphis, TN 38119
(901) 767-0216
Contact: Mr. Tom Townsend
Minimum Salary Placed: $25,000
Recruiting Specialty: General

Austin-Allen Company
Memphis, TN 38018
(901) 756-0900
Contact: C.A. Cupp
Recruiting Specialty: General

Brewer Personnel
5350 Poplar, Suite 216 Sedgewyck Center
Memphis, TN 38138
(901) 366-1400
Contact: Ms. June Johnson
Recruiting Specialty: General

Bright Professionals
1028 Oakhaven Road, Suite 101
Memphis, TN 38119
(901) 767-7007
Contact: Ms. Glenda Rust
Recruiting Specialty: General

Careers Unlimited
2500 Mt. Moriah, Suite H240
Memphis, TN 38115
(901) 367-9999
Contact: Ms. Bertha Miller
Recruiting Specialty: General, office support, and accounting

Consultant Exchange
1355 Lynnfield Road
Memphis, TN 38119
(901) 682-5663
Contact: Mr. D. Marzahl
Minimum Salary Placed: $25,000
Recruiting Specialty: General

Cornerstone Service
5100 Poplar Avenue
Memphis, TN 38137
(901) 767-4000
Contact: Mr. G. Craig
Minimum Salary Placed: $25,000
Recruiting Specialty: General

Corporate Image Group
3145 Hickory Hill, Suite 204
Memphis, TN 38115
(901) 360-8091

Contact: Mr. Joseph Knose
Minimum Salary Placed: $30,000
Recruiting Specialty: General

Dempsey Personnel, Inc.
2099 Hallwood Drive
Memphis, TN
(901) 722-2147
Contact: Ms. Dot Gilbertson
Recruiting Specialty: Information systems

Dunhill Personnel System, Inc.
5120 Stage Road, Suite 2
Memphis, TN 38134
(901) 386-2500
Contact: Mr. Eugene Rhodes
Minimum Salary Placed: $25,000
Recruiting Specialty: General

Frye/Joure & Associates Inc.
4646 Poplar Avenue, Suite 335
Memphis, TN 38117
(901) 683-7792
Contact: Ms. Leslie Mink
Minimum Salary Placed: $40,000
Recruiting Specialty: High technology, chemicals and utilities

Gateway Group
1770 Kirby Parkway, Suite 216
Memphis, TN 38138
(901) 756-6050
Contact: Mr. Charles Haddad
Minimum Salary Placed: $25,000
Recruiting Specialty: Accounting, finance, data processing and banking and some general

Healthcare Concepts
633 Monroe
Memphis, TN 38103
(901) 527-7701
Contact: Ms. Susan Oglesby
Recruiting Specialty: Healthcare

Randall Howard & Associates, Inc.
320 Walnut Bend Road, Suite 11
Memphis, TN 38183
(901) 759-1000
Contact: Mr. Randall Howard
Minimum Salary Placed: $50,000
Recruiting Specialty: General

Information Systems Group
6363 Poplar Avenue
Memphis, TN
(901) 684-1030
Recruiting Specialty: Data processing

Interim Personnel
5118 Park Avenue
Memphis, TN 38117
(901) 761-6009
Contact: Pat Busey
Recruiting Specialty: General

J & D Resources Inc.
6555 Quince Road, Suite 425
Memphis, TN 38119
(901) 753-0500
Contact: Ms. Jill Herrin
Minimum Salary Placed: $25,000
Recruiting Specialty: MIS

Madison Personnel
1864 Poplar Crest Cv.
Memphis, TN 38119
(901) 761-2660
Contact: Mr. David White
Recruiting Specialty: Manufacturing

Management Recruiters
5495 Winchester Road, Suite 5
Memphis, TN 38115
(901) 794-3130
Contact: Mr. Wally Watson
Minimum Salary Placed: $25,000
Recruiting Specialty: Managed healthcare

Memphis Legal Personnel
1 Commerce Square, Suite 1190
Memphis, TN 38103
(901) 527-3573
Contact: Ms. Mary Walpole
Recruiting Specialty: Legal

Miriam Leffler Personnel Services
4990 Poplar
Memphis TN 38119
(901) 761-9778
Contact: Ms. Miraim Leffler
Recruiting Specialty: Administrative and
office support

PIRC
1028 Cresthaven Road
Memphis, TN 38119
(901) 685-2042
Contact: Mr. J. Murrell
Recruiting Specialty: Physicians, insurance and healthcare

Pearce Personnel
3246 Scheibler Road, Suite 1
Memphis, TN 38128
(901) 377-2264
Contact: Ms. Doris Pearce
Recruiting Specialty: Accounting and
data processing

Quarles and Kelly Associates
813 Ridge Lake Boulevard
Memphis, TN 38120
(901) 682-5352
Contact: Ms. K. Kelly
Minimum Salary Placed: $25,000
Recruiting Specialty: General

Randstad Staffing
6151 Poplar
Memphis, TN 38119
(901) 767-7000
Contact: Ms. Linda Galipeau
Recruiting Specialty: General

Sales Consultants
5865 Ridgeway Center
Parkway Suite 300
Memphis, TN 38120
(901) 761-2086
Contact: Mr. Wayne Williams
Minimum Salary Placed: $20,000
Recruiting Specialty: Sales

Allen Schoenberger and Associates
2129 S. Germantown Road, Suite 212
Memphis, TN 38118
(901) 755-0441
Recruiting Specialty: Consumer product
sales

Senior Achievement
1790 Kirby Parkway, Suite 125
Memphis, TN 38138
(901) 758-8777
Contact: Mr. Ron Cook
Recruiting Specialty: General

Sims & Company
6780 Pecan Hill
Memphis, TN 38135
(901) 373-4805
Contact: Mr. Joe Sims
Recruiting Specialty: Consumer goods,
soft drinks, beer

Snelling & Snelling
5050 Poplar Avenue
Memphis, TN 38119
(901) 767-5835
Contact: Ms. Sharon Jordon
Recruiting Specialty: Office support and
light industrial

Staffing Solutions
6363 Poplar
Memphis, TN 38119
(901) 761-9595
Contact: Mr. Steve Borden
Recruiting Specialty: Accounting, banking, and finance

Summerfield Associates, Inc.
6555 Quince Road, Suite 311
Memphis, TN 38119
(901) 753-7068
Contact: Ms. Dotty Summerfield-Beall
Minimum Salary Placed: $25,000
Recruiting Specialty: General

The Williams Company
5628 Murray Road
Memphis, TN 38119
(901) 761-1070
Contact: Mr. Floyd Williams
Recruiting Specialty: Beverage industry

MORRISTOWN

Career Professionals, Inc.
P.O. Box 1223
Morristown, TN 37816-1223
(423) 587-4363
Contact: Mr. Jim Beelaert
Recruiting Specialty: Manufacturing

NASHVILLE

Accountants On Call
1101 Kermit Drive, Suite 600
Nashville, TN 37217
(615) 399-0200
Contact: Mr. Milton Ellis
Minimum Salary Placed: $20,000
Recruiting Specialty: Accounting and finance

Adia Personnel Services
3401 West End Ave., Suite 305
Nashville, TN 37203
(615) 292-5757
Contact: Ms. Laura Coverstone
Recruiting Specialty: Office support

Amicus Staffing
1900 Church Street, Suite 425
Nashville, TN 37203
(615) 320-7700
Contact: Mr. Joe Freedman
Recruiting Specialty: Legal, office support

Arvie Personnel Services, Inc.
1719 West End Avenue, Suite 116-W
Nashville, TN 37203
(615) 321-9577
Contact: Ms. Janice Sawyers
Recruiting Specialty: General

B.K. Barnes & Associates
475 Metroplex Drive
Building 400, Suite 405
Nashville, TN 37211
(615) 832-9935
Contact: Mr. B. K. Barnes
Minimum Salary Placed: $30,000
Recruiting Specialty: General

Bishop Placement Services
1321 Murfreesboror Pike, Suite 600
Nashville, TN 37217
(615) 367-6177
Contact: Mr. Otis Bishop
Recruiting Specialty: Restaurant management, retail, computer, and some general

Burton Personnel Resources, Inc.
611 Commerce Street, Suite 2915
Nashville, TN 37203
(615) 255-0005
Contact: Ms. Georgia Burton
Recruiting Specialty: Office support

Educational Management Network
5143 N. Stanford Drive
Nashville, TN 37215
(615) 665-3388
Contact: Mr. Gary Posner
Minimum Salary Placed: $50,000
Recruiting Specialty: Non-profit, education and healthcare

Executive Development Inc.
404 James Robertson Parkway,
 Suite 1120
Nashville, TN 37219
(615) 244-8484
Contact: Ms. Karen Saul
Minimum Salary Placed: $25,000
Recruiting Specialty: Finance

Growth Consultants of America
Box 150928
Nashville, TN 37215
(615) 383-0550
Contact: Mr. John Haggard
Minimum Salary Placed: $40,000
Recruiting Specialty: Healthcare

Helfer Executive Consultants
628 Harpeth Trace Drive
Nashville, TN 37205
(615) 356-2777
Contact: Mr. Frederick Helfer
Minimum Salary Placed: $40,000
Recruiting Specialty: General

Dorothy Johnson's Career Consultants
21st Fl. - First American Center
Nashville, TN 37238
(615) 244-4060
Contact: Ms. Dorothy Johnson
Recruiting Specialty: Office support and accounting

Kaludis Consulting Group
2505 Hillsboro Road, Suite 302
Nashville, TN 37212
(615) 297-3880
Contact: Mr. George Kaludis
Minimum Salary Placed: $50,000
Recruiting Specialty: Education and non-profit

Leeds and Leeds
7003 Chadwick Drive, Suite 238
Nashville, TN 37209
(615) 371-1119
Contact: Mr. Jerry Leeds
Minimum Salary Placed: $25,000
Recruiting Specialty: General

WR McLeod & Associates, Inc.
201 Thompson Lane, Suite 8-A
Nashville TN 37211
(615) 333-2969
Contact: Mr. Bill McLeod
Recruiting Specialty: General

Morgan Group
2126 21st Avenue South
Box 121153
Nashville, TN 37212
(615) 297-5272
Minimum Salary Placed: $25,000
Recruiting Specialty: Accounting and finance

PCA, Inc.
P.O. Box 140410
Nashville, TN 37214-0410
(615) 399-0026
Contact: Mr. Gregory Beatty
Recruiting Specialty: General

Remedy Personnel Service
2817 W. End Avenue
Nashville, TN 37203
(615) 320-9290
Recruiting Specialty: Office support and light industrial

Robert Half International
15 Century Boulevard, Suite 407
Nashville, TN 37214
(615) 871-4900
Contact: Mr. R. Hibray
Recruiting Specialty: Accounting and finance

Sales Consultants
1101 Kermit Drive, Suite 426
Nashville, TN 37217
(615) 367-0300
Contact: Mr. Lou Jumonville
Minimum Salary Placed: $20,000
Recruiting Specialty: Sales

Snelling Personnel Services
1808 West End Ave., Suite 1217
Nashville, TN 37203
(615) 329-0223
Contact: Ms. Janice Bobbit
Recruiting Specialty: Clerical, sales, and management

Snelling Search
4721 Trousdale Drive, Suite 202
Nashville, TN 37220
(615) 331-0980
Contact: Ms. B. Clark
Minimum Salary Placed: $35,000
Recruiting Specialty: Plant engineering in manufacturing

Southwestern Professional Services
P.O. Box 305140
Nashville, TN 37230
(615) 391-2716
Contact: Mr. Carl Roberts
Minimum Salary Placed: $30,000
Recruiting Specialty: Outside sales, sales management, and general

OLD HICKORY

Robert Walker Associates
P.O. Box 166
Old Hickory, TN 37138
(615) 847-2311
Contact: Mr. Bob Walker
Recruiting Specialty: General

PULASKI

Alexander & Associates
P.O. Box 321
Pulaski, TN 38478
(615) 424-3159
Contact: Mr. Bob V. Alexander
Recruiting Specialty: Manufacturing, technical, human resources, printing, manager, and accounting

SEVIERVILLE

Just Management Services Inc.
441 Forks of the River Parkway
Sevierville, TN 37864
(423) 428-0406
Contact: Mr. Jim Just
Minimum Salary Placed: $35,000
Recruiting Specialty: Apparel, home furnishings and textiles

SEYMOUR

Fortune Personnel Consultants
10339 Chapman Highway
Seymour, TN 37865
(423) 577-1313
Contact: Mr. Ken Colbourn
Minimum Salary Placed: $35,000
Recruiting Specialty: Engineering

T E X A S

AMARILLO

Recruiting Associates of Amarillo
P.O. Box 8473
Amarillo, TX 79114
(806) 353-9548
Contact: Mr. Michael Rokey
Minimum Salary Placed: $20,000
Recruiting Specialty: General

ARLINGTON

Accounting Resources International, Inc.
2261 Brookhollow Plaza, Suite 100
Arlington, TX 76006
(817) 640-8850
Contact: Mr. Tom Hinds
Minimum Salary Placed: $30,000
Recruiting Specialty: Accounting and finance

American Medical Search
815 NE Green Oaks Boulevard, Suite 120
Arlington, TX 76006
(817) 640-6406
Recruiting Specialty: Physicians

Burnett's Staffing, Inc.
2710 Avenue E East
Arlington, TX 76011-5240
(817) 649-7000
Contact: Ms. Joyce Burnett
Recruiting Specialty: General

Dunhill Personnel
1301 S. Bowen Road, Suite 370
Arlington, TX 76013
(817) 265-2291
Contact: Mr. Jon Molkentine
Minimum Salary Placed: $25,000
Recruiting Specialty: General

Hedman & Associates
3312 Woodford, Suite 200
Arlington, TX 76013
(817) 277-0888
Contact: Mr. Kent Hedman
Minimum Salary Placed: $40,000
Recruiting Specialty: General

Management Recruiters
1009 W. Randol Mill Road, Suite 209
Arlington, TX 76012
(817) 469-6161
Contact: Mr. Robert Stoessel
Minimum Salary Placed: $40,000
Recruiting Specialty: Chemical engineering, insurance and technical

Slater & Associates
P.O. Box 13531
Arlington, TX 76094
(817) 265-3396
Contact: Mr. Robert Slater
Minimum Salary Placed: $125,000
Recruiting Specialty: General

AUSTIN

Accountemps
6836 Austin Center Boulevard
Austin, TX 78731
(512) 345-0303
Recruiting Specialty: Accounting

Austin Career Consultants Inc.
3624 N. Hills Drive, Suite B205
Austin, TX 78731
(512) 346-6660
Contact: Mr. Chuck Wehling
Minimum Salary Placed: $25,000
Recruiting Specialty: High technology,
data processing, engineering and telecommunications

Austin Group International
117 Laura Lane, Suite 200
Austin, TX 78746
(512) 329-8077
Contact: Mr. Ray Holley
Minimum Salary Placed: $60,000
Recruiting Specialty: Marketing and technical disciplines in computers and high
technology

Dunhill Personnel
505 E. Huntland Drive, Suite 190
Austin, TX 78752
(512) 458-5271
Contact: Mr. Mike Ashby
Minimum Salary Placed: $25,000
Recruiting Specialty: General

Elliot Associates, Inc.
2813 Rio Grande, Suite 101
Austin, TX 78705
(512) 472-4484
Contact: Mr. Michael Guerchon
Minimum Salary Placed: $20,000
Recruiting Specialty: Hospitality

Ellis and Associates Inc.
1000 Westbank Drive, Suite SA-110
Austin, TX 78746
(512) 328-5067
Contact: Rose and Joe Ellis
Minimum Salary Placed: $40,000
Recruiting Specialty: Insurance, legal and
mortgage banking

Greywolf Consulting Service
301 Congress Avenue, Suite 510
Austin, TX 78701
(512) 320-8100
Contact: Mr. Jim McCaskill
Minimum Salary Placed: $35,000
Recruiting Specialty: General

Hardie Company
600 Sabine Street, Suite 100
Austin, TX 78701
(512) 474-4474
Minimum Salary Placed: $20,000
Recruiting Specialty: High technology

R. W. Hebel Association
4833 Spicewood Springs Road, Suite 202
Austin, TX 78759
(512) 338-9691
Contact: Mr. Robert Hebel
Minimum Salary Placed: $100,000
Recruiting Specialty: Healthcare

Houtz-Strawn Association, Inc.
11402 Bee Caves Road West
Austin, TX 78733
(512) 263-1131
Contact: Mr. William Strawn
Minimum Salary Placed: $125,000
Recruiting Specialty: Pharmaceuticals

Johnson & Associates
8308 Tecumseh Drive
Austin, TX 78753-5745
(512) 339-9000
Contact: Ms. Chloe Johnson
Recruiting Specialty: Economic development

A.T. Kearney
6701 Fort Davis, Suite B
Austin, TX 78731
(512) 343-8677
Contact: Mr. Dick Beal
Minimum Salary Placed: $100,000
Recruiting Specialty: General

Lehman & McLesky
98 San Jacinto Boulevard, Suite 330
Austin, TX 78701
(512) 478-1131
Contact: Ms. Jan Lehman
Minimum Salary Placed: $70,000
Recruiting Specialty: General

Lewis Group
P.O. Box 162726
Austin, TX 78716
(512) 327-3959
Contact: Mr. Bob McConnell
Minimum Salary Placed: $26,000
Recruiting Specialty: Food industry

Management Recruiters
1250 Capital of Texas Highway
3 Cielo Center, Suite 650
Austin, TX 78746
(512) 327-8292
Contact: Jan and Martin Hansen
Minimum Salary Placed: $40,000
Recruiting Specialty: General

Management Recruiters
8310 N. Capital of Texas Highway,
  Suite 400
Austin, TX 78731
(512) 338-0880
Contact: Ms. Lorraine Keller
Minimum Salary Placed: $25,000
Recruiting Specialty: General

National Human Resource Group
1001 Capital of Texas Highway
Building L, Suite 100
Austin, TX 78734
(512) 261-7770
Contact: Mr. Tom Bolick
Minimum Salary Placed: $25,000
Recruiting Specialty: General

O'Keefe and Associates
3420 Executive Center Drive, Suite 114
Austin, TX 78731
(512) 343-1134
Contact: Mr. J. O'Keefe
Minimum Salary Placed: $40,000
Recruiting Specialty: Data processing, software engineering, technical and marketing

Pencom Systems Inc.
9050 Capital of Texas Highway, Suite 310
Austin, TX 78759
(512) 343-1111
Contact: Mr. Tom Morgan
Recruiting Specialty: MIS and computers

Pierce & Associates, Inc.
8102 Club Court
Austin, TX 78759
(512) 345-0051
Contact: Mr. Douglas Pierce
Minimum Salary Placed: $50,000
Recruiting Specialty: General

Sales Consultants
106 E. 6th Street, Suite 430
Austin, TX 78701
(512) 476-3555
Contact: Mr. C. Jay Middlebrook
Minimum Salary Placed: $20,000
Recruiting Specialty: Sales

Shiela Smith and Associates Inc.
400 W. 15th Street, Suite 1620
Austin, TX 78701
(512) 472-1400
Contact: Ms. Sheila Smith
Minimum Salary Placed: $30,000
Recruiting Specialty: General

Strategic Associates
13915 Burnet Road, Suite 304
Austin, TX 78728
(512) 218-8222
Contact: Mr. Michael Goldman
Minimum Salary Placed: $40,000
Recruiting Specialty: Manufacturing

TAD Data Service
6101 Balcones Drive
Austin, TX 78731
(512) 458-2577
Recruiting Specialty: Data processing

Steven Williams and Associates
4309 Canyonside Trail
Austin, TX 78731
(512) 794-8600
Contact: Mr. Steven Williams
Minimum Salary Placed: $20,000
Recruiting Specialty: General

Zingaro & Company
4200 Green Cliffs Road
Austin, TX 78746
(512) 327-7277
Contact: Mr. Ron Zingaro
Minimum Salary Placed: $100,000
Recruiting Specialty: Healthcare

BEAUMONT

Allied Personnel
505 Milam
Beaumont, TX 77701
(409) 835-0700
Contact: Mr. Bobby Henderson
Recruiting Specialty: General

Pate Resources Group Inc.
595 Orleans Street, Suite 707
Beaumont, TX 77701
(409) 833-4514
Contact: Mr. W.L. Pate, Jr.
Minimum Salary Placed: $35,000
Recruiting Specialty: General

BEDFORD

Bower & Associates
P.O. Box 1206
Bedford, TX 76095
(817) 283-2256
Contact: Mr. Richard Bower
Minimum Salary Placed: $35,000
Recruiting Specialty: Sales and marketing in manufacturing, fabrication, energy and utility

BELLAIRE

Intra Tech Resource Group Inc.
6565 West Loop South
Bellaire, TX 77401
(713) 751-0100
Minimum Salary Placed: $20,000
Recruiting Specialty: MIS

Ken Hurst Hotel Search and Consultants
6750 West Loop South
Bellaire, TX 77401
(713) 660-0008
Contact: Mr. Ken Hurst
Recruiting Specialty: Hospitality

Optimal Resources Inc.
6750 West Loop South
Bellaire, TX 77401
(713) 666-2238
Minimum Salary Placed: $35,000
Recruiting Specialty: R&D, oil and gas and technical MBA recruiting

CARROLLTON

Career Connection, Inc.
1411 Lemay, Suite 402
Carrollton, TX 75007
(214) 242-4585
Contact: Ms. Joy Swallow
Recruiting Specialty: Administrative support, property management, and real estate

EPPA, Inc.
1953 Branch Hollow
Carrollton, TX 75007
(214) 394-9668
Contact: Mr. Jerry Forsyth
Minimum Salary Placed: $30,000
Recruiting Specialty: Printing

Executive Search Consultants Ltd.
3030 N. Josey Lane, Suite 101
Carrollton, TX 75007
(214) 394-4131
Minimum Salary Placed: $20,000
Recruiting Specialty: General

Snelling & Snelling
1000 E. Beltline Road, Suite 100
Carrollton, TX 75006
(214) 242-8575
Contact: Ms. Joni White
Recruiting Specialty: General

CEDAR PARK

Benchmark Professionals
2003 N. Bell Boulevard
Cedar Park, TX 78613
(512) 259-5666

Contact: Mr. J. Pearson
Minimum Salary Placed: $35,000
Recruiting Specialty: Physicians and medical

CELESTE

J. L. Nixon Consulting
Route 2, Box 380-E
Celeste, TX 75423
(903) 568-4111
Contact: Mr. Jeff Nixon
Minimum Salary Placed: $35,000
Recruiting Specialty: Insurance

CLEAR LAKE CITY

Management Recruiters
17625 El Camino Real, Suite 330
Clear Lake City, TX 77058
(713) 286-7797
Contact: Mr. Len Bird
Minimum Salary Placed: $25,000
Recruiting Specialty: General

CORPUS CHRISTI

Express Personnel Services
2820 S. Padre Island Drive, Suite 114
Corpus Christi, TX 78415
(512) 855-2900
Contact: Mr. Henry Eidenmuller
Recruiting Specialty: General

L.K. Jordan & Associates, Inc.
413 North Tancahua
Corpus Christi, TX 78401
(512) 884-9700
Contact: Ms. Linda Jordan
Recruiting Specialty: General

Snelling Personnel Services
146 American Bank Plaza
Corpus Christi, TX 78475
(512) 883-7903
Contact: Ms. Jean Cole
Recruiting Specialty: General

Unique Employment
4639 Corona, Suite 87
Corpus Christi, TX 78411
(512) 852-6392
Contact: Mr. Garry Bradford
Recruiting Specialty: General

Wilson Group
P.O. Box 346
Corpus Cristi, TX 78403
(512) 883-3535
Contact: Ms. A. Wilson
Minimum Salary Placed: $20,000
Recruiting Specialty: General

DALLAS

Accountants Inc. Personnel Service
5400 LBJ Freeway
Dallas, TX 75240
(214) 385-8811
Recruiting Specialty: Finance and accounting

**Accountants On Call/
Accountants Executive Search**
2828 Routh Street, Suite 690
Dallas, TX 75201
(214) 979-9001
Contact: Ms. Sheri Ferris
Recruiting Specialty: Finance and accounting

Accountants On Call/
Accountants Executive Search
5550 LBJ Freeway, Suite 310
Dallas, TX 75240
(214) 980-4184
Contact: Mr. Brett Schaefer
Recruiting Specialty: Finance and accounting

Acme High Technology Service
14001 Goldmark Drive
Dallas, TX 75240
(214) 480-9551 .
Contact: Mr. B. Garrison
Minimum Salary Placed: $30,000
Recruiting Specialty: High technology

Advantage Personnel, Inc.
10210 N. Central Expressway, Suite 216
Dallas, TX 75231
(214) 987-1101
Contact: Ms. Ginger G. Russell
Recruiting Specialty: Permanent administrative support, accounting, and management

All American Personnel Service
3131 Turtlecreek Blvd., Suite 610
Dallas, TX 75219
(214) 526-7699
Contact: Ms. Brenda Bodiford-Waldrip
Recruiting Specialty: Administrative support, medical and office

The Alternatives Group
4004 Beltline Road, Suite 210
Dallas, TX 75244
(214) 788-9393
Contact: Ms. Michele Benum
Minimum Salary Placed: $25,000
Recruiting Specialty: Sales and data processing

Peter W. Ambler Company
14651 Dallas Parkway, Suite 402
Dallas, TX 75240
(214) 404-8712
Contact: Mr. Peter Ambler
Minimum Salary Placed: $50,000
Recruiting Specialty: Manufacturing; general

Amicus Staffing
14881 Quorum Drive, Suite 300
Dallas, TX 75240
(214) 934-8367
Contact: Ms. JoAnne Heath
Recruiting Specialty: Legal and administrative support

Andre David & Associates, Inc.
P.O. Box 700967
Dallas, TX 75287
(214) 250-1986
Contact: Mr. Terry Patch
Minimum Salary Placed: $65,000
Recruiting Specialty: Manufacturing, food, beverage and healthcare

Arnett, Doyle, Farrah and Teague
8950 N. Central Expressway, Suite 302
Dallas, TX 75231
(214) 890-7960
Contact: Mr. H. L. Land
Minimum Salary Placed: $50,000
Recruiting Specialty: General

Babich & Associates
6060 N Central Expressway, Suite 544
Dallas, TX 75206
(214) 263-2561
Contact: Mr. Anthony Beshara
Recruiting Specialty: Administrative support, sales, accounting, data processing, and technical scientific

R. Gaines Baty Associates, Inc.
6360 LBJ Freeway, Suite 100
Dallas, TX 75240
(214) 386-7900
Contact: Mr. R. Gaines Baty
Minimum Salary Placed: $50,000
Recruiting Specialty: MIS and computers

Martin Birnbach and Associates
15150 Preston Road
Dallas, TX 75248
(214) 490-5627
Contact: Mr. M. Birnbach
Minimum Salary Placed: $30,000
Recruiting Specialty: Sales

The Howard C. Bloom Company
5000 Quorum Drive, Suite 160
Dallas, TX 75240
(214) 385-6455
Contact: Mr. Howard Bloom
Minimum Salary Placed: $30,000
Recruiting Specialty: Attorneys

The Boss Company, Personnel Consultants
17000 Dallas Pkwy, Suite 207
Dallas, TX 75248-1930
(214) 931-0335
Contact: Ms. Lynda Boss
Recruiting Specialty: Administrative support

Briggs Legal Staffing
600 N. Pearl, Suite 430
Dallas, TX 75201
(214) 720-3939
Contact: Ms. Kerri Luther
Recruiting Specialty: Legal support and paralegals

Brooklea and Associates, Inc.
12200 Ford Road, Suite 108
Dallas, TX 75234
(214) 484-9400
Recruiting Specialty: Medical, engineering, sales and architecture

Brown & Keene
14160 Dallas Parkway, Suite 450
Dallas, TX 75240
(214) 701-9292
Contact: Ngaire Keene
Recruiting Specialty: Administrative support, permanent

Bruce Woods Executive Search
4319 Oak Lawn Avenue
Dallas, TX 75219
(214) 522-9888
Contact: Mr. Bruce Woods
Minimum Salary Placed: $50,000
Recruiting Specialty: General

Buckley Group
15851 Dallas Parkway
Dallas, TX 75248
(214) 490-1722
Contact: Mr. John Karney
Minimum Salary Placed: $30,000
Recruiting Specialty: Sales and marketing in high technology

Bundy-Stewart Associates Inc.
13601 Preston Road, Suite 107W
Dallas, TX 75240
(214) 458-0626
Contact: Ms. C. Stewart
Minimum Salary Placed: $30,000
Recruiting Specialty: Engineering, data processing and some general

Calhoun & Association, Inc.
5001 Spring Valley, Suite 1155, LB33
Dallas, TX 75244
(214) 239-9000
Contact: Ms. Cindy Calhoun
Minimum Salary Placed: $30,000
Recruiting Specialty: Accounting and legal

Carpenter & Associates
8333 Douglas Avenue, Suite 875
Dallas, TX 75225
(214) 691-6585
Contact: Ms. Elsie Carpenter
Minimum Salary Placed: $35,000
Recruiting Specialty: Retail and direct mail

Casey & Associates, Inc.
3419 Westminister, Suite 222
Dallas, TX 75205
(214) 522-1010
Contact: Ms. Carol Casey
Recruiting Specialty: Data processing, technical, contractors, permanent contracts

Catterton Inc.
3001 LBJ Freeway, Suite 213
Dallas, TX 75234
(214) 934-9000
Contact: Ms. D. Catterton
Minimum Salary Placed: $20,000
Recruiting Specialty: Accounting

Comms People Inc.
3131 McKinney
Dallas, TX 75204
(214) 922-8930
Contact: Mr. Ian Raddant
Recruiting Specialty: Data processing, engineering, international technology, and telecommunications

Computers Professionals Unlimited
13612 Midway Road, Suite 333
Dallas, TX 75244
(214) 233-1773
Contact: Mr. V. J. Zapotocky
Minimum Salary Placed: $40,000
Recruiting Specialty: Computers and MIS

Cornwall Stockton
5930 LBJ Freeway
Dallas, TX 75240
(214) 458-7490
Contact: Mr. T. Pirro
Minimum Salary Placed: $20,000
Recruiting Specialty: General

Cox Dodson and Story
8041 Walnut Hill Lane
Dallas, TX 75248
(214) 750-1067
Minimum Salary Placed: $20,000
Recruiting Specialty: Data processing and computers

Dallas Employment Service
750 N. Saint Paul Street, Suite 1180
Dallas, TX 75201-3230
(214) 954-0700
Contact: Mr. Ken Sutton
Recruiting Specialty: Administrative support, management, legal, permanent

Damon & Associates, Inc.
7515 Greenville Avenue, Suite 900
Dallas, TX 75231
(214) 696-6990
Contact: Mr. Richard Damon
Minimum Salary Placed: $30,000
Recruiting Specialty: Sales

The Danbrook Group
4100 Spring Valley Road
Dallas, TX 75240
(214) 392-0057
Contact: Mr. Michael Kennedy
Minimum Salary Placed: $30,000
Recruiting Specialty: Legal, accounting,
insurance and packaging

Datapro Personnel Consultants
13355 Noel Road, Suite 2001
Dallas, TX 75240
(214) 661-8600
Contact: Mr. Jack Kallison
Recruiting Specialty: Technical and data
processing

John Davidson and Associates
3198 Royal Lane
Dallas, TX 75229
(214) 352-7800
Contact: Mr. John Davidson
Minimum Salary Placed: $20,000
Recruiting Specialty: General

Delta Dallas Personnel
14001 Dallas Parkway, Suite 400
Dallas, TX 75240
(214) 788-2300
Contact: Ms. Linda Crawford
Recruiting Specialty: Administrative support, banking, legal, and insurance

Denton-Lewis Inc.
4242 Lively Lane
Dallas, TX 75220
(214) 358-5597
Contact: Ms. C. Denton
Minimum Salary Placed: $20,000
Recruiting Specialty: General

Discovery Staffing Specialists
12000 Ford Road, Suite 245
Dallas, TX 75234
(214) 243-3200
Contact: Mr. Ron Corder
Recruiting Specialty: Customer service
and credit and collections

Eastman & Beaudine, Inc.
1370 One Galleria Tower
13355 Noel Road, LB-31
Dallas, TX 75240
(214) 661-5520
Contact: Mr. Robert E. Beaudine
Minimum Salary Placed: $70,000
Recruiting Specialty: General

Executive Restaurant Search
2925 LBJ Freeway, Suite 253
Dallas, TX, 75234
(214) 484-8600
Contact: Mr. John B. Traino
Recruiting Specialty: Food and hospitality

Executive Search International
1700 Alma Road
Dallas, TX 75075
(214) 424-4714
Recruiting Specialty: Health and beauty
products

Foster Partners
200 Crescent Court, Suite 330
Dallas, TX 75201
(214) 754-2241
Contact: Mr. William Rowe
Minimum Salary Placed: $75,000
Recruiting Specialty: General

Fox-Morris Associates, Inc.
5400 LBJ Freeway, Suite 1600
Dallas, TX 75240
(214) 404-8044
Contact: Mr. Jerry Sewell
Minimum Salary Placed: $35,000
Recruiting Specialty: General

Gillham and Associates Inc.
3400 Carlisle Street
Dallas, TX 75204
(214) 880-9040
Contact: Mr. Rick Gillham
Minimum Salary Placed: $20,000
Recruiting Specialty: Real estate

Alan Glazer Inc.
2001 Bryan Street, Suite 855
Dallas, TX 75201
(214) 696-2144
Contact: Mr. Alan Glazer
Minimum Salary Placed: $40,000
Recruiting Specialty: Investment banking

John Haley and Associates
2730 N. Stemmons Freeway
Dallas, TX 75207
(214) 634-7111
Minimum Salary Placed: $75,000
Recruiting Specialty: Physicians

Haragan Associates
8350 Meadow Road, Suite 262
Dallas, TX 75231
(214) 363-3634
Minimum Salary Placed: $20,000
Recruiting Specialty: Healthcare

Healthcare Recruiters
4100 Spring Valley Road
Dallas, TX 75244
(214) 3851-5470

Contact: Mr. J. Winberly
Minimum Salary Placed: $20,000
Recruiting Specialty: Healthcare

Heidrick & Struggles, Inc.
2200 Ross Avenue, Suite 4700E
Dallas, TX 75201
(214) 220-2130
Contact: Mr. David Anderson
Minimum Salary Placed: $60,000
Recruiting Specialty: General

Janice Hero
6116 N. Central Expressway
Dallas, TX 75206
(214) 360-0602
Contact: Ms. Jan Hero
Minimum Salary Placed: $20,000
Recruiting Specialty: General

The Horizon Healthcare Group
1501 LBJ Freeway, Suite 710
Dallas, TX 75234
(214) 484-9724
Contact: Mr. D. Shane Hunt
Recruiting Specialty: Physicians

Hunter and Michaels
7502 Greenville Avenue
Dallas, TX 75231
(214) 750-4666
Minimum Salary Placed: $20,000
Recruiting Specialty: Foods

Hyde Danforth & Wold
5950 Berkshire Lane, Suite 1600
Dallas, TX 75225
(214) 691-5966
Contact: Mr. W. Michael Danforth
Minimum Salary Placed: $50,000
Recruiting Specialty: General

IMCOR, Inc.
12201 Merit Drive, Suite 170
Dallas, TX 75251
(214) 239-7760
Contact: Mr. L.L. Cotter
Minimum Salary Placed: $75,000
Recruiting Specialty: General

IntelliSearch
17218 Preston Road, Suite 400
Dallas, TX 75252
(972) 735-3199
Contact: Mr. Bradford Hopson
Minimum Salary Placed: $40,000
Recruiting Specialty: Mortgage finance, sales, MIS and marketing

Interexec
5310 Harvest Hill Road
Dallas, TX 75230
(214) 233-1072
Minimum Salary Placed: $25,000
Recruiting Specialty: Distribution logistics, pharmaceuticals and sales

Interexec
1111 W. Mockingbird Lane
Dallas, TX 75247
(214) 637-6011
Contact: Mr. M. Rednick
Minimum Salary Placed: $20,000
Recruiting Specialty: Sales

James Galloway Inc.
14755 Preston Road, Suite 823
Dallas, TX 75240
(214) 934-1181
Contact: Mr. Jim Loose
Minimum Salary Placed: $50,000
Recruiting Specialty: General

J.G. Consultants
8350 N. Central Expressway
Dallas, TX 75206
(214) 696-9196
Contact: Mr. G. Stephenson
Minimum Salary Placed: $30,000
Recruiting Specialty: Sales and marketing in high technology

Kawa Stiewig and Edwards Inc.
12800 Hillcrest Road, Suite 201
Dallas, TX 75230
(214) 385-7757
Minimum Salary Placed: $30,000
Recruiting Specialty: Engineering and automation, both domestic and in Mexico

A.T. Kearney Executive Search
500 N. Akard Street, Suite 4170
Dallas, TX 75201
(214) 969-0010
Contact: Mr. Robert Johnson
Minimum Salary Placed: $60,000
Recruiting Specialty: General

Kenzer Corporation
3030 LBJ Freeway
Dallas, TX 75234
(214) 620-7776
Contact: Ms. Robin Russell
Recruiting Specialty: General

King Computers Search
9221 LBJ Freeway, Suite 208
Dallas, TX 75243
(214) 238-1021
Contact: Ms. Sally King
Recruiting Specialty: General

Korn/Ferry International
500 N. Akard Street
3950 Lincoln Plaza
Dallas, TX 75201
(214) 954-1834
Contact: Mr. Richard Hardison
Minimum Salary Placed: $100,000
Recruiting Specialty: General

Evie Kreisler Associates, Inc.
2720 Stemmons Freeway, Suite 812
Dallas, TX 75207
(214) 631-8994
Contact: Mr. Tony Priftis
Minimum Salary Placed: $25,000
Recruiting Specialty: Textiles, apparel,
food and beverage and consumer products

Kressenberg Associates
8111 LBJ Freeway, Suite 665
Dallas, TX 75251
(214) 234-1491
Contact: Mr. S. Kressenberg
Minimum Salary Placed: $30,000
Recruiting Specialty: Medical, semi-conductors and sales

La Barge & Associates
12770 Coit Road, Suite 900
Dallas, TX 75251
(214) 991-7713
Contact: Mrs. Una La Barge
Recruiting Specialty: General

Lamalie Amrop International
1601 Elm Street, Suite 4246
Dallas, TX 75201
(214) 754-0019
Contact: Mr. Robert Pearson
Minimum Salary Placed: $75,000
Recruiting Specialty: General

Largent Parks and Partners Inc.
12770 Coit Road
Dallas, TX 75251
(214) 980-0047
Contact: Mr. Akira Wilson
Minimum Salary Placed: $20,000
Recruiting Specialty: Insurance, healthcare and office support

Larsen International, Inc.
660 Preston Forest Center, Suite 114
Dallas, TX 75230
(214) 987-9142
Contact: Mr. Donald Larsen
Minimum Salary Placed: $70,000
Recruiting Specialty: General

Paul Ligon Company
11241 Rosser Road
Dallas, TX 75229
(214) 358-1727
Contact: Mr. T. Paul Ligon
Minimum Salary Placed: $35,000
Recruiting Specialty: Hospitality

MC Search Personnel Consultants
5429 LBJ Frwy, Suite 525 LB 101
Dallas, TX 75240
(214) 385-1171
Contact: Ms. Linda Mc Laughlin
Minimum Salary Placed: $20,000
Recruiting Specialty: Administrative support, banking, accounting, and marketing

MRC Resource Group, Inc.
5728 LBJ Freeway, Suite 460
Dallas, TX 75240
(214) 458-7880
Contact: Ms. Carylon Alexander
Minimum Salary Placed: $20,000
Recruiting Specialty: General

Management Recruiters
15400 Knoll Trail, Suite 230
Dallas, TX 75248
(214) 960-1291
Contact: Mr. John Burkholder
Minimum Salary Placed: $30,000
Recruiting Specialty: Insurance

Management Recruiters
8131 LBJ Freeway, Suite 800
Dallas, TX 75251
(214) 907-1010
Minimum Salary Placed: $25,000
Recruiting Specialty: General

Management Recruiters
8585 Stemmons Freeway, Suite 525N
Dallas, TX 75247
(214) 638-2300
Contact: Mr. Perry Smith
Minimum Salary Placed: $25,000
Recruiting Specialty: General

Maximum Results Inc.
5440 Harvest Hill Road
Dallas, TX 75230
(214) 386-4195
Contact: Brad
Minimum Salary Placed: $30,000
Recruiting Specialty: Distribution, transportation and logistics

McCall Resources
19 Turtle Creek Bend
Dallas, TX 75204
(214) 522-3737
Contact: Ms. Judith McCall
Minimum Salary Placed: $40,000
Recruiting Specialty: General

McClane Company
14643 Dallas Parkway
Dallas, TX 75240
(214) 239-1199
Contact: Mr. Gary Wright
Minimum Salary Placed: $20,000
Recruiting Specialty: General

Med-Source Executive Search
8533 Ferndal Road
Dallas, TX 75238
(800) 349-4444
Minimum Salary Placed: $20,000
Recruiting Specialty: Healthcare

Minority Search Inc.
777 South R.L. Thorton, Suite 105
Dallas, TX 75203
(214) 948-6116
Contact: Mr. Billy Allen
Recruiting Specialty: General

Murphy Search Management
18484 Preston Road, Suite 102
Dallas, TX 75252
(214) 960-7200
Contact: Ms. M. Murphy
Minimum Salary Placed: $20,000
Recruiting Specialty: Data processing

National Corporate Network/Legal Network
600 N. Pearl Street, Suite 2100
Dallas, TX 75201
(214) 777-6400
Contact: Ms. Lisa Jones
Recruiting Specialty: Legal, banking and finance, and administrative support

Odell & Associates
12700 Park Central Place, Suite 1404
Dallas, TX 75251-1502
(214) 458-7900
Contact: Mr. Steve N. Odell
Recruiting Specialty: General

Page-Wheatcroft & Company Ltd.
4420 Rawlins Street
Dallas, TX 75219
(214) 522-2700
Contact: Mr. Stephen Page
Minimum Salary Placed: $100,000
Recruiting Specialty: General

Pailin Group Professional Search
8500 N. Stemmons Freeway
Dallas, TX 75247
(214) 630-1703
Contact: Mr. David Pailin
Minimum Salary Placed: $20,000
Recruiting Specialty: General

Performance Recruiters
8080 N. Central Expressway
Dallas, TX 75206
(214) 891-8277
Contact: Mr. Robert Ritchey
Minimum Salary Placed: $20,000
Recruiting Specialty: General

Perigrine Services
4575 Westgrove Drive
Dallas, TX 75248
(214) 407-0294
Recruiting Specialty: MIS

Procounsel
1222 Commerce Street
Dallas, TX 75202
(214) 939-0929
Contact: Mr. B. Taylor
Minimum Salary Placed: $20,000
Recruiting Specialty: Construction, manufacturing, distribution and contracting

Prothero and Associates Inc.
15150 Preston Road
Dallas, TX 75248
(214) 788-0767
Contact: Mr. Bill Prothero
Minimum Salary Placed: $20,000
Recruiting Specialty: General

Paul Ray Berndtson
2200 Ross Avenue, Suite 4500W
Dallas, TX 75201
(214) 969-7620
Contact: Mr. Breck Ray
Minimum Salary Placed: $90,000
Recruiting Specialty: General

Realty Finance Staffing
15150 Preston Road
Dallas, TX 75248
(214) 701-0277
Contact: Mr. Brian Digan
Recruiting Specialty: Real estate

Resources in Food Inc.
12700 Preston Road, Suite 215
Dallas, TX 75230
(214) 980-4211
Minimum Salary Placed: $40,000
Recruiting Specialty: Food services

Resource Spectrum
5050 Quorum Drive, Suite 700
Dallas, TX 75240
(214) 484-9330
Contact: Mr. Bill Stukey
Recruiting Specialty: Accounting, data processing, technical and administrative support

Riccione and Associates
16415 Addine Road, Suite 404
Dallas, TX 75248
(214) 380-6432
Recruiting Specialty: High technology and computers

Robert Wesson and Associates
14800 Quorum Drive, Suite 440
Dallas, TX 75240
(214) 239-8613
Contact: Mr. B. McDermid
Minimum Salary Placed: $20,000
Recruiting Specialty: Hospitality

Robert Lowell International
12200 Park Central Drive, Suite 120
Dallas, TX 75251
(214) 233-2270
Contact: Mr. Robert Bryza
Minimum Salary Placed: $60,000
Recruiting Specialty: General

Roemer Bartlett and Kate
P.O. Box 741265
Dallas, TX 75734
(214) 699-1091
Contact: Mr. J. Roemer
Minimum Salary Placed: $20,000
Recruiting Specialty: General

Romac Temp
12770 Colt Road
Dallas, TX 75201
(214) 720-0050
Contact: Mr. J. Mitchell
Recruiting Specialty: Office support

Roth Young
5344 Alpha Road
Dallas, TX 75240
(214) 233-5000
Contact: Mr. V. Dickerson
Minimum Salary Placed: $30,000
Recruiting Specialty: General

Russell Reynolds Associates, Inc.
1900 Trammell Crow Center
2001 Ross Avenue
Dallas, TX 75201
(214) 220-2033
Contact: Mr. David Konker
Minimum Salary Placed: $100,000
Recruiting Specialty: General

Sales Consultants
1111 W. Mockingbird Lane, Suite 1300
Dallas, TX 75247
(214) 637-6011
Contact: Mr. Mark Rednick
Minimum Salary Placed: $20,000
Recruiting Specialty: Sales

Sandhurst Associates
4851 LBJ Freeway, Suite 601
Dallas, TX 75244
(214) 458-1212
Contact: Mr. James Demchak
Minimum Salary Placed: $60,000
Recruiting Specialty: General

M.S. Schwartz and Company
5956 Sherry Lane, Suite 1000
Dallas, TX 75225
(214) 691-3939
Contact: Mr. Michael Schwartz
Minimum Salary Placed: $40,000
Recruiting Specialty: General

Search America Consultants
12700 Hillcrest Road, Suite 172
Dallas, TX 75230
(214) 233-3302
Minimum Salary Placed: $20,000
Recruiting Specialty: Private clubs and
hospitality

Search Com Inc.
12900 Preston Road
Dallas, TX 75230
(214) 490-0300
Minimum Salary Placed: $20,000
Recruiting Specialty: Advertising, public
relations and marketing

Shisler Axley and Associates
13455 Noel Road
Dallas, TX 75240
(214) 387-8656
Contact: Mr. J. Shisler
Minimum Salary Placed: $20,000
Recruiting Specialty: General

Marvin L. Silcott & Associates, Inc.
7557 Rambler Road, Suite 1336
Dallas, TX 75231
(214) 369-7802
Contact: Mr. Marvin Silcott
Minimum Salary Placed: $60,000
Recruiting Specialty: Attorneys, account-
ing and engineering

Sink, Walker & Boltrus International
16479 Dallas Parkway, Suite 540
Dallas, TX 75248
(214) 369-6591
Minimum Salary Placed: $70,000
Recruiting Specialty: Telecommunications

Snelling Personnel Services
5151 Beltline Road, Suite 365
Dallas, TX 75240
(214) 934-9030
Contact: Mr. Sam D. Bingham
Recruiting Specialty: General

Snelling & Snelling
12770 Coit Road, Suite 250
Dallas, TX 75251-1316
(214) 701-8080
Contact: Mr. Don Lumas
Recruiting Specialty: Administrative support, engineering, and environmental

Snelling and Snelling, Inc.
12801 N. Central Expressway, Suite 700
Dallas, TX 75243
(214) 239-7575
Recruiting Specialty: Franchising

Source EDP
5429 LBJ Freeway, Suite 275
Dallas, TX 75240
(214) 387-1600
Contact: Mr. Rick Richards
Recruiting Specialty: Computer hardware and software

Source Engineering
5429 LBJ Freeway, Suite 275
Dallas, TX 75240
(214) 239-9010
Contact: Mr. Mike Varrichio
Recruiting Specialty: Engineering

Spencer Stuart
1717 Main Street, Suite 5300
Dallas, TX 75201
(214) 658-1777
Contact: Mr. O.D. Cruse
Minimum Salary Placed: $75,000
Recruiting Specialty: General

Spillman and Associates
3102 Oak Lawn Avenue
Dallas, TX 75204
(214) 528-8994
Minimum Salary Placed: $20,000
Recruiting Specialty: General

Spradley Legal Search
3131 McKinney Avenue
Dallas, TX 75204
(214) 969-5900
Contact: Mr. C. Spradley
Minimum Salary Placed: $35,000
Recruiting Specialty: Legal

Stanton Chase International
5050 Quorum Drive, Suite 330
Dallas, TX 75240
(214) 404-8411
Contact: Mr. Ed Moerbe
Minimum Salary Placed: $60,000
Recruiting Specialty: General

Steinfield and Associates
2626 Cole Avenue
Dallas, TX 75204
(214) 220-0535
Contact: Mr. D. Steinfield
Minimum Salary Placed: $20,000
Recruiting Specialty: Accounting, finance and MIS

Stephens, Little and Associates
1341 W. Mockingbird Lane, Suite 810E
Dallas, TX 75247
(214) 631-5588
Contact: Mr. Robert Trost
Minimum Salary Placed: $20,000
Recruiting Specialty: General

R.A. Stone and Associates
5495 Belt Line Road, Suite 153
Dallas, TX 75240
(214) 233-0483
Contact: Ms. Diane Owen
Minimum Salary Placed: $30,000
Recruiting Specialty: Broadcasting

Virginia Sumrall
4221 Rosser Square
Dallas, TX 75244
(214) 247-5772
Contact: Ms. Virginia Sumrall
Minimum Salary Placed: $35,000
Recruiting Specialty: Auditing

Taylor Henderson Consulting
6310 LBJ Freeway, Suite 201
Dallas, TX 75240
(214) 991-8782
Contact: Ms. J. Henderson
Minimum Salary Placed: $25,000
Recruiting Specialty: Insurance

Taylor Winfield
12801 Northcentral Parkway, Suite 1260
Dallas, TX 75244
(214) 392-1400
Contact: Ms. Nancy Albertini
Minimum Salary Placed: $80,000
Recruiting Specialty: Computers and telecommunications

Technical Careers of Dallas

12750 Merit Drive, LB 56
Dallas, TX 75251
(214) 991-9424
Contact: Ms. Cary Tobolka
Recruiting Specialty: Technical

Technical Recruiting, Inc.

4099 McEwen, Suite 230
Dallas, TX 75244
(214) 392-9473
Contact: Mr. Ron Stephens
Recruiting Specialty: Data processing

Technical Staffing Solutions

16775 Addison Road
Dallas, TX 75248
(214) 788-1771
Contact: Mr. Don Fink
Minimum Salary Placed: $30,000
Recruiting Specialty: Chemical engineering for petrochemical industry

Craig Trotman and Associates

3316 Oak Grove Avenue
Dallas, TX 75204
(214) 954-1919
Contact: Craig Trotman
Minimum Salary Placed: $30,000
Recruiting Specialty: Sales management in packaged goods and food industries

Michael Tucker Associates

5400 LBJ Freeway, Suite 1325
Dallas, TX 75240
(214) 458-2504
Contact: Mr. Michael Tucker
Minimum Salary Placed: $65,000
Recruiting Specialty: Healthcare

Tuttle, Neidhart, Semyan, Inc.

12655 N. Central Expressway, Suite 900
Dallas, TX 75243
(214) 991-3555
Contact: Mr. John Semyan
Minimum Salary Placed: $80,000
Recruiting Specialty: General

USI Dallas-Houston

4151 Belt Line, Suite 124-136
Dallas, TX 75244
(214) 385-9498
Recruiting Specialty: Sales and technical

Wachendorfer & Associates

9550 Forest Lane, Suite 112
Dallas, TX 75243
(214) 783-0999
Contact: Tom & Nancy Wachendorfer
Recruiting Specialty: Food

Ward Howell International, Inc.

1601 Elm Street, Suite 900
Dallas, TX 75201
(214) 749-0099
Contact: Mr. Ronald Evans
Minimum Salary Placed: $75,000
Recruiting Specialty: General

Wheeler, Moore & Elam Company

14800 Quorum Drive, Suite 200
Dallas, TX 75240
(214) 386-8806
Contact: Mr. Mark Moore
Minimum Salary Placed: $50,000
Recruiting Specialty: General

Williams Company

8080 N. Central Expressway
Dallas, TX 75206
(214) 891-6340
Minimum Salary Placed: $25,000
Recruiting Specialty: Retail

Witt/Kieffer, Ford, Hadelman & Lloyd
8117 Preston Road, Suite 690
Dallas, TX 75225
(214) 739-1370
Contact: Mr. Keith Southerland
Minimum Salary Placed: $75,000
Recruiting Specialty: Healthcare

M. Wood Associates
3320 Rolling Hills
Dallas, TX 75028
(817) 430-4395
Contact: Ms. M. Wood
Minimum Salary Placed: $40,000
Recruiting Specialty: High technology

The Wright Group
5902 Windmier Court
Dallas, TX 75252
(214) 733-7245
Contact: Ms. Jay Wright
Minimum Salary Placed: $30,000
Recruiting Specialty: Marketing research

DENTON

Apex Computers Placements Inc.
P.O. Box 50084
Denton, TX 76206
(817) 565-0658
Minimum Salary Placed: $20,000
Recruiting Specialty: Computers and data processing

Dunhill Professional Search
P.O. Box 50692
Denton, TX 76206
(817) 383-0700

Contact: Mr. Daniel Pajak
Minimum Salary Placed: $40,000
Recruiting Specialty: Manufacturing and R&D in plastics and rubber, and pharmaceuticals

DUNCANVILLE

LJC Cella
214 S. Main Street, Suite 212
Duncanville, TX 75116
(214) 296-9298
Contact: Mr. D. Scarborough
Minimum Salary Placed: $20,000
Recruiting Specialty: Foods

EL PASO

Accusearch
5959 Gateway Boulevard West
El Paso, TX 79925
(915) 778-9312
Contact: Mr. B. Steiner
Minimum Salary Placed: $30,000
Recruiting Specialty: Manufacturing

Betty Tanner Professional Service
4150 Pinnacle Street
El Paso, TX 79902
(915) 587-5166
Contact: Ms. Betty Tanner
Minimum Salary Placed: $20,000
Recruiting Specialty: Plant manufacturing

Career Concepts Personnel Service
6070 Gateway Boulevard E., Suite 300
El Paso, TX 79905
(915) 772-2200
Contact: Mr. D. Knippa
Minimum Salary Placed: $20,000
Recruiting Specialty: General

Corporate Search Associates
4180 N. Mesa Street, Suite 107
El Paso, TX 79902
(915) 534-2583
Contact: Mr. Tom Furnival
Minimum Salary Placed: $30,000
Recruiting Specialty: Manufacturing, medical and technical

Robert Half International
4100 Rio Bravo Street
El Paso, TX 79902
(915) 544-6699
Contact: Ms. V. Hannah
Minimum Salary Placed: $20,000
Recruiting Specialty: Accounting and finance

Pan American Search Inc.
600 Sunland Park Drive, Suite 200
El Paso, TX 79912
(915) 833-9991
Contact: Ms. S. Cooper
Minimum Salary Placed: $35,000
Recruiting Specialty: Manufacturing and engineering

Professionals Unlimited
Box 372314
El Paso, TX 79937
(915) 594-1803
Contact: Ms. L. Cobos
Minimum Salary Placed: $20,000
Recruiting Specialty: Plastics

R.A. Rodriguez and Associates
1790 N. Lee Trevino Drive, Suite 403
El Paso, TX 79936
(915) 598-5028
Contact: Mr. Fred Smithson
Minimum Salary Placed: $35,000
Recruiting Specialty: Manufacturing

SAI Executive Search
P.O. Box 220418
El Paso, TX 79913
(915) 585-1005
Minimum Salary Placed: $20,000
Recruiting Specialty: Medical and packaging

FARMERS BRANCH

H.S. Group Inc.
2925 LBJ Freeway
Farmers Branch, TX 75234
(214) 243-7037
Contact: Ms. Suzanne Hall
Minimum Salary Placed: $20,000
Recruiting Specialty: General

FORT WORTH

Corporate Search
2509 W. Berry Street, Suite 11
Fort Worth, TX 76109
(817) 429-1763
Contact: John
Minimum Salary Placed: $20,000
Recruiting Specialty: Sales

Dunhill of Fort Worth, Inc.
2906 SE Loop 826, Suite F
Fort Worth, TX 76140
(817) 572-0220
Contact: Mr. Dave Apte
Minimum Salary Placed: $20,000
Recruiting Specialty: Food and consumer products

Robert Half International
1300 Summit Avenue
Fort Worth, TX 76102
(817) 870-1200

Minimum Salary Placed: $20,000
Recruiting Specialty: Accounting and finance

Hughes & Association
718 Oakwood Trail
Fort Worth, TX 76112
(817) 496-3650
Contact: Mr. Ken Hughes
Minimum Salary Placed: $35,000
Recruiting Specialty: Insurance

Management Recruiters
6500 West Freeway, Suite 720
Fort Worth, TX 76116
(817) 731-1500
Contact: Mr. Bob Bond
Minimum Salary Placed: $25,000
Recruiting Specialty: General

Marshall Career Service Inc.
6500 West Freeway, Suite 200
Fort Worth, TX 76116
(817) 737-2645
Contact: Mr. Richard Marshall
Minimum Salary Placed: $25,000
Recruiting Specialty: Accounting and some general

Omnisearch
P.O. Box 161817
Fort Worth, TX 76161
(817) 236-7972
Contact: Ms. Janis Haile
Minimum Salary Placed: $20,000
Recruiting Specialty: Data processing, engineering, and manufacturing

O'Rourke Company, Inc.
4100 International Plaza, Suite 530
Fort Worth, TX 76109
(817) 735-8697

Contact: Mr. Dennis M. O'Rourke
Minimum Salary Placed: $35,000
Recruiting Specialty: Pulp and paper, oil and gas and some general

Paralegals Plus, Inc.
512 Main, Suite 311
Fort Worth, TX 76102
(817) 332-9005
Contact: Ms. Ann Dunkin
Recruiting Specialty: Legal, paralegals, administrative support, data entry, case clerks

Professional Advantage Inc.
4200 S. Hulen Street
Fort Worth, TX 76109
(817) 429-7886
Contact: Ms. A. Mecklenburger
Minimum Salary Placed: $20,000
Recruiting Specialty: Computer programming

Paul Ray Berndtson
301 Commerce Street, Suite 2300
Fort Worth, TX 76102
(817) 334-0500
Contact: Mr. Paul Ray
Minimum Salary Placed: $90,000
Recruiting Specialty: General

R.L. Scott Associates
307 West 7th Street, Suite 1800
Fort Worth, TX 76102
(817) 877-3622
Contact: Mr. R. Scott
Recruiting Specialty: Psychiatric and behavioral rehabilitation

Vernon Sage and Associates
4809 Brentwood Stair Road
Fort Worth, TX 76103
(817) 451-8785
Contact: Mr. T. Vernon
Minimum Salary Placed: $20,000
Recruiting Specialty: General

Whitney Smith Company
500 Throckmorton, Suite 1820
Fort Worth, TX 76102
(817) 877-4120
Contact: Mr. David Farmer
Minimum Salary Placed: $30,000
Recruiting Specialty: Banking, legal and accounting

FRIENDSWOOD

Management Recruiters
317 S. Friendswood Drive
Friendswood, TX 77546
(713) 996-0008
Contact: Mr. Louis Bellview
Recruiting Specialty: Healthcare and petroleum

Robert Shields & Associates
1550 W. Bay Area Boulevard
Friendswood, TX 77546
(713) 488-7961
Contact: Mr. Robert Shields
Recruiting Specialty: Data processing

GARLAND

Grove Employment Service
608 W. 1-30, Suite 421
Garland, TX 75043
(214) 226-1234
Contact: Ms. Margie Howard
Recruiting Specialty: General

HIGHLAND VILLAGE

Career Consultants
2300 Highland Village Road, Suite 640
Highland Village, TX 75067
(214) 317-0883
Contact: Mr. Terry Miller
Minimum Salary Placed: $35,000
Recruiting Specialty: Healthcare and engineering

HOUSTON

AA Action Recruiting Service
16800 Imperial Valley Drive
Houston, TX 77060
(713) 999-3793
Contact: Mr. Arthur Dominguez
Minimum Salary Placed: $20,000
Recruiting Specialty: Restaurant management

Accountants On Call
1990 Post Oak Boulevard, Suite 1300
Houston, TX 77056
(713) 961-5603
Contact: Ms. Bea Battistoni
Recruiting Specialty: Finance and accounting

Accounting Resources International, Inc.
15415 Runswick
Houston, TX 77289
(713) 486-7037
Contact: Mr. Dan Haller
Minimum Salary Placed: $30,000
Recruiting Specialty: Accounting and finance

Ackerman Johnson Consultants Inc.
333 N. Sam Houston Parkway E.,
  Suite 1210
Houston, TX 77060
(713) 999-8879
Contact: Mr. D. Johnson
Minimum Salary Placed: $20,000
Recruiting Specialty: Sales, marketing
and engineering

Ray Adams and Associates
P.O. Box 772714
Houston, TX 77079
(713) 952-2999
Contact: Mr. Ray Adams
Minimum Salary Placed: $50,000
Recruiting Specialty: General

A.H. Justice and Associates
P.O. Box 58345
Houston, TX 77258
(713) 280-9987
Contact: Ms. L. King
Minimum Salary Placed: $25,000
Recruiting Specialty: Lab personnel and
engineering

Alexander Group
1330 Post Oak Boulevard
Houston, TX 77056
(713) 961-7420
Contact: Ms. J. Howe
Minimum Salary Placed: $40,000
Recruiting Specialty: Attorneys

Anderson Bradshaw Association, Inc.
1225 N. Loop West, Suite 820
Houston, TX 77008
(713) 869-6789
Contact: Mr. Robert Anderson
Minimum Salary Placed: $60,000
Recruiting Specialty: Engineering, con-
struction, utility and environmental

Arend and Associates
13311 Saint Marys Lane
Houston, TX 77079
(713) 827-7800
Contact: Mr. Lewd Arend
Minimum Salary Placed: $45,000
Recruiting Specialty: General

Ashen and Associates
7322 SW Freeway
Houston, TX 77074
(713) 271-1983
Contact: Ms. D. Ashen
Minimum Salary Placed: $30,000
Recruiting Specialty: Oil and gas

Austin Group
11511 Katy Freeway, Suite 290
Houston, TX 77079
(713) 497-8595
Contact: Mr. P. Austin
Minimum Salary Placed: $20,000
Recruiting Specialty: General

Automotive Careers of Texas
15234 Beach Dr.
Houston, TX 77070-1404
(713) 444-4100
Contact: Mr. George McCormick
Recruiting Specialty: Automotive

John T. Baker and Associates
11757 Katy Freeway, Suite 507
Houston, TX 77079
(713) 556-1798
Contact: Mr. John Baker
Minimum Salary Placed: $25,000
Recruiting Specialty: General

Baldwin and Company
2401 Fountain View Drive, Suite 210
Houston, TX 77057
(713) 977-2300

Contact: Mr. G. Baldwin
Minimum Salary Placed: $20,000
Recruiting Specialty: Accounting and engineering

Barton Raben, Inc.
Three Riverway, Suite 910
Houston, TX 77056
(713) 961-9111
Contact: Mr. Gary Barton
Minimum Salary Placed: $75,000
Recruiting Specialty: General

Rhett Bigham and Associates
9801 Westheimer Road
Houston, TX 77042
(713) 777-0994
Contact: Mr. Rhett Bigham
Minimum Salary Placed: $50,000
Recruiting Specialty: Advanced process control system engineering, instrumentation and information

Brownson and Associates
5599 San Felipe Street, Suite 610
Houston, TX 77056
(713) 626-4790
Contact: Mr. B. Brownson
Minimum Salary Placed: $20,000
Recruiting Specialty: General

Don Bunting and Associates LLC
14900 FM 529 Suite 102
Houston, TX 77095
(713) 855-1755
Contact: Mr. Don Bunting
Recruiting Specialty: Medical

Burns Dunnam and Whitehead
4151 SW Freeway, Suite 200
Houston, TX 77027
(713) 622-9299

Contact: Mr. R. Burns
Minimum Salary Placed: $35,000
Recruiting Specialty: Engineering in refining and petro-chemical

Cadmus International
2900 Wilcrest Drive
Houston, TX 77042
(713) 977-1900
Contact: Mr. S. Cadmus
Minimum Salary Placed: $20,000
Recruiting Specialty: High technology

Career Consultants, Inc. of Texas
1980 Post Oak Boulevard, Suite 1950
Houston, TX 77056
(713) 626-4100
Contact: Mr. Carl Curtiss
Recruiting Specialty: Software and engineering telecommunication, and computers

Carlin Associates
6161 Savoy Drive
Houston, TX 77036
(713) 783-7111
Contact: Mr. Jim Hubenak
Minimum Salary Placed: $30,000
Recruiting Specialty: Oil, gas and refining

L. Center Enterprises Inc.
1155 Dairy Ashford Street, Suite 404
Houston, TX 77079
(713) 589-8303
Contact: Ms. Linda Center
Minimum Salary Placed: $40,000
Recruiting Specialty: Oil and gas and brokerages

The Cherbonnier Group, Inc.
3050 Post Oak Boulevard, Suite 1600
Houston, TX 77024
(713) 688-4701
Contact: Mr. L. Michael Cherbonnier
Minimum Salary Placed: $60,000
Recruiting Specialty: General

CoEnergy Inc.
5065 Westheimer, Suite 815 East
Houston, TX 77056
(713) 960-1868
Contact: Mr. Luis Hernandez
Minimum Salary Placed: $60,000
Recruiting Specialty: Utilities and energy

Computemp Inc.
5177 Richmond Avenue, Suite 260
Houston, TX 77056
(713) 623-8355
Contact: Ms. Sherol Zuniga
Recruiting Specialty: Permanent and temporary, contract, data processing, technology, and telecommunications

Continental Personnel Service
6671 Southwest Freeway, Suite 101
Houston, TX 77074
(713) 771-7181
Contact: Mr. R. Quinn
Minimum Salary Placed: $20,000
Recruiting Specialty: MIS

Corporate Search Group
12218 Sarti Street
Houston, TX 77066
(713) 893-1719
Contact: Mr. B. Moore
Minimum Salary Placed: $20,000
Recruiting Specialty: Contract furniture

Daniel Group
10575 Katy Freeway, Suite 439
Houston, TX 77024
(713) 932-9313
Contact: Mr. B. Daniel
Minimum Salary Placed: $20,000
Recruiting Specialty: Finance

Dilworth and Woolridge Inc.
5555 Morningside Drive, Suite 206
Houston, TX 77005
(713) 521-2800
Contact: Ms. Pamela Dilworth
Minimum Salary Placed: $40,000
Recruiting Specialty: Attorneys

Dougan-McKinley International
3200 Southwest Freeway, 33rd Floor
Houston, TX 77027
(713) 623-6400
Contact: Mr. James McKinley
Recruiting Specialty: General

Dunhill Personnel
5720 W. Little York, Suite 322
Houston, TX 77091
(713) 681-3669
Contact: Mr. Jack Davis
Minimum Salary Placed: $25,000
Recruiting Specialty: General

Dunhill of West Houston, Inc.
P.O. Box 773156
Houston, TX 77215
(713) 589-1291
Contact: Mr. Harvey Booker
Minimum Salary Placed: $25,000
Recruiting Specialty: General

Dunhill Personnel
6610 Harwin, Suite 125
Houston, TX 77036
(713) 952-2580
Contact: Mr. Don Fry
Minimum Salary Placed: $25,000
Recruiting Specialty: General

EDP Computers Service
4600 Post Oak Place Drive, Suite 204
Houston, TX 77027
(713) 960-1717
Minimum Salary Placed: $20,000
Recruiting Specialty: Computers and
data processing

B. Edwards Legal Search
1672 Beaconshire Road
Houston, TX 77077
(713) 496-0930
Contact: Ms. B. Edwards
Minimum Salary Placed: $40,000
Recruiting Specialty: Legal

Emjay Computer Careers
1824 Portsmouth
Houston, TX 77098
(713) 529-5000
Contact: Ms. Emma Jacobs
Recruiting Specialty: Data processing

Employee Sources Inc.
1 Pinedale Street
Houston, TX 77006
(713) 520-7446
Minimum Salary Placed: $20,000
Recruiting Specialty: General

The Energists
10260 Westheimer, Suite 300
Houston, TX 77042
(713) 781-6881
Contact: Mr. Bradford Macurda
Minimum Salary Placed: $50,000
Recruiting Specialty: Energy, chemical,
and environmental

Enertech Resource
13910 Champion Forest Drive, Suite 101
Houston, TX 77069
(713) 586-9074
Contact: Mr. Dan Westover
Recruiting Specialty: General

Executive Consulting Group
701 Post Oak Road, Suite 610
Houston, TX 77024
(713) 686-9500
Contact: Mr. David Gandin
Minimum Salary Placed: $30,000
Recruiting Specialty: Accounting, finance
and banking

Executive Group
1535 West Loop South
Houston, TX 77027
(713) 622-2061
Contact: Mr. Bob Black
Minimum Salary Placed: $30,000
Recruiting Specialty: Sales, engineering
and auditing

Expert Staffing Professionals Inc.
11767 Katy Freeway, Suite 430
Houston, TX 77079
(713) 497-0600
Contact: Mr. James McKnight
Recruiting Specialty: Accounting, engineering, and legal

Feldt Personnel Service
7211 Regency Square Blvd., Suite 210
Houston, TX 77036
(713) 781-6562
Contact: Ms. Marcia Feldt
Recruiting Specialty: Finance

Fortune Personnel Consultants
2555 Central Parkway
Houston, TX 77092
(713) 680-9132
Contact: Mr. Robert Shanley
Minimum Salary Placed: $30,000
Recruiting Specialty: Fuel and chemical
processing

S.L. Fultz and Associates
9099 Katy Freeway
Houston, TX 77024
(713) 935-9797
Contact: Ms. S. Fultz
Minimum Salary Placed: $20,000
Recruiting Specialty: MIS

General Sales and Search of Texas
12202 Moorcreek Drive
Houston, TX 77070
(713) 370-0414
Contact: Mr. Mike Roth
Minimum Salary Placed: $20,000
Recruiting Specialty: General

Gibson Arnold & Associates Inc.
550 Westcott, Suite 560
Houston, TX 77007
(713) 869-3600
Contact: Mr. Yahne Gibson
Recruiting Specialty: Legal

Robert Half International
1360 Post Oak Boulevard, Suite 1470
Houston, TX 77056
(713) 623-4700
Contact: Mr. B. Rowley
Minimum Salary Placed: $20,000
Recruiting Specialty: Accounting and finance

Harrison Personnel Services
1800 St. James Place Suite 110
Houston, TX 77056
(713) 960-9906
Contact: Mr. Jim Kraus
Recruiting Specialty: Data processing
and medical

Healthcare Recruiters
9301 SW Freeway, Suite 650
Houston, TX 77074
(713) 771-7344
Contact: Mr. J. Tipton
Minimum Salary Placed: $20,000
Recruiting Specialty: Healthcare

A. Herndon & Associates, Inc.
5100 Westheimer, Suite 200
Houston, TX 77056
(713) 968-6577
Contact: Ms. Angela Herndon
Minimum Salary Placed: $60,000
Recruiting Specialty: General

Lawrence W. Hill
One Riverway, Suite 1700
Houston, TX 77056
(713) 840-6373
Contact: Mr. Larry Hill
Minimum Salary Placed: $70,000
Recruiting Specialty: General

Hunt Patton & Brazeal, Inc.
2350 Sam Houston Parkway, Suite 210
Houston, TX 77032
(713) 590-8350
Contact: Mr. Bill Lawrence
Minimum Salary Placed: $25,000
Recruiting Specialty: General

ISC of Houston, Inc.
16800 Imperial Valley Drive, Suite 380
Houston, TX 77060
(713) 847-0050
Contact: Ms. K. Burke
Minimum Salary Placed: $20,000
Recruiting Specialty: Healthcare, environmental and real estate

J D A Professional Services, Inc.
701 N. Post Oak Road, Suite 610
Houston, TX 77024
(713) 681-0191
Contact: Mr. James Del Monte
Recruiting Specialty: MIS, data processing, everything with computers

Kahn, Richards and Associates, Inc.
6223 Richmond, Suite 103
Houston, TX 77057
(713) 781-1181
Contact: Mr. Douglas Kahn
Minimum Salary Placed: $25,000
Recruiting Specialty: Computers

Keypeople Resources, Inc.
520 Post Oak Boulevard, Suite 830
Houston, TX 77027
(7113) 877-1427
Contact: Ms. Betty Thompson
Recruiting Specialty: Accounting and data processing

Korn/Ferry International
1100 Louisiana, Suite 2850
Houston, TX 77002
(713) 651-1834
Contact: Mr. John Brock
Minimum Salary Placed: $100,000
Recruiting Specialty: General

Kors Montgomery International
1980 Post Oak Boulevard, Suite 2280
Houston, TX 77056
(713) 840-7101
Contact: Mr. R. Paul Kors
Minimum Salary Placed: $100,000
Recruiting Specialty: High technology, chemicals and construction

Kristan International
12 E. Greenway Plaza, Suite 1100
Houston, TX 77046
(713) 961-3040
Contact: Mr. B. Kristan
Minimum Salary Placed: $50,000
Recruiting Specialty: General

Lamalie Amrop International
1301 McKinney Street, Suite 3520
Houston, TX 77010
(713) 739-8602
Minimum Salary Placed: $75,000
Recruiting Specialty: General

The Leslie Corporation
10700 North Frwy, Suite 670
Houston, TX 77037-1146
(713) 591-0915
Contact: Mr. John Leslie
Recruiting Specialty: Permanent executive and senior retained search (overseas technical professionals)

Liberty Staffing Group
5599 San Felipe, Suite 1060
Houston, TX 77056-2721
(713) 961-7666
Contact: Mr. Kenneth Bohan
Recruiting Specialty: Property management and construction

George Lehman Associates Inc.
211 Highland Cross Drive, Suite 215
Houston, TX 77073
(713) 443-0044
Contact: Mr. George Lehman
Minimum Salary Placed: $25,000
Recruiting Specialty: Accounting and finance

Litchfield & Willis, Inc.
3900 Essex Lane, Suite 650
Houston, TX 77027
(713) 975-8500
Contact: Ms. Barbara Litchfield
Recruiting Specialty: General

Loewenstein & Associates
5847 San Felipe, Suite 1250
Houston, TX 77057
(713) 952-1840
Contact: Mr. Ron Loewenstein
Minimum Salary Placed: $40,000
Recruiting Specialty: Engineering, marketing and some general

Lord & Albus Company
11902 Jones Road, Suite L-185
Houston, TX 77070
(713) 955-5673
Contact: Mr. John Albus
Minimum Salary Placed: $25,000
Recruiting Specialty: General

M. David Lowe Staffing Services
P.O. Box 571947
Houston, TX 77257
(713) 784-4226
Contact: Mr. Patrick D. Layhee
Recruiting Specialty: Full service administrative

Lucas Group
5300 Memorial Drive, Suite 270
Houston, TX 77057
(713) 735-6060
Contact: Mr. Larry Austin
Minimum Salary Placed: $40,000
Recruiting Specialty: General

Lyn-Jay International, Inc.
9200 Old Katy Road
Houston, TX 77055
(713) 935-3333
Recruiting Specialty: Attorneys

M K Personnel, Inc.
4265 San Felipe, Suite 1100
Houston, TX 77027
(713) 968-9844
Contact: M. K. Stalder
Recruiting Specialty: Administrative support

Magellan International, Inc.
24 Greenway Plaza, Suite 1110
Houston, TX 77046
(713) 439-7485
Contact: Mr. Jonathan H. Phillips
Recruiting Specialty: Management consulting and domestic and international auditing

Magnum Recruiting Group
P.O. Box 42809, Dept. 401
Houston, TX 77242
(713) 729-1384
Contact: Mr. Fedell Price
Recruiting Specialty: General

Management Recruiters
911 Bankside Drive
Houston, TX 77031
(713) 772-6715
Contact: Mr. Cliff Drown
Minimum Salary Placed: $30,000
Recruiting Specialty: General

Management Recruiters
10700 Richmond, Suite 217
Houston, TX 77042
(713) 784-7444
Contact: Mr. Frank Albrecht
Minimum Salary Placed: $25,000
Recruiting Specialty: General

Management Recruiters
1360 Post Oak Boulevard, Suite 2110
Houston, TX 77056
(713) 850-9850
Contact: Mr. Rich Bolls
Minimum Salary Placed: $25,000
Recruiting Specialty: General

Manpower Personnel Services
P.O. Box 4478
Houston, TX 77210
(713) 680-2727
Contact: Mr. Ron Kapche
Recruiting Specialty: General

Ray Marburger and Associates Inc.
9800 NW Freeway, Suite 505
Houston, TX 77092
(713) 683-8798
Contact: Mr. Ray Marburger
Minimum Salary Placed: $25,000
Recruiting Specialty: General

Martin & Associates
4206 Broadleaf Street
Kingwood, TX 77345
(713) 360-4549
Contact: Mr. Ted L. Martin
Recruiting Specialty: Data processing, national recruiter for software and data communications

Medex
4801 Woodway, Suite 333W
Houston, TX 77056
(713) 623-2200
Contact: Mr. Dale McTaggart
Recruiting Specialty: Medical

Memorial City Personnel
800 Gessner, Suite 170
Houston, TX 77024
(713) 935-0009
Contact: Ms. Marsha Murray
Recruiting Specialty: Administrative support and sales

Meridian Consulting Group
5 Riverway
Houston, TX 77056
(713) 840-1870
Minimum Salary Placed: $40,000
Recruiting Specialty: General

Mims and Strain
3200 Southwest Freeway
Houston, TX 77027
(713) 626-1026
Contact: Mr. Steve Mims
Recruiting Specialty: Legal

Network/Energy Search Recruiters
7324 SW Freeway, Suite 670
Houston, TX 77074
(713) 777-1128
Contact: Mr. George Horne
Recruiting Specialty: Retained search technical, engineering and technical

Newman Johnson-King
P.O. Box 58345
Houston, TX 77258
(713) 474-7422
Contact: Mr. Jack King
Minimum Salary Placed: $40,000
Recruiting Specialty: General

John O'Rourke and Associates
1116 Bering Drive
Houston, TX 77057
(713) 266-4326
Contact: Mr. John O'Rourke
Minimum Salary Placed: $25,000
Recruiting Specialty: Technical disciplines

Patterson Personnel
10565 Katy Freeway, Suite 215
Houston, TX 77024
(713) 722-9777
Contact: Ms. Connie Patterson
Recruiting Specialty: General

Rick Peterson and Associates
333 N. Sam Houston Parkway E.
Houston, TX 77060
(713) 591-7777
Contact: Mr. Rick Peterson
Minimum Salary Placed: $35,000
Recruiting Specialty: Stockbrokers

Physicians Resources
3730 Kirby Dr., Suite 900
Houston, TX 77098
(713) 522-5355
Contact: Ms. Jolyn Scheirman
Recruiting Specialty: Physicians

Piper-Morgan Associates Personnel
3355 W. Alabama Street, Suite 1120
Houston, TX 77098
(713) 840-9922
Contact: Mr. Will Darroh
Minimum Salary Placed: $40,000
Recruiting Specialty: Energy, accounting, engineering, human resources and environmental

Practice Dynamics, Inc.
11222 Richmond, Suite 125
Houston, TX 77082
(713) 531-0911
Contact: Ms. Karen Lovett
Recruiting Specialty: Physicians, nurse practitioners and physicians assistants

Preng & Association, Inc.
2925 Briarpark, Suite 1111
Houston, TX 77042
(713) 266-2600
Contact: Mr. David Preng
Minimum Salary Placed: $60,000
Recruiting Specialty: General

Prescott Legal Search
3900 Essex Lane, Suite 200
Houston, TX 77027
(713) 439-0911
Contact: Mr. Larry Prescott
Minimum Salary Placed: $55,000
Recruiting Specialty: Attorneys

Professional Recruiting Consultants
5414 Antoine Drive, Suite C
Houston, TX 77091
(713) 957-3094
Recruiting Specialty: Physicians

Professional Search Consultants
3050 Post Oak Boulevard, Suite 470
Houston, TX 77056
(713) 960-9215
Contact: Mr. Larry Gobert
Minimum Salary Placed: $50,000
Recruiting Specialty: General

Quest Personnel Services
50 Briar Hollow, Suite 510-E
Houston, TX 77027-9305
(713) 961-0605
Contact: Ms. Carol Gallagher
Recruiting Specialty: Accounting and healthcare

Quinby Personnel Services
7324 SW Freeway, Suite 210
Houston, TX 77074
(713) 651-1266
Contact: Mr. J. Rodney Quinby
Recruiting Specialty: Administrative support

Railey & Associates
5102 Westerham Place
Houston, TX 77069
(713) 444-4346
Contact: Mr. J. Larry Railey
Minimum Salary Placed: $75,000
Recruiting Specialty: Attorneys

Recruit Express
8834 Prichett Drive
Houston, TX 77096
(713) 666-1001
Minimum Salary Placed: $30,000
Recruiting Specialty: Software engineering

Redstone and Associates
3838 N. Sam Houston Parkway E.
Houston, TX 77032
(713) 449-0197
Minimum Salary Placed: $50,000
Recruiting Specialty: Construction, engineering, legal, accounting and sales and marketing

Resource Management Group
701 N. Post Oak Road, Suite 204
Houston, TX 77024
(713) 956-0001
Contact: Mr. Jim Ford
Minimum Salary Placed: $40,000
Recruiting Specialty: Securities

Rhett Bigham and Associates
9801 Westheimer Road
Houston, TX 77042
(713) 777-0994
Contact: Mr. Rhett Bigham
Minimum Salary Placed: $30,000
Recruiting Specialty: Advanced processing controls and technical disciplines in petrochemicals

Richard Wayne and Roberts
24 E. Greenway Plaza, Suite 1304
Houston, TX 77046
(713) 629-6681
Contact: Mr. Neal Hirsch
Minimum Salary Placed: $25,000
Recruiting Specialty: General

RJR Associates
Box 580645
Houston, TX 77258
(713) 474-4208
Minimum Salary Placed: $25,000
Recruiting Specialty: General

Bart Roberson and Associates
1445 North Loop West, Suite 800
Houston, TX 77008
(713) 863-1445
Contact: Mr. Bart Roberson
Minimum Salary Placed: $20,000
Recruiting Specialty: Petrochemical, environmental, accounting and engineering

Roddy Group Executive Search
2400 Fountain View Drive
Houston, TX 77057
(713) 782-7642
Contact: Ms. Dorothy Roddy
Minimum Salary Placed: $50,000
Recruiting Specialty: General

Anne Rozelle & Associates
2323 S. Voss, Suite 125
Houston, TX 77057
(713) 783-4740
Contact: Ms. Anne Rozelle Schumacher
Recruiting Specialty: Property management

Russell Reynolds Associates, Inc.
1000 Louisiana, Suite 4800
Houston, TX 77002
(713) 658-1776
Contact: Mr. David Morris
Minimum Salary Placed: $100,000
Recruiting Specialty: General

Ryman, Bell, Green & Michaels, Inc.
6200 Savoy, Suite 1100
Houston, TX 77036
(713) 784-0565
Contact: Mr. Phillip Forman
Minimum Salary Placed: $50,000
Recruiting Specialty: General

Saber Group
5300 Hollister, Suite 100
Houston, TX 77040
(713) 462-6900
Contact: Mr. Steven LeMay
Minimum Salary Placed: $45,000
Recruiting Specialty: General

Sales Recruiters
340 E. Sam Houston Parkway, Suite 263
Houston, TX 77060
(713) 447-0309
Recruiting Specialty: Outside sales

Stephen T. Salemi Inc.
3200 SW Freeway
Houston, TX 77027
(713) 963-8870
Contact: Mr. Stephen Salemi
Minimum Salary Placed: $25,000
Recruiting Specialty: Oil and gas

Scannel and Hundley
14300 Cornerstone Village Drive
Houston, TX 77014
(713) 444-9592
Contact: Mr. P. Scannel
Minimum Salary Placed: $50,000
Recruiting Specialty: General

The Search Center Inc.
1155 Dairy Ashford, Suite 704
Houston, TX 77079
(713) 589-8303
Contact: Ms. Linda Center
Minimum Salary Placed: $60,000
Recruiting Specialty: Oil and gas

Search Consultants International, Inc.
4545 Post Oak Place, Suite 208
Houston, TX 77027
(713) 622-9188
Contact: Mr. S. Joseph Baker
Minimum Salary Placed: $50,000
Recruiting Specialty: Environmental, energy, oil and gas and chemicals

Seegers Estes and Associates, Inc.
14405 Walters Road, Suite 350
Houston, TX 77014
(713) 587-8765
Contact: Mr. David Estes
Recruiting Specialty: Engineering, chemical, environmental and human resources

Skillmaster, Inc.
5353 W. Alabama, Suite 600
Houston, TX 77056
(713) 552-9999
Contact: Mr. Christopher G. DeClaire
Recruiting Specialty: Data processing, engineering, accounting, and banking and finance

Source EDP
1800 W. Loop S., Suite 1200
Houston, TX 77027
(713) 439-1077
Contact: Mr. Allan Peterson
Recruiting Specialty: Computer hardware and software and legal

Source Finance
1800 West Loop S.
Houston, TX 77027
(713) 439-1077
Minimum Salary Placed: $20,000
Recruiting Specialty: Finance and accounting

Spencer Stuart
1111 Bagby, Suite 1616
Houston, TX 77002
(713) 225-1621
Contact: Mr. Louis Rieger
Minimum Salary Placed: $75,000
Recruiting Specialty: General

**Steverson & Company/Steverson
Accounting Professionals**
16010 Barkers Point Lane, Suite 120
Houston, TX 77079
(713) 496-5313
Contact: Tommie Steverson
Recruiting Specialty: Data processing

Peter Sterling & Company
One Riverway, Suite 1700
Houston, TX 77056
(713) 840-6363
Contact: Mr. Peter Sterling
Minimum Salary Placed: $40,000
Recruiting Specialty: General

Talent Tree Personnel Service
515 Post Oak Blvd., Suite 200
Houston, TX 77027-9407
(713) 871-8777
Contact: Ms. Kristi Johnson
Recruiting Specialty: Sales

M. L. Tawney & Association
P.O. Box 630573
Houston, TX 77263
(713) 784-9163

Contact: Mr. Mel Tawney
Minimum Salary Placed: $50,000
Recruiting Specialty: General

Taz Resources, Inc.
2616 South Loop West, Suite 620
Houston, TX 77054
(713) 660-7272
Contact: Ms. Zona Jefferson
Minimum Salary Placed: $25,000
Recruiting Specialty: General

Technical Search Inc.
6776 SW Freeway
Houston, TX 77074
(713) 343-1400
Contact: Mr. Steve Thompson
Minimum Salary Placed: $25,000
Recruiting Specialty: Technical disciplines

Terry Stukalin Health Care Service
10777 Westheimer Road, Suite 950
Houston, TX 77042
(713) 781-0184
Minimum Salary Placed: $25,000
Recruiting Specialty: Healthcare

**Thomas, Richardson, Runden and
Company**
9525 Katy Freeway, Suite 212
Houston, TX 77024
(713) 932-0381
Contact: Mr. Bill Thomas
Minimum Salary Placed: $40,000
Recruiting Specialty: General

Tricom Group, Inc.
4801 Woodway Drive, Suite 200E
Houston, TX 77056
(713) 661-8900
Contact: Ms. Peggy Thompson
Recruiting Specialty: Data processing

Unlimited Sources Inc.
1 Riverway, Suite 1626
Houston, TX 77056
(713) 621-4629
Contact: Mr. A. Levi
Minimum Salary Placed: $25,000
Recruiting Specialty: Sales

The Urban Placement Service
602 Sawyer, Suite 460
Houston, TX 77007
(713) 880-2211
Contact: Mr. Willie Bright
Minimum Salary Placed: $30,000
Recruiting Specialty: Minority, account-
ing, engineering and sales

Valpers, Inc.
8303 Southwest Freeway, Suite 750
Houston, TX 77074
(713) 771-9420
Contact: Mr. Donald Caffee
Recruiting Specialty: Manufacturing and
engineering in valve industry

Jane Vaughn and Associates
6400 Westpark Drive
Houston, TX 77057
(713) 780-7062
Minimum Salary Placed: $20,000
Recruiting Specialty: General

Darryl Vincent & Associates
12651 Briar Forest, Suite 165
Houston, TX 77077
(713) 497-5240
Contact: Mr. Darryl Vincent
Minimum Salary Placed: $30,000
Recruiting Specialty: Sales in consumer
products

W. Robert Michaels and Company
5065 Westheimer Road
Houston, TX 77056
(713) 965-9175
Contact: Mr. B. Davidson
Minimum Salary Placed: $25,000
Recruiting Specialty: Construction and
engineering

Wallace-Watkins International
3845 FM 1960 Road W., Suite 370
Houston, TX 77068
(713) 444-1993
Contact: Mr. William Wallace
Minimum Salary Placed: $40,000
Recruiting Specialty: Real estate

Denis P. Walsh & Associates, Inc.
5402 Bent Bough
Houston, TX 77088
(713) 931-9121
Contact: Mr. Denis Walsh
Minimum Salary Placed: $40,000
Recruiting Specialty: Engineering in en-
ergy, utility and construction

Ward Howell International, Inc.
1000 Louisiana Street, Suite 3150
Houston, TX 77002
(713) 655-7155
Contact: Mr. George Donnelly
Minimum Salary Placed: $75,000
Recruiting Specialty: General

Warwick Search Group
1000 Louisiana Street, Suite 620
Houston, TX 77002
(713) 739-8711
Contact: Ms. Kathy Renfro
Minimum Salary Placed: $25,000
Recruiting Specialty: General

Watkins and Associates
7322 SW Freeway, Suite 620
Houston, TX 77074
(713) 777-5261
Contact: Mr. M. Watkins
Minimum Salary Placed: $40,000
Recruiting Specialty: General

Whitaker Companies
820 Gessner, Suite 1400
Houston, TX 77024
(713) 465-1500
Contact: Mr. Bruce Whitaker
Minimum Salary Placed: $40,000
Recruiting Specialty: Insurance, pulp and paper, environmental, technical, data processing and medical

Windsor Consultants Inc.
13201 N.W. Freeway, Suite 704
Houston, TX 77040
(713) 460-0586
Contact: Mr. Daniel Narsh
Recruiting Specialty: Hospitality sales

John W. Worsham & Associates, Inc.
5851 San Felipe, Suite 770
Houston, TX 77057
(713) 266-3235
Contact: Mr. John Worsham
Minimum Salary Placed: $35,000
Recruiting Specialty: Banking

HUMBLE

Guidry, East, Barnes & Bono, Inc.
19506 Eastex Freeway, Suite 301
Humble, TX 77338
(713) 540-6070
Contact: Mr. Robert East
Minimum Salary Placed: $50,000
Recruiting Specialty: Physicians and healthcare

Pierce and Associates
1406 Stonehollow Drive
Humble, TX 77339
(713) 359-3100
Contact: Mr. Fred Pierce
Minimum Salary Placed: $25,000
Recruiting Specialty: High technology and software

HURST

Dunhill Personnel of Fort Worth
669 Airport Freeway, Suite 310
Hurst, TX 76053
(817) 282-8367
Contact: Mr. Andrew Barham
Minimum Salary Placed: $25,000
Recruiting Specialty: General

IRVING

Abacus Management Service
5215 N. O'Connor Boulevard, Suite 200
Irving, TX 75039
(214) 869-9169
Minimum Salary Placed: $75,000
Recruiting Specialty: General

Burnett's Staffing, Inc.
1200 Walnut Hill Lane, Suite 1000
Irving, TX 75038-3012
(214) 580-3333
Contact: Mr. Paul David Burnett
Recruiting Specialty: Administrative support, data processing, human resource, and insurance

ESP III Consulting Service
6311 N. O'Connor Boulevard, Suite N53
Irving, TX 75039
(214) 869-0837
Recruiting Specialty: Electronics and telecommunications

Fedco, Lifework, Inc.
5525 McArthur Blvd., Suite 525
Irving, TX 75038
(214) 550-8447
Contact: Mr. Fred Edwards
Recruiting Specialty: Engineering, manufacturing, computers, retained search

MSI Healthcare
5215 N. O'Connor Boulevard
1875 Williams Square Central Tower
Irving, TX 75039
(214) 869-3939
Contact: Ms. Laurelle Williams
Minimum Salary Placed: $25,000
Recruiting Specialty: Healthcare

Performance Recruiters of Dallas
5605 N. McArthur Blvd.
Irving, TX 75038
(214) 550-9060
Contact: Mr. Ron Ritchey
Recruiting Specialty: Data processing, management and supervisors

Snelling Personnel Services
1303 Walnut Hill Lane, Suite 103
Irving, TX 75038
(214) 258-5973
Contact: Mr. Joe Phy
Recruiting Specialty: Medical

Source EDP
4545 Fuller Drive, Suite 100
Irving, TX 75038
(214) 717-5005
Contact: Mr. John Morganto
Recruiting Specialty: Computer hardware and software

Source Engineering
4545 Fuller Drive, Suite 100
Irving, TX 75038
(214) 717-5005
Contact: Mr. John Morganto
Recruiting Specialty: Engineering

KELLER

CCR Coast-To-Coast Recruiting
1112 Garden, P.O. Box 1165
Keller, TX 76244
(817) 431-3880
Contact: Ms. Reta McCallum
Minimum Salary Placed: $45,000
Recruiting Specialty: Communications

KINGWOOD

Joseph Chris & Associates
900 Rockmead Drive, Suite 101
Kingwood, TX 77339
(713) 931-8744

Contact: Mr. Joe Ramirez
Minimum Salary Placed: $50,000
Recruiting Specialty: Construction and real estate development

Southcoast Partners
700 Rockhead Drive
Kingwood, TX 77339
(713) 358-3199
Contact: Mr. David Bowles
Recruiting Specialty: Real estate

LA PORTE

The Duncan Group
P.O. Box 1161
La Porte, TX 77571
(713) 470-1881
Contact: Mr. James Hall
Minimum Salary Placed: $50,000
Recruiting Specialty: General

LAKE WHITNEY

Wheeler Resources
Route 3, Box 592 H
Lake Whitney, TX 76692
(817) 694-7937
Contact: Mr. Bill Wheeler
Minimum Salary Placed: $50,000
Recruiting Specialty: Healthcare

LEWISVILLE

C. Michael Dixon
P.O. Box 293371
Lewisville, TX 75029
(214) 317-0608
Contact: Mr. C. Michael Dixon
Minimum Salary Placed: $35,000
Recruiting Specialty: Engineering

Management Recruiters
1660 S. Stemmons, Suite 460
Lewisville, TX 75067
(214) 434-9612
Contact: Mr. Anthony Kuehler
Minimum Salary Placed: $25,000
Recruiting Specialty: Sales in plastics and other coated materials

LUBBOCK

Action Personnel Services
2503 74th Street, Suite 106
Lubbock, TX 79423
(806) 748-1600
Contact: Ms. Margaret Hogan
Recruiting Specialty: General

Agape Personnel Agency
8200 C Nashville, Suite 109
Lubbock, TX 79423
(806) 794-5511
Contact: Ms. Frances DeWeese
Minimum Salary Placed: $20,000
Recruiting Specialty: General

Boren Personnel Service
6413 University
Lubbock, TX 79413
(806) 797-4161
Contact: Ms. Geneva Boren
Recruiting Specialty: General

Career Center Personnel
3305 81st
Lubbock, TX 79423
(806) 797-5765
Contact: Ms. Lois Terry
Recruiting Specialty: Sales

Management Recruiters
4413 82nd Street, Suite 310
Lubbock, TX 79424
(806) 794-8755
Contact: Mr. Lester Warren
Recruiting Specialty: Medical

Professions Today Personnel
2811 S. Loop 289, Suite 20
Lubbock, TX 79423
(806) 745-8595
Contact: Ms. Genell Ward
Minimum Salary Placed: $20,000
Recruiting Specialty: General

Snelling Personnel Services
2222 Indiana Avenue
Lubbock, TX 79410
(806) 797-3281
Contact: L.E. Crites
Recruiting Specialty: General

MCALLEN

Dunhill Professional Search
P.O. Box 3114
McAllen, TX 78502
(210) 687-9531
Contact: Mr. Lloyd Steele
Minimum Salary Placed: $25,000
Recruiting Specialty: General

USA Medical Placement Inc.
3604 Date Palm
McAllen, TX 78501
(210) 631-3540
Contact: Ms. Patricia Tracy
Minimum Salary Placed: $50,000
Recruiting Specialty: Healthcare

MESQUITE

Espro
18601 LBJ Freeway, Suite 510
Mesquite, TX 75150
(214) 686-4900
Contact: Mr. Oscar Salley
Minimum Salary Placed: $25,000
Recruiting Specialty: Healthcare, contract services and engineering

MIDLAND

Preferred Personnel
212 N. Main Street, Suite 100
Midland, TX 79701
(915) 684-5900
Contact: Ms. P. Bledsoe
Recruiting Specialty: Office Support

MINERAL WELLS

Management Resources
7611 Highway 180E
Mineral Wells, TX 76067
(817) 325-8455
Contact: Mr. Jim Hineman
Minimum Salary Placed: $25,000
Recruiting Specialty: Insurance and managed care

NEW BRAUNFELS

Management Recruiters
494 S. Seguin
New Braunfels, TX 78130
(512) 629-6290
Contact: Mr. Jim Rice
Minimum Salary Placed: $25,000
Recruiting Specialty: General

NEW DEAL

Forrest Recruiting
501 S. Monroe Avenue
New Deal, TX 79350
(806) 746-6694
Contact: Ms. Gwen Forrest
Minimum Salary Placed: $25,000
Recruiting Specialty: Agriculture

ODESSA

Bennett & Associates
2732 Palo Verdie
Odessa, TX 79762
(915) 550-9096
Contact: Mr. Mark Bennett
Minimum Salary Placed: $35,000
Recruiting Specialty: Engineers and technical disciplines in energy and healthcare

CG & Company
5050 E. University, Suite 9B
Odessa, TX 79762
(915) 362-7681
Contact: Ms. Cathy George
Recruiting Specialty: Technical

PEARLAND

John Domino and Associates
2121 East Broadway Street
Pearland, TX 77581
(713) 485-2595
Contact: Mr. John Domino
Minimum Salary Placed: $30,000
Recruiting Specialty: Healthcare

PLANO

Alpha Resources Group
1916 Brabant Drive
Plano, TX 75025
(214) 692-1616
Contact: Mr. S. Pappas
Minimum Salary Placed: $40,000
Recruiting Specialty: Hotels and resorts

Button Group
1608 Emory Circle
Plano, TX 75093
(214) 985-0619
Contact: Mr. David Button
Minimum Salary Placed: $60,000
Recruiting Specialty: General

Executive Search International
1700 Alma Drive
Plano, TX 75075
(214) 424-4714
Contact: Mr. E. Nalley
Minimum Salary Placed: $90,000
Recruiting Specialty: Sales and marketing in consumer products

Griffin Anderson and Associates
100 N. Central Parkway
Plano, TX 75074
(214) 516-1470
Minimum Salary Placed: $25,000
Recruiting Specialty: General

M H Executive Search Group
P.O. Box 868068
Plano, TX 75086
(214) 578-1511
Contact: Mr. Mike Hochwalt
Minimum Salary Placed: $35,000
Recruiting Specialty: Packaging and production

Jacob Group
2301 N. Central Expressway, Suite 200
Plano, TX 75075
(214) 422-3311
Contact: Mr. Don Jacob
Minimum Salary Placed: $25,000
Recruiting Specialty: Food, beverages
and consumer products

Vick & Associates
3325 Landershire Lane, Suite 1001
Plano, TX 75023
(214) 612-8425
Contact: Mr. Bill Vick
Minimum Salary Placed: $60,000
Recruiting Specialty: Sales and market-
ing, new media, internet and software

RICHARDSON

DSR Diversity Search & Recruitment
801 E. Campbell Road, Suite 155
Richardson, TX 75081
(214) 680-8282
Contact: Mr. David Crowley
Minimum Salary Placed: $50,000
Recruiting Specialty: Telecommunications

Charles Golden Company
331 Melrose
Richardson, TX 75080
(214) 680-8460
Contact: Mr. Charles Golden
Recruiting Specialty: Stock brokers

Robbie Griffin and Associates
670 International Parkway
Richardson, TX 75081
(214) 234-4464
Contact: Mr. Robbie Griffin
Minimum Salary Placed: $30,000
Recruiting Specialty: Medical sales

McKeen Melancon & Company
2350 Lakeside Boulevard
Richardson, TX 75082
(214) 231-9999
Contact: Mr. James McKeen
Minimum Salary Placed: $60,000
Recruiting Specialty: Manufacturing in
high technology

The Oxford Group
901 Waterfall, Suite 105
Richardson, TX 75080
(214) 644-5544
Contact: Mr. David Jackson
Recruiting Specialty: General and high
technology

Professional Executive Recruiters
1701 Galeway Boulevard, Suite 419
Richardson, TX 75080
(214) 235-3984
Contact: Mr. K. Roberts
Minimum Salary Placed: $30,000
Recruiting Specialty: Construction

Snelling Personnel Services
777 E. Campbell Rd., Suite 225
Richardson, TX 75081
(214) 470-9696
Contact: Ms. Sandy Mayo
Recruiting Specialty: Medical

Strategic Technologies, Inc.
2183 Buckingham Road, Suite 232
Richardson, TX 75081
(214) 699-8995
Contact: Ms. Sandi Taylor
Minimum Salary Placed: $40,000
Recruiting Specialty: Manufacturing in
chemical, metal, plastic, and high technology

TOF Ltd.
911 Blue Lake Circle
Richardson, TX 75080
(214) 437-2440
Contact: Mr. Ed Haynes
Minimum Salary Placed: $20,000
Recruiting Specialty: General

Wardrup Associates Inc.
2508 Spring Park Way, Suite 300
Richardson, TX 75082
(214) 437-1237
Contact: Ms. Diane Wardrup
Minimum Salary Placed: $25,000
Recruiting Specialty: General

Wydman & Associates, Inc.
1221 W. Campbell Road, Suite 207
Richardson, TX 75080
(214) 231-6432
Contact: Mr. Gary H. Wydman
Minimum Salary Placed: $25,000
Recruiting Specialty: General

ROCKWALL

Amerisearch
P.O. Box 427
Rockwall, TX 75087
(214) 722-8033
Contact: Mr. John Scott
Minimum Salary Placed: $30,000
Recruiting Specialty: Foods

SAN ANTONIO

ADIA Personnel Services
7330 San Pedro, Suite 150
San Antonio, TX 78216
(210) 349-4499

Contact: Mr. Don DeCotis
Recruiting Specialty: General

Automotive Careers of Texas
520 Garraty Road
San Antonio, TX 78209
(210) 822-3999
Contact: Mr. Mike Patton
Recruiting Specialty: Human resources
for auto dealers

Bexar County Medical Society Service Bureau
120 W. Ashby
San Antonio, TX 78212
(210) 734-9512
Contact: Ms. Kay Hays
Recruiting Specialty: Medical

Bullock Personnel of S.A.
1020 NE Loop 410, Suite 530
San Antonio, TX 78209
(210) 828-7301
Contact: Ms. Janet Connell
Recruiting Specialty: Accounting, sales
and marketing, and general

Burgeson Hospitality Search
13300 Old Blanco Road
San Antonio, TX 78216
(210) 493-1237
Contact: Mr. John Burgeson
Minimum Salary Placed: $20,000
Recruiting Specialty: Hospitality

Deacon Rawley Personnel Consulting
P.O. Box 17314
San Antonio, TX 78217
(210) 494-4000
Contact: Ms. Ann Bohl Deacon
Recruiting Specialty: General

DR Personnel Medical/Dental Employment
5282 Medical Drive, Suite 150
San Antonio, TX 78229
(210) 614-3886
Contact: Mr. Richard Cutter
Recruiting Specialty: Medical and dental

Dunhill Personnel Service
P.O. Box 700888
San Antonio, TX 78270
(210) 490-1744
Contact: Mr. John Webb
Minimum Salary Placed: $25,000
Recruiting Specialty: General

Dunhill Personnel
14514 Majestic Prince
San Antonio, TX 78248
(512) 492-5435
Contact: Ms. Angella Woodard
Minimum Salary Placed: $25,000
Recruiting Specialty: General

The Elsworth Group
10127 Morocco, Suite 116
San Antonio, TX 78216
(210) 341-9197
Contact: Mr. James O'Daniel
Minimum Salary Placed: $25,000
Recruiting Specialty: Aerospace, natural resources and high technology

Executive Source International
16500 San Pedro Avenue
San Antonio, TX 78232
(210) 494-0103
Contact: Mr. W. Cook
Minimum Salary Placed: $25,000
Recruiting Specialty: Pharmaceuticals

Food Pro Recruiters
14526 Jones Maltsberger
San Antonio, TX 78232
(210) 494-9272
Recruiting Specialty: Food industry

Fortune Personnel Consultants
10924 Vance Jackson, Suite 303
San Antonio, TX 78230
(210) 690-9797
Contact: Mr. Jim Morrisey
Minimum Salary Placed: $30,000
Recruiting Specialty: Engineering, health-care and consumer products

Global Telecommunications, Inc.
9901 IH 10 West, Suite 800
San Antonio, TX 78230
(210) 558-2828
Contact: Mr. Robert Ott
Minimum Salary Placed: $40,000
Recruiting Specialty: General

Robert Half International
6243 IH 10 West
San Antonio, TX 78209
(210) 736-2467
Contact: Ms. V. Hannah
Minimum Salary Placed: $20,000
Recruiting Specialty: Accounting and finance

Jordan-Sitter Associates
14080 Nacogdoches, Suite 323
San Antonio, TX 78247
(210) 651-5561
Contact: Mr. William Sitter
Minimum Salary Placed: $40,000
Recruiting Specialty: Construction, manufacturing and agriculture

Linn-Truett Inc.
13715 Player Drive
San Antonio, TX 78217
(210) 657-7395
Minimum Salary Placed: $20,000
Recruiting Specialty: Data processing

M&M Associates
11765 West Avenue, Suite 285
San Antonio, TX 78216
(210) 340-8772
Minimum Salary Placed: $85,000
Recruiting Specialty: Medical and physicians

Management Recruiters
7550 IH 10 West, Suite 1230
San Antonio, TX 78229
(210) 525-1800
Contact: Mr. Sam Goicoechea
Minimum Salary Placed: $25,000
Recruiting Specialty: General; manufacturing

Management Recruiters
8700 Crownhill, Suite 701
San Antonio, TX 78209
(210) 829-8666
Contact: Mr. James Cornfoot
Minimum Salary Placed: $25,000
Recruiting Specialty: Food, beverage and automotive industries

Mendez Bailey and Harrison
1250 NE Loop 410, Suite 810
San Antonio, TX 78209
(210) 826-1120
Contact: Mr. Myron Goldman
Minimum Salary Placed: $20,000
Recruiting Specialty: General

The Personnel Office
24127 Boerne Stage Road
San Antonio, TX 78255-9517
(210) 698-0300
Contact: Mr. Carl Hensley
Recruiting Specialty: General

Professional Recruiting Consultants
P.O. Box 4982
San Antonio, TX 78280
(210) 349-7801
Contact: Mr. Wes Looney
Recruiting Specialty: Accounting and finance, banking, data processing, engineering and technical

Stehouwer and Associates Inc.
2939 Mossrock
San Antonio, TX 78230
(210) 349-4995
Contact: Mr. Ron Stehouwer
Minimum Salary Placed: $20,000
Recruiting Specialty: General

Symcox Personnel Consultants
13750 N. US Highway 281, Suite 510
San Antonio, TX 78232
(210) 494-6674
Minimum Salary Placed: $25,000
Recruiting Specialty: General

SEABROOK

RJR Associates
P.O. Box 580645
Seabrook, TX 77586
(713) 474-4208
Contact: Mr. B. Reeves
Minimum Salary Placed: $20,000
Recruiting Specialty: Technical, engineering and accounting

SEVEN POINTS

Youngs & Company
P.O. Box 43635
Seven Points, TX 75143
(903) 778-4257
Contact: Mr. Donald Youngs
Minimum Salary Placed: $100,000
Recruiting Specialty: General

SPRING

Find
P.O. Box 3215
Spring, TX 77383
(713) 251-5488
Contact: Mr. Ken Jack
Minimum Salary Placed: $40,000
Recruiting Specialty: Geographic information systems

(1st) First Corporation
6450 Louetta Road
Spring, TX 77379
(713) 370-2233
Contact: Mr. Jim Giammatteo
Minimum Salary Placed: $20,000
Recruiting Specialty: Biotechnology

Hyman and Associates
719 Sawdust Road, Suite 202
Spring, TX 77380
(7130 292-1969
Contact: Mr. D. Hyman
Minimum Salary Placed: $60,000
Recruiting Specialty: Sales and marketing

STAFFORD

Management Recruiters
10707 Corporate Drive, Suite 120
Stafford, TX 77477
(713) 240-0220

Contact: Mr. John Gandee
Minimum Salary Placed: $25,000
Recruiting Specialty: Lumber/wood and environmental engineering

Staffing Solutions
12603 S.W. Frwy, Suite 691
Stafford, TX 77477
(713) 494-1940
Contact: Ms. Becky Luciano
Recruiting Specialty: General

TEXARKANA

Select Staff
4608 Summerhill Road
Texarkana, TX 75503
(903) 794-1411
Contact: Mr. R. Arnold
Minimum Salary Placed: $20,000
Recruiting Specialty: General

WACO

JB Management
2919 Mount Carmel Drive
Waco, TX 76710
(817) 772-3371
Contact: Mr. John Brosnan
Minimum Salary Placed: $25,000
Recruiting Specialty: Electronics

Robert William James and Associates
6321 Sanger Avenue
Waco, TX 76710
(817) 776-7782
Contact: Mr. J. Scofield
Minimum Salary Placed: $40,000
Recruiting Specialty: General

WEATHERFORD

The Inside Track
504 Hilltop Drive
Weatherford, TX 76086
(817) 599-7094
Minimum Salary Placed: $35,000
Recruiting Specialty: Telecommunications

WETMORE

Thompson Professional Recruiting
Box 63099
Wetmore, TX 78247
(210) 590-0675
Minimum Salary Placed: $20,000
Recruiting Specialty: MIS

WICHITA FALLS

Recruiting Associates
2107 Kemp Boulevard
Wichita Falls, TX 76309
(817) 723-0150
Contact: Mr. B. Palin
Minimum Salary Placed: $35,000
Recruiting Specialty: General

THE WOODLANDS

W. Robert Eissler & Associates, Inc.
1610 Woodstead Court, Suite 230
The Woodlands, TX 77380
(713) 367-1052
Contact: Mr. W. Robert Eissler
Minimum Salary Placed: $25,000
Recruiting Specialty: Instrumentation,
valves, fluid power, plastics and telecommunications

Management Recruiters
1610 Woodstead Court, Suite 495
The Woodlands, TX 77380
(713) 363-9494
Contact: Ms. Lynette Krochenski
Minimum Salary Placed: $25,000
Recruiting Specialty: General

U T A H

BRIGHTON

Dan Murphy
11261 E. Big Cottonwood Canyon
  Highway
Brighton, UT 84121
(800) 610-5566
Contact: Mr. Dan Murphy
Minimum Salary Placed: $50,000
Recruiting Specialty: Retailing and hospitality

MURRAY

Professional Recruiters
220 E 3900 S, Suite 9
Murray, UT 84107
(801) 268-9940
Minimum Salary Placed: $20,000
Recruiting Specialty: General

SALT LAKE CITY

Atlantic West International
6337 S. Highland Drive, Suite 300
Salt Lake City, UT 84121
(801) 943-9944
Contact: Mr. James Doddridge
Minimum Salary Placed: $50,000
Recruiting Specialty: Healthcare and
medical

Deeco International
710 Aspen Heights Drive
Salt Lake City, UT 84157
(801) 261-3326
Contact: Ms. Dee McBride
Recruiting Specialty: Healthcare

Execusource
4746 S 900 E, Suite 250
Salt Lake City, UT 84117
(801) 261-3179
Contact: Mr. M. Kennedy
Minimum Salary Placed: $25,000
Recruiting Specialty: General

Fielding Nelson & Assoc., Inc.
420 E. South Temple, Suite 364
Salt Lake City, UT 84111
(801) 532-2183
Contact: Mr. Randy Craig
Minimum Salary Placed: $50,000
Recruiting Specialty: General

Management Recruiters
6600 South 1100 East, Suite 420
Salt Lake City, UT 84121
(801) 264-9800
Contact: Mr. Dirk Cotterell
Minimum Salary Placed: $20,000
Recruiting Specialty: General

Price Perelson and Associates
19 E. 200 S., Suite 1000
Salt Lake City, UT 84111
(801) 532-1000
Recruiting Specialty: General

Robert Half Accountemps
50 S. Main Street
Salt Lake City, UT 84144
(801) 364-5500
Contact: Mr. J. Anderson
Recruiting Specialty: Accounting and finance

Source EDP
8 E. Broadway, Suite 735
Salt Lake City, UT 84111
(801) 328-0011
Recruiting Specialty: Finance, healthcare,
manufacturing and engineering

STM Associates
230 S. 500 East, Suite 500
Salt Lake City, UT 84102
(801) 531-6500
Contact: Mr. Gerald Cooke
Minimum Salary Placed: $60,000
Recruiting Specialty: Natural resources

Team Builders of America
3760 S. Highland Drive
Salt Lake City, UT 84106
(801) 277-8660
Minimum Salary Placed: $25,000
Recruiting Specialty: General

SANDY

Trout & Associates, Inc.
15 Gatehouse Lane
Sandy, UT 84092
(801) 576-1547
Contact: Mr. Thomas Trout
Minimum Salary Placed: $45,000
Recruiting Specialty: General

VERMONT

BURLINGTON

Management Recruiters
74 Main Street, 2nd Floor Front
Burlington, VT 05401
(802) 865-0541
Contact: Mr. Alan Nyhan
Minimum Salary Placed: $20,000
Recruiting Specialty: Finance and computers

PLYMOUTH

Jay Tracey Associates
P.O. Box 30
Plymouth, VT 05034
(802) 672-3000
Contact: Mr. Jay Tracey
Minimum Salary Placed: $25,000
Recruiting Specialty: Drives, process control (DCS), PLC, industrial controls, factory automation and plastic extrusion and blow molding

RANDOLPH

Theken Associates Inc.
Highway 66
Randolph, VT 05060
(802) 728-5811
Minimum Salary Placed: $25,000
Recruiting Specialty: Nursing administration

SHELBURNE

Candis Perrault Associates Inc.
5 Covington Lane
Shelburne, VT 05482
(802) 985-1017
Contact: Ms. Candis Perrault
Minimum Salary Placed: $65,000
Recruiting Specialty: Financial services

WARREN

Dunhill Search of Vermont
P.O. Box 204
Warren, VT 05674
(802) 496-0115
Contact: Mr. Herb Hauser
Minimum Salary Placed: $35,000
Recruiting Specialty: General

WILLISTON

Market Search Associates
P.O. Box 462
Williston, VT 05495
(802) 434-2460
Contact: Mr. Rick Lewis
Minimum Salary Placed: $25,000
Recruiting Specialty: Sales and marketing

WOODSTOCK

Eckler Personnel Network
14 Lincoln Street
Woodstock, VT 05091
(802) 457-1605
Contact: Mr. Geoffrey Eckler
Minimum Salary Placed: $30,000
Recruiting Specialty: Data processing and MIS

V I R G I N I A

ALEXANDRIA

Ability Resources Inc.
716 Church Street
Alexandria, VA 22314
(703) 548-6400
Contact: Mr. Noel Ruppert
Minimum Salary Placed: $25,000
Recruiting Specialty: General

The Barrister Group
207 W. Glendale Avenue
Alexandria, VA 22301
(703) 684-5130
Contact: Mr. Lee Emery
Recruiting Specialty: Legal

Bernstein Consulting Group Inc.
211 N. Union Street, Suite 100
Alexandria, VA 22314
(703) 739-9111
Contact: Ms. Christine Bernstein
Minimum Salary Placed: $25,000
Recruiting Specialty: General

Jeffrey Irving Associates, Inc.
216 S. Payne Street
Alexandria, VA 22314
(703) 836-7770
Contact: Mr. Jeffrey Irving
Minimum Salary Placed: 90,000
Recruiting Specialty: General

Raymond Karsan Associates
1500 N. Beauregard, Suite 110
Alexandria, VA 22311
(703) 845-1114
Contact: Mr. Michael Prencipe
Recruiting Specialty: Technical

A.T. Kearney Executive Search
225 Reinekers Lane
Alexandria, VA 22314
(703) 739-4624
Contact: Mr. Roger Sekera
Minimum Salary Placed: $60,000
Recruiting Specialty: General

Oerth Associates
601 King Street
Alexandria, VA 22302
(703) 739-1348
Contact: Ms. P. Oerth
Minimum Salary Placed: $25,000
Recruiting Specialty: General

ARLINGTON

Joe R. Batts and Associates
1317 19th Road South
Arlington, VA 22202
(703) 486-0788
Contact: Mr. Joe Batts
Recruiting Specialty: General

BJB Associates
1501 Crystal Drive, Suite 1024
Arlington, VA 22202
(703) 413-0541
Contact: Ms. Bobbi Bauman
Minimum Salary Placed: $40,000
Recruiting Specialty: Technical disciplines in disposable paper products, chemicals and plastic products

Frey & Sher Associates, Inc.
1800 N. Kent Street, Suite 1006
Arlington, VA 22209
(703) 524-6500
Contact: Ms. Florence Frey
Recruiting Specialty: Attorneys

McCormick Group Inc.
1400 Wilson Boulevard, Suite 100
Arlington, VA 22209
(800) 353-1787
Contact: Mr. Bill McCormick
Minimum Salary Placed: $30,000
Recruiting Specialty: General

Morgan & Banks
2300 Clarendon Boulevard, Suite 1211
Arlington, VA 22201
(703) 351-5600
Contact: Mr. Paul Dinte
Minimum Salary Placed: $60,000
Recruiting Specialty: General

Partners Accounting Staff
4350 N. Fairfax Drive, Suite 400
Arlington, VA 22203
(703) 351-7600
Contact: Mr. John Voigt
Minimum Salary Placed: $20,000
Recruiting Specialty: Accounting

U.S. Search
5712 N. 18th Road
Arlington, VA 22205
(703) 448-1900
Contact: Mr. Arnie Hiller
Minimum Salary Placed: $40,000
Recruiting Specialty: Plastics, chemicals
and packaging

BRISTOL

Management Recruiters
4526 Lee Highway, Suite 100
Bristol, VA 24201
(540) 466-5400
Contact: Mr. R. Michael Williams
Recruiting Specialty: General

CAPE CHARLES

Lawrence Veber and Associates
507 Tazewell Avenue
Cape Charles, VA 23310
(804) 678-5548
Minimum Salary Placed: $60,000
Recruiting Specialty: Supermarkets and
healthcare

CHARLOTTESVILLE

Hartman & Barnette
1324 Kenwood Lane
Charlottesville, VA 22906
(804) 979-0993
Contact: Mr. Robert Hartman
Minimum Salary Placed: $70,000
Recruiting Specialty: Healthcare and
pharmaceuticals

FAIRFAX

Halbrecht & Company
10195 Main Street, Suite L
Fairfax, VA 22031
(703) 359-2880
Contact: Mr. Thomas Maltby
Minimum Salary Placed: $30,000
Recruiting Specialty: MIS and management consulting

High Technology Consultants
9691 Main Street, Suite D
Fairfax, VA 22031
(703) 764-0123
Contact: Carolyn
Minimum Salary Placed: $35,000
Recruiting Specialty: High technology

Management Recruiters
4400 Fair Lakes Ct., Suite 103
Fairfax, VA 22033
(703) 222-8220
Contact: Mr. Tony Ehrenzeller
Minimum Salary Placed: $20,000
Recruiting Specialty: Outside sales

Sales Consultants of Fairfax, Inc.
9840 Main Street, Suite 201
Fairfax, VA 22031
(703) 385-6050
Contact: Mr. David Kurke
Minimum Salary Placed: $20,000
Recruiting Specialty: Sales

Technology Concepts Ltd.
4603 Luxberry Drive
Fairfax, VA 22032
(703) 591-2500
Contact: Ms. Barbara Sweig
Minimum Salary Placed: $40,000
Recruiting Specialty: Technical disciplines in high technology

FALLS CHURCH

Rupert and Associates
11401 Purple Beach Drive
Falls Church, VA 22042
(703) 620-1646
Contact: Mr. Bud Rupert
Minimum Salary Placed: $40,000
Recruiting Specialty: High technology

HERNDON

John Michael Associates
102 Elden Street
Herndon, VA 22070
(703) 471-6300
Contact: Mr. G. Fosset
Minimum Salary Placed: $100,000
Recruiting Specialty: Law partners

LEESBURG

Management Recruiters
44084 Riverside Parkway, Suite 170
Leesburg, VA 22075
(703) 729-5600
Contact: Mr. Jerry Gilmore
Minimum Salary Placed: $30,000
Recruiting Specialty: Chemicals and healthcare

LIGHTFOOT

Executive Career Search
P.O. Box 480
Lightfoot, VA 23090
(804) 564-3013
Contact: Mr. Charles Sillery
Minimum Salary Placed: $35,000
Recruiting Specialty: General

LYNCHBURG

Management Recruiters
2511 Memorial Avenue, Suite 302
Lynchburg, VA 24501
(804) 528-1611
Contact: Mr. C. David Blue
Minimum Salary Placed: $20,000
Recruiting Specialty: General

Phillips Resource Group
2900 Old Forest Road, P.O. Box 3198
Lynchburg, VA 24503
(804) 385-3940
Contact: Ms. Gale Smith
Minimum Salary Placed: $30,000
Recruiting Specialty: General

MANASSAS

Management Recruiters
8807 Sudley Road, Suite 208
Manassas, VA 22110
(703) 330-1830
Contact: Mr. Peter Rubando
Minimum Salary Placed: $20,000
Recruiting Specialty: Computers

MARTINSVILLE

Management Recruiters
212 Starling Avenue, Suite 201
Martinsville, VA 24112
(540) 632-2355
Contact: Mr. Herschel Gurley
Minimum Salary Placed: $25,000
Recruiting Specialty: Textiles and apparel

MCLEAN

Aaron-Jones Inc.
2010 Corporate Ridge
McLean, VA 22102
(703) 734-0014
Contact: Ms. Florence Aaron
Minimum Salary Placed: $25,000
Recruiting Specialty: General

Guild Corporation
8260 Greensboro Drive, Suite 460
McLean, VA 22102
(703) 761-4023
Contact: Mr. Paul Siker
Minimum Salary Placed: $25,000
Recruiting Specialty: MIS, engineering
and other technical disciplines

Glassman Associates Inc.
6603 Anthony Crest Square
McLean, VA 22101
(703) 442-8866
Contact: Mr. Larry Glassman
Minimum Salary Placed: $25,000
Recruiting Specialty: General

Management Recruiters
1568 Spring Hill Road, Suite 301
McLean, VA 22102
(703) 442-4842
Contact: Mr. Howard Reitkopp
Minimum Salary Placed: $20,000
Recruiting Specialty: General

Paul-Tittle Associates, Inc.
1485 Chain Bridge Road, Suite 304
McLean, VA 22101
(703) 442-0500
Contact: Mr. David Tittle
Minimum Salary Placed: $60,000
Recruiting Specialty: High technology

Paul T. Unger Associates
1550 McLean Commons Court
McLean, VA 22101
(703) 790-0404
Contact: Mr. Paul Unger
Minimum Salary Placed: $75,000
Recruiting Specialty: High technology

ONANCOCK

United Search
P.O. Box 21
Onancock, VA 23417
(804) 787-2332
Contact: Mr. Ed Oswald
Minimum Salary Placed: $40,000
Recruiting Specialty: Engineering

RESTON

Brault & Associates
11703 Bowman Green Drive
Reston, VA 22090
(703) 471-0920
Contact: Mr. J. P. Brault
Minimum Salary Placed: $70,000
Recruiting Specialty: General

Dahl-Morrow International
12020 Sunrise Valley Drive, Suite 100
Reston, VA 22091
(703) 648-1594
Contact: Ms. Barbara Steinem
Minimum Salary Placed: $100,000
Recruiting Specialty: General

Donmac Associates
2506 Freetown Drive
Reston, VA 22091
(703) 620-2866
Contact: Ms. Connie Anderson
Minimum Salary Placed: $25,000
Recruiting Specialty: Computers and
data processing

Hayes Research Group
11800 Sunrise Valley Drive
Reston, VA 22091
(703) 860-2456
Contact: Mr. Don Hayes
Minimum Salary Placed: $25,000
Recruiting Specialty: General

IPR, Inc.
11718 Bowman Green Drive
Reston, VA 22090
(703) 318-9600
Contact: Mr. G. Alan Thomas
Recruiting Specialty: General

Leonard Weiner and Associates Inc.
12355 Sunrise Valley Drive, Suite 625
Reston, VA 22091
(703) 264-0200
Contact: Mr. Len Weiner
Minimum Salary Placed: $100,000
Recruiting Specialty: General

RICHMOND

Accountants On Call
701 E. Franklin Street, Suite 1408
Richmond, VA 23219
(804) 225-0200
Contact: Mr. Michael Parks
Recruiting Specialty: Accounting

Blanchard and Associates
10815 Whitaker Woods Road
Richmond, VA 23233
(804) 741-3547
Contact: Mr. Tom Blanchard
Minimum Salary Placed: $50,000
Recruiting Specialty: General

The Corporate Connection, Ltd.
7202 Glen Forest Drive
Richmond, VA 23226
(804) 288-8844
Contact: Mr. Marshall Rotella
Minimum Salary Placed: $25,000
Recruiting Specialty: General

Dunhill of Greater Richmond
8100 Three Chopt Road, Suite 133
Richmond, VA 23288
(804) 282-2216
Contact: Mr. Frank Lassiter
Minimum Salary Placed: $25,000
Recruiting Specialty: General

Durill and Associates
7200 Glen Forest Drive, Suite 306
Richmond, VA 23226
(804) 282-0595
Recruiting Specialty: General

Heritage Personnel
1501 Santa Rosa Road
Richmond, VA 23229
(804) 285-2184
Contact: Ms. Kay Goode
Minimum Salary Placed: $25,000
Recruiting Specialty: General

Management Recruiters
6620 W. Broad Street, Suite 406
Richmond, VA 23230
(804) 285-2071
Contact: Mr. Jay Schwartz
Minimum Salary Placed: $20,000
Recruiting Specialty: General

Opalka Dixon Consultants
1215 Confederate Avenue
Richmond, VA 23227
(804) 358-0119
Contact: Ms. Violett Dixon
Minimum Salary Placed: $80,000
Recruiting Specialty: Direct Marketing

Preferred Personnel
300 Arboretum Place
Richmond, VA 23236
(804) 330-7765

Contact: Ms. Pat Newton
Minimum Salary Placed: $25,000
Recruiting Specialty: General

RTE Search
711 Regency Tower, P.O. Box 29668
Richmond, VA 23242
(804) 750-2088
Contact: Mr. Keith English
Minimum Salary Placed: $25,000
Recruiting Specialty: Manufacturing,
R&D and engineering

Sales Consultants
6620 W. Broad Street, Suite 406
Richmond, VA 23230
(804) 285-2071
Contact: Mr. Jay Schwartz
Minimum Salary Placed: $20,000
Recruiting Specialty: Sales

Strategic Search Inc.
5206 Market Road, Suite 302
Richmond, VA 23228
(804) 285-6100
Contact: Ms. Dorrey Steinberg
Minimum Salary Placed: $25,000
Recruiting Specialty: General

ROANOKE

Management Recruiters
1960 Electric Road, Suite B
Roanoke, VA 24018
(540) 989-1676
Contact: Mr. Paul Sharp
Minimum Salary Placed: $20,000
Recruiting Specialty: General

STAUNTON

The Talley Group
P.O. Box 2918
Staunton, VA 24402
(540) 248-7009
Contact: Mr. E.H. Talley
Minimum Salary Placed: $45,000
Recruiting Specialty: Human resources

TYSON'S CORNER

Secura/Burnett Partners
7799 Leesburg Pike, Suite 800
Tyson's Corner, VA 22103
Contact: Mr. William Isaac
Recruiting Specialty: Finance

VIENNA

Accountants Executive Search
8000 Towers Crescent Drive, Suite 240
Vienna, VA 22182
(703) 448-7500
Contact: Ms. Jean Jordan
Minimum Salary Placed: $25,000
Recruiting Specialty: Accounting, finance
and data processing

Clark Group Ltd.
8300 Boone Boulevard, Suite 500
Vienna, VA 22182
(703) 760-4127
Contact: Mr. Jim Clark
Recruiting Specialty: General

FGI
1595 Spring Hill Road, Suite 350
Vienna, VA 22182
(703) 847-0010
Contact: Mr. Fred Gloss
Minimum Salary Placed: $50,000
Recruiting Specialty: General

Heidrick & Struggles, Inc.
8000 Towers Crescent Drive, Suite 555
Vienna, VA 22182
(703) 761-4830
Contact: Mr. Michael Christy
Minimum Salary Placed: $60,000
Recruiting Specialty: General

Kincannon & Reed
2106-C Gallows Road
Vienna, VA 22182
(703) 761-4046
Contact: Mr. Kelly Kincannon
Minimum Salary Placed: $75,000
Recruiting Specialty: Food, agri-business
and biotechnology

Kirkman & Searing
8000 Towers Crescent Drive, Suite 630
Vienna, VA 22182
(703) 761-7020
Contact: Mr. J. Michael Kirkman
Minimum Salary Placed: $75,000
Recruiting Specialty: Healthcare, finance
and high technology

Logue & Rice Inc.
8000 Towers Crescent Drive, Suite 650
Vienna, VA 22182
(703) 761-4261
Contact: Mr. Raymond Rice
Minimum Salary Placed: $35,000
Recruiting Specialty: General

MSI International
1593 Springhill Road
Vienna, VA 22182
(703) 893-5660
Contact: Mr. Mark Lewicki
Minimum Salary Placed: $25,000
Recruiting Specialty: General

The Network Companies
1595 Spring Hill Road, Suite 220
Vienna, VA 22182
(703) 790-1100
Contact: Mr. Theodore Bruccoleri
Minimum Salary Placed: $30,000
Recruiting Specialty: Accounting, finance and MIS

Source EDP
8614 Westwood Center Drive
Vienna, VA 22182
(703) 790-5610
Contact: Mr. Paul Villella
Recruiting Specialty: MIS

VIRGINIA BEACH

A la Carte International, Inc.
3330 Pacific Avenue, Suite 500
Virginia Beach, VA 23451
(804) 425-6111
Contact: Mr. Michael Romaniw
Minimum Salary Placed: $60,000
Recruiting Specialty: Consumer Products

Career Dynamics II
1 Columbus Center
Virginia Beach, VA 23462
(804) 490-7837
Contact: Mr. Marvin Burgess
Minimum Salary Placed: $25,000
Recruiting Specialty: General

Career Market Consultants
1092 Laskin Road, Suite 100
Virginia Beach, VA 23451
(804) 428-8888
Recruiting Specialty: Technical and restaurants

Dunhill Professional Search
4828 Eastwind Road
Virginia Beach, VA 23464
(804) 495-8916
Contact: Mr. James Naughton
Recruiting Specialty: General

Information Specialists Company
Box 55313
Virginia Beach, VA 23471
(804) 340-0022
Contact: Mr. Hugo Schluter
Minimum Salary Placed: $25,000
Recruiting Specialty: Engineering and other technical

Management Recruiters
4092 Foxwood Drive, Suite 102
Virginia Beach, VA 23462
(804) 474-2752
Contact: Mr. James Murphey
Minimum Salary Placed: $20,000
Recruiting Specialty: Healthcare and engineering

Sales Consultants
4092 Foxwood Drive, Suite 102
Virginia Beach, VA 23462
(804) 474-2752
Contact: Mr. James Murphey
Minimum Salary Placed: $20,000
Recruiting Specialty: Sales

Search & Recruit International
4455 South Boulevard
Virginia Beach, VA 23452
(804) 490-3151
Contact: Mr. R. P. Brittingham
Minimum Salary Placed: $25,000
Recruiting Specialty: Engineering and technical

WILLIAMSBURG

Sloan & Associates, Inc.
1769 Jamestown Road
Williamsburg, VA 23185
(804) 220-1111
Contact: Mr. Michael Sloan
Minimum Salary Placed: $50,000
Recruiting Specialty: Consumer products

WOODBRIDGE

Key Banking Consultant
12779 Gazebo Court
Woodbridge, VA 22192
(703) 491-5700
Contact: Mr. Ron Miller
Minimum Salary Placed: $25,000
Recruiting Specialty: Banking, finance
and accounting

WASHINGTON

BAINBRIDGE ISLE

Moss and Company
12145 Arrow Point Loop NE
Bainbridge Isle, WA 98110
(206) 842-4035
Contact: Ms. Barbara Moss
Minimum Salary Placed: $35,000
Recruiting Specialty: Real estate development and finance

BELLEVUE

Accounting Partners
500 108th Avenue NE, Suite 1640
Bellevue, WA 98004
(206) 450-1990
Contact: Mr. Ted Macaulley
Minimum Salary Placed: $25,000
Recruiting Specialty: Accounting

Rod Asher Associates
411 108th Avenue NE, Suite 2050
Bellevue, WA 98004
(206) 646-1030
Contact: Mr. Rod Asher
Minimum Salary Placed: $25,000
Recruiting Specialty: Computers and high technology

Black and Deering
1605 116th Avenue NE
Bellevue, WA 98004
(206) 646-0905
Contact: Mr. Dewey Black
Minimum Salary Placed: $35,000
Recruiting Specialty: Healthcare

Career Specialists, Inc.
155-108th Avenue NE, Suite 200
Bellevue, WA 98004
(206) 455-0582
Contact: Ms. Pamela Rolfe
Minimum Salary Placed: $30,000
Recruiting Specialty: Technical disciplines and computers

CC Corporate Consultants
11100 NE 8th Street, Suite 610
Bellevue, WA 98004
(206) 635-0166
Contact: Mr. J. Freatman
Minimum Salary Placed: $25,000
Recruiting Specialty: General

J.F. Church Associates, Inc.
PO Box 6128
Bellevue, WA 98008
(206) 644-3278
Contact: Mr. James Church
Minimum Salary Placed: $40,000
Recruiting Specialty: Computers

Computer Group Inc.
777 108th Avenue NE, Suite 1550
Bellevue, WA 98004
(206) 455-3100
Contact: Mr. D. Kennelly
Minimum Salary Placed: $30,000
Recruiting Specialty: Computers

Consumer Connection
400 108th Avenue NE
Bellevue, WA 98004
(206) 455-2770
Contact: Mr. G. Chatwin
Minimum Salary Placed: $25,000
Recruiting Specialty: Consumer packaged goods

Devon James Associates
12356 Northup Way, Suite 118
Bellevue, WA 98004
(206) 462-0616
Recruiting Specialty: High technology

Emerge
800 Bellevue Way NE, Suite 400
Bellevue, WA 98004
(206) 649-1180
Contact: Ms. Renee Feldman
Minimum Salary Placed: $25,000
Recruiting Specialty: Sports and leisure

Executive Recruiters
600 108th Avenue NE, Suite 242
Bellevue, WA 98004
(206) 447-7404
Contact: Mr. Ronald Butler
Minimum Salary Placed: $25,000
Recruiting Specialty: General

L.W. Foote Company
110-110th Avenue, NE, Suite 603
Bellevue, WA 98004
(206) 451-1660
Contact: Mr. Leland Foote
Minimum Salary Placed: $70,000
Recruiting Specialty: General

Robert Half Accountemps
10900 NE 4th Street, Suite 1230
Bellevue, WA 98004
(206) 451-1000
Contact: Ms. Lori Beth Dalton
Recruiting Specialty: Accounting and finance

Headden and Associates
777 108th Avenue NE
Bellevue, WA 98004
(206) 451-2427
Contact: Mr. Bill Headden
Minimum Salary Placed: $75,000
Recruiting Specialty: General

Healthcare Specialists Inc.
400 108th Avenue NE, Suite 310
Bellevue, WA 98004
(206) 454-0678
Contact: Ms. Deni Sutherland
Minimum Salary Placed: $50,000
Recruiting Specialty: Healthcare

Hembree Galbraith and Associates
405 114th Avenue SE, Suite 300
Bellevue, WA 98004
(206) 453-5235
Contact: Ms. Ruth Hembree
Minimum Salary Placed: $40,000
Recruiting Specialty: Healthcare

Houser Martin Morris and Associates
110 110th Avenue, Suite 503
Bellevue, WA 98004
(206) 453-2700
Contact: Mr. Bob Holbert
Minimum Salary Placed: $30,000
Recruiting Specialty: General

Jenson Oldani and Cooper
411 108th Street Avenue NE
Bellevue, WA 98004
(206) 451-3938
Contact: Ms. J. Cooper
Minimum Salary Placed: $50,000
Recruiting Specialty: General

Kossuth & Associates, Inc.
800 Bellevue Way NE, Suite 400
Bellevue, WA 98004
(206) 450-9050
Contact: Ms. Jane Kossuth
Minimum Salary Placed: $50,000
Recruiting Specialty: General

Lorenzen Group
777 108th Avenue NE, 6th Floor
Bellevue, WA 98004
(206) 285-7123
Contact: Ms. Lori Lorenzen
Minimum Salary Placed: $25,000
Recruiting Specialty: General

MacroSearch
13353 Bel Red Road, Suite 206
Bellevue, WA 98004
(206) 641-7252
Contact: Ms. M. Peterson
Minimum Salary Placed: $35,000
Recruiting Specialty: Technical disciplines

John Mason and Associates
2135 112th Avenue NE
Bellevue, WA 98004
(206) 453-1608
Contact: Mr. John Mason
Minimum Salary Placed: $40,000
Recruiting Specialty: High technology,
electronic manufacturing and computer
programming

Parfitt Recruiting and Consulting
1540 140th Avenue NE, Suite 201
Bellevue, WA 98004
(206) 646-6300
Contact: Mr. Bill Parfitt
Minimum Salary Placed: $25,000
Recruiting Specialty: Accounting, fi-
nance, and high technology

Parsons Personnel
10900 NE 4th Street, Suite 1910
Bellevue, WA 98004
(206) 451-3920
Contact: Ms. Karen Parsons
Minimum Salary Placed: $25,000
Recruiting Specialty: General

Personnel Consultants
14042 NE 8th Street, Suite 201B
Bellevue, WA 98007
(206) 641-0657
Contact: Mr. Larry Dykes
Recruiting Specialty: General

Personnel Resource
10900 NE 8th Street, Suite 900
Bellevue, WA 98004
(206) 451-8423
Recruiting Specialty: General

Prior MarTech Associates
3245 146th Place SE, Suite 330
Bellevue, WA 98007
(206) 643-4411
Contact: Mr. Paul Meyer
Minimum Salary Placed: $50,000
Recruiting Specialty: General

Rigel Computer Resources
1611 116th Avenue NE
Bellevue, WA 98004
(206) 646-4990
Contact: Ms. Rita Ashley
Minimum Salary Placed: $30,000
Recruiting Specialty: Computers

Roth Young Personnel Service
Box 3307
Bellevue, WA 98009
(206) 455-2141

Contact: Mr. David Salzberg
Minimum Salary Placed: $50,000
Recruiting Specialty: General

Sales Consultants
275 118th Ave-SE, Suite 125
Bellevue, WA 98005
(206) 455-1805
Contact: Mr. Mark Stephens
Minimum Salary Placed: $20,000
Recruiting Specialty: Sales

Source EDP
500 108th Avenue NE, Suite 1780
Bellevue, WA 98004
(206) 454-6400
Recruiting Specialty: Engineering, finance and manufacturing

Strategic Resources Group
1611 116th Avenue NE
Bellevue, WA 98004
(206) 646-4983
Contact: Mr. R. Stryker
Minimum Salary Placed: $25,000
Recruiting Specialty: General

The Triad Group
12505 Bellevue-Redmond Road,
  Suite 208
Bellevue, WA 98005
(206) 454-0282
Contact: Mr. James Mercer
Recruiting Specialty: General

BOTHELL

Competitive Resources
19125 N. Creek Parkway, Suite 104
Bothell, WA 98011
(206) 486-2900
Contact: Mr. Marvin Smith
Recruiting Specialty: General

Pro-Active Consultants
20611 Bothell Everett Highway
Bothell, WA 98012
(206) 513-9200
Contact: Mr. Ken Brown
Minimum Salary Placed: $25,000
Recruiting Specialty: General

BURTON

Morgan Palmer Morgan and Hill
PO Box 13353
Burton, WA 98013
(206) 463-5721
Contact: Mr. Warren Hill
Minimum Salary Placed: $25,000
Recruiting Specialty: General

EDMONDS

Power Personnel Service
120 W. Dayton Street
Edmonds, WA 98020
(206) 771-3373
Recruiting Specialty: Power conversion

FEDERAL WAY

Almond and Associates
1010 S. 336th Street, Suite 310
Federal Way, WA 98063
(206) 946-2222
Contact: Tanya
Minimum Salary Placed: $45,000
Recruiting Specialty: General

James Group Inc.
33305 1st Way S
Federal Way, WA 98003
(206) 874-8919
Minimum Salary Placed: $25,000
Recruiting Specialty: General

Whittall Management
720 S. 333rd Street, Suite 102
Federal Way, WA 98003
(206) 874-0710
Contact: Mr. Perry Gorman
Minimum Salary Placed: $20,000
Recruiting Specialty: General

ISSAQUAH

K.E. Johnson Associates
4213-187th Place SE
Issaquah, WA 98027
(206) 747-4559
Contact: Mr. Karl Johnson
Minimum Salary Placed: $50,000
Recruiting Specialty: Technical disciplines in computers, semiconductors and high technology

Marshall Consultants
55 1st Place NW, Suite 5
Issaquah, WA 98027
(206) 392-8660

Contact: Ms. Judith Cushman
Minimum Salary Placed: $60,000
Recruiting Specialty: General

Pacific Search Consultants
310 3rd Avenue NE
Issaquah, WA 98027
(206) 392-4407
Contact: Ms. Paula Smith
Minimum Salary Placed: $40,000
Recruiting Specialty: Engineering

Jack Porter and Associates
24119 SE 18th Place
Issaquah, WA 98027
(206) 392-9252
Contact: Mr. Jack Porter
Minimum Salary Placed: $25,000
Recruiting Specialty: General, some engineering and manufacturing

KIRKLAND

NG Hayes Company
401 Park Place Center, Suite 207
Kirkland, WA 98033
(206) 453-1313
Contact: Ms. Nelia Hayes
Minimum Salary Placed: $60,000
Recruiting Specialty: MIS and high technology

Miller and Miller Executive Search
PO Box 3088
Kirkland, WA 98083
(206) 822-3145
Contact: Ms. Shirley Miller
Minimum Salary Placed: $35,000
Recruiting Specialty: Biotechnology and medical

Sander Associates
2011 Market Street
Kirkland, WA 98033
(206) 827-6446
Contact: Ms. Patty Jones
Minimum Salary Placed: $25,000
Recruiting Specialty: General

Schultz Group Inc.
401 Parkplace Center
Kirkland, WA 98033
(206) 822-1726
Contact: Ms. S. Schultz
Minimum Salary Placed: $25,000
Recruiting Specialty: Computers

Sussman and Associates
PO Box 2128
Kirkland, WA 98083
(206) 822-8775
Contact: Ms. L. Sussman
Minimum Salary Placed: $25,000
Recruiting Specialty: General

LONGVIEW

Beans Personnel Service Inc.
1953 7th Avenue, Suite 204
Longview, WA 98632
(360) 577-8434
Contact: Ms. Joanie Jones
Recruiting Specialty: General

LYNNWOOD

Management Recruiters
19109 W. 36th Avenue, Suite 208
Lynnwood, WA 98036
(206) 778-1212
Contact: Mr. Bud Naff
Minimum Salary Placed: $20,000
Recruiting Specialty: General

Richards Williams and Associates
20717 Highway 99
Lynnwood, WA 98036
(206) 672-3260
Minimum Salary Placed: $25,000
Recruiting Specialty: General

Robert William James and Associates
19105 36th Avenue W
Lynnwood, WA 98036
(206) 778-6810
Contact: Ms. D. Palmen
Recruiting Specialty: General

MERCER ISLAND

Management Recruiters
9725 SE 36th Street, Suite 312
Mercer Island, WA 98040
(206) 232-0204
Contact: Mr. James Dykeman
Minimum Salary Placed: $20,000
Recruiting Specialty: General

Maritime Recruiters
PO Box 260
Mercer Island, WA 98040
(206) 232-6041
Contact: Mr. B. Walton
Minimum Salary Placed: $25,000
Recruiting Specialty: Maritime

John O'Keefe & Associates, Inc.
7900 SE 28th Street, Suite 400
Mercer Island, WA 98040
(206) 236-6199
Contact: Mr. John O'Keefe
Minimum Salary Placed: $50,000
Recruiting Specialty: Consumer products

Thompson and Associates
2448 76th Avenue SE, Suite 212
Mercer Island, WA 98040
(206) 236-0153
Contact: Mr. Neal Thompson
Minimum Salary Placed: $50,000
Recruiting Specialty: High technology

MILL CREEK

Competitive Resources, Inc.
19125 N. Creek Parkway, Suite 104
Mill Creek, WA 98012
(206) 486-2900
Contact: Mr. Marvin Smith
Minimum Salary Placed: $40,000
Recruiting Specialty: General

MUKILTEO

DT Technical Services
P.O. Box 798
Mukilteo, WA 98275
(206) 369-7957
Contact: Mr. Dexter Turner
Minimum Salary Placed: $40,000
Recruiting Specialty: High technology

OLYMPIA

Management Recruiters
2633-A Parkmount Lane SW, Suite B
Olympia, WA 98502
(206) 357-9996
Contact: Mr. Jim Pitchford
Minimum Salary Placed: $20,000
Recruiting Specialty: General

REDMOND

RHO Company
4002 148th Avenue NE
Redmond, WA 98052
(206) 883-2233
Recruiting Specialty: Computers, software and high technology

Susan Stoneberg Executive Search
8350 164th Avenue NE, Suite 303
Redmond, WA 98052
(206) 882-4862
Contact: Ms. Susan Stoneberg
Recruiting Specialty: Sales

Shirley Tierney Executive Search
8350 164th Avenue NE, Suite 302
Redmond, WA 98052
(206) 883-4715
Contact: Ms. Shirley Tierney
Recruiting Specialty: Consumer products, sales and marketing

RENTON

Thomas Company
15434 SE 167th Place
Renton, WA 98058
(206) 255-7637
Minimum Salary Placed: $25,000
Recruiting Specialty: Insurance

RICHLAND

Caseley and Associates
1329 George Washington Way, Suite 16
Richland, WA 99352
(509) 943-0501
Minimum Salary Placed: $25,000
Recruiting Specialty: General

SEATTLE

Accountants On Call
601 Union Street
Seattle, WA 98161
(206) 467-0700
Contact: Ms. Jeaneen Reinhart
Recruiting Specialty: Accounting

Accounting Quest
101 Stewart Street, Suite 1000
Seattle, WA 98101
(206) 441-5600
Recruiting Specialty: Accounting

Adams and Associates Inc.
701 5th Avenue
Seattle, WA 98104
(206) 447-9200
Contact: Ms. Shirley Adams
Recruiting Specialty: General

B & M Unlimited
1218 3rd Avenue, Suite 821
Seattle, WA 98101
(206) 223-1687
Contact: Mr. Lonnie Moore
Minimum Salary Placed: $25,000
Recruiting Specialty: General

Berkana International, Inc.
3417 Freemont Avenue N., Suite 225
Seattle, WA 98103
(206) 361-1633
Contact: Mr. Paul Allen
Minimum Salary Placed: $40,000
Recruiting Specialty: Computer, telecommunications and multi-media

T.M. Campbell Company
1111 3rd Street, Suite 2500
Seattle, WA 98101
(206) 583-8355
Contact: Ms. Terry Campbell
Minimum Salary Placed: $25,000
Recruiting Specialty: General

Career Clinic
9725 3rd Avenue NE, Suite 509
Seattle, WA 98115
(206) 524-9831
Minimum Salary Placed: $25,000
Recruiting Specialty: General

Computer Personnel, Inc.
7200 Olive Way, Suite 510
Seattle, WA 98101
(206) 340-2722
Contact: Mr. Ron Meints
Recruiting Specialty: MIS and computer systems

Cooper Personnel
1411 Fourth Avenue, Suite 1327
Seattle, WA 98101
(206) 583-0722
Contact: Ms. Bonnie Cooper
Recruiting Specialty: Import and export

EKO Consulting
1511 3rd Avenue
Seattle, WA 98101
(206) 624-3161
Contact: Mr. Jerry Olson
Minimum Salary Placed: $40,000
Recruiting Specialty: Midrange ASA 4000

First Choice Search
5336 SW Lander Street
Seattle, WA 98126
(206) 938-1944
Contact: Ms. Michelle Hale
Minimum Salary Placed: $25,000
Recruiting Specialty: General

Robert Half Accountemps
18000 Andover Park W, Suite 102
Seattle, WA 98188
(206) 575-6996
Contact: Ms. E. Sinclair
Recruiting Specialty: Accounting and finance

Robert Half International
600 Stewart Street, Suite 800
Seattle, WA 98101
(206) 443-8840
Contact: Ms. J. Marzan
Minimum Salary Placed: $25,000
Recruiting Specialty: Accounting and finance

Hurd Siegel and Associates
1904 3rd Avenue
Seattle, WA 98101
(206) 622-4282
Contact: Mr. Tom Hurd
Minimum Salary Placed: $25,000
Recruiting Specialty: General

Knapp Agency
1904 3rd Avenue, Suite 1011
Seattle, WA 98101
(206) 623-2323
Contact: Ms. O. Frost
Minimum Salary Placed: $25,000
Recruiting Specialty: General

Korn/Ferry International
600 University Street, Suite 3111
Seattle, WA 98101
(206) 462-1100
Contact: Mr. E. Blecksmith
Minimum Salary Placed: $75,000
Recruiting Specialty: General

Russell Lager and Associates
Box 60111
Seattle, WA 98160
(206) 448-2616
Contact: Mr. Russ Lager
Minimum Salary Placed: $30,000
Recruiting Specialty: Sales and marketing in consumer products

Lawrence and Associates
1200 5th Avenue, Suite 1927
Seattle, WA 98101
(206) 621-1228
Contact: Mr. Terry Lawrence
Minimum Salary Placed: $25,000
Recruiting Specialty: Finance, accounting and some general

Management Recruiters
2510 East Fairview Avenue
Seattle, WA 98102
(206) 328-0936
Contact: Mr. Dan Jilka
Minimum Salary Placed: $80,000
Recruiting Specialty: High Technology

Management Recruiters
16300 Christensen Road, Suite 250
Seattle, WA 98188
(206) 242-7484
Contact: Mr. Marc Goyette
Minimum Salary Placed: $20,000
Recruiting Specialty: Telecommunications and MIS

McHale & Associates
1001 Fourth Avenue, Suite 3200
Seattle, WA 98154
(206) 684-9778
Contact: Mr. John McHale
Minimum Salary Placed: $40,000
Recruiting Specialty: MIS and computers

Middleton and Associates
10002 Aurora Avenue North, Suite 2282
Seattle, WA 98133
(206) 285-8380
Contact: Ms. Debra Middleton
Minimum Salary Placed: $30,000
Recruiting Specialty: General

Omega Attorney Placement
401 Second Avenue S.
Seattle, WA 98104
(206) 467-5547
Contact: Ms. Carol Richardson
Minimum Salary Placed: $40,000
Recruiting Specialty: Attorneys

Passage and Associates
1001 4th Avenue, Suite 3200
Seattle, WA 98154
(206) 622-3330
Minimum Salary Placed: $40,000
Recruiting Specialty: General

Pilon Management Company
1809 7th Avenue, Suite 1010
Seattle, WA 98101
(206) 682-6465
Contact: Mr. C. Pilon
Minimum Salary Placed: $25,000
Recruiting Specialty: General

Search First
2101 4th Avenue, Suite 2120
Seattle, WA 98121
(206) 728-4084
Minimum Salary Placed: $35,000
Recruiting Specialty: High technology

Seattle Recruiters
1001 Fourth Avenue, Suite 3200
Seattle, WA 98104
(206) 467-6617
Contact: Ms. Margaret McClory
Recruiting Specialty: Legal

Susan Schoos and Associates
120 Lakeside Avenue
Seattle, WA 98122
(206) 324-4942
Contact: Ms. Susan Schoos
Minimum Salary Placed: $40,000
Recruiting Specialty: Manufacturing, engineering and construction

Strain Personnel Specialists
801 Pine Street, Suite 2000
Seattle, WA 98101
(206) 382-1588
Contact: Mr. Joe Strain
Minimum Salary Placed: $40,000
Recruiting Specialty: General

Donna Svei Associates
1111 Third Avenue, Suite 2500
Seattle, WA 98101
(206) 654-9005
Contact: Ms. Donna Svei
Minimum Salary Placed: $40,000
Recruiting Specialty: General

Waldron and Company
101 Stewart Street, Suite 1200
Seattle, WA 98101
(206) 441-4144
Contact: Mr. T. Waldron
Minimum Salary Placed: $35,000
Recruiting Specialty: Non-profit

SPOKANE

Jackson Hawthorne Group
2920 S. Grand Boulevard, Suite 104
Spokane, WA 99201
(509) 458-3800
Minimum Salary Placed: $25,000
Recruiting Specialty: Banking

Management Recruiters
North 4407 Division Street, Suite 910
Spokane, WA 99207
(509) 484-0084
Contact: Mr. Darrell Cellars
Minimum Salary Placed: $20,000
Recruiting Specialty: General

Oberg Personnel Agency
416 Paulsen Pro Building
Spokane, WA 99201
(509) 624-9148
Contact: DeMaris Burke
Minimum Salary Placed: $25,000
Recruiting Specialty: General

Personnel Unlimited/Executive Search
25 W. Nora
Spokane, WA 99205
(509) 326-8880
Contact: Mr. Gary Desgrosellier
Minimum Salary Placed: $25,000
Recruiting Specialty: General

Pro-Search
8900 E. Sprague Avenue
Spokane, WA 99212
(509) 928-3151
Contact: Mr. C. Hager
Minimum Salary Placed: $25,000
Recruiting Specialty: General

TACOMA

Robert Half International
1201 Pacific Avenue, Suite 1780
Tacoma, WA 98402
(206) 272-1600
Contact: Ms. E. Sinclair
Minimum Salary Placed: $25,000
Recruiting Specialty: Accounting and finance

Snelling and Snelling
4301 S. Pine Street, Suite 91
Tacoma, WA 98409
(206) 473-1800
Minimum Salary Placed: $25,000
Recruiting Specialty: Engineering, sales and data processing

VANCOUVER

Circadian Executive Search
PO Box 942
Vancouver, WA 98666
(360) 693-1441
Contact: Mr. Gordon Stewart
Minimum Salary Placed: $25,000
Recruiting Specialty: General

Maki and Company
11818 SE Mill Palin Boulevard, Suite 3
Vancouver, WA 98684
(360) 256-8074

Contact: Mr. Lou Maki
Minimum Salary Placed: $25,000
Recruiting Specialty: General

Management Recruiters
703 Broadway Street, Suite 500
Vancouver, WA 98660
(360) 695-4688
Contact: Mr. James Poloni
Minimum Salary Placed: $20,000
Recruiting Specialty: General

Nola Worley & Associates, Inc.
8000 NE Parkway, Suite 300
Vancouver, WA 95662
(360) 604-5281
Contact: Ms. Nola Jeli
Minimum Salary Placed: $50,000
Recruiting Specialty: Banking, finance and accounting

Steven and Associates
1412 NE 152nd Avenue
Vancouver, WA 98684
(360) 896-6375
Contact: Mr. Steven Hashimoto
Minimum Salary Placed: $25,000
Recruiting Specialty: Pulp and paper

WENATCHEE

Express Temporary Service
230 N. Mission Avenue
Wenatchee, WA 98801
(509) 662-5187
Contact: Mr. G. Anderson
Recruiting Specialty: General

WEST VIRGINIA

CHARLESTON

Dunhill Professional Search
1111 Smith Street
Charleston, WV 25301
(304) 340-4260
Minimum Salary Placed: $25,000
Recruiting Specialty: Healthcare

MRI
1587 E. Washington Street
Charleston, WV 25311
(304) 344-5632
Minimum Salary Placed: $35,000
Recruiting Specialty: Chemicals, metals and sales

MORGANTOWN

Azimuth Inc.
1000 Technology Drive, Suite 3120
Morgantown, WV 26505
(304) 363-1162
Minimum Salary Placed: $35,000
Recruiting Specialty: Software

WISCONSIN

ALTOONA

ECG, Inc.
711 Hillcrest Parkway
Altoona, WI 54720
(715) 833-2393
Contact: Mr. Denny Burkhart
Recruiting Specialty: General

AMHERST

The Sauve Company, LTD.
P.O. Box 337
151 Mill Street
Amherst, WI 54406
(715) 824-2502
Contact: Mr. Gordy Sauve
Recruiting Specialty: Food industry with dairy specialization

APPLETON

Engineering Placement Specialists
P.O. Box 85
Appleton, WI 54912
(414) 739-1135
Contact: Ms. Lynn Sexton
Recruiting Specialty: Engineering, sales and marketing

Management Recruiters
911 N. Lynndale Drive
Appleton, WI 54914
(414) 731-5221
Contact: Mr. Russell Hanson
Minimum Salary Placed: $30,000
Recruiting Specialty: Engineering and purchasing

Schenck & Associates
Box 1739
Appleton, WI 54913
(414) 731-8111
Contact: Mr. Patrick Egan
Minimum Salary Placed: $35,000
Recruiting Specialty: General

BROOKFIELD

Boettcher Associates
120 Bishops Way, Suite 126
Brookfield, WI 53005
(414) 782-2205
Contact: Mr. Jack Boettcher
Minimum Salary Placed: $50,000
Recruiting Specialty: General

Financial Management Personnel
400 N. Executive Drive, Suite 460
Brookfield, WI 53005
(414) 784-9630
Contact: Mr. John Higgins
Minimum Salary Placed: $25,000
Recruiting Specialty: Accounting and finance

Fogec Consultants, Inc.
400 N. Executive Drive, Suite 455
Brookfield, WI 53005
(414) 427-0960
Contact: Mr. Thomas Fogec
Minimum Salary Placed: $40,000
Recruiting Specialty: General

Gibson & Company, Inc.
250 N. Sunnyslope Road, Suite 300
Brookfield, WI 53005
(414) 785-8100
Contact: Mr. Bruce Gibson
Minimum Salary Placed: $100,000
Recruiting Specialty: General

I.D.T. Corp.
P.O. Box 888
Brookfield, WI 53008
(414) 798-3000
Contact: Mr. James Peterson
Recruiting Specialty: Engineering

Maglio & Company, Inc.
450 N. Sunnyslope Road, Suite 130
Brookfield, WI 53005
(414) 784-6020
Contact: Mr. Charles Maglio
Minimum Salary Placed: $50,000
Recruiting Specialty: General

Staff Development Corporation
4040 N. Calhoun Road
Brookfield, WI 53005
(414) 783-0020
Contact: Ms. Mary Agnello
Minimum Salary Placed: $75,000
Recruiting Specialty: Physicians

Stanislaw & Associates, Inc.
300 N. Corporate Drive, Suite 120
Brookfield, WI 53045
(414) 784-8590
Contact: Mr. Robert Stanislaw
Minimum Salary Placed: $60,000
Recruiting Specialty: General

Jude M. Werra & Associates
205 Bishop's Way, Suite 226
Brookfield, WI 53005
(414) 797-9166
Contact: Mr. Jude Werra
Minimum Salary Placed: $60,000
Recruiting Specialty: General

Jude M. Werra and Associates
205 Bishop's Way, Suite 226
Brookfield, WI 53005
(414) 797-9166
Contact: Ms. Jude Werra
Minimum Salary Placed: $75,000
Recruiting Specialty: General

ELM GROVE

A.J. Placements/Human Resource Recruiters
P.O. Box 198
Elm Grove, WI 53122
(414) 541-1001
Contact: Ms. Jane Seefeld
Recruiting Specialty: Human resources

Koehler & Company
700 N. Pilgrim Parkway, Suite 104
Elm Grove, WI 53122
(414) 796-8010
Contact: Mr. Jack Koehler
Minimum Salary Placed: $70,000
Recruiting Specialty: Manufacturing and high technology

Management Recruiters
13000 West Bluemound Road
Elm Grove, WI 53122
(414) 797-7500
Contact: Mr. William Healy
Minimum Salary Placed: $30,000
Recruiting Specialty: Data processing, pharmaceuticals and manufacturing

FOND DU LAC

Management Recruiters
P.O. Box 1237
Fond Du Lac, WI 54936
(414) 921-1776
Contact: Ms. Judith Berger
Minimum Salary Placed: $30,000
Recruiting Specialty: General

Quality Consulting Group, Inc.
104 S. Main Street, Suite 517
Fond Du Lac, WI 54935
(414) 923-1900
Contact: Ms. Mary Gerlach
Recruiting Specialty: General

GREEN BAY

Dunhill of Green Bay, Inc.
336 S. Jefferson Street
Green Bay, WI 54301
(414) 432-2977
Contact: Mr. Kramer Rock
Minimum Salary Placed: $20,000
Recruiting Specialty: General

The H. S. Group, Inc.
2611 Libal Street
Green Bay, WI 54301
(414) 432-7444
Contact: Mr. Jack Seal
Recruiting Specialty: General

Management Recruiters
444 S. Adams Street, Suite 1
Green Bay, WI 54301
(414) 437-4353
Contact: Mr. Garland Ross
Minimum Salary Placed: $30,000
Recruiting Specialty: General

Sales Consultants
444 S. Adams Street
Green Bay, WI 54301
(414) 437-4353
Contact: Mr. Garland Ross
Minimum Salary Placed: $20,000
Recruiting Specialty: Sales

HALES CORNERS

Hunter Midwest
11101 W. Janesville Road
Hales Corners, WI 53130
(414) 529-3930
Contact: Mr. John Certalic
Minimum Salary Placed: $20,000
Recruiting Specialty: Data processing

Management Recruiters South
5307 S. 92nd Street, Suite 125
Hales Corners, WI 53130
(414) 529-8020
Contact: Mr. John Henkel
Minimum Salary Placed: $30,000
Recruiting Specialty: Medical, accounting, finance and insurance

HARTFORD

Needham Consultants, Inc.
2269 Hall Road
Hartford, WI 53027
(414) 670-6795
Contact: Mr. Mike Needham
Recruiting Specialty: Engineering, sales, MIS and human resources

HARTLAND

Conley Associates, Inc.
31191 W. Beaver Lake Road
Hartland, WI 53029
(414) 367-7300
Contact: Mr. Gordon Housfeld
Minimum Salary Placed: $60,000
Recruiting Specialty: General

JANESVILLE

Management Recruiters of Janesville, Inc.
20 E. Milwaukee Street, Suite 304
Janesville, WI 53545
(608) 752-2125
Contact: Mr. Carroll Smith
Minimum Salary Placed: $30,000
Recruiting Specialty: Automotive manufacturing and managed care

LACROSSE

The Plastics Specialists
421 Main
LaCrosse, WI 54601
(608) 791-1111
Contact: Ms. Angie Klatt
Recruiting Specialty: Plastics

LAKE GENEVA

Continental Research Search, Inc.
1190 Turnberry Court
Lake Geneva, WI 53147
(414) 241-4727
Contact: Ms. Jill Hillner
Minimum Salary Placed: $50,000
Recruiting Specialty: General and information brokering

The Rankin Group, Ltd.
P.O. Box 1120
Lake Geneva, WI 53147
(414) 279-5005
Contact: Mr. Jeffrey Rankin
Minimum Salary Placed: $80,000
Recruiting Specialty: Wealth management professionals for institutional and personal trusts

Ward Howell International
401 Host Drive
Lake Geneva, WI 53147
(414) 249-5200
Minimum Salary Placed: $25,000
Recruiting Specialty: Insurance, finance and healthcare

MADISON

Advanced Medical Placement
14 W. Newhaven Center
Madison, WI 53717
(608) 831-1718
Contact: Ms. Diane Backus
Recruiting Specialty: Nursing

Executive Recruiters, Inc.
P.O. Box 44704
Madison, WI 53744
(608) 833-4004
Contact: Mr. Gilbert Ormson
Minimum Salary Placed: $35,000
Recruiting Specialty: Engineering and manufacturing

EXUTEC Group
2801 International Lane
Madison, WI 53704
(608) 244-1088
Minimum Salary Placed: $75,000
Recruiting Specialty: General

Cathy Hurless Executive Recruiting
5713 Indian Trace
Madison, WI 53716
(608) 222-5300
Contact: Ms. Cathy Hurless
Minimum Salary Placed: $40,000
Recruiting Specialty: Media and advertising

Innovative Staff Search
Box 1769
Madison, WI 53703
(800) 799-5339
Minimum Salary Placed: $40,000
Recruiting Specialty: Pharmacists, nursing and physicians assistants

McGladrey & Pullen
434 S. Yellowstone Drive, P.O. Box 5946
Madison, WI 53705
(608) 833-2612
Contact: Mr. Jim Vellucci
Minimum Salary Placed: $30,000
Recruiting Specialty: General

Patterson Resources
700 Ray-O-Vac Drive
Madison, WI 53711
(608) 277-9400
Contact: Ms. Ellen Patterson
Minimum Salary Placed: $25,000
Recruiting Specialty: General

Snelling Personnel Service
1 Point Place, Suite 102
Madison, WI 53719
(608) 829-2229
Contact: Ms. T. Pendleton
Minimum Salary Placed: $25,000
Recruiting Specialty: General

Weitzel Employment Agency
P.O. Box 5531
Madison, WI 53705
(608) 238-6945
Contact: Ms. Janeane Weitzel
Recruiting Specialty: Manufacturing and engineering

Wojdula & Associates
700 Ray-O-Vac Drive, Suite 204
Madison, WI 53711
(608) 271-2000
Contact: Mr. Andrew Wojdula
Minimum Salary Placed: $50,000
Recruiting Specialty: General

MENOMONEE FALLS

Monarch Personnel Consultants
17015 Main Street
Menomonee Falls, WI 53051
(414) 250-9553
Contact: Ms. Betty Westen
Minimum Salary Placed: $30,000
Recruiting Specialty: Printing and packaging

Site Personnel Service Inc.
N. 48 W. 16550 Lisbon Road
Menomonee Falls, WI 53051
(414) 783-5181
Contact: Mr. Dave Aragon
Minimum Salary Placed: $35,000
Recruiting Specialty: Engineering

Trainor/Salick & Associates Inc.
16550 W. Lisbon Road
Menomonee Falls, WI 53052
(414) 783-7900
Contact: Mr. James Trainor
Minimum Salary Placed: $25,000
Recruiting Specialty: Engineering

MEQUON

J. M. Eagle Partners Ltd.
10140 N. Port Washington Road
Mequon, WI 53092
(414) 241-1113

Contact: Mr. Jerry Moses
Minimum Salary Placed: $60,000
Recruiting Specialty: Healthcare and pharmaceuticals

HR Inc.

1017 W. Glen Oaks Lane
Mequon, WI 53092
(414) 241-8588
Contact: Ms. Sunny Mehta
Minimum Salary Placed: $40,000
Recruiting Specialty: Plastics and manufacturing

Overton Group

10535 N. Port Washington Road
Mequon, WI 53092
(414) 241-8189
Contact: Mr. Justin Strom
Minimum Salary Placed: $75,000
Recruiting Specialty: General

Charles Ray Associates Inc.

1200 W. Sierra Lane
Mequon, WI 53092
(414) 241-4150
Contact: Mr. Chuck Ray
Minimum Salary Placed: $25,000
Recruiting Specialty: Healthcare

MIDDLETON

Sales Consultants

7600 Terrace Avenue, Suite 203
Middleton, WI 53562
(608) 836-5566
Contact: Mr. William Schultz
Minimum Salary Placed: $20,000
Recruiting Specialty: Sales

MILWAUKEE

Accountants Executive Search

3333 N. Mayfair Road, Suite 112
Milwaukee, WI 53222
(414) 771-1900
Contact: Ms. B. Mancos
Minimum Salary Placed: $25,000
Recruiting Specialty: Accounting and finance

Accounting Resources Inc.

10909 Greenfield Avenue
Milwaukee, WI 53214
(414) 476-4444
Minimum Salary Placed: $18,000
Recruiting Specialty: Accounting and clerical

Argus Technical Service

2835 N. Mayfair Road
Milwaukee, WI 53222
(414) 774-5996
Contact: Mr. B. Korb
Minimum Salary Placed: $25,000
Recruiting Specialty: Technical disciplines

Associated Recruiters

7144 N. Park Manor Drive
Milwaukee, WI 53224
(414) 353-1933
Contact: Mr. Maurice Pettengill
Minimum Salary Placed: $30,000
Recruiting Specialty: Packaging

BDO Seidman

Two Plaza East, 330 E. Kilbourn
  Avenue, Suite 950
Milwaukee, WI 53202
(414) 272-5900
Contact: Mr. Jim Heller
Minimum Salary Placed: $70,000
Recruiting Specialty: General

Carlson Consultants
5630 Northlake Drive
Milwaukee, WI 53217
(414) 962-1855
Contact: Mr. Rick Carlson
Recruiting Specialty: Healthcare

CTC-The Corporate Talent Company
324 E. Wisconsin Avenue, Suite 230
Milwaukee, WI 53202
(414) 277-0808
Contact: Mr. John Bach
Minimum Salary Placed: $25,000
Recruiting Specialty: General

David Neil and Associates
5225 N. Ironwood Road
Milwaukee, WI 53217
(414) 964-4666
Contact: Mr. K. Stanat
Minimum Salary Placed: $25,000
Recruiting Specialty: General

Dunhill Personnel of Milwaukee
735 N. Water Street, Suite 185
Milwaukee, WI 53202
(414) 272-4860
Contact: Mr. Bradley Brin
Minimum Salary Placed: $20,000
Recruiting Specialty: General

EDP Consultants Inc.
P.O. Box 26066
Milwaukee, WI 53226
(414) 255-9363
Contact: Mr. R. Anderson
Minimum Salary Placed: $25,000
Recruiting Specialty: Computers and
data processing

Executive Placement Service Inc.
10701 W. North Avenue
Milwaukee, WI 53226
(414) 778-2200
Contact: Mr. Anthony Kish
Minimum Salary Placed: $40,000
Recruiting Specialty: Engineering, pro-
duction and banking

Gielow Associates, Inc.
306 N. Milwaukee Street
Milwaukee, WI 53202
(800) 969-7715
Contact: Mr. Curtis Gielow
Recruiting Specialty: Physicians and
medical

Robert Half International
411 E. Wisconsin Avenue
Milwaukee, WI 53202
(414) 271-4253
Contact: Ms. B. Hammerberg
Minimum Salary Placed: $25,000
Recruiting Specialty: Accounting and fi-
nance

HPO Staffing
5205 N. Ironwood Road, Suite 209
Milwaukee, WI 53217
(800) 236-6194
Contact: Mr. David Caswell
Minimum Salary Placed: $50,000
Recruiting Specialty: Healthcare

Insurance National Search Inc.
P.O. Box 93386
Milwaukee, WI 53203
(414) 224-9399
Contact: Ms. T. Quirk
Minimum Salary Placed: $25,000
Recruiting Specialty: Insurance

Jonas, Walters & Associates, Inc.
1110 N. Old World Third Street,
 Suite 510
Milwaukee, WI 53203
(414) 291-2828
Contact: Mr. Richard Barnes
Minimum Salary Placed: $50,000
Recruiting Specialty: General

The Jordan Chase Group
10721 W. Capitol Drive, Suite 4
Milwaukee, WI 53222
(414) 536-6656
Contact: Mr. Chuck Kelly
Recruiting Specialty: Information systems and telecommunications

Kordus Consulting Group
1470 E. Standish Place
Milwaukee, WI 53217
(414) 228-7979
Contact: Ms. Lee Walther Kordus
Minimum Salary Placed: $40,000
Recruiting Specialty: Marketing, advertising, promotions and public relations

MARBL Consultants, Inc.
11270 W. Park Place, Suite 270
Milwaukee, WI 53224
(414) 359-5627
Contact: Mr. Allan Adzima
Minimum Salary Placed: $40,000
Recruiting Specialty: Manufacturing, engineering, human resources and data processing

Management Recruiters
828 North Broadway
Milwaukee, WI 53202
(414) 226-2420
Contact: Mr. Doug Lane
Minimum Salary Placed: $25,000
Recruiting Specialty: General

Management Recruiters
601 E. Henry Clay
Milwaukee, WI 53217
(414) 963-2520
Contact: Mr. Tim Lawler
Minimum Salary Placed: $30,000
Recruiting Specialty: General

Marketing Consultants
2589 N. Lake Drive
Milwaukee, WI 53211
(414) 962-6611
Contact: Ms. Carol Smolizer
Minimum Salary Placed: $35,000
Recruiting Specialty: Consumer packaged goods

P. J. Murphy & Associates, Inc.
735 N. Water Street
Milwaukee, WI 53202
(414) 277-9777
Contact: Mr. Patrick Murphy
Minimum Salary Placed: $50,000
Recruiting Specialty: General

Peck & Associates, Ltd.
4555 W. Schroeder Drive, Suite 120
Milwaukee, WI 53223
(414) 354-8700
Contact: Mr. James Peck
Minimum Salary Placed: $30,000
Recruiting Specialty: General

Roth Young Executive Search
5215 N. Ironwood Lane
Milwaukee, WI 53217
(414) 962-7684
Minimum Salary Placed: $35,000
Recruiting Specialty: Food industry

Sales Associates of America
2525 N. Mayfair Road, Suite 302
Milwaukee, WI 53226
(414) 774-9800
Contact: Mr. D. Martin
Minimum Salary Placed: $30,000
Recruiting Specialty: Sales

Sales Consultants
601 E. Henry Clay
Milwaukee, WI 53217
(414) 963-2520
Contact: Mr. Tim Lawler
Minimum Salary Placed: $20,000
Recruiting Specialty: Sales

Sales Search Inc.
8200 W. Brown Deer Road
Milwaukee, WI 53223
(414) 365-3651
Contact: Mr. R. Silberman
Minimum Salary Placed: $25,000
Recruiting Specialty: Sales

Sales Specialists Inc.
614 W. Brown Deer Road, Suite 300
Milwaukee, WI 53217
(414) 228-8810
Contact: Mr. J. Alexander
Minimum Salary Placed: $35,000
Recruiting Specialty: Sales

Smith Gilkey Associates Inc.
735 N. Water Street
Milwaukee, WI 53202
(414) 277-1033
Recruiting Specialty: General

Source EDP
1233 N. Mayfair Road, Suite 129
Milwaukee, WI 53226
(414) 475-7200

Contact: Mr. Dave Youngberg
Recruiting Specialty: Computer hardware and software

Source Finance
1233 N. Mayfair Road, Suite 129
Milwaukee, WI 53226
(414) 774-6700
Contact: Ms. D. Youngberg
Minimum Salary Placed: $25,000
Recruiting Specialty: Accounting and finance

Sullivan Associates
5215 N. Ironwood Road, Suite 107
Milwaukee, WI 53217
(414) 964-3500
Minimum Salary Placed: $100,000
Recruiting Specialty: General

Trinity Research Corporation
5050 W. Brown Deer Road
Milwaukee, WI 53223
(414) 355-8866
Contact: Mr. Bob Holton
Minimum Salary Placed: $30,000
Recruiting Specialty: General

Wallen, Beck and Associates Inc.
5626 N. 91st Street, Suite 306
Milwaukee, WI 53225
(414) 527-2400
Contact: Mr. Charles Wallen
Minimum Salary Placed: $40,000
Recruiting Specialty: General

Wegner & Associates
11270 W. Park Place, Suite 310
Milwaukee, WI 53224
(414) 359-2333
Contact: Mr. Carl Wegner
Minimum Salary Placed: $25,000
Recruiting Specialty: General

MOSINEE

Management Recruiters
1117 W. County Road
Mosinee, WI 54455
(715) 341-4900
Contact: Mr. Bradford Barick
Minimum Salary Placed: $30,000
Recruiting Specialty: Insurance and data processing

MUKWONOGO

Professional Staffing Consultants
P.O. Box 475
Mukwonogo, WI 53149
Contact: Mr. Dan Schauer
Recruiting Specialty: Fluid power, fluid handling, fluid controls

OAK CREEK

Career Builders
231 E. Rawson Avenue
Oak Creek, WI 53154
(414) 571-0402
Contact: Mr. Gary Schmidt
Minimum Salary Placed: $25,000
Recruiting Specialty: Data processing

Foodstaff 2000, Inc.
6560 S. 27th Street
Oak Creek, WI 53154
(414) 761-2500
Contact: Mr. Chuck Nolan
Minimum Salary Placed: $25,000
Recruiting Specialty: Food industry

OCONOMOWOC

Blum & Company
1412 N. Lapham Street
Oconomowoc, WI 53066
(414) 628-4533
Contact: Mr. D. L. Buzz Blum
Minimum Salary Placed: $40,000
Recruiting Specialty: General

Ehrhardt & Associates
P.O. Box 125
Oconomowoc, WI 53066
(414) 567-3366
Contact: Mr. Bob Ehrhardt
Recruiting Specialty: Engineering, technical and operations, and manufacturing and processing

Humiston & Weissgerber Associates
34625 Springbank Road
Oconomowoc, WI 53066
(414) 567-7727
Contact: Ms. Carol Humiston
Recruiting Specialty: Medical and consumer durables industries

TEMCO
P.O. Box 303
Oconomowoc, WI 53066
(414) 567-2069
Contact: Mr. Thomas Masson
Minimum Salary Placed: $30,000
Recruiting Specialty: General

ONALASKA

Career Resources
757 Sand Lake Road
Onalaska, WI 54650
(608) 783-6307

Contact: Mr. Chris Jansson
Recruiting Specialty: General

Sainte Marie International
1285 Rudy, Suite 101-A
Onalaska, WI 54650
(608) 781-7250
Contact: Mr. Mark Sainte Marie
Minimum Salary Placed: $25,000
Recruiting Specialty: General

RACINE

American Placement Services
440 Main Street
Racine, WI 53403
(414) 637-7776
Contact: Ms. Valerie Ferber
Recruiting Specialty: Insurance, finance, engineering, general manufacturing, and foundry

The Connolly Consulting Group Inc.
520 College Avenue
Racine, WI 53403
(414) 633-5333
Contact: Mr. M. Michael Connolly
Minimum Salary Placed: $50,000
Recruiting Specialty: General

Engineer Track
222 Main Street
Racine, WI 53403
(414) 637-9357
Contact: Mr. John Grady
Recruiting Specialty: Manufacturing, engineering, human resources and finance

Management Recruiters
8338 Corporate Drive, Suite 300
Racine, WI 53406
(414) 886-8000
Contact: Mr. Thomas Hurt
Minimum Salary Placed: $30,000
Recruiting Specialty: General

Market Equity Inc.
1842 College Avenue
Racine, WI 53403
(414) 637-5500
Contact: Mr. Randy Bangs
Minimum Salary Placed: $25,000
Recruiting Specialty: General

Sales Consultants
8338 Corporate Drive, Suite 300
Racine, WI 53406
(414) 886-8000
Contact: Mr. Thomas Hurt
Minimum Salary Placed: $20,000
Recruiting Specialty: Sales

REEDSBURG

Prestige Inc.
P.O. Box 421
Reedsburg, WI 53959
(608) 524-4032
Contact: Mr. James Sammons
Minimum Salary Placed: $50,000
Recruiting Specialty: General

RHINELANDER

Nicolet Employment
56 S. Brown Street
Rhinelander, WI 54501
(715) 365-1302

Contact: Mr. L. Zunker
Minimum Salary Placed: $25,000
Recruiting Specialty: General

SEYMOUR

Dieck, Mueller and Associates
1017 Orchard Drive
Seymour, WI 54165
(414) 833-7600
Contact: Mr. Daniel Dieck
Minimum Salary Placed: $50,000
Recruiting Specialty: Paper

SHEBOYGAN FALLS

John Kuhn & Associates
641 Monroe Street
Sheboygan Falls, WI 53085
(414) 467-1320
Contact: Mr. John Kuhn
Minimum Salary Placed: $50,000
Recruiting Specialty: General

SUSSEX

North Technical Search
N90 W25279 Tomahawk Drive
Sussex, WI 53089-1053
(414) 246-0765
Contact: Mr. Jeff North
Recruiting Specialty: Die cast, foundry
and metals

WALES

**The Cooper Executive Search Group
Inc.**
P.O. Box 375
Wales, WI 53183
(414) 968-9049
Contact: Mr. Robert Cooper
Minimum Salary Placed: $50,000
Recruiting Specialty: General

WATERTOWN

Martin Management, Inc.
901 Charles
Watertown, WI 53094
(414) 261-8050
Contact: Ms. Carol Martin
Recruiting Specialty: Food, quality, production, warehouse, and research and development

National Search Associates
P.O. Box 732, 206 Lafayette Street
Watertown, WI 53094
(414) 261-2100
Contact: Kris Slee
Recruiting Specialty: Chemists, personal
care, cosmetics

WAUKESHA

Corporate Search Inc.
P.O. Box 1808
Waukesha, WI 53187
(414) 542-6260
Contact: Mr. Joe Cali
Minimum Salary Placed: $25,000
Recruiting Specialty: General

Executive Resource Inc.
245 Regency Court, Suite 100
Waukesha, WI 53186
(414) 786-8790
Contact: Mr. William Mitton
Minimum Salary Placed: $25,000
Recruiting Specialty: General

Larson Associates
2727 N. Grandview Boulevard, Suite 119
Waukesha, WI 53188
(414) 695-0000
Contact: Ms. Mary Larson
Minimum Salary Placed: $35,000
Recruiting Specialty: Computers

Monarch Personnel Consultants
260 Regency Court, Suite 205
Waukesha, WI 53186
(414) 246-8466
Contact: Ms. Betty Westen
Minimum Salary Placed: $25,000
Recruiting Specialty: Printing and packaging

Placement Solutions
W270 S3979 Heather Drive
Waukesha, WI 53188
(414) 542-2250
Contact: Ms. Mary Sue Short
Minimum Salary Placed: $30,000
Recruiting Specialty: Accounting and finance

WAUSAU

Management Recruiters
P.O. Box 1165
Wausau, WI 54402
(715) 359-6715
Contact: Ms. Rebecca Knutson
Minimum Salary Placed: $30,000
Recruiting Specialty: General

WEST BEND

Egan & Associates
White House Center
128 S. Sixth Avenue
West Bend, WI 53095
(414) 335-0707
Contact: Mr. Daniel Egan
Minimum Salary Placed: $55,000
Recruiting Specialty: Manufacturing

WISCONSIN DELLS

Markent Personnel
722 Wisconsin Avenue, Box 122
Wisconsin Dells, WI 53965
(608) 254-6233
Contact: Mr. Thomas Udulutch
Minimum Salary Placed: $35,000
Recruiting Specialty: Engineering

W Y O M I N G

CHEYENNE

JDO Associates
515 E. Pershing Boulevard, Suite 1021
Cheyenne, WY 82001
(307) 634-0959
Contact: Ms. Joan Olesen
Minimum Salary Placed: $20,000
Recruiting Specialty: Defense marketing,
program management, HVAC/electrical
design and construction

Management Recruiters
1008 E. 21st Street
Cheyenne, WY 82001
(307) 635-8731
Contact: Mr. Verle Meister
Minimum Salary Placed: $20,000
Recruiting Specialty: Engineering

Spectra
1180 Happy Jack Road
Cheyenne, WY 82009
(307) 637-1276
Contact: Ms. Nicole Carlson
Minimum Salary Placed: $20,000
Recruiting Specialty: Medical and data
processing

Index of Executive Recruiters by Industry

(Generalists are not included in these listings, which are alphabetized under each specialty by state abbreviations and city)

ACCOUNTING/FINANCE

ARCHITECTURE

BIOTECHNOLOGY

CHEMICALS

COMMUNICATIONS

COMPUTERS

CONSTRUCTION/ BUILDING MATERIALS

CONSUMER PRODUCTS

EDUCATION

ENTERTAINMENT

ENVIRONMENTAL

FINANCIAL SERVICES/ INSTITUTIONS

HIGH TECHNOLOGY

HOSPITALITY

HUMAN RESOURCES

INFORMATION SYSTEMS/ DATA PROCESSING

INSURANCE

LIFE SCIENCES

LOGISTICS

MANAGEMENT CONSULTANTS

MANUFACTURING

MARITIME

MARKETING

MATERIALS (PLASTICS, RUBBER, METALS)

MEDICAL

MORTGAGE BROKERS

MULTI-MEDIA

NATURAL RESOURCES

Ashen and Associates, Houston, TX, 666

Rhett Bigham and Associates, Houston, TX, 666

Burns Dunnam and Whitehead, Houston, TX, 667

Carlin Associates, Houston, TX, 667

L. Center Enterprises Inc., Houston, TX, 667

The Energists, Houston, TX, 669

Fortune Personnel Consultants, Houston, TX, 670

Piper-Morgan Associates Personnel, Houston, TX, 674

Bart Roberson and Associates, Houston, TX, 676

Search Consultants International, Inc., Houston, TX, 677

Stephen T. Salemi Inc., Houston, TX, 677

The Elsworth Group, San Antonio, TX, 687

STM Associates, Salt Lake City, UT, 692

NEWSPAPERS

Youngs Walker and Company, Palatine, IL, 276

Gordon Wahls Company, Media, PA, 602

NON-PROFIT

The Hawkins Company, Los Angeles, CA, 62

McCormack & Associates, Los Angeles, CA, 65

Rusher, Ioscavio & Lo Presto, San Francisco, CA, 107

Howard W. Smith Assoicates, Hartford, CT, 152

Ast/Bryant, Stamford, CT, 158

Christopher Bryant, Stamford, CT, 158

Development Resource Group, Washington, DC, 168

Morrison Associates, Washington, DC, 169

Kittleman & Associates, Chicago, IL, 250

Quaintance Associates, Inc., Chicago, IL, 252

Tuft and Associates, Chicago, IL, 256

The PAR Group - Paul A. Reaume, Ltd., Lake Bluff, IL, 267

Auerbach Associates, Inc., Boston, MA, 324

Hospitality Executive Search, Inc., Boston, MA, 325

Ford Webb Associates, Carlisle, MA, 330

Educational Management Network, Nantucket, MA, 337

BCG Search, Inc., Timonium, MD, 320

Development Search Specialists, St. Paul, MN, 386

Messicci & Associates, White Bear Lake, MN, 388

Development Resource Group, New York, NY, 487

Gossage Regan Association, New York, NY, 493

Pathway Executive Search, Inc., New York, NY, 508

Joel H. Paul & Associates, Inc., New York, NY, 508

The Peck Consultancy, New York, NY, 509

Michael Laskin, Jenkintown, PA, 599

Marshall Rice Associates, Charlestown, RI, 617

Educational Management Network, Nashville, TN, 641

Kaludis Consulting Group, Nashville, TN, 641

Waldron and Company, Seattle, WA, 713

OFFICE SUPPORT

Personnel World, Inc., Birmingham, AL, 10

VIP Personnel, Inc., Homewood, AL, 11

Snelling Temporaries, Mobile, AL, 12

Finance Support, Phoenix, AZ, 16

Western Secretaries, Beverly Hills, CA, 31

Denham Temporary Service, Fresno, CA, 45

Availability Personnel Service, Modesto, CA, 74

CCIA, Personnel, San Francisco, CA, 99

Kathy MacDonald Associates, San Francisco, CA, 99

Proserv, San Francisco, CA, 106

Hall Kinton, San Jose, CA, 110

Accutemps Inc., Miami, FL, 189

Accountemps, Orlando, FL, 193

Executive Resources, Des Moines, IA, 292

Career Finders, Urbandale, IA, 295

Lloyd Personnel Consultants, Des Plaines, IL, 260

Beacon Services Inc., Grand Rapids, MI, 360

Snelling and Snelling, Livonia, MI, 363

Beacon Services Inc., St. Joseph, MI, 363

Wood Personnel Service, St. Joseph, MI, 363

Davidson, Laird and Associates, Southfield, MI, 364

Recruiting Group, Minneapolis, MN, 380

Don Richard Associates, Charlotte, NC, 537

Office Mates, Mountainside, NJ, 435

Morgan Mercedes Human Resource, Princeton, NJ, 444

Personnel Service, Waldwick, NJ, 454

Santa Fe Service, Santa Fe, NM, 458

Sigma Search Inc., Melville, NY, 472

Duncan Group Inc., New York, NY, 488

Staffing by Manning Ltd., New York, NY, 515

Allinger Personnel Inc., Rochester, NY, 525

Willard Associates, Syracuse, NY, 530

Adams and Associates, Portland, OR, 588

Remedy Personnel Service, Nashville, TN, 642

Austin Career Consultants Inc., Austin, TX, 644

Largent Parks and Partners Inc., Dallas, TX, 655

Romac Temp, Dallas, TX, 658

Preferred Personnel, Midland, TX, 683

Adams and Associates Inc., Seattle, WA, 710

PACKAGING

Alpha Associates, Birmingham, AL, 9

J. H. Dugan & Associates, Inc., Carmel, CA, 35

Management Recruiters, Citrus Heights, CA, 36

Cliff Schacht Company, Newport Beach, CA, 76

PHARMACEUTICALS/ DRUG

PHYSICIANS

PRINTING

PUBLIC RELATIONS

PUBLIC SECTOR

PUBLISHING

PULP, PAPER AND FORESTRY

REAL ESTATE/ DEVELOPMENT

RESEARCH AND DEVELOPMENT

RETAIL/WHOLESALE

SALES

SECURITY SPECIALISTS

SUPERMARKET/GROCERY

TECHNICAL

TELECOMMUNICATIONS

TEXTILES/APPAREL

TRANSPORTATION

Alphabetical Index

About the Author

Michael Betrus is president of American Research Group, Inc., a publishing company specializing in career strategies and resources for today's professionals. A graduate of Michigan State University, Mr. Betrus is currently based in West Palm Beach, Florida.

Changes for Future Editions

If you are an executive recruiter and would like to have an entry in future editions, or if you want to update an entry from the current directory, please complete the following:

Is your firm listed in this updated edition of the Guide?   Yes   No

Name of Firm: _____

Address: _____

Phone: _____

Principal Contact: _____

Minimum Salary Placed: _____

Recruiting Specialty: _____

If you are a user of this Guide and have any suggestions, please forward them as they will be integrated into future editions.

_____

_____

_____

_____

_____

_____

_____

_____

Direct all correspondence to Michael Betrus in care of American Research Group, Inc., 4632 Forest Hill Boulevard, Suite 360, West Palm Beach, FL 33415.